THE NEW INTERNATIONAL COMMENTARY ON
THE NEW TESTAMENT — F. F. Bruce, *General Editor*

PAUL'S SECOND EPISTLE
TO THE CORINTHIANS

PAUL'S SECOND EPISTLE TO THE CORINTHIANS

THE ENGLISH TEXT WITH INTRODUCTION,
EXPOSITION AND NOTES

by

PHILIP EDGCUMBE HUGHES
Th.D., D. Litt.

Wm. B. EERDMANS PUBLISHING CO.
GRAND RAPIDS, MICHIGAN

ISBN 0-8028-2186-3

First printing, March 1962
Second printing, February 1967
Third printing, March 1971
Fourth printing, June 1973
Fifth printing, July 1975

PRINTED IN THE UNITED STATES OF AMERICA

To

MALCOLM McQUEEN
Loyal Friend
Faithful Witness

CONTENTS

EDITOR'S PREFACE

By way of preface to this substantial addition to *The New International Commentary on the New Testament*, the tenth volume to be completed, the editor is happy to have the opportunity of briefly introducing the author and his work and especially of expressing his gratitude to him for his perceptive and eminently readable contribution.

Philip Hughes is widely known in the English-speaking world both as a churchman and as a scholar. Born in Australia and brought up in South Africa, his labors during his mature life have largely centered in England. He has also, however, enjoyed many fruitful contacts with the European continent and with America. Most recently he has been in the public eye chiefly because of his contributions to *Christianity Today* and he is now connected with the London office of this magazine as British Editorial Associate.

Dr. Hughes is also Editor of the influential *The Churchman*, an Anglican quarterly largely concerned with the life of the Church in which he was ordained in 1941. For a number of years he lectured on New Testament and other subjects in Tyndale Hall, Bristol, where he served as Vice-Principal, 1950–52. At that time he was also Theological Lecturer in the University of Bristol. His writings include numerous articles in such journals as *The Churchman*, *The Evangelical Quarterly*, *Philosophia Reformata* and *The Westminster Theological Journal*; contributions to Baker's *Dictionary of Theology* and the *Biblical Expositor*; and numerous monographs. His M.A. and D.Litt. degrees were awarded by the University of Cape Town, where he won various honors in Classics; his B.D. was earned at the University of London.

The author, who is a member of the *Studiorum Novi Testamenti Societas*, was given free rein to develop his exposition of II Corinthians and the result is a commentary of considerable length. Two factors seem to have contributed principally to this achievement. One is the breadth of scholarship reflected in the discussion of many exegetical points and in the wide range of literature drawn upon, including, to mention a few, the works of Chrysostom, Herveius, Windisch, and Allo. The other factor in view was the author's unswerving commitment to the production of an interesting and lucid work which, in his concern to avoid obscure or cryptic or dull expression, caused him to make generous use of the most significant utterances of others as well as to draw pervasively on his own exceptional powers of composition. While his chief interest happily has been in exposition of the sacred text, the questions of introduction are also evaluated in a thorough manner. The stout defence of the integrity of the Epistle is one of the outstanding features of the volume.

A reviewer of a recently published volume in this series appeared to offer as his chief criticism that the author had not undertaken a critical judgment of the teaching of Paul. The editor believes that in the last analysis this stricture was a compliment to the expositor, for it reflected his basic concern to let the apostle speak forth regardless of how uncongenial his point of view might appear to many in our modern world. Ultimately to be sure this concern of the expositor in question was bound up with his acceptance of the authority of the apostle. One cannot escape the question whether one may reject the authority of Paul's message and still allow it any decisive significance for the Church today in view of the fact that the feature of binding authority was an integral element of the apostolic message. At any rate, Dr. Hughes also shares the conviction as to the authority of the apostle, an ingredient of the Pauline message that is pervasively and emphatically present in II Corinthians.

Although the text of the American Standard Version is presented in this volume as in the preceding ones, this should not be interpreted as indicating a lack of concern with more recent translations and least of all manifesting a judgment of satisfaction from every point of view with this sixty-year-old version. Admittedly it is not distinguished by literary beauty; it is defective also in other respects. But it remains a highly useful translation especially to the student of the Scriptures because of its general literalness as compared with the freer, often periphrastic, quality of other versions.

As this work goes forth the editor is hopeful that it may be used far and wide to stimulate interest in and increase knowledge of the Epistle itself, the life and thought of the great apostle, and indeed the Christian message as a whole. For Paul is dealing with no extraneous or superficial issues as he speaks with the authority of an ambassador of Jesus Christ, and so also with the meekness and gentleness of Christ, entreating and beseeching men to be reconciled to God who in Christ was reconciling the world unto Himself.

NED B. STONEHOUSE
General Editor

EDITOR'S PREFACE TO SECOND EDITION

A second edition of Dr. Hughes' commentary on II Corinthians gives the General Editor an opportunity to associate himself with all that his predecessor, Dr. Stonehouse, wrote in introducing the first edition.

Of all the Pauline epistles, II Corinthians is probably the one which presents most problems to the interpreter. Its theological content, its structure, its relation to I Corinthians and to Paul's apostolic career — these and other questions call for a judicious weighing of evidence and a decision this way or that. Dr. Hughes has weighed the evidence and reached his decision at each stage in the apostle's argument with such acumen and skill that his commentary has won a secure place among serious and scholarly treatments of II Corinthians.

To bring Dr. Hughes' *curriculum vitae* up to date, it may be added that he is now Guest Professor of New Testament in Columbia Theological Seminary, Decatur, Georgia, and Vicar of St. Michael and All Angels Episcopal Church, Stone Mountain, Georgia.

November, 1966

F. F. BRUCE
General Editor

AUTHOR'S PREFACE

The scope of this commentary is exegetical rather than homiletic: it seeks to unfold the meaning of the text rather than to apply it. The hope is that it will provide a sound basis for homiletics, for good Christian preaching must be built on the foundation of good scriptural exegesis. As with the other commentaries in this series, the English text used is that of the American Standard Version (or American Revised Version). Only where this differs in important respects from the English Revised Version is attention drawn to the fact. Otherwise it is treated as identical with the English Revised Version (as indeed in the main it is). The commentary itself, however, is constructed from a careful and thorough examination of the original Greek text. Every endeavour has been made to ensure that the exegesis reflects not only the best readings of that text, so far as these may be ascertained at those points where there are variations in the documents which have come down to us, but also the great advances in our understanding of the language in common (as distinct from literary) usage during the first century of our era which have resulted from the discovery and study of contemporary non-literary evidence afforded by papyri and inscriptions. The main body of the commentary has been kept free from Greek terms; but where significant questions of exegesis turn upon the meaning of particular Greek expressions or constructions, or upon variant readings in the text, footnotes have been added which, it is hoped, will be of some value to the Greek scholar, and even also, if to a more limited degree, to the reader who has no acquaintance with the Greek language.

This epistle, more than any other, poses problems at many points to those who attempt to reconstruct the sequence of events or circumstances to which the Apostle alludes from time to time. Some of these problems, indeed, are impossible of solution and any reconstruction offered, however convincingly, must belong to the realm of conjecture. None the less, the commentator can hardly pass them by. In suggesting solutions it is necessary, firstly, to take all relevant known facts into account, giving them due weight and regarding them as fixed points; secondly, conjectures should be kept to a minimum; and, thirdly, the temptation to overelaboration should be resisted: the reconstruction which, in relation to the known facts, is simplest is likely to be nearest to the truth. In formulating the reconstructions which are offered in the course of this commentary I have endeavoured to respect these canons. Conjectures and reconstructions, however, are of only incidental importance. They should not be allowed to overshadow the exegesis as a whole. It is my earnest prayer that this commentary may in some small way be a means of blessing and strength, by God's grace, to the Church of Christ at a time when she stands face to face with momentous issues. May she be enabled to prove afresh the full sufficiency of God's grace and the power of God which is made perfect through weakness.

I should like to take this opportunity of acknowledging my indebtedness to my friends Professor Ned B. Stonehouse, for his editorial patience in waiting for the completion of my manuscript and his friendly and expert discussion of a variety of questions, and the Rev. Dr. J. D. Douglas, for his invaluable assistance in the reading of the proofs and the preparation of the indexes. I wish also to express my sincere gratitude to the many other Christian friends—among whom I would like in particular to mention the Rev. Professor C. F. D. Moule of Cambridge, the Rev. Dr. Martyn Lloyd-Jones of London, and Bishop Marcus Loane of Sydney—who have shown a helpful interest in the progress of the commentary. Their encouragement has meant much to me as I have, in the midst of the pressures and interruptions of other duties, persevered in bringing this work to its conclusion.

PHILIP E. HUGHES

INTRODUCTION

Authorship and Authenticity

That the Apostle Paul was the author of what is now known as the Second Epistle to the Corinthians is not a matter of dispute in reputable scholarly circles. The evidence, both external and internal, for the Pauline authorship of this letter is so strong as to be irrefragible. Indeed, of all the epistles in the New Testament none is, in style and temperament, more characteristic of the great Apostle. In no other letter do we find so much autobiographical information, and none is more tantalizing by reason of unexplained references to persons, situations, and events with which the writer and his readers were obviously so familiar that precise definition of names, places, and times was unnecessary. This consideration alone powerfully attests the letter's genuineness, for it is unlikely in the extreme that a pseudonymous author or forger would, in introducing professedly autobiographical details, have contented himself with bare allusions which leave the natural curiosity of the reader in suspense. As Plummer says, "a forger would at least have taken pains to make his meaning clear to those whom he wished to have as readers". What impostor would, for example, have mentioned the deadly affliction that overtook the Apostle in Asia (1:8) or his visionary rapture and subsequent "thorn in the flesh" (12:2ff.) without giving some precise information concerning the nature of these experiences, or the "brethren" who were to accompany Titus to Corinth without disclosing their names? What impostor could with such amazing naturalness have reproduced the swift changes of mood, the alternating joy, affection, and sternness, and the sudden digressions and switches of subject that characterize this remarkable epistle? Who could have been so artful as to simulate so genuine an artlessness? It would be difficult to find a composition more convincingly impressed with the personality of its author.

Yet among the major epistles of the New Testament this particular one has suffered a totally unmerited measure of neglect.

This is hard to understand. Can it be that its being designated the *second* epistle has illogically told against it, as though it were *secondary* or in some way inferior to the first epistle (which in point of fact was *not* the first of Paul's letters to the Corinthians—cf. I Cor. 5:9!)? Is it because, as we have observed, there are certain obscurities of reference, or digressions in the narrative sequence, or descriptions which are noticeable for their obliqueness—in particular the allusive, and therefore somewhat elusive, nature of Paul's animadversions, so often implicit by way of ironic rejoinder rather than explicit and frontal, to the false apostles in Corinth and their teachings? But these are factors which may be matched, even if not to the same degree, in others of Paul's letters. On the other hand, we may confidently affirm that for sublimity of doctrine, warmth of feeling, spontaneousness of expression, and elevation of spirit this epistle need not fear comparison with the others that have come from the Apostle's pen. Indeed, there is none (we do not say that reaches, for that is not the case, but) that sustains with such intensity the heights of the transcendental victory of grace in and through the everyday experience of the Christian believer in whatever circumstances, whether of exaltation or of affliction, he may find himself. It is a letter stamped with the mark of apostolic triumph in Christ.

Occasion

The circumstances which occasioned the writing of this letter may be deduced from a study of its contents. The general situation which lay behind its composition was as follows: certain false teachers, who claimed to be apostles, had infiltrated the ranks of the Corinthian church, and in promoting their own claims they had gone out of their way to discredit Paul and to call in question the genuineness of his apostleship. This letter, accordingly, was written largely with the purpose of refuting the accusations and insinuations against him with which these intruders had been poisoning the minds of the believers at Corinth. It is a defence by Paul of the integrity of his personal character and apostleship and an exposure of the intruders as impostors—dictated not by self-interest but by the necessity for protecting the church God had founded through him from forces and doctrines which were essentially inimical to the gospel committed to Paul and to the spiritual welfare of those whose lives, through response to that gospel, had been transformed and set free. Bound up, it would seem, with this situation was the need for Paul to explain the reason for the change in his itinerary as originally proposed (1:15ff.; cf. I Cor. 16:5ff.) and to advise the Corinthians to prepare themselves for the third visit to their city which he was soon to make (13:1ff.). One important manner in which they were to make ready for his arrival was by completing the collection for the poor Christians in Jerusalem, which they had begun but failed to finish (chapters 8 and 9;regarding the significance of this collection see pages 283ff. below).

The sequence of events leading up to the writing of this letter we may reconstruct in the following way. Paul had sent his former letter (our I Corinthians) from Ephesus by the hand of Titus. This letter had dealt specifically with a number of serious aberrations that had arisen in the Corinthian church: the rending of the fellowship into rival parties; the condoning of a case of incest in their midst; the taking of their petty squabbles into the law-courts of unbelievers; disorderliness at the Lord's Supper and in public worship; the lovelessness of their relationships with each other; and even the entertaining of doubts concerning the fact of the resurrection. These were matters of extreme seriousness, and Paul, after the despatch of that letter, was anxious to know how it had been received by his spiritual children in Corinth. He had had an arrangement with Titus to meet him, on his return from Corinth, at Troas. Paul, therefore, made his way northwards from Ephesus. On arrival in Troas, he found an open door for preaching the gospel; but as the expected arrival of Titus did not materialize Paul did not prolong his stay in that city but decided to travel on into Macedonia, so that he might meet Titus the sooner (2:12f., 7:5ff.). And there at last the encounter took place, probably in Philippi, or perhaps Neapolis the port of Philippi.

The news Titus brought from Corinth was reassuring, though not entirely so. The Corinthians had responded to Paul's letter with "godly sorrow unto repentance". They had treated Titus, Paul's emissary, with respect and affection and had taken steps to purge their community of the offences by which it had been disfigured. Their ready response filled Paul with joy and confirmed his confidence in them (7:5ff.).

But Titus also brought news of a less encouraging nature. There was still a recalcitrant group in the Corinthian church. Incited no doubt by the false apostles who had arrived on the scene, this minority was alleging that Paul's word was not to be trusted—that he wrote or promised one thing, but did another. In substantiation of this accusation they cited his change of itinerary. To this the Apostle replies that the alteration of his plans was explained not by fickleness or unreliability on his part (the Corinthians knew him well enough not to believe that, and especially they knew the utter reliability of Christ whom he had preached to them: the proof of the message was also the proof of the preacher) but by his desire not to come to Corinth again in severity (2:1). It was being said, further, that Paul's genuineness as an apostle was suspect because he had not come to Corinth with letters of commendation (3:1). These and other aspersions on his apostleship are answered by a reminder of all he so willingly and incessantly endured as a minister of the gospel (chapters 4 to 6). It is not improbable that this same dissident group had been responsible for slowing up the collection for the needy Jerusalem Christians, with the result that it became necessary for Paul to urge the Corinthians to bring to fulfilment what they had already commenced (chapters 8 and 9).

Finally, the false apostles who had invaded Paul's territory in Corinth, and who were intent on sowing the seeds of disaffection, had to be exposed in their true colours. They were intruders who had no right in the Corinthian church, for Corinth lay on the apostolic track which God had marked out for Paul (10:12ff.). They had come without being sent, bringing with them another Jesus, another spirit, another gospel, and flourishing the arts of rhetoric in doing so (11:2ff.). They were suggesting that Paul was brave from a distance, writing impressive letters, but, when present, was the opposite of impressive both in authority and in oratory (10:10, 11:6). They had battened like parasites on the Corinthians, and, to cover their unscrupulousness, asserted that the message preached by Paul was not worth listening to because, unlike the Greek rhetoricians, he made no charge for proclaiming it (11:7ff.). They had even whispered that Paul's unwillingness to allow the Corinthians to contribute to his material needs was an indication that he had no love for them (11:11, 12:13ff.), and had invented the shocking calumny that his financial independence was to be explained by the supposition that he was lining his own pockets with the money which he was ostensibly collecting for the relief of the Christians in Jerusalem (12:17f.).[1]

And so, with evident distaste for speaking about himself, Paul reminds the Corinthians that, as they well knew, in contrast to the pretended apostleship of these false teachers his apostleship was one of continuous suffering and self-abnegation, and that it was precisely in his own manifest weakness, which left no room for self-glorification, that the power and grace of God had been magnified (11:21–12:12). He admonishes them that he is now about to visit them for the third time and that, if necessary, he will come to them exercising the full force of his apostolic authority (12:14, 20f., 13:1ff.). But it is his hope that the interval between the receipt of this letter and his arrival in person will be seized by the subversive minority as an opportunity for putting right what is wrong (13:5ff.).

This summary of the situation revealed by the contents of II Corinthians gives a reasonably clear picture of the occasion which called forth its composition.

Scheme

In talking of the scheme of the epistle we do not mean to suggest a self-consciously devised literary schematization; but that there is a coherent plan or framework is, we believe, apparent. This consideration is, of course, closely linked with the question of the unity of the epistle, which will be discussed in the next section of the Introduction.

The key to the scheme of our epistle is to be found in the subject of Paul's itinerary with relation to Corinth. The Apostle's original intention for his next journey into Greece had been to pay the Corinthians a sort of double visit by crossing over by sea from Ephesus and staying for a short while with them before travelling north to Macedonia, and then, on his return from Macedonia, spending another period with them before journeying on to Jerusalem with the collection for the poverty-stricken believers there (1:15f.). The recently sent epistle had, however,

---

[1] For a discussion of the origin and identity of these false apostles and the nature of their teaching, see pp. 356ff. below.

advised the Corinthians that, though it was quite definite that he would come to them (I Cor. 4:18ff., 11:34), his itinerary had been altered to the extent that he now proposed, not to pay them two brief visits, but one longer one, possibly even spending the winter with them; for he would now travel north from Ephesus to Macedonia, and from there come on down to Corinth (I Cor. 16:5ff.). Then, in due course, he would continue his journey to Jerusalem, taking with him the collection completed under the supervision of Titus.

This scheme or framework may be traced through the epistle as follows: Paul affirms his personal integrity (1:12ff.) and explains the reason for the change in his itinerary (1:15–2:4). He describes how he journeyed from Ephesus to Troas, in the expectation of meeting Titus in the latter place, and how, not finding him there, he travelled on into Macedonia (2:12f.). At this point there commences an extended digression or "parenthesis" (2:14–7:4)—a digression, that is, as concerns the framework but not at all as concerns the substance of the epistle (see commentary below, pp. 76f., 264f.). The account is resumed at 7:5, where Paul tells of his long desired meeting with Titus and of the joy and comfort afforded him by the news of the Corinthians' obedient response to his letter. The ensuing chapters, 8 and 9, which are concerned with the matter of the collection for the relief of the Jerusalem Christians, are by no means unrelated to the scheme of the epistle. On the contrary, their position is properly explained only with reference to the over-all scheme of the letter: Paul's itinerary has changed, but not his purpose to visit Corinth; and it is a particular wish of his that the collection should be carried through to completion in readiness for his arrival; accordingly he announces that he is sending Titus and two other "brethren" on ahead (the bearers of the present letter) to supervise this matter. The final four chapters (10 to 13) are an exposure of the impostrous "apostles" who have invaded the Corinthian church, and who, in their attempt to undermine Paul's apostolic authority, have, amongst other calumnies, imputed mercenary motives to him, and have so far succeeded as to bring the collection to a standstill. Paul, however, repudiates their vicious slanders and warns that he will deal severely with any who continue to trouble the church, for he is quite certainly about to visit Corinth for the third time.

The scheme or "skeleton", then, to which is attached all the substance or "flesh" of the epistle concerns Paul's itinerary relative to Corinth, viewed in its various aspects: past—the change of plan (chapters 1 to 7); present—the sending on of Titus and the "brethren" to attend to the completion of the collection in readiness for Paul's coming (chapters 8 and 9); and future—the imminence of the Apostle's own arrival in Corinth, with all that that implies, especially for his adversaries (chapters 10 to 13). This may be diagrammatically depicted as follows:

PAUL'S THIRD VISIT TO CORINTH

THE CHANGE OF ITINERARY EXPLAINED (1–7)

THE PREPARATION FOR THE VISIT (8 and 9)

THE CERTAINTY AND IMMINENCE OF THE VISIT (10–13)

The evidence from both I and II Corinthians shows that the impending third visit of the Apostle to Corinth was closely bound up with the project of the collection in aid of the impoverished Christians in Jerusalem.

Unity

Because the question of the unity of II Corinthians has been hotly disputed in modern times it is necessary that we should devote some space to its consideration here. All discussion must, however, be prefaced by an emphatic reminder that this epistle has come down to us as a unity, that in the early church and throughout the succeeding centuries its unity seems never to have been doubted, and that modern denials of its unity are unsupported by any evidence of an objective or even circumstantial nature. For a time, indeed, during more recent years, to impugn the unity of II Corinthians was to be very much in the fashion; but now a swing back to the traditional view of the letter's integrity is noticeable: witness the judgment of contemporary scholars like

E. B. Allo[2], R. V. G. Tasker[3], Johannes Munck[4], Walther von Loewenich[5], and Professor Joachim Jeremias (who has kindly permitted me to mention his view, expressed to me in conversation, that II Corinthians is beyond doubt a unity).

The scheme to which we have drawn attention in the preceding section of this Introduction indicates the unitary framework of the epistle. The letter falls naturally into three major sections: chapters 1–7, 8–9, and 10–13. While these sections display diversities in subject-matter and in mood, yet their sequence is marked by logicality. As Zahn says: "In spirit the reader follows Paul from Ephesus through Troas to Macedonia (chaps. i–vii); then he lingers with him for a moment in the churches of Macedonia (chaps. viii–ix); finally, he is led to the consideration of conditions in the church at Corinth from the point of view of Paul's coming visit there"[6].

Despite, therefore, the diversity of its parts, there is a structural unity which gives coherence to the whole. Once this framework is discerned, the arguments which have been urged against the unity of the epistle lose most of their momentum.

In particular, it has been maintained, at times with excessive dogmatism, that the last four chapters of the epistle must belong elsewhere, some assigning them to an earlier, some to a later, letter. Hypotheses have also been propounded with the purpose of showing that other sections of the epistle, notably 6:4–7:1, either chapter 8 or chapter 9, and 11:32f., are dislocations from other writings (see commentary below, pp. 241ff., 283ff., 321f., 343ff., 420ff.). Plummer very rightly declares that "it must always be remembered that in every one of these four cases the doubts as to their being part of the Second Epistle, as St. Paul dictated it, *are based entirely on internal evidence*. No MS, no version, and no patristic quotation supplies any evidence that the Epistle was ever in circulation anywhere with any one of these four portions omitted"[7].

---

[2] *Saint Paul, Seconde Epitre aux Corinthiens* (Paris, 1936).
[3] *The Second Epistle of Paul to the Corinthians* (London, 1958).
[4] *Paul and the Salvation of Mankind* (London, 1959)
[5] *Paul: His Life and Work* (Edinburgh, 1960).
[6] T. Zahn, *Introduction to the New Testament*, Vol. I (Edinburgh, 1909), p. 312.
[7] ICC, p. xxiii.

Although, however, Plummer affirms the authenticity of the three shorter passages, he stringently opposes the authenticity of chapters 10 to 13. In view both of his eminence as an exegete and also of the assurance and precision with which he puts forward his case, the arguments on which his judgment rests merit our attention. It is Plummer's conviction that the concluding four chapters belong to the severe letter mentioned in 2:3. He is adamant, moreover, that I Corinthians does not fit the description of that letter as having been written "out of much affliction and anguish of heart . . . with many tears". The traditional view which identifies the severe letter with I Corinthians, though admittedly held by "scholars of great eminence", may, he says, "once for all be abandoned"; and so he embraces the hypothesis that the final four chapters belong to an "intermediate" severe epistle supposed to have been written between our present I and II Corinthians.

Plummer rests his case upon four main considerations:

(1) The abrupt change of tone at 10:1. He maintains that the placing of this outburst after instead of before the conciliatory section and the appeal for the collection involves "psychological maladroitness" and a change "in the wrong direction". But is the change of tone really so abrupt as it is made out to be? And do these four chapters really constitute an outburst? The tone of this concluding section is set by the opening words of the tenth chapter, where Paul addresses *an entreaty* to the Corinthians "by the meekness and gentleness of Christ". He is still writing as their spiritual father, moved by love and "godly jealousy" for them (11:1ff., 11, 12:14f.; cf. 6:11ff., 7:2f.). It is true that he has some severe and straight things to say, but they are said in entire conformity with the spirit that animates the earlier chapters of the letter; and, moreover, they apply in particular to the intruding false apostles and the minority faction that has associated itself with them. Nor can we agree that the position of the final four chapters in the epistle as we have received it involves psychological maladroitness. On the contrary, the earlier chapters provide an admirable preparation for what Paul has to say in chapters 10 to 13: they have left the Corinthians in no doubt concerning his love and affection for them and his pride and confidence in them as his children in the gospel, and as such they are an ideal psychological introduction to the sterner elements

of the concluding section. In chapters 10 to 13 Paul is tying up the loose ends that remain; he is addressing himself to the one serious problem that is still not fully resolved at Corinth, namely, the threat which the continued presence of the false teachers constitutes; and, with particular reference to this problem, he is giving final instructions and admonitions in readiness for his impending visit to Corinth. We can only conclude that neither psychologically nor schematically are there good grounds for deciding that these chapters are out of place.

(2) The existence of logical inconsistencies. Plummer cites the following comparisons:

1:24. "By your faith ye stand."	**13:5.** "Try your own selves, whether ye be in the faith."

There is, however, no conflict here. On the contrary, the two statements are in harmony with each other. In the former, Paul is reminding the Corinthians that it is through faith that they are established; in the latter, he invites them to prove by examination of their own hearts that this is so: hence he immediately adds, "or know ye not your own selves, that Jesus Christ is in you?" 13:5, therefore, springs not from doubt, but from confidence. (See commentary below on 13:5.)

7:16. "I rejoice that in everything I am of good courage concerning you."	**12:20f.** "I fear lest by any means there should be strife, jealousy, wraths, factions, backbitings, whisperings, swellings, tumults; lest I should mourn for many of them that have sinned heretofore, and repented not of the uncleanness and fornication and lasciviousness which they committed."
7:7. "As ye abound in everything, in faith, in utterance, and knowledge, and in all earnestness, and in your love to us."	

The contrast between these passages is, however, no greater than, for example, that in I Corinthians between, on the one hand, Paul's declaration of thankfulness that the Corinthians in everything were enriched in Christ and came behind in no gift, (I Cor. 1:4ff.) and, on the other hand, the stern rebukes and admonitions that follow in the same epistle concerning factions, strifes, unspirituality, immorality, litigiousness, disorderliness, lack of love, and false doctrine by which their fellowship was disfigured. If the sequence in our epistle is illogical, it is strange that Plummer fails to see any logical inconsistency in the comparable sequence of the earlier epistle. The problem, as is already apparent in the opening section of II Corinthians, was that at Corinth there was still a minority group intent on making trouble and on undermining Paul's authority (cf. 1:14, 2:5f.).

2:3. "My joy is the joy of you all."

7:4. "Great is my glorying in your behalf; I am filled with comfort."

7:11. "In everything ye approved yourselves to be pure in the matter."

3:2. "Ye are our epistle, written in our heart."

10:2. "I beseech you that I may not when present show courage with the confidence wherewith I count to be bold against some, which count of us as if we walked according to the flesh."

11:3. "I fear lest by any means your minds should be corrupted from the simplicity and purity that is toward Christ."

13:10. "I write these things while absent, that I may not when present deal sharply."

The same observations apply with equal force to these passages. The response of the Corinthians *as a whole* had been such as to rejoice Paul's heart. He is, however, determined to take effective steps to discipline the recalcitrant minority (cf. 10:2, "some which count of us as if we walked according to the flesh") if they persist in their perversity. Regarding 3:2, Paul reminded the Corinthians that they, in their own redeemed persons, were his epistle commendatory, written in his heart, precisely because there were some among them who were endeavouring to discredit his apostolic authority on the ground that, when he first came to Corinth, he had not brought with him the credentials afforded by letters of commendation.

(3) Plummer regards as even more decisive the occurrence in chapters 1 to 9 of passages which appear to refer to things mentioned in chapters 10 to 13. Judging that the citations from 1–9 belong to a later letter, and are to be understood by reference *back* to those from 10–13, he reverses the order of the sections:

10:1. "I have confidence *against* you" (εἰς ὑμᾶς).	**7:16.** "I have confidence *in* you" (ἐν ὑμῖν).
10:2. "With the confidence wherewith I count to be bold."	**8:22.** "By reason of much confidence to youward."

"In both of these cases", says Plummer, "St. Paul seems to be purposely repeating in a friendly sense an expression which in the former letter he had used in a stern and unpleasing sense." This judgment, however, reveals a failure to take into account the two different contexts in which these statements are set respectively. In the first place, the "confidence" mentioned in 7:16 and 8:22 relates to two different subjects: in 7:16 Paul is expressing his own confidence in the reality of the Corinthians' relationship of faith toward God and loyalty to himself, whereas in 8:22 he is speaking of the confidence which the unnamed brother, who was to go on ahead with Titus to Corinth, had in them. It is, in fact, Plummer who is lacking in consistency, since, in his Introduction, as we have just seen, he explains the "confidence" as *Paul's* in both places, while in his commentary on 8:22 he asserts that the word "no doubt means the envoy's confidence (RV) rather than the Apostle's"! Secondly, the "confidence" of 10:1 and 2 is, as the context shows, a different kind of confidence from that of 7:16 and 8:22: it is the confidence of a man in authority faced with a situation which calls for the exercise of discipline. In particular, Paul's language here is not an expression of no-confidence in the Corinthians, but is an ironical echo, and repudiation, of the calumny disseminated by the dissident faction in Corinth to the effect that he was brave from a distance but innocuous when present (see commentary on 10:1f. below).

10:6. "Being in readiness to avenge all disobedience, when your obedience shall be fulfilled."	**2:9.** "To this end also did I write, that I might know the proof, whether you are obedient in all things."

The traditional order of the text is, however, quite coherent, for the reference in 2:9 to a previous letter does not demand the postulation of an "intermediate" letter (to which *ex hypothesi* chapters 10 to 13 of our epistle belong), since Paul's impending visit to Corinth, if necessary "with a rod", has already been announced in I Corinthians (4:21, 16:3ff.), and it is in terms of this, rather than of some hypothetical intermediate letter, that Paul's words should be understood. 10:6, as an integral part of II Corinthians, refers forward to this same visit, now so close at hand (cf. 12:14, 20f., 13:1ff.).

12:16. "But being crafty I caught you with guile."	**4:2.** "Not walking in craftiness."

But, once again, 12:16 echoes one of the slanders which was being uttered against Paul by his enemies in Corinth (see commentary below), while 4:2 is not a later correction of a misunderstanding of 12:16, but a disavowal on Paul's part of the craftiness which was characteristic of his adversaries. Rightly understood, the two passages are, in fact, univocal.

12:17. "Did I take advantage of you?"	**7:2.** "We took advantage of no one."

Presumably Plummer regards 7:2 as the answer given to the question posed (12:17) in what, on his theory, was an earlier letter. In fact, however, the two statements say exactly the same thing. It is a linguistic commonplace to express a negation by putting a question to which the answer is obviously No. These two passages, therefore, accord perfectly with each other within the framework of the one epistle.

13:2. "If I come again I will not spare."	**1:23.** "To spare you I forebore to come to Corinth."
13:10. "I write these things while absent, that I may not when present deal sharply."	**2:3.** "I wrote this very thing that I might not by coming have sorrow."

It is, however, altogether unnecessary to imagine that 1:23 and 2:3 may be more satisfactorily understood by reference to 13:2 and 10 as though the latter belonged to an earlier epistle. 1:23 and 2:3 refer to Paul's change of itinerary and to the letter in which he had announced it (which we possess, namely, I Corinthians; cf. I Cor. 16:5ff.), whereas 13:2 and 10 refer to the present letter (II Corinthians) in which he is preparing the way for his forthcoming visit. It is noticeable that here (in his Introduction), once again, Plummer is so carried away with the desire to justify his hypothesis that he declares that the conjunction "if" in 13:2 indicates that "when the severe letter was written there was some doubt about Paul's returning to Corinth (*If* I come again)", in contrast to chapters 1 to 9 in which "there was no such doubt"; whereas in his commentary on 13:2 he states, very properly, that "there is no hint of hesitation in the ἐάν (cf. I Cor. 16:10; I Jn. 2:1; III Jn. 10). In such cases", he adds, " 'if' is almost equivalent to 'When' ". Such is the schizophrenia induced by a hypothesis even in the case of the best of scholars.

We prefer Plummer the exegete to Plummer the theorist, and we concur with Allo's judgment that all the correspondences which Plummer gives "between phrases in chapters 1 to 9 and 10 to 12 with the purpose of demonstrating that these last chapters are the first, and that the others make allusions to them as though to things previously said, can be interpreted in the opposite sense" (p. lvi).

(4) Plummer's fourth argument in support of his view that chapters 10 to 13 belong to a letter written prior to chapters 1 to 9 rests upon Paul's assertion in 10:16 that he looked forward to an extension of his missionary labours beyond Corinth: "so as to preach the gospel even unto the parts beyond you". Understanding the phrase "the parts beyond you" in the commonly accepted manner to mean Italy and Spain, Plummer reminds his readers that II Cor. 1–9 was written from *Macedonia*, and thereupon concludes that "a person in Macedonia would hardly use such an expression as 'the parts beyond you' in reference to Corinth, if he was thinking of Italy and Spain." It is scarcely necessary to point out how poverty-stricken this argument is, resting as it does on the naïve assumption that when thinking geographically Paul always thought in straight lines. The New Testament shows, however, that the Apostle's missionary strategy was in terms of districts and communities belonging to the northern seaboard of the Mediterranean, and presents his ministry as extending, in a general and comprehensive sense, westwards from Judea, by way of Asia Minor, across into the Macedonian and Greek peninsula, the parts beyond which in Paul's mind, whether he was writing from Ephesus or Philippi, were Italy and, yet further afield, Spain.

We are in entire agreement with Denney when he insists that II Corinthians should be explained as far as possible out of I Corinthians; and we have no difficulty in believing that I Corinthians was written "out of much affliction and anguish of heart and with many tears" (2:4), despite Plummer's categorical judgment that this identification of the "painful" letter with I Corinthians may "once for all be abandoned" or Tasker's more moderate opinion that "it is seen to be increasingly improbable".[8] How could it have been anything other than distressing in the extreme to the Apostle when it became necessary for him to rebuke the members of the church he had himself founded at Corinth because their fellowship was being torn to shreds by party strife; to admonish them because they were not spiritual but carnal and stunted in growth ("babes"); to warn them of the danger of building on the foundation of Christ with wood, hay, and stubble; to reprimand them because they were puffed up with pride against each other; to charge them to purge out the leaven of gross immorality which they had condoned in their midst; to reprove them for bringing lawsuits against each other before courts of unbelievers, instead of settling their squabbles amicably as becomes Christian brethren, or, failing that, putting up with injury and insult without thoughts of vengeance; to express his horror that in coming together for the sacrament of holy communion some exhibited greed, gluttony, and even drunkenness, while others were allowed to be in want; to warn them that to eat the bread and drink the cup of the Lord unworthily meant to eat and drink judgment; to deprecate serious disorderliness in their public worship, especially in their unedifying use of the spiritual gifts which they enjoyed; to preach them a sermon on love because theirs had become a community without love; and to abominate and correct the appalling error which some among them were propagating that there is no resurrection of the dead—how could such a letter have been written otherwise than out of much affliction and anguish of heart and with many tears? This being so, there is no need to postulate some "intermediate" severe letter, or to detach chapters 10 to 13 from II Corinthians and assign them to this hypothetical missive.

It seems to us that much of the unwillingness to identify the "painful" letter with I Corinthians rests upon a misunderstanding of II Cor. 7:8, namely, that Paul regretted having written the letter in question. Paul, however, does not say that he regretted the *writing* of the letter, as though he wished it had remained unwritten, distressing though its composition and despatch must

---

[8] *Op. cit.*, p. 18.

have been to him. It was a letter that had to be written if he was to be a faithful father in God to the Corinthians. What he *does* say is that he regretted the *sorrow* which that letter had at first caused them: paternal love does not rejoice in the sorrow which necessary correction brings; but the correction itself is not a matter for regret, especially when, as in this case, it is effective. Hence Paul's declaration that he does not now regret the sorrow caused by his letter, because it was sorrow "after a godly sort" leading to repentance "which bringeth no regret". It is not a question, then, of Paul's having regretted the writing of this particular letter as such, whether it be identified with I Corinthians or a lost "intermediate" letter or chapters 10 to 13 of II Corinthians.

The difficulty of the change of tone and content of the final four chapters is more imaginary than real. As we have shown, they fit in with the scheme of the epistle. But, what is more, it can be demonstrated that they harmonize with the pervading *theme* of the epistle—the theme, namely, of strength through weakness. In this theme is bound up the whole argument for the genuineness of Paul's apostolic authority, which has been impugned by his adversaries in Corinth. His human weakness and self-inadequacy are facts which he never seeks to deny or hide. On the contrary, he glories in them because it is precisely thus, as weak and inadequate, that God is able to use him in His service; it is only thus that it becomes inescapably apparent that the power of his ministry is entirely the power of God; it is by the amazing contrast between his own frailty and the all-conquering strength of God manifested through him that his apostleship is unshakeably authenticated to the world. Accordingly, we find Paul drawing attention in this epistle to the sufferings, perils, hardships, and debilities which he endures in the prosecution of his evangelical ministry, and at the same time to the great power of God which is manifested in and through his ministry, in order that thereby he might drive home to his readers the truth of the startling paradox that human weakness and divine strength go hand in hand; that, so far from human frailty being a handicap or a barrier, it provides the ideal opportunity and *milieu* for the triumph of divine power; that to whatever degree a minister of Christ asserts his own adequacy, to that degree does he deny and withdraw from the sole sufficiency of the grace of God.

By this standard Paul stands vindicated before the Corinthians, and his adversaries stand condemned. The essence of the assault upon his apostolic authority was a concentrated "exposure" of his weakness, leaving out of account the divine strength by which his ministry in Corinth had been sealed. As an attack on Paul, it was also an attack on the power of God. To disparage Paul was at the same time to disparage the grace of God conveyed through his ministry. It was to challenge the deepest reality of the redemptive experience into which the Corinthians had entered through his instrumentality.

This unitive theme, binding together both earlier and later parts of the epistle, may be exhibited by the extraction of the following quotations:

1:5f. "As the sufferings of Christ abound unto us, even so our comfort aboundeth through Christ. But whether we are afflicted, it is for your comfort and salvation ..."

1:8ff. "... our affliction which befell us in Asia, that we were weighed down exceedingly, beyond our power, insomuch that we despaired even of life: yea, we ourselves had the sentence of death within ourselves, that we should not trust in ourselves, but in God who raiseth the dead: who delivered us out of so great a death ..."

2:12ff. "... I had no relief for my spirit ... But thanks be unto God, who always leadeth us in triumph in Christ."

3:5f. "... not that we are sufficient of ourselves, ... but our sufficiency is from God; who also made us sufficient as ministers of a new covenant."

4:7ff. "We have this treasure in earthen vessels, that the exceeding greatness of the power may be of God, and not from ourselves; we are pressed on every side, yet not straitened; perplexed, yet not unto despair; pursued, yet not forsaken; smitten down, yet not destroyed; always bearing about in the body the dying of Jesus, that the life also of Jesus may be manifested in our body. For we who live are always delivered unto death for Jesus' sake, that the life also of Jesus may be manifested in our mortal flesh."

4:16. "Wherefore we faint not; but though our outward man is decaying, yet our inward man is renewed day by day."

5:1. "We know that if the earthly house of our tabernacle be dissolved, we have a building from God, a house not made with hands, eternal, in the heavens."

5:18. "All things are of God, who reconciled us to himself through Christ, and gave unto us the ministry of reconciliation."

6 : 4ff. " ... in everything commending ourselves, as ministers of God, in much patience, in afflictions, in necessities, in distresses, in stripes, in imprisonments, in tumults, in labors, in watchings, in fastings, ... in the power of God, ... by glory and dishonour, by evil report and good report; as deceivers, and yet true; as unknown, and yet well known; as dying, and behold, we live; as chastened, and not killed; as sorrowful, yet always rejoicing; as poor, yet making many rich; as having nothing, and yet possessing all things."

7 : 5f. " ... our flesh had no relief ... Nevertheless he that comforteth the lowly, even God, comforted us ..."

10 : 17f. "He that glorieth, let him glory in the Lord. For not he that commendeth himself is approved, but whom the Lord commendeth."

11 : 23ff. " ... in labors more abundantly, in prisons more abundantly, in stripes above measure, in deaths oft. Of the Jews five times received I forty stripes save one. Thrice was I beaten with rods, once was I stoned, thrice I suffered shipwreck, a night and a day have I been in the deep; in journeyings often, in perils of rivers, in perils of robbers, in perils from my countrymen, in perils from the Gentiles, in perils in the city, in perils in the wilderness, in perils in the sea, in perils among false brethren; in labor and travail, in watchings often, in hunger and thirst, in fastings often, in cold and nakedness. Besides those things that are without, there is that which presseth upon me daily, anxiety for all the churches. Who is weak, and I am not weak? who is caused to stumble, and I burn not? If I must needs glory, I will glory of the things that concern my weakness."

12 : 5. "On mine own behalf I will not glory, save in my weaknesses."

12 : 9f. "He hath said unto me, My grace is sufficient for thee: for my power is made perfect in weakness. Most gladly therefore will I rather glory in my weaknesses, that the power of Christ may rest upon me. Wherefore I take pleasure in weaknesses, in injuries, in necessities, in persecutions, in distresses, for Christ's sake: for when I am weak, then am I strong."

13 : 4. Christ "was crucified through weakness, yet he liveth through the power of God. For we also are weak in him, but we shall live with him through the power of God toward you."

The unitive nature of this theme is obvious, and the proof it affords of the integrity of the epistle is supported by numerous other points of affinity between the letter's earlier and later parts which in an unobtrusive manner augment the testimony to the congruity of the whole. A few examples must suffice. Others will be noticed in the course of the commentary.

1:13. "We write no other things unto you, than what ye read or even acknowledge."

1:17. "The things that I purpose, do I purpose according to the flesh?"

2:1. "I determined this for myself, that I would not come again to you with sorrow."

2:17. "In the sight of God speak we in Christ."

3:2. "Ye are our epistle" (i.e., of commendation, cf. verse 1).

6:13. "I speak as unto my children."

8:6, 18, 22. "We exhorted Titus, that as he had made a beginning before, so he would also complete in you this grace also ... And we have sent together with him the brother whose praise in the gospel is spread through all the churches ... And we have sent with them our brother, whom we have many times proved earnest in many things."

10:11. "What we are in word by letters when we are absent, such are we also in deed when we are present."

10:2. " ... some who count of us as if we walked according to the flesh."

12:14. "This is the third time I am ready to come to you."

12:21. "Lest again when I come my God should humble me before you, and I should mourn ..."

13:1f. "This is the third time I am coming to you ... I have said beforehand ... that if I come again I will not spare."

12:19. "In the sight of God speak we in Christ."

12:11. "I ought to have been commended of you."

11:2. "I espoused you (*sc.* as your father) to one husband, that I might present you as a pure virgin to Christ."

12:14. "I seek not yours, but you: for the children ought not to lay up for the parents, but the parents for the children."

12:17f. "Did I take advantage of you by any one of them whom I have sent unto you? I exhorted Titus, and I sent the brother with him."

It is, surely, a fact of some significance that, broadly speaking, those who, on the strength of the supposed internal evidence, have concluded that II Corinthians is not a unity fall into two camps: those, firstly, who hold that chapters 10 to 13 belong to a separate *earlier* letter, and, secondly, those who hold that they belong to a *later* letter (though the latter constitute a less numerous company than the former). Bernard aptly remarks that "when internal evidence leads competent scholars to such entirely divergent conclusions, it is a natural inference that the arguments on which they rely do not amount to demonstration"[9].

Regarding the hypothesis that chapters 10 to 13 belong to an earlier severe letter, Munck makes the following pointed observations: "This assumption will not hold water. The only thing that we know for certain about the severe letter is that Paul demanded the punishment of one of the church members (2:5–11; 7:11f.), and in chs. 10–13 there is not a single word about this. To deal with this objection the point has, of course, been made that the last four chapters are only a fragment of the severe letter, and that the missing part may be contained in the part that was lost. But it is more than remarkable if in a search for identification the one thing that was certain to be found in the letter is not contained in what is believed to be a fragment of it. This is particularly striking when we read the demands that Paul makes (12:14–13:10) before his visit to the church. There is nothing mentioned here about the punishment of a church member which has 'caused pain'." Munck judges as more probable the "assumption that chs. 10–13 were written later than chs. 1–9, either as part of the same letter or as a later letter or a fragment of one". If indeed there was an interval between the composition of these two sections, "the numerous points of agreement" suggest that it was "only a short interval", so much so that Munck "wonders whether the intervening period is not getting so short that after all the two parts are only one letter"[10].

Sufficient has been said, we trust, for the presentation of our case that II Corinthians as it has come down to us is indeed only one letter, diversified in its parts but none the less an integrated whole. For the rest, we would only remark that it would be a

---

[9] J. H. Bernard, *The Second Epistle of Paul to the Corinthians* (The Expositors' Greek Testament), Edinburgh, 1903, p. 24

[10] Johannes Munck, *op. cit.*, pp. 170ff.

misfortune for the Church if the profound spiritual riches of this great epistle were overlooked or passed by either because of academic contentions regarding its unity or because of certain places and passages in the course of the text the precise force of which may not be immediately apparent (and which have sometimes been rendered unnecessarily obscure by unsatisfactory translations).

Place and Date

The letter was written in Macedonia, probably at Philippi, (cf. 2:13, 7:5ff., 8:1ff.). The exact year of its composition cannot be determined with certainty, but we would suggest the year 57 A.D., and the autumn of that year. The meagre chronological evidence available to us does not permit the reaching of firm conclusions, but it is discussed at various points in the commentary below; see especially, the notes on Paul's Associations with Corinth (pp. 31ff.) and on the Mention of Aretas in 11:32 and Pauline Chronology (pp. 424ff.) and also comments on 3:10 (pp. 303f.) and 12:2 (pp. 430ff.).

Commentaries

For a comprehensive bibliography readers are advised to turn to Allo (pp. lxxi ff.). We shall do no more here than mention a selected number of commentaries.

4th century:	Ambrose (Migne, *Patr. Lat.*, Vol. XVII. I have used the Paris edition of the *Ambrosii Opera*, Vol. III, 1586).
—	Chrysostom (Migne, *Patr. Graec.*, Vol. LXI; English translation, Oxford, 1848).
5th century:	Theodoret (Migne, *Patr. Graec.*, Vol. LXXXII).
12th century:	Theophylact (Migne, *Patr. Graec.*, Vol. CXXV).
—	Herveius (Migne, *Patr. Lat.*, Vol. CLXXXI).
13th century:	Thomas Aquinas, *Expositio in Pauli Episolas* (Basle, 1475).
16th century:	Erasmus, *Opera omnia*, Vol. VII.
—	Calvin (*Corp. Ref.*, Vol. VII; English translation, Edinburgh, 1849).
17th century:	Estius, *Commentarii in Epistolas Apostolicas* (Douai, 1614–16).
18th century:	Bengel, *Gnomon Novi Testamenti* (Tübingen, 1742).
19th century:	Henry Alford, *The Greek Testament* (London, 1849–61).
—	Charles Hodge (Edinburgh, 1859).

— Christopher Wordsworth (London, 4th ed., 1866).
— B. Weiss (Leipzig, 2nd ed. 1902; Engl. tr., New York and London, 1906).
— Arthur P. Stanley, *The Epistles of St. Paul to the Corinthians* (London, 4th edn., 1876).
— James Denney in the *Expositor's Bible* (London, 1894).

20th century: J. H. Bernard in the *Expositor's Greek Testament* (London, 1903).
— H. Lietzmann, *An die Korinther* (Tübingen, 1909).
— P. Bachmann in Zahn's *Kommentar* (Leipzig, 1909).
— A. Plummer, *Critical and Exegetical Commentary on the Second Epistle of St. Paul to the Corinthians* (ICC, Edinburgh, 1915).
— H. Windisch, *Der Zweite Korintherbrief* (Göttingen, 1924).
— A. Schlatter, *Paulus Der Bote Jesu Eine Deutung Seiner Briefe an die Korinther* (Stuttgart, 1934).
— R. H. Strachan, *The Second Epistle of Paul to the Corinthians* (Moffat, London, 1935).
— E. B. Allo, *Saint Paul: Seconde Epitre Aux Corinthiens* (Paris, 2nd edn., 1956).
— F. V. Filson, *The Second Epistle to the Corinthians* (*The Interpreter's Bible*, New York, 1953).
— R. V. G. Tasker, *The Second Epistle of Paul to the Corinthians* (London and Grand Rapids, 1958).

1:1, 2 SALUTATION

1:1

Paul, an apostle of Christ Jesus through the will of God, and Timothy our brother, unto the church of God which is at Corinth, with all the saints that are in the whole of Achaia.

The proud Pharisee who as Saul of Tarsus had been a fierce opponent of the Christian Church was transformed through his conversion and divine calling into Paul the Apostle; the erstwhile persecutor now takes his stand with the persecuted followers of Christ. Various explanations have been offered of his change of name from Saul to Paul. It is first mentioned in Acts 13:9 ("Saul, who is also called Paul"), in the midst of the account of the conversion of Sergius Paulus, proconsul of Cyprus—a fact which caused Jerome to conclude that, as Scipio after his conquest of Africa had assumed the name of Africanus, so Saul adopted the name Paul (Latin: *Paulus*) as though a banner to mark the evangelical conquest of a personage as important as Sergius Paulus.[1] Augustine also, in his *Confessions*, writes that the Apostle "desired because of so notable a victory to be called Paul instead of his former name Saul".[2] A few years later, however, he expresses the opinion that Paul chose this new designation "for no other reason than because he wished to show himself *little* [3]— the very 'least of the apostles'".[4] Another possibility is that the smallness of the Apostle's physical frame led to his being called "Paul" as a sort of nickname. According to tradition, he was "a man small in size, bald-headed, bandy-legged, well built, with eyebrows meeting, rather long-nosed, full of grace—for sometimes he seemed like a man, and sometimes he had the countenance of an angel".[5] Thus to the Jew the name Paul might have suggested a ridiculous contrast between the Apostle and Saul, Israel's first king, who "from his shoulders and upward

---

[1] Jerome, Commentary on Philemon, *ad init.*
[2] Augustine, *Confessions*, VIII, 4.
[3] The Latin *paulus* means "little" or "small".
[4] Augustine, *De Spiritu et Littera*, VII.
[5] *Acts of Paul and Thecla*, *ad init.*

was higher than any of the people" (I Sam. 9:2); and the once proud Pharisee might well in his new-found humility have welcomed this derogatory sobriquet as fitting to one who saw himself as chief of sinners (I Tim. 1:15) and "less than the least of all saints" (Eph. 3:8). It may be that in any case the Greek form of the Hebrew name was considered objectionable because it was identical with the adjective meaning "waddling" or "effeminate".[6] But, whatever value there may be in these conjectures, it was customary for Roman citizens to bear a Roman name in addition to one of their own nationality, and there is no hint in the New Testament that the name Paul was ever regarded as uncomplimentary; after all, *Paulus* was the cognomen of the distinguished Roman family of Aemilius.

Yet though in himself he is nothing, Paul is a divinely appointed emissary—for such is the significance of the term *apostle* by which he designates himself. Thus, without a moment of delay, he produces his authority and indeed sets the tone for the whole epistle, which is in the main a vindication of his apostleship. Had he not, like the other apostles, encountered the risen Christ, even though at a time subsequent to the ascension (I Cor. 15:8), and been chosen and commissioned by Him to bear His name before the world (Acts 9:15)? In himself, as creature and as sinner, he has no right whatever to utter one single word on God's behalf; but as apostle, called by God's grace and charged with God's message (cf. Gal. 1:15f.; I Tim. 1:12ff.; I Cor. 1:27ff.), he not only may but must speak with the very authority of God Himself. Paul's apostleship, moreover, is not something vague and mystically ill-defined. It is inseparably and specifically associated with the person and work of Christ Jesus, Himself the unique Apostle sent from heaven (Heb. 3:1; Jn. 20:21, Greek)—with Him who is *the Christ*, God's "Anointed One", in whom all the hopes and promises of the Old Testament receive their perfect fulfilment (cf. v. 20 of this chapter), and who is *Jesus*, God in action saving His people from their sins (cf. 5:19; Mt. 1:21). Christ Jesus is his Saviour, his Master, and his Message.

Further, Paul's apostleship is not something derived from man: it has resulted from the effective operation of the Divine will. And not only Paul the Apostle but every single Christian owes

---

[6] Σαῦλος.

2

his status and calling in Christ entirely to the will of God. The new birth, as the writer of the Fourth Gospel declares, is "not of blood, nor of the will of the flesh, nor of the will of man, but of God" (Jn. 1:13; cf. Eph. 2:8). But apostleship is something more than the new life in Christ which is common to all believers, and it surpasses the level of a mere ministerial function within the Church. The apostolate, as K. H. Rengstorf says, "is not an office created by the community or a synonym for its leaders, but an appointment of Jesus creating the Church".[7] It is upon the foundation of the apostles and prophets (who are the apostles of the Old Testament, similarly appointed by the sole and sovereign will of God[8]) that the holy temple of Christ's Church is built (Eph. 2:20ff.). In accordance with the eternal purposes of God, Paul formed a vital part of this sacred foundation, not, however, in virtue of innate ability or even Christian zeal, but only in virtue of the apostleship entrusted to him.

Paul associates Timothy with himself in the opening greeting of this epistle, as he does also when writing to other churches.[9] But it would be a mistake to conclude that this association extends either to Paul's apostleship or to the authorship of the letter. Paul's epistles were written in the authority of his own received apostleship; and this he could not share with another. Indeed the distinction between Paul and Timothy in this respect is marked by the fact that, while the former introduces himself as "an apostle of Christ Jesus", the latter is described simply as "the brother".[10] The use of the definite article in this designation indicates that Timothy is well known to the Corinthians (cf. v. 19); hence the sense is rightly given in our English version by rendering it "our brother", that is, "our fellow-Christian". So far as Paul is concerned, however, Timothy is not only his brother in the faith, but he is also his son, for the Apostle had been the instrument in God's hands of his conversion (cf. I Cor. 4:17; I Tim. 1:2; II Tim. 1:2). Consequently the closest bonds of

---

[7] K. H. Rengstorf, *Apostleship* (No. VI in the series *Bible Key Words* from Kittel TWNT, London, 1952), p. 29.

[8] Cf., e.g., the striking parallel between Paul (Gal. 1:15) and Jeremiah (Jer. 1:5).

[9] See I Thess. 1:1, II Thess. 1:1, Phil. 1:1, Col. 1:1, Philem. 1; and cf. Rom. 16:21 where Timothy is included in the final salutation.

[10] Ὁ ἀδελφός.

affection and spiritual understanding united them, and they delighted to labour together in the cause of the Gospel.

The term "brother" was in fact currently employed in pagan cults.[11] But Christian brotherhood involves something far more than a confraternity of initiates, for its very heart and essence is the objective mystical fact of oneness with and in Christ, who is the unique Son of God. The basis of Christian brotherhood is identification with the Redeemer, which means incorporation into His Sonship. Having received the Spirit of adoption and being one in Him who is the everlasting Son and Heir, believers participate also in His eternal Sonship and heritage (cf. Rom. 8:14ff.; Gal. 3:28); and accordingly they are brethren in the profoundest possible sense.

The epistle is addressed to "the church of God which is at Corinth". The Church [12] may be defined as "that group of human beings which is called out of the world by God".[13] The Corinthian church is indeed *localized*, but it would do less than justice to scriptural reality to envisage it as isolated and fragmentary in character. The Holy Spirit is not fragmented, but dwells in fulness equally in the individual believer as in the Church as a whole. The church at Corinth is none the less *the* church and also the church *of God*. It is at Corinth but not of Corinth; nor is it the church of an apostle or a sect: for it is *God's* Church, not man's. God has called it into being; God sustains and sanctifies it; and God it is who will bring it to ultimate glory. In the designation of our text K. L. Schmidt finds strong support for "the contention that the Church is not a great community made up of an accumulation of small communities, but is truly present in its wholeness in every company of believers, however small.... When it is said that in such a gathering anyone is despised (I Cor. 6:4), that people come together (I Cor. 11:18; cf. 14:23 and Acts 14:27), that women must keep silence (I Cor. 14:34), or that it must not be burdened (I Tim. 5:16),

---

[11] See A. Deissmann, *Bible Studies* (Edinburgh, 1909), pp. 87f.

[12] Ἐκκλησία—root: ἐκ-καλέω, to call out.

[13] K. L. Schmidt, *The Church* (No. II in the series *Bible Key Words* from Kittel TWNT, London, 1950), p. 58. Schmidt, however, inclines to the opinion that the term ἐκκλησία should be understood "even without any conscious emphasis on the preposition, like the original qᵉhal Yahwe, in which no preposition is expressed".

it is not the local congregation, but the Church as a whole that is in view".[14]

But the letter is addressed also to "all the saints that are in the whole of Achaia". Achaia here is not the small territory of classical times, but the Roman province of that name comprising the whole Peloponnesus, the greater part of Hellas proper, and the coastal islands—in other words, the whole area south of the province of Macedonia. Paul's words imply that there were Christians scattered over this area who because of their distribution were not ordinarily able to meet together for congregational worship. It must not be thought, however, that he implies that they were therefore outside of the Church of God. On the contrary, they are "saints", that is, "holy ones",[15] persons who know the regenerating and sanctifying power of the Holy Spirit, and it is precisely of such that the Church of God is composed. All who are Christ's are holy, not in themselves—for the inconsistencies and deficiencies of their daily life and witness remove any ground for such presumption—but in Christ, the Holy One of God, in whom they have been chosen and with whom they have become one. Christ has been made their sanctification (I Cor. 1:30). Here the important distinction must be observed between what they are in Christ by the free grace of God and what they are in themselves. In the practical realm of everyday life the Christian should experience the steady growth in Christlikeness which is a mark of the healthy child of God (cf. Eph. 4:15). What is his potentially and really in Christ should become his more and more experimentally in the daily walk—Christ increasing, he decreasing (Jn. 3:30). In fine, as the Christian pursues his earthly pilgrimage the state of his sanctification (which is the measure of his Christlikeness) should ever advance towards the state of his justification (which, being complete from the moment of conversion, is the measure of the perfection of Christ). But it is only in the state of glorification, in the new heavens and the new earth, that sanctification and justification will at last become one in the completeness of Him who fills all in all.

This opening verse, then, indicates clearly enough the elevated concept which the Apostle entertained of the Christian Church. Despite all the reprehensible excesses and aberrations which had

---

[14] K. L. Schmidt, *op. cit.*, p. 10.
[15] Ἅγιοι.

been tolerated within their ranks, he does not hesitate to call the Corinthian Christians by the name of saints and to assign to them the noble title of Church of God. The divine act in choosing and calling them cannot be undone by human frailty or reversed by satanic forces at work within the very ranks of the believers. "What ground did Paul have for recognizing the Church of Corinth?" asks Calvin; and answers as follows: "Just this, that he discerned among them the doctrine of the Gospel, Baptism, and the Lord's Supper, the tokens by which the Church ought to be judged. For although some had begun to have doubts concerning the resurrection, yet since that error had not spread through the whole body the name and genuineness of the Church are not on that account forfeited. Although some faults had crept into the administration of the Supper, and discipline and probity had largely collapsed; although through contempt of the simplicity of the Gospel they had given themselves up to ostentation and arrogance, and because of the ambition of their ministers were rent into various parties; yet since they retained fundamental doctrine, since the one God was adored among them and invoked in the name of Christ, and since they placed the confidence of their salvation in Christ and had a ministry that was not altogether corrupted, the Church still continued to exist there. Accordingly, wherever the worship of God remains intact and that fundamental doctrine of which I have spoken persists, there we should conclude without hesitation that the Church exists".[16]

1 : 2

Grace to you and peace from God our Father and the Lord Jesus Christ.

In this typically Pauline salutation (cf. the salutations in all his other epistles, with the exception of I and II Timothy) God is set before the Corinthians as the sole true source of grace and peace. As Charles Hodge says, "grace and peace, the favour of God and its fruits, comprehend all the benefits of redemption". This is no mere perfunctory combination of the Greek "greetings" or "good wishes" and the Oriental "salaam".[17] The Apostle is

---

[16] Calvin, Commentary on I Corinthians, *sub* 1:2.

[17] "The favourite Pauline greeting χάρις καὶ εἰρήνη may have been suggested by the union of the ordinary Greek and Hebrew forms of salutation,

dealing with souls, not ciphers, and the superficial formalities of polite society would have been uncongenial to himself and out of place in a letter of spiritual counsel. Not, of course, that Paul is at all uncouth or impolite: these introductory verses show the opposite to be true. But one of the constant joys of the Christian life is the discovery that even common every-day things are transformed by the Master's touch. So here, the unthinking formality of a worldly greeting is transformed into the deeply significant desire of the Apostle that those to whom he is writing may be enriched by those special blessings which God bestows through Christ Jesus.

It should be noticed that the deity of Jesus Christ is plainly implied by the language of this verse. In the first place, the Lord Jesus Christ is united with God our Father as the source of grace and peace, which shows Him to be one with the Father in deity and dignity. This could not be so were He a created entity and not the co-eternal and consubstantial Son.[18] And in the second place, Jesus Christ is distinguished by the title "Lord" (*Kyrios*),[19] the very term which is used in the Septuagint version of the Old Testament to translate the sacred four-letter name of God (*Yahweh*).[20] In the judgment of Moulton and Milligan, Paul's usage of this title "was doubtless primarily influenced by the LXX", and his insistence upon the name *Kyrios* "which is above every name" (Phil. 2:9, 11) is seen as "a protest against the worship of the 'gods many and lords many' [21] (I Cor. 8:5), with which Christianity found itself confronted".[22]

---

but both are deepened and spiritualized, χαίρειν (cf. Acts 15:23, 23:26, Jas. 1:1) giving place to χάρις, and εἰρήνη (cf. Ezra 4:17, Dan. 4:1) pointing to the harmony restored between God and man (cf. Jn. 14:27)": Moulton and Milligan, *The Vocabulary of the Greek Testament* (London, 1949), p. 685.

[18] The phrase ἀπὸ θεοῦ πατρὸς ἡμῶν καὶ Κυρίου Ἰησοῦ Χριστοῦ could also be rendered: "from God, the Father of us and of the Lord Jesus Christ", but the most natural and, in view of the context, only satisfactory way of reading the Greek is reflected in our English version. In any case, it would have been superfluous for Paul to have spoken of God as the Father of our Lord Jesus Christ here as he is about to do so in the very next sentence (v. 3).

[19] Κύριος.

[20] יהוה.

[21] Θεοὶ πολλοὶ καὶ κύριοι πολλοί.

[22] Moulton and Milligan, *op. cit.*, p. 366. "Soon after the Resurrection", says J. H. Bernard, "the title began to imply that larger and deeper meaning of ὁ κύριος as the representative of יְהֹוָה which is frequent in Paul and is

7

Rudolf Bultmann, however, does not concur with this judgment. "It is highly improbable", he says, "that the title 'Kyrios' as applied to Jesus is derived from the LXX, in which it is the usual translation for Yahweh ... Rather, the term Kyrios used of Christ is derived from the religious terminology of Hellenism, more specifically from that of oriental Hellenism, in which Kyrios was the Greek translation of typical terms in various languages which denoted the deity as 'Lord'." He maintains that "this origin of the Kyrios-title comes clearly into view in the antithesis of 'one Lord Jesus Christ' to the 'many lords' in I Cor. 8:5f." [23]

But it may well be that the application of the title Kyrios to Christ should be explained as the result of the twofold influence of the Septuagint on the one hand and Hellenistic religion on the other. It is by no means necessary that the one should be viewed as excluding the other. Be that as it may, however, it is agreed that in the apostolic Church the title "Lord" as assigned to Christ implies His deity. Thus the prophecy of Isa. 40:3 is fulfilled in the ministry of John the Baptist whose voice cries in the wilderness, "Make ye ready the way of the Lord" (Mk. 1:3). Christ Himself foretells that in the day of final judgment many will vainly address Him as "Lord, Lord" (Mt. 7:21ff.). Thomas calls the risen Saviour "My Lord and my God" (Jn. 20:28). The identical title is used of God the Father (e.g. Lk. 2:26; Mt. 11:25; I Tim. 6:15). Christ, indeed, is Lord of all (Acts 10:36; Rom. 10:12) and King of kings and Lord of lords (Rev. 19:16; 17:14); and confession of Him as Lord is essential to salvation (Rom. 10:9; I Cor. 12:3; Phil. 2:11).[24] These and many other references leave no room for doubt concerning the fundamental significance of the title "Lord" when used in conjunction with the name of Jesus Christ.

---

found in the Acts (2:36, 9:11). That 'Jesus is Lord' (I Cor. 12:3; cf. Phil. 2:11) has become the central thought of the Christian profession; but now the predicate means more than 'Master', for it expresses the doctrine of the Incarnation. Perhaps we may say that the passage from the lower to the higher sense begins with the citation of Ps. 110:1 by the Master Himself (Mk. 12:36)": *Commentary on the Gospel according to St. John* (ICC. Edinburgh, 1928), Vol. I, pp. 132f.

[23] R. Bultmann, *Theology of the New Testament* (London, 1952), Vol. I, p. 124.

[24] For extensive references see Arndt and Gingrich, *Greek-English Lexicon of the New Testament and other Early Christian Literature* (Cambridge, 1957), sub κύριος. See also commentary on 4:5 below.

8

1:3–11 THANKSGIVING FOR COMFORT
IN AFFLICTION

1 : 3, 4

> Blessed be the God and Father of our Lord Jesus Christ, the
> Father of mercies and God of all comfort; who comforteth
> us in all our affliction, that we may be able to comfort them
> that are in any affliction, through the comfort wherewith we
> ourselves are comforted of God.

The import of this section, verses 3 to 11, seems to have been
missed by many commentators. It is no mere amiable preamble
intended only to cushion the sterner matters which the Apostle
is shortly to broach. On the contrary, it is very much of a piece
with the major theme of the opening portion of this epistle,
namely, Paul's vindication of his own integrity. Having raised
their hopes of a visit from himself (see I Cor. 16:5ff.), he had
failed to come to them, with the result that some in Corinth had
permitted themselves to listen to insinuations that he had treated
them with fickleness (v. 17). A little later on (v. 23) he will tell
them that the main reason why he forbore to come was that he
might spare them. But there was another good reason, stated
indirectly and with remarkable tenderness in this present passage:
he had suffered such severe affliction in Asia that he had even
despaired of life. An incapacitating experience of this kind
explained much, and called for sympathy rather than censure.
Nor was there cause for anyone at Corinth to whisper that Paul's
affliction was a judgment of God upon him because he had
proved untrustworthy; for God, so far from frowning on him,
had graciously delivered him and granted him unfailing comfort
and consolation through it all. Anyone who is preparing to find
fault, says Chrysostom, "cannot for shame drag to the bar one
who is thanking God for deliverance from such great calamities,
and bid him clear himself of loitering". Chrysostom also gives
it as his opinion that, while the leading object of this introduction
is to excuse himself for his delay, Paul is at the same time by
implication censuring the false apostles who had invaded Corinth
(cf. 11:13ff.), "those vain boasters who sat at home and lived in
luxury".

9

Paul's use of the expression "the God and Father of our Lord Jesus Christ" may seem surprising [1]; but it is not an isolated expression, for it can be matched elsewhere in the writings both of Paul and of others of the Apostles (cf. 11:31; Eph. 1:3, 17, Rom. 15:6; I Pet. 1:3; Rev. 1:6; Jn. 20:17). In view of the deity of the Son, how is it possible to speak of the God of our Lord Jesus Christ? The answer to this problem is to be found in the mediatorial office of Christ. God is not the God of the Son as God, but His Father. As Mediator, however, the Son humbled Himself and in the incarnation assumed our human nature. As Mediator He is our Lord Jesus Christ, God's anointed servant, the divine Son suffering as Man for man, and thereby bridging the gulf between man and God. In partaking of our nature the Mediator placed Himself in a position of dependence on God, a dependence of which prayer was a natural and necessary expression (cf. Jn. 17, etc.). On the cross He could appropriate to Himself the psalmist's cry of dereliction: "My God, my God, why hast Thou forsaken me?" (Mk. 15:34). To Him the prophetic words of Psalm 40: "Lo, I come to do thy will, O God", were rightly applied (Heb. 10:7). And after His resurrection it is the Mediator in His theanthropic person, still man as well as God, who sends Mary Magdalene to the disciples with the message: "I ascend unto my Father and your Father, and my God and your God" (Jn. 20:17). As Hodge says,[2] "our Lord had a dependent nature to which God stood in the relation of God, and a divine nature to which He stood in the relation of Father, and therefore to the complex person Jesus Christ God bore the relation of both God and Father".

God is not only *our* Father (v. 2), but the Father of our Lord Jesus Christ; indeed, in the economy of redemption He is *our* Father solely because He is the Father of our Lord Jesus Christ. Were He not the latter, He would not be the former, for in scriptural thought all divine sonship is vested in the one person

---

[1] Ὁ θεὸς καὶ πατὴρ τοῦ Κυρίου ἡμῶν Ἰησοῦ Χριστοῦ could be rendered, as in AV, "God, even the Father of our Lord Jesus Christ"; cf. Col. 1:3, where, however, there is no καί: "God the Father of our Lord Jesus Christ". But it is more natural to render καί as "and" here, as in fact AV does when the expression occurs elsewhere (cf. 11:31; Mk. 15:34; Jn. 20:17; Eph. 1:3, 17; I Pet. 1:3; Rev. 1:6), with the exception of Rom. 15:6.

[2] Commenting on 11:31.

10

of Jesus Christ, the eternal Son of God. Christians, being united to Christ through faith, are one with Him in sonship also; their standing and acceptance before God are *in Christ* alone, as the New Testament makes abundantly clear, and especially Paul's writings. No man comes to the Father but by Him (Jn. 14:6). "God the Father is indeed Creator", says P. T. Forsyth, "but it is not as Creator that He is Father.... We are sons by an election rather than by a creation. We are sons not by heredity but by adoption; not by right but by redemption.... We are sons 'begotten in the Gospel'. God is, directly, the Father of Christ alone. He is our Father only in Christ. God has but one Son; the many sons are sons in Him; and He is Son in none".[3]

But our God is also "the Father of mercies" or pityings:[4] from Him loving compassions flow to His children when they are being tested by affliction. Paul may have had in mind the words of Ps. 103:13f.: "Like as a father pitieth his children, so Jehovah pitieth them that fear him; for he knoweth our frame, he remembereth that we are dust". And, further, this God of ours is "the God of all comfort", that is, the divine fount of all consolation to His people—the "all" both excluding any other source of comfort and also emphasizing the complete adequacy of that comfort for every circumstance that may arise (cf. Phil. 4:19). No suffering, however severe, can separate the believer from the tender care and compassion of his Heavenly Father. On the contrary, it is precisely in the extremity of the believer's weakness that the supreme power and grace of Almighty God are magnified —and this is, indeed, a theme which is central to the thought of our epistle. Thus here, in this opening passage, Paul blesses the Father above for the precious consolations received in the midst of affliction.

The word "comfort", whether as a noun or a verb, occurs no less than ten times in verses 3 to 7, building up in a characteristically Pauline manner a compelling impression of the comfort which God bestows upon His children. Paul employs the term here in its basic (Greek) sense of standing beside a person to encourage him when he is undergoing severe testing.[5] This work

---

[3] P. T. Forsyth, *Positive Preaching and the Modern Mind* (London, 1907), p. 215.

[4] Οἰκτιρμοί. The expression ʽΟ πατὴρ τῶν οἰκτιρμῶν is probably influenced by the Semitic form of thought, = "the compassionate Father".

[5] Παρα+καλέω.

of encouragement is indeed a work of the blessed Trinity: as Paraclete,[6] the Father comforts and consoles us; as Paraclete, the Holy Spirit strengthens and guides us (Jn. 14:16, 26; 15:26; 16:7—Greek); and as Paraclete, Jesus Christ the righteous is our Advocate with the Father and our Helper in the hour of temptation (I Jn. 2:1; Heb. 2:18—Greek). The present tense of the verb shows that this God of ours comforts us constantly and unfailingly, not spasmodically and intermittently; and He does so in *all* our affliction, not just in certain kinds of affliction. If any one person knew the experimental proof of this great assurance it was the Apostle Paul, who later in this same epistle justly speaks of himself in comparison with others as "in labors more abundantly, in prisons more abundantly, in stripes above measure, in deaths oft" (11:23). And the comfort God gives enables the Christian not only to *endure*, but even to *rejoice* "in weaknesses, in injuries, in necessities, in persecutions, in distresses, for Christ's sake" (12:10), so dynamic and vitalizing is its effect.

Nor is the comfort received from God intended to terminate in the recipient: it has a further purpose, namely, to fit the Christian for the God-like ministry of comforting and encouraging others, whatever the affliction they may be suffering.[7] Those who are continually experiencing comfort from God are particularly fitted to minister to others who stand in need of comfort. This is one of the principles of Christian service: the Christian receives in order that he may pass on that which he has received; he is blessed so that he may be a blessing to others. Accordingly, it is Paul's wish to be a channel of comfort to the Corinthians (v. 6). Whether the latter were in need of comfort because of some specific affliction which they had been called upon to endure is not clear. Plummer suggests that "Paul is here thinking of the affliction which the Corinthians had recently been experiencing

---

6 The title *Paraclete (παράκλητος)* is not as such used of the Father in the New Testament, but its application to the Father is fully justified by Paul's terminology here, for ὁ παρακαλῶν = "the Comforter", "the One who constantly comforts"—a timeless present participle; cf. ὁ σπείρων, "the sower" (Mt. 13:3) and see note on τῷ ἐγείροντι, v. 9, below.

7 "Who comforteth us in all our affliction *(ἐπὶ πάσῃ τῇ θλίψει ἡμῶν)*, that we may be able to comfort them that are in any affliction *(ἐν πάσῃ θλίψει)*": the two uses of πᾶς, (i) with the article and (ii) without the article, indicate different shades of meaning, the former signifying "the whole of" and the latter "every kind of".

in their agony of self-reproach and remorse when the severe letter of the Apostle and the remonstrances of Titus, who had brought the letter to them, had convinced them that they had treated their spiritual father abominably in listening to the misrepresentations and slanders of the Judaizing teachers and in rebelling against him". What is certain, however, is that he wishes them to share with him in all the blessings and consolations which flow from God. However deplorable their attitude to him may have been, he wants them to be assured that his heart is enlarged with love toward them (6:11).

1:5

For as the sufferings of Christ abound unto us, even so our comfort also aboundeth through Christ.

No matter how great the sufferings a Christian is called upon to endure, they are matched, and more than matched (cf. 4:17), by the comfort which God bestows. The comfort is never outweighed by the suffering. But what does Paul mean here when he speaks of the *sufferings of Christ* abounding to him? He does not mean suffering merely *for* Christ, though this is an important aspect of his discipleship (cf. Mt. 5:11; Acts 9:16, etc.). Far less does he mean that Christ's sufferings in their redemptive efficacy are in any sense extended or amplified in those of the Church. Christ's work of redemption is unique, complete, once-for-all; on its absolute perfection depend the repentant sinner's acceptance with God and the believer's eternal security. For the Christian, however, as Paul explains elsewhere, there is such a thing as the fellowship of Christ's sufferings (Phil. 3:10; cf. I Pet. 4:13), that is, a sharing or partnership with Christ in suffering. To follow Christ is to follow Him into suffering. In this also the disciple must expect to be identified with the Master. Hence our Lord's admonition: "Remember the word that I said unto you, A servant is not greater than his lord. If they persecuted me, they will also persecute you" (Jn. 15:20). Those who are one with Christ must be prepared to drink His cup (Mt. 20:23). As with Him suffering was the prelude to glory, so also those who wish to share in His glory must first be willing to share in His sufferings (cf. Rom. 8:17f.; Acts 14:22; II Tim. 2:12).

13

It is important to observe that the Apostle is speaking here of the sufferings *of Christ*, and not sufferings in general. Suffering which is the consequence of disobedience and selfishness has no blessing in it and cannot possibly be described as "of Christ". Likewise the compensating comfort abounds only *through Christ*. Christ is the beginning, the centre, and the end of all things to the Christian. Apart from Him, suffering leads to despair, not consolation. But Christ, let it be remembered, is no longer suffering in humiliation, for He is now exalted in glory. If we are called to fellowship in the sufferings of the Christ of humiliation, it is the Christ of glory who mediates an abundance of comfort to us—one and the same Christ. Allo follows Bachmann in pointing out that to separate the "spiritual" and glorified Christ from the "historic" Christ who suffered is anti-Pauline.[8]

1:6

> But whether we are afflicted, it is for your comfort and salvation; or whether we are comforted, it is for your comfort, which worketh in the patient enduring of the same sufferings which we also suffer.

Not only is the believer bound to Christ, but he is also bound, in Christ, to every other believer. He cannot act as an isolated individualist, for he is an integral member of an organic whole. If one member suffers, all the members of the body suffer with it —a truth of which it had been necessary for Paul to remind the Corinthians in an earlier letter (I Cor. 12:26ff.). Lack of sympathy on their part betrayed an unspiritual insensitivity; but, more than that, it betrayed a failure to appreciate that Paul's afflictions had in a special sense been endured *on their behalf*— "for your comfort and salvation". Not, again, that the Apostle intended them to understand that his afflictions on their behalf were in any sense redemptive: his meaning is that his sufferings were endured in the course of bringing them the Gospel, the Good News which to every believing heart conveys the supreme

---

[8] Cf. P. T. Forsyth: "To divide up the personality, and detach the heavenly Christ from the earthly Jesus, is not a feat of criticism so much as a failure of religion, or an intellectual freak and a confession of unfaith"—*The Person and Place of Jesus Christ* (London, 1909), p. 177. See also commentary below on 4:10.

comfort of sins forgiven and eternal salvation. As their messenger of salvation he had passed through the severest affliction. To the sufferings of their own Apostle, borne for their sakes, they should have been particularly sensitive; and when he received comfort in his afflictions they themselves should have been comforted to a special degree. How deeply they should have felt their Apostle's sufferings to be their sufferings! How zealously they should have emulated his selflessness in propagating at all costs this same message of salvation! But the reciprocity of loyalty and mutual responsiveness which should exist between every faithful pastor and his flock was deficient in their case.

1:7

And our hope for you is stedfast; knowing that, as ye are partakers of the sufferings, so also are ye of the comfort.

Yet, despite the deficiency of their love and loyalty, Paul regards them with an unshakeable hope. How could he do otherwise, seeing that the work being performed in their midst, and which had already brought about a marvellous change in them, was a work of God, not of man, a work of the Gospel of Jesus Christ, not of human philosophy? If it is *God's* work it cannot fail; it will be brought to completion (cf. Phil. 1:6). In the service of Christ, therefore, there may be disappointments, but there cannot be despair; there may be conflicts, but never doubt; there may be afflictions, but never without comfort. Our epistle, indeed, is pervaded by this spirit of a faith which abides serene and stedfast no matter how much the outward circumstances of life may tempt to the shadow of distrust. Paul is assured that, though a number of the Corinthian Christians have been misled by the malicious slanders of false apostles who have been seeking to usurp his authority, yet the root of the matter is within them. He has confidence that the appeal which this epistle constitutes will call forth a true and loving response, as from those who are his own children in the Gospel (cf. 6:11f.; 7:2, 16; 8:8, 24). Therefore, knowing [9] them to be, at heart, sharers both of his

---

[9] *Καὶ ἡ ἐλπὶς ἡμῶν βεβαία ὑπὲρ ὑμῶν· εἰδότες κτλ.* — Strictly speaking, the participle should have been in the genitive plural *(εἰδότων)*, agreeing with the *ἡμῶν* of the preceding clause. But it would then more properly have been construed with the immediately antecedent *ὑμῶν*. The nominative plural is

sufferings and of his comfort, he anticipates their fellow-feeling with him as he is about to mention an exceptionally severe affliction which he suffered in Asia and the goodness of God in delivering him from it.

1:8

For we would not have you ignorant, brethren, concerning our affliction which befell us in Asia, that we were weighed down exceedingly, beyond our power, insomuch that we despaired even of life.

PAUL'S AFFLICTION IN ASIA

This epistle presents the modern reader with a number of problems to which, because of the imprecise nature of the information available, no certain solution can be discovered; and it is at this point that we are confronted with the first of these questions. What exactly was the affliction that overtook Paul in Asia? Conjectures have been, and no doubt will continue to be, numerous and conflicting. Whether they are helpful in the task of exegesis is debatable; but it can hardly be maintained that they are illegitimate. In any case, we are bound to examine such information as the text affords, and in doing so it will not be without interest to draw attention to some of the solutions which have been proposed at different times by a variety of scholars.

There are, to begin with, certain positive conclusions which may be put forward:

(i) The Corinthian Christians were ignorant not of the character, but of the *intensity* of Paul's affliction. Hence Paul writes to tell them not *what* it was, but *how* it had oppressed him beyond endurance.

(ii) It occurred after the writing of I Corinthians; otherwise it would have been mentioned in the earlier epistle. And this implies that it had happened within recent months.

---

no doubt influenced by those implied in the verbs θλιβόμεθα, παρακαλούμεθα, and πάσχομεν of the previous verse. The break is so slight that it reads not unnaturally, and in addition it serves, whether intentionally or not, to remove any ambiguity, i.e. as to whether ἡμεῖς or ὑμεῖς is implied. It should probably not be classified as an absolute participle, standing here for an indicative, though such usage is not foreign to this epistle; see note below on θλιβόμενοι, 7:5.

(iii)   It came upon him *in Asia*, which indicates that its occurrence was prior to his crossing from Troas to Macedonia (where II Corinthians was written) in order to await the arrival from Corinth of Titus (2:12f.).   The somewhat general designation "in Asia" would further seem to imply that it was unnecessary for Paul to be more precise about the locality, as this was already known to the Corinthians.

(iv)   It was an affliction of such severity that, apart from divine intervention, he could not hope to survive it.

(v)   It is classified as among "the sufferings of Christ" which abounded to Paul (v. 5).

The earliest explanation of this affliction that we possess is found in Tertullian, who connects it with an experience of fighting with wild beasts at Ephesus.[10]   This, however, rests upon a literal interpretation, which is strongly disputed, of I Cor. 15:32. Calvin, Paley, Neander, Olshausen, and others, identify the affliction with the uproar stirred up against the Apostle by Demetrius the silversmith in Ephesus (Acts 19:23ff.).   This event, however, probably took place prior to the writing of I Corinthians (as also did Paul's fighting with wild beasts at Ephesus, if an historical occurrence), and, besides, Luke gives no indication in his account that Paul's life was then in danger.   Plummer suggests that "there may easily have been a much worse outbreak at Ephesus somewhat later, and even a plot to kill St Paul", reminding us that in Ephesus he had "many adversaries" (I Cor. 16:9). Hodge thinks it probable that there is a more general allusion to "trials of different kinds, and especially to plots and attempts against his life"; while Lietzmann and others envisage a succession of persecutions in Asia, touched off by the Ephesian uproar. Windisch entertains the possibility of an attempt to lynch the Apostle, a view with which Strachan seems disposed to concur. Hofmann is one of those who conjecture an experience of shipwreck followed by a night and a day in the deep (see 11:25); but it is difficult to understand how that could be described as having taken place *in Asia*.   Stanley and Rendall suppose that it may have been agonizing anxiety concerning the state of the Church at Corinth which incapacitated the Apostle, rather than outward persecution (see 2:13; 7:5).   Alford concludes that it

---

[10]   Tertullian, *De Resurrectione Carnis*, XLVIII.

17

was a deadly sickness, and a similar opinion is held by Lightfoot [11] and Allo who associate the affliction with the "thorn in the flesh" referred to in 12:7. To link 1:8 with 12:7 is certainly an attractive proposal, but whichever way one turns it is impossible to escape from the realm of speculation. Is there justification for classifying physical malady or internal anguish among "the sufferings of Christ"? On the other hand, if, as Allo and others affirm, the affliction in question was lasting or recurrent in its effect (see commentary below on vv. 9 and 10), the reference can hardly be to some particular external persecution, especially as, wherever he went, it was the Apostle's lot frequently to pass through severe persecutions. As things are, we must be content to remain ignorant regarding the precise nature of the affliction mentioned here, remembering, as Denney remarks, that "it is elsewhere than in its accidental circumstances that the interest of the transaction lies for the writer and for us".

Whatever it may be that Paul is referring to, it was an experience that weighed him down to excess [12] and beyond the normal power of endurance,[13] so much so that he could see no possibility of survival.[14] And this terrible affliction, though experienced in Asia, was in some way endured on behalf of the Corinthians (v. 6). It was of a piece with his sufferings as their chosen Apostle. This was something they had failed to appreciate because of the narrow-heartedness induced by the false apostles in their midst. When this letter was read in Corinth there must have been some who were thoroughly shamefaced!

1 : 9, 10

Yea, we ourselves have had the sentence of death within ourselves, that we should not trust in ourselves, but in God who raiseth the dead: who delivered us out of so great a death, and will deliver: on whom we have set our hope that he will also still deliver us.

Paul was conscious within himself that he was a man upon

---

[11] J. B. Lightfoot, *Epistle to the Galatians* (London, 1865), p. 190.

[12] *Καθ' ὑπερβολήν.*

[13] *Ὑπὲρ δύναμιν.* Note the effect produced by the double use of *ὑπέρ.*

[14] *Ὥστε ἐξαπορηθῆναι ἡμᾶς καὶ τοῦ ζῆν.* The verb *ἀπορέω* means "to be in doubt"; *ἐξαπορέω* is an intensive compound with the sense of "to be utterly at a loss". Cf. 4:8, *ἀπορούμενοι, ἀλλ' οὐκ ἐξαπορούμενοι,* "perplexed,

18

whom, humanly speaking, sentence of death had been passed.[15] The question arises as to whether this consciousness related only to what he had experienced in Asia, or whether it was from then on continuous. Does he mean, "I had the death-verdict then in Asia", or, "I not only had it then but still have it now within myself"?[16] If the former, the reference may be to a particular persecution or misfortune which, but for the divine deliverance, would have proved fatal—similar, perhaps, to the savage violence of the mob at Lystra, when it was thought that he had been stoned

---

yet not unto despair"—which does not contradict what Paul says here. There he is speaking of the problems which assail him; here of the apparent inevitability of death.

[15] Ἀπόκριμα is a rare word, found only here in biblical Greek. Elsewhere it occurs only in Polybius (*Excerpta Vaticana*, XII, 26b), in Josephus (*Antiq.*, XIV, x, 6), and in inscriptions. Its meaning seems to be an official decision or verdict in response to an inquiry or deputation, rather than a judicial sentence. But the line of separation between the two ideas is slender. See Arndt and Gingrich, Moulton and Milligan, and Deissmann, *Bible Studies*, p. 257.

[16] The question turns on the interpretation of ἐσχήκαμεν. Allo is emphatic that it "should be taken in the full force of the perfect, of a past act which has not been cancelled, and the consequences of which still continue, and not in a weakened aoristic sense". This understanding of the term lends support to his view that Paul's affliction in Asia should be identified with the incidence of his "thorn in the flesh" and was a form of recurrent fever, every attack of which threatened to be fatal (see commentary below on 12:7). Plummer, however, while suggesting that the perfect here (and in 2:13) may be explained on the grounds of a present vivid recollection of a past experience, draws attention to a "purely aoristic use of the perfect", especially in late Greek, and points out that aorist and perfect are found in combination in the Apocalypse (3:3; 5:7; 8:5; 9:17). J. H. Moulton (*Grammar of New Testament Greek*, Vol. I, Edinburgh, 1908, pp. 144f.) classifies ἐσχήκαμεν here, ἔσχηκα in 2:13, and ἔσχηκεν in 7:5, among the "genuinely aoristic perfects" to be found in the New Testament, remarking that he can see "an excellent reason why ἔσχηκα should have been used as an aorist". "There is no Greek for *possessed*, the constative aorist", he explains, "since ἔσχον is almost (if not quite) exclusively used for the ingressive *got, received*. Ἔσχον occurs only 20 times in the NT, which is about 3 per cent of the whole record of ἔχω. There is not one place where ἔσχον *must* be constative . . . The similarity of ἔσχηκα to the aorists ἔθηκα and ἀφῆκα gave a clear opening for its appropriation to this purpose, and the translation 'possessed' will generally suit the case". Allo's theory concerning the implication of ἐσχήκαμεν here may, of course, be correct; but he is over-violent when he insists that "the perfect (ἐσχήκαμεν) indicates an act which continues all the time" and that "it is nothing but an evasion (for those who are unwilling to admit that the reference is to an illness) to give it the far from usual aoristic sense of an event entirely past".

to death (Acts 14:19). If the latter, the reference may be, as Allo maintains, to the onset of a chronic and extremely malignant illness, the recurring spasms of which were a persistent reminder of the sentence of death within himself. If the former, his confident hope of future deliverance relates to persecutions and misfortunes yet to be endured; if the latter, to further attacks of his illness. What is certain is that the deliverance God had granted him had been tantamount to a resurrection from the dead: it was not merely from illness or violence but from *so great a death* that he had been snatched.

His feelings must have been not unlike those of Abraham when faced with the offering up of Isaac, the very one in whom, according to God's promise, the line of future and universal blessing was to be carried forward. Paul's appointed task was not yet fulfilled, his fight not over, his course unfinished—though the day would arrive when he would be ready to be offered, knowing that the time of his departure had come and that his earthly pilgrimage was at an end (II Tim. 4:6f.). However much he may have desired to depart and be with Christ, he realized that until the apostolic work for which he had been chosen and called was completed to abide in the flesh was more needful for the sake of those to whom he had been sent (cf. Phil. 1:23f.); and so this sentence of death in Asia must have come upon him with the terrifying and shattering effect of a thunderbolt. But he learnt also to have a faith similar to that of Abraham, who accounted "that God is able to raise up, even from the dead" and who did also in a figure receive back his son from the dead (Heb. 11:17-19). The great lesson of this overwhelming affliction which had befallen him was that he (and all who are Christ's) should trust, not in self, but in God "the Raiser of the dead".[17]

This is, indeed, a theme which provides a key to the whole epistle. Is Paul assailed by anguish of spirit? It is God who always leads him in triumph in Christ (2:13f.). Do we have the treasure of divine glory in earthen vessels? It is that it may be seen that the exceeding greatness of the power is of God, and not of self (4:7ff.). Is the Apostle always delivered unto death for Jesus' sake? It is that the life also of Jesus may be manifested in his

---

[17] *Τῷ θεῷ τῷ ἐγείροντι τοὺς νεκρούς* As Plummer observes, *ἐγείροντι* is a "timeless present participle expressing a permanent attribute". See also note on *ὁ παρακαλῶν, verse 4*, above.

mortal flesh (4:10f.). Is the outward man decaying? Yet the
inward man is renewed day by day (4:16). Though our earthly
tabernacle suffer dissolution, we are to put on an eternal heavenly
habitation (5:1ff.). All things are of God, both in the work of
reconciliation which He has effected through Christ and in the
ministry of reconciliation which He has entrusted to His servants
(5:18f.). The climax is reached in the twelfth chapter where
Paul explains how through the endurance of a "thorn in the
flesh" he was taught that God's grace is all-sufficient and that
His power is made perfect in weakness (12:7ff.). This was a
principle to which even our Lord submitted in procuring our
salvation, for He was crucified through weakness, but is alive
through the power of God (13:4). It is a theme, therefore, which
points to the unity of this epistle, and which in particular links
the concluding to the opening chapters.[18]

Chrysostom makes the interesting suggestion that in these
verses Paul is reminding the Corinthians of the doctrine of the
resurrection about which he had said so much in the earlier
epistle. "Notwithstanding that the resurrection is a future event,
he shows that it happens every day; for when God raises up again
a man whose life is despaired of, and who has been brought to
the very gates of hell, He shows nothing other than a resurrection,
snatching from the very jaws of death the one who had fallen
into them". Even though it may be objected that Paul's thought
here is not primarily eschatological, yet the logic of what he says
inevitably leads to the postulation of an ultimate resurrection.
The Apostle had already written at length on the eschatological
doctrine in I Cor. 15, and he will expound a particular aspect
of it later in this present epistle (5:1ff.). In any case, the whole
doctrine is implied in the single expression "God the Raiser of
the dead".

The AV rendering: "who delivered..., and doth deliver...,
will yet deliver us", which gives the attractive tense-sequence of
past-present-future, must be rejected on the textual evidence now
available.[19] Our own version reflects the best attested reading,

---

[18] On the question of the unity of II Corinthians see *Introduction*, pp. xxiff.

[19] Instead of ῥύεται, "doth deliver" (*textus receptus*), p[46] א BC etc. read
ῥύσεται, "shall deliver", and there is really no question as to which enjoys
the stronger attestation. Despite the evidence, however, Allo prefers ῥύεται,
"regarding the other as an assimilation which slipped in—as does happen—

substituting "and will deliver" for "and doth deliver" in the middle clause. This means that we have a past followed by two futures. But it is not necessary to conclude, as Plummer does, that the second clause is "superfluous, anticipating and somewhat spoiling the next clause"; for in this setting the former has a force equivalent to that of a present. The whole may be paraphrased in the following manner: "In Asia God delivered me from so great a death, and He will continue to deliver me in my present circumstances; I am confident, moreover, that He will also still deliver me through all that lies ahead". This interpretation is confirmed by the consideration that the second future is distinguished from the first by the addition of the qualification "still": He will deliver (in the present and near future) and He will *still* deliver (in the more remote future).

1 : 11

Ye also helping together on our behalf by your supplication; that, for the gift bestowed upon us by means of many, thanks may be given by many persons on our behalf.

Though the Apostle's hope is firmly fixed on God, yet he also relies on the prayers of fellow-believers on his behalf, especially of those to whom, like the Corinthians, his ministry of the Gospel has closely linked him. Their supplications play an important role in his expectation of deliverance. Prayer is indeed a mystery, but it is stressed over and over again in the New Testament as a vital prerequisite for the release and experience of God's power. It is true that it is *God* who delivers, and that God stands in no need of human prayers before He can act on behalf of His afflicted

---

under the pen of good witnesses". Some commentators have proposed the omission of the middle clause, but this is a desperate measure and quite unwarranted. Weiss, more constructively, punctuates after ἠλπίκαμεν, giving the sense: "who delivered us out of so great a death, and he in whom we have set our hope will deliver; and he will still deliver us while you also help together by your supplication on our behalf". This requires the dropping of ὅτι after ἠλπίκαμεν; and the ὅτι is, in fact, omitted by p46BD* Origen, etc., which in our judgment is sufficient evidence to authorize its exclusion. Weiss's reading and punctuation seem to us to be quite the best, and there is the added attraction that the repeated καί is thereby permitted in both cases to act as the natural copula linking the sequence of clauses: ὃς ἐρρύσατο . . . καὶ ῥύσεται . . . καὶ ἔτι ῥύσεται.

servants. Yet there is the manward as well as the Godward aspect of such deliverance, and the manward side is summed up in the duty of Christians to intercede in prayer for their fellow-believers who are enduring affliction. But prayer is not a second "force" in competition with or supplementary to divine grace, for its function and very attitude is precisely to emphasize the utter dependence and resourcelessness of man and the absolute sovereignty of the Father of mercies. In prayer, human impotence casts itself at the feet of divine omnipotence. Thus the duty of prayer is not a modification of God's power, but a glorification of it. Supplication for others is, further, one practical form of expressing the communion of the saints; another which receives particular attention in this epistle is that of liberality towards those who are in need (chs. 8 and 9).

Supplicatory prayer not only expresses but also promotes the communion of the saints: the end to which it leads is joy and thanksgiving because of the Heavenly Father's goodness in hearing and answering the petitions of His children. The exact significance of one or two terms in the latter part of this verse is open to dispute, but the general meaning is clear: You Corinthians help together [20] by your supplication, exhorts Paul, "to the end that God's gracious favour of deliverance granted to us through the prayerful co-operation of many persons may cause many to give thanks to God on our behalf". If many intercede, many will have cause for thanksgiving.[21] Ideally, the "many" here should

---

[20] Συνυπουργούντων καὶ ὑμῶν: the reference of the prefix συν- has been variously explained. It may mean (i) together with me (Paul), i.e. uniting your supplication to mine; or (ii) together with Christians elsewhere, i.e. uniting your prayers with those of other churches; or (iii) together with each other in Corinth. There is something to be said for each of these, and perhaps the three should be held in combination, rather than as alternatives. If a choice is necessary, the last mentioned is preferable, firstly, because, except when the person or persons with whom there is to be co-operation are explicitly stated (as e.g. in Rom. 15:30), it is more natural to understand the verb in a reflexive sense; and, secondly, because of the particular need for true unity at Corinth, where the Christians had been divided by party strife and disloyalty.

[21] The main exegetical problem in the latter part of this verse revolves round the significance of the expression ἐκ πολλῶν προσώπων, which may mean either (i) "from many faces" or (ii) "from many persons". Allo, Plummer, Bachmann, Stanley, and others, both ancient and recent, favour the former. Plummer explains that "the Apostle, as he dictates, sees in thought the many upturned faces, lighted up with thankfulness, as praises for this preservation

be taken to stand for "all": for *all* to be united in supplication would lead to *all* being united in thanksgiving, which would in turn be a notable demonstration to themselves and to the world of the communion of the saints. Nor should it be thought that the Apostle imposes the responsibility of supplication on the Corinthians without himself accepting a reciprocal responsibility toward them. "I thank my God upon all my remembrance of you, always in every supplication of mine on behalf of you all making my supplication with joy...", he writes to the Philippians (1:3f.); and the same sacred bond of spiritual energy keeps him in dynamic union with every convert won and every church founded (cf. Rom. 1:9; Eph. 1:16; Col. 1:3; I Thess. 1:2f.; Philem. 3f.). So also in the case of the Corinthians he gladly spends and is spent for their souls (12:15); and this self-expenditure includes the labour of intercession.

---

rise up from their lips." On this interpretation πρόσωπα is used as the equivalent of "mouths, whence prayer bursts towards the heavens" (Allo). Such a sense, however, is without parallel. If there is one particular feature which the word πρόσωπον may legitimately be said to suggest, it is not the mouth, but the eyes *(πρός + ὤψ)*, which are the portals of personality. We do not dispute that in the New Testament πρόσωπον usually means "face"; but that fact cannot be taken as determinative of its meaning on every occasion on which it is found, for it is also an indisputable fact that πρόσωπον in the sense of "person" is, as Plummer acknowledges, "abundantly illustrated in the Greek of the period". Thus Moulton and Milligan draw attention to "the frequent use of the word in the Κοινή as practically equivalent to our 'person' ". There is, therefore no ground whatever for supposing that this was a meaning which Paul could not have intended. As both meanings were common in his day, our task is to decide which of them accords best with the particular context in which the word occurs. It is certainly surprising to find Plummer affirming that "it is difficult to explain ἐκ, if persons are meant", for ἐκ is used precisely in this manner in association with persons (God, us, you, countrymen, Gentiles), as the source of the thing spoken of, with some frequency in this very epistle (cf. 2:17; 3:1; 3:5 *bis*; 4:7; 5:1; 5:18; 7:9; 8:7; 11:26 *bis*; 12:6), and it is far more probable that Paul had in mind *persons* rather than *faces* as the source of the thanksgiving in question. In view of these considerations we find it difficult to doubt that πρόσωπα in this instance means "persons"—and this is the judgment also of Arndt and Gingrich, Windisch, Lietzmann, and others, both ancient and recent.

1:12-2:4 PAUL'S INTEGRITY OF MOTIVE
AND CONDUCT

1 : 12

For our glorying is this, the testimony of our conscience, that in holiness and sincerity of God, not in fleshly wisdom but in the grace of God, we behaved ourselves in the world, and more abundantly to you-ward.

The conjuction "for" indicates that there is a logical transition from the preceding to the present paragraph: the claim that Paul makes upon the prayers and thanksgivings of the Corinthians on his behalf rests not only on the fact that he had suffered affliction for their sakes (v. 6), but also on his and their knowledge of his disinterestedness of purpose and transparency of life, whether in their midst or elsewhere. The testimony of a clear conscience [1] is indeed something in which to glory. He is content at this stage to leave his readers to draw their own conclusions from the contrast between the blameless consistency of his conduct and the behaviour of the upstart adversaries who had spawned the calumnies against his good name. The glorying of the latter was marked by insincerity and carnal pride. But Paul's glorying is in the Lord (cf. 10:17); he attributes nothing to self, but all to the grace of God (cf. I Cor. 15:10). The holiness and sincerity [2] to which his conscience testifies are *of God*, that

---

[1] It is only in the New Testament that συνείδησις, "inner self-knowledge", comes to receive the full force of what we understand by "conscience", though in classical authors it is not lacking in moral implications. Cremer defines it as "the consciousness a man has of himself in his relationship to God" (*Biblico-Theological Lexicon of New Testament Greek*, Edinburgh, 1883, p. 234). Paul uses the term frequently.

[2] The reading ἐν ἁγιότητι, "in holiness", is strongly attested and must be retained. Although ἁγιότης is a rare word in biblical Greek, its use here is (*pace* Plummer) not inappropriate. The variant reading of the *textus receptus*, ἐν ἁπλότητι, "in simplicity", undoubtedly accords well with the context—simplicity being contrasted with duplicity, though it could be said that it is practically tautologous with "sincerity" with which (if the reading ἐν ἁπλότητι is accepted) it is coupled. Ἁπλότης is used by Paul four times later in this epistle, viz. 8:2; 9:11, 13; 11:3, and in the place last mentioned it is coupled with ἁγνότης, "purity" (the reading, however, is not universally attested).

is, they have their origin in God, not in himself. Fleshly wisdom he had shunned from the very first moment of his arrival in Corinth (cf. I Cor. 2:1ff.). The Christian's wisdom is from God and its concentration is in Christ (I Cor. 1:30); whereas fleshly wisdom is the expression of sinful man's revolt against the sovereignty of God in being and knowledge. Fleshly wisdom is, therefore, the expression of the deepest folly. And to a particular degree it had become characteristic of the Greek mind (cf. I Cor. 1:18ff.; Rom. 1:22). Paul, says Calvin, "gives the name of fleshly wisdom to everything apart from Christ which procures for us the reputation of wisdom". The Apostle's life was lived, by contrast, in the grace of God before the world, in all places and at all times, but "more abundantly" in the presence of the Corinthians. This, of course, does not indicate that his integrity had been greater in Corinth than elsewhere, for there are no degrees of integrity and genuineness, and holiness and sincerity that are of God do not vary. But the Corinthians had had a better opportunity of assessing and appreciating the Apostle's holiness of life and sincerity of purpose, both because against the dark background of all the vice and wickedness which made their city notorious the purity of his conduct had stood out in unmistakeable relief, and also because he had spent no less than eighteen months continuously in their company, so that they could not excuse

Rückert suggests that the true reading in our present verse should be ἐν ἁγνότητι, "in purity", the term ἁγιότητι being attributed to a scribal error. But the latter gives excellent sense. Holiness is God-given no less than sincerity; ἁγιότης would refer to the "moral purity" (Arndt and Gingrich) of Paul's conduct and εἰλικρίνεια to the genuineness of his motives.

Εἰλικρίνεια, "sincerity" (a term which Paul uses again in 2:17; see also I Cor. 5:8), relates to the Apostle's inner motives, as ἁγιότης relates to his outward behaviour. The derivation of the word is disputed, but it is probably a compound of εἴλη, "the heat of the sun", and κρίνειν, "to judge". The difference in the breathing should be compared with the variation between ἥλιος (Attic) on the one hand and ἠέλιος (Epic) and ἀέλιος (Doric) on the other. The word would then suggest the state of an object which has successfully passed the test of examination by the sun's pure light, a state, that is, of spotless purity. The correctness of this etymology is doubted by Liddell and Scott, *Greek-English Lexicon* (7th edition, Oxford 1883), who regard the fact that εἴλη means the heat rather than the light of the sun as telling against it. The difficulty hardly exists, however, when it is remembered that the sun's light and heat are inseparably associated with each other. The derivation suggested is favoured by E. Boisacq, *Dictionnaire Etymologique de la Langue Grecque* (Paris 1916).

26

themselves by saying that they did not know him and the quality of his living well. Besides, the absolute antipathy between the wisdom of carnal man and the grace of God, between the flesh and the Spirit, is familiar to every heart; and the members of the Corinthian Church were being tempted to walk after the flesh, instead of after the Spirit (cf. Rom. 8:4ff.; Gal. 5:16ff.). That is something which cannot be done with a good conscience.

1:13, 14

> For we write no other things unto you, than what ye read or even acknowledge, and I hope ye will acknowledge unto the end: as also ye did acknowledge us in part, that we are your glorying, even as ye also are ours, in the day of our Lord Jesus.

No man can be called upright unless his uprightness embraces every aspect of his activity. Honour and sincerity relate to the whole of life, not to a part of it. And so it is with Paul: the integrity of his character informs his conduct in its entirety. It extends therefore to his letter-writing; and it has become necessary for him to refer to this because his detractors in Corinth had been alleging that his letters were documents of insincerity, that he wrote one thing and meant another, that the man who was so impressive in his letters showed up very differently when present in person (cf. 10:10f., a further indication of the coherence between the earlier and later chapters of this epistle). If the Corinthians are honest with themselves, they must acknowledge from first-hand observance that his conduct in their city was marked by transparent genuineness: well, so it is also with his letters; they can trust the plain meaning of what they read; there is no *double entendre*, no subtle misdirection. What they read from him is not incompatible with what they know with certainty about him.[3]

---

[3] The play on words, ἀναγινώσκετε ... ἐπιγινώσκετε, cannot successfully be reproduced in English. 'Αναγινώσκετε refers to what they read in his letters and ἐπιγινώσκετε to what they know through personal contact with him. They are being assured that the two are in complete harmony. Paul is fond of using ἐπιγινώσκειν as an intensive compound, "to know fully" or "to know with certainty", and the verb is best understood in this sense here, for he is referring to the certainty of the Corinthians' knowledge of his character through first-hand experience. He uses the same compound with a clearly

The punctuation of these two verses can be much improved and the sense clarified, as Allo, Denney, Hofmann, Hodge, and others agree, by placing a semicolon instead of a comma after the first "acknowledge" and treating the clause "as also ye did acknowledge us in part" as parenthetical. The statement will then read as follows: "For we write no other things unto you, than what ye read or even acknowledge; and I hope ye will acknowledge unto the end (as also ye did acknowledge us in part) that we are your glorying..." Paul, in fact, desires that their glorying should coincide with his glorying. He glories in the testimony of his conscience to the holiness and sincerity of his behaviour, so well known to them through prolonged personal contact, and it is his hope that they will continue in this certainty of knowledge and thus that, in this respect, he may be their glorying too. But already the shadow under which this epistle is written is becoming apparent: their acknowledgment of his integrity, founded on the assurance of personal fellowship, is but partial. They should *all* have complete confidence in him who is their divinely appointed Apostle; but the calumnies and insinuations of the false apostles who have invaded his territory have caused some to waver and others even to transfer their allegiance. He longs that all who are Christ's in Corinth should unanimously acknowledge him as their genuine Apostle—not for the sake of his own reputation (as the whole of this epistle shows) but for their sakes and the Gospel's. Paul, however, may also have intended them to understand that their knowledge of him, though certain (no matter what his opponents might say), was

---

intensive significance in two other places in this epistle: 6:9, ὡς ἀγνοούμενοι καὶ ἐπιγινωσκόμενοι, "as unknown and yet well known"; and 13:5, ἢ οὐκ ἐπιγινώσκετε ἑαυτούς, "or do you not know your own selves fully?" (self-knowledge at least should be full knowledge!). The classic example of this intensive force of ἐπιγινώσκειν is found in I Cor. 13:12, ἄρτι γινώσκω ἐκ μέρους, τότε δὲ ἐπιγνώσομαι καθὼς καὶ ἐπεγνώσθην, "now I know in part; but then shall I know fully even as also I was fully known (*sc.* by God)". There is a similar play on words in 3:2, γινωσκομένη καὶ ἀναγινωσκομένη, "known and read"; cf. Acts 8:30, γινώσκεις ἃ ἀναγινώσκεις; The suggestion that ἀναγινώσκειν in our present verse and in 3:2 is an intensive, meaning "to admit" or "to acknowledge", is unacceptable, for the current sense of the verb in New Testament times is undoubtedly "to read", and this sense is naturally appropriate to both these passages. Cf. C. F. D. Moule, *An Idiom Book of New Testament Greek* (Cambridge, 1953), p. 89.

partial in the sense of not being complete: there were still things for them to learn concerning him, for example, the truth about his "thorn in the flesh" (ch. 12). They must learn that physical weakness does not imply moral weakness. And the certainty of his integrity will be confirmed, not shaken, the more complete their knowledge of him becomes.

"Unto the end" should not be given an eschatological connotation, but should be understood in the sense of "unto completion", in contrast to the expression "in part" in the following clause.[4]

The last part of verse 14 is best treated as almost parenthetical in character, added to forestall any misunderstanding of what Paul has just written about himself being the Corinthians' glorying, for there is no question of this glorying being merely one-sided (cf. 5:12; 9:3). They also are his glorying, his joy and crown (Phil. 4:1), in the day of the Lord Jesus. This affirmation of affection not only corroborates the complete genuineness of his own attitude towards them, but attests his confidence regarding the genuineness of their profession of faith in the Gospel. In that great ultimate day they will be there in the company of the redeemed, and he, their Apostle, with them. What delight for him to see them then (as he sees them now in anticipation), his children in the Gospel, "unreprovable in the day of our Lord Jesus Christ" (I Cor. 1:8)—no further need for letters of reproof and admonition!— the work of grace completed at last within them. What better commentary on Paul's brief sentence here could be desired than the words he had written some five years previously to his Thessalonian converts: "For what is our hope, or joy, or crown of glorying? Are not even ye, before our Lord Jesus at his coming? For ye are our glory and our joy" (I Thess. 2:19f.)?

Chrysostom rightly draws our attention to the great humility disclosed by what the Apostle writes here, in that he addresses

---

[4] Commenting on ἕως τέλους, Allo says: "Those who wish to understand it in an eschatological sense, 'to the end of the world' or 'of time' or 'of your lives' [*Plummer, Sickenberger, Windisch*, etc.] are not only misled by the mistaken idea that Paul and the Corinthians were expecting the end of the world as near at hand . . ., but they also commit a serious error of literary judgment in failing to notice the intentional antithesis between ἀπὸ μέρους and ἕως τέλους."

himself, "not as a master discoursing to disciples, but as a disciple to fellow-disciples of his own rank".[5] They, equally with him, are sinners saved and transformed by the same free grace of God. He lives constantly in the light of that day, the day of Christ's appearing, when every man will be revealed as he truly is, in himself, and not as he has appeared to be to others (cf. 5:10-12). It is the *day* of our Lord Jesus, which dawns with the rising of the Sun of Righteousness (Mal. 4:2) to dispel for ever the darkness of sin and to usher in the eternal heavenly sabbath. For Christians, nothing can be more humbling and levelling than the expectation of that day when before the sole and supreme glory of Christ all the glory of man will sink into judgment and oblivion. There will be no place for deception, disunity, and self-esteem in that day.

1 : 15, 16

And in this confidence I was minded to come first unto you, that ye might have a second benefit; and by you to pass into Macedonia, and again from Macedonia to come unto you, and of you to be set forward on my journey unto Judaea.

"In this confidence", that is, in the confidence that he was their glorying, their trusted and loyally acknowledged Apostle, Paul had formulated the plan of paying the Corinthians a double visit: to come to them first before proceeding north to Macedonia, and then to return to them from Macedonia. In this way they would have had "a second benefit", which may mean that they would have had two opportunities, not one, of receiving spiritual communications from him in person (cf. Rom. 1:11), or, more simply, that they might enjoy the pleasure of his presence with them twice during the same itinerary instead of once.[6] As has

---

5 As Plummer observes, the καθάπερ ("even as") "brushes away all idea of his claiming superiority".

6 The evidence is somewhat equally divided between the readings χάριν and χαράν. The former is followed by our English version ("benefit"), also AV and Vulgate (*gratiam*), and is adopted by Allo, Nestlé, Souter, etc. The latter ("joy") is favoured by Plummer, Westcott and Hort, etc. Allo understands χάρις here in the sense of a "mark of consideration", which approximates to the sense given by Theodoret who, though reading χαρά, interprets it as human χάρις = "favour". Chrysostom on the other hand reads χάρις but

been said, the intention was conceived at a time when Paul was confident that he was their glorying, as they also were his; but subsequently news had reached him of such a nature as to shake this confidence and cause him to modify this project. One result of this change of plan on his part had been that (as the verses that follow show) certain persons intent on alienating the loyalties and affections of the Corinthians from their Apostle had used it as an occasion for denouncing him as fickle, unreliable, and insincere. It is against this calumny that Paul now finds it necessary to defend himself.

PAUL'S ASSOCIATIONS WITH CORINTH

Biographical information concerning Paul's movements and actions is so incomplete, and the gaps in our knowledge are so considerable, that it is impossible to establish with any real certainty the sequence of his associations with the Corinthian Church, whether by personal visit or by letter. Every attempt at reconstruction must inevitably be conjectural—a consideration which in itself is sufficient to explain the wide divergence of opinion amongst those who have tried to work out a chronology of Paul's life. II Corinthians, more than any other epistle, poses the most puzzling questions, and in particular: how many visits had he previously paid to Corinth? and how many letters had he previously written to the Christians there? and precisely at what points in the history of his life as we know it are these visits and letters to be located? These are questions to which a commentator on this epistle is bound to attempt some answer. Accordingly, we shall set forth what in our judgment is the most reasonable reconstruction of those events which, up till the time of the composition of this epistle, had brought Paul and the Corinthians into special contact with each other. Certain aspects of the picture given here will be amplified at later stages in this commentary, as occasion demands.[7]

From what he says in 12:14 and 13:1f. it is evident that Paul

---

interprets it as χαρά = "pleasure", and we are inclined to think that he is right. Both nouns come from the same root and so it is not surprising if, as Arndt and Gingrich remark, "it seems that χάρις is not always clearly differentiated in meaning from χαρά". (See also note on χάρις above, v. 2.) To expound δευτέραν χάριν here as though it supported the "second blessing" teaching held by certain perfectionist or near-perfectionist groups is entirely unwarranted.

7 See also Introduction, pp. xvi ff.

had already been in Corinth on two separate occasions.[8] The first of these was his original visit during which the Church was founded in that city (Acts 18:1ff.), and it lasted eighteen months (Acts 18:11), probably from the autumn of A.D. 52 to the spring of A.D. 54. This was followed by a second visit about which we have no information, except that it was for Paul a sorrowful event: "I determined this for myself", he now writes to the Corinthians (2:1), "that I would not come again to you with sorrow". Luke omits all mention of it in the Acts, just as he is silent also concerning a number of other events to which Paul alludes in this epistle.[9] No doubt this second visit took place within the period of his third missionary journey, and it may well have been hurriedly undertaken during the course of his long stay in Ephesus (Acts 20:31) upon the receipt of disturbing news about the state of affairs across the water at Corinth. Such indications as there are suggest that serious moral problems had arisen in the Church there, and that what he found on his arrival occasioned him much sorrow. Subsequently, he wrote them a letter, now lost, in which he admonished them "to have no company with fornicators" (I Cor. 5:9). Possibly during the second visit or possibly in this lost letter he had intimated to them his hope of being able to pay them a double visit by seeing them both on his way to and on his return from Macedonia. But thereafter further grievous news, and in particular the report that a case of incest had actually been condoned within the Corinthian Church (I Cor. 5:1ff.), caused him to reconsider this intention and occasioned the writing of what is now known as the First Epistle to the Corinthians. In this epistle he advises his readers that he will shortly be visiting them again, and that it depends on them whether he comes to them "with a rod or in love and a spirit of gentleness" (I Cor. 4:18–21; cf. 11:34; 16:2ff.). But he also explains that he will now see them only *after* he has travelled through Macedonia, for his proposal to see them "by the way", that is, in passing, on his journey northwards, has been abandoned (I Cor. 16:5–7). The original plan would have meant voyaging from Ephesus to Corinth, followed by a trip to and from Macedonia. As things are, however, his itinerary will take him northwards from Ephesus to Troas, from there into Macedonia, and then south to Corinth.

---

[8] Some commentators have attempted to explain 12:14 and 13:1f. in such a way as to avoid the necessity for postulating two previous visits. For discussion of this view see commentary below on those passages and also on 2:1.

[9] See commentary below on 11:23ff.

The purpose of this alteration in his plans was to spare the Corinthians (1:23), to give them time to set their house in order in readiness for his arrival; for he is fully prepared to exercise, if necessary, the sternest discipline when he comes (13:2). But it is his hope that their response will be such that it will not be necessary. Besides, in view of what had transpired, a hurried visit in passing would have served no good purpose, and it is now Paul's intention to prolong his stay during the impending visit, perhaps even to spend the winter with them (I Cor. 16:6). He had further informed them that he would remain in Ephesus, where he was writing I Corinthians, until Pentecost (I Cor. 16:8). From this it can be deduced that I Corinthians was written after the winter and before Pentecost, that is, some time in the spring of, probably, A.D. 57, and that II Corinthians was written (from Macedonia—cf. 2:13 and 7:5) before the onset of winter in that same year. Thus the latter would have been composed only some six months after the former, and it was occasioned by the news which Titus brought of conditions in Corinth and of the manner in which I Corinthians had been received.[10]

Paul's plan as originally envisaged had a threefold structure: (i) he would cross from Ephesus to Corinth in order to pay the Corinthians a visit *en route* to Macedonia; (ii) he would come again to them after completing his business in Macedonia; (iii) thereafter in due course they were to set him forward on his journey, by which he means that they were to provide companions to escort him on his way, which was then a common practice among friends (cf. I Cor. 16:6, 11; Acts 15:3; 20:38; 21:5; Rom. 15:24; Tit. 3:13; III Jn. 6).[11] Of these projects, only the first was in fact abandoned (cf. I Cor. 16:5ff.). The other two remained as originally proposed. But the alteration was greedily seized upon by the Apostle's adversaries in Corinth and brandished by them as evidence of bad faith on his part. The sad thing is that any of his friends should ever have allowed themselves to be persuaded to entertain such a calumny, especially when their intimate knowledge of his character should have assured them that any change of plan must have been prompted by the best of reasons. (See comments below on Paul's use of the verb determined in 2:1.)

---

[10] See commentary below on 2:1ff. and 7:8, also Introduction, pp. xxviii ff. for discussion of the hypothesis that in between the writing of I Corinthians and II Corinthians a severe letter had been sent by Paul to Corinth.

[11] In each of these references the verb is προπέμπω, the meaning of which is as given above.

1 : 17, 18

When I therefore was thus minded, did I show fickleness? or the things that I purpose, do I purpose according to the flesh, that with me there should be the yea yea and the nay nay? But as God is faithful, our word toward you is not yea and nay.

Paul finds it incredible that any at Corinth could really have thought that a change in plan pointed to a change in character.[12] Nor was it a question of the abandonment of his original project, but only a modification of it; as Stanley says, "although he had apparently given up his original plan, he still in fact and in spirit adhered to it; that, for the two short visits which they had lost, they would now (see I Cor. 16:7) be compensated by one long visit at the end of his whole journey". Indeed, as they well knew, it was in themselves, not in him, that the real cause of the change in plan lay: it was they, not he, who were guilty of inconstancy and fickleness; it was they who, after having responded to him with so clear a yea, had admitted into their fellowship false apostles whose object was to persuade them to say nay to their true Apostle. Had they remained stedfast and loyal, the plan as originally conceived would have been carried through. His decision, moreover, had not been governed by selfish motives, but by consideration and affection for them (v. 23). For him to plan and purpose "according to the flesh",[13] which is the opposite of "according to the Spirit", would be the absolute negation both of his whole profession in Christ and also of all that they knew of him through close personal association.

In fact, the import of their accusation went even further than that, for it really had the effect of bringing into question the faithfulness and trustworthiness of God Himself, who by revelation had entrusted His word to Paul as to a chosen vessel (cf. Gal. 1:11ff.; Acts 9:15). But that God is faithful is a truth they cannot gainsay, for, as they had previously been reminded, it was through Him and His faithfulness that they were "called into

---

[12] The formula μήτι ἄρα which introduces the twofold question of verse 17 shows that the only possible answer is a negative: ". . . did I really show fickleness? Of course not! Do I really purpose according to the flesh? Of course not!"

[13] Regarding the significance of the expression "according to the flesh" see commentary below on 5:16.

34

the fellowship of His Son Jesus Christ our Lord" (I Cor. 1:9). When God speaks His positive does not carry a hidden negative. And so it is also with His chosen Apostle: his word to the Corinthians is not a mixture of yea and nay at the same time, but a faithful yea—sincere, honest, unambiguous. It is not an emphatic yes which may be expected to turn into an equally emphatic no (this is the force of the repetition in the expression "the yea yea and the nay nay"), as some had been scornfully asserting.   There is no nay coupled with his yea.[14]

1 : 19

> For the Son of God, Jesus Christ, who was preached among you by us, even by me and Silvanus and Timothy, was not yea and nay, but in him is yea.

In Jesus Christ, faithful God's Son, whom Paul, together with Silvanus and Timothy, preached to them, the Corinthians have a further compelling proof of his personal integrity.   Not only had his preaching proved true and trustworthy, but Jesus Christ Himself in whom, through his preaching, the Corinthians had believed, was not yes-and-no; on the contrary, in Him one unequivocal affirmative has become the great and lasting reality of their experience.[15]   Nothing could be more incongruous than to suspect of insincerity the Apostle whose entire being was dedicated to the service and proclamation of Him who is the Truth and the Same yesterday, today, and for ever. The veracity of the Christ, by faith in whom, in accordance with the word of God, their lives had been completely transformed, was evidence conclusive to them of the veracity of him who had endured so much in order to bring the message to them.   They know their Apostle,

---

[14]   By the time when Paul was writing the classical distinction between the consecutive force of ὥστε and the final force of ἵνα was not always maintained. We agree with Allo and Plummer in assigning to ἵνα in verse 17 a consecutive force: "The things that I purpose, do I purpose according to the flesh, *with the result that* with me there is the yea yea and (simultaneously) the nay nay?" J. H. Moulton, however, is of the opinion that ἵνα should be treated as final here: "Paul", he explains, "is disclaiming the mundane virtue of unsettled convictions, which *aims* at saying yes and no in one breath" (*Grammar of New Testament Greek*, Vol. I, p. 210).
[15]   Ναὶ ἐν αὐτῷ γέγονεν — "In Him yes was and continues to be a reality". The force of the perfect γέγονεν must not be overlooked.

as they know his Master, to be not yes-and-no, but sincere and trustworthy in both word and character.

Silvanus (= Silas) and Timothy were closely associated with Paul on his second missionary journey. Silas, who was a leader of the Church at Jerusalem, had been one of the delegates appointed by the Council of Jerusalem to accompany Paul to Antioch with the decree of the Council (Acts 15:22ff.). Paul and Barnabas had remained in Antioch, "teaching and preaching the word of the Lord"; but after the break with Barnabas the Apostle chose Silas to accompany him as he set out on his second missionary journey (Acts 15:36ff.). On reaching Lystra they were joined by Timothy, whom they found there (Acts 16:1ff.). In due course they came to Macedonia and proclaimed the Gospel there, but later Paul journeyed on into Greece without his two companions. After preaching in Athens, he then moved on to Corinth, where he stayed with Aquila and Priscilla, and Silas and Timothy arrived from Macedonia and assisted in the work of evangelization there (Acts 17:14ff.; 18:1ff.); it is to this occasion that he refers in this present verse. Both Silas and Timothy are associated with the Apostle in the opening greetings of the two epistles to the Thessalonians, and Peter speaks of Silas as "our faithful brother" (I Pet. 5:12). It is not irrelevant to observe that in doing so the latter applies to Silas the same epithet—"faithful" = "trustworthy"—as Paul applies to God here (v. 18) and, by implication, to himself and his two fellow-labourers in the Gospel cause.

1:20

> For how many soever be the promises of God, in him is the yea: wherefore also through him is the Amen, unto the glory of God through us.

In Christ is the yes, the grand consummating affirmative, to all God's promises. He is the horn of salvation raised up for us by God, "as He spake by the mouth of His holy prophets which have been since the world began" (Lk. 1:69f.). In Him all things "which are written in the law of Moses, and the prophets, and the psalms" achieve their fulfilment (Lk. 24:44). The covenant promises addressed to Abraham and his seed are realized in His single person (Gal. 3:16). To the believer, therefore,

Christ is all, not merely as fulfilling a word of the past, but as Himself being the very living Word of God, faithful and eternal. In Him all fulness dwells (Col. 1:19): wisdom, righteousness, sanctification, redemption are to be found in Him alone (I Cor. 1:30). There is nothing which is not in Him, who is the First and the Last, the Beginning and the End (Rev. 22:13).

This being so, the Christian's every need is supplied by God "according to His riches in glory in Christ Jesus" (Phil. 4:19). It follows, therefore, that the concluding "Amen" of the Christian's prayers and petitions, in which he invokes the promises of God, is also through Christ. The ancient prayer-ending, ". . . through Jesus Christ our Lord. Amen." is something far more than a mere formula or a convenient formality; on the contrary, it is the true and profoundly significant keystone of all Christian prayer. It is not only primitive, it is pristine. Our Lord Himself taught that requests were to be made in His name (Jn. 14:13f.), and the apostolic Church offered prayer to God "through the name of our Lord Jesus Christ" (Eph. 5:20). That the final "Amen" was in current liturgical use in the New Testament Church is shown from what Paul has already written in I Cor. 14:16. This word "Amen" is a term which helps to proclaim the continuity of the Christian with the Jewish Church, for in the latter it had been used liturgically from time immemorial (cf. Deut. 27:15ff.; I Chron. 16:36; Ps. 106:48; Jer. 28:6; Neh. 5:13; 8:6, etc.). The Hebrew root from which it is derived conveys the idea of *firmness* and *reliability*, and the utterance of "Amen" in public or private worship after prayers and thanksgivings expresses confidence in the faithfulness of God and the certainty of His promises. It is, in short, the voice of faith, setting to its seal that God is true (Jn. 3:33).

Our Lord employed the term in a unique manner when He placed it *at the beginning*, either singly or in repetition, of many of His most solemn utterances — "Amen, amen, I say unto you. . ."—, thus in a most arresting manner emphasizing for His hearers the absolute authenticity and immutability of His teaching. The application of the term to Christ as a title in Rev. 3:14 is particularly significant: "These things saith the Amen, the faithful and true witness". The "Amen" is through Him who is Himself the Amen. There could be no greater assurance of the divine faithfulness than that! [16]

The "Amen" is, naturally, affirmed "unto the glory of God", for thereby man confesses his own abject resourcelessness and magnifies the sovereign grace of his Creator and Redeemer. It is, moreover, through Paul and his companions ("through us"[17]) as God's instruments not only that Jesus Christ was preached among the Corinthians (v. 19), but also, consequently, that they are in that blessed position of being able to affix their "Amen" to all that God offers in Christ. How illogical, then, while by their "Amen" attesting the trustworthiness of God, to suspect the trustworthiness of the Apostle who taught them to do so! Any charge of inconsistency must be levelled at them, not him.

1 : 21, 22

> Now he that establisheth us with you in Christ, and anointed us, is God; who also sealed us, and gave us the earnest of the Spirit in our hearts.

The question of Paul's sincerity and reliability might so easily

---

[16] In a monograph entitled *Reisepläne und Amen-Sagen, Zusammenhang und Gedankenfolge in 2 Korinthier 1:15–24*, published in *Studia Paulina* (in honorem Johannis De Zwaan septuagenarii) (Haarlem, Holland, 1953), pp. 215–234, W. C. van Unnik propounds the view that the key to the understanding of this passage (verses 15–24) is to be found in the realization that the construction is built on the Semitic root אמן. By a careful comparison of passages from the Old and New Testaments he shows that the keywords of these verses —πιστός (v. 18), ναί (vv. 19 and 20), ὁ βεβαιῶν (v. 21), πίστις (v. 24)—may properly be associated with this root. But when he concludes that it is only through the detection of this subjacent אמן-motif that Paul's thought is seen to follow on in a logical succession we must object that this is tantamount to introducing a form of esoteric exegesis which certainly would have been far from the Apostle's intention, and which would besides have been lost on the majority of the Corinthian Christians for whom Semitic roots and vocables held no significance whatever. Whether, as van Unnik further concludes Paul thought, and perhaps wrote, in Aramaic is an open question. But there is, in our judgment, every reason to believe that the Apostle was thoroughly bilingual, at home in Greek no less than in Semitic forms of thought and speech. Van Unnik, however, holds that Aramaic was the controlling partner in this combination (see also his *Aramaeismen bij Paulus* in *Vox Theologica*, vol. XV [1943], pp. 117–126). He has at least shown as an interesting possibility that the Apostle may have had the root אמן, with its wealth of connotation in mind—perhaps in the back of his mind?—when composing this passage.

[17] "By us" in verse 19 should read "through us", as in margin—δι' ἡμῶν.

have degenerated into an unprofitable wrangle with an exchange of accusations and recriminations, but the Apostle approaches it in such a manner as to place it on a level far above that of any mere personal grievance. By penetrating beyond such superficialities to the very heart of the matter, namely, the believer's dynamic status in Christ, he makes it plain that his concern is not simply with the opinion which others may hold of him personally. He does not lay claim to integrity as a personal achievement; all is attributed to the redeeming and recreative activity of the Holy Trinity. It is *God*, firstly, who *establishes* him, together with the Corinthian believers, into Christ—the present tense showing that this is a *constant* experience, and the graphic "into" [18] that it is a *progressive* experience: in the purpose of God the stability is not only continuous, but is ever being intensified. Placed by grace into dynamic union with Christ, "the Amen, the faithful and true witness", how should the Apostle be anything but stable, trustworthy, consistent? The Corinthians themselves know this same stabilizing and progressive irreversibility of the work of grace in their own lives, for, as Paul had reminded them in his earlier letter, God, who established the testimony of Christ within them, would also establish them to the end so that they would be unreprovable at the last day (I Cor. 1:6, 8).[19] Thus he is speaking of something which is concrete in their own experience. To suspect his reliability was, in fact, to cast a shadow over their own stability, for it is a case of "us with you in Christ", not "us different from you", but all dynamically united in the unchanging Son of God.

But God, further, had also *anointed* Paul, thereby declaring another respect in which he was closely bound to Christ; for the title "Christ" means precisely "the Anointed One".[20] The anointing, as Plummer observes, does not imply any actual ceremony of unction, but is an anointing with the Spirit. The anointing which Christ received for the fulfilment of His mediatorial office was an anointing with the Spirit of the Lord Jehovah. Accordingly He appropriated to Himself the words of Isa. 61:1f.:

---

[18] *Εἰς.*

[19] The same verb *(βεβαιόω)* is used by Paul in I Cor. 1:6, 8 *(ἐβεβαιώθη ... βεβαιώσει)* as here *(βεβαιῶν)*. Regarding the significance of *βεβαιόω* here see note 30 below.

[20] The juxtaposition: *εἰς Χριστόν, καὶ χρίσας* should be noticed.

"The Spirit of the Lord is upon me, because he anointed me to preach good tidings to the poor: he hath sent me to proclaim release to the captives, and recovering of sight to the blind, to set at liberty them that are bruised, to proclaim the acceptable year of the Lord" (Lk. 4:18f.). So, too, Paul was sent by Christ to the nations "to open their eyes, that they may turn from darkness to light and from the power of Satan unto God, that they may receive remission of sins and an inheritance among them that are sanctified by faith" in Christ (Acts 26:17f.). Truly it is a case of "as the Father hath sent me, even so send I you" (Jn. 20:21); and for this sacred commission the Apostle (that is, the sent one) received an anointing with the same Holy Spirit. To all whom He chooses and commissions to be His witnesses and servants God grants the unction of the Spirit, so that, in a subordinate and derivative sense—and not in any mediatorial sense, for there is but *one* mediator between God and men (I Tim. 2:5)—it is possible to speak of them as God's "messiahs" or "christs" = "anointed ones". Thus when God says in Ps. 105:15 (= I Chron. 16:22), "Touch not mine anointed ones", the Hebrew term is "my messiahs", which in the Greek (Septuagint) version is rightly rendered "my christs".[21]

Chrysostom draws attention to the fact that in Old Testament times it was customary for prophets, priests, and kings to be anointed for the performance of their particular offices, whereas all three diginities are combined in the believer, who is a prophet to whom things that eye hath not seen nor ear heard have been revealed (I Cor. 2:9) and whose duty it is to proclaim the message of the Gospel (Acts 1:8); a priest whose spiritual service is to present his body a living sacrifice, holy, acceptable to God (Rom. 12:1; cf. I Pet. 1:5); and a king over whom sin shall not have dominion (Rom. 6:12, 14) and whose destiny is to reign with Christ (II Tim. 2:12; cf. also I Pet. 2:9; Rev. 1:6; 5:10; 20:6). Eusebius also explains how prophets, priests, and kings of old were, by virtue of their anointing, christs in type, who in their offices pointed forward to "the true Christ, the divinely inspired and heavenly Word, who is the only High Priest of all, and the only King of every creature, and the Father's only

---

21 Hebrew: עַל־תִּגְּעוּ בִּמְשִׁיחָי

Greek: μὴ ἅψησθε [ἅπτεσθε] τῶν χριστῶν μου.

40

supreme Prophet of prophets".[22] God's anointing, which abides in the believer, "and is true, and is no lie" (I Jn. 2:27), is therefore a further guarantee of Paul's sincerity and trustworthiness.

Paul, moreover, had been *sealed* by God. The affixing of the royal seal to an object gave it complete security (cf. Dan. 6:17; Mt. 27:66); letters and legal documents that had been sealed were proof from interference and forgery (cf. I Kings 21:8; Jer. 32:10–14; Esther 3:12); so, too, God has set His seal upon those who are His: they are known to Him and in Him they are secure for all eternity (cf. II Tim. 2:19). And it is with the Holy Spirit of promise that they are sealed (Eph. 1:13); and as God's promise carries with it the absolute certainty of fulfilment, under the seal of the Holy Spirit they are preserved inviolate unto the day of redemption (Eph. 4:30). The bearing of the divine seal conveys a twofold advantage: identification and protection (cf. Rev. 9:4; 7:2ff.). In our epistle Paul speaks of believers as letters of Christ (3:3) and as those who have heavenly treasure in earthen vessels (4:7). Under both metaphors the idea of sealing, the mark of authenticity and security, is highly appropriate. The sealing itself, however, is neither metaphorical nor external: as a sealing with the Holy Spirit of God, it is a stamping of the divine character upon the human personality, a fresh and indestructible communication to the believer of the image of God which was defaced through the fall (cf. 3:18). He who carries the impress of the seal of the Spirit of truth (Jn. 14:17; 15:26; 16:13) is not faithless and insincere.

There is yet more, however, for God had also given Paul the *earnest* of the Spirit in his heart. The term "earnest" [23] means a deposit which is in itself a guarantee that the full amount will be paid later. It is important to notice that, as Lightfoot observes, "the thing given is related to the thing assured—the present to the hereafter—as a part to the whole. It is the same in kind".[24]

---

[22] Eusebius of Caesarea, *Hist. Eccles.* I, iii; cf. *Demonstr. Evang.* IV, xv.

[23] The term ἀρραβών, translated "earnest" here, is precisely the same word, transliterated, as the עֵרָבוֹן of Gen. 38:17, 18, 20, which is derived from the root עָרַב meaning "to interlace", thence "to exchange", and thus "to pledge". Suidas explains it as "the deposit given in advance by the purchasers for the things purchased, as security", Chrysostom as "a part of the whole", and Theodoret as "a small part of the whole". The word is generally believed to have been taken over from the trading vocabulary of the Phoenicians.

[24] J. B. Lightfoot, *Notes on the Epistles of St. Paul* (London, 1895), p. 323.

Hence it is not simply a pledge, which may be different in kind,[25] but a deposit, a first instalment. The sense of "the earnest of the Spirit" is well illustrated in Rom. 8:23 where Paul speaks of "the firstfruits of the Spirit"—the Christian already possesses here and now the first of the fruits of the complete harvest which he is destined ultimately to enjoy. While, therefore, the word "earnest" denotes something given for the present, it also looks to the future and carries a strong eschatological overtone. To quote Lightfoot again, "the actual spiritual life of the Christian is the same in kind as his future glorified life; the kingdom of heaven is a present kingdom; the believer is already seated on the right hand of God.... Nevertheless the present gift of the Spirit is only a *small fraction* of the future endowment. This idea also would be suggested by the usual relation between the earnest-money and the full payment".[26] Accordingly, it is not surprising to find Paul using this same expression, "the earnest of the Spirit" later in our epistle in a distinctly eschatological setting (5:5), while in Eph. 1:13f. (where, as here, he conjoins the idea of the sealing with that of the earnest) he speaks of the Holy Spirit as "an earnest of our inheritance", a foretaste, that is, or down payment, which guarantees the final possession in its fulness of that "inheritance incorruptible, and undefiled, and that fadeth not away, reserved in heaven" for those "who by the power of God are guarded through faith unto a salvation ready to be revealed in the last time" (I Pet. 1:4f.). Few things could be more incongruous than that one to whom such an earnest has been granted should himself be lacking in seriousness when formulating plans or making promises for the future, for good faith is absolutely central to the concept of such a transaction.

In the thought of the New Testament, then, the Christian

---

[25] As Vulgate: *pignus*. Cf. *Five Books in Reply to Marcion* (attributed to Tertullian but almost certainly a spurious work) which speaks of Christ as having "from His own Spirit poured a pledge (*pignus*)" (II, 1. 346). Augustine (Serm. 378) remarked on the inadequacy of the word *pignus* as a rendering of ἀρραβών: "It is better rendered *arrha* (i.e. *arrhabon*) than *pignus*; for these two seem to be similar to each other, but yet they possess a certain difference which should not be overlooked". Jerome had expressed himself to the same effect, but still failed to alter *pignus* in his Vulgate version. In Gen. 38:17ff., however, the term is used in the sense of "pledge", something different in kind being given as a guarantee.

[26] J. B. Lightfoot, *op. cit.*, p. 324.

experiences of anointing, sealing, and receiving the earnest are all associated with the operation of the Holy Spirit: the first connotes separation and commissioning for service, the second recognition and safe-keeping, and the third the authentic guarantee of the full inheritance of the glory yet to be revealed. Although these blessings are the privilege of every believer, it is preferable to take the first person plural here as referring specifically to Paul—in accordance with his practice of using "I" and "we" interchangeably of himself (cf. vv. 8ff., 15ff., 23f., etc.); for it is his own integrity which he is intent on affirming in this passage. The consideration that he is established, together with them, in Christ, and has been anointed, sealed, and given the earnest of the Spirit, should convince the Corinthians how groundless are the charges of fickleness and instability which certain ill-disposed persons have been muttering against him. This is the thrust of his argument; but at the same time it is evident from the expression "us with you", and also from the plural "our hearts", that Paul's outlook is in no way exclusive or self-centred.

The question arises as to whether there is in these verses an allusion to particular ecclesiastical rites or sacraments. The aorist tense of the verbs "anointed", "sealed", and "gave" [27] points to an event or events of the past. In our judgment all three verbs point back to different aspects of the Holy Spirit's operation in the one crucial event of conversion: anointing, sealing, and the receipt of the earnest are together the experience of the converted man. But many scholars have seen in the mention of being sealed a more or less direct reference to the sacrament of baptism. In this connection, it is an interesting fact that in Rom. 4:11 Paul describes as a *seal* the Old Testament sacrament of circumcision, of which the New Testament sacrament of baptism is the counterpart, and that in the early Church (from the second century onwards) it became customary to refer to baptism simply as "the seal". There can be no doubt that for Paul his baptism, though an event of the past, was an experience of tremendous significance, marking, externally at least, the irreversible turning of his back on the old life without Christ. Baptism need not, and indeed should not, be excluded from the picture here, for its impact and importance for the believer are

---

[27] Χρίσας, σφραγισάμενος, δούς.

not to be belittled; but we cannot agree that the rite of baptism is in the forefront of Paul's mind at this point. For one thing, both the crisis on the Damascus road and, it would seem, the coming of the Holy Spirit upon him preceded his baptism (Acts 9:17f.; cf. also the sequence in the case of Cornelius: Acts 10:44–48); and for another, if the sealing refers to the rite of baptism, it becomes necessary to indicate the rites to which the anointing and the giving of the earnest refer.

But this is a difficult, if not impossible, task, for the New Testament makes no mention of any external ceremony of anointing or chrism (apart from the anointing of the sick with oil, Jas. 5:14, where, however, a different verb is used.[28]) In the early Church, it is true, certainly from Tertullian onwards, chrism was employed at baptism and at confirmation; the latter, indeed, followed closely on the former. Accordingly, various commentators have wished to identify the anointing and the sealing of which Paul speaks in this passage either separately or conjointly with the rites of baptism or with confirmation. Yet more problematical, at least from the point of view of the New Testament, is the identification of the giving of the earnest with any particular rite. Allo favours the view that the "anointing" is baptism, whence results the continuous "establishment" which God grants to those who have been baptized, while the "sealing" is confirmation, whereby the "earnest" of the Spirit is given. That such an interpretation is open to dispute is apparent from what has already been said.[29]

It would have seemed to us a more satisfactory arrangement to identify the anointing, sealing, and giving of the earnest with

---

28 Ἀλείφω.

29 R. Bultmann, *Theology of the New Testament*, vol. I (London, 1952), p. 137, affirms that the sealing here and in Eph. 1:13 "undoubtedly alludes to baptism" and wishes to attribute the later use of the noun σφραγίς as a synonym for baptism to the idea which he supposes to be implicit in Paul's use of the verb σφραγίζεσθαι. In the opinion of Lightfoot, however—*The Apostolic Fathers*, pt. I, vol. II (London, 1890), p. 226—"it may be questioned whether S. Paul (σφραγισάμενος 2 Cor. i. 22, comp. Ephes. iv. 30) or S. John (Rev. ix. 4 τὴν σφραγῖδα τοῦ θεοῦ ἐπὶ τῶν μετώπων) used the image with any direct reference to baptism"; and T. K. Abbott, commenting on ἐσφραγίσθητε in Eph. 1:13—*The Epistles to the Ephesians and to the Colossians* (ICC, Edinburgh, n.d.)—says: "In later writers σφραγίς is used simply for 'baptism'; but there is no reason to suppose such a reference here, which would be too obscure."

the single event of baptism, and the continuous establishing with the other and constantly repeated New Testament sacrament of the holy communion—assuming that in the exposition of this passage it is desirable to seek some outward and visible sign with which to associate the inward and spiritual graces of which Paul speaks. But as far as we are aware, and to our surprise, such an identification does not seem to have been proposed hitherto, though it harmonizes well with what we know of the apostolic Church. We are not convinced, however, that these verses demand an understanding of this kind, unless it be in a secondary sense.[30]

Finally, the trinitarian implications of these two verses should be noticed. The sequence "... Christ ... God ... the Spirit" shows how naturally and without any trace of embarrassment the Apostle spoke of the three Persons of the Godhead, not because those to whom he was writing were adepts in theological learning (far from it! cf., e.g., I Cor. 3:1f.), but because to those who have experienced the redeeming work of the Triune God, Father, Son, and Holy Spirit, in the heart, the doctrine of the Trinity is one which needs no apology. Origen's pupil, Gregory Thaumaturgus, cites this passage, together with 13:14 and 3:15–18 of this same epistle, as evidence that "the Holy Trinity is to be worshipped without either separation or alienation".[31]

---

[30] Deissmann, *Bible Studies*, pp. 104ff., offers some interesting observations on the terminology of this verse. He suggests that Paul is using with some precision the technical language of legal contract. The word βεβαίωσις (cf. βεβαιῶν here) was employed in Attic jurisprudence to denote the definite obligation of the seller, who "did not only make over the thing to the buyer, but assumed the *guarantee* to defend the validity of the sale against any possible claims of a third party". The term implied the guarantee or safeguarding of a bargain which had been struck. The giving and receiving of earnest-money came to be closely linked with this conception: "in technical usage, ἀρραβών and βεβαιοῦν stand in an essential relation to each other. It is exactly in this way that Paul speaks —his indestructible faith representing the relation of God to believers under the image of a legally indisputable relation". Deissmann cites a patristic comment on this passage to the effect that the earnest used to confirm the whole contract *(ὁ γὰρ ἀρραβὼν εἴωθε βεβαιοῦν τὸ πᾶν σύνταγμα),* as showing "how a Greek reader could fully appreciate the specific nature of the metaphor".

[31] Gregory Thaumaturgus, *A Sectional Confession of Faith,* XX. This, however, is among the works dubiously attributed to him.

1 : 23, 24

> But I call God for a witness upon my soul, that to spare
> you I forbare to come unto Corinth. Not that we have
> lordship over your faith, but are helpers of your joy: for
> in faith ye stand fast.

Paul has been showing how the accusation of insincerity and
fickleness is entirely incompatible with the Corinthians' own personal knowledge of him and his word, as well as with the character
of one to whom God has given stability, anointing, sealing, and
the earnest of the Spirit. Now he explains why it was that he
had found it desirable to make an alteration in his plans: it was
to spare them—and the explanation is fortified by a solemn oath.
The taking of oaths would be superfluous were it not for the
presence of sin in the world and the satanic debasement of
language into a vehicle of falsehood instead of truth. Thus Holy
Scripture speaks even of God as confirming His word by an oath
(cf. Lk. 1:73; Heb. 6:13ff. = Gen. 22:16; Acts 2:30; Heb.
7:20f. = Ps. 110:4) and of an oath as being final for confirmation
of an utterance (Heb. 6:16). Our Lord's prohibition of swearing
in Mt. 5:33ff. is directed against the casuistry that was prevalent
among the Jews of His time, in accordance with which not only
was swearing frequent in ordinary speech, but also oaths were
regarded as not binding provided the Divine Name had not been
invoked and even lies were condoned if unaccompanied by an
oath. Such a situation was a grave scandal in the name of religion
and truth. It is due to the effect of evil, or the evil one, that
there should be any necessity for adding the emphasis of an oath
to a pronouncement (Mt. 5:37). Thus our Lord Himself was
accustomed to reinforce particularly important sayings of His
with the preface "Verily, verily, I say unto you", which, as
Origen has observed, was a form of oath. An oath is legitimate,
therefore, when the occasion demands that special weight should
be given to the truthfulness of some specific affirmation or promise,
or when it is necessary to vindicate the truth in opposition to
error and falsehood; and there can be no more solemn form of
oath than that, such as the Apostle employs here, whereby God
is invoked as a witness against one's soul.[32] It is essential that the

---

[32] It is preferable to understand ἐπὶ τὴν ἐμὴν ψυχήν as meaning "against
my soul" (Vg: in animam meam) = "against my life", that is, "may my life be
forfeit if I am not speaking the truth". 'Επί is used in this sense in Lk 9:5

Corinthians should be in no doubt as to what were the true motives behind his change of plan, for, as he is an apostle of Christ Jesus through the will of God to them (v. 1), it is ultimately the honour of God, no less, which is at stake. And so Paul reinforces his explanation with an oath.

His motive was one of love and concern for them, not for self. To have fulfilled his original intention would have meant coming to them in sorrow and with a rod (cf. I Cor. 4:21); but for their sakes, and because of his overflowing affection for them, he has delayed his coming so that they may have a prolonged opportunity for repentance and setting things in order. This is not a sign of weakness any more than the delay in the second coming of our Lord is a sign of weakness or inability on God's part to give substance to the judgment that has been threatened against the ungodly. Paul's attitude is, indeed, a reflection of his Master's, who "is not slack concerning his promise, as some count slackness, but is longsuffering ..., not wishing that any should perish, but that all should come to repentance" (II Pet. 3:9). An unusually interesting parallel to this situation is found in a letter written by Augustine to the nuns of a monastery founded by him where a spirit of insubordination and insurrection had been stirred up against the one who had succeeded his sister as prioress. "As severity is ready to punish the faults which it may discover", he writes, "so charity is reluctant to discover the faults which it must punish. This was the reason of my not acceding to your request for a visit from me, at a time when, if I had come, I must

---

and Acts 13:51, and frequently, of course, in classical authors from Homer onwards. To render it, as the ASV does, "upon my soul" weakens the force of the expression. "Against my soul" is also better suited to the Hebrew form of oath: "The Lord do so to me and more also, if ...", with which Paul was naturally familiar (cf. Ruth 1:17; I Sam. 14:44; II Sam. 3:35; I Kings 2:23, etc.). W. C. van Unnik (*Studia Paulina, ut supra*, p. 220) regards the expression as "ein deutlicher Semitismus: ἐπὶ τὴν ἐμὴν ψυχήν = על נפשי = mich selbst", and therefore as further evidence that Paul thought—and perhaps wrote—not in Greek, but in Aramaic.

Augustine observes that in the discourses of which we possess a record Paul "never used an oath, lest he should ever fall unawares into perjury from being in the habit of swearing", whereas in his writings, "where he had more leisure and opportunity for caution, we find him using oaths in several places to teach us that there is no sin in swearing truly, but that, on account of the infirmity of human nature, we are best preserved from perjury by not swearing at all" (*Contra Faustum Manichaeum*, XIX, 23).

47

have come not to rejoice in your harmony, but to add more vehemence to your strife. For how could I have treated your behaviour with indifference, or have allowed it to pass unpunished, if so great a tumult had arisen among you in my presence as that which, when I was absent, assailed my ears with the din of your voices, although my eyes did not witness your disorder? For perhaps your rising against authority would have been even more violent in my presence, since I must have refused the concessions which you demanded — concessions involving, to your own disadvantage, some most dangerous precedents, subversive of sound discipline; and I must thus have found you such as I did not desire, and must myself have been found by you such as you did not desire.[33] The Apostle, writing to the Corinthians, says: Moreover, I call God for a witness upon my soul, that to spare you I forbare to come unto Corinth. Not that we have lordship over your faith, but are helpers of your joy. I also say the same to you; to spare you I have not come to you. I have also spared myself, that I might not have sorrow upon sorrow, and have chosen not to see you face to face, but to pour out my heart to God on your behalf, and to plead the cause of your great danger not in words before you, but in tears before God, entreating Him that He may not turn into grief the joy wherewith I am wont to rejoice in you, and that amid the great offences with which this world everywhere abounds I may be comforted at times by thinking of your number, your pure affection, your holy conversation, and the abundant grace of God which is given to you ...".[34] It is evident that in writing these words Augustine had very much in mind the situation in which Paul found himself at the time of writing II Corinthians.

The Apostle, clearly, is so painfully conscious of the facility with which his statements, even in their most amicable form, are prone to be misconstrued by those who wish to present him in a bad light in Corinth that, having said that his reason for not coming was that he might spare the Corinthians, he immediately feels the need for anticipating any derogatory use which might be made by his detractors of this explanation. These cavillers would readily draw from his wish to spare them the inference that he claimed to exercise a lordship or dictatorship over their

---

[33] Cf. II Cor. 12:20.
[34] Augustine, Letter CCXI (A.D. 423).

faith: he who spares is also the master who punishes and disposes in accordance with his arbitrary decision. And so Paul explains further that there is no question of his lording it over the Corinthians in the realm of their faith.[35] There is but one Lord and one faith (Eph. 4:5),[36] and that one Lord alone has lordship over the faith of every Christian. It is not Paul's office to lord it over the servant of another; to his own lord each man stands or falls (Rom. 14:4), and the Christian's Lord and Master is Christ, not an apostle, nor any other creature. As Christ is the object of faith, so also He is the Lord of faith. He alone has lordship over [37] both the dead and the living (Rom. 14:9); it is before *His* judgment-seat that all must stand (Rom. 14:10; II Cor. 5:10). Lording it over others is, in fact, a mark of the potentates of this world, who arrogantly attempt to assert their own lordship to the exclusion of the Lordship of God. Christian greatness, however, is not of this kind, but displays itself in the humility of service (Lk. 22:25f.). And, no matter what may be the appearance of things in this fallen world, Christ is and will ultimately prove Himself to be "the Lord of those who act the lord" (I Tim. 6:15).[38]

There is, then, no scriptural warrant for hierarchical domination or overlordship in the Church of Christ. Absolute authority is invested not in any supposed apostolic office or succession, but in the person and office of Christ who is the only Apostle and High Priest of our confession (Heb. 3:1) and the one Shepherd and Bishop of our souls (I Pet. 2:25). Peter, upon whom so oppressive a burden of overlordship has been heaped during the intervening centuries, regarded himself as an ecclesiastical lord no more than did Paul. The elders, with whom he classes himself as a fellow-elder, he exhorts not to lord it over [39] the charge allotted to them (I Pet. 5:1, 3), for no man, even though he be an apostle, has dominion over the faith of another man.

To claim such dominion is to manifest oneself as a false apostle and minister of Satan (and Paul may well have intended his disclaimer here as a thrust against those intruders who had sought to usurp his position in Corinth). Faith, as Calvin ob-

---

35 Οὐχ ὅτι κυριεύομεν ὑμῶν τῆς πίστεως.
36 Εἷς Κύριος, μία πίστις.
37 Κυριεύσῃ.
38 Κύριος τῶν κυριευόντων.
39 Μηδ' ὡς κατακυριεύοντες.

serves, "acknowledges no subjection except to the Word of God and is not at all liable to the rule of men". The Christian is justified by faith (Rom. 5:1), and therefore his standing is in faith (cf. Eph. 2:8; Phil. 3:9; II Tim. 3:15); and this standing is entirely before God, not before man. If the standing of the Corinthians is in any doubt, it is they, and not some-one else, who must examine and test themselves to see whether they are in the faith (13:5). This does not mean that the Apostle wields no authority. On the contrary, the object of his writing is to affirm his authority. But his is a delegated, not an absolute, authority; it is exercised over those who already profess faith; and it expresses itself in the discipline of error, the punishment of misconduct, and the correction of disorder. It is given for the purpose of the edification and well-being of the Church, not for making absolute pronouncements concerning the state of the souls of others; for it is to God alone that the heart is made manifest (cf. 5:10f.). Paul, moreover, so far from wishing, like some despot, to oppress and subjugate the Corinthians by the relentless imposition of authority, desires to be a helper of their joy—that is, that he may assist them to arrive at that state of unclouded communion with God and fellowship with each other, in which their overflowing and constant experience will be one of joy unspeakable and full of glory (cf. Phil. 4:4; I Pet. 1:8). How can he, whose whole standing, altogether equally with them, is in faith, have lordship over their faith? How can he, as their Apostle, not long that their faith may be of such deep genuineness that their joy, like his, may be full in the Lord?

2:1

But I determined this for myself, that I would not come again to you with sorrow.

This, as Calvin and others have remarked, is an inept chapter division, for there is no break in the Apostle's argument at this point. What he says here should be compared with what he has already written in 1:15. There he states that he "was minded", that is, had formed the wish,[40] to pay the Corinthians a double visit, the implication being that no fixed decision had then been reached on this matter. Here he explains that he "determined",

---

[40] Ἐβουλόμην — Vg: volui.

that is, formed the judgment,[41] not to come again to them with sorrow. This was the settled decision at which he subsequently arrived, and the verb indicates that this decision was not the result of capriciousness on his part, but of a careful and deliberate weighing up of the situation. It was dictated by responsible judgment, no less than was his determination,[42] upon first coming to Corinth, to know nothing among them save Jesus Christ, and Him crucified (I Cor. 2:2). There was, therefore, no question of irresolution or irresponsibility where he was concerned.

When Paul declares that he had determined not to come again to the Corinthians in sorrow the plain inference is that there had been a previous occasion on which a visit to Corinth had caused him sorrow. This being so, he cannot be referring to his original visit during which the church at Corinth was founded, but to some later visit when the state of affairs found by him in the church already in existence there had grieved his heart. This in turn implies that there must have been at least two visits to that city prior to the writing of this present epistle. That there had in fact been just two such visits—that is, the original visit and a subsequent one—is evident from what we read in 12:14 and 13:1f. Luke's silence in Acts concerning a second visit prior to the writing of II Corinthians should not be taken as being in conflict with or as demanding some other, less natural, interpretation of what Paul says here, for his annals are highly selective, with the result that many things are omitted by him, presumably because he considered them not relevant to the purpose and scheme of his treatise (compare in particular the catalogue of experiences given by Paul in 11:23ff. below). Calvin, surprisingly, expresses the opinion that Paul's previous sorrowful coming to the Corinthians had not been in person, but by letter. If letters are to be understood as comings then the whole issue becomes hopelessly confused. Equally unsatisfactory is the proposal of Stanley and others that Paul should be taken to mean here that his impending visit will be only his second one to Corinth: "I determined that when I come to you again, that is, for the second time, it will not be in sorrow"; for this then requires that the references to an impending third visit in 12:14 and 13:1 must be explained by the hypothesis that the second visit

---

41 Ἔκρινα.
42 Ἔκρινα.

implied in such terminology was in intention only, but in actual fact never took place. For Paul to mean that a coming in intention should be counted as equivalent to a coming in person would be disruptive of the whole thrust of the argument he has been elaborating. As Denney says, the natural meaning of Paul's words here is that he "had once visited Corinth in grief, and was resolved not to repeat such a visit".

Many modern scholars have favoured the hypothesis that this second or intermediate visit (intermediate, that is, between the original visit and the impending third visit) took place during the interval between the writing of the two canonical epistles, and that it was occasioned by the arrival of news, possibly brought by Timothy, to the effect that there had been a revolt against the Apostle's authority in Corinth. It is further supposed that during this brief visit Paul had been grossly insulted by a certain unnamed individual and that, on his return to Ephesus, he had written a severe and sorrowful letter, the main part of which is, according to the view of most who adopt this theory, to be identified with the last four chapters (10–13) of our present epistle. On these questions we shall have more to say in the commentary on 2:3ff. and 7:8ff. below. For our present purposes it is sufficient to state that we are in agreement with the opinion of Alford, Denney, Lightfoot, Bernard, Sanday, Zahn, and numerous others that the intermediate visit took place prior to the writing of I Corinthians (see pp. 45ff. above), and that we concur with the judgment of those who identify the epistle in question with the letter which is now known as I Corinthians. Since Paul's revised itinerary is plainly outlined in I Cor. 16:5ff. it is difficult to believe that he would not have explained the reasons for his change of plan during a subsequent visit and also, if necessary, in a subsequent letter. The fact that he takes trouble to explain the circumstances in our present epistle tells against the supposition that there had been either a visit or a letter to Corinth during the interval between the composition of our two canonical epistles.

2:2

> For if I make you sorry, who then is he that maketh me glad but he that is made sorry by me?

Considered by itself, this verse could mean, as Chrysostom and others have supposed, that for Paul's rebuke to have caused the Corinthians to experience sorrow would have made him glad, on the ground that such a reaction would have been clear evidence of the love and esteem in which they hold him; and in this sense it would correspond to 7:9 where Paul declares that he rejoices that they were made sorry unto repentance. But this interpretation is quite unsuited to the context, for the point the Apostle is making is that he adjusted his plan precisely for the purpose of avoiding a sorrowful encounter with them—sorrowful in that he would find them disobedient and recalcitrant and that he would have to correct them with a rod. In 7:9, however, he rejoices because their response to the letter he had sent means that his impending visit will be one of gladness, not pain, for both himself and them. His object is to be a helper of their joy (1:24), and accordingly his desire is that they through the unclouded fellowship of their love and loyalty may make him glad. The sense of this verse is that he cannot be made glad by those whom he has made sorry; for their sorrow is his sorrow, just as their joy is his joy.[43] The sorrow envisaged here is that produced by unrepentance on their part, resulting for him in disappointment (see next verse) and for them in chastisement; whereas the sorrow with which Paul is concerned in 7:9f. is that godly sorrow which works repentance.

2:3, 4

> And I wrote this very thing, lest, when I came, I should have sorrow from them of whom I ought to rejoice; having confidence in you all, that my joy is the joy of you all. For out of much affliction and anguish of heart I wrote unto you with many tears; not that ye should be made sorry, but that ye might know the love which I have more abundantly unto you.

Paul had written a letter to the Corinthians and his purpose in doing so was twofold. In the first place, he had hoped thereby to ensure that what was amiss in Corinth would be set right, so that there might be no necessity for him to come to them in severity. This in itself was an expression of confidence in those

---

[43] As Alford remarks, καί prefixed to a question, as here (εἰ γὰρ ἐγὼ λυπῶ ὑμᾶς, καὶ τίς ὁ εὐφραίνων με . . .;), "denotes *inconsequence on*, or *inconsistency with*, the foregoing supposition or affirmation".

who were, after all, his children in the Lord. As their spiritual father he had a right to expect joy from them, not sorrow, when present in their midst, and he trusted that a letter from him, whose joy should be their concern no less than theirs was his, would be sufficient to obviate the prospect of an unhappy encounter. In the second place, the letter was designed to be an expression of the surpassing love which he had for them. Its motive was not recrimination or vindictiveness, but overflowing love [44]—the love which they had been deceived into doubting, the love which, unseen by them, had called forth "much affliction and anguish of heart ... with many tears" in the writing of the letter. Genuine love always experiences profound grief when it perceives those who are loved falling into error and disloyalty; it always manifests itself in deep concern for their best and highest interests. By writing, rather than immediately coming to them in person with a rod, he lovingly afforded them an opportunity for self-examination, repentance, and reformation. This passage, as Denney says, "reveals, more clearly perhaps than any passage in the New Testament, the essential qualification of the Christian minister—a heart pledged to his brethren in the love of Christ.... Depend upon it", he counsels, "we shall not make others weep for that for which we have not wept; we shall not make that touch the hearts of others which has not first touched our own".

The Identity of the Epistle mentioned in 2:3f.

But to which letter is the Apostle referring, and when was it written? To these questions there is no unanimous answer. Olshausen and others have followed Chrysostom in taking "I wrote" to be an epistolary aorist, equivalent, that is, to "I am

---

[44] In the Greek the word "love" is in a position of particular emphasis, τὴν ἀγάπην being placed *before* the conjunction ἵνα—ἀλλὰ τὴν ἀγάπην ἵνα γνῶτε ἣν ἔχω περισσοτέρως εἰς ὑμᾶς. In view of the extreme affection which Paul expresses in his letters to other churches, it seems unwarranted to understand (as do Chrysostom, Theophylact, Alford, Hodge, etc.) περισσοτέρως here to imply that the Apostle's love for the church at Corinth was greater than his love for any other of the churches he had founded. The force of this adverb here is intensive rather than strictly comparative, corresponding to our "exceedingly": cf. τῇ περισσοτέρᾳ λύπῃ, "with overmuch sorrow", in verse 7; 7:13, where περισσοτέρως is used to intensify another comparative—περισσοτέρως μᾶλλον; and the notes on the significance of περισσοτέρως in 7:15 and 11:23.

writing". They therefore understand Paul to be alluding to our present epistle, which he was then in process of composing.[45] This opinion, however, is unsatisfactory both because "I wrote" here must properly be co-ordinated with "I determined"[46] in verse 1, the force of which is that of a genuine aorist (verse 2 forming, as Allo observes, a sort of parenthesis), and also because in 7:8ff. the *effects* produced in Corinth by the letter in question are described, which would be quite impossible had the letter not yet been sent and received. Therefore the view is unacceptable that the letter intended by the Apostle was the one which he was then actually in process of writing, namely, our present II Corinthians.

It has most commonly been supposed that the reference is to the first of our two canonical epistles. Many modern scholars, however, have rejected this judgment on the ground that the character of I Corinthians is not such that it could with appropriateness be described as written "out of much affliction and anguish of heart" and "with many tears". Accordingly, the composition of another epistle, intermediate in time between our two canonical epistles, is postulated. But among those who accept this conclusion opinion is divided as to whether or not the text of this intermediate letter is still extant, either in part or in its entirety. Those who answer in the affirmative contend, for the most part, that the last four chapters (10–13) form an inept appendage to our present epistle, but that they answer excellently to the letter described by Paul here; and consequently they are in favour of identifying the intermediate epistle, or a portion of it, with these chapters. In disallowing this theory we shall only say here [47] that, apart from the fact that there is no shred of external evidence nor breath of tradition to suggest that the concluding four chapters were ever anything but an integral part of our epistle, for Paul to have written affirming the imminence of his coming to Corinth and warning that he will not spare, but will take a strong line with any who withstand his authority (10:1ff., 12:14, 13:1ff.), and now, some time later (*ex hypothesi*), to write again without having made the promised visit, saying that it was to spare the Corinthians that he had forborne

---

45 The use of the epistolary aorist was an accepted literary procedure. Definite examples in this epistle may be seen in 8:17f., ἐξῆλθε and συνεπέμψαμεν, and 9:3, ἔπεμψα (though Allo disagrees: see note below on 12:18); cf. also ἔπεμψα in Eph. 6:22 and Phil. 2:28, and ἀνέπεμψα in Philem. 12.

46 Ἔκρινα . . . ἔγραψα.

47 The question is discussed more fully in the Introduction, pp. xxii ff.

to come since he had determined not to come again to them with sorrow (1:23, 2:1ff.), not only fails to make sense but lays him open to those very charges of pusillanimity, fickleness, and weakness which he is intent on repudiating.

There are others, however, Lietzmann, Bachmann, Windisch, Allo, and, most recently, Tasker among them, who, while adopting the hypothesis of an intermediate letter, maintain that the letter in question is now entirely lost—thus constituting the second epistle to which Paul refers that is no longer extant (the first being mentioned in I Cor. 5:9). This theory is certainly, to our mind, simpler and more plausible than that which was outlined in the last paragraph.

But we believe that it is unnecessary in this case to add to the number of "unknown" and "lost" documents, since it is possible to give a reasonable and satisfactory explanation of Paul's reference here to an earlier letter by connecting it with the earlier of our two canonical epistles. This indeed was the understanding of the Church throughout many centuries (apart from a minority opinion which, as we have seen, interpreted Paul's words to refer to this present epistle, but which otherwise expounded the allusions of the next section—verses 5–11—in terms of what the Apostle had previously written in I Corinthians). The further we are removed in time from the original event, the more we should, as a matter of principle, hesitate to entertain novel theories in the face of a strong tradition of interpretation and in the absence of anything fresh in the way of external evidence. In a case of this kind the probability is all in favour of the earlier exegesis being correct rather than the later conjecture.

Yet today it is becoming fashionable to state in a quite categorical manner that the letter written "out of much affliction and anguish of heart ... with many tears" cannot be identified with I Corinthians, thereby implying that, though the evidence which was before it was certainly not less than that which is before us, the Church of old was quite mistaken in its interpretation at this point (which is, we grant, a possibility) and also failed to see what should have been obvious (which is much less likely). Thus Plummer, who strongly advocates the "four-chapter-letter" hypothesis, declares that the traditional view, though favoured by more recent "scholars of great eminence", may "once for all be abendoned as untenable"; and Allo, who no less strongly advocates the "lost-letter" hypothesis, gives it as his judgment that the character attributed by Paul to the letter in question "forbids absolutely its identification with the First

Epistle". But though their judgment is concurrent in this respect, we are entitled to question whether either can with confidence be followed as a reliable guide in the debate which the theories they favour have aroused, since the one holds that the final four chapters are quite incompatible with the earlier part of our epistle but answer admirably to, and therefore are to be identified with, the "intermediate" letter which the Apostle is supposedly describing, whereas the other contends that the final four chapters form an integral and coherent part of our epistle and certainly do *not* correspond to the character of the letter mentioned here.

For our part, the view that it would have been inappropriate for Paul to describe I Corinthians as a letter written "out of much affliction and anguish of heart" and "with many tears" is quite unacceptable. Sorrow and anguish are precisely the emotions we would have expected him to experience when it became necessary for him to write to those whose father he was in the faith, and for whom he had so overwhelming a love, in terms of reproof and condemnation because of the manner in which they had lapsed into serious error, disorder, and immorality: their church, so far from being a centre of unity in Christ, had become an arena of warring factions and rivalries; they had shown themselves to be yet carnal, immature and stunted in spiritual growth, and all too easily deceived by the wisdom of this world; not only were they defiling the temple of God by succumbing to the lusts of the flesh, but they had condoned the sin of incest in their midst, an enormity which even the Gentiles abhorred; they were puffed up with self-esteem and arrogance; they were animated by a spirit of litigiousness which caused them to take their squabbles before the courts of unbelievers, thereby bringing the Church of Christ into disrepute; by their misuse of the gifts of the Spirit with which they had been enriched public worship in Corinth was marred by unedifying scenes of disorderliness; the sacrament of the Lord's Supper was profaned by gluttony and uncharitableness; and they had even called in question a fact so cardinal for their faith as the resurrection of Christ from the dead. Any one of these things would have been sufficient to cause Paul real distress; taken together, they could not have failed to occasion one who felt as deeply as the Apostle did the severest grief. Nothing, surely, should surprise us less than the information that such an epistle had been written out of much affliction and anguish of heart and to the accompaniment of many tears. We cannot agree, therefore, that there is any inappropriateness in the identification of the letter mentioned by Paul here with the earlier of our two canonical epistles.

Since the Apostle's primary purpose in this passage is to explain the reason for his change of plan, his words "I wrote this very thing" are most suitably understood as a direct reference to I Cor. 16:5ff. where he has plainly told the Corinthians of his revised itinerary. This is more satisfactory than taking them, as some commentators have done, to refer in a more general sense to the whole contents of the letter in question.[48]

---

[48] Erasmus understood τοῦτο αὐτό as meaning "for this very reason"—a rendering which is certainly admissible and which may be matched in the classical authors. But it is preferable to translate τοῦτο αὐτό as the direct object of the verb ἔγραψα, both because it gives added point to the sentence when taken in this way, and also because it is Paul's custom elsewhere to employ the preposition εἰς when he wishes to say "for this reason"—as in verse 9 where he has εἰς τοῦτο . . . ἔγραψα (cf. also εἰς τοῦτο in I Thess. 3:3 and I Tim. 4:10, and εἰς αὐτὸ τοῦτο in 5:5, Rom. 9:7, 13:6, and Col. 4:8).

2:5

> But if any hath caused sorrow, he hath caused sorrow, not
> to me, but in part (that I press not too heavily) to you all.

That Paul is referring here to one particular offender at
Corinth is plain from the verses that follow: he had been punished
through the discipline imposed on him by the church in accordance
with the instructions given in a previous letter of Paul's, and
now he was to be forgiven and afforded the comfort of the
Corinthians' love.   Until modern times it was the practically
universal conclusion of the Church that the offender in question
was to be identified with the man mentioned in I Cor. 5 who
had been guilty of the sin of incest. But that opinion is now widely
dismissed as untenable.   It is maintained that the Apostle, who
had previously condemned the incestuous Corinthian in such
extreme terms, could hardly now with consistency speak so
indulgently of him, even though he had repented, and that, in
any case, the language of our text indicates that he is referring
to an offence of a quite different category involving himself and
his authority. Accordingly, many modern commentators (among
them Godet, Moffatt, Plummer, Lietzmann, Bachmann, Robertson [1], Strachan) suppose that, probably during the hypothetical
"intermediate" visit, Paul had been wantonly affronted to his
face and his authority resisted by a particular member of the
Corinthian church, who may also have been the ringleader of
an insubordinate faction, and thereafter had written the hypothetical severe "intermediate" letter demanding the punishment
of this offender.   It must be said, however, that if this theory is
correct then there would seem to be some real justification for
the caustic criticism of his opponents to the effect that, while
his letters are weighty and threaten strong action, yet when
present in person his supposed authority vanishes into weakness
and incompetence (cf. 10:10ff.).
The force of this objection has led some scholars to propose
a modification of the theory, whereby it is supposed that it was

---

[1]   A. Robertson, *HDB*, Vol. I, p. 493.

not Paul personally but someone closely associated with him who, as the representative of his authority, suffered the injury of a gross insult after the Apostle's departure from Corinth. Thus Allo writes: "For our part, we are unable to believe that the Apostle was affronted to his face or that the offence took place during the course of the intermediate journey. To us it would seem strange if the community, as a whole, had not immediately reacted, or that, if it had shown this inconstancy, Paul should have left them with such conciliatory feelings, promising them an early and well-disposed return. ... But above all we cannot imagine such a man placing himself at a safe distance in order to repulse an outrage which would have affected not only his person but also his dignity as an Apostle, and daring to censure or punish only by letter; there would then have been reason for the ironical accusations of his adversaries that he was courageous only from a distance".

Who, then, was the person involved in the presumed incident in which not merely his own dignity but even the authority of Paul was affronted? Among those who have thought that they could identify the offended individual the name of Timothy has had most favour. G. G. Findlay, for example, suggests the following sequence of events: "Appearing at Corinth on Paul's behalf about the time of the arrival of the 1st Ep. (4:17–21; 16:10, 11), and perhaps taking the initiative in the trial of the incestuous man, Timothy received a gross insult from 'some one' of note in the Church, the injury thus inflicted striking the apostle through his representative, and, not improbably, involving an angry reflexion upon him for sending a stripling in his place". This thesis is somewhat wildly supported by the assertion that the attack on Timothy accounts for the "emphatic and continuous" (!) identification by Paul of his young helper in the first seven chapters of our epistle and for the "subtle interchanges" (?) between the first person plural and singular in the passages relating to the offender and the person offended.[2]

Allo, however, shows more good sense in pointing out that it is impossible to know whether Timothy had ever fulfilled his mission to Corinth and in concluding that "in the whole of our present epistle there is nothing, apart from his name in the

---

[2]   G. G. Findlay, *HDB*, Vol. III, p. 711.

salutation and the recollection of his co-operation, with Silas, in the foundation of the Church (1:19), to suggest that he had had a personal role in the most recent events". And so Allo, content to leave this "secondary point" in its obscurity, takes his stand with those who suppose that the offence in question was committed against some person other than the Apostle whose identity is now unknown.

We must not overlook the fact that in the early Church an important voice, that of Tertullian, was raised against the traditional interpretation of this passage. This consideration has not, of course, escaped the attention of those modern commentators who hold that the ancient view is untenable. (Plummer, indeed, declares that "Tertullian's vigorous argument almost suffices without any others".) Tertullian maintains [3] that the case in point concerned "some *moderate* indulgence" which could not conceivably have been granted so readily to one guilty not simply of fornication but of incest, and whom, moreover, the Apostle had previously (I Cor. 5:5) commanded to be handed over to Satan for the destruction of the flesh. Tertullian's exegesis, however, is governed by the premise that the sin of incest is *irremissible*, involving the "loss of baptism" and the impossibility of the restoration of the sinner to a state of grace and salvation. Accordingly, he insists that "it was not with a view to emendation but with a view to perdition that Paul delivered the incestuous fornicator to Satan, to whom he had already, by sinning above a heathen, gone over"; the condemned offender "had already perished *from the Church* at the moment when he had committed such a deed".

But is Tertullian right in affirming that the Apostle's sentence means that the guilty man was irretrievably lost? The very terms of the sentence itself show that Tertullian's conclusion cannot be accepted by those who come to the text with an open mind, for Paul had enjoined that the offender was to be delivered to Satan for the destruction of the flesh, "*that the spirit may be saved in the day of the Lord Jesus*". In short, as Robertson and Plummer explain, "the purpose of the suffering is not mere destruction; it is remedial".[4] The exegesis offered by Tertullian

---

[3] Tertullian, *De Pudicitia*, XIII–XVI.
[4] Robertson and Plummer, *Commentary on the First Epistle of St Paul to the Corinthians* (ICC, Edinburgh, 1911), *sub* 5:5.

—that Paul's meaning was "that *that* Spirit which is accounted to exist *in the Church* must be presented 'saved', that is, untainted by the contagion of impurities in the day of the Lord, by the ejection of the incestuous fornicator"— was no more likely to commend itself in his day than it does in ours. As Allo (who also rejects the identification of the offender with the incestuous Corinthian) observes, "at the time when the passionate African was occupying himself with our question he had already fallen into heresy, and he was concerned to remove from the catholics, who acknowledged the Church's power to reconcile repentant fornicators, the right to invoke the example of St. Paul and to say that in the Second Epistle to the Corinthians the Apostle had lifted the excommunication imposed on the incestuous man in the First... In all this discussion", he continues, "Tertullian completely falsifies the spirit of St. Paul by giving him the severity and rigorism of a Montanist sectary". We would add that Tertullian's distinction between the remissibility of certain sins committed *before* baptism and the irremissibility of those same sins, though repented of, when committed *after* baptism, together with the teaching then gaining currency in the Church to the effect that the blood of Christ no longer avails for the cleansing away of sin once baptism has been received, is quite out of harmony with the reality of the New Testament situation, in accordance with which the *baptized Christian* has the assurance that the blood of Jesus still cleanses from *all* sin and that, upon repentance and confession, God is faithful and righteous to forgive him his sins and to cleanse him from *all* unrighteousness (I Jn. 1:7, 9).

The presuppositions by which Tertullian's exegesis of this text is governed are, therefore, unacceptable. But this positive conclusion may at least be drawn from what he writes, that the traditional interpretation was established in his day, not much more than a century after the apostolic age. And it is interesting to find that, in what is by no means a brief treatment of the subject, he makes no mention at all of any other interpretation, apart from the explanation which he himself offers. Had he had any knowledge of a tradition or even hypothesis that a scandalous affront had been offered to Timothy or some other delegate of Paul's shortly after the delivery of I Corinthians, or that Paul himself had paid an intermediate visit to Corinth during the course of which his authority had been treated with contempt, and that he had subsequently written an intermediate letter demanding the punishment of the offending person, it is incredible that he should have made no mention of this knowledge and indeed that he should not have welcomed it as affording corroboration of his own view that the Apostle could not have been alluding to the incestuous Corinthian here. Tertullian's silence in this respect tells strongly against the modern theory in its various forms. So also does the fact that he shows no hesitation in identifying the epistle mentioned in this passage with our present I Corinthians. His opinion, however, that the offender whom Paul had in mind was some individual guilty of being "puffed up" (see I Cor. 4:18f.) is altogether unconvincing.

Despite the sweepingly categorical assertions of many modern commentators to the effect that it is now absolutely certain that, whoever the offender may be, the Apostle is not referring to the incestuous Corinthian of I Cor. 5, we believe that no compelling reason has been advanced for the abandonment of the traditional understanding of this passage. In holding this judgment we keep company not only with such scholars of the ancient Church as Chrysostom, Ambrosiaster, Theodoret, and Theophylact, but also with modern exegetes of the calibre of Hodge, Stanley, Lightfoot, Denney, Weiss, and Zahn. In the Christian Church there must always be room for repentance and restoration, no matter how grievously a member may have sinned. Hence the apostolic injuction: "Brethren, even if a man be overtaken in any trespass, ye who are spiritual, restore such a one in the spirit of gentleness; looking to thyself, lest thou also be tempted" (Gal. 6:1). Lightfoot, in fact, believes that there is a definite connection between this admonition to the Galatians and the problem that had but recently arisen over the offence committed in Corinth. "A grievous offence had been committed in the Christian community at Corinth", he explains. "In his first Epistle to the Church there, St Paul had appealed to the brotherhood to punish the guilty person. The appeal had not only been answered, but answered with so much promptness, that it was necessary to intercede for the offender. He commended their indignation, their zeal, their revenge; they had approved themselves clear in the matter [2 Cor. vii. 11]; and now they must forgive and comfort their erring brother, lest he be swallowed up with overmuch sorrow [2 Cor. ii. 7]. It was the recollection of this circumstance that dictated the injunction in the Galatian Epistle".[5]

Concurring with Denney's judgment that "it is natural and justifiable to explain the Second Epistle as far as possible out of the First", and that in view of certain significant verbal resemblances between the two epistles "it becomes extremely difficult to believe that in 2 Cor. ii. 5ff. and 2 Cor. vii. 8ff. the Apostle is dealing with anything else than the case of the sinner treated in 1 Cor. v",[6] we feel bound to conclude that what was for centuries the all but universal understanding of this passage is still the only one of substantial worth.

The traditional interpretation receives further confirmation from Paul's declaration that it was not to him but to the Corinthians that the offender had caused sorrow. He could hardly have written this had he himself been affronted, either directly in his own person or indirectly in the person of his delegate.[7] There could be no question, therefore, of the discipline he had

---

[5] J. B. Lightfoot, *Saint Paul's Epistle to the Galatians* (London, tenth edition, 1902), p. 54.

[6] James Denney, *The Second Epistle to the Corinthians* (*The Expositor's Bible*, London, 1894), pp. 2f. He draws attention to the correspondence "between ἁγνὸς ἐν τῷ πράγματι, 2 Cor. vii 11 (cf. the use of πρᾶγμα in 1 Thess. iv. 6), and τοιαύτη πορνεία in 1 Cor. v. 1; between ἐν προσώπῳ Χριστοῦ, 2 Cor. ii. 10, and ἐν τῷ ὀνόματι τοῦ Κ. ἡμῶν 'I.X., 1 Cor. v. 4; between the mention of Satan in 2 Cor. ii. 11 and 1 Cor. v: 5; between πενθεῖν in 2 Cor. xii. 21 and 1 Cor. v. 2; between τοιοῦτος and τις in 2 Cor. ii. 6f., 2 Cor. ii. 5, and the same words in 1 Cor. v. 5 and 1 Cor. v. 1".

[7] Alford, Plummer, Allo, and others are not correct in asserting that ἀλλά, "but", cannot have the sense of εἰ μή, "except", for ἀλλά is occasionally found with the meaning of "except" in the classical authors (cf. Homer, *Odys.*, XII, 404f.; Sophocles, *Oed. Tyr.*, 1331; Aristotle, *Nichom. Ethics*, X, v, 10). This means that the rendering of Tertullian, Theodoret, the Vulgate, Luther, Bengel, AV, etc., to the following effect: "he has not caused sorrow to me, except to a partial extent (that I press not too heavily on you all)", is possible. Yet it is certainly preferable to take ἀλλά here in its normal sense of "but", as in our version, and as do almost all recent commentators and editors. Paul is then saying: "it is not to me, but to you all (with certain exceptions) that he has caused sorrow". There would seem to be no instance in the New Testament of ἀλλά being used with the meaning of "except". In Mk. 10:40, as Swete points out, "the true complement of the sentence" — τὸ δὲ καθίσαι ἐκ δεξιῶν μου ἢ ἐξ εὐωνύμων οὐκ ἔστιν ἐμὸν δοῦναι, ἀλλ' οἷς ἑτοίμασται—"is δοθήσεται, not ἐμόν ἐστιν δοῦναι"; consequently here too ἀλλά retains its full adversative force. Concerning the expression, "that I press not too heavily", see next note.

demanded having been prompted by a spirit of rancour or injured pride on his part. The shame and injury belonged, rather, to the Church of Christ at Corinth, which by failing to take action against the offender had given the impression of condoning the offence. Even now the sorrow evinced in Corinth was only "in part"; there were some there who set themselves in resistance to the authority of Paul, as was shown by the fact that the sentence of condemnation passed on the offender had not been unanimous (see next verse; also Chapters 10 to 13).[8]

2:6—8

Sufficient to such a one is this punishment which was inflicted by the many; so that contrariwise ye should rather forgive him and comfort him, lest by any means such a one should be swallowed up with his overmuch sorrow. Wherefore I beseech you to confirm your love toward him.

The punishment imposed on the offending Corinthian had been consequent on a resolution passed by a majority of the

---

[8] The precise significance of the parenthetical "that I press not too heavily" (ἵνα μὴ ἐπιβαρῶ) is uncertain. Chrysostom, Calvin, and many others have treated ἐπιβαρῶ as transitive and have understood the offender to be the object: "that I press not too heavily *on him*". Others have taken the Corinthians to be the object: "that I press not too heavily *on you*". Olshausen follows Mosheim in preferring to include πάντας in the parenthesis: " . . . he hath caused sorrow, not to me, but in part (that I press not too heavily on all) to you"—ἀλλ᾽ ἀπὸ μέρους (ἵνα μὴ ἐπιβαρῶ πάντας) ὑμᾶς. But this arrangement leaves ὑμᾶς in unnatural isolation, and, in any case, if this had been Paul's meaning, he would surely have placed the ὑμᾶς immediately after ἀπὸ μέρους. It is true that the verb ἐπιβαρεῖν is used transitively on the two other occasions, both in Paul, on which it occurs in biblical Greek, namely, I Thess. 2:9 and II Thess. 3:8. But it is more satisfactory to understand it, with most modern scholars, as intransitive here, so that the expression ἵνα μὴ ἐπιβαρῶ means either "in order not to say too much" or, perhaps better still, "in order not to exaggerate" (see Arndt and Gingrich): that is, to say that the offender had caused sorrow to "all" without the qualification "in part" would be to exaggerate, for there is still a minority group who resist the Apostle's authority. Denney is of the opinion that, if ἐπιβαρῶ is in fact transitive (though he prefers to treat it as intransitive), "the object must be the partisans of the offender. It would 'bear hardly' on them, to assume that *they* had been grieved by what Paul considered an offence. They had not been grieved. That is why he excludes them from πάντας ὑμᾶς by ἀπὸ μέρους". But it is unlikely that Paul intended such a note of sarcasm in this context.

church members.[9] There had been some dissentient voices (cf. the qualification "in part" in the previous verse), but as a body the church had passed judgment in obedience to their Apostle's instructions. This passage, coupled with I Cor. 5:3ff., throws an interesting light on the earliest form of church government. "We have first of all", writes Lightfoot in his famous essay on the Christian Ministry, "the Apostles themselves exercising the superintendence of the churches under their care, sometimes in person and on the spot, sometimes at a distance by letter or by message. The imaginary picture drawn by St Paul, when he directs the punishment of the Corinthian offender, vividly represents his position in this respect. The members of the church are gathered together, the elders, we may suppose, being seated apart on a dais or tribune; he himself, as president, directs their deliberations, collects their votes, pronounces sentence on the guilty man [1 Cor. v. 3sq.]. How the absence of the apostolic president was actually supplied in this instance, we do not know. But a council was held; he did direct their verdict 'in spirit though not in person'; and 'the majority' condemned the offender [2 Cor. ii. 6]." [10]

Now, however, the punishment has proved sufficient,[11] for the reason that it has successfully effected the primary end for which all discipline within the Christian community should be exercised, namely, the reformation and thereupon the restoration of the guilty person. Discipline which is so inflexible as to leave no place for repentance and reconciliation has ceased to be truly Christian; for it is no less a scandal to cut off the penitent sinner from all hope of re-entry into the comfort and security of the fellowship

---

9 ‘Υπὸ τῶν πλειόνων = "by the majority". "By the many" is an awkward and not strictly accurate rendering.

10 J. B. Lightfoot, *St Paul's Epistle to the Philippians* (London, second edition, 1869), p. 196.

11 ‘Ικανόν in the sentence ἱκανὸν τῷ τοιούτῳ ἡ ἐπιτιμία αὕτη is commonly explained as a substantival use of the neuter adjective, similar in form to ἀρκετόν in Mt. 6:34 (ἀρκετὸν τῇ ἡμέρᾳ ἡ κακία αὐτῆς) and πλεῖον in Lk. 12:23 (ἡ ψυχὴ πλεῖόν ἐστιν τῆς τροφῆς). This may well be; but we are of the opinion that ἱκανόν here is more likely to be a simple latinism (= *satis*; cf. Lk. 22:38, ἱκανόν ἐστι, and Mk. 15:15, τὸ ἱκανὸν ποιῆσαι = *satisfacere*). Stanley suggests that ἱκανόν may be used here "possibly in the legal sense of 'satisfaction', as in Acts xvii. 9, λαβόντες τὸ ἱκανόν". This, however, is improbable. For the use of ἱκανόν in this technical sense of "security" or "bail", as well as in other senses, see Arndt and Gingrich, and Moulton and Milligan.

of the redeemed community than it is to permit flagrant wickedness to continue unpunished in the Body of Christ. The Christian who falls into sin, however deplorable his sin may be, may still look to Jesus Christ the Righteous as his Advocate with the Father (I Jn. 2:1). How thoroughly Christlike, then, is Paul's role here as he acts as advocate on behalf of the repentant offender at Corinth, urging the Corinthians now to reverse ("contrariwise") the disciplinary process by receiving the offender back in a spirit of forgiveness and love. And so, as Stanley remarks, Paul throws "the whole weight of his apostolical authority into this act of 'loosing', by the Christian society, as he had before thrown it (in 1 Cor. v. 4) into the act of 'binding'".

The danger which the Church, with its desire for a pure and unsullied membership, must avoid is that of a discipline so inflexible and so inexorable that it thereby sets a false limit to the grace of God. To deny a penitent fellow-Christian all hope of divine mercy and restoration is indeed to allow Satan to gain an advantage (v. 11). Hence the Apostle's fear lest the Corinthian offender, now repentant, should be engulfed [12] by an excess [13] of despairing sorrow, and his exhortation to the members of the Corinthian church to confirm their love towards him. By this latter it is probable that he means them to enact a ratification of their love by an official resolution re-admitting the penitent brother to the benefits and privileges of church membership.[14]

---

[12] Μήπως . . . καταποθῇ ὁ τοιοῦτος. The intensive force of the compound καταπίνειν should be brought out: "to swallow up completely" or "engulf". This force is well illustrated by its use elsewhere in the New Testament; see Mt. 23:24, I Cor. 15:54, II Cor. 5:4, Heb. 11:9, I Pet. 5:8, Rev. 12:6.

[13] Τῇ περισσοτέρᾳ λύπῃ: "by his excessive sorrow". It is not necessary to give the adjective a strictly comparative sense, such as "by sorrow more excessive than hitherto" or "by the increase of sorrow" (Meyer, Alford; cf. Vg., abundantiore tristitia). See note on περισσοτέρως, verse 4, above. The force of the definite article is conveyed by translating it as "his", as in our version: "his overmuch sorrow"; it is the sorrow which the penitent offender feels.

[14] The verb κυρόω, "ratify" or "confirm", was commonly used with a legal connotation, as is clear from Gal. 3:15 (the only other place in which it occurs in the New Testament) where Paul points out that a will which has been ratified—κεκυρωμένη διαθήκη—can be neither set aside nor added to. Hence the likelihood that the use of this term here implies an official or formal ratification of the Corinthians' love by resolution of the congregation or church to re-admit the repentant offender to their fellowship. For examples from the papyri of the use of κυρόω in legal documents, see Moulton and Milligan.

It should be noticed that the Apostle *exhorts*, but does not order, them to display their love, for love cannot be commanded. True Christian love (*agapé* [15]) must be spontaneous and unforced, else it ceases to be what it professes to be.

The dissentient minority, who failed to vote with the rest for the punishment of the offender, may with perfect naturalness be identified with that faction in Corinth which, under the leadership of the intruding false apostles, by its contemptuous opposition was seeking to undermine Paul's apostolic authority in that city (see chs. 10 to 13). Indeed, this is one of the links in the chain of internal evidence which points to the unity and coherence of our epistle. Such is the tyranny of a theory, however, that Plummer, who stoutly contends for the hypothesis that the last four chapters belong, not to this epistle, but to an earlier severe letter, is led into a quite self-contradictory position. Rather than identify the minority with the anti-Paul faction, he proposes an exegesis whereby the term *contrariwise* in the clause "so that contrariwise ye should rather forgive him" is taken to imply that "hitherto they had refused to forgive him", as though Paul were at this point addressing the dissenting minority. This enables him to conclude that "it is more likely that the minority were the Paul party (1 Cor. i. 12, 13), who thought that one who defied the Apostle ought to be much more severely punished". But it

---

[15] The primary importance of ἀγάπη in the thought of Paul (not to mention the New Testament as a whole) must not be overlooked. Love is the fulfilment of God's law (Rom. 13:10). Of the fruit produced by the Spirit in Christian character it receives pride of place (Gal. 5:22). Love, as he has already told the Corinthians, is the way of excellence (καθ' ὑπερβολὴν ὁδός—I Cor. 12:31). Of the three qualities that abide—faith, hope, and love—it is the greatest (I Cor. 13:13). "Love", as E. Stauffer says, "is the greatest of the gifts of the Spirit, 'the more excellent way'; it not only stands at the centre of the triad, faith, love, hope [Why Stauffer places it in the centre of the triad is not clear, since Paul's order is faith, hope, love.], but is more than faith, more than hope. Faith and hope are under the sign of this passing age; 'Love never faileth'. Love is the power of the coming age already breaking into this world. For Paul, as for Jesus, love is the only life-force that has a future in this age of death" (*Love*: No. I in the series *Bible Key Words* from Kittel TWNT, London, 1949; p. 59). The challenge to the Corinthian Christians is to manifest this power of the coming age in their own relationships at Corinth, and in particular towards the brother who has now repented of his sin, and thereby to repulse the god of this age (4:4; cf. Jn. 12:31, 14:30, 16:11), who otherwise will gain an advantage over them (v. 11).

must be objected that the context makes it plain, firstly, that Paul is addressing the Corintian church *as a whole* (the "ye" of v. 7 corresponds with the "you all" of v. 5), and not the minority, whose existence is not directly mentioned, but only implied; and, secondly, that the term "contrariwise" refers back, not forward, (as the consequential "so that" shows), giving the sense: "You who have punished him should now contrariwise, since the discipline has proved adequate, discontinue the punishment and rather forgive him". But, further, Plummer is guilty of contradicting himself; for in commenting on verse 5 he describes the minority as "a few who were *not* distressed by the scandalous treatment of the Apostle". This contrasts oddly with the explanation in the commentary on the next verse that "the minority were the Paul party" who were so distressed at the scandalous treatment of their Apostle that they thought the offender ought to be much more severely punished! If, to preserve Plummer's consistency, we suppose that he envisages Paul to be referring to two altogether distinct minorities in these two contiguous sentences, it still exhibits the tyranny which a theory may exercise over the thinking even of the best of exegetical scholars.

2:9—11

For to this end also did I write, that I might know the proof of you, whether ye are obedient in all things. But to whom ye forgive anything, I forgive also: for what I also have forgiven, if I have forgiven anything, for your sakes have I forgiven it in the presence of Christ; that no advantage may be gained over us by Satan: for we are not ignorant of his devices.

Paul states a *further* reason for his having written as he had done to the Corinthians, namely, to test their obedience to his authority. This is the force of "also" in verse 9; it does not mean that he had also written as well as spoken to them, or that the purpose of that letter was also the same as the purpose of this, as various commentators have suggested; nor can "did I write" be interpreted as an epistolary aorist = "I am writing", as others have wished.[16] Paul has already declared, in verse 3, that one reason for the writing of his previous letter was lest he should

---

[16]   See comments above on the siginificance of "I wrote" in verse 3.

have sorrow from them of whom he ought to rejoice. Now he adds another reason: that by their response to it he might have proof [17] of their obedience. But it is not considerations of self-interest or self-importance that have prompted him to desire their obedience in all things—he has already repudiated the suggestion that he has lordship over their faith (1:24)—but, on the contrary, the knowledge that their own best interests will be served by loyalty to him as the Apostle of Christ to them. All his dealings with them are directed to the end of their edification (12:19).

The Apostle does not, indeed cannot, take from the Corinthians the initiative in forgiving the offender, although, because of their sluggishness he took the initiative in demanding his condemnation. Their obedience in condemning gives him confidence that they will spontaneously forgive, now that the punishment has produced the fruit of humility and repentance. Chrysostom rightly draws attention to the fact that here, in this act of forgiving, Paul "assigns the second part to himself, showing them as beginning, himself following". This could hardly have been so had the offence been an affront to Paul personally, for in that case he would have been the proper person to take the initiative. The whole tenor of this passage indicates that the offence in question was, in its primary impact, an offence against the church within which it was committed. Hence the hypothetical manner in which the Apostle speaks of his own part—"if I have forgiven anything" = "if there is anything for me to forgive"—and hence also the assertion that it is for their sakes, not his own, that he has already forgiven anything that there may be for him personally to forgive. Moreover, that it is in no merely formal or polite sense that he forgives, but in a manner that is at once profound and spiritual, is shown by his declaration that he does so "in the presence of Christ".[18] It is his constant endeavour to live the

---

17 The word δοκιμή, translated "proof" in our version, is a term of which we possess no examples prior to Paul (who uses it seven times—four of them in our epistle). Otherwise, with the exception of the second century physician Dioscurides, it is found only in subsequent Christian writers. In the judgment of Moulton and Milligan, "δοκιμή is a new formation of the Hellenistic age"; but Paul, although the earliest authority, is "certainly not the coiner, unless we are to make the medical writer dependent on him". The term indicates that proof which is the result of testing (cf. δοκιμάζειν).

18 Ἐν προσώπῳ Χριστοῦ: literally, "in the face of Christ". The word πρόσωπον may mean "face", "person", "presence", or "outward appearance",

whole of his life, both in private and in public, "in the sight of God" (2:17; 4:2), as already standing before the ultimate tribunal of Him to whom the secrets of all hearts are open (5:10f.). The Apostle's manifest humility and sincerity cannot but act as a spur to the Corinthians to be in earnest about the spirituality and genuineness of their own daily walk. The admonition of his example to them is that given, in a later age, by Richard Baxter to his congregation at Kidderminster: "Live now as you would wish you had done at death and judgment".[19] And so even to exercise forgiveness for their sakes, without concern for self, is not by itself enough, for it must be done within the framework of that ultimate reality which is defined in the expression "in the presence of Christ".

The restraint and consideration with which Paul writes here are most noteworthy: he leads the Corinthians, now obedient, by example rather than by command; he spares the offender, now penitent, by speaking of him only in indefinite terms as "any person" and "such a one"; and, finally, he says that he is animated by a spirit of forgiveness for fear lest Satan should gain an advantage over *him* (that is, Paul himself).[20] The Apostle has

according to the context. Cf., in this epistle, 3:7, 13, 18 and 11:20 where it means "face"; 1:11 where, used in the plural, it means "persons" (see note there); 5:12 and 10:7 where it means "outward appearance"; and 10:1 where it means "personal presence". In 4:6 it almost certainly means "face" rather than "person" (see commentary there); and here (2:10) and in 8:24 it is probable that it means "presence". The Vulgate, Estius, Luther, Alford, AV, RV (one of the places where the latter differs from ASV) render ἐν προσώπῳ Χριστοῦ here "in the person of Christ", implying that Paul forgave the offender "acting as Christ" (Alford). But the authoritarian note of such a rendering is out of harmony with the context. There is little to commend Chrysostom's hesitating suggestion that by this expression Paul means "according to the will of God or unto the glory of Christ". In our judgment, ἐν προσώπῳ Χριστοῦ here is best explained as a semitism: ἐν προσώπῳ = לִפְנֵי, meaning simply "in the presence of" (similarly εἰς πρόσωπον τῶν ἐκκλησιῶν, 8:24). Cf. Prov. 8:30 where לְפָנָיו is rendered ἐν προσώπῳ αὐτοῦ in the Septuagint (Vg., *coram eo*). Corresponding expressions in our epistle may be seen in 2:17, κατέναντι θεοῦ, and 4:2, ἐνώπιον τοῦ θεοῦ.

[19] Richard Baxter, *Practical Works* (London, 1830), Vol. XXII, p. 6.

[20] We believe it is correct to understand the first person plural throughout this epistle of Paul himself as an individual, as distinct from the Corinthians to whom the second person plural is applied. This contrast is clearly shown in 1:8, 3:1, etc., etc. When he wishes to associate the Corinthians directly with himself Paul speaks of "we *all*", as in 3:18 and 5:10. The change here,

sufficient confidence in the Corinthian Christians to leave it to them to *infer* that, if for him to show an unforgiving spirit would be to grant Satan [21] an entry where he has no right, much more, in this particular case, would it be so with them. Discipline, as the Reformers recognized, is a proper mark of Christ's Church; but to bring a fellow-Christian to a state of blank despair because of discipline which, despite manifest repentance, is applied with unrelenting rigour is to yield ground to the Enemy and to allow him to seize what does not belong to him.[22] "To take by sin is his proper work", Chrysostom reminds us; "by repentance, however, is more than his due; for ours, not his, is that weapon". If Paul is not ignorant of the Adversary's devices,[23] neither are the Corinthians. Every Christian soldier is familiar with his cunning designs, of which not the least is to suggest that a desirable end (e.g., the purity of the Church) may be attained by unworthy and indeed wrongful means (e.g., a harsh and unforgiving spirit); whereas, in reality, a wrong means always leads to a wrong end (cf. the character of our Lord's temptations in the wilderness). In the case in question, the end achieved by Satan would have been the abandonment of a penitent brother to despair and the disruption, through this spirit of harshness, of that fellowship in love which should distinguish the Church as the community of salvation.

---

however, from the first person singular of verse 10 to the first person plural of verse 11 may perhaps be intended to have the effect of a gentle invitation to the Corinthians to participate with him in denying Satan an opportunity for gaining an advantage.

[21] The appellation "Satan", ὁ Σατανᾶς, is taken over from the Hebrew שָׂטָן (Aramaic סָטָנָא), which means "adversary" and in the Bible is used always as a proper title of the devil, who is the great Adversary. The term is found again in our epistle at 11:14 and 12:7.

[22] The verb πλεονεκτεῖν, translated in our version "to gain an advantage", is compounded of πλέον and ἔχειν, and means to have or to grasp more than one's due, hence to defraud for the purpose of gaining what belongs to another. In this epistle it occurs again in 7:2 and 12:17f.

[23] "His devices", αὐτοῦ τὰ νοήματα. The word νόημα signifies the function of the intellective faculty (νοῦς). Its meaning varies between mind, understanding, thought, purpose, and design. Here, in the plural, it bears a sinister connotation: devices, wiles, or plots, i.e. evil schemings. Elsewhere in this epistle Paul uses it of the mind or understanding of man: 3:14, 4:4, and 11:3, and once of every thought or purpose: 10:5. Its only other occurrence in the New Testament is in Phil. 4:7.

2 : 12, 13

> Now when I came to Troas for the gospel of Christ, and
> when a door was opened unto me in the Lord, I had no
> relief for my spirit, because I found not Titus my brother:
> but taking my leave of them, I went forth into Macedonia.

Paul now returns to the theme of his itinerary and sets before
the Corinthians further proof that his change of plan is in no
way attributable to lack of love for them (cf. 1:15ff., 23ff.). On
the contrary, at the very time when it was being whispered that
his attitude was one of irresponsibility and unconcern they
occupied the main horizon of his thought and his heart was
tormented with anxiety for news of them. Chrysostom links
Paul's words here with what he had written earlier in 1:8. There
the Apostle mentioned the grievous affliction which had overtaken him in Asia and had even threatened his life; here he shows
that that was not the only anguish which he had suffered then,
for, on his arrival in Troas, he was disappointed not to find Titus
there on his way back with the eagerly awaited news of the state
of affairs at Corinth, with the result that the agony of his suspense
was greatly intensified. As Calvin remarks, "the fact that he
was so anxious about them that he had no rest anywhere, even
when a large prospect of usefulness presented itself, until he had
learned how things stood with them, argues a singular degree of
attachment to the Corinthians".

Paul's coming to Troas [1] had been with a view to proclaiming

---

[1] *Εἰς τὴν Τρῳάδα.* Stanley suggests that the article may suggest the region
of "the Troad", rather than the city; but it was common for the names of
cities to be accompanied by the article, and Paul almost certainly means the
city here. In II Tim. 4:13 he writes the name without the article; and in
Acts 20:5f., where the reference is clearly to the city, the name occurs twice,
once without and once with the article. The city, as Ramsay points out
(HDB, IV, pp. 813f.), was more accurately called *'Αλεξάνδρεια ἡ Τρῳάς,*
i.e. "the Troas Alexandria" as distinct from other places with the name of
Alexandria (cf. Livy XXXV, xlii, and XXXVII, xxxv, "Alexandria Troas").
Pliny (*Nat. Hist.,* V. 33) and Strabo (XIII, p. 593) refer to it simply as
"Alexandria". Its situation on the Aegean coast was opposite the isle of
Tenedos, some miles to the south of the Troy of the *Iliad* with which it should
not be confused. The city had been founded by Antigonus and named by

the Gospel of Christ [2]—that is, the Good News whose content is Christ. No doubt his expectation had been, first, of finding Titus at Troas and having all his questions concerning matters at Corinth answered, and then of engaging in a period of missionary activity in that part. How long he remained in Troas he does not say, but it was sufficiently long for him to discover that there was an open door for the evangelical message. This door of opportunity was apparently still open on his return to Troas the following spring, as the incident recounted in Acts 20:6–12 indicates. The metaphor of the door is both natural and graphic, and one for which Paul seems to have had some partiality. He had already used it in an earlier letter to the Corinthians (I Cor. 16:9) with reference to the work at Ephesus, and it occurs again in the Epistle to the Colossians (4:3) where he asks his readers to pray that God may open to him "a door for the word, to speak the mystery of Christ". The opening of a door has a twofold effect: it enables the evangelist to enter with the message of the Gospel, and it also makes possible the entry of that message into the minds and hearts of his hearers. Thus Paul and Barnabas explained to the church at Antioch how God had "opened a door of faith unto the Gentiles" (Acts 14:27).

---

him Antigonia Troas, but in 300 B.C. it was refounded and renamed Alexandria Troas by Lysimachus. In 133 B.C. it fell under Roman dominion. Because of their cherished belief in their Trojan origin, the Romans regarded it with special favour. Augustus Caesar bestowed on it the status of a Roman *Colonia* with the title *Colonia Augusta Alexandria Troas*, and it was granted the *ius Italicum*, which conveyed privileges of property-ownership, exemption from poll and land tax, and freedom from the command of the provincial governor. Julius Caesar, according to Suetonius (*De Vita Caes.*, Julius, 79), was reputed to have had thoughts of removing himself and his seat of government from Rome to Alexandria Troas (*Alexandria vel Ilium*); and Constantine is said to have favoured this city for his new imperial centre before finally deciding on Byzantium (= Constantinople; see Zosimus II, 30 and Zonarius XIII, 3). In this connection it is interesting, as Ramsay remarks, "to observe that the modern name is Eski-Stamboul, 'Old Stamboul', while Constantinople is Stamboul simply". The district of the Troad in which Troas was placed constituted the north-western corner of the province of Mysia. Troas was an important Aegean port. From it Paul had set sail for Macedonia (Acts 16:8, 11) during the course of his second missionary journey which later brought him to Corinth for the first time (Acts 18:1). On that memorable occasion the Spirit had not permitted him to carry through his plan for taking the gospel into Bithynia, and a vision had constrained him to cross over from Troas to Macedonia.

[2] Εἰς τὸ εὐαγγέλιον τοῦ Χριστοῦ.

In each case, it will be observed, it is God, not man, who opens the door [3]; and when God opens the door it is not for the sake of the preacher only, but for the sake also of his hearers. Again, the door that God opens no man can shut: "Behold, I have set before thee a door opened, which none can shut" (Rev. 3:8; cf. Isa. 45:1f.).[4] Augustine points to the opening of the door for Paul at Troas as "a most manifest demonstration that even the very beginning of faith is the gift of God" [5]

Yet Paul could find no relief from the intense anxiety by which he was harassed while he awaited news of the outcome of the visit of Titus to Corinth, for he realized that the crisis at Corinth was of such a kind that, unless satisfactorily resolved, it would seriously threaten the well-being and progress of the whole apostolic Church. Vital issues were at stake. And so, after waiting in vain for Titus to arrive in Troas, he said farewell to the disciples there ("To whom", asks Augustine, "did he bid farewell but to those who had believed,—to wit, in whose hearts the door was opened for his preaching of the Gospel?") [6] and pressed on into Macedonia, where at last he found his envoy and gratefully received the comfort of the encouraging news which the latter had brought from Greece (7:5ff.). Till then he had no relief for his spirit.[7]

---

3   This may be explicitly stated, as in Col. 4:3 and Acts 14:27, or implied by the use of the passive voice, as in verse 12 here and in I Cor. 16:9.

4   This force is conveyed by Paul here by the use not only of the passive voice but also of the perfect tense: θύρας μοι ἀνεῳγμένης—a door which has been opened (sc. by God) and remains open. Μοι is a dative of advantage, "for me", not, however, in any egocentric sense; for the thought is thoroughly Christocentric: the door had been opened in the Lord (ἐν Κυρίῳ). The Lord Christ is both the content of the Apostle's message and also the sphere of his opportunity.

5   Augustine, De Praedest. Sanct., ch. 41.

6   Loc. cit.

7   Οὐκ ἔσχηκα ἄνεσιν τῷ πνεύματί μου—"I had no relief for my spirit". Ἔσχηκα is probably to be explained as an aoristic perfect (see note above on ἐσχήκαμεν in 1:9). But we cannot rule out the possibility that it may, as a perfect, "denote the nearness of the impression, as though it still continued" (Allo), or that it may suggest "the continuous expectation of relief, which was always anew disappointed" (Denney). Cf. also Stanley's opinion that "the perfect has here the same force as the praesens historicum, in giving a living image of what is past". Τῷ πνεύματί μου, "for my spirit", dative of advantage. A similar usage is found in the LXX version of Gen. 8:9—οὐχ εὑροῦσα ἡ περιστερὰ ἀνάπαυσιν τοῖς ποσὶν αὐτῆς.

Titus

The New Testament provides us with little biographical information concerning the person of Titus. We know that he was a Gentile by birth (Gal. 2:3, where the term "Greek" is used broadly for Gentile as distinct from Jew). Plummer expresses the opinion that "his acceptability among the Corinthians, and his success in the delicate mission which St Paul entrusted to him, are evidence of his being by race a Greek". There is no specific mention of Titus in the Acts, unless, which is most improbable, the Titus Justus of Acts 18:7 is the same person. If we are right in thinking that Acts 15:2 and Gal. 2:1 refer to the same occasion, it follows that Titus accompanied Paul and Barnabas to the Council of Jerusalem. It is plain that Paul held him in high esteem and affection: he calls him "my brother" here (2:13); he speaks warmly of his devotion and care for the Corinthians (7:15, 8:16); later on, Paul left Titus in Crete (Titus 1:5) entrusted with an exacting and responsible task of ecclesiastical oversight, which in itself was a notable tribute to the strength and reliability of his character; and the reference to him in II Tim. 4:10 indicates that he was with Paul for a while during his last imprisonment in Rome. Paul, indeed, calls him his "true child" (Titus 1:4 [8]), an expression which can only mean that it was through his ministry that Titus was brought to faith in Christ. Tradition has it that Titus, having become first bishop of Crete, died there in advanced years. His successor, Andreas Cretensis, eulogized him in the following terms: "The first foundation-stone of the Cretan church; the pillar of the truth; the stay of the faith; the never silent trumpet of the evangelical message; the exalted echo of Paul's own voice".[9]

2:14

But thanks be unto God, who always leadeth us in triumph in Christ, and maketh manifest through us the savour of his knowledge in every place.

This is the start of what may be regarded as an extended digression. Suddenly and characteristically Paul breaks off from his account in order to praise God for His unfailing goodness which remains constant through all the changing circumstances

---

[8] $Γνήσιον\ τέκνον$.

[9]   For a discussion of the associations of Titus with the church at Corinth, see commentary below on 8:6, 10, also 12:18.

and tensions of human experience. And one thought leads on to another in an outpouring of spiritual wealth unsurpassed in any other of his epistles. The theme of his journey into Macedonia and meeting with Titus is not resumed until 7:5. How very much poorer we should be without Paul's "digressions", and not least without chapters 3 to 6 of this epistle! Indeed, we have here an excellent illustration of the fact that in the activity of inspiration the Holy Spirit does not violate, far less obliterate, the personality of the human instrument, but develops and enhances it to the full extent of its redeemed potentiality. When, moreover, we view the epistle as a whole we discover that this digression, prolonged though it is, is in no way lacking in relevance, but is of a piece with the rest. Viewed in its full perspective, it is more properly described as the living, pulsating flesh which is attached to the bony skeleton. The latter, of course, is also important, for it provides an essential structural framework, and to it the account of the journey from Troas to Macedonia and of the encounter with Titus belongs.

Paul, then, in describing the acute anxiety which he experienced as he awaited news from Corinth, hastens to forestall any misunderstanding which might arise from what he has said by explaining that, anxious though he was, there was no question of his having been in a state of spiritual defeat. It is this corrective "but" by which the digression is initiated; and it is in full harmony with the major theme of our epistle, which is that of the triumph of God's grace over and through human frailty. The Apostle remembers how unfailingly he has been led in a progress of triumph at all times, and how the savour of the knowledge of Christ has been made manifest through him in every place, even in Troas when his mind was preoccupied with concern for the Corinthians. This means that he did not neglect to pass through the door that the Lord had opened for him there—that the suspense of those days did not succeed in inhibiting him from proclaiming the message of life with which he had been entrusted. That was indeed a triumph! And so he bursts out spontaneously into thanksgiving to God, through whom alone such victory, always and in every place, is possible.

The metaphor introduced by Paul here is particularly graphic. The picture he conjures up is that of the splendour of a Roman triumphal procession, in which the victorious general led his cap-

77

tives as a public spectacle before the multitudes of onlookers. We who were God's former enemies (Rom. 5:10) have been overcome and taken captive by Him and are led and displayed by Him to the world, not just on one passing occasion, but every day and everywhere. From justification until glorification the redeemed sinner is on exhibition as a trophy of divine grace. But Paul is speaking more particularly of himself and his apostolic ministry. For him, the triumphal procession in Christ's train began at Damascus and continued without cessation through all his labours and journeyings to his martyrdom at Rome. And this victorious progress is "in Christ". This inclusion of the believer in Christ is fundamental to Paul's conception of the state of salvation. Christ alone is accepted before God. Through faith in Christ's perfect work of atonement the Christian is justified and incorporated into Him; but the believer has no standing before God except in Christ. To be "in Christ" is not merely to be within the sphere of His influence, but is to be mystically and really in Him. There is no context for redemption apart from this mystery. Thus it is only "in Christ" that God triumphs over us and exhibits us to the world as His captives, subdued (unlike the prisoners of Rome) by the power of mercy and grace.[10]

It was, moreover, customary for the triumphal processions of Paul's day to be accompanied by the release of sweet odours from the burning of spices in the streets. So, too, the knowledge of Christ, whom to know is life eternal, is manifested like a pervading fragrance through the Apostle wherever he is led. It is important to notice that the operation is wholly of God: it is *God* who leads His servant in triumph, and it is *God* who manifests the savour of the knowledge of Christ; Paul is nothing but the vessel or the

---

[10] The verb θριαμβεύειν means "to lead in triumph", not, as in AV, "to cause to triumph". Paul uses it again in Col. 2:15, though with a different emphasis, for there it is the defeated forces of evil which are paraded in chains behind the Victor. Those who do not submit to Christ's triumph in mercy must submit to His triumph in judgment (cf. I Cor. 15:25ff., Phil. 2:10f.). A similar metaphor is used, though again with differing application, in I Cor. 4:9, where the apostles are pictured as bringing up the rear of the triumphal procession, which was the position of those who were appointed to die in the arena. Our English word "triumph" (Latin *triumphus*) is derived from the Greek θρίαμβος, which was a hymn sung in honour of Bacchus in festal processions.

instrument *through* whom the fragrance is released.[11] To know Christ was for Paul the sum of the vital experience of salvation, in comparison with which all things else dwindled into unimportance. For the excellency of this knowledge he counted all things to be loss (Phil. 3:8, 10). But how different is this knowledge (*gnosis*) from that of the gnosticism and mystery religions of the first century! The latter was arcane, esoteric, communicated only to the favoured few who were capable of initiation; whereas the knowledge of Christ is diffused, like a fragrant odour, through God's messengers in every place and to all people. Christ's disciples are commanded to carry the knowledge of him into all the world and to every creature, so that it may become a *universal* savour.

2 : 15, 16a

For we are a sweet savour of Christ unto God, in them that are saved and in them that perish; to the one a savour from death unto death; to the other a savour from life unto life.

Paul emphasizes that it is *of Christ* that he is a sweet savour [12] —the human vessel being identified with its contents (fragrance).[13] In the first place, this sweet savour directs itself Godwards, and as the savour of that unique grace of which He is Himself the Author it is acceptable to Him, not only in those who are being saved, but also in those who are perishing[14]; for grace, even when it is rejected, does not cease to be grace. It is this grace, more-

---

[11] T. W. Manson, writing in *Studia Paulina* (*ut supra*, p. 157), understands "the savour of his knowledge" (τὴν ὀσμὴν τῆς γνώσεως αὐτοῦ) to mean Christ. The sense then is: "Through us God manifests Christ, who is the savour of his (God's) knowledge". To explain the expression in this way as a circumlocution for Christ seems to us, however, unwarranted; nor do we concur with Manson and others who take αὐτοῦ "as referring back to τῷ θεῷ earlier in the verse". Were this so, Paul would have been more likely to use the reflexive pronoun: "God makes manifest through us the savour of the knowledge of Himself". The αὐτοῦ is more naturally associated with τῷ Χριστῷ: it is God who both leads us in triumph in Christ and also manifests through us the savour of the knowledge of Christ. This, in our judgment, is the proper balance of the twofold statement.

[12] Ὅτι Χριστοῦ εὐωδία ἐσμέν. The position of Χριστοῦ is emphatic.

[13] A similar metathesis occurs in I Cor. 11:26, "as often as ye ... drink the cup", where the vessel (the cup) is used for its contents (wine).

[14] Or, as in ARSV, "among [ἐν] those who are being saved and among those who are perishing".

over, which is the dynamic formative principle of the kingdom of God, of the new or renewed creation, which is already a reality in Christ, but which in its final form of perfection will be introduced only at the conclusion of this present age. It is, therefore, a savour that is wholly pleasing to God. In the Old Testament the concept of a burnt offering being "a sweet savour unto the Lord" [15] is frequently encountered, and the sacrifice of Christ, of which the Old Testament offerings were typical, is spoken of by Paul in identical terms (Eph. 5:2 [16]). Elsewhere (for example, Rom. 12:1) the same concept is applied to the self-offering of Christians to God. But in our present passage the Apostle's thought is not primarily that of sacrifice, but of the effects produced through the ministry of the Gospel.

These effects are twofold and, further, they are alternative and antithetical effects: either death, or life. For those who refuse to receive the evangelical message the consequence of its proclamation is death; but for those who believe it is life. The effect of Christ's coming is either falling or rising (Lk. 2:34). Thus those that believe on the Son have eternal life; whereas those who do not obey the Son shall not see life, but the wrath of God abides on them (Jn. 3:36). "To whom is there the savour of death unto death", asks Irenaeus, "unless to those who believe not, neither are subject to the Word of God?" [17] The force of the Gospel, then, is such that, as Calvin well points out, "it is never preached in vain, but is effectual, leading either to life or to death". At the same time, however, the Reformer reminds us that we must distinguish between "the proper office of the Gospel", which is the proclamation of salvation to all who believe, and its "accidental" office whereby, through their own fault, it becomes an occasion of condemnation to unbelievers, "so that for them life is turned into death".[18]

---

[15] Ὀσμὴ εὐωδίας Κυρίῳ.

[16] Παρέδωκεν ἑαυτὸν ὑπὲρ ἡμῶν προσφορὰν καὶ θυσίαν τῷ θεῷ εἰς ὀσμὴν εὐωδίας.

[17] Irenaeus, Adv. Haer., IV, xxviii, 3.

[18] The precise significance of the expressions "from death unto death" (ἐκ θανάτου εἰς θάνατον) and "from life unto life" (ἐκ ζωῆς εἰς ζωήν) is difficult to determine. An exegesis of the latter in isolation would probably have suggested itself along the lines that he who is himself regenerate becomes the instrument of regeneration in others—life leading to life in a continuous evangelical sequence. But the former expression can hardly be expounded

Whether there is any connection between Paul's thought here and the rabbinical concept of the Law as a drug whose effect, depending on the manner of its reception, is either deadly or life-giving, it is impossible to say.[19] It is, however, important to recognize that, although it is possible for him, because of the universality of human sin (that is, the breaking of God's law), to describe the giving of the law as "the ministration of death" (3:7), yet Paul is no opponent of the law. On the contrary, he perceives that the law is holy, not evil, and that love is precisely the fulfilment of the law (Rom. 7:12; 13:10). The significant question of the relation of the Law to the Gospel is introduced, in one of its aspects, in the next chapter of our epistle.

---

in any parallel manner. The interpretation of Alford, Hodge, and others to the effect that to those who are perishing Christ is seen only as dead and powerless, yielding nothing more than a savour of death, whereas to those who are saved Christ is seen as risen and living, and therefore yielding a savour of life, is unsatisfactory, if only because it involves too much explanation. Stanley is probably nearer the mark when he proposes that the expressions are "Hebrew superlatives", corresponding to the Semitic idiom whereby emphasis is conveyed through the repetition of a word.

[19] Strack–Billerbeck (*Kommentar zum Neuen Testament aus Talmud und Midrash*, III, pp. 498f.) gives the rabbinical texts in which the Torah or law is viewed as a drug whose effect may be either fatal or vitalizing. As T. W. Manson points out, "the beneficial or lethal effect of the Torah does not depend on anything in the Torah itself, but simply on the nature of the people who come into contact with it" (*op. cit.*, p. 157). It is his opinion that, "if . . . the Rabbinical mind could think of the Torah as the divinely appointed remedy against the evil inclination and call it the 'perfect medicine' (סם תם) or 'the medicine of life' (סם החיים), there is no reason why the pupil of Gamaliel should not have thought in a similar way of Christ as the remedy against the evils that arise from the presence of Ἁμαρτία in the flesh. From this point of view [he continues] Christ may truly be called the 'perfect remedy' (סם תם), for, as Paul insists often enough elsewhere, he does what the Law fails to do. This thought of Christ as a cleansing and purifying influence is expressed in the word ὀσμή, which is used by Paul in much the same way that סם is used by the Rabbis" (pp. 160f.). Whether or not, however, Paul's mode of expression is influenced, consciously or subconsciously, by his rabbinical training, his thought as a Christian is essentially practical rather than academic, and it possesses a dynamic character unknown to the Rabbis. Returning to the framework of the New Testament, it is interesting to notice the twofold effect of the sacrament: when worthily received it is indeed a true spiritual eating and drinking of Christ's body and blood unto everlasting life (cf. Ignatius' description of it in the next century as the "medicine of immortality" —φάρμακον ἀθανασίας—*Ephes.*, XX); but when unworthily received it is an eating and drinking of judgment (I Cor. 11:27ff.).

Dr. H. Clavier's suggestion that in these verses Paul may be alluding to one of the unpleasant manifestations of a malady which would have been offensive not only to the sight but also to the smell [20] is the product of a lively imagination rather than of sound exegetical reasoning.

2 : 16b, 17

And who is sufficient for these things? For we are not as the many, corrupting the word of God: but as of sincerity, but as of God, in the sight of God, speak we in Christ.

The mention of the awful and ultimate effects, either in salvation or in damnation, of the ministry of the Gospel causes the Apostle to exclaim "Who is sufficient for these things?" How can any frail and fallible mortal fail to be conscious of his own utter inadequacy when charged with so stupendous a responsibility? Paul certainly makes no claim to self-sufficiency; but neither does he disown the responsibility and the authority which are his by virtue of his being Christ's chosen apostle to the Corinthians. The question asked here is answered in 3:5, where he affirms that his sufficiency is *of God*. It is a sufficiency, therefore, which is far beyond and very different from mere human self-sufficiency; and this consideration at once places Paul in a category totally different from that of those false apostles who had invaded his territory at Corinth. That "the many" to whom he refers should primarily be understood of these unauthorized invaders is generally agreed, and the pointed allusion to them here is of a piece with the more protracted denunciation of them in the concluding chapters of the epistle. The expression "the many" is no doubt used in a comparative sense—many as compared with the small number of authentic apostles [21]—and it is probably meant to include others who were troubling churches elsewhere than at Corinth—"teachers without author-

---

[20]   H. Clavier, *La Santé de l'Apôtre Paul*, in *Studia Paulina (ut supra)*, p. 78.

[21]   Strachan suggests "too many" as a possible translation of οἱ πολλοί here. Moffatt renders it "most". But better than either is ARSV: "so many", which conveys the meaning well. The variant reading οἱ λοιποί, which is attested by p46 and the Byzantine text and also Marcion, demands consideration; according to it Paul is saying, "We are not as *the rest*", i.e. the others in Corinth who, as distinct from Paul, claim to be apostles, but are not.

ity", says Allo, "as are, in the midst, alas, of many others who infest the churches, his adversaries in Corinth".

It is characteristic of these intruders that they go about hawking or peddling [22] the word of God, cheapening and degrading the message by the illegitimate admixture of foreign elements, judaistic or pagan, as a dishonest merchant adulterates wine with water; they seek only their own gain, irrespective of the effect of their teaching on others and careless of the momentous issues which are at stake; self-interest governs their outlook; accordingly they are unconscious of any sense of insufficiency for the task which they profess to fulfil, nor do they hesitate to batten like parasites on the all too gullible members of the church. They have taken up "apostleship" as a business, and so long as it brings quick returns they are not particularly scrupulous as to how they conduct it. In unmistakeable contrast, Paul, who is the Corinthians' genuine apostle, exercises a ministry which, subjectively,

---

[22] *Καπηλεύοντες,* which is rendered, somewhat colourlessly, "corrupting" in our version, is an expressive term. The noun *κάπηλος* means a retail-dealer, a hawker or pedlar, and thus indicates somebody who is intent on dispensing his goods for the sake of gain. In general the term carried a pejorative implication. An illuminating passage is found in Plato, *Protagoras* 313DE, where Socrates warns against those who hawk about *(καπηλεύοντες)* their wares, whether material or intellectual, and who, to effect a sale, praise their whole stock, irrespective of whether the articles offered are good or bad for the purchaser. Hence the adjectival form *καπηλικός* signified "mercenary", "cheating", that is, characteristic of the petty trader. The Latin *caupo* and English "chaffer", "chapman", "cheap" are probably derived from the same root. In Isa. 1:22, LXX, the *κάπηλοι* adulterate wine with water *(οἱ κάπηλοι σου μίσγουσι τὸν οἶνον ὕδατι).* The noun also occurs in Ecclus. 26:29, LXX *(οὐ δικαιωθήσεται κάπηλος ἀπὸ ἁμαρτίας).* The verb *καπηλεύω* occurs only here (II Cor. 2:17) in biblical Greek. Calvin, Alford, Plummer, etc., favour its translation by "adulterate". This, however, fails to convey the primary force of the word, namely, the seeking of cheap gain, whether by adulteration or by other means (cf. the examples given in Moulton and Milligan). The marginal alternative of our version, "making merchandise of the word of God", is much nearer the graphic original. We would suggest as better still "hawking the word of God"; cf. ARSV "peddlers of God's word". Gregory Nazianzen paraphrases this passage as follows: "For we are not as the many, able to corrupt the word of truth, and mix the wine, which makes glad the heart of man, with water, mix, that is, our doctrine with what is common and cheap and debased and stale and tasteless, in order to turn the adulteration to our own profit, and accomodate ourselves to those who meet us, and curry favour with every one ..." (*Defence of his flight to Pontus,* xlvi).

is stamped with complete sincerity [23] and, objectively, is derived from God (cf. 1:1). It is exercised, moreover, in the sight of God, that is, humbly and tremblingly, and without thought of selfish gain or of the praise of men (cf. 4:2); and, as with everything else, it is fulfilled in Christ, that is, by real incorporation, a union so complete that it can best be described in our Lord's own words, "he in me and I in him" (Jn. 15:5), but which no analogy from the physical realm is adequate to explain.[24] This contrast between the true apostle and the false is one that becomes increasingly clear as the epistle proceeds, for it has become essential for Paul to remind the Corinthians of the genuineness of his own ministry as compared with the impostures of the gospelmongers who have sought to usurp the leadership in their church.

---

[23] Εἰλικρίνεια. See note on 1:12 above.

[24] The structure of the sentence ἀλλ' ὡς ἐξ εἰλικρινείας, ἀλλ' ὡς ἐκ θεοῦ, κατέναντι θεοῦ ἐν Χριστῷ λαλοῦμεν would be better conveyed in English by placing the verb at the beginning: "But I speak as (a man) of sincerity, indeed as (one whose authority is) of God, before God in Christ". As Plummer observes, "the repetition of ἀλλά gives emphasis in an ascending scale; vii. 11; I Cor. vi. 11". This we have indicated by the insertion of "indeed". For a similar usage of ὡς see Mt. 7:29: ἦν γὰρ διδάσκων αὐτοὺς ὡς ἐξουσίαν ἔχων —"He taught them as (one) having authority".

3:1–11 AN EPISTLE OF CHRIST

3:1

Are we beginning again to commend ourselves? or need we, as do some, epistles of commendation to you or from you?

Having affirmed his own sincerity, in contrast to the many gospel-hawkers who were troubling the Church, Paul is aware that what he has said will be seized on by his calumniators, and not least by those impostors who were peddling the word of God in Corinth, and twisted by them into evidence of egotism and self-advertisement on his part. No utterance of his was safe from perversion at their hands. When he asks whether he is *again* beginning to commend himself, it does not imply that he had actually on some earlier occasion been guilty of the indiscretion of self-laudation, but rather that the charge of commending himself had already been made against him—very probably in connection with some of his statements in an earlier letter, such, for example, as those in I Cor. 4:16 and 11:1 where he urges the Corinthians to be imitators of him. And so here he forestalls his critics by anticipating the repetition of this charge, and indeed turns it with nice irony against them.

The irony is pointed by the effective, almost sarcastic, use of the anonymous "some".[1] The intruders thus designated had succeeded in penetrating the ranks of the Corinthian church on the strength of certain letters of commendation which they had produced on their arrival. They would require similar letters too on their departure from Corinth ("to you" and "from you"), for they were largely dependent on these bills of clearance for the profitable marketing of their merchandise in spiritual things. There was, however, an element of the ludicrous in any suggestion that the Apostle Paul might stand in need of epistles commendatory or that his ministry and personal character should require to be boosted by self-commendation (cf. 4:2, 5:12, 10:12). The quality of his work was such that it spoke for itself. The nature

---

[1] Τινές. Cf. 10:2 where Paul again refers to his adversaries as "some" (τινες)—another link between the earlier and the later chapters of our epistle. Cf. also I Cor. 4:18; 15:12; Gal. 1:7; I Tim. 1:3, 19.

of the work of the false apostles who had invaded Corinth will become increasingly apparent as Paul proceeds with the writing of this epistle.

Yet it would be rash to conclude that Paul regarded the provision of letters of commendation as a deplorable practice. In writing I Corinthians he had taken the opportunity of speaking strongly on Timothy's behalf (16:10f.); this present letter of II Corinthians is itself in part a commendation of Titus and his companions who carried it to Corinth (8:22ff.); in Rom. 16:1f. he commends [2] Phoebe to the Christians in the imperial capital; and in Col. 4:10 he reminds the Colossians that they had received injunctions [3] to welcome Barnabas if he came to them. Epistles commendatory became customary and indeed necessary in the early Church because of the appearance of large numbers of sanctimonious charlatans who sought to lead a parasitic existence by imposing themselves on local churches as itinerant teachers or preachers. In the middle of the fifth century the Council of Chalcedon found it expedient to decree that "strange and unknown clerics were under no circumstances whatever to minister in another city without epistles commendatory [4] from their own bishop". Paul's implication here is that those to whom he is referring are unworthy adventurers with unreliable credentials.

3:2

Ye are our epistle, written in our hearts, known and read of all men.

Paul indeed has a letter of commendation the validity of which is beyond dispute, but it is a *human* letter: none other than the Corinthian believers themselves. This is a letter engraved in his heart, not flourished in his hand or carried in his luggage. It is something far more intimate than an external document of

---

[2] The same verbal root is used there as here: Rom. 16:1, συνίστημι δὲ ὑμῖν Φοίβην ... II Cor. 3:1, ἢ μὴ χρῇζομεν, ὥς τινες, συστατικῶν ἐπιστολῶν πρὸς ὑμᾶς ἢ ἐξ ὑμῶν; In fact, συστατικὴ ἐπιστολή (or συστατικὰ γράμματα) was quite a technical expression, and was not confined to the religious world.

[3] Sc. from Paul: "The natural inference", says Lightfoot, *ad loc.*, "is that they were sent by St. Paul himself, and not by anyone else".

[4] Δίχα συστατικῶν γραμμάτων.

paper and ink, and at the same time far more permanent.[5] It could not be forgotten, nor mislaid. This letter of his, moreover, is "known and read of all men".[6] By no means least are the Corinthians themselves aware of its complete authenticity, for it is the transformation of their lives by the power of the gospel which, in striking contrast to their former manner of existence, presents incontrovertible testimony to the world at large of the genuineness of Paul's apostleship. By implication, the authenticity of the letters produced by the invading "apostles" is suspect and will not stand close scrutiny. An interesting echo of this Pauline metaphor is found in Polycarp (martyred c. A.D. 156) who addresses the members of the Philippian church as those "among whom the blessed Paul laboured, who were his letters in the beginning".[7] Archbishop Cranmer (who suffered martyrdom just 1400 years after Polycarp) alludes in impressive terms to this same verse in a letter to Thomas Cromwell: "I pray God never to be merciful unto me at the general judgment", he says, "if I perceive in my heart that I set more by any title, name, or style that I write, than I do by the paring of an apple, farther than it shall be to the setting forth of God's word and will. ... But I would that I, and all my brethren the bishops, would leave all our styles, and write the style of our offices, calling ourselves *apostolos Jesu Christi*: so that we took not upon us the name vainly, but were so even indeed; so that we might order our diocese in such sort, that neither paper, parchment, lead, nor wax, but the very Christian conversation of the people might be the letters and seals of our offices, as the Corinthians were unto Paul, to whom he said: *Literae nostrae et signa apostolatus nostri vos estis*".[8]

---

[5] The perfect tense of ἐγγεγραμμένη indicates that it was a letter which remained permanently written in his heart.

[6] The play on words in the phrase γινωσκομένη καὶ ἀναγινωσκομένη cannot be effectively reproduced in translation. Calvin is inclined to render ἀναγινώσκειν here as "acknowledge" rather than "read"—a letter "known and acknowledged by all men", and therefore unquestionably trustworthy. But all the evidence more recently accumulated goes to show that in Paul's day ἀναγινώσκειν ordinarily meant "to read". Cf. the similar play on words in 1:13, ἢ ἃ ἀναγινώσκετε ἢ καὶ ἐπιγινώσκετε.

[7] Polycarp, *Epistle to the Philippians*, XI.

[8] Thomas Cranmer, *Miscellaneous Writings and Letters* (Parker Society, Cambridge, 1846), p. 305. Cranmer's concluding quotation is a conflation of II Cor. 3:2 and I Cor. 9:2.

The heart is the centre of love and devotion, and it is in the heart of Paul, their true apostle, that the Corinthian believers are written. They are secure in his affection, and he should be also in theirs. Thus later on he assures them that his heart is enlarged to them, that they are in his heart, and entreats them to enlarge and open their hearts to him (6:11–13, 7:2f.); so sacred, so inward, so vital, is the epistle which they are. If on coming to Corinth inquiry should be made as to whether he carries with him letters commendatory, his answer is: "You yourselves, new men in Christ Jesus through my ministry, are my credentials"; and if on leaving them he should request of them a testimonial to his faithfulness, their answer should be: "We, transformed as a result of the gospel you preached to us, are your letter of commendation, carried always and everywhere in your heart, a letter whose authenticity none can honourably deny".

3:3

> Being made manifest that ye are an epistle of Christ, ministered by us, written not with ink, but with the Spirit of the living God; not in tables of stone, but in tables that are hearts of flesh.

They are manifest, open for all to read, as a letter possessing no less an author than Christ Himself. The character imprinted upon them is that of Christ. The fundamental humility of the Apostle Paul shines through these words: he makes no claim to be the author of this living letter; it is the writing of Christ, and he is merely the instrument used by the Divine Author ("ministered by us"); "not I, but Christ" is the key-note of all he says and does. There is here, then, a further rebuttal of those calumniators who were alleging that Paul was in the habit of commending himself.

In quite characteristic fashion Paul now permits the perspective of the picture to alter: he has just been considering the matter from the point of view of the Corinthians' relationship to him, as his letter of commendation, engraved in *his* heart (see previous v.); but now he contemplates them more particularly from the standpoint of their relationship to Christ, whose letter they are, and whose handwriting is in *their* hearts. The mention of a letter written in the heart is, in fact, sufficient to suggest the graphic imagery of the ancient promises concerning the new covenant and to remind Paul that these have their fulfilment in Christ. The thought at this point, therefore, provides a natural bridge to the comparison between the Mosaic and the Christian dispensations which follows (vv. 6ff.). God had assured His people, through the prophets, that the time was coming when He would put His law in their inward parts and write it in their heart (Jer. 31:33), a time when He would take the stony heart out of their flesh and give them a heart of flesh (Ezek. 11:19 and 36:26). This prophecy had come to realization with the pentecostal outpouring of the Holy Spirit and the subsequent apostolic proclamation of the gospel. The change of heart that the Corinthian believers had experienced as a result of Paul's ministry among them was proof inescapable of its fulfilment.

Paul, indeed, introduces a bold metaphor when he says that, as Christ's epistle, they are written "not with ink, but with the Spirit of the living God"—that is, that the medium of writing is not perishable ink but Divine Spirit. The presence of the eternal age of Christ's kingdom is discernible, even amid the shadows of our fallen and temporal world, in the redeeming and sanctifying operation of the Sovereign Spirit, whose writing is dynamic and permanent. This letter, comments Herveius, "has not been written with ink, that is, in such a way that it may be deleted, as is the case with things written with ink; but with the Spirit of the living God, that is, in order that it may abide eternally and vitally in our hearts, just as He who has written it lives and is eternal. Since the things which have been promised us are eternal, therefore this epistle is said to have been written with God's Spirit, who ever exists. But temporal things are written with ink, which fades and is lost to memory".[9]

But, further, it is written "not in tables of stone, but in tables that are hearts of flesh"[10]: the writing, in other words, is not external to them, but internal, within their innermost being. It is evident that Paul has in mind the contrast between the

---

[9]   Herveius (12th century), Migne PL, Vol. 181.

[10]   'Εν πλαξὶν καρδίαις σαρκίναις is somewhat clumsy, but its attestation is overwhelmingly strong. Its force would appear to be, "on tables (hearts) of flesh", and this is suitably paraphrased in our version. An alternative reading, καρδίας for καρδίαις, is an early one, and this certainly simplifies the phrase: "on the fleshy tables of the heart"; but it must be assumed to be a scribal

giving of the law to Moses on Mount Sinai and the establishment of the new covenant prophesied by Jeremiah. At Sinai the law had been written by the finger of God on tablets of stone (Ex. 31:18); but this was an external law-giving, whereby sinful man was confronted with his awful inability to fulfil the just requirements of his holy Creator. Jer. 31:33, however, promises a law-giving that is internal, namely, the writing by God of His law in the very heart itself. It is most important to realize that it is the selfsame law which was graven on tables of stone at Sinai that in this age of the new covenant is graven on the tables of the human heart by the Holy Spirit. The gospel does not abrogate the law, but fulfils it. There is no question, as Augustine points out, of Paul finding fault with the dispensation of the Old Testament.[11] The Christian is still under solemn obligation to keep the law of God, but with this vital difference, that he now has the power, the power of Christ by the Holy Spirit within himself, to keep it. The law, therefore, is neither evil nor obsolete, but, as Paul says elsewhere, "the law is holy, and the commandment holy, and righteous, and good" (Rom. 7:12). Nor is the law opposed to love; on the contrary, love of God and love of one's neighbour are the sum of the law, as our Lord Himself taught (Mk. 12:28–31): love, the Apostle affirms, is precisely "the fulfilment of the law" (Rom. 13:8–10). To overlook these considerations leads to the postulation of an erroneous and unscriptural antithesis between law and gospel, which by its equation of divine love with divine "injustice", or disregard of law, undermines the whole structure of the Christian redemption.

To the Manicheans, who had suggested that Paul's approving mention of flesh in the expression "hearts of flesh" afforded excuse for fleshly or carnal living on the part of Christians,

---

simplification of an otherwise awkward expression. Westcott and Hort suggest that πλαξίν is "probably a primitive interpolation". An early scribe might well have inserted πλαξίν a second time by mistake. If the second πλαξίν is omitted, a natural balance results: "... not on tables of stone, but on hearts of flesh". Christopher Wordsworth suggests "that the true reading may be simply ἐν πλαξὶ σαρκίναις and that the substantive καρδίας was only an explanatory gloss, imported from v. 2, ἐγγεγραμμένη ἐν ταῖς καρδίαις ὑμῶν, and that this was corrected by other copyists into καρδίας". There is little to choose between these two suggestions of Wordsworth and Westcott and Hort; but the problem still remains that neither is supported by any external evidence.

[11] Augustine, *Contra Faustum*, XV, iv.

Augustine replies that "by the heart of flesh and the fleshy tables is not meant a carnal understanding; but as flesh feels, whereas a stone cannot, the insensibility of stone signifies an unintelligent heart, and the sensibility of flesh signifies an intelligent heart".[12] And in another work he writes as follows: "We must not, of course, suppose that such a phrase as this is used as if those might live *carnally* who ought to lead spiritual lives; but inasmuch as a stone has no feeling, with which man's hard heart is compared, what was there left Him to compare man's intelligent heart with but the flesh, which possesses feeling?"[13]   There is little to commend the view of Irenaeus who, seeming to understand the flesh here in a physical sense, contends that its association in this passage with the Spirit of the living God argues for the veracity of the doctrine of the ultimate resurrection of the flesh.[14]   Herveius rightly points out that Paul's concept is of that which is living and sensitive in comparison with a stone, which is without sense.[15] The contrast is between the vital and dynamic responsiveness of the regenerate heart and the dullness, indeed deadness, of the heart of unbelief.

It is the opinion of Olshausen that Paul is not alluding here to the law written on tablets of stone given to Moses at Sinai, but to the breastplate of the high priest, in which were set twelve precious stones inscribed with the names of the twelve tribes of Israel and which was worn upon the heart of Aaron and his successors when they went "in unto the holy place, for a memorial before Jehovah continually" (Ex. 28:15-30).   The Apostle, he suggests, bore their names engraven in his heart and brought them continually before God in prayer, while at the same time the pictorial concept of the breastplate, worn outwardly and with each of the twelve stones bearing a separate inscription, explains Paul's description of them as an epistle "known and read of all

---

12 Augustine, *loc. cit.*

13 Augustine, *De Gratia et Libero Arbitrio*, XXIX.

14 Irenaeus, *Adversus Haereses*, V, xiii, 4.

15 Cf. R. Bultmann, *Theology of the New Testament*, Vol. I (London, 1952), p. 222: "The description of 'hearts' as 'fleshly' which means 'living hearts' (in contrast to the 'tablets of stone') is derived from Ezek. 11:19; 36:26. At any rate, 'heart' is clearly regarded to be that inward sphere which is the seat of life". Cf. also Olshausen who gives a similar interpretation: "σαρκινός has in this passage, as the antithesis to λιθινός, only the signification of 'living', without reference to the idea of weakness which is otherwise found in the σάρξ".

men" (v. 2). But we have no hesitation in dismissing this interpretation, interesting though it is, as unacceptable, both because it is certainly far more natural to understand the "tables of stone" to mean the stony tablets of the law rather than the precious stones of the high-priestly breastplate, and also because verses 7ff. show beyond question that it is the receiving of the law by Moses at Sinai that is in Paul's mind here.

3:4, 5

> And such confidence have we through Christ to God-ward: not that we are sufficient of ourselves, to account anything as from ourselves; but our sufficiency is from God.

Though it is apparent that these two verses are closely linked in thought and expression with 2:16f., it does not follow that, as Strachan supposes, the intervening verses (3:1-3) constitute a parenthesis. The latter, on the contrary, declare the precise ground of the confidence which the Apostle now affirms. His confidence rests upon the sure knowledge that the Corinthian believers are an epistle *of Christ*, written *with the Spirit of the living God*. With such a letter to show for his credentials he had good cause to be confident. The assurance with which he speaks is not arrogance; it is entirely compatible with genuine humility. The Apostle claims nothing for himself: his confidence is *through Christ*, directed not to self but *to God*. Indeed, as though to silence his accusers finally and completely, he disclaims in the plainest terms any measure of self-competence and asserts that such competence as was apparent in his ministry is derived solely *from God*. He is saying in effect what he had said explicitly on a previous occasion: "not I, but the grace of God which was with me" (I Cor. 15:10). Only a man who, like the Apostle, is humbly awake to his own utter weakness can know and prove the total sufficiency of God's grace. This great truth echoes and re-echoes through our epistle (cf. 4:7ff.; 5:18f.; 6:4ff.; 7:5f.; 11:23ff.; 12:9f.; 13:3f.). He who has, through Christ, received all things from God looks with confidence, through Christ, to God.[16]

---

[16] "By a fanciful derivation, El Shaddai, as a name for God, was sometimes interpreted as meaning 'The Sufficient One'. In Ruth i. 20, 21, ὁ Ἱκανός, and in Job xxi. 15, xxxi. 2, xxxix. 32 [xl. 2], Ἱκανός is used as a Divine name. It is just possible that St Paul had this in mind here; 'Our sufficiency comes from the Sufficient One'."—Plummer.

3:6a

Who also made us sufficient as ministers of a new covenant.

The past tense [17] implies significantly that Paul, unlike his rivals in Corinth, could actually point back to a definite occasion when God had called him to the office of an apostle and granted him sufficiency for this ministry. He is referring beyond doubt to all that took place at the time of his conversion: his encounter with the risen Lord and the impartation of the Holy Spirit through the laying on of Ananias' hands. Paul's meaning here is fully elucidated by the words of Christ to him then: "To this end have I appeared unto thee, to appoint thee a minister and a witness both of the things wherein thou hast seen me, and of the things wherein I will appear unto thee; delivering thee from the people, and from the Gentiles, unto whom I send thee, to open their eyes, that they may turn from darkness to light and from the power of Satan unto God, that they may receive remission of sins and an inheritance among them that are sanctified by faith in me"; and also by the confirmatory words of Ananias: "The God of our fathers hath appointed thee to know his will, and to see the Righteous One, and to hear a voice from his mouth; for thou shalt be a witness for him unto all men of what hast seen and heard" (Acts 9:3ff.; 26:16–18; 22:14f.). That God should have placed His hand upon him and commissioned him in this remarkable manner never ceased to be a source of wonder and gratitude to the Apostle. "I thank him that enabled [18] me, even Christ Jesus our Lord", he writes to Timothy, "for that he counted me faithful, appointing me to his service" (I Tim. 1:12). The ministry to which the false apostles at Corinth pretended was one of arrogant self-appointment and usurpation. The whole foundation and sole justification of Paul's apostleship was, by contrast, his appointment in unmistakeable circumstances by Christ Himself, and none other.

THE NEW COVENANT

The Christian ministry is essentially the ministry of the new covenant. This covenant, promised in the Old Testament, is

---

[17] Ἱκάνωσεν, aorist.

[18] Ἐνδυναμώσαντι (aorist), the equivalent of ἱκάνωσεν here. The variant reading ἐνδυναμοῦντι (present) may, as Souter suggests, be the result of an assimilation to Phil. 4:13.

realized in the gospel of Jesus Christ, the effect of which is the writing of God's law in the hearts of His people (see commentary on v. 3 above and the references given there). As the writer of the Epistle to the Hebrews points out, the introduction of a *new* covenant presupposes that it is a *better* covenant, since if the earlier covenant had been faultless there would have been no need for a second; and the arrival of the new means the outmoding of the old (Heb. 8:6–13). The old was necessarily temporary and imperfect inasmuch as it looked forward to the establishment of that which is perfect and permanent. The blood of the ancient sacrifices, oft-repeated, could not take away sins; but the blood of Christ's sacrifice, offered once for all, is the blood of the *eternal* covenant (Heb. 10:4ff.; 13:20).

The establishment of the new covenant, however, implies neither the abrogation nor the depreciation of the Mosaic law. This is plainly shown by the terms in which God announces His new covenant: "I will put *my law* in their inward parts" (Jer. 31:33), and by the object it is intended to achieve: "that they may walk in *my statutes*, and keep *mine ordinances*, and do them" (Ezek. 11:20). There is no question of a new law or of no law. Neither God changes nor His law. The difference between the old and the new covenants is that under the former that law is written on tablets of stone, confronting man as an external ordinance and condemning him because of his failure through sin to obey its commandments, whereas under the latter the law is written internally within the redeemed heart by the dynamic regenerating work of the Holy Spirit, so that through faith in Christ, the only law-keeper, and inward experience of His power man no longer hates but loves God's law and is enabled to fulfil its precepts. (There were, of course, lovers of the law in the Old Testament period, but as such they did not differ radically from believers of the New Testament era: their love of the law was by reason of divine grace granted to them, not by reason of any self-adequacy; and, as Fathers and Reformers have repeatedly emphasized, they were men and women of faith whose trust was centred in the same Christ whom the New Testament proclaims, but in an anticipatory manner, as looking forward to the coming of Him in whom all the promises of the new covenant would find their fulfilment.) Of this new and better covenant with its better promises Christ Himself is the Mediator by virtue of His propitiatory sacrifice of Himself, offered upon the foundation of a life lived in unfaltering conformity to the requirements of the divine law.

It must be emphasized that throughout Scripture the covenant is *God's* covenant, for it is always the manifestation of His sovereign goodness in action. He, and none other, is its author and initiator. All is of grace. Thus God announces His covenant to Noah in these terms: "*I*, behold, *I* establish *my* covenant with you, and with your seed after you"; and to Abraham He says: "*I* will establish *my* covenant between me and thee and thy seed after thee"; and through Jeremiah He declares: "*I* will make a new covenant ..." (Gen. 9:9; 17:7; Jer. 31:31).

This important truth is corroborated by the Greek word *diathēkē*,[19] which is the term exclusively used in the New Testament for "covenant". Ordinarily it has the meaning of "last will and testament"; indeed, in the papyri and inscriptions of the Hellenistic period this is its sense "with absolute unanimity, and such frequency that illustration is superfluous" (Moulton and Milligan). Since a testator disposes of his goods in accordance with his own personal wishes and decisions, the appropriateness of the term when applied to God's sovereign covenant is apparent. Its proper significance, as Moulton and Milligan explain, is "*dispositio*, an 'arrangement' made by one party with plenary power, which the other party may accept or reject, but cannot alter. ... A covenant offered by God to man was no 'compact' between two parties coming together on equal terms".[20]

The covenant is in fact viewed under the analogy of a will or testament in Heb. 9:15ff., the purpose of the author being to display the truth that as apart from the death of the testator a will cannot come into force, so death and the shedding of blood were closely associated with both the old and the new covenants —in the former the sacrifice of animals, in the latter the sacrifice of Christ Himself. Hence the expression "the blood of the covenant" (Ex. 24:8; Heb. 9:20; 10:29), and "the blood of the eternal covenant" (Heb. 13:20). This concept is also integral to the full comprehension of the terminology used by Christ at the institution of the Lord's Supper: "This is my blood of the covenant" (Mk. 14:24; Mt. 26:28), and, "This cup is the new covenant in my blood" (Lk. 22:20; I Cor. 11:25), in which in the word "covenant" the overtone of "testament" must also be discerned.

---

[19] Διαθήκη.

[20] See also Arndt and Gingrich, *sub* διαθήκη. The term for a "compact", or agreement mutually reached between two parties, is συνθήκη. In derivation, of course, our word "covenant" (*cum* + *venire*) corresponds to this meaning. In its biblical usage διαθήκη certainly involves the *coming together* of two parties, God and man, but on the terms appointed by only one of them, namely, God.

In speaking of himself as a minister of the new covenant it is most probable, as Herveius suggests, that Paul also had the false apostles in mind, implying that they, by contrast, were ministers of the old covenant, or judaizers. Hence the care with which in the passage which follows he expounds the difference between the Mosaic and the Christian dispensations.[21]

3:6b

Not of the letter, but of the spirit: for the letter killeth, but the spirit giveth life.

THE LETTER AND THE SPIRIT

Paul sums up the crucial difference between the ministries of the old and new covenants by declaring that the former is a ministry of the letter, whereas the latter is a ministry of the spirit. We must now examine the significance of this distinction which he makes between the letter which kills and the spirit which gives life. The Apostle does not mean that the law is in and of itself something evil and death-dealing. On the contrary, he taught that it was holy and good, and indeed "unto life" (Rom. 7:10ff.), and he approved the doctrine of the Old Testament Scriptures that "the man that doeth the righteousness which is of the law shall live thereby" (Rom. 10:5; Gal. 3:12; cf. Lev. 18:5; Neh. 9:29; Ezek. 20:11, 13, 21; Prov. 4:4; 7:2; also Rom. 2:13). It is, moreover, the plain teaching of our Lord (cf.

---

[21] This distinction is implied in the expression "new covenant", καινὴ διαθήκη. The difference in meaning between the two Greek words for "new" —καινός and νέος—is explained by Lightfoot as follows: "Of the two words νέος and καινός, the former refers solely to time, the other denotes quality also; the one is new as being *young*, the other as being *fresh*: the one is opposed to long duration, the other to effeteness" (*Commentary on Colossians*, London, 1892, p. 213). "The covenant", says Plummer, "is fresh and effective, with plenty of time to run, in contrast to the old covenant, which is worn out and obsolete. This is the constant meaning of καινός as distinct from νέος, so that καινός always implies superiority to that which is not καινός, whereas what is νέος may be either better or worse than what is not νέος." In Heb. 12:24, however, the expression διαθήκη νέα occurs; here Jesus is spoken of as "the Mediator of a new covenant", that is, a covenant recently introduced by His incarnation, death, and resurrection. But it is perhaps more probable that Heb. 12:24 affords an indication that at the time when the New Testament was being written the distinction between καινός and νέος was becoming blurred. Cf. Moulton and Milligan, *sub* καινός.

Mt. 19:17; Lk. 10:28). Paul is a faithful follower of his Master in that he nowhere speaks of the law in a derogatory manner. Christ, in fact, proclaimed that He had come to fulfil the law, not to destroy it (Mt. 5:17). So also the effect of Paul's doctrine was to establish the law (Rom. 3:31). There is no question of an attack by him on the law here, since, as we have previously seen, the law is an integral component of the new no less than it is of the old covenant.

Nor is it Paul's intention here to suggest that it is necessary to go deeper than the letter and to observe the spirit of the law —though this attitude certainly has its place, for, as our Lord again declared, to entertain hatred and lust in the heart, without actually committing murder or adultery, is to be guilty of breaking the sixth and seventh commandments (Mt. 5:21–27).

Far less is the Apostle proposing that the law may be understood in two senses: a literal and inferior sense and a spiritual and superior sense. This was, of course, the view of Philo and of the Christian theologians of Alexandria of the third and fourth centuries.[22] The Christian cabalists of a later age, indeed, adopted the tradition of Jewish theosophy that, concealed under the rough exterior of the written words, a secret esoteric revelation had been communicated to God by Moses. Thus Pico della Mirandola, writing towards the close of the fifteenth century, says that "apart from the law which God gave to Moses on the mount, and which he left written within the compass of five books, there was also revealed to the same Moses by God Himself the true exposition of the law, together with the manifestation of all the mysteries and secrets which were contained beneath the shell and crude surface of the words of the law: in short, that on the mount Moses received a double law, the one literal and the other spiritual; that he wrote down the former and at God's command communicated it to the people; but that as regards the latter he was enjoined by God not to write it down, but to communicate it only to the wise men ...."[23] This concept of Scripture as possessing a superficial sense accommodated to the limited capacities of the common multitude and a mystic arcane sense accessible to none but a select few violates the fundamental

---

[22] Cf., for example, Origen, *Con. Cels.*, VII, xx and *De Princ.*, I, i.
[23] Pico della Mirandola, *Apologia*, in *Opera* (Basel, 1572).

principles of the biblical view of revelation, in accordance with which God's Word, whether incarnate in Christ or spoken through prophets and apostles, is addressed to all without discrimination.[24]

In his *Obedience of a Christian Man* William Tyndale makes a vigorous attack on the four senses of Scripture (literal, tropological, allegorical, and anagogical) which the Schoolmen had sought to distinguish. "The Scripture", he affirms, "hath but one sense, which is the literal sense. And that literal sense is the root and ground of all, and the anchor that never faileth, whereunto if thou cleave, thou canst never err nor go out of the way. And if thou leave the literal sense, thou canst not but go out of the way". Not that the allegorical use of Scripture (the tropological and anagogical senses being but different forms of the allegorical) is illegitimate; but, insists Tyndale, it must be proved by the literal, and borne by it, as a house is borne by its foundation. "The greatest cause of ... the decay of the faith", he complains, "and this blindness wherein we now are, sprang first of allegories." In his own day there was an abundance of adept allegorizers—"sophisters with their anagogical and chopological sense, and with an antitheme of half an inch, out of which some of them draw a thread of nine days long. Yea", he continues,

---

[24] Bishop Lightfoot's comments on the terms τέλειος ("perfect", Col. 1:28) and ἀπόκρυφοι ("hidden", Col. 2:3) are of interest in this connection. "While employing the favourite Gnostic term", he says of the former, "the Apostle strikes at the root of the Gnostic doctrine. The language descriptive of the heathen mysteries is transferred by him to the Christian dispensation, that he may thus more effectively contrast the things signified. The true Gospel also has its mysteries, its hierophants, its initiation: but these are open to all alike. In Christ every believer is τέλειος, for he has been admitted as ἐπόπτης of its most profound, most awful secrets" (Commentary on Colossians, p. 169). And on the latter term he writes: "As before in τέλειος (i. 28), so here again in ἀπόκρυφοι the Apostle adopts a a favourite term of the Gnostic teachers, only that he may refute a favourite doctrine. The word apocrypha was especially applied to those esoteric writings for which sectarians claimed an *auctoritas secreta* (Aug. *c. Faust.* xi. 2, VIII. p. 219) and which they carefully guarded from publication after the manner of their Jewish prototypes the Esseness ... Thus the word *apocrypha* in the first instance was an honourable appellation applied by the heretics themselves to their esoteric doctrine and their secret books; but owing to the general character of these works the term, as adopted by orthodox writers, got to signify 'false', 'spurious'. The early fathers never apply it, as it is now applied, to *deutero-canonical* writings, but confine it to *supposititious* and *heretical* works" (*ibid.*, p. 172).

"thou shalt find enough that will preach Christ, and prove whatsoever point of the faith that thou wilt, as well out of a fable of Ovid or any other poet, as out of St John's gospel or Paul's epistles. Yea, they are come unto such blindness, that they not only say the literal sense profiteth not, but also that it is hurtful, and noisome, and killeth the soul". In support of this conclusion it was their custom to cite the verse which is now before us.

When considered in its context, however, it is evident that this verse is not concerned with any supposed distinction between two different senses of Scripture, the literal and the spiritual. "God is a Spirit, and all His words are spiritual. His literal sense is spiritual", declares Tyndale.   "Paul", he rightly explains, "maketh a comparison between the law and the gospel; and calleth the law the letter, because it was but letters graven in two tables of cold stone: for the law doth but kill, and damn the consciences, as long as there is no lust in the heart to do that which the law commandeth. Contrariwise, he calleth the gospel the administration of the Spirit and of righteousness or justifying. For when Christ is preached, and the promises which God hath made in Christ are believed, the Spirit entereth the heart, and looseth the heart, and giveth lust to do the law, and maketh the law a lively thing in the heart".[25]

Augustine similarly emphasizes that "the Apostle's words, 'the letter killeth, but the spirit giveth life', have no reference to figurative phrases", but "must be understood in the sense... that the letter of the law, which teaches us not to commit sin, kills, if the life-giving spirit be absent, forasmuch as it causes sin to be known rather than avoided, to be increased rather than diminished, because to an evil concupiscence there is now added the transgression of the law". Contrasting Sinai and Pentecost, he says: "*There* it was on tables of stone that the finger of God operated; *here* it was on the hearts of men. *There* it was outwardly that the law was registered, so that the unrighteous were terrified by it; *here* it was inwardly given, so that we might be justified by it. ... When the works of love are written on tables to alarm the carnal mind, there arises the law of works and 'the letter which killeth' the transgressor; but when love itself is shed abroad

---

[25] William Tyndale, *The Obedience of a Christian Man*, in *Doctrinal Treatises* (Parker Society, Cambridge, 1848), pp. 303ff.

in the hearts of believers, then we have the law of faith, and the spirit which gives life to him that loves".[26]

In our day, Rudolf Bultmann, though so radical a critic of the cardinal doctrines of the New Testament, has shown that he none the less has at this point an excellent understanding of the mind of Paul. "Though the Christian in a certain sense is no longer 'under Law' (Gal. 5:18; Rom. 6:14)", he writes, "that does not mean that the demands of the Law are no longer valid for him; for the *agape* demanded of him is nothing else than the fulfilment of the Law (Rom. 13:8–10; Gal. 5:14). ... The reason why man's situation under the Law is so desperate is not that the Law as an inferior revelation mediates a limited or even false knowledge of God. What makes his situation so desperate is the simple fact that prior to faith *there is no true fulfilment of the Law*.... That is why the 'ministration of the Law' is a 'ministration of death' or 'of condemnation' (II Cor. 3:7, 9); that is why 'the written code kills' (II Cor. 3:6); that is why the Law is 'the law of sin and death' (Rom. 8:2). The reason why man under the Law does not achieve 'rightwising' and life is that he is a transgressor of the Law, that he is guilty before God".[27]

The distinction here, then, between the letter and the spirit indicates the difference between the law as *externally* written at Sinai on tablets of stone and the *same* law as written *internally* in the heart of the Christian believer. Under the former dispensation it was an external ordinance by which the unrighteous (and that means all: cf. Rom. 3:9ff.) were confronted and condemned. "It was added because of transgressions" (Gal. 3:19). Sin, which is the breaking of the law, is shown up by the commandments of the law in its true light. And the verdict pronounced over the lawbreaker is death (cf. Ezek. 18:4, 20; Prov. 11:19; Rom. 5:12; 6:23). Hence Paul is able to speak startlingly of the letter which kills. The grace of the new covenant, however, is life-giving, in that Christ, who as God is the Law-Giver and as Man is the *only* law-keeper, vicariously endured the sinner's death penalty, ridding us, as it were, of the legal document with its accusing ordinances and nailing it to His cross for all to see (Col. 2:14f.), and also, by the Pentecostal outpouring of the

---

[26] Augustine, *De Spiritu et Littera*, V and XVII. The whole treatise will repay study.

[27] Rudolf Bultmann, *Theology of the New Testament*, Vol. I, pp. 262f.

Holy Spirit, communicated His life and obedience to every trusting heart.

Paul's language is by no means theoretical: he knew from first-hand experience how true it is that the letter kills whereas the spirit makes alive. He knew only too well what it was to be a self-righteous observer of the letter of the law—"circumcised the eighth day, of the stock of Israel, of the tribe of Benjamin, a Hebrew of Hebrews; as touching the law, a Pharisee; as touching zeal, persecuting the church; as touching the righteousness which is in the law, found blameless" (Phil. 3:5f.). Yet at the same time he had been "a blasphemer and a persecutor and injurious" (I Tim. 1:13), that is, a law-breaker under judgment, and in particular a fierce enemy of Jesus the Messiah and only Saviour, God's own Son (Acts 26:9ff.). Outward conformity to the law had been a hypocritical cloak covering the inward corruption of his heart. It was only through the exceeding abundance of the grace of God in Christ Jesus that he had been enabled to become a "minister of the new covenant, not of the letter, but of the spirit" (cf. I Tim. 1:12ff.). It was by faith in Christ alone and the operation of the Holy Spirit's grace in his heart that it became possible for him to conform inwardly, in spirit, as well as outwardly, in letter, to the demands of the law—or, as he puts it in another epistle, to "serve in newness of the spirit, and not in oldness of the letter" (Rom. 7:6).

The American Revised Standard Version, in taking "spirit" here to mean the Holy Spirit and therefore spelling it with a capital S ("Spirit"), has the support of numerous scholars from the earliest centuries onwards, including Chrysostom, Jerome, Augustine, Theodoret, Theophylact, and Tyndale. But, while it is entirely true that the blessings of the new covenant may be experienced only through the operation of the Holy Spirit, "the Lord and Giver of life", within the heart of man, yet it is unlikely that a direct reference to the Spirit is intended. The contrast is still (as in verse 3) between what is external and what is internal; and the interpretation which we have offered is confirmed by the Apostle's use of similar terminology in Romans 2:28f., where he writes: "He is not a Jew who is one *outwardly*; neither is that circumcision which is *outward* in the flesh: but he is a Jew who is one *inwardly*; and circumcision is that of the heart, *in the spirit not in the letter*".

101

Let Herveius sum up the whole question for us: "The letter kills in that it causes us to sin knowingly; ... but the spirit gives life in that it causes us to fulfil what is commanded.... Let the spirit be added therefore to the letter, and the letter to which the spirit gives life no longer kills. Accordingly, we ought not to regard the letter as condemned or reprehensible.... The letter alone, forbidding evil and commanding good, kills the souls of those who transgress it. But the Spirit, who through the grace of the new covenant is in the hearts of believers, now gives life to their souls by justifying them, and hereafter will also cause their bodies together with their souls to live everlastingly".

3 : 7, 8

But if the ministration of death, written, and engraven on stones, came with glory, so that the children of Israel could not look stedfastly upon the face of Moses for the glory of his face; which glory was passing away: how shall not rather the ministration of the spirit be with glory?

The contrast between "the ministration of death" and "the ministration of the spirit" corresponds to and carries on the thought of the contrast already made between the letter and the spirit. In this context "letter" is equivalent to "death" and "spirit" to "life", so that "death" and "spirit" may fittingly be opposed to each other, as here. The ministration of death was given through the mediation of Moses, the ministration of the spirit through Christ (cf. Heb. 8:6; 9:15; 12:24); but the giver in both cases was God—hence the glory with which each was accompanied. The Apostle is particularly careful not to give the impression that the law is in itself something evil or inglorious. It is true that it consists of the letter which kills and is engraved externally on stone. But it is not designed to kill: on the contrary, the keeping of the law is the way of life and the way of love (cf. Rom. 10:5; 13:10). "By the *ministration of death* he means the law", says Chrysostom. "And mark too what great caution he uses in the comparison, so as to give no handle to the heretics; for he did not say, 'which causeth death', but 'the ministration of death'; for it ministers unto, but was not the parent of, death; for that which caused death was sin; but the law brought in the punishment and showed the sin: it did not cause it. For it more distinctly revealed the evil, and punished it: it did not impel unto the evil; and it did not minister to the existence of sin or death, but to the suffering of retribution by the sinner—so that in this way it was even destructive of sin".

Thus Paul gives due weight to the truth that the law came into being in glory.[28]   As coming *from God*, it was necessarily glorious.   This was apparent to the people by the glory with which the countenance of Moses was suffused when he came down from the mount after receiving the law from God—a glory so bright that they were unable to maintain their gaze upon his face (Ex. 34:29f.). This, then, is a sufficient contradiction of the calumnies of those adversaries who were suggesting that Paul, who rejoices in his calling as an apostle of grace and a minister of the new covenant, is a despiser of the law. He is concerned, however, to expose the grave error of the false apostles who were exalting the law at the expense of the gospel. Theirs is in fact a ministry of death, for by the works of the law sinful (that is, law-breaking) man cannot be justified (cf. Gal. 2:16; 3:11).   In a later century Augustine found it necessary to join issue with opponents of this kind who affirmed the adequacy of the law for salvation. "What, therefore, do those very vain and perverse persons who follow Pelagius mean by saying that the law is that grace of God which helps us to avoid sin?" he asks. "Do they not, by making such an allegation, unhappily and beyond all doubt contradict the great apostle? He, indeed, says that through the law sin received its strength and power against man; and that man, through the commandment, although it be holy and just and good, dies, death working in him through that which is good, from which death there could be no deliverance unless the Spirit quickened him, whom the letter had killed".[29]

The Apostle accordingly reminds his readers that the glory of the old covenant is not to be compared with that of the new. The former was external, radiant on Moses' face, resplendent in the *shechinah* cloud of God's presence in the camp; the latter is intimate and internal. "What", asks Charles Hodge, "was a bright cloud overhanging the cherubim, to the light of God's presence filling the soul?" The former was a transient, imper-

---

28   'Εγενήθη ἐν δόξῃ.
29   Augustine, *De Gratia et Libero Arbitrio*, XI.

manent glory [30]—in course of time it faded from Moses' face, and in course of time Moses, the mediator of the law, himself was removed from their sight by death; the latter is a glory which does not fade—the light, in every believing heart, of the knowledge of the glory of God in the face of Jesus Christ (4:6), who is the ever-living Mediator of the new covenant (Heb. 7:24f.; 8:6). The law is distinguished from grace, as Herveius explains, "because the one is good in that it commands good things, the other in that it confers good things; the one makes a hearer, the other a doer, of righteousness". And Calvin writes: "The office of the law is to show us the disease in such a way that it shows us no hope of a cure; whereas the office of the gospel is to bring a remedy to those who are past hope. For the law, since it leaves man to himself, necessarily condemns him to death; whereas the gospel, by bringing him to Christ, opens the gate of life". From whatever aspect it is considered, the glory of the gospel is seen to excel that of the law.

3:9—11

> For if the ministration of condemnation hath glory, much rather doth the ministration of righteousness exceed in glory. For verily that which hath been made glorious hath not been made glorious in this respect, by reason of the glory that surpasseth. For if that which passeth away was with glory, much more that which remaineth is in glory.

The terms which Paul now uses—"the ministration of condemnation" and "the ministration of righteousness"—as he pursues his comparison between the law and the gospel clearly imply that in the new covenant the law is neither disparaged nor discarded. Condemnation is the consequence of breaking the law; righteousness is precisely the keeping of the law. The gospel is not lawless. It is the ministration of righteousness to those who because of sin are under condemnation. And this righteousness is administered to men solely by the mediation and merit of Christ, who alone, as the incarnate Son, has perfectly obeyed God's holy law. Christ is the believer's righteousness (I Cor. 1:30): first of all in justification, whereby Christ's obedience is reckoned to the sinner on the ground that the penalty of the

---

[30] Τὴν δόξαν ... τὴν καταργουμένην. Cf. τὸ καταργούμενον, verse 11.

sinner's disobedience has been borne by Christ, who suffered the Righteous for the unrighteous (I Pet. 3:18); and then in sanctification, whereby the Holy Spirit causes the believer to grow more and more in obedience and likeness to Christ (Eph. 4:13, 15; Gal. 4:19). In accordance with the promises of the new covenant, as we have already seen, God's law is written on the believing heart and the power is granted—the dynamic of Christ's perfect law-keeping—to fulfil it. Thus the letter of condemnation is transformed by God's grace into the way of love and of life. Before the law the sinner is guilty and powerless, shut up to condemnation and judgment; but in the gospel he is offered forgiveness and power and an everlasting inheritance, in Christ (cf. Rom. 3:19–26; 8:16ff.).

The ministration of righteousness so far surpasses in glory the ministration of condemnation that in comparison with it the latter may be said to be no longer glorious: in this respect,[31] that which has been made glorious has been made not glorious [32] —just as the brightness of the sun altogether transcends and supersedes the brightness of the moon, or the advent of the day causes the brilliance of a lamp to fade away.[33] The impermanence of the earlier dispensation is confirmed by the fact that it was "with", or, more literally, "through glory"[34]: that is, it was

---

[31] Ἐν τούτῳ τῷ μέρει—cf. 9:3 where the expression is used again with the same meaning.

[32] Οὐ δεδόξασται τὸ δεδοξασμένον — an example of oxymoron.

[33] Cf. Herveius: " . . . sicut ortu solis caecatur lumen lucernae, quod antea videbatur magnum habere fulgorem". The following passage from Archelaus (third century) is worth quoting: "Even though my Lord Jesus Christ excels Moses in glory, as a lord excels his servant, it does not follow from this that the glory of Moses is to be scorned . . . Thus, although a person kindles a lamp in the night time, after the sun has once risen he has no further need of the paltry light of his lamp, on account of that effulgence of the sun which sends forth its rays all the world over; and yet, for all that, the man does not throw his lamp contemptuously away, as if it were something absolutely antagonistic to the sun; but rather, when he has once found out its use, he will keep it with all the greater carefulness. Precisely in this way, then, the law of Moses served as a sort of guardian to the people, like a lamp until the true Sun, who is our Saviour, should arise" (Disputation with Manes, xliii). Cf. also Basil, De Spiritu Sancto, xxi: "Lamps are made needless by the advent of the sun; and, on the appearance of the truth, the occupation of the law is gone, and prophecy is hushed into silence".

[34] Διὰ δόξης. C. F. D. Moule suggests that the usage with διά here is "all but adjectival", so that "διὰ δόξης practically = glorious" (An Idiom Book of New Testament Greek, Cambridge, 1953; p. 58).

accompanied with the manifestation of the divine glory at mount Sinai when it was mediated to the people through Moses, whose face also shone with that glory. The permanence of the gospel dispensation, on the other hand, is confirmed by the fact that it is "in glory": [35] that is, it is established in the sphere of glory.[36] Its glory is the glory that surpasses; and it is *all* glory, glory leading to glory, without a shadow of condemnation (see v. 18 below). What unspeakable comfort and security there is for the Christian in the knowledge that his is an everlasting gospel (Rev. 14:6), an everlasting covenant (Heb. 13:20), an everlasting salvation (Heb. 5:9)!

---

[35] Ἐν δόξῃ.

[36] It is true that the phrase ἐν δόξῃ was used of the giving of the law above (verse 7); there, however, as the context shows, it is descriptive of the attendant circumstances, whereas here, now used of the gospel ("the ministration of righteousness"), it is descriptive of the abiding element within which the gospel is set.

3:12-4:6 WITH UNVEILED FACE

3 : 12, 13

Having therefore such a hope, we use great boldness of
speech, and are not as Moses, who put a veil upon his face,
that the children of Israel should not look stedfastly on the
end of that which was passing away.

What is the "hope" of which Paul speaks at the beginning
of verse 12?   Some—for example, Denney, Stanley, Hodge,
Olshausen—regard it as equivalent to the "confidence" of verse 4,
and a resumption of what was said there, though now the use
of the term "hope" shows that the Apostle's confidence extends
into the future.[1] Alford relates it to the hope implied in verse 8,
that the ministration of the spirit will surpass the ministration of
condemnation. On this basis we would suggest that it is worth
considering whether Paul's meaning, when he says "having such
a hope", is not just this: possessing the fulfilment of this hope.
Tasker and Allo take it in a primarily eschatological sense as
referring to the fulness of the glory and of the gospel harvest
which is yet to be revealed. Ambrose holds a similar opinion,
explaining it as the hope of seeing the glory, not such as shone
on the face of Moses, but that which the three apostles beheld
on the mount when Christ was transfigured. Theophylact understands it to mean the hope that we who believe have been
accounted worthy of greater blessings than was Moses. Others—
for example, Filson, Plummer, Weiss, Bengel, Herveius—connect
the hope with the immediately preceding thought of verse 11,
namely, that the surpassing glory of the gospel is also a glory
that is abiding and permanent. Of these interpretations the last
mentioned seems to us the most natural and therefore preferable
to the rest.

Paul reminds his readers that the openness of his ministry of
the gospel is in contrast to the ministry of the law by Moses, who
had found it necessary to place a veil over his face (see Ex. 34:32ff.).
Moses, in other words, was unable to use complete openness. It

---

[1]   Denney points out that "in the LXX ἐλπίζω is often used as the rendering
of בָּטַח, *confidere*".

is unfortunate that the rendering of Ex. 34:33 in the AV ("And *till* Moses had done speaking with them, he put a veil on his face") has given rise to a general misconception of what actually took place. The text of this version would lead one to conclude that Moses had covered his face with a veil *while* he was speaking with the people of Israel. The correct rendering of the Hebrew original is given, however, in the RV: "*when* Moses had done speaking with them, he put a veil on his face"; that is, it was not during but *after* his speech with them that he covered his face.[2] This accords well with what is said in verse 35 (both AV and RV). While Moses spoke to them the people saw the glory shining from his uncovered face. Then, as soon as he had finished speaking, he covered his face with a veil. This he removed again when he went into the holy of holies to speak with the Lord (Ex. 34:34). Paul's language suggests that this procedure became customary: "Moses *used to place*[3] a veil over his face". The Apostle also indicates the purpose and significance of this veiling of his face by Moses: it was with the object that[4] the Israelites should not look right on to[5] the end of that which was transient— that they should not see even that impermanent glory without interruption. The glory, since it was of God, was entirely incompatible with the wickedness of a rebellious and stiffnecked people (cf. Ex. 32). They were permitted to look upon it when Moses was speaking the words of God to them because it afforded irrefutable proof of the authenticity of his ministry and leadership. But, reflected and temporary though it was, the sinful Israelites could not sustain their gaze upon that splendour. And so Moses used to veil his face when he had done speaking with them—not so much for the convenience of the people as to show them, by a kind of enacted parable, that it was their iniquities which rendered them unable, and unworthy, to behold such glory. The veiling of Moses' face was a condemnation of the people.

Modern commentators explain verse 13 to mean that Moses veiled his face in order that the Israelites might not gaze upon

---

[2] Cf. also LXX: καὶ ἐπειδὴ κατέπαυσεν λαλῶν πρὸς αὐτούς, ἐπέθηκεν ἐπὶ τὸ πρόσωπον αὐτοῦ κάλυμμα, and Vg.: *impletisque sermonibus, posuit velamen super faciem suam*.

[3] Ἐτίθει, iterative imperfect.

[4] Πρὸς τό + infinitive.

[5] Μὴ ἀτενίσαι ... εἰς.

the end, that is, according to them, the fading away and final vanishing, of the passing glory with which it was radiant. Thus Plummer, for example, affirms that "the Apostle's main point is this fading of the glory, which he treats as symbolizing the temporary nature of the Mosaic Law"; and, according to Moffatt's version, Moses "used to hang a veil over his face to keep the children of Israel from gazing at the last rays of a fading glory". But, apart from the noteworthy consideration that this interpretation finds no support in the exegesis of the patristic authors, it is an interpretation which confuses the issue at this stage in Paul's argument by proposing that it was not the glory but the *fading* of the glory which Moses was intent on hiding from the people. It also raises a moral problem; for, despite disclaimers to the contrary on the part of many who advocate this understanding of the text, it attributes to Moses the practising of a subterfuge, and this to Paul would have been unthinkable. In any case, why should Moses have wished the children of Israel to believe that a fading glory was not fading? How could so notable a minister of God have been party to an untruth of this nature? And are we to imagine that day after day during all the years in the wilderness he kept his face covered with a veil, the only exceptions being the occasions when he addressed the people as the messenger of God and when, alone, he went in before the Lord? The children of Israel, rather, must have been well aware that the glory shining from Moses' face was a fading glory, for in course of time when this glory, so insupportable to their eyes, had faded away Moses would remove the veil. It was through speaking with the Lord in the holy of holies that the glory was renewed, so that when he emerged from the tabernacle the assembled people witnessed the divine splendour radiating from his countenance and knew that he was about to announce to them the words of God. We understand Paul to mean, therefore, that Moses placed a veil over his face so that the people might not gaze right to the end of the glory which was passing away, that is, that they might not behold it without interruption or concealment.[6] It is the interruption and conceal-

---

[6] *Eἰς τὸ τέλος* indicates *duration* here—"right on to the end"—rather than the ultimate vanishing point—"on the end". Theodoret and other commentators since his day have connected the phrase, "to the end of that which was passing away", with Rom. 10:4, where Christ is spoken of as "the end of the

ment of that glory, rather than its fading, with which Paul is now primarily concerned.[7]

In this respect, then, the ministry of Moses was marked by concealment; and the Apostle draws attention to this fact in order to emphasize that, by contrast, his own ministry of the gospel has the character of great *openness*.[8] He uses no veil. His is not a message of condemnation and death, but of grace and mercy and life to every sinner who repents and believes. The eye of faith may gaze upon the everlasting glory of Christ without interruption.

3 : 14 — 16

> But their minds were hardened: for until this very day at the reading of the old covenant the same veil remaineth, it not being revealed to them that it is done away in Christ. But unto this day, whensoever Moses is read, a veil lieth upon their heart. But whensoever it shall turn to the Lord, the veil is taken away.

Even when confronted with the glory shining from Moses' countenance the Israelites were unwilling to receive what God had to communicate to them through him; and in consequence

---

law", and have accordingly understood Paul to mean that Moses veiled his face to prevent the children of Israel perceiving that his dispensation was to have its end or consummation in Christ. This interpretation, however, is consistent neither with the context of Ex. 34:33 nor with good exegesis. Moses' purpose in veiling his face was hardly mystical and eschatological —however significant it now appears in retrospect—but *ad hoc*, related to the immediate necessity for concealing the divine glory from the eyes of a sinful people. Paul, as Plummer points out, "could not mean that Moses veiled his face to prevent the Israelites from seeing Christ". Had this been his purpose, it would be legitimate to ask, firstly, why the interposition of a piece of material should have been thought adequate to interrupt an essentially spiritual and eschatological vision, and, secondly, why Moses should have wished to prevent their enjoying so praiseworthy and desirable a perspective.

[7] According to rabbinical tradition, the glory continued to shine unabated from Moses' face up till the day of his death and even after death in his tomb (cf. Strack–Billerbeck, *Kommentar zum Neuen Testament aus Talmud und Midrasch*). By traditions of this sort the rabbinical doctrine of the supreme glory of the law was bolstered up—a doctrine which Paul, the former rabbinist, refutes by showing that the glory of the law was a transient glory which is surpassed and superseded by the abiding glory of the gospel.

[8] The basic meaning of παρρησία, translated "boldness of speech" in our English version, is indeed *outspokenness*. Hence it came to mean *openness* as opposed to secrecy. Thus in Jn. 7:4 ἐν κρυπτῷ, "in secret", is used as the

their minds were hardened: their understandings were dulled and deadened. This is always the result of refusing and suppressing the revelation of divine truth. A veil of intellectual darkness hides the glory which has been deliberately rejected. The epitaph of the rebellious Israelites and of all hardened sinners is simply this: "Knowing God, they glorified Him not as God, neither gave thanks; but became vain in their reasonings, and their senseless heart was darkened" (Rom. 1:21). We are warned, therefore, of the terrible possibility of intellectual hardening when face to face with the glorious revelation of divine truth; and the responsibility is proportionately greater of those who are confronted, not with the partial and transient glory of the law, but with the surpassing and permanent glory of the gospel of Jesus Christ.

Paul introduces a bold transference of thought when he affirms that *the same veil* remains when the old covenant is read; but he is fully justified in doing so because he is thinking historically: the placing by Moses of a veil over his face was in itself an action symbolical of the veil of rebellion and unbelief which curtained the hearts of the people from the true apprehension of God's glory. During the succeeding centuries that veil has never been removed from the understanding of the nation as a whole. Moses, to be sure, is dead and the material veil which he used has perished; but the same veil, the inward veil of which the outward veil was the symbol, is still keeping the hearts of the Israelites in darkness whenever they are confronted afresh, as it were, with Moses in the form of the Old Testament Scriptures. Now that Christ has come, however, it has the added effect of blinding them also to the splendour and significance of the new covenant. The same veil shuts out from their gaze not only the reflected glory of Moses but also the full glory of Christ and His gospel. This, indeed, was precisely the import of our Lord's condemnation

---

opposite of ἐν παρρησίᾳ, "in public". Paul uses the expression ἐν παρρησίᾳ with precisely the same force in Col. 2:15. In Jn. 7:13, 26; 11:54; 18:20 the dative παρρησίᾳ has a similar force, that is, "openly" or "in public" (cf. also 10:24; 11:14; 16:25, 29; Mk. 8:32). Arndt and Gingrich render μετὰ πάσης παρρησίας, Acts 28:31, as "quite openly". *Openness* (which for a minister of the gospel naturally involves outspokenness) is undoubtedly the principal significance of παρρησία here in our present verse, in contradistinction to the concealment resulting from the veiling of Moses' face.

of His Jewish critics when He said to them: "If ye believed Moses, ye would believe Me; for he wrote of Me. But if ye believe not his writings, how shall ye believe My words?" (Jn. 5:46f.). These words of Christ confirm that, as we have explained earlier, there is no contradiction between old and new covenants. The one is preparatory; it leads to Christ (cf. Gal. 3:24; Rom. 10:4; Mt. 5:17); it is fulfilled in and therefore superseded by the other. Belief in Moses would have prepared the heart of Israel for belief in Christ, as was in fact the case, for example, with Simeon and Anna (Lk. 2:25ff., 36ff.) and the Jews who responded to Peter's preaching on the day of Pentecost (Acts 2:5ff.).

Of course, now that the old covenant has given way to the new, the passing glory to the surpassing, it is only by turning in faith to Christ that the veil over the reading of Moses is removed. The shining of the moon can be understood only in terms of the shining of the sun, of which it is a less glorious reflection. It is one and the same light. Nor is Paul speaking theoretically; he is speaking from experience. Hebrew of the Hebrews though he had been (Phil. 3:5), the same veil had remained unremoved over his heart until the day when he submitted himself to the will of God in Christ.[9] And this is the practical issue with which all

---

[9] The sentence, τὸ αὐτὸ κάλυμμα ἐπὶ τῇ ἀναγνώσει τῆς παλαιᾶς διαθήκης μένει μὴ ἀνακαλυπτόμενον, ὅτι ἐν Χριστῷ καταργεῖται, has been understood in different ways. Of these, there are three which deserve mention. (i) "At the reading of the old covenant the same veil remains unlifted, which veil is done away in Christ". This interpretation is adopted by AV, RV, and Souter; but it involves dividing ὅτι to read ὅ τι and treating it as a simple relative pronoun, = ὅ,—a procedure which grammatically is neither necessary nor satisfactory. (ii) "At the reading of the old covenant the same veil remains, it not being revealed to them that (ὅτι) it is done away in Christ". This rendering, which is favoured by our own English version (American Standard Version), and also by Nestlé, Allo, Moffatt, Bachmann, Stanley, Alford, etc., requires the placing of a comma after μένει and treats μὴ ἀνακαλυπτόμενον as a nominative or accusative absolute. In our judgment, however, this is an awkward and improbable construction. (iii) "At the reading of the old covenant the same veil remains unlifted, because it is in Christ that it is done away". This is the interpretation preferred by Westcott and Hort, Plummer, Weiss, Hodge, Calvin, Luther, etc.,—also the Vulgate, which is very clear: *idipsum velamen in lectione veteris testamenti manet non revelatum, (quoniam in Christo evacuatur)*—and it is certainly the most natural way of taking the words. There is also a difference of opinion regarding the implied subject of the verb καταργεῖται. Some, including those who adopt interpretation (ii) above, take "the old covenant", which in Christ has been superseded, to be the

his fellow-Israelites are faced: unless and until they also turn to Christ they will continue to be shut out from the apprehension of the glory of God's revealed truth. It is not merely the intellect over which the veil lies, but *the heart*, which, in the scriptural view of man, is the centre of his being, the spring of will and activity, the seat of the affections and the understanding, the focal prism of the personality. Israel must turn to the Lord, *the same Lord* to whom Moses turned in the tabernacle and in whose presence the veil was removed from his face so that he beheld with unimpeded vision the divine glory.[10] The terminology used by Paul in verse

---

subject, but in that case we should have expected the verb to be in the aorist or perfect, rather than the present, tense. Others make "the veil" the subject, and this accords well with the two present tenses—ἀνακαλυπτόμενον (understood as qualifying the preceding κάλυμμα) and καταργεῖται — which both indicate a present reality: the state of the veil being unremoved (where there is unbelief) and, its counterpart, the state of the veil being done away in Christ.

[10] Verse 16, ἡνίκα δ'ἀν ἐπιστρέψῃ πρὸς Κύριον, περιαιρεῖται τὸ κάλυμμα, has received a variety of interpretations, particularly with regard to the unexpressed subject of the verb ἐπιστρέψῃ.

(i) "When *a man* shall turn to the Lord the veil is taken away". Thus Augustine comments: "The Old Testament, from Mount Sinai, which genders to bondage, profits nothing unless because it bears witness to the New Testament. Otherwise, however long Moses is read, the veil is put over their heart; but when any one shall turn thence to Christ, the veil shall be taken away" (*Civ. Dei*, XVII, 7).

(ii) "When *Israel* shall turn . . ." The words, according to Tertullian, "properly refer to the Jew, over whose gaze Moses' veil is spread, to the effect that, when he is turned to the faith of Christ, he will understand how Moses spoke of Christ" (*Adv. Marc.* V, xi).

(iii) "When *Moses* shall turn . . ." "Who does not see that this is said of Moses, that is, of the law?" asks Calvin. "For since Christ is the end of the law, to whom it ought to be referred, it was turned away in another direction when the Jews excluded Christ from it".

(iv) "When *their heart* shall turn . . ." (Allo, Alford, etc.). Grammatically, this last would seem to be the best, because "their heart", occurring towards the end of the preceding clause, provides the nearest subject for the verb ἐπιστρέψῃ. But whether it is the correct subject, that is, the subject which was in Paul's mind, it is difficult to say, and the diversity of opinion on this point is unlikely to be resolved. Fortunately, however, the force of the Apostle's argument is not in dispute, namely, that the veil will be removed from the Jewish heart only when there is a turning to Christ (whether it be a turning of the individual, or of the nation, or of the law metaphorically, or of the heart).

On the verb περιαιρεῖται Wordsworth comments as follows: "*The veil is being removed.* By the *present* tense he indicates what is always going on; and he intimates the *certainty* of the *future total removal* of the veil from the Jewish

113

16 affords us a significant insight into the christological doctrine of the Apostolic Church; for the implication is unmistakeable, that the Lord (Yahweh, LXX *Kyrios*) before whom Moses went in (Ex. 34:34) is one and the same Lord (= Christ) to whom the people are invited to turn even now.[11] Thus it is apparent that, as Article VII of the Church of England says, "the Old Testament is not contrary to the New: for both in the Old and New Testament everlasting life is offered to mankind by Christ, who is the only Mediator between God and man".

Further light is thrown on this passage when we consider what took place on the occasion of the transfiguration of Christ.[12] On that mountain height Moses and Elijah appeared with Christ, but it was *Christ alone* who was transfigured with heavenly radiance before the eyes of Peter, James, and John. It was *His* face that shone as the sun and *His* garments that became white and dazzling. It was of *Him alone* that the voice from the cloud said. "This is My beloved Son, in whom I am well pleased; hear ye Him". And thereafter the disciples saw no one, *save Jesus only*. It is He who abides. The glory in which Moses and Elijah appeared was not their own but Christ's glory—the glory which

---

heart, when it will turn to Christ. Rom. xi. 26". This exegesis is perhaps supported by the view of J. H. Moulton that περιαιρεῖται here is an intensive compound, which might suggest the translation, "is being completely removed" (*Grammar of N. T. Greek*, Vol. II, p. 321). A. M. Ramsey is interested by the suggestion that περιαιρεῖται may be middle rather than passive, the meaning then being: "He (the Lord) takes away the veil" (see *The Glory of God*, etc., p. 52). In favour of the verb being middle is the fact that in the LXX of Ex. 34:34 it is the middle of the same verb which is used: "But when Moses went in before the Lord to speak with Him, he took the veil off" (περιῃρεῖτο τὸ κάλυμμα). If the parallel is to be maintained here, however, we should have to understand the subject of περιαιρεῖται as "the Jew" or "Israel": "whenever the Jew (or Israel) shall turn to the Lord, he (the Jew or Israel) takes off the veil". But it is perhaps more natural to take περιαιρεῖται as a passive.

The occurrence of ἐπιστρέφειν in this context is interesting because it is used elsewhere in the New Testament of the experience of conversion (see, for example, Acts 3:19). In ἐπιστρέψῃ here a double force should be discerned: firstly, a graphic parallel to the account in Ex. 34 where Moses turned from the people and went in before the Lord, thereupon removing the veil from his face; and, secondly a deeper significance, for the act of turning to the Lord here involves the experience of evangelical conversion.

[11]   See commantary above on 1:2.
[12]   Mk. 9:2ff. and parallel passages.

He had had with the Father before the world was (Jn. 17:5). Just as in the wilderness the glory which shone from Moses' face was the reflected glory of Yahweh, so too on the mount of transfiguration the glory with which he was surrounded was the glory of the same Yahweh. Christ's alone is the full, the abiding, the evangelical glory. To turn to Him is to turn to the Light of the world. To follow Him is not to walk in darkness, but to have the light of life (Jn. 8:12).

3:17

Now the Lord is the Spirit: and where the Spirit of the Lord is, there is liberty.

The exegetical problem in this verse revolves around the significance of the term "spirit". Many commentators from the early centuries onwards have understood the Apostle to be referring specifically to the Holy Spirit, the Third Person of the Trinity. By them the first clause has been interpreted to mean either that "the Holy Spirit is Lord (= God)"—indicating unequivocally the Godhead of the Holy Spirit—or that "the Lord (= Christ) is the Holy Spirit"—indicating the unity of the Second and Third Persons of the Trinity. Accordingly, this verse has been adduced as a proof-text attesting the truth of the trinitarian doctrine and the deity of the Holy Spirit. We do not hesitate to give it as our judgment that such an understanding of this passage is neither required by the words nor congruous with the context. In this passage Paul's concern is with the relationship and contrast between the old and new covenants, not with the ontology of trinitarianism. There is no warrant for supposing that at this point he is interrupting his theme. Already in verse 6—"the letter killeth, but the spirit giveth life"—he has set "the spirit" in contrast to "the letter".[13] Now here, in verse 17, he says that "the Lord is the spirit"; that is, Christ[14] is the source of light and life: to turn to Him is to have the veil of misunderstanding removed and to pass from death to life. Apart from Christ, Moses the law-giver is a minister of condemnation; but in Christ, the sole Law-Keeper, the letter springs to life. This

---

[13] On the significance of verse 6 see commentary above.
[14] Cf. the use of "the Lord" (*ὁ Κύριος*) as a distinctive title of Christ in verses 16 and 18, and throughout the New Testament.

interpretation is confirmed by what the Apostle has previously written to the Corinthian Church, in I Cor. 15:45, where he uses identical terms:

I Cor. 15:45: "The last Adam (=Christ) became life-giving spirit".
II Cor. 3:6,17: "The spirit giveth life. ... Now the Lord (= Christ) is the spirit".[15]

The second part of the verse—"and where the spirit of the Lord is, there is liberty"—is a proper consequence of the first. It is also what Paul had proved by his own experience of conversion and life in Christ. The Jews were in bondage to the letter which kills, but Christians have entered into the liberty of Christ—the dynamic liberty of the spirit as opposed to the mere letter. And it is important that the man who has been made free in Christ should not return into any kind of unevangelical bondage. Hence the apostolic reminder to the Romans that the spirit they had received was the spirit of adoption, not of bondage again to fear (Rom. 8:15), and the admonition to the Galatians: "For freedom did Christ set us free: stand fast therefore, and be not entangled again in a yoke of bondage" (Gal. 5:1). Throughout this passage, then, we would write the word "spirit" with a small and not a capital initial letter. Although, however, there is in our judgment no *direct* reference to the Holy Spirit here, yet there can be no doubt that the operation of the Holy Spirit is implicit in Paul's argument, especially in view of his plain teaching elsewhere that it is the Holy Spirit's office to apply the work of Christ to the believing heart.[16] The distinction

---

[15]   I Cor. 15:45—Ἐγένετο ... ὁ ἔσχατος Ἀδὰμ εἰς πνεῦμα ζωοποιοῦν.

II Cor. 3:6, 17—Τὸ δὲ πνεῦμα ζωοποιεῖ ... ὁ δὲ Κύριος τὸ πνεῦμα ἐστιν.

[16]   Plummer translates οὗ δὲ τὸ πνεῦμα Κυρίου, ἐλευθερία: "he who possesses the spirit of Christ has liberty", taking οὗ as the genitive of the relative pronoun and not as an adverb. This, however, is a less natural rendering of the Greek.

Westcott and Hort suggest that Κυρίου is "probably a primitive error for κύριον", that is, a neuter nominative adjective agreeing with πνεῦμα. The sense would then be: "Where the spirit is sovereign, there is liberty". Another conjecture, likewise unsupported by any evidence, is that of Dobschütz, who proposes Κύριος for Κυρίου, which would mean that the second clause of the verse is a repetition and expansion of the first: "The Lord is the spirit; but where the spirit is the Lord, there is liberty". The text as it is, however, is clear enough, from the standpoint of exegesis as well as grammar, without requiring conjectural emendations of this sort. Besides, the sense of Κύριος in verse 17 is determined by its force in verse 16, which is virtually a quotation of Ex. 34:34, where (in the LXX) it stands for Yahweh.

between "spirit" and "Spirit" accordingly becomes a fine one and explains the division of the commentators over this point. The use of the term in this verse in particular is felt by many to be applicable only to the Third Person of the Trinity. It is perhaps one of those matters which is unlikely to be resolved until we attain to that fulness of knowledge of which Paul speaks in the earlier epistle (I Cor. 13:12).

3 : 18

> But we all, with unveiled face beholding as in a mirror the glory of the Lord, are transformed into the same image from glory to glory, even as from the Lord the Spirit.

The expression "we all" signifies all Christians without exception. Erasmus, Bengel, and some others have taken it to indicate only ministers of the Gospel rather than all believers without discrimination; but, as Calvin remarks, it is evident that Paul is speaking of an experience which is common to all believers. In the old dispensation only one man, Moses, gazed with unveiled face on the divine glory. Now, in the gospel age, however, this is the blessed privilege of all who are Christ's, whether great or small, well known or unknown, while the mass of the Jews who continue in unbelief continue also in darkness. For him who has turned in faith to Christ the veil which shuts off the glory from his apprehension has been removed for good and all. The evangelical glory is abiding, without intermission; so also the believer's beholding of that glory is uninterrupted.[17]

The glory is "the glory of the Lord", and we behold it "as in a mirror". To gaze by faith into the gospel is to behold Christ, who in this same passage is described as "the image of God" (4:4) and elsewhere as "the image of the invisible God" (Col. 1:15) and "the effulgence of the Father's glory and the impress of His substance" (Heb. 1:3). To see Him is to see the Father, and to behold His glory is to behold the glory as of the only begotten from the Father (Jn. 14:9; 1:14). And to contemplate Him who is the Father's image is progressively to be transformed into

---

[17]   In the phrase "with unveiled face"—$\dot{a}\nu\alpha\varkappa\varepsilon\varkappa\alpha\lambda\nu\mu\mu\dot{\varepsilon}\nu\omega$ $\pi\varrho\sigma\sigma\dot{\omega}\pi\omega$—the perfect participle indicates that the veil, once lifted, *remains* lifted, while the present participle $\varkappa\alpha\tau\sigma\pi\tau\varrho\iota\zeta\dot{\sigma}\mu\varepsilon\nu\sigma\iota$ ("beholding as in a mirror") shows that the beholding is continuous and free from interruption.

that image. The effect of continuous beholding is that we are continuously being transformed [18] "into the same image", that is, into the likeness of Christ—and increasingly so: "from glory to glory". In contrast to the glory seen on Moses' face, there is no prospect of the evangelical glory fading or diminishing, but only of its increasing more and more until the coming in person of the Lord of glory Himself. Then at last the glory will be revealed to us in all its fulness (Rom. 8:18). Till then we behold it by faith, "as in a mirror" (cf. I Cor. 13:12). But then, when He appears, we shall behold Him face to face and our transformation into His image will be complete. Thus John writes: "When He is manifested we shall be like Him, for we shall see Him even as He is" (I Jn. 3:2).[19]

---

[18] Μεταμορφούμεθα, present tense; see also the preceding note. It is worthy of notice that the verb μεταμορφεῖν is the same as is used to describe the transfiguration of Christ on the mount (Mk. 9:2; Mt. 17:2). The heavenly glory with which He was then transfigured is the heavenly glory with which those who are His are even now being progressively transfigured. The significance of the element μορφή in μεταμορφούμεθα is indicated by Lightfoot's comment on the noun in Phil. 2:6, that "the possession of the μορφή involves participation in the οὐσία also: for μορφή implies not the external accidents but the essential attributes". Similarly A. M. Ramsey points out with reference to our text that "μορφή means real being in contrast with outward appearance; it is in respect of our real being that we are changed. It is a transformation of the essential man". And he draws attention to Rom. 12:2, which he renders: "be not outwardly fashioned (συνσχηματίζεσθε) according to this world; but be ye changed in real being (μεταμορφοῦσθε) by the renewing of your mind" (The Glory of God, etc., p. 54). This distinctive significance should, however, be attributed to μορφή with caution when dealing with the language of the first century A.D. There is evidence to suggest that μορφή and εἰκών were on occasion treated as equivalent terms (see, for example, R. P. Martin, Μορφή in Philippians ii. 6, in The Expository Times, Vol. LXX, No. 6 [March, 1959], pp. 183f.). This being so, Paul's language in the clause τὴν αὐτὴν εἰκόνα μεταμορφούμεθα may well take on added significance.

[19] The rendering of κατοπτριζόμενοι in our version ("beholding as in a mirror") is similar to the AV ("beholding as in a glass"); but RV translates it "reflecting as a mirror". Either rendering is permissible on linguistic and exegetical grounds. If the former is adopted, then it is Christ who mirrors the glory of God (and our exposition above is based on this sense); if the latter, then it is *we* (Christians) who mirror the glory of God, and as we reflect Him who is the Father's image so we ourselves become more and more like that image. Allo suggests that "as Moses reflected *temporarily* the glory of Yahweh which he had seen, our faces reflect continually the brilliance of Christ". The Vulgate has *speculantes*, which, though it can only mean "beholding" and never "reflect-

This process of transformation into the image of Christ is none other than the restoration of the image of God which was marred through the fall of man. "In Christ", says Archbishop Ramsey, "mankind is allowed to see not only the radiance of God's glory but also the true image of man. Into that image Christ's people are now being transformed, and in virtue of this transformation into the new man they are realizing the meaning of their original status as creatures in God's image".[20] The image of Christ is the true seal of the Spirit with which the believer is impressed.[21] Indeed, as Calvin explains, the design of the gospel is precisely this, "that the image of God, which had been defaced by sin, may be repaired within us"; and he adds that "the progress of this restoration is continuous through the whole of life, because it is little by little that God causes His glory to shine forth in us". A significant passage in this connection is Col. 3:10, where Paul explicitly affirms that the Christian has

---

ing", may perhaps be thought (with the Greek original in mind) to carry the suggestion of a mirror. Hence the comment of Herveius: "*speculantes*, id est per speculum intuentes . . .". The following passage from Clement of Rome may be adduced in favour of the sense "beholding as in a mirror": "Through Him (Christ) we behold as in a mirror *(ἐνοπτριζόμεθα)* His faultless and most excellent visage; through Him the eyes of our hearts were opened; through Him our foolish and darkened mind springeth up unto [His marvellous] light . . ." (*Epistle to the Corinthians*, XXXVI. Lightfoot's translation). Here we clearly have an echo of II Cor. 3:18; indeed, ἐνοπτριζόμεθα probably represents a faulty reminiscence of κατοπτριζόμενοι, and there can be little doubt that it indicates the sense in which Clement understood this Pauline passage. Ἐνοπτρίζεσθαι means to look into a mirror; hence the comment of Lightfoot that "Christ is the mirror in whom is reflected the faultless countenance of God the Father". In view of the fact that Clement was personally acquainted with the Apostles and a disciple of theirs, and that in writing to the Corinthians the use of this metaphor of "beholding in a mirror" would have been all the more significant because Paul had used the same figure of speech in writing to them a generation previously, it may be supposed that Clement's words represent the contemporary understanding of what Paul had written. It is possible, however, that Paul's meaning is simply "beholding" (so ARSV), without the concept of a mirror at all. With this understanding of the term κατοπτριζόμενοι Tertullian would seem to concur, for in *Adv. Marc.*, V, xi, he gives *contemplantes* as its Latin equivalent. This observation would apply also to the use of the word by Philo, Paul's contemporary, in a passage which is concerned with precisely the same Old Testament context (*Legis Alleg.*, III, 33).

[20] A. M. Ramsey, *op. cit.*, p. 151.
[21] See commentary above on 1:22.

"put on the new man, that is being renewed unto knowledge after the image of Him that created him". In justification, through faith *into* Christ [22] the sinner is accepted *in* Christ (cf. 5:17) who Himself is the pure and perfect Image of God, and that divine image is freely *imputed* to the believer. In sanctification, through the operation of the Holy Spirit who enables the believer constantly to behold the glory of the Lord, that image is increasingly *imparted* to the Christian. In glorification, justification and sanctification become complete in one, for that image is then finally impressed upon the redeemed in unobscured fulness, to the glory of God throughout eternity.

In origin, process, and consummation this whole work of redemption is "of the Lord the Spirit"—that is, "of the Lord who is spirit".[23] The expression must be interpreted by its context, and in particular in terms of the contrast which Paul has drawn between "letter" and "spirit" (v. 6). It is the Lord, Christ, who transmutes the letter that kills into the spirit that makes alive; and He does so because He Himself is spirit and life (cf. Jn. 4:24; 14:6). The words that He speaks are spirit and are life (Jn. 6:63). No more, then, than in the preceding verse is there a direct mention here of the Third Person of the Trinity, though the very title *Holy Spirit* implies and embraces all that may be said of the significance of the term "spirit" in this setting. "There is no transforming power so effectual as spirit", writes Plummer, "and in this case it is the Lord Christ Himself who is the transforming power. Spiritual agency is here at its highest. The most wonderful changes are not only possible but natural, when such a cause is operating. But the conditions must be

---

[22] Πίστις εἰς Χριστόν—cf. Jn. 3:16, etc.

[23] The different ways of taking the phrase καθάπερ ἀπὸ Κυρίου πνεύματος may be listed as follows:

i. "Even as by the Spirit of the Lord" (AV).

ii. "Even as from the Lord (who is) the Spirit" (Vulgate, RV, ARSV, Souter).

iii. "Even as from the Spirit which is the Lord" (RV margin).

iv. "Even as from sovereign spirit" (Nestlé, Westcott and Hort—treating κυρίου as an adjective).

v. "Even as from the Lord who is spirit" (Allo, Plummer).

The last is most in harmony with Paul's thought and language in this passage. For a parallel form of expression see Gal. 1:3, ἀπὸ Θεοῦ πατρός, and cf. 3:3 above, ἐν πλαξὶν καρδίαις.

observed, and they are mainly three. There is the turning to the Lord; every veil that might hide Him must be removed; and it is His glory and no other that is reflected. When these three things are secured, by continual reflexion of the Lord's glory Christians are transfigured into the very image of Him whose glory they have caught and retained, and step by step the likeness becomes more and more complete—'unto the full measure of the maturity of the fulness of Christ' (Eph. iv. 13)".

4:1

Therefore seeing we have this ministry, even as we obtained mercy, we faint not.

"This ministry" of Paul's is that of the new covenant, which is the ministration of the spirit and of life and righteousness and liberty and glory, so vividly described in the preceding passage (3:6–18). Having a ministry of such splendour, there is no place for faint-heartedness or concealment, but only for boldness and outspokeness (cf. 3:12). However severe the opposition, and however intense the conflict, Paul is ever urged forward by the stimulus and exhilaration of the task committed to him of making known Christ as the Mediator of the new covenant. For him who ministers the eternal riches of the gospel there can be no question of abandoning the struggle. This great theme is developed more fully from verse 7 onwards, leading up to verse 16 where Paul repeats his affirmation "therefore we faint not", and from there on into chapter 5 where, with his eye fixed on the future consummation, he confidently proclaims that he is always of good courage (5:6), which is the opposite of being faint.[24]

In saying that he has or possesses this ministry the Apostle is making no arrogant claim to self-sufficiency (cf. 3:5). Any such criticism, readily as his opponents would have uttered it, is

---

[24] Ἐγκακεῖν (or ἐνκακεῖν) is found in the New Testament twice in this chapter—verses 1 and 16—and also in Lk. 18:1; Gal. 6:9; Eph. 3:13; and II Thess. 3:13. In each case there is a variant reading ἐκκακεῖν. Lightfoot suggests that the latter 'arose in the first instance from a faulty pronunciation, rather than as a distinct compound" (*Notes on the Epistles of St. Paul*, p. 132). Ἐκκακεῖν is found also in Philo (*De Confus. Ling.*, 13) and in some of the Greek fathers. The earliest use of ἐγκακεῖν seems to be in Polybius (IV, xix, 10). Elsewhere it occurs in 2 Clem., ii, and in the versions of the second century writers Symmachus (Gen. 27:46; Num. 21:5; Isa. 7:16) and Theodotion (Prov. 3:11). It is now accepted by scholars as the correct form.

disarmed by the addition of the clause, "even as we obtained mercy". The evangelical ministry is by virtue of the evangelical mercy which he had experienced. It is not an achievement of human ability but a consequence of divine mercy. Paul, in fact, is making an acknowledgment of his own utter unworthiness: mercy is shown only to the guilty, the condemned, the hopeless. This relationship between Paul's ministry and God's prevenient mercy is brought out more fully in I Timothy 1:12–17. There the Apostle thanks the Lord for enabling him and appointing him to the ministry, who previously had been a blasphemer and a persecutor and injurious. 'Howbeit", he says, "I obtained mercy". He had indeed proved for himself the faithfulness of the saying that Christ Jesus came into the world to save sinners —"of whom I am chief", he adds; and then repeats: "howbeit I obtained mercy" (cf. I Cor. 7:25). Against this background of mercy his ministry is seen in its true perspective as something from which self-esteem is entirely excluded.

4:2

> But we have renounced the hidden things of shame, not walking in craftiness, nor handling the word of God deceitfully; but by the manifestation of the truth commending ourselves to every man's conscience in the sight of God.

While Paul speaks of the purity and candour of his ministerial conduct, it is evident from the whole context of this epistle that he does so not out of concern for his own reputation, but rather that by implication he is contrasting himself with others whose behaviour has been inconsistent with their claims to be ministers of Christ. "These things", says Herveius, "are spoken against the false apostles, who did not have the unveiled face, nor the ministration of the new covenant". And Allo comments aptly as follows: "Plainly he has someone in view—and in such a manner that he will not fail later on to disclose who it is. It is in chapters 10 to 13 that this will be done. These rumblings of polemic, still vague and muffled, certainly have the air of preparing the way for a decisive explanation rather than of recalling one which had already been given". At the time of his conversion Paul renounced once and finally [25] those shameful things which

---

[25] Ἀπειπάμεθα should be given a genuine aoristic force (like ἠλεήθημεν in the previous verse).

are done in secret or surreptitiously: the moment of obtaining mercy was also a moment of renunciation. This does not necessarily indicate that he had previously practised such things, but that there are certain things to which every Christian has said a decided No. Where, as with the false apostles, there is no such renunciation, it must be questioned whether there has been any experience of obtaining mercy. By "the hidden things of shame" are meant secret practices which are dishonourable, deceitful, and perhaps, as Stanley supposes, sensual, and which can only result in shame when brought to the light. "You", says Paul to the Ephesians, "were once darkness, but are now light in the Lord: walk as children of light—for the fruit of the light is in all goodness and righteousness and truth—... for the things which are done by them in secret it is a shame even to speak of" (Eph. 5:8ff.). Paul walked, that is, conducted himself day by day, as a child of light, and this meant, among other things, that there could be no place in his life for "craftiness" in his dealings with others. The word signifies a cunning readiness to adopt any device or trickery for the achievement of ends which are anything but altruistic.[26] Craftiness, indeed, is characteristic of Satan, the arch-deceiver (11:3), and also, not surprisingly, of those who, like the false apostles, are Satan's ministers (11:13–15). From 12:16 it would appear that Paul had actually been accused by his calumniators of being a crafty trickster. This being so, it is likely that his denial here was directed against this particular slander.

If by "the word of God" Paul means the Old Testament Scriptures, the deceitful handling of it would refer to the wresting of passages from their context and their misapplication, probably in a judaizing manner. But it seems preferable to understand "the word of God" here to mean the message of Jesus Christ, in which case the deceitful handling of it would refer to the falsification of the gospel, probably by robbing it of its unique glory and essential content in such a way as to suggest that the old covenant was still in force. For this sense of the expression "the word of God", compare, for example, the following passages: I Thess. 2:13—" ... ye received from us the word of the message,

---

rather than treat it, as Plummer and Tasker do, as an example of a timeless or ingressive aorist.

[26] The man who practises πανουργία (πᾶν + ἔργον) is ready to do anything, up to every trick.

... not as the word of men, but, as it is in truth, the word of God"; Heb. 13:7—"Remember them that had the rule over you, men that spake unto you the word of God"; Rev. 1:9— "I John ... was in the isle that is called Patmos, for the word of God and the testimony of Jesus".

So far from being marked by subterfuge, self-interest, and deceit, however, Paul's ministry was one in which the truth was manifested, openly displayed, outspokenly proclaimed (cf. 3:12f.), in such a manner that none could gainsay the genuineness and sincerity of his motives. The internal forum of every conscience bore witness to this. Herein lay his impregnable commendation, not in external written testimonials, which might be, as with the false apostles, counterfeit and valueless (cf. 3:1ff.). Paul, in fact, expresses himself rather more graphically than our English versions show: "commending ourselves", he says, "to every conscience of men",[27] that is, to every type and variety of the human conscience, whether clear or dull, whether of friend or of adversary—no conscience (in other words, no man conscientiously) could pronounce against the authenticity of his ministry. The Apostle's ministry, moreover, and above all, was conducted "in the sight of God" (cf. 1:12; 2:17), to whom every creature is manifest, and before whose eyes all things are naked and laid open (Heb. 4:13). There is a higher scrutiny than that of the human conscience: it is to *God* that every minister of the gospel is ultimately and eternally answerable. In the light of the divine presence the true is infallibly separated from the false. In contrast to those who shun the light because of the shameful character of their conduct, "he that doeth the truth cometh to the light, that his works may be made manifest, that they have been wrought in God" (Jn. 3:20f.). Such a minister was the Apostle Paul.

4:3, 4

> And even if our gospel is veiled, it is veiled in them that perish: in whom the god of this world hath blinded the minds of the unbelieving, that the light of the gospel of the glory of Christ, who is the image of God, should not dawn upon them.

At this point Paul turns to the objection that the gospel,

---

[27] *Πρὸς πᾶσαν συνείδησιν ἀνθρώπων*. This form is preserved in the Vulgate: *ad omnem conscientiam hominum.*

124

for which he claims so unique a power, has patently been ineffective in the case of many, no doubt the majority, of those to whom he proclaimed it; large numbers have entirely failed to perceive its superlative glory of which he has spoken with such enthusiasm. This Paul concedes.[28] The fault, however, is not in the gospel, but in those who have failed to discern its glory. The unveiled gospel, openly proclaimed, has been veiled *to* them because it is veiled *in* them: the veil is over their hearts and minds (3:14ff.), not over the gospel.[29] It is not Paul's gospel but they who stand condemned. The absence of its saving effects in their lives shows that they are perishing in blind unbelief, while its glory continues undiminished. "The blindness of unbelievers in no way detracts from the clearness of his gospel", comments Calvin; "for the sun is no less resplendent because the blind do not perceive its light".

Paul's characteristic confidence in the authenticity of *his* gospel ("our gospel" here and in II Thess. 2:14 = "my gospel" in Rom. 2:16 and II Tim. 2:8) is not an indication of arrogance, for, so far from being the pretentious construction of a religious philosopher, his gospel was not of man at all, but had been received by revelation (Gal. 1:11ff.) and was in accordance with the divinely given Scriptures (I Cor. 15:1ff.). No more does his mode of expression indicate that his gospel was in important respects at variance with that proclaimed by Christ or by others of the Apostles. Throughout the New Testament Christ is the unique and only Mediator and trust in His perfect person and work is the sole way of salvation. Thus our Lord described Himself as The Way apart from whom no man can come to the Father (Jn. 14:6), Peter declared that there is salvation in none other and that His is the only saving Name given among men (Acts 4:12), and Paul affirmed that He is the one Mediator between God and men (I Tim. 2:5). Hence Paul's assurance that

---

[28] The force of the phrase εἰ δὲ καί is concessive: "Even if, as I grant, my gospel is veiled in the case of some..." Cf. notes on 4:16, 5:16, 7:8, 12:11 below, where εἰ καί occurs again.

[29] Weiss gives ἔστιν κεκαλυμμένον a full perfect force: "is and remains veiled"; but the opinion of Moule (*An Idiom Book of New Testament Greek*, p. 18) is preferable that this is an instance of a periphrastic perfect which is "perfect in form more than in meaning", so that κεκαλυμμένον here is virtually an adjective.

his gospel is the one *true* gospel, identical with that proclaimed by Christ and his fellow-apostles; and hence also his unequivocal denunciation of any who preach a different gospel, which, in the nature of the case, cannot but be a spurious gospel (cf. 11:4; Gal. 1:6ff.). John writes with the same absolute certainty of the truth: "We are of God", he says; "he that knoweth God heareth us; he who is not of God heareth us not. By this we know the spirit of truth and the spirit of error" (I Jn. 4:6).

But there is another power at work besides the wills of those whose hearts are veiled against the gospel light—the god, namely, of this world, to whom, in turning away from the one true God, those who are perishing have submitted themselves, and by whom their unbelieving minds are blinded. It is plain that by "the god of this age" [30] Satan is meant. The nearest parallel to this title in the New Testament is that used by our Lord: "the prince of this world" (Jn. 12:31; 16:11), which is equivalent to "the prince of the world" (Jn. 14:30). Closely associated with this is the statement in I John 5:19 that "the whole world lieth in the evil one". Satan is also called "the prince of the power of the air" (Eph. 2:2) and "the prince of the demons" (Mk. 3:22 = Mt. 9:34; 12:24; Lk. 11:15). The temporal designation ("of this age") in our text must be understood in terms of the scriptural distinction between two different ages, namely (i) what is variously described as "this age" (I Cor. 1:20; 2:6, 8; 3:18; Rom. 12:2; Eph. 1:21), "the present age" (I Tim. 6:7; II Tim. 4:10; Tit. 2:12), "the present season" (Rom. 3:26; 8:18; 11:5), "the age of this world" (Eph. 2:2), and, more graphically still, "the immediate evil age" (Gal. 1:4) on the one hand, and (ii) "the future age" (Eph. 1:21; Heb. 6:5), "the age that is coming" (Lk. 18:30), or simply "that age" (Lk. 20:35, as opposed to "this age") on the other hand.[31] Satan holds a certain sway over the world during this present age—a consideration which adds point to our Lord's third temptation in the wilderness (as recorded in Mt. 4:8f.). But it is a sway that is usurped, temporary, and in

---

[30] ῾Ο θεὸς τοῦ αἰῶνος τούτου is literally "the god of this age", and it is preferable to translate it thus so that the distinction between the terms αἰών, "age", and κόσμος, "world", may be retained.

[31] In 2 Clem., vi, we find the interesting comment: "This age and the future one are two enemies"—ἔστιν δὲ οὗτος ὁ αἰὼν καὶ ὁ μέλλων δύο ἐχθροί. Cf. *Clem. Hom.*, XX, 2.

no sense absolute. The satanic world sovereignty is in fact apparent rather than real; for God alone is "the King of the ages" (I Tim. 1:17, Greek [32]), that is, of every age, past, present, and future.

How, then, is it possible to ascribe the name of "god" to him who is the great adversary of Almighty God? The answer is that Satan wishes, albeit vainly, to set himself up as God, and sinners, in rebelling against the true God, subject themselves to him who is the author of their rebellion. The unregenerate serve Satan as though he were their God. They do not thereby, however, escape from the dominion of the one true God. On the contrary, they bring themselves under His righteous judgment; for Satan is a creature and not a God to be served (cf. Rom. 1:18, 25). Just as there is only one gospel in the world and every pretended alternative to it is a false no-gospel, so there is only one God of the universe and every other "deity" whom men worship and serve is a false no-god. Thus Psalm 96:5 affirms that "all the gods of the peoples are things of nought" [33]; and the Song of Moses speaks of the Israelites' having "sacrificed to demons, which are no-gods" (Dt. 32:17). Similarly, Paul tells the Corinthians that "the things which the Gentiles sacrifice, they sacrifice to demons, even to a no-god" (I Cor. 10:20), and reminds the Galatian Christians that prior to their conversion, "not knowing God, ye were in bondage to them which by nature are no gods" (Gal. 4:8; cf. I Cor. 8:4ff.). It is not the existence of demons which is denied, but their status as gods. In this respect they are indeed no-gods, nothings. And, *a fortiori*, this is true also of Satan, the prince of the demons. This age, in rebelling against the one true God and submitting to Satan, offers homage to one who is aptly, though ironically, called "the god of this age", even though he is in fact a no-god, and himself a rebellious creature under the judgment of Almighty God. This situation reveals both the appalling folly of sin and also its extreme wickedness.

In the early centuries of the Church those heresiarchs who propounded a dualistic view of the universe seized upon Paul's

---

[32] Ὁ βασιλεὺς τῶν αἰώνων.

[33] All the *elohim* (אֱלֹהִים) of the peoples are *elilim* (אֱלִילִים)—an effective play upon words.

127

mention of "the god of this age" as a confirmation of their doctrine, as though the Apostle supported their distinction between a malevolent creator-demiurge and the benevolent God of the New Testament. The Church Fathers, of course, rebutted this teaching; but it is an admonitory fact that in doing so it became customary to force upon this verse a meaning which could not be justified by the natural sequence of the words. Instead of linking the phrase "of this world" with the noun "god", which it immediately followed, many sought to link it with the noun "unbelievers", thereby achieving the following sense: "in whom God (that is, the true and only God) has blinded the minds of the unbelievers of this world". This exegesis is found in Irenaeus, Tertullian, Origen, Chrysostom, Ambrose, Theodoret, and Augustine (who speaks of its acceptance with most of his contemporaries—*plerique nostrum*—that is, at the beginning of the fifth century), and it persists in Theophylact (eleventh century) and Herveius (twelfth century). That it was uncalled for is apparent from the facility with which its exponents were able to explain the text in accordance with its more natural significance. Thus Tertullian admits that a simpler answer is available by interpreting "the god of this world" of the devil, who once said, "I will exalt my throne above the stars of God; I will make myself like the Most High" (Isa. 14:13f.). "The whole super-stititon of this world has got into his hands, so that he blinds effectually the hearts of unbelievers".[34] And Chrysostom, though also adopting the current interpretation, none the less comments most appropriately that "Scripture frequently uses the term *god*, not in regard of the dignity that is so designated, but of the weakness of those in subjection to it; as when it calls mammon lord and belly god: but the belly is neither therefore God nor mammon Lord, save only of those who bow down themselves to them". Calvin effectively remarks: "We see what the heat of controversy does in the midst of disputes. If all those men had read Paul's words with a calm mind, it would never have occurred to any of them to twist them in this manner into a forced meaning; but because they were harassed by adversaries, they were more concerned to refute them than to investigate Paul's meaning. ... The devil is called the god of this age in

---

[34] Tertullian, *Adv. Marc.*, V, xi; cf. V, xvii.

no other way than Baal was called the god of those who worshipped him or the dog the god of Egypt".

The dreadful consequence, then, of unbelief, of bowing down to "the god of this age" instead of to the only true God, is that the mind is blinded. This effect is attributed to Satan as the initiator of sin and therefore of its consequences; but it should not be overlooked that, despite the satanic revolt, God is still sovereign and that this blindness resulting from sin also has the nature of a judgment upon the wilful and persistent rebelliousness of the human heart. This, in turn, is attended by the inability to perceive and rejoice in the surpassing splendour of the gospel, and that means perdition. The tempter, in fact, sets in motion a kind of chain-reaction: sin leads to blindness, and blindness leads to destruction. Impelled by hatred of the gospel, he has been a liar (= a blinder of men's minds) and a murderer (= a destroyer of men's souls) from the beginning (Jn. 8:44f.).

Unbelievers, their minds blinded by that no-god the devil, are incapacitated from "gazing upon [35] the light of the gospel of the glory of Christ"—a characteristically splendid verbal sequence which rings with the thrill of personal experience: Paul had full knowledge of what it meant to be blinded by sin, and he knew

---

[35] The verb αὐγάζειν has two main meanings: (i) to see distinctly or to gaze upon; (ii) to illumine or beam upon, the latter being used of the sun (αὐγή = the light of the sun, and in general any bright light). This is the only occurrence of the verb in the New Testament. In classical Greek the verb, in both its senses, is transitive, being followed by an accusative (see, for example, Sophocles, *Philoctetes*, 217, and Euripides, *Hecuba*, 635f.). That, in post-classical times at least, the verb could have an intransitive sense is suggested by the use of the present participle in Lev. 13 (seven times) and 14 (once) with the meaning "to appear bright". If it is to be treated as intransitive in our present verse, then the accusative τὸν φωτισμόν must be taken as the subject of the infinitive αὐγάσαι, and this is how the majority of translators and commentators have interpreted it—for example, Marcion, Chrysostom, Vulgate (*ut non fulgeat illis inluminatio*), AV, RV. This interpretation explains the addition of αὐτοῖς to the text, which must be regarded as a gloss. RV margin and ARSV, however, treat αὐγάσαι as transitive, and in this case its subject is an implied αὐτούς, that is, the unbelievers of the preceding clause: the purpose of their being blinded is that they should not gaze upon the light. This seems to us the more satisfactory way of understanding it, and it certainly harmonizes well with Paul's use of ἀτενίσαι ("look stedfastly on") in 3:13, where, as Allo observes, the sense is analogous. But whichever way it is taken, the effect of the unbeliever's blindness is the same: his unseeing heart remains in darkness, unillumined by the Sun of Righteousness.

also, through his own history, that the all-prevailing power of God alone could dispel that darkness (see v. 6). From the moment of his conversion onwards the transcendental light of the gospel unceasingly suffused the whole of his existence and, as the Apostle to the Gentiles, it became his consuming mission "to open their eyes that they might turn from darkness to light and from the power of Satan unto God" (Acts 26:18). For the gospel light is the glory of the Messiah, who Himself is God's image.[36] Into that image the believer is transformed (3:18), so that in the re-creation of the new birth the image of creation (Gen. 1:26f.), marred by the fall, is perfectly restored.[37] In Him who is "the radiance of God's glory and the impress of His substance" (Heb. 1:3) we are confronted with the true likeness of God. Hence our Lord's own assurance: "He that hath seen Me hath seen the Father" (Jn. 14:9). In Him the invisible God becomes visible: "No man hath seen God at any time; the only begotten Son, who is in the bosom of the Father, He hath declared Him" (Jn. 1:18). Therefore He is described as "the image of the invisible God" (Col. 1:15). As Redeemer and Mediator, He is at the same time the image of man—man in his true essence and stature according to the purposes of God his Creator. In His theanthropic person the divine and the human meet and are reconciled.

4:5

> For we preach not ourselves, but Christ Jesus as Lord, and ourselves as your servants for Jesus' sake.

It is true that Paul has spoken of the gospel as *his* gospel (v. 3), but that in no way confirms the calumnies of his opponents who had charged him with self-commendation (cf. 3:1; 5:12), for, as he has just said, his gospel is the gospel of the glory *of Christ* (v. 4). It is not, therefore, himself that he preaches, nor at

---

[36] "The word εἰκών means 'that which resembles' (ἔοικα), and in particular the resemblance of something to a prototype from which it is derived and in whose essence it shares. Christ is 'the image of the invisible God' (Col. 1:15) in that He shares in God's real being and hence can be a perfect manifestation of that being"—A. M. Ramsey (*op. cit.*, p. 150).

[37] It is interesting that in Alexandria the *imago Dei* of Gen. 1:26 was interpreted as referring to the Logos (cf. Philo, *De Mund. Op.*, 6, where the first man is spoken of as εἰκὼν εἰκόνος, "the image of the Image").

any time had he been found seeking the glory of men (I Thess 2:5f.). So incompatible was self-aggrandisement with the character of his apostleship that from the very first he had determined to know nothing among the Corinthians "save Jesus Christ, and Him crucified" (I Cor. 2:2). In his gospel the glory is of Christ, and accordingly the burden of its proclamation is Christ Jesus *as Lord* (*Kyrios*), for the Lordship of Christ is central and altogether indispensable to the evangelical message (Phil. 2:11; Acts 2:36). Confession of Jesus as Lord is essential to salvation (Rom. 10:9). And it is only in the Holy Spirit that a man can say "Jesus is Lord" (I Cor. 12:3). Accordingly the church at Corinth is Paul's work *in the Lord* and the seal of his apostleship *in the Lord* (I Cor. 9:1f.). Moreover, just as the designation of Christ in the preceding verse as the image of God implies true and essential likeness to God, so, as Werner Foerster has pointed out, "the name of *kyrios* involves equality with God".[38]

The force of the concluding clause of this verse is: "and as for myself, I am your bondservant for Jesus' sake". This is the only mention of himself that is permissible in his preaching—a mention which by declaring the humility of his station ascribes all the glory to God and focuses the attention of the hearers entirely upon Christ. Paul is a minister, not a master; a bondservant, not an ecclesiastical lord. He is nothing, but God who gives the increase is all. How could there be room for misunderstanding among the Corinthians when he who had lived humbly in their midst, selflessly ministering the gospel to them, had also in writing repeatedly emphasized this aspect of his relationship with them (see I Cor. 3:4ff.; 4:1, 9ff.; 15:10, etc.)? What humbler view of himself could a messenger of the gospel take than to regard himself not only as a bondservant of Jesus Christ (as Paul delights to call himself; cf. Rom. 1:1; Gal. 1:10; Phil. 1:1) but even as the bondservant of those to whom he ministers? Does not this place Paul in unmistakeable contrast to the false apostles who had invaded the church at Corinth? It is the exact antithesis of posing as their lord, and, it may be added, is an utter condemnation of the prelatical pomp and authori-

---

[38] Werner Foerster: *Lord* (No. VIII, *Bible Key Words* from Kittel TWNT, London, 1958), p. 98.

tarianism by which the Church has in subsequent centuries been so much disfigured, as though it were an institution of this world (cf. Mk. 10:42ff.).

Paul is not suggesting, however, that those to whom he ministers are his masters. There is but one Master, and so he affirms that it is *for Jesus' sake* that he assumes the role of the servant of others. The servant of Jesus is also the servant of his fellow-men, but always for the sake of Him who is his sole Master. Here, then, there is not a contradiction but rather a corroboration of the admonition given by Paul in his earlier epistle to the Corinthians that they "become not bondservants of men" (I Cor. 7:23)— that is, as though the mastership belonged to men and not to Christ, who has bought them with a price. Christ's bondservant, indeed, is for this reason free from all men, but in order to win others to the acknowledgment of Christ's sovereignty he brings himself under bondage to all (I Cor. 9:19). The expression "for Jesus' sake" is significant, further, because the name *Jesus* is properly associated with our Lord in His state of humiliation, as incarnate for our redemption. As Jesus, the eternal Son "emptied Himself, taking the form of a bondservant" (Phil. 2:7). Thus the Apostle's language and attitude here are consonant with his own injuction, namely: "Let this mind be in you which was also in Christ Jesus", in that same passage where he speaks so memorably of our Master's humbling of Himself for our sakes (Phil. 2:5). His was a true following of the Master.

4:6

> Seeing it is God, that said, Light shall shine out of darkness, who shined in our hearts, to give the light of the knowledge of the glory of God in the face of Jesus Christ.

The clinching reason why there is no place in a genuine evangelical ministry for self-esteem and self-proclamation is that in the believer's experience of salvation all is of God, nothing of self. This truth Paul emphasizes in the clearest terms a little later in the epistle, when he writes: "All things are of God, who reconciled us to Himself through Christ, and gave unto us the ministry of reconciliation" (5:18). Unbelievers are helplessly blinded by the god of this age so that they cannot see the light of the gospel (v. 4); spiritual sight and enlightenment can come, if they are to come at all, only through the intervening grace of Almighty God, for, left to himself, the sinner can only stumble in darkness. The evil work of Satan is sovereignly counteracted by the redeeming activity of God, who by delivering us out of the power of darkness makes us partakers of the inheritance of the saints in light (Col. 1:12f.). The divine action ever declares the divine character, for, as John affirms, "God is light, and in Him is no darkness at all" (I Jn. 1:5). Thus, as Paul reminds us here, at the dawn of creation the darkness was dispelled by the word of Almighty God (see Gen. 1:2f.); and it is the same God who, in the spiritual sphere, drives back the darkness of sin and unbelief from the hearts of men. Indeed, by asserting that the God who commanded light to shine at the creation is the same God who shines in our hearts at the new birth, Paul shows beyond dispute that there is absolutely no place for any kind of gnostic dualism in the Christianity he proclaims, and that those who, on the strength, for example, of his mention in verse 4 of "the god of this age", seek to attribute such a dualism to him do so entirely without justification. The Creator God of the Old Testament is one and the same with the Re-Creator God of the New Testament. It should be noticed, however, that at creation God's word, "Let there be light", was a divine fiat uttered from heaven; whereas in re-creation God's effective word is not a mere fiat, but the Living Word of His only-begotten Son, made flesh here on earth (Heb. 1:2). "Then indeed He said, 'Let it be', and it was", comments Chrysostom; "but now He said nothing, but Himself became light for us: for the Apostle does not say, 'hath also now commanded', but 'hath *Himself* shined'."

This is no case of academic theorizing: Paul whose mind had before been spiritually dark had by divine grace been enabled to rejoice in the full clear splendour of the evangelical sunshine. How could he ever fail to remember and be filled with wonder at that great transforming encounter with the glorified Christ on the Damascus road when, at midday, the time of the sun's intensest light, he saw "a light from heaven above the brightness of the sun" (Acts 26:13)—the light, in other words, which he defines in our present passage both as "the light of the gospel of the glory of Christ", who is the image of God, and as "the light of the knowledge of the glory of God in the face of Jesus Christ"? It is in the face of Him who is the true image of God that the glory of God is manifested. So, too, John testifies: "We beheld His glory, glory as of the only begotten from the Father" (Jn. 1:14).

The past tense, "shined",[39] points back to the moment of conversion. The shining, moreover, is *in the heart*, that is, in its scriptural significance, the centre of man's whole being, moral, intellectual, and spiritual. It is this reality which guarantees that the man in Christ is nothing less than a new creature (5:17). This shining in the heart takes place when the veil that lies on the heart is removed (3:15f.)—by God: it was God who, according to His good pleasure, revealed His Son in Paul (Gal. 1:15f.)—; and it corresponds to the writing by God of His law upon the tables of the heart (3:3). The light resulting from this shining is the light of genuine *gnosis* or knowledge, as distinct from all false gnostic pretensions, precisely because it is the revelation of the Father in the Son, who is the image of the omniscient God and in whom all the treasures of wisdom and knowledge are hidden (Col. 2:3). It is, therefore, the knowledge of ultimate truth, and as such it is everlastingly glorious. It is true that the believer's knowledge of the glory of God is as yet partial and incomplete; but it is none the less accurate and authentic, and, moreover, it is knowledge which is advancing from glory to glory until at last, in the heavenly perfection, he will know even as he is now known by God and his glory will be that of complete assimilation to the image of Christ Himself (3:18; I Cor. 13:12; I Jn. 3:2). In this grand perspective of redemption the abiding and transcendental character of "the glory of God in the face of Jesus Christ" is displayed, in contrast to the transient and fading glory of the old covenant that shone from Moses' face (3:7ff.).

---

[39] Ἔλαμψεν, aorist.

4:7–16a TREASURE IN EARTHEN VESSELS

4:7

> But we have this treasure in earthen vessels, that the exceeding greatness of the power may be of God, and not from ourselves.

The conjunction "but" introduces the startling contrast between the splendour of which Paul has just been speaking and the poor vessels in which it is contained. The treasure in question is "the light of the knowledge of the glory of God" (v. 6) rather than, as some have suggested,[1] the ministry mentioned in verse 1 —though the thought of the main clause of verse 1 ("we faint not") is taken up and elaborated in this and the following verses, leading up to the conclusive repetition, "wherefore we faint not" in verse 16. There could be no contrast more striking than that between the greatness of the divine glory and the frailty and unworthiness of the vessels in which it dwells and through which it is manifested to the world. Paul's calumniators had contemptuously described his bodily appearance as weak and his speech as of no account (10:10; cf. 10:1, 11:6, 12:7), hoping thereby to discredit his authority. But it is one of the main purposes of this epistle to show that this immense discrepancy between the treasure and the vessel serves simply to attest that human weakness presents no barrier to the purposes of God, indeed, that God's power is made perfect in weakness (12:9), as the brilliance of a treasure is enhanced and magnified by comparison with a common container in which it is placed.

In the opinion of T. W. Manson, the *earthen vessels* from which the Apostle draws his analogy here "are the small pottery lamps, cheap and fragile, that could be bought in the shops of Corinth. The followers of Christ may be likened to such fragile lamps, since they bear about in their frail mortal bodies a light derived from the central source of light in the face of Jesus Christ".[2] It may well be, however, that Paul had in mind earthenware vases or urns rather than lamps. It was not unusual for the most precious

---

[1] Linking "we have this ministry" with "we have this treasure".

[2] T. W. Manson, *Studia Paulina (ut supra)*, p. 156. Cf. Denney: ". . . the lamp of frail ware in which the light of Christ's glory shines for the illumination of the world".

treasures to be concealed in mean and valueless containers. In Roman triumphal processions, also, it was customary for gold and silver to be carried in earthen vessels. Thus Plutarch describes how, at the celebration of the Macedonian victory of Aemilius Paulus in 167 B.C., three thousand men followed the wagons carrying silver coin in seven hundred and fifty earthen vessels, each containing three talents and borne by four men.[3] Paul has already shown his fondness for graphic similes taken from the spectacle of a Roman triumph (see 2:14 and I Cor. 4:9), and it was very possibly his intention here to suggest a picture of the victorious Christ entrusting His riches to the poor earthen vessels of His human followers.

The conception of God as the Potter and man as the clay vessel moulded by His hands is characteristic of scriptural thought. It occurs especially in Isaiah and Jeremiah and is forcefully propounded by Paul in his letter to the Romans.[4] Through it the absolute sovereignty of God as Creator and the fragile dependence of man as creature are effectively emphasized. Basic to the biblical concept, of course, is the description of man as formed by God from the dust of the ground (Gen. 2:7; cf. Job. 33:6). Hence Paul's statement in I Cor. 15:47: "The first man is of the earth, earthy".

Paul's language concerning the "exceeding greatness" of divine power as compared with human weakness suggests a confrontation, as it were, of two opposite forces, the one positive, the other negative, the one abundant, the other deficient. Weakness is a challenge to power. The extent of God's power is such that it overcomes and transcends all man's weakness: the former is not merely sufficient to counterbalance the latter, but it goes beyond and far exceeds it.[5] Indeed, as Paul perceives, there is a particular

---

[3] Plutarch, *Life of Aemilius*, XXXII.

[4] Rom. 9:20ff. Cf. Isa. 29:16; 30:14; 45:9; 64:8; Jer. 18:6; 19:1, 11; Lam. 4:2; Job. 10:9. The ἀγγεῖα ὀστράκινα of Lam. 4:2 (LXX) correspond to the ὀστράκινα σκεύη here, as do also the ἀγγεῖον ὀστράκινον and the ἄγγος ὀστράκινον of Isa. 30:14 and Jer. 19:11 respectively. It is evident that in Rom. 9:20 Paul is echoing the thought of Isa. 29:16 and 45:9. In the next verse: "Hath not the potter a right over the clay, from the same lump to make one part a vessel unto honour, and another unto dishonour?" he uses the same noun, σκεῦος, as he does here in II Cor. 4:7.

[5] "Exceeding greatness" is the translation of the single word ὑπερβολή, which means literally "a throwing beyond", and hence a transcending or

purpose behind the almost incredible contrast between the brilliance of the treasure and the meanness of the vessel, namely, that the surplus or excess of power may be, that is, may be apparent as being, of God (entirely God's) and not from himself (as something for which he could claim any credit). "By speaking of earthen vessels", says Ambrose, "he signifies the infirmity of human nature, which can do nothing unless it has received strength from God; and God proclaims Himself to His own praise through those that are weak, in order that the glory may be given to Him, not to man who is formed from clay". Theophylact suggests that Paul had an eye on the false apostles, since they ascribed everything to themselves.

Paul is speaking here primarily of himself and his apostleship. But the great truth he is affirming is applicable to every genuine servant of Christ. In all their abject weakness and in every crushing affliction Christians are not only conquerors but *more than conquerors*, always, however, and solely by virtue of the all-transcending grace and love of God (Rom. 8:27). It was the exceeding greatness of this same power that enabled Gideon with his contemptible handful of followers to advance in the darkness against the hosts of Midian and, by the breaking of their earthen pitchers and the consequent shining forth of the light, to turn to flight the alien army (Judg. 7:15ff.; Heb. 11:34). So also for the Christian (as the succeeding verses show) the breaking up of the outward man, the daily dying to self, allows the divine life and glory within to burst forth and drive back the powers of darkness, to the praise of Almighty God. It is precisely the Christian's utter frailty which lays him open to the experience of the all-sufficiency of God's grace, so that he is able even to rejoice because of his weakness (12:9f.)—something that astonishes and baffles the world, which thinks only in terms of human ability.

---

exceeding of ordinary limits. In 12:7 the noun is used by Paul to describe the altogether extraordinary nature of the revelations granted to him. The adverbial phrase καθ' ὑπερβολήν (1:8; I Cor. 12:31; Gal. 1:13; Rom. 7:13) means "to an excessive degree" and is equivalent to ὑπερβαλλόντως (11:23), an adverb formed from the present participle of the verb ὑπερβάλλειν. The present participle occurs in 3:10; 9:14; Eph. 1:19; 2:7; and 3:19, and in each instance is used to describe the surpassing quality of some divine attribute (glory, grace, power, love). In verse 17 of our present chapter we find the intensified adverbial expression καθ' ὑπερβολὴν εἰς ὑπερβολήν (see note below *ad loc.*).

4 : 8, 9

We are pressed on every side, yet not straitened; perplexed, yet not in despair; pursued, yet not forsaken; smitten down, yet not destroyed.

These two verses are illustrative of the great principle that the excess of power working in the Christian is all of God. The Apostle is speaking the language of experience, and, what is more, of *constant* experience (as the present tenses and the "always" of v. 10 show)—the experience simultaneously of his own incapacity and of God's transcending power which transforms every situation. Hostile forces press in upon him from all sides and threaten to crush and immobilize him, but a way out of the desperate straits in which he finds himself is always provided; contrary to all human probability, God brings him safely through. Moreover, there is always the inner secret, the treasure of divine grace within the earthen vessel of his physical frame, which ensures that, no matter how straitened his outward circumstances, his heart is not narrowed and confined, but enlarged and expanded by the liberating love of Christ (see 6:11ff.). A particular example of what Paul means is found in 7:5ff., where he describes how on arriving in Macedonia he was unremittingly pressed on every side,[6] but how the good news brought by Titus from Corinth afforded him such joy and comfort that every restriction of his circumstances was transcended.

As problems and oppositions close in on him from all sides the Apostle is perplexed, at bay, not knowing which way to move; but, notwithstanding this, he is never in a state of hopeless despair.[7] To be at the end of man's resources is not to be at the end of God's resources; on the contrary, it is to be precisely in

---

[6] Paul uses the identical expression—ἐν παντὶ θλιβόμενοι—in 7:5 as in verse 8 here.

[7] The original: ἀπορούμενοι, ἀλλ' οὐκ ἐξαπορούμενοι, is difficult to reproduce as a correspondingly effective epigram in English. Ἀπορεῖσθαι is to be without means or resources, and so to be in a state of perplexity. Ἐξαπορεῖσθαι is an intensive compound meaning to be perplexed to a hopeless degree. Among attempts to convey something of the epigrammatic form of the original the following may be mentioned: "at a loss, but not at a loss that matters" (Tasker); "in despondency, yet not in despair" (Plummer); "put to it, but not utterly put out" (Denney). We would suggest, "confused, but not confounded". See also note on ἐξαπορηθῆναι, 1:8.

the position best suited to prove and benefit from them, and to experience the surplus of the power of God breaking through and resolving the human dilemma.

Paul speaks of being hunted.[8] He knew very well the intense agony of being hated and pursued like a quarry by his fellow-men; but he also knew that, however savage their hatred, he was never forsaken and left as a prey to his enemies. The divine promise, "Under no circumstances whatever will I forsake thee" (Heb. 13:5),[9] was unfailingly fulfilled in his daily experience, even though friends and fellow-workers should forsake him (cf. II Tim. 4:10,16). He was able, moreover, to prove the truth of the paradox (as the world sees it) that those who are hunted for Christ's sake are blessed, and through everything should rejoice and be exceeding glad (Mt. 5:11). Thus also John Chrysostom, the golden-tongued preacher, driven by unscrupulous enemies from his cathedral in Constantinople, was hunted like a beast through the inhospitable wastes of Armenia, until, after enduring extreme torments of mind and body, he succumbed to his sufferings on 14 September, 407. He too, though hunted for Christ's sake, rejoiced in the knowledge of not being forsaken, as his dying words attest: "Glory to God for all things. Amen." And William Tyndale, whose only crime was a determination to obey his call from God to translate Holy Scripture into the English tongue, was another who, hounded into exile, again by fierce adversaries of the truth from within the Church, and hunted from place to place on the Continent, was enabled, like Paul and Chrysostom and numberless others in every age, including our own, to finish his course with joy as a martyr for the sake of his Redeemer, on 6 October 1536.

There are indeed times when Christ's servants seem to be overtaken and struck down by their pursuers and when it appears that they and the truth they proclaim are destroyed. But Paul knew, both by assurance and by experience, that the reality differed from the appearance. He who without exaggeration could speak of himself as being "in deaths oft" (11:23) was well qualified to declare that even to be smitten to the ground was not to be destroyed. The Lord was constantly at hand to deliver

---

8 In this terse, graphic passage διώκειν has the strong force of *to hunt*.

9 Οὐ μή σε ἐγκαταλίπω—the same verb, answering to ἀλλ᾽ οὐκ ἐγκαταλειπόμενοι here.

(1:10). The most remarkable instance known to us of his being, in a literal sense, hunted and struck down by the enemies of the gospel was the occasion when hostile Jews from Antioch and Iconium pursued him to Lystra, stoned him, and, after dragging his apparently lifeless body out of the city, left him for dead; but he was miraculously raised up and restored to vigour (Acts 14:19f.). The fact that he, like so many others before and since, was at length put to death for the testimony of Jesus Christ does not indicate a failure of the principle which he here enunciates; on the contrary, and more than ever despite every appearance, that was the consummating moment of its truth, since for the Christian the sting of death has been removed by Him who vicariously bore his sins (I Cor. 15:56; I Pet. 2:24), and to die is not to be destroyed but to enter into everlasting bliss and to receive a crown of righteousness (II Tim. 4:6-8). Allo, in fact, suggests that the Apostle was deliberately "thinking ahead here to the end of his earthly course, when enemies and misfortunes would at last, in appearance, get the better of him, but when less than ever he would be 'destroyed', since then he would enter into his glorious rest". The sequence of present tenses argues against this as being Paul's sole meaning, but that it was very clearly within the perspective of his faith there can be no doubt. In the ultimate view, indeed, the Christian is indestructible. His life is hid with Christ in God (Col. 3:3). His death, like Christ's, is indissolubly linked to resurrection. At Christ's appearing his ransomed soul will be eternally clothed with a glorified and incorruptible body (5:1ff.; I Cor. 15:42ff.). Therefore he does not fear man who is able to destroy only his body but not his soul; but he fears and serves God who can and will destroy the unbeliever, both body and soul, in hell (Mt. 10:28). As death is the culminating moment of the Christian's weakness, so also it is the point at which the all-transcending power of God is most marvellously displayed. The death-resurrection-glorification experience is the climax of the triumph of God's power working in us.[10]

---

[10] The grammatical construction of these two verses should be noticed. They consist of a sequence of four pairs of participles, of which the second of each pair is construed with the negative οὐ, thus: ἐν παντὶ θλιβόμενοι, ἀλλ' οὐ στενοχωρούμενοι . . . etc. Two explanations may be offered:

(i) that the participles should be linked with ἔχομεν in verse 7—"we have

4:10, 11

Always bearing about in the body the dying of Jesus, that the life also of Jesus may be manifested in our body. For we who live are always delivered unto death for Jesus' sake, that the life also of Jesus may be manifested also in our mortal flesh.

Here we have the summing up and also the explanation of the paradoxical experiences mentioned in the two preceding verses. The afflictions endured may best be described as a perpetual carrying around [11] in the body of the dying [12] of Jesus. *The body* in which this dying is borne is still the frail human frame and is identical with the *mortal flesh* in which the life also of Jesus is manifested. The theme of this constant dying is indeed integral to Paul's thought and experience. Thus in I Cor. 15:30f. he reminds the Corinthians that he stands in jeopardy every hour and dies daily; in Rom. 8:36 he appropriates to himself the psalmist's declaration, "For Thy sake we are killed all the day

---

this treasure in earthen vessels, ... being pressed on every side, yet not straitened . . ."—in which case the οὐ, instead of μή which normally is used with forms of the verb other than the indicative, would serve to bring into relief an indisputable *fact* of Christian experience (for other instances where οὐ is found with a participle in the New Testament, see J. H. Moulton, *Grammar*, Vol. I, pp. 231f., and cf. Moule, *Idiom Book*, p. 105);

(ii) that these are examples of absolute participles, standing here for the indicative, in which case it is the participial form and not the use of οὐ that is abnormal. This is the more satisfactory way of understanding the construction, especially as Paul uses participles absolutely on a number of other occasions in this epistle (see 5:12; 7:5; 8:19, 20, 24; 9:11, 13; 10:5, 15; 11:6). "The absolute participle", says Lightfoot, commenting on Col. 3:16, "being (so far as regards mood) neutral in itself, takes its colour from the general complexion of the sentence. Thus it is sometimes indicative (e.g. II Cor. 7:5, and frequently), sometimes imperative . . ., sometimes optative". On the usage of the participle for the indicative, see J. H. Moulton, *Grammar*, Vol. I, pp. 222ff., who observes that "the participial use we are discussing is in the papyri not at all a mark of inferior education".

[11] Περιφέροντες.

[12] Νέκρωσις here retains its proper significance of an actual *process*, of dying, in contrast to Rom., 4:19 where it is used of a *state* of deadness. Weiss and Stanley, however, take it in the latter sense here. Stanley, indeed, envisages a continual descent from the Cross for Paul, who consequently carries with him, "like Joseph and Nicodemus", the weight of the dead corpse. But the context surely requires the thought rather of a continual *ascent to* the the Cross, that is, as verse 11 puts it, a constant experience of being "delivered unto death" of suffering the pains and rigours of a dying man.

long" (Psa. 44:22); and in Gal. 6:14 he asserts that through the cross of our Lord Jesus Christ the world has been crucified to him and he to the world. Christ, it is true, has left the Christian an example of patience and perseverance in suffering (I Pet. 2:21; Heb. 12:3); so that they who wish to come after Him must *daily* take up their cross and follow Him (Lk. 9:23). But Paul is speaking of something more than example. Between Master and follower there is a certain unity of experience and destiny. There is an inclusiveness of the latter in the former. It was Christ Himself who said: "A servant is not greater than his lord; if they have persecuted me, they will also persecute you" (Jn. 15:20). There is a fellowship of Christ's sufferings which means a conformity to His death (Phil. 3:10). Martyrdom, for Paul, was not confined to the hour of his death in Rome; it was expressed daily and constantly in his dying-living existence.

But this perpetual dying is not solely the expression of the earthen vessel's frailty. It is taken up into and transformed by the divine power and purpose, so that it becomes precisely the opportunity for the display of the life of Jesus in that same body which carries about the dying of Jesus. The qualification "of Jesus" is of central importance, for the dying *of Jesus* cannot be divorced from the life *of Jesus*, who, as the Prince of Life, cannot be overcome by death (Acts 3:15; 2:24). The dying *of Jesus* is essentially the seed of resurrection: His own and the believer's (Jn. 12:24; I Cor. 15:20). Conformity to the death of Jesus in the fellowship of His sufferings is experienced in the power of His resurrection (Phil. 3:10). It is in this way that the all-sufficiency and sole-sufficiency of God's grace is demonstrated to the world and that the Christian finds that God's power is made perfect in his weakness (12:9), the life of Jesus in his dying.

This is indeed a glorious reality in the present this-worldly experience of the believer; but it is a reality which at the same time points beyond the present to a still more glorious consummation. The "life of Jesus" in the believer will be revealed in its entire fulness only at the appearing of Christ when at last our present earthen vessels will be transformed into the likeness of His glorified body (Phil. 3:20f.). Union with Christ extends from suffering to glorification, and the sufferings of this present time are not worthy to be compared with the glory which will be revealed to us (Rom. 8:17f.). He who has died with Christ

142

will also live with Him, and he who endures will also reign with Him (II Tim. 2:11f.). Passages such as these sum up the Apostle's outlook, an outlook fixed unfalteringly on the heavenly glory. Where Christ, the Christian's treasure, is, there his heart is also.

In speaking of himself as being constantly delivered, while living, unto death Paul conjures up the picture of a man being thrown alive to the wild beasts in the arena—a fate experienced by many Christians in the apostolic age. The qualification *for Jesus' sake* must not be overlooked. Suffering and death are not in themselves meritorious, and their endurance for any motive other than "for Jesus' sake" is not commended. The time would soon come when professing Christians would afflict their own bodies with stripes and indignities, vainly thinking to gain favour with God thereby, and would even rashly court the death of martyrdom because they had been induced to imagine that the "baptism" of martyrdom automatically cleansed from all sin and ensured an immediate entrance into heavenly bliss. Conceptions of this kind, which were to become so prevalent in the Church, disclosed a seriously inadequate understanding of the fulness and freeness of the believer's justification through the death of Christ on his behalf, and opened the way for the intrusion of motives of self-interest under the guise of an unscriptural sanctity. This misguided piety, however well intentioned, can only mean a debasement of the motive *for Jesus' sake*, which alone has the sanction of the New Testament and alone is compatible with the logic of Christian faith and service (cf. Mt. 5:11; 10:39, etc.).

There are two further points that should be noticed:

(i)   Not only the dying of Jesus but also the life of Jesus is manifested *in the body*. There is no contempt for the body either here or elsewhere in the New Testament, such as we find in the idealism of the Greek philosophers and in the cognate dualism of the Docetic (Gnostic) cult which threatened the Church in the first century. The body is respected as coming from God's creative hand, and therefore as an honourable and integral part of man as God intended him to be. When their salvation is completed, that is, when justification and sanctification merge in glorification, the redeemed will not find themselves in a disembodied state; for to be disembodied is to be less than fully man, and therefore to be not properly human. And fulness of humanity is realized only when at last man's body is conformed to the body

143

of Christ's glory (Phil. 3:21). Man in the heavenly state is the fullgrown man who has attained to the measure of the stature of the fulness of Christ (Eph. 4:13). God saves man as man: accordingly the redemption procured through Christ extends to and includes the body (I Cor. 15:35ff.). The dignity of the human body is apparent, therefore, both in creation and in redemption, and the very fact that our Lord at His coming assumed a human body confirms to us the truth that He came to save us, body as well as soul. To this every aspect of the Christ-event bears witness—His incarnation, circumcision, baptism, transfiguration, suffering, death, burial, resurrection, ascension, glorification, and future appearing: none is dissociated from the body.

(ii) It has become fashionable in modern theology to make a distinction between "the historic Jesus" and "the risen Christ", as though the history of Jesus ended with the cross and the tomb. But, as Plummer observes, from the repetition of the words "of Jesus" in the expressions "the dying of Jesus" and "the life of Jesus" we see that "Paul does not separate the historic Jesus from the glorified Christ. To him it is the same Jesus" (cf. the testimony of Peter on the day of Pentecost: "This Jesus did God raise up, whereof we all are witnesses", Acts 2:32). "The life of Jesus can only mean the life which Jesus lives now at God's right hand", says Denney; "and these repeated escapes of the Apostle, these restorations of his courage, are manifestations of that life; they are, so to speak, a series of resurrections. Paul's communion with Jesus is not only in His dying, but in His rising again; he has the evidence of the Resurrection, because he has its power, present with him, in these constant deliverances and renewals. Nay, the very purpose of his sufferings and perils is to provide occasion for the manifestation of this resurrection life". So, too, Tasker comments that the Apostles were "witnesses in deed as well as in word to the truth of their Lord's resurrection". To call in question the historicity of the bodily resurrection of Jesus from the dead is necessarily to undermine the Christian's assurance of resurrection to everlasting glory. The two stand or fall together, as Paul has already shown in I Corinthians (15:12ff.), and as he emphasizes again in verse 14 of our present chapter: the Christian *knows* that He who raised up the Lord Jesus will raise him up also with Jesus.

4:12

So then death worketh in us, but life in you.

The Corinthian believers are themselves an assurance to the Apostle that his severe sufferings, his constant "dying", are not fruitless. Through his endurance the gospel had been brought to them, and by believing its word they had passed from death to life. To see repentant sinners entering into newness of life in Christ makes every affliction borne for Jesus' sake and in His service a thousand times worth-while. And this is the joy of all Christian witness. It is the unconquerable life of the risen Jesus within that enables His servants willingly and perpetually to be handed over to death for His sake, in order that the same life of Christ may be kindled in the hearts of others, enabling them in turn to win others. This is the chain of faith which, in a true succession from the Apostles, is unbroken through the ages. It is the outworking of our Lord's admonition and exhortation uttered as the hour of His own supreme suffering was approaching: "In the world ye have tribulation: but be of good cheer; I have overcome the world!" (Jn. 16:33). The wonder of all this is enhanced by the consideration that it is those who are weak, despised, and persecuted by the world, those who in the eyes of the world are losing their life, who yet are mighty in the Holy Spirit—a reality very evident to the Corinthians in the person of Paul, their Apostle, in whose body death was working as he laboured on so that his limitations and afflictions were obvious to all and despised by some, but through whose ministry none the less the life of eternity was working in them.

Most recent commentators (Tasker, Allo, Plummer, Denney, Hodge, Alford, etc.) rightly question the opinion of Calvin that Paul is speaking ironically here, in a manner comparable to I Cor. 4:8ff., implying that the Corinthians wanted a Christianity without the cross and a life of ease rather than hardship for Christ's sake. It is certainly true that Paul, in comparison with others, suffered to an unusual degree in the cause of the gospel. It was a mark of the authenticity of his apostleship, as this epistle makes particularly clear. But irony is not appropriate to the present context, where the *life* of which he is writing refers not to ease and freedom from suffering, but to the life *of Jesus*, resurrection life. It is that life which is working actively in the Christian believers at Corinth. In other words, Paul is reminding them again that he, who through many afflictions brought them this transforming message, is their genuine Apostle.

4 : 13, 14

> But having the same spirit of faith, according to that which is written, I believed, and therefore did I speak; we also believe, and therefore also we speak; knowing that He that raised up the Lord Jesus shall raise up us also with Jesus, and shall present us with you.

The Apostle has the same spirit of faith as animated the author of Psalm 116. The structure of his argument may be amplified as follows: "The spirit of faith that I have is according to what has been written by the Psalmist, I believed, therefore I spoke; I also, as well as the Psalmist, believe and therefore I also speak".[13] As usual with the New Testament use of the Old Testament, not only the quotation but also its context is appropriate. This indicates an important principle of biblical exposition: a text is not to be isolated without respect to its context, for the whole is of more importance than the parts, and the parts take on their proper significance from the whole. An outstanding illustration of this is found in the account of Christ's temptation in the wilderness: our Lord's three quotations from Deuteronomy are taken from contexts that accord perfectly with His own situation, whereas Satan's quotation from Psalm 91 is employed in a manner incompatible with its context and therefore is illegitimate and irrelevant (Mt. 4:1ff.).

It is particularly fitting that at this point Paul should quote from Psalm 116 precisely because it is a hymn of thanksgiving for deliverance from death: "The cords of death compassed me. ... I found trouble and sorrow. Then called I upon the name of Jehovah. ... I was brought low and He saved me. ... Thou hast delivered my soul from death, mine eyes from tears, and my

---

[13] The quotation agrees exactly with the LXX of Psa. 116:10. The Hebrew original הֶאֱמַ֗נְתִּי כִּ֣י אֲדַבֵּ֑ר seems to mean: "I believed, for I spoke", but the sense, as the commentators allow, is obscure. The LXX rendering (= Paul's here): ἐπίστευσα, διὸ ἐλάλησα, is also supported by the Vulgate: *credidi, propter quod locutus sum.* Whether or not Paul is consciously quoting the LXX here, we may take it that he is giving the accepted understanding of Psa. 116:10.

feet from falling. ... I believed, and therefore I spoke. ... Praise ye Jehovah". Paul, as Chrysostom says, "has reminded us of a psalm which abounds in heavenly wisdom and which is especially fitted to encourage in dangers; for that just man uttered this saying when he was in great dangers, from which there was no possibility of recovery except by the aid of God".

Many of the old commentators understood the expression "the spirit of faith" as a direct reference to the Holy Spirit. Hodge, concurring with this opinion, remarks that the Holy Spirit is often designated from the effects which He produces, being called elsewhere the Spirit of adoption (Rom. 8:15), the Spirit of wisdom (Eph. 1:17), the Spirit of grace (Heb. 10:29), and the Spirit of glory (I Pet. 4:14).[14] Starting from this premiss, Chrysostom deduces from Paul's words the equal inspiration of Psalmist and Apostle, or, more widely, of Old Testament and New Testament. Calvin, Alford, and others discern in the expression an indirect reference to the Holy Spirit, taking "the spirit of faith" to imply that faith is a gift of the Holy Spirit. True though it is that saving faith and the operation of the Holy Spirit may not be dissociated, the term "spirit" as it is used by Paul here is best understood in the general sense of "disposition" or "impulse".[15]

Herveius, in an interesting passage, interprets "the same spirit of faith" in a credal sense, as teaching a unity of belief between the fathers of the Old Testament and the fathers of the New. "The same faith", he says, "governed the hearts of those who preceded (Christ) as filled the hearts of those who followed. Indeed, those spiritual fathers believed that the omnipotent God is a Trinity in just the same way as the new fathers openly proclaimed the same Trinity. Moreover, the same faith of Christ's incarnation saved them as that by which we are saved; for, just as we believe that He came, suffered, and rose again, so they also believed that He would come, would suffer, and would rise again. The times have changed, but not the faith; for we have the same spirit of faith which they had".

---

[14] It is doubtful whether the first two of these four texts should be taken to refer directly to the Holy Spirit.

[15] For a usage of πνεῦμα by Paul which seems to be parallel to πνεῦμα πίστεως here, see I Cor. 4:21 and Gal. 6:1 where he speaks of πνεῦμα πραΰτητος, "a spirit of meekness", that is, a meek disposition.

Believing and speaking, or open confession, are in fact two essential aspects of salvation, as Paul stresses in Rom. 10:9f. Belief in the heart that God has raised Jesus from the dead must be and inevitably is accompanied by confession with the mouth that Jesus is Lord; and intimately involved in this belief is the knowledge, of which Paul speaks here in verse 14, "that He who raised up the Lord Jesus will raise up us also with Jesus". The inward operation of belief is manifested by the outward operation of speaking (witness), which in turn leads to the experience of being delivered unto death for Jesus' sake—but always with the certain assurance that physical death, when at length it overtakes and immobilizes the believer's body, will be followed by resurrection to endless glory. "By believing they laid hold of life, and by speaking they found death", comments Herveius, with particular reference to Christ's martyrs: "but death in which a corruptible body is sown and incorruption is harvested".

God, moreover, will raise up us, who believe and speak, *with Jesus*. By this Paul does not of course mean simultaneously with Jesus (for He is the firstborn from the dead: Col. 1:18; Rev. 1:5), but by reason of our identification with Jesus in whom we are elected to everlasting life. Paul's meaning is to be sought in the teaching which he has already given in his earlier letter to the Corinthians, where he shows (I Cor. 15:12ff.) that *apart from* the resurrection of Jesus from the dead there is *no* resurrection to life for us. To die, albeit trusting in Christ, would then be to *perish*. But Christ has indeed been raised from the dead, and His resurrection is the *firstfruits* whereby that great harvest is guaranteed in which all who are His will be gathered in to participate in the eternal inheritance of His glory. The deepest ground of our salvation and security is, indeed, our present mystical, but none the less real and objective, union with Christ, whereby we are even now one with Him in His crucifixion, burial, resurrection, ascension, and heavenly session (Rom. 6:3ff.; Eph. 2:5f.; Col. 2:13; 3:1ff.). The sum of the whole new creation is *in Christ* (5:17); for it is with the beloved Son alone, and with no one else, that the Father is well pleased (Mt. 3:17; 17:5). It is, therefore, only as we are one with Christ and in Christ that we can be pleasing and acceptable to God; it is only as His death for sin is also, by union with Him, our death to sin that we may know, with complete certainty, that His resurrection, ascension, and glorification are ours also. The Christian has no other destiny than the destiny of Jesus.

Not only will believers be raised up to heavenly glory, but they will also be *presented*; and this experience of "presentation" will be common to all the redeemed without distinction: "us ... with you", affirms Paul. Though the term is not further defined or qualified here, its significance is plain enough: Christians are to be presented before the King of kings. For the analogical concept on the human plane of the presentation of a subject before a ruler, cf. Acts 23:33, which describes how the soldiers presented Paul to the governor of Caesarea. Later in our epistle Paul uses the same term when he says to the members of the Corinthian church: "I espoused you to one husband, that I might present you as a pure virgin to Christ" (11:2). This picture of a bride being presented to the bridegroom is found again in Eph. 5:27 where Christ is spoken of as presenting the Church to Himself as His bride. The ultimate purpose of Christ in redemption is explained in Col. 1:22 as being to present His redeemed holy and without blemish and unreprovable before God; and the Apostle's ministry is closely bound up with this purpose, for his preaching and teaching are animated by the desire to "present every man perfect in Christ" (Col. 1:28). But he is no more than a servant, labouring to perform his Master's will. As the passages mentioned above show, the presentation is essentially by God and to God, who both initiates our salvation and also brings it to completion in Himself (5:18; Heb. 12:2), and to whom accordingly all praise is to be given. All this is included in Jude's ascription of glory, majesty, dominion, and power through Jesus Christ our Lord to the only God our Saviour, who is able to set us before the presence [16] of His glory without blemish in exceeding joy (Jude 24f.).

Some modern commentators have maintained that a change or adjustment in Paul's eschatological expectations is discernible in the passage before us. Previously, it is said, the Apostle had had no thought that he might die before the return of Christ (cf., e.g., I Cor. 15:51, "we all shall not sleep", and I Thess. 4:15, 17, "we that are alive, that are left unto the coming of the Lord"); whereas now he is speaking in terms of being raised from

---

[16] Στῆσαι κατενώπιον is synonymous with παραστῆσαι (to cause to stand, στῆσαι, in the presence of, παρά), the verb which is used in all the other references given above.

the dead. This hypothesis, however, is the consequence of a misconception of the Apostle's outlook. In the first place, Christ's own teaching concerning this culminating event had stressed not only its imminence but also the unpredictability of its day and hour (cf. Mt. 24:42ff., etc.). This necessarily leaves the whole question of the time of its occurrence open: it might be soon or it might be long delayed; it might be within the lifetime of the Apostles or it might be many generations later. Paul was well aware of this. Thus in I Thess. 4:13ff., written some years before the composition of our present epistle, his purpose is to assure his readers that believers who die prior to the return of Christ suffer no loss or disadvantage with respect to His appearing; and he very properly speaks of himself and his readers as "we that are alive, that are left unto the coming of the Lord", since every Christian while still alive should watch and be ready for his Lord's coming. But to live in this state of expectancy does not mean to conclude (for Paul or anyone else) that one will quite definitely not be overtaken by death. The very context is against such a categorical conclusion. Indeed, shortly afterwards Paul wrote again to the Thessalonians, whom false notions of an *immediate* return of Christ (that is, they had misconstrued the significance of the event as *imminent*) had beguiled into inactivity and disorderliness, to remind them that there were certain things which would take place (and which had not yet taken place) *before* the day of the Lord (II Thess. 2:1ff.; 3:5ff.; cf. the instruction given by Christ in Mk. 13:3ff.; Mt. 24:3ff.).

If the Apostle is speaking in terms of death and resurrection at this point in our epistle, we find, a few sentences further on (5:1ff.), that the question whether or not he will be alive at the return of Christ is still an open one.[17] In any case, we do not have to go outside the pages of the New Testament to see that the imminence of Christ's return continued to be a reality for the Church, despite the passage of time and the consequent removal by death from the earthly scene of more and more Christians, apostles included (see, for instance, I Jn. 2:28; 3:2; Rev. 22:20; II Pet. 3:10ff.). Allo rightly dismisses as "fanciful" the view that recent painful experiences had, shortly before the composition of our epistle, caused Paul to lose the hope of being still alive at

---

[17] See commentary below on 5:1ff.

the time of Christ's second coming. Alford is, in fact, probably correct in his opinion that the verb "shall raise up" here, "having respect rather to the contrast of the future glory with the present suffering, does not necessarily imply one or other side of the alternative of being quick or dead at the Lord's coming, but embraces all, quick and dead, in one blessed resurrection-state". The certainty of Christ's return is not impaired by the delay in its fulfilment (cf. II Pet. 3:8ff.); but in the meantime successive generations of Christians should continue to be conscious of that same element of tension which characterized the outlook of the Apostolic Church: the day of the Lord, as the great eschatological event which will bring to its conclusion this present era of grace, will come suddenly, at a time known to no man, and consequently it is an event which is always imminent. It is final, but always at hand. The proper effect of this tension is to be sought, not in the realm of curious speculation, but in the sphere of Christian ethics: in the light of this impending consummation Christians are to be watchful, pure, joyful, and diligent in the work of the Lord, so that they may not be ashamed before Him at His coming. They are, in short, to conduct themselves in a manner befitting those who live in the constant expectancy of Christ's appearing.

4:15

> For all things are for your sakes, that the grace, being multiplied through the many, may cause the thanksgiving to abound unto the glory of God.

What Paul has been saying in the preceding verses makes it plain that by "all things" here he means all the sufferings and afflictions involved in his experience of being constantly delivered unto death: all are endured for the sakes of the Corinthian Christians, and of course for those also in every place who through his ministry of the gospel are brought to faith in the Saviour. This does not conflict with his assertion in verse 11 that it is for *Jesus*' sake that he is always being delivered unto death. Indeed, as we contemplate the Apostle's willing and continual endurance of all these things (so incomprehensible to the world), "for your sakes" can be adequately comprehended only within the setting of "for Jesus' sake". Just as Christ's coming and sufferings were for our sakes, so he who lives and labours for Jesus' sake by that very fact lives and labours also for the sake of mankind. There is no hint of self-interest: in view of the perfect atoning sacrifice of Christ offered once-for-all on our behalf, no other suffering can in any degree contribute to man's salvation. And there is no suggestion of self-centredness or of isolating individualism: the true follower of Christ is Christ-centred and for Jesus' sake, and after His example, gladly spends himself and is spent for the sake of his fellow-men (12:15).

The latter part of the verse, which in form and thought is not dissimilar from 1:11, has been interpreted in a variety of ways.[18] The sense seems to be as follows: All things are for your sakes, in order that the grace which increased through the increase in the number of believers may cause thanksgiving to abound to the glory of God—or, as Tasker paraphrases it, "the more people who come to know the grace of God through the gospel Paul preaches, the more numerous will be the thanksgivings that will be evoked, and the greater the praise that will be offered to God". Calvin remarks that "when Paul makes the overflowing of God's gift to consist in gratitude, to the glory of its Author, he admonishes us that every blessing which God confers on us perishes through our carelessness, if we are not prompt and active in returning thanks".

4:16a
Wherefore we faint not.

Here Paul resumes the "we faint not" of verse 1. The argument is rich and cumulative: in verse 1 the statement looks back to the preceding section but also extends onwards to what is to follow; and now here again the same statement looks back to the intervening passage from verse 1 onwards, but also prolongs its application to the next stage of the argument. Paul has been speaking of his continual dying-while-living experience, and now he is about to consider the implications of the total dissolution of the earthen vessel of his body by death, with special reference to the heavenly body with which every believer is to be clothed at Christ's return. We are, in fact, on the threshold of one of the most important eschatological passages of the New Testament.

---

[18] See, for example, Plummer and Alford, who discuss the different renderings which have been proposed.

4:16b–5:10   THE PROSPECT OF DEATH AND ITS CONSEQUENCES

4:16b

But though our outward man is decaying, yet our inward man is renewed day by day.

The "outward man", which corresponds to the "earthen vessels", the "body", and the "mortal flesh" mentioned by Paul in verses 7, 10, and 11, must not be confused with the "old man" of which Paul speaks in Rom. 6:6, Eph. 4:22,. and Col. 3:9, which the Christian is enjoined to "put off" and to reckon as having been crucified with Christ on the cross. The connotation of the latter is strongly ethical, referring to the old unregenerate nature and its desires; whereas the connotation of the "outward man" here is not moral but physical, referring to man's, and in particular the Apostle's, mortal frame which is undergoing decay and moving towards the grave. The present tense ("is decaying") indicates a steady and irreversible process; and this process is especially and even startlingly marked in the case of the Apostle because of the extreme severity of his sufferings.[1] But the "outward man" should not be understood in a merely material sense, for it indicates the human constitution with all its faculties and energies, mental as well as muscular, perceptive as well as practical. Indeed, there is no doubt that the significance of the expression is to be found most simply and adequately in terms of that aspect of Paul's being which, being *outwardly* manifested, is *visible* to his fellow-men: it is what they see of him. Similarly, the significance of the expression the "inward man" should not be sought in terms of anatomy or psychology: it indicates that which is hidden from the gaze of the man of this world and inaccessible to his analysis. Paul is speaking of a great *Christian* reality, of the remarkable fact that the advance, evident to all,

---

[1] The construction εἰ καί . . . διαφθείρεται should be noticed, for, as Alford points out, "εἰ καί with the indicative asserts the *fact*, as in εἰ καί σπένδομαι, Phil. 2:17". In Paul's case the the decay of his outward man was a very obvious fact. See also notes on verse 3 above and on 5:16, 7:8, and 12:11 below.

in outward decay is accompanied, day after day,[2] by the experience of an inward renewal. The outward is the paradox of the inward (6:9f.). The light of eternity shines in the Christian's heart (v. 6), a light which no affliction can extinguish. The earnest of the Spirit within (1:22, 5:5) assures him that present sufferings are not even comparable with the glory to be revealed at last (Rom. 8:18). His path, however rough and dark externally, is as the morning light which shines more and more unto the full noonday (Prov. 4:18).

For the unbeliever, of course, the decay of the outward man is also a fact of experience; but his heart is darkened, he knows no inward renewal, and his way becomes more and more confined until it brings him to the narrow limits of the grave and the grim reality of judgment. "In the reprobate also the outward man decays, but without anything to compensate for it", says Calvin. So, too, Denney observes that "the decay of the outward man in the godless is a melancholy spectacle, for it is the decay of everything".

It was customary for philosophical thought—Pythagorean, Stoic, Neoplatonic—to distinguish in a dualistic manner between the inward man of the rational soul and the outward and evil covering of the material body in which the former was confined during this earthly existence.[3] Such a dualistic concept is, however, entirely alien to the thought both of Paul and of Scripture as a whole. It constituted, indeed, a serious threat to the theology of the early Church under the forms of Docetism, Gnosticism, and Philonism during the first century, and later on in the Neoplatonism which flourished especially in the schools of Alexandria, and in the extravagances of Manichaeism. Thus we find Augustine replying to Faustus the Manichaean that,

---

[2] Ἡμέρᾳ καὶ ἡμέρᾳ may be a semitism, the equivalent of יוֹם וָיוֹם, as in Esther 3:4, which is rendered καθ᾽ ἑκάστην ἡμέραν in LXX (cf. καθ᾽ ἑκάστην ἡμέραν, Heb. 3:13). The expression is also found, but without the copula, in Psa. 68:20 — יוֹם יוֹם which is rendered ἡμέραν καθ᾽ ἡμέραν in LXX.

[3] Cf. Plato, *Republ.* IX, 588Dff., who speaks of the inward man (ὁ ἐντὸς ἄνθρωπος) enveloped by an outward sheath (τὸ ἔξω ἔλυτρον); Plotinus, *Enn.* I, i, 10, who speaks of the inward man (ὁ ἔνδον ἄνθρωπος or ὁ εἴσω ἄνθρωπος); Philo, whose anthropology likewise postulates two men, material and immaterial; and the Stoic writers Epictetus, Seneca, and Marcus Aurelius who propounded a similar concept.

although Paul speaks here of both an outward and an inward man, "we nowhere find him making these two different men, but one, which is all made by God, both the inward and the outward. ... The whole of this man", he continues, "both the inward and the outward part, has become old by sin and liable to the punishment of death. There is, however, a restoration of the inward man when it is renewed after the image of its Creator in the putting off of unrighteousness, that is, the old man, and the putting on of righteousness, that is, the new man. But when that which is sown a natural body shall rise a spiritual body, the outward man too shall attain the dignity of a celestial character; so that all that has been created may be created anew, and all that has been made be remade by the Creator and Maker Himself".[4]

Paul's terminology in this verse, then, affords no indication that he has come under the influence of contemporary philosophical modes of thought, as some scholars have suggested.[5] It is, indeed, by no means certain that the Apostle was even deliberately making use of current philosophical expressions, though there can be little doubt that he was well aware of the dualism prevalent in the Hellenistic thinking of his day. It may well be, however, that he was consciously removing certain terms and expressions from the erroneous context of paganism and transferring, and thereby transmuting, them into the sphere of Christian truth within which alone they can take on a valid significance, as he seems to have done, for example, in his earlier letter to the Corinthians (I Cor. 2:6ff.). Among the more recent commentators, Allo inclines to the view that Paul's terminology here was influenced by a distinction current in Greek and Hellenistic philosophy. "Only", he says, "he has changed its sense in order to adapt it to Christian doctrine; he has transported the distinction into the spiritual domain in order to oppose what man in the state of grace truly is and is becoming in his profound and enduring reality to what he appears to be and to be becoming in the sensible world. Among the Greeks, it was a question only of a psychological distinction; thus in Plato 'the inward man'

---

[4] Augustine, *Con. Faust.*, XXIV, 2. Herveius comments to the same effect.
[5] See, for example, R. Bultmann, *Theology of the New Testament*, Vol. I, pp. 201f.

is the rational *part* of the soul, as opposed to his animal parts. This gave occasion incidentally, for example among the Stoics, for fine ethical sentiments; but with Paul ... it is not at all a question of different parts or functions, but of an *indivisible personality, seen from without or seen from within,* after the experience of regeneration. We are able therefore to conclude, with Bachmann, that these verses, far from proving a profound influence of Hellenism on Paul, display his independence with respect to this Hellenism—even though he may have adopted (or let us rather say adapted) its terminology". This judgment we consider to be eminently sensible and fully in accord with the facts as they are set before us in the New Testament.

4:17

For our light affliction, which is for the moment, worketh for us more and more exceedingly an eternal weight of glory.

In this verse we find a series of extreme contrasts. Paul, as Chrysostom remarks, "sets side by side the things present with the things to come, the momentary with the eternal, the light with the weighty, the affliction with the glory". The conjunction "for" shows that what Paul says here is explanatory of what has immediately preceded: the astonishing fact that the decay of the outward man is accompanied by the renewal of the inward man is not merely an experience; it has an inner logic. The affliction endured is itself in process of achieving or making effective [6] the surpassing glory. It must be stated quite emphatically that no ground is offered here for the doctrine that merit is acquired through suffering, though this verse has been claimed in support of such teaching.[7] Merit implies a correspondence of effort and reward. How can something that is light and momentary be said to *merit* what is eternal and weighty and "beyond all comparison" (ARSV)? Nothing could be more vain than to spin distinctions, as do the Roman Catholic theologians, between merit of condignity and merit of congruity; for Paul is speaking here of contrast, not of correspondence. In other words, it is his purpose to extol the inexpressible magnitude of the grace

---

[6] *Κατεργάζεται,* present tense.
[7] See, for example, *Canons and Decrees of the Council of Trent,* Sess. VI, xvi.

of God, which, so far from being bestowed because of man's deserts, is bestowed solely because of God's mercy.

No more does the Apostle mean that all suffering is productive of glory, as though it were an infallible means to this end. The history of the Church has shown that such a concept leads to an unscriptural self-interest and to a misconception of the true character of Christian suffering. Paul is concerned here with suffering *for Jesus' sake* (v. 11; cf. Acts 9:16), which means suffering in which there cannot possibly be any self-interest. It is precisely as the "I" decreases that Christ increases (Jn. 3:30). This is the sense in which the Apostles learnt that "through many tribulations we must enter into the kingdom of God" (Acts 14:22). The burning flames of affliction are also flames resplendent with glory. Paul's theme throughout this epistle is that the frailty of the human frame and the afflictions which it sustains in the cause of the gospel magnify, by reason of the astonishing contrast, and provide the opportunity for experiencing, the all-transcending glory and power and grace of Almighty God.

Paul is writing of *real* suffering. Because he describes it as "light affliction" it should not be concluded that the tribulations he endured were inconsiderable in the intensity of their force and duration. On the contrary, they were exceptionally severe and virtually unremitting during the length of his ministry, as he indicates in general terms in verses 8ff. of this chapter and more specifically in the remarkable, but not exhaustive, catalogue of 11:23ff. below. The language he uses must, as we have said, be interpreted by way of contrast: Christian suffering, however protracted it may be, is only for this present life, which, when compared with the everlasting ages of the glory to which it is leading, is but a passing moment; affliction for Jesus' sake, however crushing it may seem, is in fact light [8], a weightless trifle, when weighed against the mass of that glory [9] which is the inheritance of all who through grace have been made one with

---

[8] Cf. Mt. 11:30, where our Lord uses the same word *(ἐλαφρός)* of the burden which His followers are called to take upon themselves.

[9] It is a matter of interest that the Greek noun δόξα ("glory") is the LXX rendering of the Hebrew noun כָּבוֹד, which comes from a root meaning to be heavy, and thence to be wealthy, prosperous, honoured, or mighty. Far closer to כָּבוֹד in its root meaning is the Greek βάρος, "weight" or "heaviness". Both כָּבוֹד and βάρος could also carry the sense of "abundance."

the Son of God. And this is a present reality, even though it is only hereafter that it will be experienced in its fulness. The afflicted Apostle finds, moreover, that the inward glory is constantly advancing in intensity towards the measure of its eschatological completeness—"more and more exceedingly", or, as Alford renders it, "in a surpassing and still more surpassing manner".[10]

4 : 18

> While we look not at the things which are seen, but at the things which are not seen: for the things which are seen are temporal; but the things which are not seen are eternal.

The verb translated "to look at" here [11] has the force "to fix one's gaze upon" or "to concentrate one's attention upon" some object. The gaze of faith is focused upon eternal realities which are no less real because they are unseen (cf. Heb. 11:1). The things seen of which Paul is speaking are precisely his obvious human frailty and suffering (the outward man that is decaying)—the very things that the man whose values are of this world alone most wishes to forget and to avoid, since they cast a haunting

---

In writing $\beta\acute{\alpha}\varrho o\varsigma$ $\delta\acute{o}\xi\eta\varsigma$ "weight (or abundance) of glory", was Paul consciously combining the two significances of the Hebrew כָּבוֹד ? Attractive though the suggestion must be to those whose business is with words, we do not hesitate to answer in the negative, since an etymological refinement of this kind, being irrelevant to his main purpose, which is doctrinal and certainly not philological, would not consciously have been devised by the Apostle—least of all at a point like this where his visionary ardour reaches a summit of spontaneous utterance. Whether there was a link in his subconscious mind, who can say?

10   The expression $\varkappa\alpha\theta'$ $\acute{\upsilon}\pi\varepsilon\varrho\beta o\lambda\grave{\eta}\nu$ $\varepsilon\grave{\iota}\varsigma$ $\acute{\upsilon}\pi\varepsilon\varrho\beta o\lambda\acute{\eta}\nu$ is probably a combination, for the purpose of intensifying the force, of two adverbial phrases, $\varkappa\alpha\theta'$ $\acute{\upsilon}\pi\varepsilon\varrho\beta o\lambda\acute{\eta}\nu$ and $\varepsilon\grave{\iota}\varsigma$ $\acute{\upsilon}\pi\varepsilon\varrho\beta o\lambda\acute{\eta}\nu$, and may answer to the Hebrew device of intensification by repetition (for example, מְאֹד מְאֹד). Whether this is so or not, the $\varepsilon\grave{\iota}\varsigma$ in this combination is so placed as to indicate clearly that there is a constant *increase* in the intensity of the experience. The expression should be linked exegetically with the $\acute{\upsilon}\pi\varepsilon\varrho\beta o\lambda\acute{\eta}$ of verse 7, for the reference here is similar, namely, the excess of the glory (there, the power) of God—an ever increasing excess—over the frailties and afflictions of the present.

11    $\Sigma\varkappa o\pi\varepsilon\tilde{\iota}\nu$, "to fix one's gaze upon" or "concentrate one's attention upon" some object, whereas the sense of $\beta\lambda\acute{\varepsilon}\pi\varepsilon\iota\nu$, "to see", is weaker and more general. The construction of $\mu\grave{\eta}$ $\sigma\varkappa o\pi o\acute{\upsilon}\nu\tau\omega\nu$ $\acute{\eta}\mu\tilde{\omega}\nu$ is that of a genitive absolute. The dative, $\sigma\varkappa\acute{o}\pi o\upsilon\sigma\iota$, agreeing with the immediately preceding $\acute{\eta}\mu\tilde{\iota}\nu$, might have been expected here, but genitive absolutes of this kind (which are not strictly "absolute") are not infrequent in the New Testament.

shadow over all his ambitions. In the world's estimation the Apostle's life was an unenviable failure—his conversion when in the full course of a brilliant career, his counting as loss the things that had been gain to him, his labours, journeyings, hardships, persecutions, and, finally, his ignominious death as a despised martyr—for it is only the outward man that the world beholds.[12] But Paul's estimate is totally different, because his values are the direct antithesis of the world's values. So far from being a disappointed man, his way is one of joy and power and hope beyond description. Despite afflictions, perplexities, and catastrophes, the Christian's gaze is concentrated on the glory within and beyond; his treasure is not on earth, but in heaven, and there accordingly his heart is also; he knows himself to be united in destiny with his risen and glorified Saviour, the supreme Sufferer, now everlastingly exalted above all principalities and powers. It is true that these imperishable verities are known by the Christian only imperfectly as yet; but he rejoices in the certainty that the day is coming when, seeing his Redeemer face to face, he will be like Him, transfigured into the image of His glory, and will know even as he is known (3:18; I Jn. 3:2; I Cor. 13:12). Persuaded that nothing whatsoever, not even death, can separate him from the love of God which is in Christ Jesus our Lord (Rom. 8:38f.), he presses on toward the heavenly goal (Phil. 3:14)[13], gladly enduring the present tribulations in the assurance that they are, in contrast to the prize, temporary, fleeting, transient:[14] they are the things seen, the *affliction* of the preceding verse which is only for the passing moment; whereas the things not seen are in one word the *glory* of the preceding verse, and like that glory they are eternal. "A moment is long", says Calvin, "if we look at the things around us; but once we have raised our minds to heaven a thousand years begin to be like a moment".

---

[12] In the next sentence (5:1) Paul describes the "outward man" as "our earthly tent-dwelling" *(ἡ ἐπίγειος ἡμῶν οἰκία τοῦ σκήνους)*, and in Phil. 3:19 he speaks of those "whose concern is with earthly things" *(οἱ τὰ ἐπίγεια φρονοῦντες*—where *φρονεῖν* has exactly the same force as *σκοπεῖν* here). To be concerned with earthly things is precisely to fix one's attention on the things which are seen.

[13] The goal *(σκοπός)* of Phil. 3:14 is that on which he fixes his gaze *(σκοπεῖν)* here.

[14] *Πρόσκαιρα:* "temporary" rather than "temporal" (A.V., R.V.).

5 : 1

> For we know that if the earthly house of our tabernacle be dissolved, we have a building from God, a house not made with hands, eternal, in the heavens.

The knowledge of which the Apostle is speaking here is a particular knowledge which has been granted to Christian believers. As Calvin says, it "does not spring from the human intellect, but takes its rise from the revelation of the Holy Spirit".[15] A belief, in one form or another, in the immortality of the soul is, of course, found in a variety of non-Christian religions and philosophies; but Paul is teaching something which far exceeds any of the tentative aspirations of paganism, for his perspective is enriched by the assurance that the Christian's body is to be redeemed and glorified as well as his soul. He rejoices in the certainty that the frailty, the limitations, and the gravitational pull of sin associated with his present bodily experience will hereafter become entirely a thing of the past. The believer, accordingly, entertains the certain hope of an incomparably better life beyond the grave, in contrast to the unbeliever whose values are all of this world, and for whom consequently death is the personification of uncertainty and the inexorable frustration of all for which he has lived.

There is, indeed, for Paul one note of uncertainty, introduced by the conditional clause: "if the earthly house of our tabernacle be dissolved". This, however, is in no sense an uncertainty about the unclouded future blessedness of all who are Christ's, but only concerning the question whether or not he would be overtaken by death. The reason why Paul treats this as only a possibility and not an inevitability is because it is balanced by another possibility, namely, that of the prior return of Christ, in which case he will not experience death, but immediate bodily translation and transformatiion.

The theory, propounded by many modern scholars, that our present passage indicates that Paul's eschatological outlook had undergone a radical alteration or adjustment since the writing of I Corinthians is more specious than substantial. It is suggested

---

[15] Οἴδαμεν is used here in its proper sense of to know as the result of perceiving or seeing (root εἰδ-) a truth by intuition or revelation, in contrast to the acquiring of knowledge by instruction or research (γινώσκειν).

that disappointed hopes of Christ's return without delay, coupled with his own increasing physical frailty and especially the all but fatal affliction experienced in Asia (1:8), had forced him, however reluctantly, to set aside his earlier confidence that he would still be alive at the time of the parousia. But this theory ignores the significant fact that Paul's earliest epistle (I Thessalonians) was occasioned by the need to reassure those to whom he was writing that Christians who die before the second advent are quite definitely at no disadvantage in comparison with those who are alive at the coming of the Lord (I Thess. 4:13ff.). This possibility of dying rather than remaining alive was no less real for the Apostle than for his hearers. Besides, it became necessary for him to write again shortly afterwards to the same church in order to remind its members that Christ's return would not take place before the occurrence of certain historical developments (II Thess. 2:1ff.)—a consideration which, incidentally, increased the possibility of being carried off by death before the great eschatological event. In the famous eschatological passage of his previous letter to the Corinthians the same twofold possibility is again present, either of dying before the parousia or of being alive at the parousia (I Cor. 15:40ff.). It is fitting that, so long as he is alive, the Apostle should associate himself with the expectation of those who will still be living when Christ returns rather than with the prospect of those who have died, without in any way presupposing that he would not be overtaken by death.

This double possibility has been present to the minds of Christ's faithful followers in every age. It has at all times been a powerful incentive to holy living: neither the day nor the hour of the Bridegroom's coming is known to us; therefore it is an event which is always imminent for the Church; it is always probable that death will be forestalled by the parousia of Christ; and, in accordance with our Lord's admonition to watch, we should live now and every moment as we would wish to be found living at the sudden instant of His return or, should that be delayed, in the hour of death. "Every one that hath this hope set on Him purifieth himself, even as He is pure" (I Jn. 3:3).

"The earthly house of our tabernacle", or, as it may better be rendered, "our tent-dwelling on earth" (cf. RSV: "the earthly tent we live in"), is an expression which effectively emphasizes the fragile impermanence of our present bodies, for in ancient times a tent was a familiar picture of what was transitory and without foundations. Although it is true, as Alford points out, that this similitude was common to Greek as well as Hebrew writers, it is none the less probable that Paul had in mind the wilderness experiences of the children of Israel. As Bishop Lightfoot says (commenting on Phil. 1:23), "the camp-life of the Israelites in the wilderness, as commemorated by the annual feast of tabernacles, was a ready and appropriate symbol of man's transitory life on earth: while the land of promise with its settled abodes, the land flowing with milk and honey, typified the eternal inheritance of the redeemed". And L. S. Thornton writes to the same effect: "The contrast between an 'earthly tent-house' and a heavenly temple has its biblical background in the story of Israel. The tabernacle belonged to the wilderness wanderings, whereas the temple upon Mount Zion was associated with the triumphs of David and the splendours of Solomon's reign".[16] Another striking illustration of this reality, equally appropriate to Paul's theme here, is seen by the New Testament in the story of Abraham who, at the call of God, became a sojourner "as in a land not his own, dwelling in tents", for he was looking towards the heavenly city "which has foundations, whose builder and maker is God" (Heb. 11:8ff.). The life of the tent-dweller is never settled: his outlook is that of a sojourner and pilgrim, and this should be characteristic of every Christian (cf. I Pet. 2:11). In Jn. 1:14, indeed, the tent-metaphor is used of our Lord's incarnation and earthly sojourn: "the Word became flesh and pitched His tent [17] among us".

Even if the Christian's tent-dwelling is dismantled by death,[18]

---

[16] L. S. Thornton, *Christ and the Church* (*The Form of the Servant*, Vol. III; London, 1956), p. 119.

[17] Ἐσκήνωσεν.

[18] The tent metaphor is preserved in the use of the verb καταλυθῇ which is descriptive of the act of dismantling. In general, καταλύειν and ἀναλύειν are synonymous verbs, and the latter was sometimes used of the operation of striking camp, that is, the dismantling of tents (cf. Polybius, V, xxviii, 8; II Macc. 9:1). Was Paul employing the same figure of speech when, with specific reference to death, he said: ὁ καιρὸς τῆς ἐμῆς ἀναλύσεως ἐφέστηκε — "the time of my departure (the dismantling of my tent?) is at hand" (II Tim. 4:6)—and again: τὴν ἐπιθυμίαν ἔχων εἰς τὸ ἀναλῦσαι—"my own inclination being to depart (to dismantle my tent?)" (Phil. 1:23)?

this does not alter the fact that he, in common with all other believers, has [19] "a building from God", that is, a permanent structure with foundations [20], "eternal, in the heavens", in strong contrast to his temporary tent-abode here on earth.[21]   Paul is not, of course, suggesting that our present bodies are not from God the Creator (cf. I Cor. 12:18, 24), but that the resurrection body, as part of God's *new creation*, will be entirely glorious, free from sin and its corruption, and fitted by God for unbroken fellowship with Himself.   It belongs to that free gift of grace in Christ Jesus which is altogether of God and from God.

It is, furthermore, "a house not made with hands".   This expression, too, must not be misunderstood, for it certainly does not imply that our present "dwelling" *is* made with hands. There may be a hint of the thought that man, by virtue of his faculty of procreation, has a hand in the miracle of the formation of the earthly body, whereas the new dwelling comes immediately from God.   The expression may also be interpreted in part by reference to Paul's own particular *handicraft*, namely, *tent-making*: tents, with the *manufacture* of which he was so familiar, he naturally thought of as made with hands.   This description, however, which is distinctive to the New Testament, must be understood as a synonym, almost a technical term, for that which is heavenly

---

[19]   Taking account of the passage as a whole, with its clear contrast between the present body and the resurrection body, the present tense of the verb "have" is understood, with most commentators, as referring to a future possession which is so real and assured in the apostle's perspective that it is appropriately spoken of in the present tense.   For examples of the use of the present denoting future time cf. J. H. Moulton, *Grammar*, Vol. I, p. 120; Moule, *Idiom Book*, p. 7.

[20]   Οἰκοδομή: a late form of οἰκοδόμησις—the act or process of building, which is its sense in I Cor. 3:9—or οἰκοδόμημα—which is properly the finished product and fits the sense better here.

[21]   Ἐπίγειος. This adjective does not mean "made of earth", as though corresponding to the ὀστραχίνοις of 4:7; nor is it the equivalent, as Olshausen suggests, of ἐκ γῆς as opposed to the ἐκ θεοῦ of the main clause, for Scripture teaches throughout that our present bodies are also ἐκ θεοῦ. The meaning of ἐπίγειος is "on earth" *(ἐπὶ γῆς)*, that is, belonging to this earthly state, and its opposite is ἐπουράνιος, or, as we have in this verse, ἐν τοῖς οὐρανοῖς, "in heaven", that is, belonging to the heavenly state (cf. Heb. 11:16; Phil. 2:10; I Cor. 15:40; Jn. 3:12). In Job. 4:19 the ideas of the ἐπίγειος οἰκία here and the ὀστράχινα σκεύη of 4:7 are combined in the expression "houses of clay" (LXX, οἰκίας πηλίνας): men are those "who dwell in houses of clay, whose foundation is in the dust".

and spiritual in contradistinction to what is earthly and physical. Thus in Col. 2:11 we read of a "circumcision not made with hands" (cf. Rom. 2:28f.) and in Heb. 9:11 of a "tabernacle not made with hands" (cf. Heb. 9:24). In fact, the latter of these two references defines the phrase precisely for us by adding the explanation, "that is to say, not of this creation". And this provides us with the proper understanding of its meaning in the passage which is before us. The origin of the expression in its distinctive Christian significance may well be discovered in Mk. 14:58 where it is declared that it had been used by our Lord Himself—in a manner, moreover, with which Paul's usage of it here completely harmonizes. In fact, the obvious affinities between our Lord's utterance (so readily seized upon by His uncomprehending enemies) and Paul's terminology here make it virtually certain that the Apostle had this dominical saying in mind when he was writing these words.[22] This probability is corroborated by John who, in his account of the occasion when Jesus must have uttered these words, is careful to explain that our Lord was speaking about the temple of His body (Jn. 2:19ff.). This in turn suggests that there was in Paul's mind a definite connection between the resurrection body of Christ and that of the believer—a connection which is explicitly asserted in Phil. 3:21, where the Apostle states that the Lord Jesus Christ "will fashion anew the body of our humiliation (our earthly tent-dwelling), that it may be conformed to the body of His glory (the temple or building not made with hands)". Thus Ambrose comments on our verse: "This house signifies the immortal body in which, when we rise again, we shall ever be, and the form of which is already made clear in the body of the Lord in heaven".

The special significance for the members of the Corinthian Church of Paul's instruction here on the resurrection should not be overlooked, for, as Chrysostom reminds us, they had shown themselves to be particularly unsound respecting this doctrine.

Some commentators, ancient as well as modern—Ephraem,

---

[22] Mk. 14:58—"I will destroy (ἐγὼ καταλύσω) this temple that is made with hands (χειροποίητον), and in three days I will build (οἰκοδομήσω) another made without hands (ἀχειροποίητον)".

II Cor. 5:1—"For we know that if the earthly house of our tabernacle be dissolved (καταλυθῇ), we have a building (οἰκοδομήν) from God, a house not made with hands (ἀχειροποίητον)".

Herveius, Aquinas, Hodge, Stanley, and Tasker among them—, understand the "house not made with hands, eternal, in the heavens" to refer to the heavenly home or abode of God's people after death (cf. Jn. 14:2ff.), rather than to the glorified body which they will receive at the return of Christ. Thus Stanley states that Paul "speaks rather of a habitation into which he is to enter, than of a body which he is to assume". But this interpretation requires the term "house" to be taken in two quite different senses in one and the same sentence, which throws Paul's meaning into doubt and seriously weakens his argument. Sound exegesis surely demands that the word "house" as used by the Apostle here should signify "body", both when he speaks of the present earthly house (as is universally agreed) and also when he speaks of the house in the heavens. The terminology he uses in the verses that follow confirms this conclusion, as we shall hope to show. He is concerned with the same great theme as that about which he has already written in I Cor. 15:35ff., but viewed from a different angle. He is, in a sense, filling in a gap in the instruction he has previously given. There he is speaking of the sowing (in death) of this present frail physical body and of its being reaped (in resurrection) in power as a glorified body at Christ's coming. Here his attention is focused upon the intermediate period between the sowing of the earthly and the reaping of the heavenly body.

Hodge, with unwonted inconsistency, though arguing against the interpretation of the "house not made with hands" as meaning the resurrection body, and explaining it as "a mansion in heaven into which believers enter as soon as their earthly tabernacle is dissolved", none the less, in a manner ill becoming his use of language, has to regard this place or abode as in fact a body (that is, an interim body—a most inappropriate confusion of the term "house" in its literal and in its metaphorical senses), since he strongly maintains that it is impossible for the soul to exist apart from a body.[23] Calvin takes the passage to mean that "the blessed state of the soul after death is the beginning of this building, and the glory of the final resurrection its consummation".

---

[23] Regarding the present tense of ἔχομεν, Hodge says that it "is used because the one event immediately follows the other: there is no perceptible interval between the dissolution of the earthly tabernacle and entering on the heavenly house. As soon as the soul leaves the body it *is* in heaven".

Others have held that the eternal body is received by the Christian in this life at his baptism, with the consequence that the intermediate state between death and Christ's return is not one of nakedness (verse 3 then being expounded in that sense). Thus a recent writer has affirmed that "those who have been baptized into Christ have already put on a new Body—that of Christ (cf. Gal. 3:27; I Cor. 12:13) and can never again be naked".[24] And he says, further: "The Christian is already clothed with Christ (Gal. 3:27) and has already 'put on the new man' (Eph. 4:24). He already knows what it is to 'walk in newness of life' in the power of Christ's Resurrection (Rom. 6:4; Col. 2:12) and to be raised up to heavenly places (Col. 3:1-3; Eph. 2:6). It is true, of course, that the full realization of this new life waits upon the Parousia even in the latest of the Pauline writings (Col. 3:4; Eph. 1:13, 14); but in the light of his emphasis upon the truth that Christians share in the Resurrection in this life, St. Paul can hardly have regarded death as an interruption of that incorporation—as nakedness".[25] But this interpretation must be rejected, firstly, because it would be entirely incongruous for the Apostle to long to be clothed upon with his habitation which is from heaven (v. 2) if in fact he already possesses that habitation —a man does not long for that which he already has—, and, secondly, because when he speaks of the Christian as being even in this life raised with Christ and seated with Him in heavenly places, the experience he is describing cannot be explained as or equated with a *bodily* resurrection and ascension. The latter, for Paul, is always the eschatological experience, which will be realized only at Christ's parousia. Meanwhile his body is earth-bound. The nakedness which his soul experiences through being divested of the body at death in no sense implies an interruption of his incorporation in Christ; indeed, it is precisely that incorporation which explains the present experience, though still in this earthly tent-dwelling, of being risen and ascended with

---

[24] R. F. Hettlinger, article on "2 Corinthians 5:1-10" in *The Scottish Journal of Theology*, June, 1957, p. 185. See also J. A. T. Robinson, *The Body* (London, 1952), pp. 80f. This view of the "clothing" as something which takes place at baptism is mentioned by Ambrose as being held by some in his day (fourth century). It is a view which interprets the present tense of ἔχομεν as implying the *presentness* of the possession of which Paul is speaking.

[25] *Ibid.*, pp. 188f.

Christ (and also, let it be remembered, of having died and been buried with Him—Rom. 6:3ff.) and the future eschatological experience of bodily resurrection and ascension.[26]

5:2

For verily in this we groan, longing to be clothed upon with our habitation which is from heaven.

Opinion is divided as to whether "in this" means "in this tent-dwelling" or "in this, namely, that we are longing ..." [27] The *groaning* of which Paul speaks here is mentioned again in Rom. 8:19–23, where he explains that not only the Christian, but also the whole creation groans, the former in expectation of the redemption of the body (the theme with which the Apostle is dealing here), and the latter in expectation of its consequent deliverance "from the bondage of corruption into the liberty of the glory of the children of God".[28] The work of Christ, while it is primarily directed towards the salvation of man, also necessarily involves the whole created order, for in his fall man, inasmuch as he is the crown of creation, brought a curse upon the realm over which he had been given dominion, and the redemption of man, likewise, will in its consummation mean the blessing and restoration of the whole of creation. Thus God's purposes in creation will not experience frustration, but will (inevitably so, because they are *God's* purposes) be brought to full fruition. The scope of salvation in Christ is *cosmic*: the new man in Christ is himself a new creation (v. 17) and his ultimate setting is the new heavens and the new earth wherein righteousness dwells (II Pet. 3:13). True, the believer already possesses the

---

[26] For further discussion of these and other interpretations of this passage, see Allo, pp. 137ff.

[27] Those who understand ἐν τούτῳ to mean "in this body" take it as referring back to σκῆνος in verse 1, and find in verse 4 a parallel *(οἱ ὄντες ἐν τῷ σκήνει στενάζομεν)* to ἐν τούτῳ στενάζομεν here. On the other hand, it is perfectly common usage for οὗτος to refer forward to what follows. We venture to offer the suggestion that the expression ἐν τούτῳ should be allowed to stand by itself here, with the excellent sense of "meanwhile". We may then render as follows: "For in the meantime indeed we groan, longing to be clothed upon...". On the significance of ἐπενδύσασθαι see note 31 below.

[28] It is surprising to find Hodge affirming that Rom. 8:22 is not parallel to our present passage. Had he given attention to the very next verse (Rom. 8:23), he would surely have had to revise this opinion.

earnest of the Spirit in his heart (1:22), which accounts for his experience, even here and now, of sharing in the glory of Christ's resurrection and ascension; but it is this very fact which causes him to groan and long for the day when he shall receive the payment in full. He who has the firstfruits of the Spirit yearns for the full harvest, which involves the redemption of his body (Rom. 8:23).

At this point Paul varies his metaphor, though in a manner that is not at all unnatural: he has been speaking of the heavenly body as a dwelling, but now he describes it, still as a habitation,[29] as though it were also a garment to put on. In II Pet. 1:13f. we find a corresponding garment-dwelling simile, where death is depicted as the putting off (like a garment) of the tent (of one's earthly body).[30] But Paul's language here indicates something more than the mere putting on of a garment: he is talking of putting on one garment *over* another.[31] The picture conveyed is that of the heavenly body being put on, like an outer vesture, over the earthly body, with which the Apostle is as it were clad, so as not only to cover it but to absorb and transfigure it. In this way the ideas both of continuity and of transformation,

---

[29] Τὸ οἰκητήριον, Plummer remarks, "denotes a permanent abode or home", and "the difference between οἰκία and οἰκητήριον is that the latter implies an οἰκητήρ, and inhabitant, while the former does not".

[30] Ἡ ἀπόθεσις τοῦ σκηνώματος.

[31] This is beyond doubt the correct meaning of ἐπενδύσασθαι. The prefix ἐπι signifies the putting on of an *additional* or *outer* garment. We cannot agree with Tasker, Hodge, and others that Paul is using the compound and simple forms *(ἐπενδύσασθαι ... ἐνδυσάμενοι)* indiscriminately as synonyms. On the contrary, that a precise distinction in meaning is intended is confirmed by the terminology of verse 4, where he says that it is not that he wishes to put off a garment *(ἐκδύσασθαι)*, that is, his present earthly body, but to put on over it another garment *(ἐπενδύσασθαι)*, that is, the glorified body which will be provided at Christ's parousia. The usage of the same compound verb in Herodotus (*Hist.*, I, 195), Josephus (*Ant. Jud.*, V, i, 12), and Plutarch (*Pelop.*, 11) establishes yet further that it bears this specific sense. To this evidence may be added that of the cognate nouns ἐπένδυμα (Plutarch, *Alex.*, 32) and ἐπενδύτης (Sophocles, Frag. 391, Pseudo-Thespis in Pollux, VII, 45, Nichochares, *Her.* 1, and, in biblical Greek, I Sam. 18:4, II Sam. 13:18, and Jn. 21:7) which are used to signify an outer garment. Thus Suidas explains that ἐπενδύτης is τὸ ἐπάνω ἱμάτιον in contrast to ὑποδύτης, which is τὸ ἐσώτερον ἱμάτιον. Consistently with the above, the Vulgate renders ἐπενδύσασθαι by *superindui* (verse 2) and by *supervestiri* (verse 4)—though it is incorrect in giving passives for the middle (as do also A.V. and R.V.).

which are also prominent in the great resurrection chapter of I Cor. 15, are effectively communicated. Indeed, the very same metaphor is employed in the earlier epistle when it is said that "this corruptible must *put on* incorruption and this mortal must *put on* immortality" (I Cor. 15:53).

The Apostle's language indicates that it is still his earnest desire to be alive at the time of Christ's return so that, without undergoing the interposition of death and the intermediate state, he may experience the instantaneous change (I Cor. 15:51f.) effected by the putting on of the abode from heaven over the earthly tent-dwelling. According to biblical history, this change had already been experienced under special circumstances by two individuals of the Old Testament period, namely, Enoch, who "was translated that he should not see death" (Heb. 11:5; Gen. 5:24), and Elijah, who also was taken up bodily into heaven (II Kings 2:11). The clothing, at the coming of Christ, with the building not made with hands both of those believers who are living and of those who have died was prophetically enacted or prefigured on the occasion of our Lord's transfiguration, when Moses and Elijah appeared with Him and partook of His glory —Moses representing those who have died (Deut. 34:5) and Elijah those for whom the day of the Lord will anticipate death. It is Paul's wish to be numbered amongst the latter; and the reason for this is suggested in the next two verses.

5 : 3, 4

> If so be that being clothed we shall not be found naked. For indeed we that are in this tabernacle do groan, being burdened; not for that we would be unclothed, but that we would be clothed upon, that what is mortal may be swallowed up of life.

Paul's meaning is as follows: "Of course if [32] we have the garment of the body on we shall not be found naked, that is, in a disembodied state, by the Lord at His appearing. For it is a fact that [33] we who are in the tent-dwelling groan, being burdened by its frailties and limitations; which does not mean

---

[32] This is the force of εἰ γὲ καὶ. The correct reading may well be εἴπερ καὶ (P⁴⁶BDG), which would seem to introduce a note of greater certainty.

[33] Καὶ γάρ. It has the same force in verse 2 above.

169

that we wish to divest ourselves of the body, but to put on over it the transforming heavenly garment, so that the present mortal frame may be completely absorbed [34] by Life".[35] The Apostle is saying, in other words, that if he is still alive at Christ's return then he will be found by Christ clothed with a body (this present body)[36] and not in a disembodied state. To be without a body is to be "naked"—a manner of speech well established in Paul's day. The same figure is found in Plato, who speaks of "the soul naked of the body"[37], but for whom soul-nakedness was welcomed as a desirable state.[38] The Pythagorean doctrine, that the body is the prison-house of the soul from which the soul of the wise longs to be liberated so that without restraint it may soar upwards and be reunited to the supreme soul of the world, was characteristic not only of Platonism and of the contemporary Philonism but also of Gnosticism which, in its various forms, presented so serious a threat to the early Church. The Apostle's teaching, however, is anything but Pythagorean. Rudolf Bultmann, indeed, affirms that "the arguments of 5:1ff. contain indirect polemic against a Gnosticism which teaches that the naked self soars aloft free of any body".[39] Paul clearly does not regard the soul which has no body as being, for that reason, in an enviable state, for the body, so far from being a dungeon of the soul, is essential, in accordance with the scheme of creation, for the full expression of the personal and potential faculties of humanity. The soul of man is able to express itself adequately only in conjunction with the specially prepared instrument of

[34] Καταποθῇ is an intensive compound which emphasizes the completeness of the swallowing up.

[35] Ὑπὸ τῆς ζωῆς = by Life as the agent, not as the instrument—an indication that it is the action of God, who is Life (cf. Jn. 14:6).

[36] The aorist ἐνδυσάμενοι presents no difficulty since with a verb meaning "to put on" neither the present nor the perfect participle would have been appropriate. Plummer suggests that the reading ἐκδυσάμενοι (in place of the much better attested ἐνδυσάμενοι) is "an early alteration to avoid apparent tautology".

[37] Plato, Crat., 403B (ἡ ψυχὴ γυμνὴ τοῦ σώματος); cf. Republ., 577B, Gorg., 523D, 524D, also Paul's contemporary Philo, Virt., 76 (τῆς ψυχῆς ἀπογυμνουμένης) and Leg. All., II, 57, 59 (ἀεὶ γυμνός ἐστι καὶ ἀσώματος).

[38] Plato, Phaedo, 67DE, cf. 81C. See also the similar concept in Wisd. Sol. 9:5: φθαρτὸν γὰρ σῶμα βαρύνει ψυχήν, καὶ βρίθει τὸ γεῶδες σκῆνος νοῦν πολυφροντίδα, and in the Neoplatonic writings.

[39] R. Bultmann, Theology of the New Testament, Vol. I, p. 202.

the body. Without a body, man ceases to be truly and properly man. "We are burdened with this corruptible body", says Augustine; "but knowing that the cause of this burdensomeness is not the nature and substance of the body, but its corruption, we do not desire to be deprived of the body, but to be clothed with its immortality".[40] "If Adam had not sinned", he says again, "he would not have been divested of his body, but would have been clothed upon (superinvested) with immortality and incorruption, that his mortal (body) might have been absorbed by life; that is, that he might have passed from his natural body to the spiritual body." [41]

At death the soul is separated from the body, and man's integral nature is disrupted. This important aspect of the disintegrating character of death explains the Apostle's desire that Christ should return during his lifetime so that he might experience the change into the likeness of Christ's body of glory (Phil. 3:21) without first having to undergo the experience of "nakedness" which results from the separation of soul and body at death. There is, of course, no question of death separating the believer from Christ, but only the soul from the body; for nothing, not even death, can separate us from the love of God which is in Christ Jesus our Lord (Rom. 8:39). It is also true that for the Christian to die is gain, because to depart this life is to be with Christ (Phil. 1:21–23; and cf. verses 6–8 below) and his state after death is consequently one of peace and bliss.[42] This, however, is not the consummating gain, but only that of an intermediate state in which he still awaits the glorious reintegration of soul and body in an incorruptible union.

True though it is that for the Christian the sting of death has been removed (I Cor. 15:55ff.), yet death in itself is not something in which he takes pleasure. It still means a state of nakedness and a period of waiting until he is clothed with his resurrection body. Like the souls of the martyrs in the Apocalypse, there is a sense in which he cries "How long?" (Rev. 6:9ff.). Death, although no longer feared, is still repulsive to the Christian; it is still a disruptive event; it is still the reminder that he has not yet come to that *ultima thule* where there will be no more death.

---

[40] Augustine, *Civ. Dei*, XIV, 3.
[41] Augustine, *De Peccatorum Meritis et Remissione*, I, 2.
[42] See commentary on 12:3 below.

171

The correctness of the interpretation we have offered is further
confirmed by the language of the concluding clause of verse 4,
where Paul speaks of what is mortal being swallowed up by life,
or, to put it negatively, not being swallowed up by death. Of
particular significance is the expression "what is mortal",[43] for
a comparison with I Cor. 15:50–54 shows that Paul uses it to
indicate in a precise manner the physical frame of the man who
is still alive at the time of Christ's return. In I Cor. 15:50–54
(as in I Thess. 4:13–18) it is evident that Paul has two categories
of Christians in mind, namely, those who are alive and those who
have died when the parousia occurs. Thus the following classification may readily be discerned:

I Cor. 15	LIVING	DEAD
verse 50	Flesh and blood	Corruption
verse 51	All shall not sleep (=die)	All (dead as well as living) shall be changed
verse 52	We (who remain alive)	The dead
verses 53f.	This mortal	This corruptible

The distinction drawn by the Apostle there between "mortal"
and "corruptible" provides a key to the right exegesis of our
present passage; and the appropriateness of this distinction, which
predicates mortality of those who are living and corruption of
those who have died, is obvious. The expression "what is mortal",
therefore, should be understood of the body which has not been
dismantled by death. It follows, moreover, that the swallowing
up of what is mortal by life, of which Paul speaks here, is only
one part of what he means by the swallowing up of death in
victory in I Cor. 15:54, for the latter refers to the resurrection
of the dead as well as to the transformation of the living, and
points to the complete and consummating conquest of death at
the parousia of Christ—to the despoiling of death not only of
those who would otherwise have come into its grip, but also of
those who are already in its grip.[44]

In their exegesis of verse 3 Calvin and Olshausen have under-

---

[43] Tὸ θνητόν.

[44] See J. Jeremias, " 'Flesh and blood cannot inherit the kingdom of God'
(I Cor. xv, 50)", *New Testament Studies*, Vol. II, No. 3 (Feb., 1956), pp. 151ff.,
and J. N. Sevenster, "Some Remarks on the ΓΥΜΝΟΣ in II Cor. V. 3" in
Studia Paulina (ut supra), pp. 202ff. Cf. also Tertullian, *Con. Marc.*, V., xii.

stood the expression "being clothed" by taking it to refer to a clothing with righteousness, and, accordingly, interpreting "naked" to mean the condition of those who are not clothed with righteousness.[45]   But Paul's concern in this passage is, as we have endeavoured to show, with *the body* as though a garment and the nakedness of the soul when separated from the body in death.[46] None the less, however, the righteousness of Christ is very vitally connected with the putting on of the glorious heavenly body; for Christ is our righteousness (I Cor. 1:30), whereas all our own righteousnesses are "as a polluted garment" (Isa. 64:6), so that only whose who have *put on* Christ (Rom. 13:14; Gal. 3:27) are covered with righteousness before God.   It is they who constitute the great multitude of the redeemed who have "washed their robes and made them white in the blood of the Lamb" (Rev. 7:9, 14); and it is this enduement with the Lord our Righteousness (Jer. 23:6, 33:16) which alone prepares and capacitates the Christian for the enduement with the body not made with hands.[47]

5:5

Now he that wrought us for this very thing is God, who gave unto us the earnest of the Spirit.

In the Greek of this sentence the word "God" is in a position of emphasis: "But it is *God* who fashioned us for this very thing",

---

[45]   Cf. also Irenaeus, *Adv. Haer.*, IV, xxxvi, 7: "He has made it clear that we ought, according to our calling, to be adorned with works of righteousness, so that the Spirit of God may rest upon us; for this is the wedding garment, of which also the Apostle speaks, 'We do not wish to be unclothed, but super-invested, so that what is mortal may be swallowed up by immortality' ".

[46]   "It is the *body*, therefore, that is in view through all these verses, the body which belongs to the present existence, and the body which is in reserve for the future existence ... The idea of an *interim* body, with qualities intermediate between the earthly body and the glorified body, is, as Meyer justly observes, something entirely strange to the New Testament" —S. D. F. Salmond, *The Christian Doctrine of Immortality* (Edinburgh, fifth edition, 1913), p. 453.

[47]   L. S. Thornton, *Christ and the Church*, pp. 129ff., even suggests that the white robes of Rev. 7:9, 13f., "represent the risen bodies of the saints", and that the fact that these are their own garments which have been washed and made white in the blood of the Lamb indicates not only the transformation of the earthly garment of the body, but also its continuity with the heavenly one.   The admissibility of this interpretation must, however, be regarded as extremely doubtful.

that is, for the ultimate investiture with the glorified body. Paul has been speaking of putting it on, but he now characteristically takes care to explain that this process of "clothing" is in no sense the product of man's workmanship. This, the crowning experience of God's work of grace in the believer, is entirely of God. The good work begun in the Christian by God will be carried through to completion by God, until it reaches perfection in the day of Jesus Christ (Phil. 1:6). Not only is everything attributed to grace, but it is towards this glorious goal that God's redemptive activity is all along directed. What confidence and certainty the assurance should give us that this work is altogether of God, and not in any measure of man! As it is *God's* work, it will be done. There can be no place for failure or frustration.

But we are doubly assured of this great reality, for we have not only the (so to speak) external assurance of the apostolic word, but also the internal assurance of the earnest of the Spirit (a genitive of apposition) which God has granted us here and now —we already have the deposit which guarantees the payment in full in due course.[48] Chrysostom rightly says that at creation man was fashioned by God, not for death, but for immortality. This purpose has been reaffirmed in the new creation through Christ, so that the consummation of redemption is also the fulfilment of God's will and plan in creation. The experience of this revolves around the gift of the Holy Spirit. The particular association of the Holy Spirit with the theme which the Apostle is here expounding is clarified by the significant statement of Rom. 8:11: "If the Spirit of Him who raised up Jesus from the dead dwells in you, He who raised up Christ Jesus from the dead will quicken also your mortal bodies through His Spirit that dwells in you". From this it becomes apparent that "the earnest of the Spirit" is not a mere static deposit, but the active vivifying operation of the Holy Spirit within the believer, assuring him that the same principle of power which effected the resurrection of Christ Jesus from the dead is also present and at work within him, preparing his mortal body for the consummation of his redemption in the glorification of his body. This earnest of glory is, further, bound up with the internal witness of the Spirit (*testimonium Spiritus*

---

[48] See the note above, 1:22, on the "earnest of the Spirit" (ἀρραβὼν τοῦ Πνεύματος).

Sancti internum) within the believer to his heirship with and in Christ: "The Spirit Himself bears witness with our spirit that we are children of God; and if children, then heirs, heirs of God and joint-heirs with Christ; if so be that we suffer with Him, that we may be also glorified with Him" (Rom. 8:15f.). This life-giving earnest of the Spirit explains, then, the daily renewal of the inward man which the Christian experiences and which is producing a weight of glory far in excess of the afflictions which he endures in the outward man (4:16, 17). On the believer's horizon there are no clouds: shadow and suffering there may be here, but it is all glory hereafter. There is nothing of which he is more certain, and he has this unshakable assurance because God has given him the earnest of the Spirit. It is the Holy Spirit who, as Paul says elsewhere, is "the earnest *of our inheritance*" (Eph. 1:14). "The future is never considered in the New Testament in a speculative fashion", observes Denney; "nothing could be less like an apostle than to discuss the immortality of the soul. The question of life beyond death is for Paul not a metaphysical but a Christian question; the pledge of anything worth the name of life is not the inherent constitution of human nature, but the possession of the Divine Spirit".

5:6–8

Being therefore always of good courage, and knowing that, whilst we are at home in the body, we are absent from the Lord (for we walk by faith, not by sight); we are of good courage, I say, and we are willing rather to be absent from the body, and to be at home with the Lord.

There is no question of the Apostle showing a craven face towards death. On the contrary, he is full of confidence because the earnest of the Spirit which he has received witnesses unfailingly to the indescribable glory that awaits all those who are Christ's. Despair, comments Tasker, is "an experience to which he does not submit; for to despair is to disown the Spirit, and to disown the Spirit is not to be a Christian at all". (In v. 6 the "therefore" points back to what has just been said, while the following clause "and knowing ..." adds a further ground of confidence. Hence it is wrong to understand "and" here as the equivalent of "because", as though giving the ground for the conclusion introduced by the preceding "therefore"—*sc.* we are confident because we know—as Chrysostom, Calvin, Olshausen, and others have taken it.) This confidence, moreover, is constant ("always"); it is not dependent on moods or circumstances, nor on whether the Lord comes before or after death; certainly not on a resigned stoical acceptance of whatever the future may bring.[49] The good courage that animates the Apostle is as permanent and serene as the Spirit dwelling within. And it is enhanced by the knowledge ("knowing") that to be at home in the body—that is, the present tent-dwelling, the metaphor of the preceding verses being maintained here in the idea of being "at home"—is to be away from our real home which is with the Lord, whereas to depart from the bodily tent (in death) is to go home to the Lord.[50]

By saying that while at home in the body we are absent from the Lord Paul is not moralizing, as though to suggest that those who feel "at home" in this life are not living close to Christ (true though this may be); nor does he mean to question the fact that in this life Christ is already very really present with believers, for the gift of the Holy Spirit ensures the Saviour's presence in every believing heart, and one of the great themes of the Pauline epistles is that of the mystical union of the believer here and now with Christ—Christ in me and I in Christ. It is precisely for the purpose of averting misunderstanding that the parenthesis of verse 7 is inserted: "for we are at present walking [51] by faith and not by appearance".[52] "This is manifest", says Ambrose, "because we are now with the Lord through faith, not through presence;

[49] The verb θαρρεῖν, to be of good courage, was popular with the Stoics.

[50] Ἐκδημεῖν means to be or go away from home, and thus to be abroad or to emigrate (cf. Herodotus, *Hist.*, I, 30, Sophocles, *Oed. Tyr.*, 114, Plato, *Laws*, 864E); ἐνδημεῖν, to live in a place or to be at home, is rare in classical literature.

[51] Περιπατοῦμεν, present tense, indicating our walk during this life.

[52] Οὐ διὰ εἴδους. The noun εἶδος applies to the thing seen, the form or appearance of an object, rather than to the act of seeing, sight, and accordingly, as Allo remarks, is not intended here as specifically opposed to faith, but is rather, in Hodge's words, "the object of faith, the form and fashion of the things believed". Thus Luke describes how the Holy Spirit descended on Christ at His baptism in bodily form (σωματικῷ εἴδει) (Lk. 3:22), and speaks also of the appearance of Christ's face (τὸ εἶδος τοῦ προσώπου αὐτοῦ) being altered at His transfiguration (Lk. 9:29), and John records how our Lord told the Jews that they had never seen the form or appearance of the Father (εἶδος αὐτοῦ) (Jn. 5:37).

176

and for this reason we are absent from Him, not in faith, but in appearance. ... For when we do not see Him, although He is present, we are absent from Him". In this life it is faith that gives reality to things which are still hoped for and assurance concerning things which are not yet seen (Heb. 11:1). Hereafter, however, "faith will vanish into sight". If absence from the body means to be at home with the Lord, then death cannot but be welcome, even though it involves a period of "nakedness" in a disembodied state. Hence, were there a choice between the present life in this body and departing in death to be at home with Christ, the Apostle would willingly choose the latter. But even more he would wish for his earthly tent-dwelling to be superinvested and absorbed by the habitation from heaven.

Again, there is no question of the Apostle courting death in a spirit of rashness. The wonder and sacredness of the ministry with which he had been entrusted never faded. It was a source of joy and encouragement to him (4:1); and he clearly saw himself as a runner with an earthly course *to finish*, not to abandon (see commentary below on 10:13ff. and cf. II Tim. 4:7), and a steward with a ministry *to accomplish* which he had received from the Lord Jesus, "to testify the gospel of the grace of God" (Acts 20:24; I Cor. 9:23ff.). His outlook is nowhere more aptly and tersely summed up than in the words which he wrote to the Christians at Philippi: "To me to live is Christ, and to die is gain"; and though it is true that he has "a desire to depart and be with Christ, which is very much better", yet he realizes, as he tells them, that "to abide in the flesh is more needful for your sake" (Phil. 1:21–23). We believe with Denney that "it would be an incalculable gain if we could recover the primitive hope in something like its primitive strength. It would not make us false to our duties in the world, but it would give us the victory over the world".

"Do you see", says Chrysostom, "how keeping back what was painful, the names of death, and the end, he has employed instead of them such as excite great longing, calling them presence with God; and passing over those things which are accounted to be sweet, the things of life, he has expressed them by painful names, calling the life here an absence from the Lord? Now this he did, both that no one might fondly linger amongst present things, but rather be weary of them, and that no one when about to die might be disquieted, but might rejoice even, as departing unto greater goods".[53]

5 : 9

Wherefore also we make it our aim, whether at home or absent, to be well-pleasing unto him.

"Wherefore"—that is, because of his desire to be with the Lord—it is only natural that Paul should also wish to live in such a way as to please Him. This, indeed, is his consuming ambition, the motive force behind all that he does.[54] To be well-pleasing to Christ is, indeed, the sum of all ambition which is truly Christian. In arresting contrast to the ambition of this world, it is centred, not on self, but on the Saviour; its goal is to please Him. Hence Paul's injunction to the Colossians: "Whatsoever ye do, in word or in deed, do all in the name of the Lord Jesus, ... heartily, as unto the Lord, and not unto men" (Col. 3:17, 23). And this is his ambition, "whether at home or absent"—that is, whether at Christ's parousia he is found still alive ("at home in the body") or, through the experience of death, in a state of "nakedness" ("absent from the

---

[53] The structure of the sentence (verses 6–8) as originally intended by Paul was probably as follows: θαρροῦντες οὖν πάντοτε, καὶ εἰδότες ὅτι ..., εὐδοκοῦμεν μᾶλλον, κτλ — "Being therefore always of good courage, and knowing that ..., we are willing rather, etc." But the characteristically spontaneous interpolation of an explanatory parenthesis arrested momentarily the sequence of thought, and so θαρροῦμεν δέ, though strictly redundant, is added indicating the resumption of the thought introduced by the participle θαρροῦντες at the beginning of the sentence. Θαρροῦμεν then becomes a main verb in series with εὐδοκοῦμεν, which is accordingly preceded by καί.

The phrase πρὸς τὸν Κύριον is probably an instance of that pregnant mode of thought which is characteristic of the Greek language, combining the idea of going to the Lord ('linear' motion) and that of being in His presence thereafter ('punctiliar' rest). It may, however, be an example of the usage which is found in Jn. 1:1, where the Word is spoken of as having been πρὸς τὸν θεόν (cf. I Jn. 1:2, πρὸς τὸν πατέρα), the notion being, it would seem, that of intimate fellowship with God. Some, for example J. Rendel Harris and C. F. Burney, have suggested that the expression is an Aramaism. For further comments and other New Testament references see J. H. Moulton, *Grammar of New Testament Greek*, Vol. II, p. 467, and C. F. D. Moule, *An Idiom Book of New Testament Greek*, pp. 52f.

[54] The verb φιλοτιμεῖσθαι means to love honour, and hence to be ambitious, to devote oneself zealously to a cause.

body"). That the Apostle is in no sense suggesting that the conflict between good and bad within the individual continues in the intermediate state between death and resurrection is confirmed in the next verse which declares that at the tribunal of Christ it is the things done *in the body* (that is to say, in this life as distinct from the disembodied intermediate state) which will be taken into account. Besides, as Filson points out, the idea "of the intermediate state as one in which moral striving and responsibility continue" is one which Paul "never elsewhere suggests; the thought here is rather that it is not important whether the final day finds us *at home* in the physical body *or away*, i.e., already separated from that body by death; what counts is that while we have time we should make every effort *to please* the Lord".

Alford rightly dismisses as "the most absurd" Meyer's merely literal interpretation of Paul's language as meaning "whether at home or on travel", the symbolism of the preceding verses being entirely disregarded. "But all else aside, *can he tell us where Paul's home was*, subsequently to Acts ix?" Alford inquires.

5:10

For we must all be made manifest before the judgment-seat of Christ; that each one may receive the things done in the body, according to what he hath done, whether it be good or bad.

Paul was no withdrawn mystic or cloistered visionary passively devoting his days to the rapt contemplation of the divine essence and the world to come. All that he writes is intensely practical and has vital bearings upon this present life. To have the glorious hope of being transformed into the likeness of Christ at His appearing in no way absolves us from responsibility for the manner in which we conduct ourselves now. If our deepest longing is for that consummating moment when we shall at last be transfigured into His image, then it should be our present concern to progress daily, by the grace of God, towards the goal of Christlikeness. Love for the Master because of His matchless love for us should be sufficient incentive for us to follow devotedly in His steps. But there is a further consideration, to which the Apostle draws attention here, namely, that even for the Christian there is to be a day of reckoning. We must all, apostles and the rest, whether living or dead at Christ's coming, be made manifest before the tribunal of Christ.

To be made manifest [55] means not just to appear, but to be laid bare, stripped of every outward façade of respectability, and openly revealed in the full and true reality of one's character. All our hypocrisies and concealments, all our secret, intimate sins of thought and deed, will be open to the scrutiny of Christ—a clear indication, incidentally, of the absolute Deity of the Redeemer, for it is only the divine gaze which penetrates to the very essence of our personality: "man looks on the outward appearance, but the Lord looks on the heart" (I Sam. 16:7). The conduct of our lives should constantly be influenced by the solemn remembrance that "there is no creature that is not manifest in God's sight, but all things are naked and laid open before the eyes of Him with whom we have to do" (Heb. 4:13; cf. I Cor. 4:5). In that day of manifestation both the hypocritical and the hypercritical will be shown for what they really are.

"Because much is required of those to whom much has been given", comments Tasker, "the thought of the judgment seat of Christ has for the Christian a peculiar solemnity. It is not meant to cloud his prospect of future blessedness, but to act as a stimulus". The incentive is to Christian living that is marked throughout by complete integrity, both in what is apparent and in what is not apparent to one's fellow-men, so that the outward, instead of concealing the inward person, corresponds to it. It is only in Christ, through the gracious operation of the Holy Spirit, that this wholeness of being, free from division and dissimulation, can be realized. "Let us then imagine Christ's judgment-seat to be present now", urges Chrysostom, "and reckon each one of us with his own conscience, and account the Judge to be already present, and everything to be revealed and brought forth. For we must not merely stand, but also be manifested. Do you not blush? Are you not dismayed?"

The tribunal of Christ serves the purposes of absolute justice. It vindicates the holiness and impartiality of God. It is a salutary reminder to the Christian that, although it is true that he has been justified by faith, and is no longer under law but under grace, yet the moral values of God's universe have not therefore

---

[55]   *Φανερωθῆναι.*

ceased to be his concern. On the contrary, it is precisely the Christian, on the fleshy tables of whose heart the law of God has been inscribed (3:3), whose life should display the fruit of moral consistency. In view both of the grace of God, whereby his body has been redeemed, and of the justice of God, in accordance with which "the things done in the body" will be recompensed, no service of his could be more reasonable than that in which he presents his body "a living sacrifice, holy, well-pleasing [56] to God" (Rom. 12:1). He is, indeed, under obligation to glorify God *in his body* (I Cor. 6:20).

The impartiality of Christ's tribunal is stressed by the assurance that each individual will receive as his own the things done in his body,[57] according to what he did,[58] whether good or worthless.[59] It is important to see that the purpose of this tribunal is not positively penal, but properly retributive, involving the

---

[56] Εὐάρεστον—the same adjective as Paul uses in our passage (verse 9): "we make it our aim . . . to be well-pleasing *(εὐάρεστοι)* unto Him".

[57] In the New Testament the middle κομίζεσθαι seems to have the particular meaning "to receive back" or "to receive what is one's own". For instances of the verb with this significance in the papyri see Moulton and Milligan. It is certainly a sense which is very appropriate in the context of our passage. There is an important variant reading which instead of διά has ἴδια, and which enjoys the support of early authorities (p46 Lat. (vt. vg.) Goth. Arm. Origen, Ambrosiaster, Cyprian, Theodoret, etc.). It is very probably the correct reading, and, if so, intensifies the retributive force of the verb κομίζεσθαι. The clause will then read: ἵνα κομίσηται ἕκαστος τὰ ἴδια τοῦ σώματος—"in order that each one may receive back *his own things of the body*" (Vulgate, *propria corporis*), instead of "the things (done) in the body" *(τὰ διὰ τοῦ σώματος)*. Whichever reading we adopt, the meaning is not affected.

[58] Πρὸς ἃ ἔπραξεν—"with reference to what he did". The aorist is interesting: looking back from Christ's tribunal, the whole life of the individual Christian is seen as a unity. This concept is strengthened by the rather unexpected addition in the neuter singular (following the neuter plural) of εἴτε ἀγαθόν, εἴτε φαῦλον—"whether it be good or whether it be worthless". "The change to the neuter singular is significant", says Plummer. It seems to imply that, although persons will be judged one by one and not in groups, yet conduct in each case will be judged as a whole. In other words, it is character rather than separate acts that will be rewarded or punished. It is a mistake to suppose that any act, however heroic, can secure eternal life. We must ask, not τί ποιήσας κληρονομήσω; (Lk. x. 25), but τί με δεῖ ποιεῖν; (Acts xvi. 30). It is habitual action that will be judged. And this explains the aorist; it is what he did during his lifetime that is summed up and estimated as a total".

[59] The proper meaning of φαῦλον.

disclosure not only of what has been worthless but also of what has been good and valuable in this life. The judgment pronounced is not a declaration of doom, but *an assessment of worth*, with the assignment of rewards to those who because of their faithfulness deserve them, and the *loss* or withholding of rewards in the case of those who do not deserve them. Commentators in general have spoken too facilely of punishments in connection with this tribunal of Christ, and in doing so have been in danger of falling out of harmony with Paul's thought. The Apostle is not suggesting here the punishment of sin, as though there were some imperfection in the justification imputed to the believer in Christ; for every believer is justified from all things (Acts 13:39) and "there is therefore now no condemnation to them that are in Christ Jesus" (Rom. 8:1). No more is he proposing a doctrine of merit as an aid or adjunct to justification, as though the Christian's ability to stand before God depended in some measure upon himself and not entirely upon the divine mercy and grace. Paul's meaning becomes admirably clear in the light of what he has already written to the Corinthians in his earlier letter: every believer is building upon the one foundation that has been laid, namely, Jesus Christ; upon this foundation he is secure for all eternity; but he is to take heed how he builds on this foundation, for his work of building will be made manifest [60] on "the day", that is, the day of Christ's tribunal. The picture used is that of a trial by fire, and the materials envisaged are such as are either destroyed by fire (wood, hay, stubble) or resistant to and indeed purified by fire (gold, silver, precious stones). The Christian whose work abides after the test will receive a reward, whereas he whose work is consumed will suffer loss—"but he himself shall be saved" (I Cor. 3:10–15). The declaration of Christ's judgment-seat is not the ultimate sentence of salvation or damnation; for it is the redeemed alone who stand before it, and their doing so results either, on the one hand, in their hearing the Lord's "well done" and the receiving of a reward, or, on the other hand, in their suffering loss, that is, through failing to receive a reward. The rewards themselves vary in proportion to the faithfulness and diligence of each individual (cf. Lk. 19:16ff.). All the implications and consequences of being made

---

[60] Φανερὸν γενήσεται, corresponding to φανερωθῆναι here.

manifest before the judgment-seat of Christ will not be known until the day itself arrives; but meanwhile the Christian is left in no doubt that he is regarded by God as fully answerable for the quality of his present life in the body.

It is worth remarking that a passage like this shows that, so far from there being discord, there is an essential agreement between the teaching of Paul and that of James on the subject of faith and works. The justification of the sinner, it is true, is by faith in Christ and not by works of his own; but the hidden root of faith must bring forth the visible fruit of good works. This fruit is expected by Christ, for it brings glory to the Father and is evidence to the world of the dynamic reality of divine grace. And it is especially in the bearing of *much* fruit that the Father is glorified (Jn. 15:8).

This passage indicates, further, both that the limits of this present earthly life ("the things done in the body") are, so far as the judgment-seat of Christ is concerned, the limits also of our time of opportunity and responsibility, and that there is a quite definite continuity between this earthly body and the future glorified body, however much the latter may transcend the former in splendour and power. Thus to certain heretics who affirmed that it is a different body which is raised Chrysostom offers the rejoinder: "How so? Tell me. Has one sinned, and is another punished? Has one done virtuously, and is another crowned?" Christopher Wordsworth also speaks to the same effect.

The appearance of an article on *II Corinthians v.* 1–10 *in Pauline Eschatology* by Dr. E. Earle Ellis in *New Testament Studies*, Vol. 6, No. 3 (April 1960), pp. 211ff., calls for some comment, especially in view of the author's contention that this particular passage "simply does not deal with the intermediate state". This is not the first time that this opinion has been propounded; and Dr. Ellis is, of course, fully justified in maintaining that if the analysis he offers is correct "II Cor. v. cannot be used at all to illustrate a changed Pauline theology of the intermediate state". "Paul's primary thought", he says, "is not of individual bodies at all, but of corporate solidarities which inhere in Adam and in Christ, the old aeon and the new aeon". He acquiesces in the judgment of Dr. J. A. T. Robinson that "whenever Paul uses the word οἰκοδομή (except in the purely figurative sense of 'edification'), it means the Body of Christ, the Church (I Cor. iii. 9; Eph. ii. 21; iv. 12, 16), not an individual body".[61] This conclusion, however, begs the question. The fewness of the other references shows that they cannot be determinative of the interpretation here, where, in our judgment, the context leaves no doubt that Paul is speaking of the individual body (cf. 4:7, "earthen vessels"; 4:10, "our body"; 4:11, "our mortal flesh"; 4:16, "our outward man"; 5:6, "at home in the body"; 5:8, "absent from the body"; 5:10, "the things done in the body").

If it is true that our Lord's prophecy in Mk. 14:58 "refers to the corporate body of Christ", it is true only in a secondary and as it were extended sense. In the apostolic understanding, which surely is decisive, the immediate and primary reference of this saying is to the individual body of Christ, as Jn. 2:21f. makes clear: "He spake of the temple of His body. When therefore He was raised from the dead, His disciples remembered that He spake this; and they believed the scripture and the word that Jesus had said". It was Christ's bodily resurrection on the third day that caused them to remember and understand and believe this word. Again, to maintain that "the 'tent-house' (II Cor. v. 2) envisions primarily not the individual self (although this is included) but the whole ἐν ᾿Αδάμ corporeity which stands under death" is to impose a theological doctrine (true and Pauline though it may otherwise be) which is not specifically present in this passage. We cannot doubt that Paul would explicitly have introduced the

---

[61] J. A. T. Robinson, *The Body* (London, 1952), p. 76.

teaching concerning the "corporate solidarities which inhere in Adam and in Christ" had it been his intention that his readers should understand this passage primarily in that sense.

Dr. Ellis's failure to mark any distinction in significance between the verbs ἐνδύειν (to put on) and ἐπενδύειν (to put on over or superinvest) is disappointing and exegetically unsatisfactory. It is precisely in the light of these compounds, together with the other cognate ἐκδύειν (to put off or divest), that the adjective γυμνός (naked) requires to be interpreted as descriptive of that state of nakedness which results from being divested at death of one's body, and we do not agree that this interpretation "presupposes an anthropological dualism". The exegesis of γυμνός as related to the fate of unbelievers who are "naked" before God, in the sense that they have no covering for their sin, is attractive, but, we believe, inapplicable to this passage because it is not the general eschatology of both believers and unbelievers that Paul has in mind here, but the particular eschatology of believers only, all of whom will be "made manifest before the judgment-seat of Christ" (v. 10)—a concept which should be distinguished from that of the judgment throne of God before which unbelievers will appear.

Another misconception is apparent in Dr. Ellis's enlistment of ἀλλαγησόμεθα ("we shall be changed") in I Cor. 15:52 in support of his view that at death "a psychosomatic organism ... envelops and pervades the whole personality and finds its fulfilment in the deliverance of the whole man at the resurrection"; for in I Cor. 15:52 Paul is not speaking of what happens *at death* but of that change which will be experienced at the sounding of the last trump, that is, at the parousia. Indeed, ἀλλαγησόμεθα in verse 52 applies, if anything, in particular to those Christians who are *alive* at Christ's coming, whereas ἀλλαγησόμεθα in verse 51 applies to all Christians, both those who have died and those who are alive, at that consummating event. In any case, what is the significance of resurrection for the dead except precisely the recovery of bodily existence which was lost at death—a psychosomatic union, however, of incomparable glory and power?

5:11

> Knowing therefore the fear of the Lord, we persuade men, but we are made manifest unto God; and I hope that we are made manifest in your consciences.

As the "therefore" shows, this verse must be interpreted in close connection with what has immediately preceded, namely, the teaching concerning the judgment-seat of Christ before which all believers will be made manifest. Paul himself has a deep consciousness [1] of the awe which should be inspired in the heart of every servant who will be required to give an account of his stewardship to his master. The recollection of this fact fills him with a wholesome reverence for his divine Master and causes him to treat the ministry which has been entrusted to him with the utmost seriousness. In the light of the ultimate realities of which he has been speaking every genuine follower of Christ should apply himself earnestly to "the perfecting of holiness in the fear of God" (7:1). By "the fear of the Lord", then, the Apostle does not mean that terror (A.V., Ambrose, Herveius, Beza) which the ungodly will experience when they stand before God's judgment throne (cf. Rev. 6:15ff.), but that reverential awe which the Christian should feel towards the Master whom he loves and serves and at whose hand he will receive "the things done in the body".

Accordingly, when Paul speaks of "persuading men" here he is not referring to the evangelical duty of warning the ungodly of the wrath to come and pleading with them (as in v. 20 below) to be reconciled to God,[2] but rather to the necessity which has regrettably been laid upon him of persuading certain members of the Corinthian church of the integrity of his personal character (see 1:12ff., 4:1f., 6:3ff., 7:2ff.) and of the authenticity of his status as their apostle (see 3:1ff., 10:1ff.). There is, indeed, a sense in which this whole epistle may be described as a vindication

---

[1] Εἰδότες.

[2] Πείθειν, "to persuade", is of course used in this sense in the New Testament (e.g., Acts 17:4; 18:4; 19:26; 26:28; 28:23).

of his genuineness in face of the false reports and calumnies that were being circulated about him.

While, however, the Apostle feels himself obliged to persuade men, because of their perversity and prejudice, of his personal uprightness and apostolic authority, yet there is no question of his having to persuade God, for his whole life, including the depths of his personality and the motives of his behaviour, lies open to God who discerns all things. Paul possesses that priceless and unassailable bulwark of the soul, the testimony of a clear conscience before God (1:12; cf. Acts 23:1, 24:16). He also has every reason to expect that he—that is, his true and integral self—has been and continues to be manifested [3] in the consciences of the Corinthians: whatever they or others might be saying about him, he believes [4] that in their heart of hearts they know that he is sincere and genuine. This corresponds closely to what he has already written: "... by the manifestation of the truth commending ourselves to every conscience of men in the sight of God" (4:2). If a man rebels against the truth as it is revealed in his conscience, he does so in the sight of God, his ultimate and inevitable Judge; for a man's conscience is not the source of calumnies and prejudices, but the seat of his awareness of the absolute demands of a holy God. As a man is in his conscience so he is before God. And what he knows in his conscience he knows with candour in sharp contrast to the hypocrisies and dissimulations which may disfigure his personality. Accordingly, the Apostle here appeals once again to the consciences of the Corinthian Christians: they really know, deep down, what God knows about him, namely, that his ministry is whole-hearted and free from duplicity.

5:12

> We are not again commending ourselves unto you, but speak as giving you occasion of glorying on our behalf, that ye may have wherewith to answer them that glory in appearance, and not in heart.

Paul realizes that what he has just written is likely to be seized on by his adversaries in Corinth and brandished by them

---

[3] This is the force of the perfect πεφανερῶσθαι.
[4] A common meaning of ἐλπίζειν.

as further proof (cf. 3:1) of arrogance and boastfulness on his part. Self-glorying is, however, as we have seen, far from the Apostle's mind. In fact, it is to his children in the faith at Corinth that he is giving [5] an incentive [6] to speak up boldy on his behalf in refutation [7] of those who were making false charges against him. If, as many commentators think, there is a suggestion of irony in what Paul writes here, the irony is not harsh but gentle, and tinged with disappointment that there should be any need for him to incite his own children in the faith to rally to his defence. Certainly, the false charges of his opponents could not harm him in himself, for he has a clear conscience before God (hence the absence of all self-concern); but they were harmful to the unity of the Church and hindered the progress of the apostolic ministry that had been entrusted to him. His concern, in brief, is not with what men may think or say about him, but with the well-being and edification of the Church of Christ. "We are taught here", says Calvin, "that Christ's servants ought to be concerned for their own reputation only in so far as it is for the advantage of the Church", and "that in the ultimate issue a minister's true praise is that which is common to him with the whole Church, rather than peculiar to him alone".

Paul is doing no more than remind the Corinthians that the knowledge which they have of him, both outwardly by personal acquaintance and inwardly through the testimony of their own consciences, is adequate for them to rebut the calumnies against his person of those "who glory in appearance and not in heart". By describing his opponents in this way the Apostle means, it

---

[5] Διδόντες—another instance of an absolute participle, used for the indicative. See note on 4:8 above.

[6] For the various meanings of ἀφορμή see Moulton and Milligan. "He is supplying them with an incentive to go proudly into the attack, and also with ammunition with which to fight, when they hear others running their apostle down. This interpretation", says Tasker, "is suggested by the word translated *occasion, aphorme*, which means both a starting point for an operation and the resources with which an operation can be launched".

[7] "Ἵνα ἔχητε πρός . . . , literally: "in order that you may have against . . ." The idiom is clear and means simply: "in order that you may have a rejoinder to or a refutation of those who glory in appearance and not in heart". It is unnecessary to supply καύχημα as the object of ἔχητε: "that you may have something to boast against those . . ." (Chrysostom, Alford, Hodge, Stanley), or ἀφορμήν: "that you may have this resource ready to your hand" (Plummer).

188

would seem, that their glorying is entirely outward and fails to correspond to their true inward state; they put on a bold face and appear to be thoroughly confident of the things which they teach, but in reality, in their hearts, they are anything but confident, and indeed care little for the spiritual issues which they profess to defend, for their glorying is only a façade, a pretence designed to impress and deceive men and directed towards their own material advantage. Paul's glorying, however, is not in things which the world might reckon to be to his advantage: the things which were, in this sense, gain to him he had counted loss for Christ (Phil. 3:7). His outward glorying, as this epistle repeatedly shows, is in his infirmities and sufferings, because it is precisely through them that the grace and power of God are magnified. Accordingly, his concern is not to serve self or to impress men, but to fulfil the ministry entrusted to him (Acts 20:24) in obedience to the heavenly vision (Acts 26:19). Unlike his opponents, then, his glorying may truly be described as "in heart and not in appearance"—deeply genuine and not superficial; for it is centred on Him who is Himself the Light and the Truth. And this should be true of all Christ's ministers.

Does not what Paul says in this verse afford an internal indication of the unity and coherence of this epistle? Allo offers the following comment: "It is plain, as Windisch has well observed, that this as yet vague allusion to a subject which will be treated with such great precision and emphasis in the concluding chapters shows that those chapters were not yet written. When they read or hear them the Corinthians will no longer need that "something by way of rejoinder" should modestly be suggested to them. The eagle is beginning to cast its gaze from on high on the martens and foxes; but the moment has not yet come to swoop down in vertical descent".

5:13

> For whether we are beside ourselves, it is unto God; or whether we are of sober mind, it is unto you.

Whatever his state or disposition, Paul, in contrast to his critics, is entirely free from self-interest: if in an ecstatic condition, it is to God; if sober-minded, it is for the Corinthians' sakes. The question as to what precisely Paul meant by being

189

beside himself, or in a state of ecstasy, is one which we are not in a position to answer with assurance. It is at least clear, however, that the two verbs which he uses [8] stand in contradistinction to each other as opposites, and it is also apparent that the former describes a state which is directed towards God, while the latter is related to those to whom he ministers. This is the only occasion on which the verb here translated "to be beside oneself" [9] is found in the epistles, and it does not occur at all in the Johannine writings. In the synoptic Gospels and Acts its most frequent meaning is "to be amazed" [10]. The same applies to the noun "ecstasy",[11] which occurs seven times in Mark, Luke, and Acts and in four of these instances means "amazement". On the remaining three occasions (Acts 10:10, 11:5, 22:17) it is used of a state of trance in which a vision is seen—a state, that is, in which the mind as it were stands aside from the body. The verb is also applied to those who make what are judged to be extravagant claims and who are therefore said to be beside themselves, in a state of hallucination or mental aberration. Thus we find that at a particular juncture of His ministry our Lord's relatives attempted to remove Him from the public scene on the ground that He was beside Himself,[12] that is, mentally deranged —a charge which was supplemented by the scribes from Jerusalem who declared that He was Satan-possessed (Mk. 3:21ff.).

In our present passage the verb is in the aorist tense, and some commentators have therefore taken it to point back to a particular event in the past, the most likely of which would be Paul's experience of conversion on the Damascus road; his rivals in Corinth might have suggested that on that occasion he was the victim of a great hallucination and had then gone out of his mind. Less probable is the proposal that it refers to the ecstatic experience, mentioned in 12:1ff., of being caught up to the third heaven and hearing unspeakable words. This, however, was essentially a *private* experience, not mentioned elsewhere nor commonly known, and concerning which he uses the most guarded and indeed cryptic terms.

---

8   'Εξέστημεν and σωφρονοῦμεν.
9   'Εξίστημι.
10   In the middle voice—a usage which is not classical.
11   "Εκστασις.
12   'Εξέστη, Mk. 3:21.

It is more likely, however, that the verb, rather than referring to some past event or experience, conveys an allegation concerning Paul's present state of mind.[13] This is how it is understood by the majority of scholars, and it would indicate that the Apostle, as had been the case with his Master before him, was said by his enemies to be out of his senses. On a later occasion the Roman procurator Festus would make a similar charge ("Paul, you are mad;[14] much learning turns you to madness." [15]); though this must be distinguished from the present case in that Festus, unlike Paul's critics at Corinth, did not profess to be a Christian and also because the accusation had reference only to the gospel which Paul preached, and not, as far as we can judge, to anything exceptional in the Apostle's behaviour. Accordingly, it is a charge which he immediately repudiates: his proclamation of the gospel to others, whether Festus or the Corinthians, is essentially sober-minded ("I am not mad,[16] most excellent Festus, but speak forth words of truth and soberness" [17]). In other words, Paul's preaching of the gospel is at all times thoughtful, intelligible, balanced, directed to the mind as well as to the heart, and entirely free from any suggestion of "mania" or "ecstasy".

Yet, though his evangelism is marked by sobriety, he does not here reject the charge of "ecstasy"; and this would suggest that there was indeed another side to the Apostle which his opponents seized on in order to insinuate that there existed a contradiction in his personality—that his was a Jekyll-and-Hyde character. The hypothesis that this charge of mental aberration (if such it was) was connected with the epilepsy to which some have supposed the "thorn in the flesh" of 12:7 to refer [18] is in our opinion quite unacceptable. Apart from other considerations, it is a case of building an hypothesis on an hypothesis. We prefer to understand it as an accusation of *religious mania*: it was objected

---

[13] Ἐξέστη in Mk. 3:21 provides an exact parallel, which J. H. Moulton explains as a timeless aorist, perfect in force: "he has gone out of his mind" (*Grammar of New Testament Greek*, Vol. I, p. 134). In our passage, the present tense of the Vulgate conveys the same sense: *Sive enim mente excedimus.*

[14] Μαίνη.

[15] Μανίαν. Acts 26:24f.

[16] Οὐ μαίνομαι.

[17] Σωφροσύνης.

[18] On the significance of the "thorn in the flesh" see commentary on 12:7 below.

that Paul went to extremes, that he was unbalanced, fanatical, senseless (cf. 11:1, 16), that he courted hardships and hazards beyond all reason (cf. 11:16ff.), that his conduct was characteristic of the religious maniac. "If this is madness and fanaticism", says Paul in effect, "then I acknowledge myself to be mad and fanatical—but it is a matter between me and God; what concerns you is the undeniable fact that I was sober-minded in bringing you the good news of Jesus Christ and in all my dealings with you".[19]

5 : 14, 15

For the love of Christ constraineth us; because we thus judge, that one died for all, therefore all died; and he died for all, that they that live should no longer live unto themselves, but unto him who for their sakes died and rose again.

The objectivity and therefore the disinterestedness of Paul's outlook is nowhere better seen than in this passage. The great compelling motive force in his life since conversion is that of love; not, however, love originating, far less ending, in himself, but the love which originates and ends with God in Christ. His conduct, however it be judged, is dictated by the love of Christ (not so much his love for Christ—though that inevitably is involved—as Christ's love for him, which is prior to and the explanation of his love for Christ, and which is supremely manifested, as is clear from what immediately follows, in Christ's atoning sacrifice of Himself for mankind). It is this love (*agape*) and none other, that shuts him in, confines him as between two walls,[20] to one purpose which may be summed up in the terms of the preceding verse as being to live selflessly "unto God" and, within the framework of that supreme allegiance, to his fellowmen ("unto you"). "God has the first word", says Stauffer. "It is He who founds the relationship. That is established once for all in Romans viii. His design, His choice, His calling—these are decisive. All that Agape can mean proceeds from Him. When men love God, that is the immediate reflection of the love

---

[19] Plummer observes that "all that is certain is that ἐξέστημεν refers to exceptional, and σωφρονοῦμεν to ordinary conditions, and that these two cover the whole of his behaviour, which, therefore, is never self-seeking".

[20] Συνέχει.

which streams down from heaven upon the elect".[21] The constraining power of the divine love of Christ is the explanation of another famous statement of Paul's: "To me to live is Christ" (Phil. 1:21); it is the logic which demands his willingness to suffer the loss of all things for Christ's sake; and it is the reason for his overmastering ambition to win Christ, to be found in Christ, and to know Christ (Phil. 3:7ff.). In Christ, his Redeemer and Lord, lay the deep springs of all his conduct.

The Apostle, however, is not speaking merely of the response of love to Love, as though the spectacle of the cross were sufficient by itself to move us to repentance and faith. The theology of salvation is far more profound than that. The death of Christ for us has an inner consequence which can be understood only in terms of substitution; and this consequence is tersely propounded by Paul when he declares: "One died for all, therefore all died". This is his considered judgment, the conclusion he had reached,[22] the rational ground of his security in Christ. Although it is true that the preposition "for" or "on behalf of"[23] does not by itself necessarily convey the idea of substitution, yet this sense is fully appropriate when the context requires it, and Paul's language here has meaning only if it is understood in this sense. The substitutionary force of the preposition here is plainly indicated by the conclusion, "therefore all died"; for this conclusion cannot be valid except on the understanding that Christ died in the stead of all, as their substitute. On this ground alone is there justification for speaking as Paul does here of a logical identification of all with Christ in His death; and on this ground alone is there an adequate explanation of the constraining power of Christ's love. To interpret Christ's death as being merely exemplary or in some general sense as for the advantage of man, as an assurance of God's good will notwithstanding man's rebellion, is to destroy the mainspring of the Apostle's argument.[24]

---

[21] E. Stauffer, *Love* (No. I in the series of *Bible Key Words* from Kittel's TWNT, London, 1949), p. 56.

[22] The aorist participle κρίναντες properly points to a judgment formed in the past, perhaps at or soon after his conversion.

[23] Ὑπέρ.

[24] Categorical statements to the effect that ἀντί is the only "substitutionary" preposition and is used no more than once in the New Testament of Christ's sacrifice (MK. 10:45 = Mt. 20:28), and that ὑπέρ is not and cannot be a

In the scheme of salvation the doctrine of Christ's vicarious atonement for man's sin is of cardinal importance. It is central in the soteriology of the New Testament, and, as is generally acknowledged, is an essential element of Paul's teaching in this passage. Thus Tasker says that "Christ's death was the death of all, in the sense that He died the death they should have died; the penalty of their sins was borne by Him; He died in their place". "There can be little doubt", observes Strachan, "that the words *One has died for all* bear a substitutionary meaning. . . . Paul means that Christ bore voluntarily a doom that should have been ours". Denney comments: "Plainly, if *Paul's* conclusion is to be drawn, the 'for' must reach deeper than this mere suggestion of our advantage: if we all *died*, in that Christ died *for* us, there must be a sense in which that death of His is *ours*; He must be identified with *us* in it: there, on the cross, while we stand and gaze at Him, He is not simply a person doing us a service; He is a person doing us a service *by filling our place and dying our death*". That Christ died on behalf of all means, affirms Alford, "not only, for the *benefit* of all, as Meyer,—but *instead of* all, suffered death in the root and essence of our humanity, as the second Adam". "Taking a body like our own", writes Athanasius, clearly with this passage in mind, "because we all were liable to

---

"substitutionary" preposition, argue for prejudice rather than detachment. The context in which a word occurs cannot be ignored. As Plummer says, "the ideas of representation and substitution easily run into one another, as in ἵνα ὑπέρ σοῦ μοι διακονῇ (Philem. 13), and in the formula, which is frequent in papyri, ἔγραψα (or ἔγραψεν) ὑπὲρ αὐτοῦ, the nominative of the verb being the name of the scribe who wrote the letter for some person who was unable to write". See examples given in Moulton and Milligan. In classical literature, there is an interesting and significant passage in Euripides in which ὑπέρ is used repeatedly with a substitutionary meaning—that of dying instead of someone else: ὀφείλω δ' οὐχ ὑπερθνῃσκειν σέθεν . . . μὴ θνῇσχ' ὑπὲρ τοῦδ' ἀνδρός . . . κατθανεῖν . . . ὑπὲρ σοῦ (*Alcestis*, 682, 690, 700f.). The relevance of this usage to the New Testament doctrine with which we are concerned is obvious. Other references will be found in Liddell and Scott and in Arndt and Gingrich. In I Tim. 2:6, where Paul is propounding the same doctrine as here, ἀντί and ὑπέρ are used conjointly: Christ Jesus "gave Himself a ransom for all" *(ἀντίλυτρον ὑπὲρ πάντων)*. Commenting on our verse, Olshausen says: "The ὑπέρ plainly stands here = ἀντί, for only upon this supposition does the ἄρα κ.τ.λ. acquire significance"; and Bishop Wordsworth asserts: "It is unquestionable that ὑπέρ is sometimes used to signify *in the stead of* by St. Paul . . . St. Paul's argument here would fail if ὑπέρ does not signify *in the place of*". Cf. also the note below on 5:20.

the corruption of death, He surrendered His body to death instead of all,[25] and offered it to the Father. This He did out of sheer love for us, so that, as all died in Him, the law relating to the corruption of men might be abolished." [26]   And again: "The death of all was consummated in the Lord's body, and both death and corruption were utterly destroyed through the Word who was present in it; for death there had to be, and death for all,[27] so that the debt of all might be paid. Wherefore, as I said before, the Word, since it was not possible for Him to die, assumed a body that was capable of dying, so that He might offer it as His own in place of all".[28]

The two aorist verbs—"One died ... all died" [29]—point back to the one event, namely, the crucifixion of Christ. A passage which is complementary to this is Rom. 5:12ff., where the Apostle teaches that when the *one* man, Adam, sinned death, the penalty of sin, passed on to *all* men on the ground that *all* sinned,[30] that is, were identified with Adam in his sin. In the case of both Adam and Christ, one action has had consequences of universal significance, and the involvement of all men in the action of each is a real involvement. As Thomas Goodwin has quaintly said: "There are but two men standing before God, Adam and Christ, and these two men have all other men hanging at their girdles" [31] (cf. I Cor. 15:22). The same aorist occurs in Col. 3:3 ("you died" [32]) and, in a much more extended context, in Rom. 6:1–11 (which, of course, supplements the argument of Rom. 5:12–21). In Paul's doctrine the death of Christ has a twofold significance for the believer, which is implicit in the verses we are considering: firstly, Christ died *for* me (cf. Rom. 5:6, 8), and, secondly, I died *with* Christ (cf. Rom. 6:8). On His dying for me, His meeting the demands of God's justice in my stead, depends the reality of my justification; and on my dying with Him depends the whole

---

[25]   Ἀντὶ πάντων.

[26]   Athanasius, *De Incarn.*, VIII.

[27]   Ὑπὲρ πάντων.

[28]   Ἀντὶ πάντων. Athanasius, *op. cit.*, XX.

[29]   Ἀπέθανεν ... ἀπέθανον.

[30]   Πάντες ἥμαρτον—the aorist points back to the one original sin of Adam, and is parallel to the aorist here *(πάντες ἀπέθανον)* which points back to the one event of the death of Christ.

[31]   Thomas Goodwin,   quoted from memory;   reference not located. I am indebted to the Rev. John Kidd for calling my attention to a passage where Goodwin speaks to the same effect, namely, *Christ set forth in His Death, Resurrection*, etc. (1651), p. 38.

[32]   Ἀπεθάνετε.

195

possibility of my sanctification. He who died with Christ must reckon himself to be dead to sin, but, in Christ Jesus the risen Lord, alive unto God (Rom. 6:6, 11). So also here: He died for all so that we should no longer live to ourselves (the old self-life having been crucified with Him on the cross), but unto Him who for our sakes died and rose again. This theme, so fundamental to all the Apostle's thinking and acting, is admirably summed up in the notable affirmation of Gal. 2:20: "I have been crucified with Christ; it is no longer I who live, but Christ lives in me; and the life I now live in the flesh I live in faith, the faith which is in the Son of God who loved me and gave Himself up for me".

In the New Testament the death of Christ is always, and necessarily, associated with His resurrection. Death without resurrection spells only hopeless defeat; a dead saviour is a contradiction in terms. Only a risen, victorious Saviour has the power to communicate His redemption to those on whose behalf He has acted. Accordingly, Paul speaks here of living unto Him who died and rose again for our sakes.[33] "By the sacrifice of His body He did two things", says Athanasius: "He put an end to the law of death which barred our way; and He made a new beginning of life for us, by giving us the hope of resurrection".[34] The implications of Christian baptism are closely bound up with the teaching we have been considering. They are well brought out in the following prayer from the baptismal service in the Book of Common Prayer of the Church of England: "... humbly we beseech Thee to grant, that he, being dead unto sin, and living unto righteousness, and being buried with Christ in His death, may crucify the old man, and utterly abolish the whole body of sin; and that, as he is made partaker of the death of Thy Son, he may also be partaker of His resurrection; so that finally, with the residue of Thy holy Church, he may be an

---

[33] There has been some dispute as to whether the phrase ὑπὲρ αὐτῶν in the expression τῷ ὑπὲρ αὐτῶν ἀποθανόντι καὶ ἐγερθέντι should be connected with both ἀποθανόντι and ἐγερθέντι, or with the former alone. Some, indeed have held that it is incorrect to speak of Christ rising for us. While it is possible, technically, to limit the words "for them" to the nearer participle ἀποθανόντι, yet as the Greek reads it is more natural to associate them with ἐγερθέντι as well. Rom. 4:25, where the Apostle speaks of Jesus as having been "delivered up for (διά) our trespasses and raised for (διά) our justification", may be adduced as a corresponding and fuller doctrinal statement.

[34] Athanasius, ut supra, X.

inheritor of Thine everlasting kingdom"; and, more concisely, in the exhortation that "as He [Christ] died and rose again for us, so should we, who are baptized, die from sin and rise again unto righteousness".

5 : 16

Wherefore we henceforth know no man after the flesh: even though we have known Christ after the flesh, yet now we know him so no more.

The consequence ("wherefore") of what Paul has just said, namely, that Christians no longer live to self but to Him who died and rose again for them, is that he now knows nobody according to the flesh. "Henceforth" doubtless means from the time when he formed the judgment or conclusion expressed in the preceding two verses, that is, the time of his conversion and enlightenment by the Holy Spirit. His knowledge, by which he means his appraisal and acknowledgment, of persons is no longer, as it once was, after the flesh—in other words, in accordance with the estimate formed of people by the unregenerate man and by the world in general. The world's standard of value is respect of persons in their outward appearance (cf. v. 12 above, "that glory in appearance and not in heart"). But with God there is no such respect of persons [35] (Rom. 2:11; Eph. 6:9; Col. 3:25); and it follows that the faith of our Lord Jesus Christ is not to be held with respect of persons (Jas. 2:1). In the teaching of Paul the flesh (in its ethical, not its material, connotation) is the antithesis and the enemy of the Spirit (Gal. 5:16ff.). Between the two there is a sharp dividing line separating mankind into two distinct categories according as a person's conduct and standard of values is dictated either by the flesh or by the Spirit. Hence Paul declares that "they that are after the flesh mind the things of the flesh, but they that are after the Spirit the things of the Spirit" (Rom. 8:5). Typically worldly distinctions, such as those of race, social status, wealth, and title, should no longer govern the Christian's estimate of his fellow-men (cf. Gal. 3:28). This, surely, was the lesson our Lord wished to teach when, on being told that His mother and brethren were seeking to speak

---

[35] Προσωποληψία (cf. ἐν προσώπῳ, verse 12)—acceptance of persons because of their outward showing.

with Him, He stretched out His hand towards His disciples and said: "Behold, My mother and My brethren! For whosoever shall do the will of My Father who is in heaven, he is My brother, and sister, and mother" (Mt. 12:46ff.). The absolutely vital question, as the next verse shows, is whether a person is a new man in Christ Jesus. Yet it is sadly possible for those who profess the faith of Christ to estimate others according to the flesh; for this fault Paul had found it necessary to rebuke the Corinthians when writing to them on a previous occasion: they had shown themselves to be carnal, "fleshly",[36] conducting themselves after the manner of unregenerate men,[37] indeed, in their schismatic jealousy and strife, followers of men, albeit apostles (I Cor. 3:3ff.). And the calumnies urged against him by the false apostles who have invaded Corinth in his absence have obliged him to protest, in our present epistle, that his intentions are not according to the flesh (1:17).

But what does Paul mean when, in one of the most arresting sentences of the New Testament, he affirms that even if he has known Christ according to the flesh yet now he no longer knows Him in this way?[38] In the Greek, the construction[39] indicates that he concedes as a fact what he states in hypothetical form: "even if, as is indeed the case, I have known Christ after the flesh ..." The question then arises as to the sense in which Paul wished it to be understood that he had formerly known Christ "after the flesh". Does his language imply that he had actually seen and had some form of contact with Christ during His earthly ministry? There is no inherent impossibility in such a contingency, and it has been variously suggested that Paul when a disciple of Gamaliel in Jerusalem (see Acts 22:3) must have enjoyed ample opportunity for hearing Jesus and even meeting with Him, that he had been a witness of the crucifixion of Christ, or that he was the rich young ruler who had questioned Christ (Mk. 10:17ff.).

---

[36] Σαρκικοί.

[37] Κατὰ ἄνθρωπον.

[38] It is unnecessary to seek for an exegetical explanation of the change from οἴδαμεν in the preceding clause to ἐγνώκαμεν here; the reason may be seen in the fact that οἶδα, a defective verb, is perfect in form but present in force, with the result that when it is desired to express a perfect force γινώσκω has to do duty, as here. It is only natural that as ἐγνώκαμεν has been used in the protasis γινώσκομεν should follow in the apodosis, rather than οἴδαμεν.

[39] Εἰ καί + the perfect indicative. See note on 4:2 above.

But, whether or not Paul had had some such personal contact with Jesus in the past, the significance of what he says here is determined by the immediate context: prior to his conversion his knowledge of Christ had been after the flesh, formed in accordance with external and mistaken standards; but his conversion had meant the transformation of his knowledge of Christ. A man in Christ is a creature entirely renewed, for whom the old judgments after the flesh have become a thing of the past (v. 17). He now knows Christ as He truly is.

We reject as altogether incongruous with all that we know of Paul the view of Baur, Stanley, and others that this verse indicates that during the earlier part of his ministry—and therefore subsequently to his conversion—the Apostle had held and propounded opinions concerning Christ which later he had abandoned, that his outlook had been narrow and nationalistic, similar in this respect to the outlook of the Pharisees of whose party he had once been a zealous adherent, but that he had experienced a "second conversion" whereby he was led to embrace a view of the gospel as universal in scope and to set aside his strong Jewish prejudices as being "after the flesh". This supposed second conversion of Paul is justly dismissed by Allo as "pure imagination, unsupported by a single word, properly understood, of the Epistles or Acts". Our knowledge of the Apostle, from his remarkable conversion on the road to Damascus onwards, militates against it. One of the purposes of this present epistle is, as we have seen, to remind the Corinthians of the constancy and consistency of his life and doctrine; and there is his own very emphatic declaration in Gal. 1:6ff. that there is only *one* gospel, which he had received not from man but through revelation of Jesus Christ and which he had faithfully proclaimed ever since his conversion. Paul had never preached "a different gospel" nor had he ever during the course of his ministry believed that there was "another gospel".

Contemporary theologians of the dialectical and existentialist camps have pressed this verse into service as a support for their depreciation of objective historical truth. The great acts and facts of the Christ of history are treated by them (in so far as they accept them at all) as peripheral rather than central to the essence of Christianity; judgments of value must rest upon experience that is subjective, existential, and of the present moment; "Christ-after-the-flesh",[40] that is, according to this interpretation, Christ considered as an objective figure of the past, is not and cannot be known by modern man and therefore is irrelevant to him. But that such a meaning was very far from Paul's mind is plain from all his writings and not least from the concluding section of this present chapter (vs. 18 to 21). For him, Christian truth, involving all the facts of Christ's person and work, is in the first place, *a priori*, objective; the truth as it is in Christ Jesus confronts mankind as an objective reality initiated and revealed by God who is its Author. The subjective (existential) experience of this truth through the grace of the Holy Spirit always and necessarily follows upon a prior apprehension of the objectivity of redemption as an act of God within history.

Among the factions in the Corinthian church there was a "Christ" party, led, presumably, by some who claimed to have known Christ during the period of His earthly ministry and who prided themselves on this as though it constituted a right to superior status in the Christian Church (cf. I Cor. 1:12ff.). It may well be that the leaders of this particular faction were identical with the false apostles who had infiltrated the ranks of the Christians in Corinth and that they had alleged Paul's failure to follow Christ during His earthly ministry as a ground for challenging his apostolic authority. Their attitude, however, was that of men who glory in what is merely outward and superficial, and, for Paul, their claim was, in itself, not only beside the point, but quite valueless. The fact, that, in our judgment, the radical change in his thought concerning Christ is specifically related to the crisis of his conversion need not, as some commentators have held, eliminate any reference to a personal contact with Christ prior to Good Friday. On the contrary, it seems to us that such a reference is implicit in what Paul says here, but that, being an element in his former knowledge of Christ after the flesh, he cannot regard it as a matter of consequence. It is a rejoinder to those who have sought to discredit him by alleging that he had no first-hand knowledge of Christ, and also at the same time an exposure and repudiation of their

---

[40] Associating κατὰ σάρκα closely with Χριστόν, although it goes far more naturally with the verb ἐγνώκαμεν. As the more general statement in the first half of the verse shows, Paul is talking of *knowing* after the flesh: this refusal to know after the flesh extends even to his knowledge of Christ.

false standards of judgment.   To have known Christ in this way was a guarantee of nothing.   Great numbers had followed Christ in person who afterwards deserted Him and demanded His crucifixion.   Even the privileged inner circle of His disciples, despite their intimate association with the Master, had failed to grasp the true significance of what He taught them; their knowledge of Him was distorted by misconceptions and by this-worldly considerations.   They wrangled among themselves as to who was to be given the place of honour in His kingdom; Peter who had confessed Him so remarkably was also the one who denied Him; Judas, who had enjoyed equal privileges of intimacy with Christ, betrayed Him to His enemies; and all fled at His arrest.   Their knowledge of Christ *in* the flesh, pregnant with blessing though it was, was far from being unmixed with knowledge of Him *after* the flesh.   It was not until the great enlightenment of Pentecost that they at last came to know Him fully after the Spirit.   Then we find them no longer dull of understanding, cowardly, despondent, of little faith, but wise in the things of God, bold, outspoken, and full of joy and power.   To know Christ after the flesh, in accordance with the standards of this world, is not to know Christ at all.   Paul, like Peter and like Thomas, had to learn that it is not having seen Christ, nor knowing *about* Him, that matters, but loving Him and believing on Him (I Pet. 1:8; Jn. 20:29).   Our Lord's accusation against the Pharisees who criticized Him with such rancour was that they had no real knowledge of Him, precisely because they judged Him after the flesh (Jn. 8:14f.).   The same had been true of Paul, the proudest and most prejudiced of them all, until that unforgettable moment when he encountered Jesus as Saviour and acknowledged Him as Lord (Acts 9:4ff.).

5:17

Wherefore if any man is in Christ, he is a new creature: the old things are passed away; behold, they are become new.

Paul now propounds a further consequence ("wherefore", *cf.* preceding v.) of the Christian's identification with Christ in His death and resurrection (vv. 14, 15): not only does he no longer know any man according to the flesh (v. 16), but also as a man-in-Christ he is in fact a new creation—a reborn microcosm belonging to the eschatological macrocosm of the new heavens and the new earth—for whom the old order of things has given place to a transcendental experience in which everything is new. The expression "in Christ" sums up as briefly and as profoundly as possible the inexhaustible significance of man's redemption. It speaks of security in Him who has Himself borne in His own body the judgment of God against our sin; it speaks of acceptance in Him with whom alone God is well pleased; it speaks of assurance for the future in Him who is the Resurrection and the Life; it speaks of the inheritance of glory in Him who, as the only-begotten Son, is the sole heir of God; it speaks of participation in the divine nature in Him who is the everlasting Word; it speaks of knowing the truth, and being free in that truth, in Him who Himself is the Truth. All this, and very much more than can ever be expressed in human language, is meant by being "in Christ". No wonder that the Apostle describes it in absolute terms as a "new creation". Redemption in Christ is nothing less than the fulfilment of God's eternal purposes in creation, so radical in its effects that it is justly called a new creation (cf. 4:6 where Paul has already related the enlightenment of regeneration to the activity of God at creation). In the experience of this new creation the standards and pretensions of this world sink into insignificance. Hence Paul tells the Galatians that, through the cross of our Lord Jesus Christ, the world having been crucified to him and he to the world, former distinctions, such as that between circumcision and uncircumcision, are of no consequence, but only a new creation (Gal. 6:14f.). And to the Ephesians he says, combining the two concepts of "in Christ" and "new creation" in a single phrase: "We are His workmanship, *created in Christ Jesus* for good works, which God afore prepared that we should walk in them" (Eph. 2:10). Again, a Christian is one who has "put on the new man which is after God", in contrast to the old man which is after the flesh, "created in righteousness and holiness of truth" (Eph. 4:24). These considerations lead us to think that the most effective rendering of the first part of our verse is given in the R.V. (= R.S.V.) margin: "Wherefore if any man is in Christ, there is a new creation".[41]

---

[41] The Vulgate, Tertullian (*Adv. Marc.*, V. 12), and some others impair the force of this verse by including καινὴ κτίσις in the protasis of the condition and making τὰ ἀρχαῖα παρῆλθεν the apodosis, thus: *si qua ergo in Christo nova*

When Paul declares that for the Christian old things have passed away, the tense of the verb (aorist) [42] points back to a definite moment or event, namely, the experience of the new birth. It is then that the old things—the distinctions, prejudices, misconceptions, and enslavements of the former unregenerate way of life—assume the character of pastness. "Behold, they are become new": note the tense again (this time perfect) [43], indicating that the old things became and continue to be new; for the newness of God's new creation is not a newness that in course of time palls and grows old and outmoded; it is a newness that is everlastingly new.

The exclamation "behold!" sounds an unmistakeable note of spontaneous jubilation. In its "sudden note of triumph", says Denney, "we feel, as it were, one throb of that glad surprise with which he (Paul) had looked out on the world after God had reconciled him to Himself by His Son". This response of delight and wonderment cannot fail to be evoked in the hearts of those to whom the miracle of God's new creation is revealed. It is present in prediction—"Remember ye not the former things, neither consider the things of old: behold, I will do a new thing!" (Isa. 43:18f.)—and it is present in fulfilment—"The first things are passed away. ... Behold, I make all things new!" (Rev. 21:4f.). And meanwhile it is present in the hearts of all who, though still in this world, have already become by God's grace members of the world to come.

It should be noticed, too, that while the new is so different from the old that the latter can be said to have passed away, yet there is a radical continuity between them, so that it is also possible to say that the old has become new. This truth, which, as we have already seen, applies to the relationship between the believer's present earthly body and his future glorified body, operates on a cosmic scale. The redeeming work of Christ is effective not only in the experience of the believer but also

---

creatura, vetera transierunt (Vg) — "If therefore there is any new creation in Christ, the old things have passed away".

[42] Παρῆλθεν. The verb παρελθεῖν is used elsewhere in the New Testament in connection with the passing away of an old order and its replacement by a new order; see Mt. 24:35; II Pet. 3:10. In Rev. 21:4 the verb is ἀπελθεῖν (τὰ πρῶτα ἀπῆλθαν).

[43] Γέγονε.

throughout the whole order of God's creation: the consummation of all things is not merely a renewed humanity, but new heavens and a new earth, a renewed cosmos. The believer, in his capacity as the re-created man-in-Christ, is the dynamic guarantee that all God's purposes in creation are unfailingly being brought to full fruition.

5 : 18

> But all things are of God, who reconciled us to Himself through Christ, and gave unto us the ministry of reconciliation.

As in the original creation all things were brought into being by the Word of God, so also in the new creation God through His Son, who is The Word, is the sole Author of all things. "Nothing is of ourselves", says Chrysostom in a fine passage; "for remission of sins, and adoption, and unspeakable glory are given to us by Him. ... But, behold, a new soul (for it was cleansed), and also a new body, and a new worship, and new promises and covenant and life and table and dress, and all things absolutely new. For instead of the Jerusalem below we have received that mother city which is above, and instead of a material temple we have seen a spiritual temple; instead of tables of stone, fleshy tables; instead of circumcision, baptism; instead of the manna, the Lord's body; instead of water from a rock, blood from His side; instead of Moses' and Aaron's rod, the Cross; instead of the promised land, the kingdom of heaven; instead of a thousand priests, one High Priest; instead of a lamb without understanding, a spiritual Lamb. ... But *all* these things are of God by Christ, and His free gift." Paul's words here confirm that God is not only the Initiator but also the Finisher of our faith (Heb. 12:2): it is *He* who reconciles us, and it is *to Himself* that He reconciles us. Reconciliation proceeds from God and returns to God. Thus all begins and ends in God. And all is performed *through Christ*, who is the sole Mediator between God and men (I Tim. 2:5), with the result that it is by Him alone that we may come to the Father (Jn. 14:6) and in His name alone that there is assurance of salvation (Acts 4:12). These are essential elements in the message of reconciliation.

The need for this message is seen against the background of man's alienation from God; and the cause of this alienation is, in a word, sin. By sin man sets himself in rebellion against God; he becomes an enemy of God. It is not a question of some minor misunderstanding which could easily be put right; it is a case of mutiny, and mutiny of a kind far more radical in its nature and effect than anything that is known in purely human relationships; for the essence of sin is seen in the desire of the creature to set himself up in the place, not of another creature, but of his Creator, the wish to be even as God, the attempt to place himself, instead of God, at the centre of reality as the arbiter and controller of all things. Sin is the revolt of man both against God his Creator and also against his own constitution as creature.

But man's rebellion, though it is the originating factor, is not the sole factor in the alienation between man and God: it is met and matched by the wrath of God against sin. God, in other words, is not the helpless victim of the mutiny of man. His supremacy as sovereign Governor of the universe is unimpaired, and His government of it is in conformity with those absolute moral principles which constitute an essential framework of an orderly world. It is of particular importance to emphasize that the wrath of God is by no means a contradiction of the love of God. For God to have permitted sin to flourish unchecked and unpunished, and passively to have watched the world degenerate into a dung-heap of corruption and violence, would have been very far removed from an expression of love, apart from the fact that it would have argued the impotence of His purposes in creation and the incompetence of His hand to control the affairs of men, which would mean in turn that He was not God at all. Those who speak sentimentally of the love of God as though it were incompatible with the wrath of God show that they have entirely failed to grasp the realities of the situation.

The rebellion of man, however, is also met and matched by the love of God in Christ Jesus. If there is no wrath of God against sin, then the love of God in Christ Jesus is deficient of all moral content; the Cross, however sentimentally it may be viewed, then becomes an exhibition of cruelty and injustice, which as such cannot be the action of a truly loving, let alone perfectly holy, God. But when the Cross is seen to be the place where God-become-Man bears for man and as Man the sin of man, endures the just penalty of sin, and therefore exhausts the wrath of God against sin, and all this because of God's surpassing

205

love for man, then alone will it be seen that at the Cross love and wrath meet in a common purpose, that mercy combines with truth and righteousness and peace kiss each other (Psa. 85:10; Rom. 3:26).

In Christ God's holy and loving work of reconciliation has been accomplished once and for all.[44] It is because the way of reconciliation now stands wide open that the ministry of reconciliation has been committed by God to His servants. There is no service to mankind more crucial and urgent than the exercise of this ministry. As God does not cease to be the sovereign Creator and man does not cease to be His creature in desperate need of redemption, and as all things are of God who, even while we were yet enemies, graciously acted on our behalf (Rom. 5:10), this ministry with its message of reconciliation is, in the ultimate issue, the *one thing needful* for our world in all circumstances and in every generation.

5:19

> To wit, that God was in Christ reconciling the world unto himself, not reckoning unto them their trespasses, and having committed unto us the word of reconciliation.

The expression "to wit, that ..."[45] introduces the terms of the ministry of reconciliation and shows in particular that it is a ministry of proclamation, involving the announcement to the world of a message of good news, the declaration of what God in His royal grace has done for the rescue of His fallen creatures.

---

[44] Its unique and once-for-all character is implied in the aorist participle καταλλάξαντος.

[45] ῾Ως ὅτι is an unusual combination, which is found again in 11:21 and II Thess. 2:2. Winer (ed. W. F. Moulton) says that when ὡς is immediately followed by ὅτι, "ὡς properly indicates that the clause with ὅτι expresses the thought of another, a thought which is merely reported, or even feigned". This certainly seems to be the force of ὡς ὅτι in II Thess. 2:2: "We beseech you ... that ye be not troubled ... as that (ὡς ὅτι = as by a report that) the day of the Lord is now present"; and possibly also in II Cor. 11:21: "I speak by way of disparagement, as though (as by a report that) we had been weak" (but see the note on 11:21 below). Lightfoot, commenting on II Thess. 2:2 (*Notes on the Epistles of St. Paul*, p. 110), renders ὡς ὅτι by "representing that"; the ὡς, he says, "points to the subjective statement as distinguished from the objective fact, and thus this idea of untruth is frequently implied". But he refers to our present verse as evidence that this is not in-

Christ's ministers are, in fact, His *messengers*: declarers of reconciliation, not agents of it. Hence Paul speaks here of the *word* of reconciliation which God has deposited [46] in His ministers. This divine act of depositing implies two things: firstly, that those who minister have themselves been made recipients of the grace of reconciliation, and, secondly, that they are under obligation to proclaim that grace to the world (cf. Rom. 1:14ff.; I Cor. 9:16). Paul's fondness for the term "word" (*logos*) as a synonym for the message of the gospel (cf., for example, Eph. 1:13," ... having heard the word of truth, the gospel of your salvation"; Col. 1:5," ... the word of the truth of the gospel"; I Cor. 1:18," ... the word of the cross") and John's application of the term to Christ as a title (Jn. 1:1, 14; cf. Rev. 19:13) take on extra significance in view of the consideration that in Greek thought *logos* indicates what is true and trustworthy as opposed to the term "myth" (*mythos*) which is descriptive of what is fictitious and spurious. Socrates, for example, declares that a particular story is "no fictitious myth but a true logos".[47] Hence the term "logos" carries with it, like a kind of overtone, the implication of truth and genuineness, and is accordingly peculiarly appropriate as a synonym for the gospel, which is "the word of truth".

There has never been unanimity as to how the opening clause of this verse should be understood. It may be taken to mean either (i) that "God was in Christ, reconciling the world to Himself" (Origen, Ambrose, Ambrosiaster, Herveius, Erasmus, Luther, Calvin, Beza, Bengel, Bachmann, Allo, etc.), or (ii) that "in Christ God was reconciling the world to Himself" (Chrysostom,

---

variably the implication. In our verse the force seems to be directly epexegetic or declarative of what has immediately preceded: " ... the ministry of reconciliation, namely, that ..." (cf. A.V., R.V., "to wit, that"; A.R.S.V., "that is"), or even more literally, "how that ..." (Alford). J. H. Moulton draws attention to the fact that "in the vernacular at a rather later stage it meant merely 'that' " (*Grammar of New Testament Greek*, Vol. I, p. 212). The Vulgate has *quoniam quidem* here, thus giving ὡς ὅτι a quasi-causal force: "since" or "because". In this it has been followed by many commentators. It has even been conjectured, despite the absence of any textual evidence, that the ὅτι was originally a marginal explanation of ὡς which later became incorporated in the text.

46　Θέμενος ἐν ἡμῖν means "having deposited in us"; cf. Vulgate, *posuit in nobis*, and R. V. margin, "placed in us".

47　Plato, *Timaeus*, 26E.

Theodoret, Theophylact, Estius, Meyer, Alford, Olshausen, Hodge, Denney, Plummer, Strachan, Filson, R.S.V. mg., etc.). We need not here examine the arguments which have been put forward by either side concerning the possible or probable associations and significances of the words which constitute the Greek text. Of the alternatives mentioned above, the former would convey the interpretation that in reconciling the world to Himself God the Father was not only acting through Christ, as an instrument (see previous v.), but was also *in* Him, united with Him in being and act. God-in-action on our behalf is essentially God-in-Christ. The unanimity of Father and Son flows from their eternal unity (Jn. 10:30), and on the fact that Christ acting for us is no less than God acting for us hangs the whole efficacy and security of our salvation. "It is", says Allo, "this presence of God in Christ, in the man Jesus, which gives to the sacrifice of the cross its infinite value; the doctrine of redemption depends on that of the hypostatic union, a doctrine with which these verses are impregnated". Denney, however, maintains that "it is safe to say that 'God was in Christ' is a sentence which neither St. Paul nor any other New Testament writer could have conceived". The merits of this assertion need not be discussed here; but he, and others who with him favour the second of the alternatives given above, lay stress on the past tense of the verb and understand it to point back specifically to the completed historical event on which our reconciliation depends; in other words, the verb "was" is not regarded as standing alone, but is closely associated with the participle "reconciling" in a periphrastic construction, giving the sense that God, at the historic moment of the Cross, was reconciling the world to Himself in Christ who suffered there for us.

Thus Paul effectively emphasizes the identity of Christ's work with God's work. Here, as before, God is still viewed as the end as well as the beginning of reconciliation: it is He who reconciles, and He does it to Himself; but the scope of the reconciliation is now extended from "us" (previous v.) to "the world". This should not be understood in the sense of an indiscriminate universalism, nor is it legitimate to interpret it narrowly, as Augustine does,[48] as having reference only to the

---

[48] Augustine, *In Joann.*, Tract. LXXXVII, 2, 3; CX, 4.

elect who have been predestined to salvation. The implication is, rather, that reconciliation is *cosmic* in its effects: it is applied in the first place to mankind; but since man, as the crown of God's creation, in his fall brought a curse upon the subordinate realm also, so in man's restoration the whole created order (*cosmos*) will also be restored. What the first Adam dragged down the second Adam raises up. This grand perspective of reconciliation is more explicitly affirmed in Col. 1:20, where Paul declares that it is God's purpose through Christ "to reconcile all things unto Himself, having made peace through the blood of His cross, ... whether things upon the earth or things in the heavens". The method whereby this is achieved is now briefly mentioned by the Apostle: "not reckoning unto them their trespasses" (a statement which is further explained in v. 21). The pronoun "them" (which corresponds to the pronoun "us" in the previous v.) indicates again that the cosmic rehabilitation is brought about through the salvation of fallen mankind. This God effects, not by overlooking the trespasses of men, for His mercy cannot be vindicated by injustice, but by *not reckoning* their trespasses to them. There is a reckoning of sins; they are reckoned, however, not to the sinner but to Christ, the sinner's substitute. In the truest sense, for the man in Christ old things have passed away; his sin and its judgment have been borne by Jesus the Lamb of God who takes away the sin of the world (Jn. 1:29).

5:20

> We are ambassadors therefore on behalf of Christ, as though God were entreating by us: we beseech you on behalf of Christ, be ye reconciled to God.

An ambassador acts and speaks not only on behalf of but also in the place of [48] the sovereign from whom he has received

---

[48] The preposition used on both occasions in this verse is ὑπέρ. That it may not unnaturally bear a vicarious sense, "in the place of", is shown not only by the appropriateness of this sense to the context but also by the fact that a Greek father like Chrysostom understood ὑπὲρ Χριστοῦ here to mean "in the place of Christ", ἀντὶ τοῦ Χριστοῦ (see the fuller note on v. 14 above). Many other commentators point out the appropriateness of this sense here; for example, Herveius: *pro Christo, id est, vice Christi*, and Alford who renders it "in Christ's stead". A.V. has "in Christ's stead" in the second instance only.

his commission. It is his duty to proclaim faithfully and precisely the message entrusted to him by his sovereign. Accordingly there is a real sense in which the voice of the ambassador may be said to be the voice of the sovereign he represents. Here, therefore, Paul boldly urges this analogy: when Christ's ambassador entreats it is equivalent to the voice of God entreating through him. His message, his authority, his power are all imparted to him by his Lord. Paul, however, is not proposing an analogy which only more or less fits the situation; what he says here is factual: Christ's messengers are really His ambassadors; God does actually entreat through them.[50] It is, moreover, evident, once again, as Allo remarks, that the Apostle makes no difference between Christ and God, Christ Himself being the Second Person of the eternal Godhead.

The message of reconciliation is not something which Christ's ambassador announces with impersonal detachment. He has been entrusted with vital news for people in desperate need. It is for this reason that he *beseeches* his hearers. We cannot fail to detect the strong note of urgency and compassion in the Apostle's language. He sees men as God sees them, in a lost state; he has the word which, because it is a word of reconciliation, above all else they need to hear; and, because he is proclaiming what God in His mercy and grace has already done for them in Christ, his voice has the authority of the voice of God. As with Paul, "so", says Origen, "would we in the same spirit and language earnestly desire to be ambassadors for Christ to men, even as the Word of God beseeches them to the love of Himself, seeking to win over to righteousness, truth, and the other virtues those who, until they receive the doctrines of Jesus Christ, live in darkness about God and in ignorance of their Creator".[51]

It is generally assumed that Paul is addressing the words of

---

[50] Plummer translates ὡς here as "seeing that", pointing out that ὡς with the genitive absolute may be used to express a view the correctness or otherwise of which is shown by the context. In I Cor. 4:18, I Pet. 4:12, and Acts 27:30 the view expressed is the wrong one, and is fittingly introduced by the translation "as though". In II Pet. 1:3, however, a factual statement is made, hence "seeing that" (R.V.) is in this case an appropriate rendering of ὡς. Plummer accordingly suggests "seeing that" for ὡς here. The force then is: "We are ambassadors for Christ, seeing that God does in fact entreat through us".

[51] Origen, *Contra Celsum*, VIII, 1.

this verse in a particular manner to the Corinthians, as though, because of their misdemeanours, they were in need of a fresh experience of reconciliation. Hence Stanley even speaks (though in a relative sense) of a "second conversion" which Paul, so he thinks, desired for them, and Hodge points to the daily need of the believer "to avail himself of the offer of peace with God through Jesus Christ". Similarly, Calvin explains that the Christian, as he daily sins, must turn to Christ for daily remission. Hence also the insertion in the English versions of the pronoun "you", although it is not present in the Greek text, implying that Paul intended his appeal specifically for the members of the Corinthian church. In our judgment, however, this is a mistaken interpretation. At this point the Apostle is concerned with the ministry of reconciliation for the world at large rather than with its application to the special circumstances of the church in Corinth. He is referring, not to the requirements of believers, but to the evangelistic duty of Christ's ambassadors to go into all the world and announce the good news of reconciliation to every creature, pleading with men to receive as their own what God has freely provided in His Son. His specific appeal to the Corinthian believers comes shortly, in the first verse of chapter 6, but not here. For the present, the concise economy of the terms in which he effectively describes his universal missionary entreaty is best reproduced without resort to the introduction of inessential pronouns, as follows: "We beseech on behalf of Christ: 'Be reconciled to God!'"

5:21

Him who knew no sin he made to be sin on our behalf; that we might become the righteousness of God in him.

In these few direct words the Apostle sets forth the gospel of reconciliation in all its mystery and all its wonder. There is no sentence more profound in the whole of Scripture; for this verse embraces the whole ground of the sinner's reconciliation to God and declares the incontestable reason why he should respond to the ambassadorial entreaty. Indeed, it completes the message with which the Christian ambassador has been entrusted. To proclaim: "Be reconciled to God" is not good news unless it is accompanied by a declaration of the ground on which reconciliation has been effected and is available. Preaching from which

211

the exposition of this ground is omitted is neither scriptural nor evangelical. Thus it is important to see that the statement of this verse is an inseparable part of the announcement made by Christ's ambassador and must not be isolated from the immediately preceding exhortation of the previous verse: "Be reconciled to God: [ground] Him who knew no sin God made sin for us in order that we might become the righteousness of God in Him". The true nature of this ambassadorial ministry of reconciliation is admirably explained by Calvin in his *Reply to Cardinal Sadolet*: "Then" (that is, when a man has been brought under conviction of his sin and its deserts), he writes, "we show that the only haven of safety is in the mercy of God, as manifested in Christ, in whom every part of our salvation is complete. As all mankind are, in the sight of God, lost sinners, we hold that Christ is their only righteousness, since, by His obedience, He has wiped off our transgressions, by His sacrifice appeased the divine anger, by His blood washed away our stains, by His cross borne our curse, and by His death made satisfaction for us. We maintain that in this way man is reconciled in Christ to God the Father, by no merit of his own, by no value of works, but by gratuitous mercy".

Christ is described here as not having known sin. The significance of this is made clear in other New Testament passages, especially Heb. 4:15 ("one that hath been in all points tempted like as we are, yet without sin"), I Pet. 2:22 ("... who did no sin"), I Jn. 3:5 ("in him is no sin"), and Heb. 7:26 ("holy, guileless, undefiled, separated from sinners"). The sinlessness of which these passages speak refers to our Lord's incarnate life. To wish, as some commentators (Windisch, for example) have done, to move it back to His pre-existent state prior to the incarnation is not only unwarranted but also pointless. That as God He is without sin goes without saying; but what is of vital importance for us and our reconciliation is that *as Man*, that is, in His incarnate state, Christ knew no sin, for only on that ground was He qualified to effect an atonement as Man for man. Nor is the sinlessness of Christ merely a verdict pronounced by His followers *post eventum* (though that it was an integral part of the apostolic *kerygma* is apparent from what Paul says here and from the other passages to which we have alluded); it was a fundamental element of His own human consciousness. To His adversaries He issues the challenge: "Which of you convicteth me of sin?" (Jn.

212

8:46). Both at His baptism and on the mount of transfiguration the voice from heaven declares: "This is my beloved Son in whom I am well pleased" (Mt. 3:17, 17:5). His freedom from sin is the secret of His unbroken unity and fellowship with the Father—"I and the Father are one", "I am in the Father and the Father in me" (Jn. 10:30, 14:10f., 17:11, 21f.). Even His earthly judge had perforce to protest publicly that he found no fault in Him (Lk. 23:4, 14, 22). And those who witnessed His dying— the malefactor crucified at His side, the centurion standing by the cross, and also the gazing multitude—were constained to testify to His blamelessness (Lk. 23:41, 47, 48). Only He who had completely and uninterruptedly obeyed the law of God was fitted to suffer the punishment due to those who have wilfully disobeyed that law. Only He who was entirely without sin of His own was free to bear the sin of others. And only God-become-Man could achieve this unblemished victory over Satan and death for our fallen and rebellious race. Such a Mediator was absolutely essential for our reconciliation to God. None other could suffer for our sins, "the Righteous for the unrighteous, that He might bring us to God" (I Pet. 3:18). As Bengel says, He alone, who did not know sin, had no need of reconciliation, whereas we, who did not know righteousness, were bound to be destroyed unless reconciliation were found. It is found in Christ who stood in our place so that His righteousness might be exchanged for our sin. Chrysostom, indeed, graphically expounds "Him who knew no sin" as signifying "Him who was Righteousness-Itself" [52] (cf. Acts 3:14).

God, declares Paul, made the Sinless One sin for us. It is important to notice that he does not say that God made Him a *sinner*; for to conceive of Christ as sinful, or made a sinner, would be to overthrow the very foundation of redemption, which demands the death of an altogether Sinless One in the place of sinful mankind. But God made Him *sin*: that is to say that God the Father made His innocent incarnate Son the object of His wrath and judgment, for our sakes, with the result that in Christ on the cross the sin of the world is judged and taken away. In this truth resides the whole logic of reconciliation. The believer's security, moreover, is fully summed up in the brief expression

---

[52] Αὐτοδικαιοσύνη.

"in Him", which the Apostle uses here. As it is on Him that the full force of God's judgment against sin has fallen, so it is *in Him*, our Ark, that the sinner finds shelter from that judgment. It is *in Him*, precisely because He is Righteousness-Itself, that the sinner is made the righteousness of God. "He was wounded for our transgressions, He was bruised for our iniquities, the chastisement of our peace was upon Him, and with His stripes we are healed; ... and Jehovah hath laid on Him the iniquity of us all" (Isa. 53:5f.)—that is the meaning of Christ's having been made sin for us. Not for one moment does He cease to be righteous, else the radical exchange envisaged by the Apostle here, whereby our sin is transferred to Him and His righteousness is transferred to us, would be no more than a fiction or an hallucination.

It should be noticed, further, that, just as Paul does not say that Christ was made sinful, but sin, for us, so also he does not say that in Him we are made righteous, as though henceforth untouched by sin, but *righteousness*, indeed, even more expressly, the righteousness *of God*—that righteousness, namely, which, being of God, is complete and inviolable for evermore. It is, in a word, the sinner's *justification* of which the Apostle is speaking, whereby our trespasses are reckoned to Christ and the absolute and spotless perfection of His righteousness is reckoned to us, with the consequence that "there is now no condemnation to them that are in Christ Jesus" (Rom. 8:1). Justification, indeed, does not preclude sanctification, whereby the believer increasingly becomes that which judicially he already is; on the contrary, justification presupposes sanctification; and the two become one at last in the consummating experience of glorification. But meanwhile they must be kept distinct, since the former is instantaneous and complete, while the latter is gradual and progressive. And both are in Christ our Righteousness.

Although it is perfectly true that Christ as the Lamb of God was a sin-offering (a doctrine which in particular is elaborated in the epistle to the Hebrews), yet it is not legitimate to interpret "Him who knew no sin He made to be sin" as meaning that God made Christ a sin-offering. This rendering was favoured by Ambrose, Augustine, Cyril of Alexandria, Herveius, Erasmus, and others, who had in mind passages such as Lev. 4:24ff., Num. 8:8, Psa. 40:6, and possibly Gen. 4:7 where the Hebrew word for sin [53] may mean "sin-offering". That this is not a permissible rendering of the Greek term here is evident, firstly, from the fact that the noun, which occurs twice in this clause, must mean the same on both occasions and cannot mean sin-offering on the former ("Him who knew no sin ..."), and, secondly, from the fact that on the latter occasion ("... made to be sin") the term "sin" corresponds antithetically to "righteousness" in the following clause, which again would not be congruous if "sin" meant "sin-offering". For the same reasons, "sin" can, on the second occasion, mean neither "flesh", as the seat of sin (Gregory of Nyssa), nor "sinner" (Meyer and others).

There is, of course, no question of the Son being an unwilling victim of the Father's wrath. Not only is such a thought scandalous; it is also entirely foreign to the teaching of Scripture. The freedom of Christ's action and the harmony of mind and purpose which He enjoyed with the Father are concisely conveyed in the words of Psa. 40:7f., which are applied to our Lord in Heb. 10:7ff.: "Lo, I come to do Thy will". His emptying is voluntary *self*-emptying; His humiliation, *self*-humiliation (Phil. 2:7f.). The power of dying and living rests in His own hands: "Therefore doth the Father love me, because I lay down my life, that I may take it again. No one taketh it away from me, but I lay it down of myself. I have power to lay it down, and I have power to take it again" (Jn. 10:17f.). There is, and can be, no tension within the Godhead, no disturbance of the divine unity.

It is plain, finally, that reconciliation is the result of expiation. Forgiveness follows satisfaction. Restoration is achieved through the vicarious endurance of punishment. The cross, therefore, is not an exhibition that all is well, but the proof that all is not well, and the place where God in pure grace and mercy deals with the surd of sin in a manner commensurate with His own holiness and justice. "The New Testament at least cannot sever Atonement from Reconciliation", writes P. T. Forsyth. "The greatest passage which says that God was in Christ reconciling says in the same breath that it was by Christ being made sin for us. The reconciliation is attached to Christ's death, and to that as an expiation. For reconciliation there means more than changing the temper

---

[53] חטאה = LXX ἁμαρτία.

of individuals; it means changing the relations between God and the race".[54] And of this same verse Denney speaks as follows: "It is not the puzzle of the New Testament, but the ultimate solution of all puzzles; it is not an irrational quantity that has to be eliminated or explained away, but the key-stone of the whole system of apostolic thought. It is not a blank obscurity in revelation, a spot of impenetrable blackness; it is the focus in which the reconciling love of God burns with the purest and intensest flame".

6:1

> And working together with him we entreat also that ye receive not the grace of God in vain.

The words "with him" are not in the original, with the result that the question as to precisely with whom Paul envisaged himself as a fellow-worker has been open to dispute. Some commentators (for example, Chrysostom, Theodoret, Bengel, Olshausen, Bachmann, Allo) take it to mean the Apostle working together with the Corinthian believers—that is, "working together *with you* ..."—and therefore an expression of humility and graciousness on his part. Others, however, (for example, Herveius, Alford, Godet, Hodge, Stanley, Weiss, Denney, Plummer, Tasker) understand Paul to mean "working together *with God*"—an interpretation which is also favoured by the English versions (in which the insertion "with him" = either "with God" or "with Christ"). This latter interpretation is to be preferred. For one thing, it is matched by what Paul has said in his previous letter to the Corinthians: "We are God's fellow-workers" (I Cor. 3:9)[55], which shows that the concept of working together with God was not foreign to Paul's thought. For another thing, and more particularly, it harmonizes better with the context: he has just said (5:20) that his ambassadorial delivery of the gospel message was in effect *God entreating* through him; now he adds: "working together (with God who entreats) *I also entreat* you...", in this way emphasizing the co-operation of the minister with God in the work of evangelical entreaty. The former entreaty

---

[54] P. T. Forsyth, *The Cruciality of the Cross* (2nd edn., London, 1948), p. 68.
[55] The terminology is cognate: I Cor. 3:9, Θεοῦ γάρ ἐσμεν συνεργοί. II Cor. 6:1, συνεργοῦντες.

was to receive the grace of reconciliation; whereas the present entreaty is to receive that grace in such a way that it is not received in vain.

But, it may well be asked, is it really possible for the grace of God, once received, to prove ineffective and fruitless? and if so, precisely in what sense does Paul envisage such a possibility? This is an important question, and there are four different answers which merit consideration. (1) Paul has in mind a receiving of God's grace which is not genuine but, so to speak, merely external. It was just such a possibility that our Lord Himself spoke of when, in the parable of the good seed, He taught that there are some who hear and receive the word of the kingdom with joy, and who yet, having no root, that is, having received it only in a superficial manner, fall away in times of difficulty and persecution (Mt. 13:20f.). It is unlikely, however, that the Apostle is thinking here in terms of a spurious profession of faith or of final perseverance. (2) Olshausen, indeed, seizes on this verse as proof that Paul "unquestionably considers the possibility of the grace received by the individual being again lost", and goes on to make the extraordinary declaration that "the dangerous error of predestination, which asserts that grace cannot be lost, is unknown to Scripture"—a declaration which can only have been dictated by prejudice, since wherever else the doctrine of predestination may be unknown it is certainly not unknown in Scripture, and least of all in the writings of the Apostle Paul! In any case, Paul is not speaking at this point of predestination but of human responsibility. That the grace of salvation once bestowed could thereafter have been abandoned would, for Paul, have been unthinkable. The work of God in the believing heart, precisely because it is the work *of God*, cannot fail and come to nothing. It is this which explains Paul's confidence, when writing to the Philippian Christians, that God who had begun a good work in them would carry it through to perfection until the day of Jesus Christ (Phil. 1:6). Nor is such teaching peculiar to Paul, for it is in complete harmony with that of the other apostles, as also with that of Christ Himself who so plainly affirmed that to His sheep He gives eternal life and that they shall never perish and no one shall snatch them out of His hand (Jn. 10:28). The everlasting life, which is so frequently promised in the New Testament to the believer, is with singular inappropriateness described as everlasting if it may be lost and thus, in those who have enjoyed and then lost it, does not after all last for ever. (3) Hodge understands Paul's entreaty in this verse not as directed to the Corinthians in particular, but (conformably with the terms of 5:20f. which immediately precede) as part of his proclamation of the message of reconciliation to mankind in general, so that his entreaty not to receive the grace of God in vain is equivalent to an exhortation to all men "not to reject this great salvation". It must be objected, however, that "to receive in vain" is not the same thing as "to reject", for the former expression necessarily implies that a receiving does take place,[56] whereas on Hodge's premises "to reject" means not to receive at all. The personal pronoun "ye" which is now introduced (it was absent from the original in 5:20), and which in the Greek is in an emphatic position, would seem to indicate, moreover, that it is the members of the Corinthian church whom Paul is now specifically addressing. (4) The explanation which in our judgment is most satisfactory, and which seems best to fit the broad context in which this verse is found, is that Paul is here thinking in terms of the judgment-seat of Christ, before which the works of every Christian will be made manifest (5:10). He had brought the Corinthians the full and glorious gospel of reconciliation, and they had believed that Christ who knew no sin was made sin for them that they might become the righteousness of God in Him; but false apostles had come into their midst, who had made merchandise of the word of God (2:17), corrupting their minds from the simplicity and purity that is toward Christ, preaching another Jesus whom Paul did not preach, and proclaiming a different gospel—"a gospel", says Paul, "different from that which you received" (11:4).[57] For them to receive the grace of God in vain meant that their practice did not measure up to their profession as Christians, that their lives were so inconsistent as to constitute a denial of the logical implications of the gospel, namely, and in particular, that Christ died for them so that they might no longer live to themselves but to

---

[56] The force of the aorist infinitive δέξασθαι may well be present, but, as Plummer says, "the aorist may have the force of a past tense", in which case "the reference is to the time of their conversion."

[57] 'Εδέξασθε—the same verb as here, where he is exhorting them not to receive, or to have received (δέξασθαι), the grace of God in vain.

His glory (5:15). This is a matter of which Paul had written more fully and graphically in his earlier letter: as recipients of the grace of God they were securely placed upon Jesus Christ, the only foundation, but they were in danger of building on that foundation with wood, hay, and stubble—a structure which would be made manifest and destroyed in the day of the Lord, though they themselves will be saved (I Cor. 3:10–15). It is in this sense that the grace of God may be received in vain. The Apostle goes on to remind them with what care under every circumstance he seeks to ensure that his own practice is consistent with his profession, his personal conduct with his public ministry; but first he interposes a quotation from the Old Testament.

6:2

For he saith, At an acceptable time I hearkened unto thee, and in a day of salvation did I succour thee: behold, now is the acceptable time; behold, now is the day of salvation.

"He saith", that is, *God* says, for Isa. 49:8, from which the first part of this verse is quoted, is introduced by the words: "Thus saith Jehovah".[58] The quotation in its present setting may be applied in a variety of ways: firstly, to the Corinthians who in receiving the message of reconciliation had proved the reality of God's grace in Christ Jesus and His readiness to attend to their prayers; secondly, to Paul who in carrying the gospel to Corinth had experienced the power and help of God as sinners responded to his preaching; and, thirdly, to Christ Himself concerning whom, as the Servant of Jehovah, the words of Isa. 49:8 were originally spoken. The quotation, accordingly, serves to remind the Corinthian believers of those wonderful days of repentance and conversion when they had received the gift of salvation under Paul's ministry, of the demonstration of Spirit and of power that had accompanied his preaching, weak though he was in himself (I Cor. 2:3f.), and of the transforming reality of the Saviour, God's Accepted One, in whom they had then trusted. In the

---

[58] Λέγει without a stated subject is comparatively frequent in the epistles (cf. Rom. 9:25, 10:8, 15:10, Gal. 3:16, Eph. 4:8, 5:14, Heb. 8:8, 13, Jas. 4:6), φησίν less so (cf. I Cor. 6:16, Heb. 8:5), and may mean either "He (God) says" or "it (Scripture) says", being practically equivalent, as Plummer observes, to inverted commas.

faithful discharge of his apostolic office Paul, the servant of the Servant, had made himself their servant, and they had been brought into the participation of the eschatological messianic kingdom and all its blessings. This is a fact which, being a fact of their own experience, none of them could deny.

Paul drives home this truth by adding a comment of his own to the quotation: "Behold, now is the acceptable time; behold, now is the day of salvation",[59] thereby explaining and calling the attention of the Corinthians to the fact that they themselves, through his ministry and their response, possessed first-hand knowledge of the actual fulfilment of this ancient prophecy. The "now" is the season of this present age of grace, bounded, on the one hand, by the advent in humiliation of the incarnate Son and, on the other, by His future coming in glory. It is the gospel "now", the "now" of the new man in Christ, the "now" of their own rebirth.

Plummer suggests that "acceptable" here means acceptable *to man*, and cites in support Lk. 4:19: "... to proclaim the acceptable year of the Lord", where he says "acceptable" has this meaning. In holding this opinion, however, he is almost certainly wrong. Lk. 4:19 is a quotation of Isa. 61:2 where the Hebrew means "the year of acceptance to Jehovah" or "Jehovah's year of grace",[60] and in our present verse, too, the original of which it is a quotation (Isa. 49:8) means "in a season of acceptance" or "in a season of grace".[61] Paul's thought must be interpreted in accordance with the consistent viewpoint of Scripture that the gospel era is a season acceptable *to God* because it is the "day of salvation" *appointed by Him*. The acceptability of this time is dependent, not on the uncertainties of human nature, but on the firm decree and gracious activity of Almighty God. The fact that it is God's appointed period of grace places man in a position of favour and opportunity, which is at the same time a position of answerability; not only is he called upon to be reconciled to God, but he is also to attend to it that he does not receive God's grace in vain.

---

[59] E. E. Ellis, *Paul's Use of the Old Testament* (Edinburgh, 1957), p. 143, regards this verse as an example of the employment by Paul of the *pesher* method, whereby the quotation of a scriptural passage was combined with an explanatory interpretation.

[60] שְׁבַת־רָצוֹן לַיהוה

[61] בְּעֵת רָצוֹן

6 : 3, 4a

> Giving no occasion of stumbling in anything, that our ministration be not blamed; but in everything commending ourselves, as ministers of God.

Grammatically, this verse continues the construction of verse 1, verse 2 having been of a parenthetical nature; the participles are in series: "working together with God we entreat ..., giving no occasion of stumbling ..., but in everything commending ourselves ..." The Greek verb translated "to blame" here [62] also conveys the suggestion of mocking and ridicule. *Momus* (from the same root) was the name given by the Greeks to the god of mockery and ridicule. Plummer suggests that the verb may here include the thought of being made a laughing-stock, and it may well be that Calvin had this implication of the term in mind when commenting that "nothing is more ridiculous than striving to maintain your reputation before others, while you invite reproach upon yourself by a shameful and base life".

If it is a matter of seriousness to Christians in general that their profession of Christ should not be in conflict with their daily conduct, it is even more so to ministers of the gospel who as the leaders of Christ's flock are called to set an example of consistent and godly living. "It is an artifice of Satan", writes Calvin, "to seek some misconduct on the part of ministers which may tend to the dishonour of the gospel; for when he has been successful in bringing the ministry into contempt all hope of progress is destroyed: therefore the man who wishes to serve Christ with usefulness must apply himself with all possible diligence to preserve the honour of his ministry." This was the reason why the apostle Paul was so scrupulously careful to avoid giving even the slightest occasion of stumbling [63] in any respect in all his labours for Christ. The preaching of the cross, it is true, inevitably gives offence to the unregenerate mind which is governed by pride and self-esteem (cf. I Cor. 1:23, Gal. 5:11); but for the

---

[62] *Μωμάομαι*—a classical word which occurs only here and in 8:20 in the New Testament.

[63] *Προσκόπη*, a hapax legomenon in biblical Greek, is elsewhere found a few times in Polybius. The cognate noun *πρόσκομμα* is more usual (Rom. 9:32, 33, 14:13, 20 I Cor. 8:9, I Pet. 2:8). Cf. Paul's use of *ἐγκόπη*, another biblical hapax legomenon, in I Cor. 9:12.

messenger of reconciliation to place a stumblingblock in the way of unbelievers by behaviour which is improper and inconsistent with his message is quite another thing, and altogether inexcusable. Nothing is more likely to cause the name of God to be blasphemed and mocked by unbelievers than the example of a minister whose conduct of himself is evidently a contradiction of the transforming power of God in Christ which he advocates in his preaching. Paul was constantly concerned lest for unworthy reasons the ministry should become a laughing-stock to the world, lest the message of the cross, which is the power of God unto salvation to all that believe (Rom. 1:16; I Cor. 1:18, 24), should be emptied of meaning and effectiveness because of the misbehaviour of its bearer (cf. I Cor. 1:17; 9:27). Even as Paul wrote, the Corinthian church was confronted with the formalism and hypocrisy of certain would-be apostles whose lives denied the power of the godliness which they professed (cf. II Tim. 3:5). But Paul was not one of them, and the Corinthians knew it. He enjoyed the blessed testimony of a clear conscience in the fulfilment of his evangelical commission; he had given no cause of stumbling to any one of them; on the contrary, his conduct had been marked by holiness, sincerity, and consistency (cf. 1:12ff.). In everything, as he says here, he had commended himself in the way that God's minister should do (cf. 4:2; 12:11)—and that too without having to rely on the doubtful support of specious letters of reference of the kind which his adversaries had produced when they had invaded his territory in Corinth (cf. 3:1.)

6:4b
In much patience, in afflictions, in necessities, in distresses.

In much patience. Perhaps this phrase should be taken with what precedes: Paul commended himself, as a minister of God should, in much patience. Certainly the necessity for *much* patience is illustrated by the list of trials which follows. As Bengel and many other commentators have pointed out, this list falls quite naturally into three groups of three trials each, the first triplet (afflictions, necessities, distresses) mentioning his hardships in general terms, the second (stripes, imprisonments, tumults) drawing attention to specific persecutions, and the third (labours, watchings, fastings) describing tribulations not so much

222

imposed on him from without as voluntarily endured. The value of the patient enduring of sufferings has already been mentioned in the opening section of this letter (1:6). For the Christian, indeed, tribulation should bring forth patience (Rom. 5:3; Jas. 1:3), whereas in the natural man it gives rise to despair or embitterment. Paul does not go into details here, but more precise information concerning some of the things he suffered is given in the famous catalogue which is found later on in this epistle (11:23ff.), and also of course by Luke in the Acts of the Apostles. It is this quality of patient endurance which Clement of Rome particularly mentions in his eulogy of the Apostle: "Paul by his example pointed out the prize of patient endurance. After that he had been seven times in bonds, had been driven into exile, had been stoned, had preached in the East and in the West, he won the noble renown which was the reward of his faith, having taught righteousness unto the whole world and having reached the farthest bounds of the West; and when he had borne this testimony before the rulers, so he departed from the world and went unto the holy place, having been found a notable pattern of patient endurance".[64]

In afflictions. Paul starts with the most general term and then goes on to speak with increasing definition of the things that a faithful minister of Christ may expect to endure. Those who follow Christ must expect to follow Him in the experience of affliction; yet at the same time they know that they will be participants of His victory. "In the world you have affliction", our Lord advises His disciples: "but be of good cheer", He adds; "I have overcome the world" (Jn. 16:33). In turn, Paul and Barnabas admonish their converts that "through many afflictions we must enter into the kingdom of God" (Acts 14:22). On the moving occasion of his farewell meeting with the Ephesian elders at Miletus Paul disclosed to them that, although he was uncertain what things would befall him in Jerusalem, yet the Holy Spirit testified to him in every city that bonds and afflictions awaited him (Acts 20:23). But throughout everything he was fully assured, as every Christian should be fully assured, both by promise and by experience, that no affliction, however severe or prolonged, can separate the believer from the love of Christ (Rom. 8:35).

---

[64] Clement of Rome, *Ep. ad Cor.*, 5; Bishop Lightfoot's translation.

In necessities. The minister of God has duties and obligations which are binding and may not be disavowed, and which will involve him in testing circumstances which cannot be avoided. His great and overruling necessity, by which every other necessity is conditioned, is the preaching of the gospel: "Necessity is laid upon me", declares the Apostle; "for woe is unto me if I preach not the gospel" (I Cor. 9:16). All other necessities are subordinate to this supreme necessity, and are endured because of it. (In I Thess. 3:7 the order is reversed: "... in all our necessity and affliction".)

In distresses. These distresses are literally "straits",[65] situations of utter perplexity in which Christ's servant is faced with difficulties which, humanly speaking, appear to be insoluble. Viewed from God's side, however, he is never in hopeless straits (which is Paul's meaning in 4:8), for he looks to God, with whom all things are possible (Mk. 10:27), to make a way through for him (I Cor. 10:13). To be in straits (anguish) can separate us from the love of Christ no more than can affliction (Rom. 8:35). Indeed, realizing that his weakness is the opportunity for Christ's strength, the believer is able even to take pleasure in afflictions, necessities, and straits, provided they are borne for Christ's sake (12:10). That is one of the great lessons of this epistle.

6:5

> In stripes, in imprisonments, in tumults, in labours, in watchings, in fastings.

In stripes. In 11:23ff. Paul speaks of having received "stripes above measure", and in particular mentions that five times he received thirty-nine stripes from the Jews and that on three occasions he was beaten with rods (that is, by order of Gentile civic authorities). One of these latter floggings is recounted in Acts 16:23, when the Philippian magistrates caused Paul and Silas to be beaten with many stripes—an occasion distinguished not only by the patient endurance displayed by the two companions, but also by the manner in which, though cruelly injured, cast into the inner prison, and clamped in the stocks, they found it in themselves to pray and sing hymns triumphantly to God. It should be remembered that this epistle was written in the mid-

---

[65] Στενοχωρίαι.

224

course of Paul's apostolic career: there were still many more sufferings for him to endure.

In imprisonments. Paul speaks, in 11:23 again, of having been "in prisons more abundantly". One such occasion known to us is that of Acts 16:23ff., to which reference was made in the preceding paragraph. No other instance is precisely recorded in the Acts, in which, however, only a comparatively few incidents from the many that befell the Apostle as he journeyed from place to place are described. There is no reason to doubt that on numerous occasions he endured the indignity of imprisonment.

In tumults. Of these we have considerably more information of a precise nature. The malice of the Jews against their erstwhile leader was such that they lost no opportunity of inflaming the mob against him. Uprisings against Paul took place at Pisidian Antioch (Acts 13:50, at Iconium, in which the Gentiles joined the Jews (Acts 14:5), at Lystra (Acts 14:19), at Philippi—a Gentile tumult (Acts 16:22), at Thessalonica (Acts 17:5), at Corinth (Acts 18:12), at Ephesus (Acts 19:23ff.), and at Jerusalem (Acts 21:27ff.). The last of these had not taken place at the time when this letter was written.

In labours. Paul has in mind those labours for Christ and the gospel which involve great effort and weariness. The Greek word might suitably be translated "fatigues".[66] The servants of God, however, have the certainty that their labour is not in vain in the Lord (I Cor. 15:58). In writing to the Thessalonians the Apostle uses the term of his manual labour for the purpose of earning his daily bread, that he might not prove a burden to them (I Thess. 2:9; II Thess. 3:8); but it is unlikely that he intends this form of toil to be included in the labours here, except in a secondary sense.

In watchings. By "watchings" we should understand times of sleeplessness—not, however, bouts of insomnia, but the occasions, no doubt frequent, when Paul voluntarily went without sleep or shortened his hours of rest in order to devote more time to his evangelical work, to his care of all the churches, and to prayer. In 11:27 he says that he was "in watchings often".

---

[66] The noun κόπος implies toil unto fatigue. It means "not so much the actual exertion which a man makes, as the lassitude or weariness which follows on this straining of all his powers to the utmost": R. C. Trench, *Synonyms of the New Testament* (12th edn., London, 1894), p. 379.

In fastings. The reference is not to some formal religious practice of fasting (cf. Mt. 6:16f.), but to the times, which were frequent (11:27), when Paul spontaneously went without meals rather than interrupt his work. This interpretation is confirmed by the distinction that is made between "fastings" and "hunger and thirst" in 11:27, where the latter seems plainly to indicate the involuntary deprivation of food and drink. There is reason to conclude too that another reason for Paul's having to endure fastings was his determination to preach the gospel for nought (11:7, 9) rather than exercise his right to have his daily needs supplied by those to whom he ministered (I Cor. 9:12ff.).

6:6

> In pureness, in knowledge, in longsuffering, in kindness, in the Holy Spirit, in love unfeigned.

Having drawn attention to the various kinds of tribulation and vicissitude in which the faithful prosecution of his ministry of reconciliation has involved him, Paul now sets down a list of the spiritual qualities, graces, and means whereby he has been enabled triumphantly to endure all these things.[67]

In pureness. It is probably purity of life and motive in a comprehensive sense that Paul is speaking of here, rather than chastity in particular, though doubtless the latter is included in the former [68] (cf. I Thess. 2:10).

---

[67] In these verses we have a remarkable indication of the excellent ear which Paul had for words and phrases in combination. To seek for some special inner significance in the sequence of expressions here is futile; the structure is not so much according to sense as according to sound. Thus the single terms: ἐν ἁγνότητι, ἐν γνώσει, ἐν μακροθυμίᾳ, ἐν χρηστότητι carry on the impetus of the single terms of verses 4 and 5 and then are succeeded by a series of double terms: ἐν Πνεύματι Ἁγίῳ, ἐν ἀγάπῃ ἀνυποκρίτῳ, ἐν λόγῳ ἀληθείας, ἐν δυνάμει Θεοῦ. These in turn lead to a series of antitheses each introduced by διά and coupled together by καί, and, finally, to a further such series, now adjectival or participial in form, each introduced by ὡς and coupled again by καί. The mounting effect of this structure on the mind of the reader is evident even in translation. Yet throughout the writing is unstudied and free from any suspicion of artificiality. Paul's use of his literary gifts is entirely spontaneous. The effect he desires upon his readers is that of truth, not of verbal bravura.

[68] Ἁγνότης occurs only here in the New Testament and in 11:3, though in the latter instance the reading is not unanimously attested.

In knowledge. The Apostle has no doubts about the validity of the knowledge he possesses (cf. 11:6), for it is knowledge of the truth as it is in Christ Jesus, revealed from above—"wisdom such as is given from God" (Chrysostom). Therefore it is ultimate knowledge; it is summed up in the Saviour, "in whom all the treasures of wisdom and knowledge are hidden" (Col. 2:3); and it is enshrined for us in Holy Scripture (II Tim. 3:15ff.). There is never, however, any suggestion of its being a *gnosis* accessible only to the intellectual élite, for it is available, in Christ, to every believer, however humble, without respect to innate ability or social status. In short, it is *saving* knowledge freely offered to sinners.

In longsuffering. Plummer defines this longsuffering as "the forbearance which endures injuries and evil deeds without being provoked to anger (Jas. i. 19) or vengeance (Rom. xii. 19)". We would suggest, further, that it must be distinguished from the *patience* mentioned in verse 4, which is descriptive of the Apostle's reaction to indignities inflicted by the enemies of the Church, as it were from without, whereas longsuffering here is a virtue displayed as between Christians, within the redeemed community. We know, for example, and the Corinthians knew, that the calumnies and injustices imposed upon their apostle by certain members of the Corinthian Church had called for the exercise of the greatest measure of longsuffering on his part. This understanding of the term accords with its setting in Eph. 4:2, where Paul exhorts his fellow-believers to walk worthily of their calling, "with all lowliness and meekness, *with longsuffering forbearing one another in love,* giving diligence to keep the unity of the Spirit in the bond of peace" (cf. Col. 3:12f.). The Corinthians were also well aware from the shame of their own experience that a deficiency of longsuffering in the Church of Christ leads to jealousies, backbitings, and divisions amongst the very persons who ought to be displaying to the world their brotherly unity and forbearance in Christ.

In kindness. In Gal. 5:22 kindness is coupled, as it is here, with longsuffering. There they are amongst the fruits of the Spirit, which serves to confirm that the qualities of pureness, knowledge, longsuffering, and kindness which occur together here are considered by Paul as *Christian graces.* Longsuffering and kindness, moreover, are linked together in I Cor. 13:4 as expres-

227

sions of Christian *love*: "Love is longsuffering and is kind". Christian kindness is the right and logical consequence of the kindness of God toward us in Christ Jesus (Eph. 2:7; Tit. 3:4). The interrelated significance of kindness, longsuffering, and love is admirably brought out in Paul's exhortation to the members of the church at Colossae to put on "a heart of compassion, kindness, lowliness, meekness, longsuffering, forbearing one another, and forgiving each other, if any man have a complaint against any. Even as the Lord forgave you", he ·continues, "so also do ye; and above all these things put on love, which is the bond of perfectness" (Col. 3:12f.).

In the Holy Spirit. Plummer offers the opinion that "it is scarcely credible that St Paul would place the Holy Spirit in a list of human virtues and in a subordinate place, neither first to lead, nor last to sum up all the rest". He therefore takes Paul to mean here "a spirit that is holy", that is, "the spirit of holiness which distinguishes true ministers from false". But it is not to be disputed that the natural rendering of this expression in its specific New Testament setting is "in the Holy Spirit"—a direct reference, that is, to the Third Person of the Trinity. The reason for the occurrence of this phrase at this particular point is suggested, at least in part, in our comment on the structure of this passage in Note 67 above. The great majority of editors and commentators are agreed in understanding the Apostle to be referring to God the Holy Spirit here,[69] while at the same time acknowledging that the Holy Spirit cannot be separated from the gifts and graces He imparts. Calvin, for example, remarks that "the Spirit is taken, by metonymy, to denote spiritual graces", and Allo similarly supposes that Paul here intends "the charismatic gifts communicated by the Spirit". Swete grants that it is surprising at first sight to find the Holy Spirit placed in the midst of the gifts He conveys, but rightly offers the reminder that "St Paul is as far as possible from the conventionalities of the professed theologian; he writes, especially in this epistle, as the words offer themselves, with the freedom of the informal letter which pays little regard to the logical requirements of the sentence". He adds that "it is not the person of the Spirit but

---

[69]   In any case, it is likely that had Paul meant simply "a spirit of holiness" he would have written ἐν πνεύματι ἁγιωσύνης, comparably with Rom. 1:4 (κατὰ πνεῦμα ἁγιωσύνης), and not ἐν πνεύματι ἁγίῳ.

the gift that is intended", and concludes that the Holy Spirit here "is nearly equivalent to the spirit of holiness which ought to be the central feature of the ministerial character, the spirit which is common to all true ministers of God, distinguishing them from *false apostles*".[70] This being so, then Plummer is right in effect, though not in principle.

In love unfeigned. Paul speaks here, literally, of unhypocritical love.[71] Love that is not entirely genuine, that is admixed with insincerity or self-seeking, is not Christian love, and especially, in this context, it falls short of that pure love by which the minister of Christ should be animated in all his dealings with those to whom he ministers. The mention of the Holy Spirit is, as Bengel observes, immediately followed by that of love, "which is the primary fruit of the Spirit and governs the use of the spiritual gifts". In writing to the Christians at Rome Paul also enjoins them to display that love which, as here, is unhypocritical (Rom. 12:9): how can he, Christ's apostle, require this of others unless he himself is a consistent example of such love? Peter uses the same adjective, "unhypocritical" (I Pet. 1:22), to describe that love which ought always to bind together those who are brethren in Christ (*philadelphia*). This characteristically Christian love (*agape*) is God's manifestation of Himself as He essentially is (13:11; I Jn. 4:8, 16); it is God in action, first of all for us (5:14; Jn. 3:16), and then through us (I Jn. 4:11); it is the more excellent way which the members of the Corinthian Church had such need of learning and following (I Cor. 12:31; 13:1ff.); it is, as Ethelbert Stauffer has said, "the power of the coming age breaking into this world".[72]

6:7ab

In the word of truth, in the power of God.

In the word of truth. Paul frequently uses "word" (*logos*) in the sense of "message" or "proclamation" (see commentary on 5:19 above); and this is probably its meaning here. "The word of truth" is then the message of truth which he proclaimed. Thus in Eph. 1:13 "the word of the truth" is explained as "the gospel

---

70   H. B. Swete, *The Holy Spirit in the New Testament* (London, 1909), pp. 196f.
71   'Εν ἀγάπῃ ἀνυποκρίτῳ.
72   E. Stauffer, *Love* (Kittel TWNT), *ut supra*, p. 59.

of your salvation" (cf. Col. 1:5, "the word of the truth of the gospel", and Jas. 1:18). It is possible, however, that Paul is here alluding to the sincerity and truthfulness of his own words, either in speech when present or in letters when absent (cf. 1:12f.; 2:17; 4:2; 10:11).

In the power of God. This power of God by which the genuineness of Paul's ministry was confirmed may most appropriately be associated with the divine power manifested in his preaching of the truth and experienced by his Corinthian converts. To the point is the autobiographical note contained in his earlier letter to them: "I was with you in weakness, and in fear, and in much trembling; and my speech (*logos*) and my preaching (*kerygma*) were not in persuasive words of wisdom, but in demonstration of the Spirit and of power: that your faith should not stand in the wisdom of men, but *in the power of God*" (I Cor. 2:3ff.). Power experienced becomes power communicated. As this epistle makes so plain, it is precisely human weakness which is fitted to receive and to carry divine power, and, by virtue of the startling contrast between the two, to magnify the superabundance of the latter's sufficiency (4:7ff.; 12:9f.).

6:7c — 8b

By the armour of righteousness on the right hand and on the left, by glory and dishonour, by evil report and good report.

By the armour of righteousness on the right hand and on the left. The Apostle is fond of military metaphors, doubtless because they are so well suited to illustrate the fact that the Christian is engaged in a stern and unremitting conflict with the powers of darkness. The armour (literally "weapons") of righteousness is that with which the believer is endued from above for the successful prosecution of this warfare. Once endued with the armour of light (Rom. 13:12), the Christian is equipped, and indeed is under obligation, to present his own members, not to sin as instruments (literally "weapons") of unrighteousness, but to God as instruments of righteousness (Rom. 6:13). Later in our epistle (10:4) Paul reminds the Corinthians that the weapons of our warfare are not of the flesh. The classic passage is Eph. 6:13ff., where "the panoply of God" is described, weapon by weapon (cf. I Thess. 5:8; Isa. 59:17). The description of these weapons of righteousness as being "on the right hand and on the left" has been variously explained to mean: (i) that one so equipped is prepared to meet attack from any quarter; (ii) that the Christian soldier is armed both with weapons of the right hand, which are for offence (such as the sword of the Spirit, Eph. 6:17), and with weapons of the left hand, which are for defence (such as the shield of faith, Eph. 6:16); or (iii) that as in ancient times the right was considered to be the side of good fortune and the left the side of ill fortune, so some of the older commentators, such as Chrysostom, Theodoret, Theophylact, and Herveius, supposed Paul to mean that the weapons of righteousness must be wielded by the Christian both in prosperity and in adversity. Paul, however, is unlikely to have had such a thought in mind, if only because of the suggestion it carries of pagan superstition. Of these explanations the first commends itself as the simplest.[73]

By glory and dishonour. The Greek word rendered "glory" [74] in our version has the meaning here of good opinion or esteem which is common in the classical authors (cf. Jn. 5:44, "How can ye believe, who receive glory one of another, and the glory that cometh from the only God ye seek not?" and Jn. 12:43, "They loved the glory that is of men more than the glory that is of God", where "glory" has this same sense). The general force of the word as used by Paul here might be conveyed by rendering it "popularity". The minister of Christ is not immune from the fluctuating fashions and fickle judgments of this world; that is the point of this catalogue of opposites, of which this is the first (unless "right" and "left" in the immediately preceding clause are interpreted as opposites). He will have bitter enemies as well as devoted friends; some will hold him in high esteem, while others will heap insult and dishonour upon him; even the

---

[73] The change of the preposition from ἐν to διά at this point is natural: ἐν would not have been so suitable here, though it might well have been resumed for the next two phrases. The διά, however, helps to break the monotony of the repetition of ἐν, which has now occurred consecutively no less than 18 times; and having changed to διά it was natural to retain it in the two following clauses, besides being stylistically advantageous—though it would almost certainly be wrong to suggest that questions of style were in the forefront of the Apostle's thinking.

[74] Δόξα properly is what others think of one (δοκεῖν), thus opinion or reputation. The sense of "glory" presupposes that a person is held in high repute among his fellows.

same people may show a complete alteration of attitude towards him. But, whether popular or despised, he must be careful to commend himself as a minister of God should do, always keeping in mind the words of his Master: "If the world hate you, you know that it hated Me before it hated you. ... A servant is not greater than his lord" (Jn. 15:18ff.).

By evil report and good report. Plummer's comment is to the point: "This is not a repetition of the preceding clause. That refers to personal treatment of the Apostle; this refers to what was said behind his back. It was during his absence from Corinth that the worst things were said about him". Few things are more provoking than for false and malicious calumnies to be spread within the Christian community against a minister of God while he is absent. Yet even in these circumstances God's minister should calmly and consistently show forth the spirit of Christ, "who when He was reviled, reviled not again; when he suffered, threatened not; but committed Himself to Him that judgeth righteously" (I Pet. 2:23). On the other hand, the desire to be well spoken of is a temptation which readily assails Christian ministers and which, if not resisted, leads to pride and complacency. His task is to steer a straight and undeviating course, giving heed only to the word of his one Master, regardless of what men may say about him. So long as he is doing that, no evil report, however false, can harm him and no good report, however true, can distract him.

In the preceding pair of opposites what was pleasant (glory) was placed first and what was unpleasant (dishonour) second; but here and in the succeeding pairs that order is reversed (evil report : good report; deceivers : true; etc.). That Paul sustains neither the same order nor a series of chiasmic contrasts throughout is an indication that he is writing spontaneously and from the heart and not with an eye to artificial considerations of style and polish. At the same time, as this passage and many others show, the Apostle's natural literary ability, so far from being inhibited, is exercised with impressive effectiveness.

6:8c — 9

As deceivers, and yet true; as unknown, and yet well known; as dying, and behold, we live; as chastened, and not killed.

As deceivers, and yet true. One of the evil reports which was being circulated against Paul was that he was a deceiver, an impostor, a false apostle. But he responds to the slander with calmness, for he has that priceless inward strength which the testimony of a clear conscience before God affords: he knows, as in fact the Corinthians do also in their hearts, that he is no deceiver, but the messenger of everlasting truth (cf. 4:2). Had not the same slander been falsely charged against his Master whom he had been called to follow (Mt. 27:63)? It has always been the work of Satan and his servants to attempt to overthrow the truth of God by calling it falsehood. Thus our Lord told the Pharisees who withstood His teaching that their father was not Abraham but the devil, who is the father of all lying (Jn. 8:44; cf. Gen. 3:4). The antichrist, Satan's agent on earth, is precisely described as *the deceiver* (II Jn. 7). Such a one seeks to present truth as error and error as truth; but the truth is self-vindicating and ultimately impregnable. Of this Paul needed no persuading.

Of course, the calumny that Paul was a deceiver did not cease with his death, but has been repeated through the succeeding centuries and continues to be active in our day (cf., for example, the strongly anti-Pauline animus of the Clementine literature of the second century and the attempts of various theological schools of modern times to dismiss Paul's teaching as being at variance with that of Christ or the other apostles, or as being inimical to the essence of genuine Christianity).

As unknown, and yet well known. It may well have been a further evil report that Paul was "not known", that is, not recognized as having the credentials of an apostle (cf. 3:1), that he was a self-intruding upstart who had no first-hand knowledge of Christ (cf. 5:16). We think it preferable, however, to understand the language here in a wider and more general sense: as Saul of Tarsus, the brilliant and ambitious young Pharisee, he had achieved a considerable measure of fame, at least among his own compatriots; but as Paul the Apostle he had turned his back on all those things which, from the worldly point of view, were gain to him, and he became the despised preacher of a crucified Messiah, ignored by the world at large, indeed, unnoticed. This unknownness of Paul is vividly illustrated by what he has previously written to the Corinthians: "Even unto this present we both hunger, and thirst, and are naked, and are buffeted, and have no certain dwelling-place; and we toil, working with our own hands: being reviled, we bless; being persecuted, we endure; being defamed, we entreat: we are made as the filth of the world, the offscouring of all things, even until now" (I Cor. 4:11ff.).

And yet he was "well known". Despite the opinion of many commentators, it seems to us inadequate and unworthy to understand Paul to mean that from those who could appreciate him—those, that is, who had experienced the power of the gospel he preached—he received recognition and acknowledgment. It is true that the same verb [75] is used in 1:13f. in the sense of "acknowledge", but its proper force here is indicated by its use in I Cor. 13:12: "Now I know in part, but then I shall know fully [76] even as also I am fully known (*sc.* by God)" [77]. Thus we understand Paul to mean here that, though unknown and unacknowledged in the world, he is fully known *by God*. This accords well with what he subsequently wrote to Timothy: "The firm foundation of God standeth, having this seal, *The Lord knoweth them that are His*" (II Tim. 2:19), and also with the words of our Lord: "I am the Good Shepherd, and I know mine own" (Jn. 10:14). To be unknown to the world matters nothing; it is to be known of God as His own that is all important.

As dying, and behold, we live. Because of the severe perils and antagonisms to which he was constantly exposed the Apostle could justly describe his experience as one of hourly jeopardy and daily dying (I Cor. 15:30f.). His recovery from the affliction which had recently struck him down in Asia was virtually a resurrection from death (1:8f.). And the threat to his physical existence came not only from illness, but also from violence and adventure—from the fury of the mob, from floggings, from imprisonments, from shipwrecks—which caused him to be "in deaths often" (11:23ff.). There is nothing surprising, therefore, in his assertion that he was being always delivered unto death for Jesus' sake that the life of Jesus might be manifested in his mortal flesh (4:11). Nothing could detract from the wonder of this cheating of death; hence the spontaneous and exulting exclamation "behold!": "as dying, and *behold!* we live". We can well imagine Paul ejaculating words similar to these after

---

[75] Ἐπιγινώσκειν.

[76] Ἐπιγνώσομαι.

[77] Ἐπεγνώσθην. The verb is an intensive compound appropriate for conveying the notion of that full knowledge which belongs to God.

his terrible experience at Lystra when, after being stoned by the mob, he was dragged out of the city as dead, and then suddenly was enabled to arise full of life and vigour (Acts 14:19ff.). Even the eventual dissolution of the body and its faculties in death can be contemplated without misgiving, because the Christian rests under the assured hope of resurrection from the dead to everlasting life in the presence of Christ's heavenly glory (4:14; 5:1; I Cor. 15:54ff.; II Tim. 4:6ff.). To believe in Christ is, as He Himself declared, to pass out of death into life, to have, and to experience the power of, eternal life, here and now as well as hereafter (Jn. 3:16, 36; 5:24; 11:25f.).

As chastened, and not killed. In Scripture, chastening indicates the discipline which God, as Heavenly Father, imposes upon His children for the purpose of their correction and training. Though unpleasant to bear, it is a sign of God's loving concern in controlling and directing the way of those who are His, and it is productive of the valuable fruit of righteousness (cf. Prov. 3:11f.; Job 5:17; Ps. 94:12; 119:67, 75; Jer. 31:18f.; Rev. 3:19; etc., and especially Heb. 12:5–13). Paul, the once proud and ambitious Pharisee, had needed and received much chastening at God's hands. No doubt his opponents had proclaimed that it was a mark of divine wrath upon him, ready as they always were to interpret everything to his disadvantage. But he had proved that it was a mark of divine love, designed for his own spiritual benefit, and had learnt that the Lord did not smite to kill, but to bless, and therefore he endured it without fainting (cf. 4:1, 16; Heb. 12:5, 12). The close affinity between Paul's thought and language here and Psalm 118:17f. should be noticed. Indeed, it may well be that the previous clause ("as dying, and behold, we live") had put the Apostle in mind of the psalmist's words: "I shall not die, but live. ... Jehovah hath chastened me sore; but He hath not given me over unto death".

6:10

As sorrowful, yet always rejoicing; as poor, yet making many rich; as having nothing, and yet possessing all things.

As sorrowful, yet always rejoicing. Although the Christian minister has the deep abiding joy of Christ in his heart, he is not immune to sorrows and disappointments. Friends may fail, converts may falter, and the work which he has built up with

much toil and devotion may be threatened by heresy or world-
liness. The Apostle Paul had a full measure of such griefs, as
his two letters to the Corinthians alone are adequate to show:
divisions and feuds, incontinence, denial of Christ's resurrection
from the dead, contempt and calumny of his person and his
ministry, and many other things within the church he had
founded crowded upon him to make him sorrowful. He had
found it necessary to pay them a visit with sorrow, and he had
written a letter to them out of much affliction and anguish of
heart, and with many tears (2:1, 4). Anxiety not only for the
church at Corinth but for all the churches pressed upon him
daily (11:28). There was also great pain and unceasing sorrow in
his heart because of the rejection of the gospel by his fellow-
countrymen (Rom. 9:2). But no sorrow, no disappointment,
however severe, could ever interrupt, let alone extinguish, the
joy of his salvation with its vision of unclouded glory to come,
for this joy was founded upon the sovereign supremacy of God,
who overrules all things and causes them to work together for
good for those He has called (Rom. 8:18, 28). Had his work
been a mere work of man, the Apostle might have had frequent
cause for despair; but as it was *God's* work the end was assured,
and the ultimate perspective allowed room only for joy and
confidence and victory. Hence the constancy and permanence
("always") of the Apostle's rejoicing; and hence also his clarion
call to his fellow-believers: "Rejoice in the Lord always; again
I will say, Rejoice!" (Phil. 4:4; cf. Rom. 5:3-5; Phil. 2:17; 3:1;
I Thess. 5:16). Did not our Lord Himself teach that, for His
followers, tribulation and good cheer are not mutually exclusive
(Jn. 16:33)?

As poor, yet making many rich. The Apostle's poverty in this
world's goods was obvious to all, and no doubt those who judged
according to worldly values regarded him as a figure to be pitied,
or at any rate not to be envied. But that was not Paul's view of
himself. Having learnt that it is not according to human resources
but "according to His riches in glory in Christ Jesus" that God
supplies our every need (Phil. 4:19), he considered no man
richer than himself. The salvation he had experienced through
faith in Christ had caused him to know what it means to be *rich
toward God* (Lk. 12:21). This was to be rich to excess; accordingly
he attributes all to "the exceeding riches of God's grace in Christ

Jesus" (Eph. 2:7f.; cf. 1:7). There was no question, of course, of these spiritual riches being enjoyed selfishly or with complacency. He had received them in order that, as God's steward, he might communicate them to others. To him, the minister of the gospel, had been entrusted the sacred task of "preaching to the Gentiles the unsearchable riches of Christ" (Eph. 3:8). So it was that he was able to thank God for the grace which had been given to the Corinthian saints in Christ Jesus, with the result that in everything they were enriched in Him (I Cor. 1:4f.). The apostolic attitude is well illustrated in the account of the healing of the lame beggar at the Beautiful Gate of the temple: "Silver and gold have I none", declared Peter; "but what I have, that I give thee". And thereupon the man was made whole through faith in the name of Jesus Christ of Nazareth (Acts 3:1ff.). The ministry of the gospel effects the restoration of sinful men and women to wholeness in Christ Jesus, to their everlasting enrichment.

So far from claiming any virtue or merit for his poverty (few things could have been more out of character), Paul is emphasizing rather the all-sufficiency of God's grace. The only poverty to which merit attaches and from which virtue proceeds is that which the Son of God voluntarily assumed for our sakes—a truth which is beautifully expressed later in our epistle: "For ye know the grace of our Lord Jesus Christ, that, though He was rich, yet for your sakes He became poor, that ye through His poverty might become rich" (8:9). That, and that alone, is the fount of the whole wealth of the Christian.

Suggestions that the Apostle may be referring here to the collection and distribution of alms, that is, material riches, for the poverty-stricken Christians in Jerusalem (Chrysostom, Theodoret, Theophylact) are completely beside the point and out of harmony with the spiritual exaltation of this passage.

As having nothing, and yet possessing all things. With this clause the passage reaches both its conclusion and its climax. To the uncomprehending onlooker the Apostle Paul must have presented the picture of destitution—without home, without money, without possessions, hated and hunted by his own countrymen, proclaiming a message despised by Jew and Gentile alike. But at the same time the observer must have been arrested and puzzled to mark the other-worldly gleam in the Apostle's eye, his utter dedication

to the mission he had espoused, his disregard of suffering and discomfort, his exalted view of life, his compassionate love for
others, and the joy and peace which constantly sustained his
spirit. It was indeed true that this remarkable man, who lacked
the very things which most regard as necessary to make life
tolerable, conducted himself as though he were the possessor of
all things. And so in fact he was. He who no longer claimed
even himself as his own, for he had been bought at infinite cost
(I Cor. 6:19f.), could yet claim all things as his own. The logic
of this is unfolded always and only in the believer's position in
Christ: to have Christ is to have all, for Christ is all. "All things
are yours", the Apostle has previously said to the Corinthian
believers, "whether Paul or Apollos or Cephas or the world or
life or death or things present or things to come: all are yours,
and ye are Christ's, and Christ is God's" (I Cor. 3:21ff.). The
stupendous magnitude of God's act in delivering up His Son for
us is in itself the assurance that with Him He also freely gives
us all things (Rom. 8:32). A man may have an abundance of
this world's goods, but he does not possess them; empty-handed
he will go out of this world, as he came into it (I Tim. 6:7).
All that a man has in Christ, however, he possesses, for ever; it
is treasure laid up eternally in heaven (Mt. 6:19–21).[78]

This movingly beautiful hymn-like passage flows from the deep
heart of the Apostle's knowledge and experience. Its almost
lyrical intensity, its structural balance, and its genuine spontaneity
have called forth the response of admiration and gratitude in all
generations. In the judgment of Erasmus, its effect is such that
nothing could be lovelier or more fervent. It is certainly one
of the high peaks not only of this remarkably human epistle but
of all Paul's writings. It displays without any trace of artificiality
all the ardour and devotion and sincerity of his regenerated
nature. And it challenges every serious reader to re-examine as
before God his own relationship to the crucified, risen, and
ascended Lord and with redoubled earnestness to dedicate his
life and talents afresh to the singleminded prosecution of the cause
of Christ.

---

[78] In the Greek the play upon the words $\check{\epsilon}\chi o\nu\tau\epsilon\varsigma$ ... $\kappa\alpha\tau\acute{\epsilon}\chi o\nu\tau\epsilon\varsigma$ should be
noticed. The latter is an intensive compound, and the meaning accordingly is:
"as having nothing, and yet having all things to the full". Cf. the use of the
same compound in I Cor. 7:30.

6:11–7:4 A SPIRITUAL FATHER'S APPEAL TO HIS CHILDREN

6:11

Our mouth is open unto you, O Corinthians, our heart is enlarged.

At the conclusion of this fervent outpouring of spirit the Apostle pauses and addresses the Corinthians directly by name. As Chrysostom says, "the addition of their name is a mark of great love and warmth and affection".[1] It is as though the uninhibited nature of the passage he has just dictated has confirmed to Paul the fulness of his love for the Corinthians: freedom in speaking is evidence of an unconfined heart. Only to dearly loved friends does one express oneself freely and without restraint as he has just done, for openness of speech goes with, indeed flows from, warmth and enlargement of heart. Here, then, is a further proof, if they need it, of the genuineness and wholeheartedness of his affections for them. "Out of the abundance of the heart the mouth speaks" (Mt. 12:34). The absence of inward barriers and reservations leads to outward spontaneity. How can the Corinthians possibly doubt that Paul's heart is anything but enlarged with love toward them to such a degree that there is a special and permanent place for them within it?

6:12

Ye are not straitened in us, but ye are straitened in your own affections.

Paul's heart was not narrowed or pinched by suspicions and misconceptions of the Corinthians. Though he knew their failings and though their attitude to him had been marked by a deplorable lack of generosity, yet his love for them remained unaffected; there was no question of their being squeezed out of his heart. No, it was in their own affections that they were confined and restricted; they had permitted a spirit of meanness to close or

---

[1] Only on two other occasions (Gal. 3:1 and Phil. 4:15) does Paul address those to whom he is writing directly by name.

at least to narrow their heart towards him; they had found room for calumnies and suspicions, implanted by enemies and impostors, rather than for love and loyalty to the one who had devotedly given himself to them in bringing them the Good News of Jesus Christ.[2]

6 : 13

Now for a recompense in like kind (I speak as unto my children), be ye also enlarged.

The Apostle utters no note of censure, though he might very justly have done so, but with grace and simplicity pleads for a response of love from their own hearts. They cannot cavil if he requests from them an affection no more than equivalent to his own.[3] But this touching appeal rests not merely upon, so to speak, the justness of legal equivalence; it has deeper roots than that, the roots that unite a father to his children. Here is an affinity that cannot be gainsaid. Nothing is more natural than that a father should enjoy a primary place in the affections of

---

[2] Καρδία ("heart") and σπλάγχνα ("affections") were used interchangeably to denote the seat of the emotions. Hence they are to be treated as synonymous in these verses. The σπλάγχνα properly were the contents of the thorax or breast (heart, lungs, liver) as distinct from the ἔντερα or lower organs (entrails or viscera).

[3] 'Αντιμισθία means a *quid pro quo*, a requital, and the idea of just equivalence is strengthened by the addition of αὐτήν, "the same, i.e., the exact recompense". The term is not classical and is confined to Christian writers—in the New Testament only here and in Rom. 1:27, and also in some patristic authors; but it may be assumed that it was a word in general usage in Paul's day, as with most other words examples of which have so far not been discovered outside of the New Testament and subsequent Christian literature. As for the construction here, Alford understands it as an accusative of a remoter object, and suggests that the sense is compounded of τὸν αὐτὸν τρόπον and ἀντιμισθιαν, "in the same manner, as a return of my largeness of heart to you". C. F. D. Moule, somewhat similarly, suggests that τὴν δὲ αὐτὴν ἀντιμισθίαν "may be an instance of an adverbial phrase made up upon a basis other than that of a neuter noun: it looks like a subtle blend of τὸ δὲ αὐτό, *in the same way*, and κατ' ἀντιμισθίαν, *by way of recompense*, and, on this showing, might be rendered *and accordingly, by way of recompense on your part*", or that it may be an accusative in apposition to the whole sentence, or, more simply still, an accusative of respect (*Idiom Book*, pp. 34–36; 160f.). Others again have regarded the construction as broken, the verb which governs the accusative ἀντιμισθίαν having been omitted—"after the affectionate parenthesis ὡς τέκνοις λέγω, he forgets the opening construction" (Plummer, so also Allo).

his children. It is in the nature of things that paternal love should meet with the response of filial love. Paul was the spiritual father of the Corinthian believers, and in grudging him a place in their hearts they were behaving unnaturally. Both Paul and his fellow-apostle John were accustomed to call those whom they had won for Christ their children or their little children (cf. I Cor. 4:14, 17; Gal. 4:19; I Tim. 1:2, 18; II Tim. 1:2; 2:1; Tit. 1:4; Philem. 10; I Jn. 2:1, 28; 3:7, 18; 4:4; 5:21). This sense is preserved in our English version by the addition of "my" (which is not in the original): "I speak as unto *my* children". To understand Paul to mean that he is speaking to those who are young in the faith is inappropriate in this context, and still more so, in our judgment, to take "children" in a literal sense as, for example, Tasker does: "He appeals to them, as he would appeal to children who have an innate sense of fair-play".[4]

THE AUTHENTICITY OF THE SECTION 6:14–7:1

For many years now this paragraph has provided a focus of controversy in academic circles. Various scholars have argued that, as it is here placed, it is quite incongruous with the context, both in substance and in sentiment. Some have rejected it as being a non-Pauline interpolation; others, while not disputing its Pauline origin, have conjectured that through some mischance it became dislocated from its original position, either in this or in some other letter, and was wrongly inserted in the place where it now appears. Before considering some of the theories that have been advanced, it must be admitted that 6:14, with its strong prohibition of compromise, has the appearance of following on abruptly after the moving appeal of 6:11–13 by the Apostle for a response of affection from the Corinthians; and it must further be admitted that 7:2, which reinforces this appeal, would, if the intervening paragraph were omitted, form an apt continuation of 6:13, giving the sequence: "Our heart is enlarged; be ye also enlarged; open your hearts to us". The proposal that 6:14–7:1 is an interpolation from elsewhere has, accordingly, proved irresistibly attractive to many commentators.

Those who affirm that this section could not have come from the pen of the Apostle Paul rely, in the main, upon the following

---

[4] This interpretation no doubt lies behind Moffatt's rendering of the parenthesis by "as the children say"; but it is scarcely admissible as a translation of ὡς τέκνοις λέγω.

arguments: (i) the noticeably large number of *hapax legomena* within so brief a space; (ii) the spirit of exclusivism it displays, which is said to be incompatible with the teaching of one who had himself been liberated from the narrow outlook of Pharisaism and who elsewhere is so ardent an advocate of Christian freedom; and (iii) the conjunction, in the expression "defilement of flesh and spirit" (7:1), of the terms "flesh" and "spirit", which are said to be antagonistic to each other in the theology of Paul. With respect to these three points it is sufficient to say (i) that in a repetitive rhetorical passage like 6:14–16 a rich diversity of vocabulary is not at all surprising, especially when we bear in mind the Apostle's academic training and linguistic abilities and the fact that, so far from being unusual, scores of *hapax legomena* are to be found in his epistles (there are some 50 in II Corinthians alone!); (ii) that this passage is not to be understood in the sense of a rigorous exclusivism of the Pharisaic type but in accordance with Paul's teaching elsewhere which preserves the balance between the extremes of isolationism and promiscuity (see commentary below); and (iii) that, even though there are important passages in which Paul uses the terms "flesh" and "spirit" in a theologically technical and antagonistic sense, this is by no means always the case, and there is no justification for the charge of incongruity because of their combination here (see commentary below). There is, in short, no *prima facie* evidence that this passage could not have been written by the Apostle Paul.

But there are those who, though accepting it as an authentic Pauline composition, still regard the paragraph as a fragment which in some way became dislocated from another of his writings and was imported into II Corinthians. Moffatt, for example, supposes that we have here an extract from "some other part of Paul's correspondence with the Corinthian Church". It has further been suggested that its contents would accord most appropriately with the purpose of the lost "precanonical" letter mentioned in I Cor. 5:9, where Paul says: "I wrote unto you in my epistle to have no company with fornicators". The attractiveness of this hypothesis is understandable, but as it belongs entirely to the realm of conjecture it is lacking in corroboration of any kind. Its advocates, moreover, (and also, of course, those who conclude that the passage is an intrusion from a non-Pauline source) are faced with the difficult task of offering some reasonable explanation as to how such an interpolation might have taken place—a task all the more formidable when it is remembered that the current form of document in apostolic times was of the papyrus scroll variety, so that the question of separate leaves or sheets of paper being accidentally transposed does not arise. As Allo says: "There is no justification for believing that Christians made use of papyrus codices composed of separate leaves before the second century, by which time the manuscript text of each of Paul's epistles had had a chance of becoming sufficiently well fixed to ensure that any accident occurring to a particular 'codex' would hardly have been likely to alter the general transmission of an epistle and to affect all the manuscripts of the fourth and following centuries".

Other scholars, again, have attempted to rearrange the existing material in such a way that the passage we are considering may enjoy what may on the face of it be a more logical and harmonious location in Paul's communications to the Corinthians. In the prosecution of this purpose considerable ingenuity (though not unanimity) has been exhibited, but otherwise there is little to commend it. No doubt, smoother and more logical sequences may be devised here and elsewhere in the Apostle's writings through manipulations of the text, but in doing so it is all too easy to forget that, after all, what we are dealing with is a spontaneously dictated *letter* and not an academically sophisticated essay in logic. It is, besides, characteristic of Paul to "digress" either briefly, as here, or at some considerable length, and then to take up his previous theme again at the point where, whether premeditatedly or not, he had left it. (See, for example, the commentary on 7:5 below.)

Denney (not to mention others) has suggested that "it is always possible that, on reading over his letter, the Apostle himself may have inserted a paragraph breaking to some extent the closeness of the original connexion". This conjecture is, of course, as unsubstantial and as unsupported by any shadow of evidence as are the others that have been offered; and, in any case, if Paul wrote in this passage as an afterthought, either it was extremely remiss of him to have done it at so (supposedly) inappropriate a point as this, or he must have had good reasons for choosing this place. If the latter—which is obviously by a long way the more probable alternative—then the conjecture loses its force, since it is apparent that the passage may more sensibly be allowed as an integral part of the epistle in its original form.

There is, indeed, an impressive array of exegetes (Zahn, Plummer, Lietzmann, Allo, Filson among them) whose judgment has been that this section is by no means out of place. Paul is perturbed about the peril to the Corinthian church of stultifying compromise with the forces of unbelief, so much so that he entreats the Corinthians not to receive the grace of God in vain (6:1).

He proceeds to remind them of the blamelessness of his own ministry in their midst and of the suffering and privation which he had endured in the cause of the gospel (6:3–10). This affords more than proof sufficient of the undiminished warmth of his affection towards them and shows how groundless are the suspicions respecting himself which they have allowed to narrow the response of their hearts (6:11–13). And now, having reassured them that their place is still within his heart and having established his authority as their spiritual father (6:13), he is in a position to warn them unequivocally against the sin of the unequal yoke, showing them how unscriptural and how contradictory to their profession such a state is (6:14–18). But, while this admonition is direct and to the point, it is still administered in the spirit of love, not of censoriousness (7:1). That this is so is reinforced by the resumption, at this juncture, of his plea of 6:13 that they should make room in the affections of their hearts for him—for him who had wronged none of them and from whose heart they could never be ousted (7:2–4). Seen in its setting, then, the section 6:14–7:1, with its plainly worded warning against the danger of compromise, is most skilfully and graciously cushioned by the loving passages on either side of it, while at the same time it itself is prompted by this same spirit of affection. In fact, it provides a valuable object lesson to the Christian pastor of the manner, animated by love yet none the less plainspoken, to the point but not crushing and harsh, in which to deal with those who through lack of discernment are placing themselves in a position of the gravest spiritual peril.

Finally, were it the case that this passage is an interpolation from elsewhere, it is almost incredible that there should be no tradition in the Church, however faint, to this effect; but, as Plummer remarks, "there is no evidence in MS, or version, or quotation that any copy of the Epistle ever lacked this passage".

6:14

Be not unequally yoked with unbelievers: for what fellowship have righteousness and iniquity? or what communion hath light with darkness?

The metaphor employed by the Apostle here is that of a double yoke under which two animals work side by side. It is almost certain that he had in mind the prohibition of Deut. 22:10: "Thou shalt not plough with an ox and an ass together", and Lev. 19:19 where it is forbidden to cross-breed animals of different kinds.[5] This principle is adapted and applied by Paul with the purpose of emphasizing the incongruity of believers being paired with unbelievers. Indeed, the biblical teaching that the ultimate and radical division of persons before God is that between believers and unbelievers, between those who are in Christ and those who are not, is strongly propounded here. Paul does not state in specific terms what he means by being unequally yoked with unbelievers, but already in the earlier epistle there are indications of some of the things he must have had in mind, namely, marriages between Christians and non-Christians (I Cor. 7:12–15), eating meat that had been offered to idols in the home of an unbeliever (10:27f.), speaking in tongues when unbelievers were present at the service (14:24), and instituting legal proceedings against a Christian brother before unbelievers (6:5ff.).[6] The negative injunction of course carries with it the opposite and positive implication, that believers should be equally and harmoniously yoked with fellow-believers, so that in marriage, Christian service, and public witness they may walk and work worthily of the Lord. True Christian partnership is that which exists between (to use another Pauline expression) *genuine yokefellows*,[7] and that can apply only to those who already are one in Christ Jesus.[8]

It would be a serious mistake to conclude that Paul is here condemning all contact and intercourse with non-Christians: isolationism of this sort would, as he has previously written (I Cor. 5:10), logically necessitate departure from the world. In other words, it is a position of absurdity. The pharisaical attitude of exclusiveness was discarded by him once for all at his conversion, and his whole ministry and manner of life was

---

5 Ἑτερόζυγοι, LXX—cf. ἑτεροζυγοῦντες here.

6 "Be not" is the rendering of μὴ γίνεσθε, which means literally "do not become". Bengel suggests that "do not become" is a gentle way of saying "do not be" (*ne fiatis:* molliter pro *ne sitis*). The proper force, however, of μὴ γίνεσθε κτλ (μή plus present imperative) is "do not go on becoming unequally yoked with unbelievers, as you are already doing".

7 Phil. 4:3 — γνήσιοι σύζυγοι.

8 Ζύγον can also mean the beam of a pair of balances, and hence the balance itself. Theophylact interprets μὴ γίνεσθε ἑτεροζυγοῦντες with reference to the idea of an unequal balance, that is, of believers being unduly inclined towards unbelievers. But this weakens the sense and in any case, not least in view of the Old Testament allusions to which we have drawn attention, has little to commend it.

a denial of any policy of total withdrawal for fear of contamination from unbelievers. He, if anyone did, sought unremittingly to fulfil our Lord's commission to go *into all the world* and preach the gospel *to every creature*. He made it his practice to conform to the pattern of the society in which he found himself, without, however, in any way compromising the integrity of the faith or lowering the high standards of Christian morality, and all with the great objective of winning others for Christ. To the Jews he became as a Jew; to those under law, as one under law, though he himself was not under law; to those without law, as one without law, though he himself was not without law to God. "I am become all things to all men, that I may by all means save some; and I do all things for the sake of the gospel, in order that I may partake of it with others" (I Cor. 9:20–23). It may even be that some of the Corinthian Christians had misinterpreted and misused these words of the Apostle as an excuse for entering into unholy alliances with unbelievers. The metaphor of the yoke which he uses here shows that he is thinking of close relationships in which, unless both parties are true believers, Christian harmony cannot be expected to flourish and Christian consistency cannot fail to be compromised.

For what fellowship have righteousness and iniquity? The conjunction "for" shows that there is a logical and obvious incongruity about the unequal yoke, and the pairs of opposites which it introduces illustrate the absolute and ultimate antithesis that exists between the believer and the unbeliever. Each question is pointed and rhetorical; no answer is stated because the answer in each case is obvious. It is almost as though we can in this passage catch an echo of Paul the preacher: the series of rhetorical questions, the notable variety of vocabulary and construction,[9] the quotations from the Old Testament Scriptures, and the application of the biblical promises to those he is addressing (7:1)—all these together conjure up a vivid picture of the power and effect of the Apostle's preaching.

Righteousness is placed in antithesis here to iniquity, or, more

---

[9] Notice the variations in the succession: μετοχή + dative + καί + dative, κοινωνία + dative + πρός + accusative, συμφώνησις + genitive + πρός + accusative, μερίς + dative + μετά + genitive, συγκατάθεσις + dative + μετά + genitive. Notice also the terms ἑτεροζυγεῖν, μετοχή, συμφώνησις, βελίαρ, συγκατάθεσις, and μολυσμός, all of which are *hapax legomena* in the New Testament.

literally, lawlessness.[10]   The same antithesis is found again in
Heb. 1:9 (= Ps. 45:7): "Thou hast loved righteousness and
hated lawlessness"—a verse which presents the divine attitude,
through the Messiah, to these two opposites.   John, indeed,
declares that "sin is lawlessness" (I Jn. 3:4); and Paul particularly
associates "the mystery of lawlessness", of which he writes to the
Thessalonians, with "the man of sin, the son of perdition", who
is himself "the lawless one" [11] through whom Satan works
(II Thess. 2:3-10).   Christ's offering of Himself for us was "that
He might redeem us from all lawlessness" (Titus 2:14).   Accordingly, His final word to those who continue in unbelief is: "Depart
from me, ye that work lawlessness" (Mt. 7:23).   To the believer,
however, as Paul has previously told the Corinthians, Christ has
been made righteousness (I Cor. 1:30); and the fundamental
contrast between a man's way of life before and after his conversion
should be apparent in the fact that, whereas formerly he presented
his members as servants to uncleanness and to lawlessness unto
lawlessness, now he presents his members as servants to righteousness unto sanctification (Rom. 6:19).   Righteousness and
lawlessness stand therefore in completely radical opposition to
each other as two contradictory states.

Or what communion hath light with darkness? No antithesis in the
daily experience of man is more fundamental than that between
light and darkness; and this antithesis provides a parable of the
fundamental incompatibility of belief and unbelief.   It is out of
"the power of darkness" that sinful man needs to be delivered
(Col. 1:13).   Christ is "the Light of the world" (Jn. 8:12; 9:5)
and His advent meant the shining of a great light for those sitting
in darkness (Mt. 4:16 = Isa. 9:2; Lk. 1:79; Jn. 1:4f.).   The
essence of unbelief is that, though the Light has come into the
world, men love darkness rather than light (Jn. 3:19).   The latter
end of the unbeliever is to be cast into "outer darkness" (Mt.
8:12; 22:13; 25:30), for "God is light and in Him is no darkness
at all" (I Jn. 1:5).   Believers have been called "out of darkness
into His marvellous light" (I Pet. 2:9).   Paul was sent by God
to the Gentiles precisely "to open their eyes, that they might
turn from darkness to light" (Acts 26:16ff.).   Thus, in our epistle,
he has already reminded the Corinthian believers that the same

10   Ἀνομία.
11   Ὁ ἄνομος.

God, who in creation caused light to shine out of darkness, in re-creation has shined in their hearts, giving them "the light of the knowledge of the glory of God in the face of Jesus Christ" (4:6).

6:15

And what concord hath Christ with Belial? or what portion hath a believer with an unbeliever?

Now the captains themselves of the hosts of light and darkness are placed in juxtaposition: Christ, the Lord our Righteousness, the Light of the world, and Belial, the prince of lawlessness and darkness. Between these two no harmony is possible, but only the deadliest antagonism. The devil, whose dark and lawless character is revealed in the fact that he is a liar and a murderer from the beginning (Jn. 8:44), has always made it his supreme objective to oppose and overthrow the purposes of God. Hence he is known as *Satan*, "the adversary". He it was who entered into Judas and induced him to betray the incarnate Son of God into the hands of wicked men to be put to death (Lk. 22:3; Jn. 13:27). It was through death, however, that Christ, God's chosen and anointed One, brought to nought "him that had the power of death, that is, the devil", so that He might deliver "all them who through fear of death were all their lifetime subject to bondage" (Heb. 2:14f.). The antithesis, once again, is absolute: "He that doeth righteousness is righteous, even as Christ is righteous; he that doeth sin is of the devil, for the devil sinneth from the beginning". The Son of God was manifested for this very purpose, "that He might destroy the works of the devil" (I Jn. 3:7f.).

Some (for example, Bengel, Lietzmann) have taken Belial here to denote Antichrist. But had Paul intended Antichrist—who in the New Testament is set forward as animated by the spirit of Satan rather than as Satan himself—it is likely that he would have used that term here, rather than Belial which in his day was recognized as a name for Satan.[12]

---

[12] Βελίαρ represents the Hebrew בְּלִיַּעַל which is not uncommon in the Old Testament. Though the Vulgate and AV often treat it as a proper name, that does not seem to be in accordance with its Old Testament usage. The precise significance and derivation of the term בליעל, however, is a matter of uncertainty. The following derivations have been suggested:

This text is cited in the Encyclical Letter of the Council of Sardica (c. 343 A.D.) in support of the prohibition of fellowship of any kind with the Arian heretics: "For they who separate the Son and alienate the Word from the Father ought themselves to be separated from the Catholic Church and to be alien from the Christian name. Let them therefore be anathema to you, because they have adulterated the word of truth. ... Charge your people that no one hold communion with them, for there is no communion of light with darkness; put away from you all these, for there is no concord of Christ with Belial. And take

(i) בְּלִי, "without", plus עוֹל, "yoke". This was Jerome's understanding of the term — "Belial, absque jugo, quod de collo suo Dei abjecerit servitutem" (on Eph. 4); cf. Judg. 19:22 Vg., "filii Belial (id est absque jugo)". Thus explained, Belial signifies rebelliousness, lawlessness, unrestraint. (ii) בְּלִי, "without" plus the root עלה, "to ascend", giving the meaning "without ascent", so that the term would signify degradation, debasement. In this connection mention may be made of Cheyne's suggestion (*Expositor*, June, 1895) that the word is a mythological survival, signifying "the subterranean watery abyss" which was regarded as "the depth which lets no man return" (בְּלִי יַעֲלֶה).

(iii) More generally accepted than either of the foregoing is the linking of בְּלִי with the root יעל, "to profit" or "to benefit", giving the sense "worthlessness". Yet it is important to notice that the LXX rendering of בְּלִיַּעַל frequently seems to support the first of these suggestions (i.e., that *Belial* = a state of being without yoke, lawlessness). Thus "sons of Belial" is translated ἄνδρες παράνομοι, "lawless men" (Deut. 13:13), and *Belial* is rendered ἀνόμημα, "lawless act", in Deut. 5:9, and ἀνομία, "lawlessness" in II Sam. 22:5 (= Ps. 18:4). It is of particular interest to find the term occurring twice in the first chapter of Nahum, in the first instance in the impersonal sense which is customary in the Old Testament (= "wickedness", RV, v. 11), and in the second as the designation of a person (= "the wicked one", RV, v. 15: literally, "Belial shall no more pass through thee; he is utterly cut off"). This is cited by Cheyne as an illustration of the transition to the use of the word absolutely as a title for Satan, which becomes normal in the apocryphal literature (and is the sense in which Paul uses it in the passage before us). Βελίαρ is the spelling most strongly attested here, though besides Βελίαλ the variants Βελίαν and Βελίαβ are found. As there is a tendency in language for *l* and *r* to become interchangeable, it has been suggested that this is what has happened with the final consonant of *Belial* (Meyer, Alford, Plummer, and others). A New Testament example of this phenomenon of dissimilation is found in the terms φραγελλόω, φραγέλλιον, which are taken over from the Latin = *flagello*, *flagellum* (Mt. 27:20; Mk. 15:15; Jn. 2:15), and in which the substitution of *l* for *r* is plainly displayed. (A Hebrew transliteration, פרגל, is also found.) So also two forms of the same word may occur: for example, κλίβανος, κρίβανος, and φαῦλος, φαῦρος. Somewhat in the same manner as the

heed, dearly beloved, that ye neither write to them nor receive letters from them; but desire rather, brethren and fellow-ministers, as being present in spirit with our Council, to assent to our judgment by your subscriptions, to the end that concord may be preserved by all our fellow-ministers everywhere".[13] Augustine adduces this same text when denouncing the superstitious wearing of amulets: "As for the accursed superstition of wearing amulets", he writes, "... it is practised with the view not of pleasing men but of doing homage to devils. But who can expect to find in Scripture express prohibition of every form of wicked superstition, seeing that the Apostle says generally, 'I would not that ye should have communion with devils', and again, 'What harmony is there between Christ and Belial?' ... Meanwhile, let those unhappy people be admonished that, if they persist in disobedience to salutary precepts, they must at least forbear from defending their impieties and thereby involving themselves in greater guilt. But why should we argue at all with them if they are afraid to take off their earrings, and are not afraid to receive the body of Christ while wearing the badge of the devil?"[14]

Or what portion hath a believer with an unbeliever? This resumes the opening warning against being unequally yoked with un-

---

Chinese are popularly supposed to pronounce *r*'s like *l*'s when speaking English, Alcibiades is represented by Aristophanes as pronouncing his *r*'s as *l*'s: ὁρᾷς as ὁλᾷς, Θέωρος as Θέωλος, and κόραξ as κόλαξ, because of some disability of speech (*Vespae*, 44f.). A contemporary example of the tendency for *l* to become *r* is found in the neighbouring Spanish and Portuguese languages, in which, for example, *blanco* (Spanish) = *branco* (Portuguese), "white", and *iglesia* (Spanish) = *igreja* (Portuguese), "church". It must be said, however, that if this form of dissimilation were to take place with the word *Belial*, it is far more likely that the first rather than the final *l* would be altered to *r*. (The form Βερίαλ is in fact found.) The number of textual variants indicates, moreover, that there was considerable uncertainty about the last consonant. With regard to the Greek form Βελίαρ, which receives the best attestation in the New Testament, J. H. Moulton felt that "some Semitic etymology need not be excluded" (*Grammar*, II, p. 103), and Cheyne was of the opinion that, if it is not to be ascribed to the harsh Syriac pronunciation of the word Βελίαλ, it "must be derived from בְּל יַעַל, lord of the forest". It is our view that there is no good warrant for abandoning the traditional association of the term with the בְּלִיַּעַל of the Old Testament and apocryphal writings.

[13] The text is given in Athanasius, *Apol. cont. Arian.*, 49.
[14] Augustine, *Ep.* CCXLV, to Possidius.

believers. The unbeliever's life is centred on self, the believer's on Christ; the treasure of the one is here on earth, of the other in heaven; the values of the one are those of this world, of the other those of the world to come; the believer seeks the glory of God, the unbeliever the glory of men. The antithesis, however, must not be interpreted as though it encouraged pharisaic concepts of contamination or invited to eremitic and monastic attempts at segregation from "the world". As Calvin wisely observes, "when Paul says that the Christian has no portion with the unbeliever he is not referring to food, clothing, estates, the sun, and the air, ... but to those things which are peculiar to unbelievers, from which the Lord has separated us".

6:16

> And what agreement hath a temple of God with idols? for we are a temple of the living God; even as God said, I will dwell in them, and walk in them; and I will be their God, and they shall be my people.

To the Jew, with his strictly spiritual and monotheistic knowledge of God, idols were an abomination (cf. Rom. 2:22), for idolatry was not only the infringement of the second commandment of the decalogue, but also the deletion of the absolute distinction between the Creator and His creatures. The temple at Jerusalem was, accordingly, entirely free of any kind of graven image or idol. The Jewish abhorrence of idols was spontaneously demonstrated by the display of open consternation when, some twenty years before the writing of our epistle, the Emperor Caligula promulgated an edict requiring his bust to be set up and worshipped in the temple and in all synagogues. Submission to such a demand would for the Jew have been an act of inconceivable blasphemy, such as to cause the temple to cease from being *God's* temple and to become a centre of profanity. The antipathy between God's temple and idols was radical and absolute.

The background of the Gentile was, of course, very different; but, once converted, his opposition to idols could hardly be less pronounced, for becoming a Christian meant for him a complete break with his religious past, which was one of idol-worship (cf. Acts 17:16), in contrast to the Jew in this respect. Thus Paul reminds the Thessalonian believers that they had "turned unto

God from idols, to serve a living and true God" (I Thess. 1:9); and the Council of Jerusalem had found it necessary to enjoin that Gentile converts should "abstain from the pollutions of idols" (Acts 15:20). As for the Corinthians, Paul had already, in his earlier letter, had occasion to warn them to flee from idolatry and indeed not even to keep company with any professing fellow-Christian who was found to be an idolater; for idolaters are among those who have no part in the kingdom of God (I Cor. 10:7, 14; 5:10f.; 6:9f.).

That the Apostle is not, however, speaking merely in general terms of church worship, but intends his admonition to be understood by his readers as applying to them in a personal sense, is shown by his adding of the explanation: "for we are a temple of the living God". If it was unthinkable for a temple of wood and stones to have any association with idols, how much more so a temple constructed of living stones! This simile had already been employed in the earlier letter, with a twofold application: (i) corporately, to believers, who together form the Church of Christ (I Cor. 3:16f.), and (ii) individually, to the separate believer, whose body is a temple of the Holy Spirit (I Cor. 6:19f.). In our present passage Paul's language indicates the corporate figure, but the responsibility of the individual to keep himself pure is both implicit and later emphasized (7:1). The corporate temple is built of individual persons. The same temple-image is found again in Eph. 2:20ff.: "Ye are ... built upon the foundation of the apostles and prophets, Christ Jesus Himself being the chief corner stone, in whom the whole building, fitly framed together, groweth into a holy temple in the Lord; in whom ye also are builded together for a habitation of God in the Spirit"; and in I Pet. 2:5: "Ye also, as living stones, are built up a spiritual house, to be a holy priesthood, to offer up spiritual sacrifices, acceptable to God through Jesus Christ". It is, indeed, a figure of speech which had first received the sanction of Christ Himself, who spoke of the temple of His body (Jn. 2:21). God's true dwelling-place,[15] so far as His relation to men is concerned, is

---

[15] The term ναός, translated "temple" in our version, was properly used of the innermost sanctuary of a temple where the divine presence was supposed to be located. Being cognate with the verb "to dwell", it signified the dwelling-place of a god.

in believing hearts, and not in temples made with hands—a truth expressed in the Acts of the Apostles by the lips both of Stephen (7:48) and of Paul (17:24). Indeed, it may well be that Paul, who witnessed Stephen's martyrdom, had also been one of those who listened to his defence and had been strongly though unwillingly impressed with the significance of this particular truth. Whether that is so or not, the temple-concept stands out as a favourite element of his apostolic teaching.

Paul confirms what he has just been saying with a chain of quotations from the Old Testament Scriptures. Here and elsewhere it is abundantly clear that the Scriptures are for him the authoritative Word of God, the absolute truth of which is not open to dispute. Yet a comparison of texts reveals that he did not feel himself bound to quote slavishly word for word, but rather according to the sense and with the purpose of applying and showing the relevance of the revelation to the circumstances of his readers.[16]

To begin with, he cites Lev. 26:11f., which reads: "I will set my tabernacle among you ..., and I will walk among you, and will be your God, and ye shall be my people". The change in the pronouns from the second to the third person plural is explained by reference to Ezek. 37:26f. (see below). It in no way affects the sense. Nor does the change from "I will set my tabernacle among you" to "I will dwell in them"; for to set one's tabernacle among signifies precisely to dwell in or among: the tabernacle of the Lord, and in particular the ark of the covenant which was within the innermost sanctuary of the Holy of Holies, was a guarantee to the Israelites of the presence of God in their midst. As verse 9 of Lev. 26 demonstrates, this promise was

---

[16] "In some twenty quotations in which the LXX and M. T. agree and Paul's text varies, the evidence of *pesher* quotation is more certain", says E. E. Ellis. "In almost all of these the variation seems to be a deliberate adaptation to the N.T. context; in some cases the alteration has a definite bearing on the interpretation of the passage. Changes in person and number are especially prevalent. The deviations in the *catena* in II Cor. vi. 16ff. are evidently designed for a messianic-age interpretation of the prophecies. God's command to Israel regarding Babylon *(αὐτῆς)* is now applied to the relation of Christians with unbelievers *(αὐτῶν)*; the promise given to Israel 'personified' in Solomon *(αὐτῷ ... αὐτός)* is fulfilled in the true Israel, the members of Christ's body *(ὑμῖν ... ὑμεῖς)*"—*New Testament Studies*, Nov. 1955, p. 130. Cf. also *Paul's Use of the Old Testament*, pp. 90ff., by the same author.

intimately bound up with God's age-old covenant of grace which had originally been established with Abraham (Gen. 17:7ff.). It is, further, an integral element of God's new covenant, which is essentially one with the Abrahamic covenant, and which finds its ultimate fulfilment in Christ and in the pentecostal gift of the Holy Spirit. Accordingly, Paul almost certainly also had in mind the promise of Ezek. 37:26f.: "I will make a covenant of peace with them: it shall be an everlasting covenant with them; ... and I will set my sanctuary in the midst of them for evermore. My tabernacle also shall be with them, and I will be their God, and they shall be my people" (cf. Jer. 31:31ff.). This great covenant promise is realized in three stages: (i) at the incarnation of the Son of God, when "the Word became flesh and tabernacled among us" [17] (Jn. 1:14); (ii) during this present and final age between the two comings of Christ, when God in Christ by the Holy Spirit tabernacles again as it were in flesh, dwelling within the hearts of His people (Eph. 3:17); and (iii) hereafter, in the glorious and crowning experience of the heavenly perfection, the consummation of our redemption, when the voice from the throne declares: "Behold, the tabernacle of God is with men, and He shall dwell with them, and they shall be His people, and God Himself shall be with them and be their God" (Rev. 21:3). To know Christ is indeed to know Him who is truly and fully Immanuel, "God with us" (Mt. 1:23), and in whom all God's covenant promises receive their affirmation (1:20).

The following passage from the *Martyrdom of Ignatius* is worth quoting at this point. Ignatius is standing face to face with the Emperor Trajan.

"Who art thou", said Trajan, "thou wretch of a devil, that art so ready to transgress our orders, whilst thou seducest others also, that they may come to a bad end?" Ignatius said: "No man calleth one that beareth God a wretch of a devil; for the devils stand aloof from the servants of God..." Trajan said: "And who is he that beareth God?" Ignatius answered: "He that hath Christ in his breast". Trajan said: "Dost thou not think then that we too have gods in our heart, seeing that we employ them as allies against our enemies?" Ignatius said: "Thou art deceived, when thou callest the devils of the nations gods. For there is one God who made the heaven and the earth and the sea and all

---

[17] Ἐσκήνωσεν ἐν ἡμῖν.

254

things that are therein, and one Christ Jesus His only-begotten Son, whose friendship I would fain enjoy". Trajan said: "Speakest thou of him that was crucified under Pontius Pilate?" Ignatius said: "I speak of Him that nailed on the cross sin and its author, and sentenced every malice of the devils to be trampled under foot of those that carry Him in their heart". Trajan said: "Dost thou then carry Christ within thyself?" Ignatius said: "Yes, for it is written, 'I will dwell in them and will walk about in them'." Trajan gave sentence: "It is our order that Ignatius who saith he beareth about the crucified in himself shall be put in chains by the soldiers and taken to mighty Rome, there to be made food for wild beasts, as a spectacle and a diversion for the people".[18]

6 : 17, 18

Wherefore, Come ye out from among them, and be ye separate, saith the Lord, And touch no unclean thing; and I will receive you, and will be to you a Father, and ye shall be to me sons and daughters, saith the Lord Almighty.

Scripture is reinforced by Scripture. The implications of the quotation Paul has just given (Lev. 26:11f. + Ezek. 37:26f.) are pressed home ("wherefore") by the use of further quotations in combination. Verse 17 combines the thought of two passages from the prophetic writings of the Old Testament: Isa. 52:11, "Depart ye, depart ye, go out from thence, touch no unclean thing, go ye out of the midst of her" (cf. Jer. 51:45, "My people, go ye out of the midst of her ..."), and Ezek. 20:34, "I will bring you out from the peoples and will gather you out of the countries wherein ye are scattered ..." Paul has admonished the Corinthians negatively by telling them not to be unequally yoked with unbelievers; but, in view of the absolute incompatibility of the kingdom of Christ with that of Satan, and in view, further, of the covenant promise cited in the preceding verse, positive action is also required: they must take steps to separate themselves from all that is unclean and to be free from unholy compromise. The Old Testament passages to which allusion is now made were originally addressed to God's people who,

---

[18] *Martyrdom of Ignatius*, iii (Bishop Lightfoot's translation). For a discussion of the question concerning the authenticity of the Antiochene Acts of Martyrdom, from which the quotation above is taken, see J. B. Lightfoot, *Apostolic Fathers*, Part II, Vol. II (London, 1889), pp. 383ff.

because of their sin, had been taken captive by their enemies and led into circumstances of gross wickedness and idolatry. Isa. 52:11 is, in fact, addressed in particular to those "that bear the vessels of the Lord", that is, the priests of God's temple. That such passages are with appropriateness applied to Christian believers is shown by the following considerations: (i) Christians are the people of God, ransomed from the captivity and defilement of sin by the blood of Christ; (ii) they are all members of a royal priesthood (I Pet. 2:9; Rev. 1:6); and (iii) the vessels of the Lord which they bear are their own bodies (cf. Acts 9:15; Rom. 9:21ff.; II Cor. 4:7; I Thess. 4:4; II Tim. 2:20f.). There was a grave danger that, through carelessness and compromise, the Corinthian believers would be carried away, as it were, into a Babylonian captivity of the soul. It is no idle injunction, there-fore, (which Paul offered to the members of the church in another city) that they who were once darkness, but are now light in the Lord, should "walk as children of light ... and have no fellow-ship with the unfruitful works of darkness" (Eph. 5:7ff.). Calvin rightly points out, however, that we who have been redeemed and rescued from the pollutions of the world are not meant to turn our backs on life, but only to avoid all participation in the world's uncleanness. Christians, indeed, as our Lord taught, are the light *of the world*; this they cannot be if their light is hidden or withdrawn. Thus they are to let their light shine before men (Mt. 5:14ff.), though at the same time shunning the depravities of unregenerate society and of unchristian worship.

Paul's sequence of quotations from the Scriptures is completed (in v. 18) by giving, once again, the thought of more than one Old Testament passage in combination. Thus in Isa. 43:6 God speaks of His sons and daughters being brought back from the ends of the earth (cf. Hos. 1:10), and in II Sam. 7:8, 14, which seems mainly to have been in the Apostle's mind at this point, we read: "Thus saith the Lord of hosts, ... I will be his Father and he shall be my son".[19] The words of II Sam. 7:8ff. were

---

[19] The similarity of grammatical structure between the LXX of II Sam. 7:8, 14 and II Cor. 6:18 is particularly interesting, as the following comparison shows:

II Sam. 7:8, 14 — τάδε λέγει Κύριος παντοκράτωρ ... ἐγὼ ἔσομαι αὐτῷ εἰς πατέρα καὶ αὐτὸς ἔσται μοι εἰς υἱόν.

II Cor. 6:18 — ἔσομαι ὑμῖν εἰς πατέρα, καὶ ὑμεῖς ἔσεσθέ μοι εἰς υἱοὺς καὶ θυγατέρας, λέγει Κύριος παντοκράτωρ.

originally spoken to David concerning his son who was to succeed him. The manner in which Paul adduces this passage here is of a piece with the attitude of the rest of the New Testament to the promises of the Old Testament, namely, that they have both a proximate fulfilment in Christ (see Heb. 1:5, where II Sam. 7:14 is explicitly applied to Christ) and, as is natural, in those who are one with Him. Christ is unique as the eternal Son of God and, after the flesh, as the messianic Son of David. Before God, all sonship is concentrated in Him. Accordingly, it is only by union with Christ, through redeeming grace and the response of faith, that men and women may so participate in His Sonship as to become the sons and daughters of God the Heavenly Father (cf. Jn. 1:12). It should be noticed that, as always, it is God who takes the initiative in the work of grace. The one who utters the promise is God, the Sovereign Lord of all,[20] whose word is creative and cannot fail to perform what it promises. It is God who, by His reconciling act in Christ Jesus, presents Himself to us as a Father, even while we are enemies and rebels against His goodness (Rom. 5:6, 8, 10), and opens wide the door into the home of His love.

7:1

Having therefore these promises, beloved, let us cleanse ourselves from all defilement of flesh and spirit, perfecting holiness in the fear of God.

In applying the plain lessons of these promises Paul addresses the members of the Corinthian church with the tenderest affection as "beloved"—a form of address which is all the more significant of the warmth of his love towards them because he employs it with comparative infrequency: it occurs only on six other occasions in his letters (once more in our epistle, 12:19, and also in I Cor. 10:14; 15:58; Rom. 12:19; Phil. 2:12; 4:1). The affectionate tone of this earnest exhortation is amplified by his saying "let us", rather than (as with every reason he might have done) "do you". He exhorts not only them, but himself also. Despite the disgraceful way in which they have treated him and the grievous moral lapses they had condoned, he reaffirms his loving oneness with them. These considerations go to show that the section 6:14–7:1

---

[20] Κύριος παντοκράτωρ.

is not in reality out of character with the affectionate appeals of 6:11–13 and 7:2–4 on either side of it.

The promises which Paul has cited are not vague and general in their application; they are specific and wonderful promises attached to God's everlasting covenant, and as such they belong to the Christian believer as his own proper possession and heritage (cf. Gal. 3:22, 29). The logical consequence ("therefore") of possessing such promises is that Christ's followers should make a complete break [21] with every form of unhealthy compromise—the necessity for a thorough cleansing is emphasized both by declaring that it should be from *all* defilement and also by the addition of the words "of flesh and spirit", that is, all defilement of every possible kind, both external and internal, both seen and unseen, both public and private—and not only that, but that they should also advance constantly in holiness.[22] Not only are our members *not* to be presented unto sin as instruments of unrighteousness, but they *are* to be presented as instruments of righteousness unto God (Rom. 6:13). We are intended to press on towards the goal of perfection (Heb. 6:1). And this is to be done "in the fear of God"—that is, in reverence and devotion towards Him to whom we owe everything, in awe of Him at whose judgment-seat we shall have to give an account of the things done in the body (5:10f.), and in dread lest, through carelessness and disloyalty, we should be ashamed before Christ at His coming (I Jn. 2:28). Not that the perfection of holiness will be attained in this life; for holiness is synonymous with Christlikeness, and that will be realized only at Christ's appearing, when, seeing Him even as He is, we shall at last become fully like Him. John, accordingly, is saying precisely the same thing as Paul says here when he writes that every one who has this hope in Christ purifies himself, even as He is pure (I Jn. 3:2f.). Thorough cleansing from defilement involves also continual progress in holiness.

Some scholars have formed the opinion that the expression "defilement of flesh and spirit" could never have been written by the Apostle Paul. It is, however, demonstrably incorrect to

---

[21] This is the force of the aorist καθαρίσωμεν. The combination of καθαρίζειν ἀπό is found again in Heb. 9:14 and also in some inscriptions (see Deissmann, *Bible Studies*, pp. 216f.).

[22] This is the force of the present participle ἐπιτελοῦντες.

suppose that "flesh" and "spirit" are always technical and opposite terms when used by him. Of course, there are occasions when the two words stand in strong contradistinction to each other (as, for example, in Rom. 8:12ff. and Gal. 5:16ff.); but they do not cease to be common words of everyday language, and consequently the context in which they are placed must be allowed to determine their significance on each occasion of their use. Their force in the passage before us is, as Bachmann points out, psychological, not ethical. This is quite obviously also the case in Col. 2:5: "... though I am absent in the flesh, yet I am with you in the spirit"—a statement which corresponds exactly to that of I Cor. 5:3 where Paul speaks of "being absent in body but present in spirit". In Gal. 2:20, again, the Apostle declares that the life which he now lives "in the flesh" is a life lived in faith. In these instances, then, it is clear that "the flesh" is used as a synonym for the body. The term "flesh", indeed, is found again in a non-technical sense just a little later in the chapter on which we have now entered, when, Paul, referring to the afflictions he had endured in Macedonia, says, "our flesh had no relief", significantly (for our present discussion) adding that there were fightings without and fears within—indicating that in this instance "flesh" implies the whole bodily existence, inward as well as outward (see commentary below on 7:5). We may point also to I Cor. 7:34: "... holy both in body and in spirit", as corresponding closely to the concept here of cleansing "from all defilement of flesh and spirit". These examples are sufficient to demonstrate that there is no justification for the conclusion that the expression "defilement of flesh and spirit" is un-Pauline. Such a judgment can be based only on the assumption that in Paul's thought "flesh" and "spirit" inevitably represent an absolute dualistic antithesis, as though dictated by Pythagorean, or even Gnostic, preconceptions. To judge in this way, however, betrays a fundamental misunderstanding of the New Testament doctrine of the constitution of man as God's creature.

The reading found in Tertullian: "defilement of flesh and blood",[23] probably reflects a Gnostic "correction" of "spirit" to "blood". Another early attempt to resolve the supposed difficulty of the expression "defilement of spirit" is apparent in the sugges-

---

[23] Tertullian, *Adv. Marc.*, V, 12.

tion that the term "spirit" here should be taken with what follows, not with what precedes it. Thus, instead of "let us cleanse ourselves from all defilement of flesh and spirit, perfecting holiness in the fear of God", the sentence would read: "let us cleanse ourselves from all defilement of the flesh, perfecting holiness of spirit in the fear of God". Augustine classed this as an ambiguity of punctuation, which might be decided either way in accordance with the reader's discretion.[24] But there can be no doubt that our version conveys the more natural understanding of the Greek text and that endeavours to disconnect the terms "spirit" and "flesh" from each other display an exegetical embarrassment which is the result of philosophical rather than scriptural presuppositions.

7:2

Open your hearts to us: we wronged no man, we corrupted no man, we took advantage of no man.

This is clearly a resumption of the appeal of 6:11–13: "O Corinthians, our heart is enlarged... Be ye also enlarged". As there is spacious accommodation for the Corinthians in his heart, so the Apostle desires them to respond by making room for him in their hearts.[25] A threefold denial is now added, that no person had been unjustly treated, ruined, or made a source of personal enrichment by him;[26] and it seems likely that it is in fact a threefold repudiation of charges which had been made against him, and the tenor of which had been conveyed by Titus when he and Paul met in Macedonia (cf. vv. 5ff.). Was it being said (by the false apostles) that some had suffered injury or injustice at his hands because of an alleged overbearing and dictatorial abuse of the authority he claimed?—that by his severe judgments he had destroyed or ruined some, for example, the man guilty of incest whom he had declared should be delivered to Satan for

---

24 Augustine, *De Doct. Chr.*, III, 2.

25 The verb χωρεῖν means "to make room for", "to provide a place for" (cf. Mk. 2:2; Mt. 19:11; Jn. 8:37; 21:25). Though χωρήσατε ἡμᾶς here is literally "make room for us", the implication, brought forward from 6:11–13, is "in your hearts". Hence our version, "open your hearts to us", conveys Paul's meaning.

26 The three aorists ἠδικήσαμεν, ἐφθείραμεν, ἐπλεονεκτήσαμεν point back to a definite occasion, no doubt the time when he was in Corinth. On the significance of πλεονεκτεῖν see note on 2:11.

the destruction of the flesh (I Cor. 5:5)?—that he had defrauded them to his own material advantage, for example, by collecting money for the poverty-stricken saints at Jerusalem and then spending it on himself (cf. the clear allusion to a similar charge in 12:16–18 below; also Acts 20:33)?

Chrysostom, Herveius, and others, however, understand Paul to be referring here not so much to accusations made against himself as to the malpractices of the false apostles, who, coming into their midst, had been the cause of injury, corruption, and impoverishment to the members of the Corinthian church. His conduct, in contrast to theirs, had been blameless, as the Corinthians well knew.

7:3

I say it not to condemn you: for I have said before, that ye are in our hearts to die together and live together.

It is not Paul's purpose to indulge in recriminations, though the assumption is that he might with justification have spoken to their condemnation had that been his wish. This would appear to indicate that his denials in the previous verse were written with reference to specific accusations that had been made against himself, rather than with reference to the activities of the false apostles. His purpose, however, is to establish, or re-establish, the relationship of true Christian love and mutual confidence that should exist between the Apostle and the church he has founded. He is impelled by love, not bitterness. Hence his reminder to them of what he had already said earlier on, that they were in his heart, undoubtedly referring to 6:11 where he had affirmed that his heart was enlarged toward them. But his language now is even more intense; he speaks with the utmost devotion of the true lover: not only does he declare that they are in his heart, but that they are in his heart "to die together and live together"—so far as he is concerned, they will be one in true love, one in death as well as in life. This is not the language of romanticism but of Christian reality. That genuine love which is the expression of communion and fellowship in Christ is the greatest of those things which abide (I Cor. 13:13) and can neither be destroyed by death nor impaired by the changing circumstances of life. Could there be greater openness of speech and affection than is displayed here? And the authenticity of this protestation of his love is proved by the afflictions which Paul so willingly, and so constantly, endured for their comfort and salvation (1:6; 6:3ff.; 11:23ff.).

"It is worth noticing", says Tasker, "that the words *I have said before* may be taken to imply that Paul is deliberately making a reference back to vi. 11–13 after what he is conscious has been an abrupt diversion. If this deduction is legitimate, it is an argument against the view that vi. 14–vii. 1 is an interpolation from another letter".

7:4

> Great is my boldness of speech toward you, great is my glorying on your behalf: I am filled with comfort, I over-flow with joy in all our affliction.

Paul's mention of his great boldness of speech relates to the free manner in which he has just declared the warmth and constancy of his love for the Corinthians, and corresponds to the earlier statement in 6:11, "our mouth is open unto you". The Greek word here, however,[27] though its root meaning is that of outspokenness or boldness of speech, may also be used to signify boldness or confidence in a more general sense (as, for example, in Eph. 3:12; I Tim. 3:13; Heb. 3:6; 4:16; 10:19, 35: I Jn. 2:28; 3:21; 4:17; 5:14), and this sense has been preferred here by many commentators (cf. Vg., *fiducia*, and ARSV, "I have great confidence in you"). But, whichever rendering is favoured, the meaning of the passage is not vitally affected, for boldness of speech is indicative of confidence of heart.

Not only is Paul bold towards the Corinthians, but he also boasts because of them to others. One of those to whom he had spoken proudly of them, even at a time when they were allowing their attitude to him to be influenced by his detractors, was Titus (see v. 14 below). That was a triumph of love indeed! His glorying on their behalf openly demonstrates his fundamental confidence in them. As with true love, again, this glorying, this pride in each other, is reciprocal: they also have occasion to glory on his behalf (5:12); he is their glorying, even as they are his (1:14). The pride, however, which the Apostle takes in his

---

[27] Παρρησία.

converts is not that of self-congratulation, but that of joy and gratitude before God because of the manifestation of His saving and transforming grace, even through so unworthy an instrument as himself, in the lives of men and women who previously were in bondage to Satan. Such selfless glorying is characteristic of Paul, not least in this epistle (cf. 7:14; 8:24; 9:2–4; also I Thess. 2:19; II Thess. 1:4). In contrast to the ministers of Satan (11:15) who had invaded his territory at Corinth, his glorying is always and entirely glorying *in the Lord* (10:17).

Paul, moreover, is filled with comfort [28] with respect to the Corinthians, and he is more than filled with joy, for his joy overflows—and that too in the midst of all his affliction. The power of the Christian's consolation and joy is greater than that of any tribulation he may have to endure. This reality believers are constantly proving (cf. 1:3ff.). Here, of course, Paul is referring in particular to the comfort and joy he experienced upon hearing, through Titus, the news of the favourable response at Corinth to the letter he had written—as is evident from the explanatory conjunction "for" with which the next verse is introduced and from the whole following passage, which is one full of comfort and joy. Our present verse, in fact, constitutes a transition to the resumption of the account of the Apostle's meeting with Titus in Macedonia.

---

[28] Πεπλήρωμαι τῇ παρακλήσει. Ordinarily πληρόω is construed with a genitive, but the construction here with the dative is also classical, though rare. Paul uses it with the dative again in Rom. 1:29.

7:5

> For even when we were come into Macedonia our flesh
> had no relief, but we were afflicted on every side; without
> were fightings, within were fears.

At this point the Apostle takes up again the account (which
was interrupted at 2:14) of his movements and emotions prior
to the writing of this letter, so that the section 2:14 to 7:4 may
in this respect be regarded as an extensively developed parenthesis
or digression. This digressive propensity is characteristic of his
writing, and to it we owe, under God, some of the richest treasures
of New Testament theology. The case in point is no exception;
indeed, were the intervening four chapters missing from our
Bibles some of the mountain peaks of spiritual doctrine and
consolation would be covered from our view.

It will be understood, then, that to speak of digressions of
some length in Paul's epistles in no way implies that their contents
should therefore be regarded as only of incidental or secondary
importance. They are, in fact, digressions in no more than a
relative sense, that is, in relation to a particular theme which is
taken up, set aside for a while, and then, sooner or later, resumed.
That that theme is not necessarily the chief theme of the epistle
is evident from the instance which we are now considering:
Paul's travels, especially his crossing from the Troad to Macedonia,
and his meeting there with Titus, while highly relevant and
integral to the whole, may none the less be described (as we have
previously described it—see commentary on 2:14 above) as part
of the skeletal framework to which the flesh of the epistle is
attached. A digression of this kind, furthermore, serves to remind
us that Paul is composing a spontaneous *letter*, that he is writing
in his capacity of apostle and pastor, not as a self-conscious
logician or essayist—though himself deficient neither in logical
skill nor in literary ability.

In 2:12f. the Apostle was explaining how, in the cause of
Christ's gospel, he came to Troas, but, failing to find Titus there
(whom he was expecting with news direct from Corinth), had
no relief for his spirit and so travelled on into Macedonia (in the

hope, that is, of encountering Titus in that place with the news which he so urgently desired to hear). He now resumes this narrative, explaining further how even after his arrival in Macedonia his flesh had no relief, for there he was distressed by outward contentions (which would seem to indicate a state of disharmony within the Macedonian church) and inward anxieties—not, however, anxieties concerning his own safety, since nothing would have been more out of character for one who counted not his life dear to himself (Acts 20:24) and who looked forward to the time when he would be at home with the Lord (5:8; Phil. 1:21, 23), but concerning the spiritual well-being of his converts at Corinth.

It is of interest to compare Paul's mode of expression here with that which he uses in 2:13. There he says that in Troas he had no relief for his *spirit*, because he failed to find Titus in that place. Here he says that even when Macedonia had been reached his *flesh* had no relief prior to the arrival of Titus. Now, it is apparent that the relief of his spirit in 2:13 and the relief of his flesh here are intended by him as generally synonymous expressions, for the latter expression is in effect a resumption of the former—the relief that he lacked in Troas was still lacking in Macedonia, until the moment of his meeting with Titus. We have, then, in these expressions (which, though separated from each other by a prolonged digression, are none the less, so far as Paul's narrative of his movements is concerned, used in close conjunction with each other) a further example of a non-technical usage of the terms "flesh" and "spirit". In 7:1 the two terms in combination signify the entirety of human existence and experience, outward and inward. In the two instances which we are now considering the part is used for the whole: "spirit" in 2:13 and "flesh" here, as though the one implies the other; for it is the spirit which animates the flesh and co-ordinates its experiences, and it is the flesh which is the vehicle of the spirit and the means of its expression. Hence the comprehensive association of the flesh here with inward as well as outward experiences.[1] It is worth noticing that Tertullian enlists this verse in support of his argument from Scripture for the ultimate glorification of the body together with the soul: as the outward man is not exposed to sufferings apart from the inward man, "both will be

---

[1] On the significance of the perfect ἔσχηκε here, see notes above on ἔσχηκα, 2:13, and ἐσχήκαμεν, 1:9

glorified together, even as they have suffered together; parallel with their participation in troubles must necessarily run their association also in rewards".[2]

7 : 6

Nevertheless he that comforteth the lowly, even God, comforted us by the coming of Titus.

It is an appellation especially attributable to God that He is "the One who comforts those who are cast down";[3] whence as Calvin remarks, "a most profitable doctrine may be inferred, namely, that the more we are afflicted, so much the greater is the consolation prepared for us by God". This, indeed, as we have already had cause to observe more than once, is one of the dominant notes of this epistle, the whole of which affords a noble proof that the ascription with which it opens—"Blessed be the God and Father of our Lord Jesus Christ, the Father of mercies and God of all comfort, who comforteth us in all our affliction" (1:3f.)—is not a piously framed formality, but the expression of the emotion of the Apostle's gratitude surging up from the deep wells of his own experience of divine consolation. Paul's description of God, as though by a familiar title, as "the One who comforts those who are cast down" seems to betray an echo of Isa. 49:13—a passage which was very probably in his mind while he was writing.[4] It was the arrival of Titus, bringing the longed-for news from Corinth, which God used to drive away the Apostle's anxious misgivings and to replace them with joy and comfort.

7 : 7

And not by his coming only, but also by the comfort wherewith he was comforted in you, while he told us your longing, your mourning, your zeal for me; so that I rejoiced yet more.

To remove any possible misunderstanding on the part of the Corinthians, Paul makes it plain that it was not simply the joy

---

[2] Tertullian, *De Resurr. Carn.*, XL.

[3] The force of ταπεινός here is psychological, = "downcast", "depressed", rather than ethical, = "lowly", "humble".

[4] Compare the LXX rendering of the last clause of Isa. 49:13, καὶ τοὺς ταπεινοὺς τοῦ λαοῦ αὐτοῦ παρεκάλεσεν, with ὁ παρακαλῶν τοὺς ταπεινοὺς παρεκάλεσεν ἡμᾶς here.

of reunion with his friend and fellow-labourer Titus that had brought him such comfort—as though his thoughts were for Titus and not for them—but rather the joy of discovering that Titus himself had been comforted and encouraged by them and had brought back such welcome news from their city. The report he gave had described their longing, their mourning, and their zeal on behalf of him who was their true apostle. Their longing doubtless denotes an earnest desire to see Paul again and to have the old harmony and confidence restored between themselves and him; their mourning, the sorrow and regret they had evinced for the wrong and ignoble things they had themselves done or condoned in others and for the unworthy manner in which they had caused him so much grief; and their zeal, the recaptured fervour and enthusiasm, displayed in their conduct, which was the evidence of the genuineness of their repentance and of their determination not to be the occasion of further grief to the one who had so selflessly brought the gospel of Jesus Christ to them in Corinth.

The position in the Greek of the thrice-repeated "your" seems to lend it a special emphasis,[5] suggesting, as Denney observes, a contrast and a counterpart to Paul's longing over the Corinthians, his deploring of their lapses, and his zeal for the integrity and advancement of their Christian living. Hitherto the longing, the mourning, and the zeal had been all on his side, but now, to his joy, it has become "*your* longing, *your* mourning, *your* zeal".

In consequence of all this Paul "rejoiced yet more". By this most modern commentators take him to mean that, great as was his delight at meeting with Titus, it was exceeded by the delight he experienced on receiving from him the good news of the Corinthian church. Another interpretation, which, however, is somewhat lacking in point, is that he rejoiced yet more than he was comforted. Others again have understood it to imply that the extent of his previous distress was exceeded by the extent of his present joy. But the connection in Paul's mind seems rather to be with the comfort and joy which Titus experienced during his visit to Corinth: the news that Titus had been well received

---

[5] In each case the ὑμῶν is placed between the article and the noun—τὴν ὑμῶν ἐπιπόθησιν, τὸν ὑμῶν ὀδυρμόν, τὸν ὑμῶν ζῆλον. For other examples of ὑμῶν in this position see 1:6, ὑπὲρ τῆς ὑμῶν παρακλήσεως (twice) and 12:19, ὑπὲρ τῆς ὑμῶν οἰκοδομῆς.

by the Corinthians, and had been comforted himself through their response, was a cause of increased rejoicing to the Apostle. This understanding of Paul's words is confirmed a little further on in verse 13, where he says that in his comfort he "he joyed the more exceedingly for the joy of Titus, because his spirit hath been refreshed by you all"; for it is apparent that verse 13 is a recapitulation of what he has said in our present verse. Thus, characteristically, Paul's own joy was enhanced and enlarged as a result of the joy of his friend whose mission to Corinth had produced so happy an outcome.

7 : 8, 9

> For though I made you sorry with my epistle, I do not regret it: though I did regret it (for I see that that epistle made you sorry, though but for a season), I now rejoice, not that ye were made sorry, but that ye were made sorry unto repentance; for ye were made sorry after a godly sort, that ye might suffer loss by us in nothing.

Paul has already assured the Corinthians that the purpose of his writing the letter in question was not that he might cause them sorrow, but that they might know his more abundant love for them (2:4)—for genuine love cannot remain silent when it sees those that are loved in danger, and therefore in need of urgent warning. Indeed, it was only "out of much affliction and anguish of heart, and with many tears" that he had written it at all (*ibid.*). Moreover, the sending of that letter had occasioned him regret because of the sorrow its contents would cause them. Genuine love, again, cannot fail to feel regret at the necessity for causing sorrow, even though that sorrow is but temporary and directed towards a beneficial end. Both Chrysostom and Calvin liken the Apostle's feelings to those experienced by a father: the former to a father who finds regret, not pleasure, in seeing his son suffering pain under the surgeon's knife, but pleasure, not regret, in the cure that the operation is producing; the latter to a father who is grieved when he finds it necessary to punish his son severely, but none the less approves the action because it is directed towards his son's welfare. The aptness of this simile is attested by Paul's earlier statement that his object in writing this stern letter to the Corinthians was that he might have proof of them, whether (like sons) they were obedient in all things (2:9; cf. 6:13). And now that he has received the good news of the beneficial effects of the sorrow he had induced, his regret is replaced by joy and comfort.[6]

Regret had given place to rejoicing; but Paul, careful to remove any possibility of misunderstanding or misrepresentation (so eager were his opponents in Corinth to distort his words), immediately and gently explains that it was not their sorrow that had occasioned him joy (on the contrary, he has just shown that their sorrow was the cause of his regret), but the fruit of their sorrow, namely, repentance. The impulse of the natural man upon receiving such a letter would have been to indulge in hypocritical self-vindication, and even in embittered recrimination; but the Corinthians, contentious though they had shown themselves to be in the past, had not responded in man's way: their sorrow had displayed itself in God's way,[7] which is the more excellent way of love (I Cor. 12:31, 13:1ff.)—without unkindness, self-vaunting, unseemliness, or readiness to be provoked. Had Paul not faithfully fulfilled his painful duty of writing in stern terms to them, and had they not responded with repentance, they would have suffered loss. If he had not fulfilled his part, difficult though it was, then they would have suffered loss as the result

---

6 The fact that the Vulgate renders βλέπω by the present participle *videns* caused Lachmann and Hort to suspect that the original reading was in fact the present participle βλέπων. Hort, indeed, having regard to the scribal practice of contracting the ending -ων to -ῶ, was of the opinion that this accounted for our present reading βλέπω and that the Vulgate had accordingly preserved the true reading. Since the proposal of this conjecture, moreover, and since the appearance of Westcott and Hort's edition of the Greek New Testament (in which they express the suspicion that βλέπω is "probably a primitive error for βλέπων"), the reading βλέπων has received the significant attestation of a document no less important than P46 (beginning of the third century). That it is the correct reading is almost certainly confirmed by the consideration that the conjunction γάρ must on the evidence available be rejected as unauthentic—an importation, doubtless, to smooth over the awkwardness of βλέπω by itself. Βλέπω γάρ ("for I see . . ."), however, suitably conveys the force of the participle βλέπων here. The participial clause is rightly regarded as parenthetic, and the main structure of the sentence is as given in our version: " . . . even though I did regret it (seeing that the letter in question caused you sorrow, even though only for the time being), yet now I rejoice . . ."

7 Κατὰ θεόν—"i.e. in a manner agreeable to the mind and will of God" (Hodge). For a similar usage of this expression cf. Rom. 8:27.

of his negligence.[8] The meaning of to "suffer loss" is well illustrated in what he had already said to them in his earlier letter. In building upon the foundation of Jesus Christ, which he as a wise master-builder had laid, it was his earnest desire that they should build with enduring and precious materials—gold, silver, precious stones—and not with perishable and worthless materials—wood, hay, stubble, which would be consumed in the day of testing and cause them to suffer loss, by which he means the loss not of salvation but of reward (I Cor. 3:10–15). Not content with having laid the saving foundation, he is aware of his solemn responsibility, as a diligent pastor and apostle, for the care and guidance of those whom he had brought to a knowledge of the gospel. Accordingly he was determined, by God's grace, to allow neither concern for their feelings nor unwillingness to give offence to preponderate in such a way as to make him keep silence, instead of dealing with them as a faithful father, and thereby to jeopardize their spiritual well-being.

THE IDENTITY OF THE EPISTLE MENTIONED IN 7:8

For a discussion of the different theories concerning the identification of the letter in question, see the commentary on 2:3f. above. From what has been said there it will be evident that we concur with Denney's judgment: "The letter is, on the simplest hypothesis, the First Epistle; and though no one would willingly speak to his friends as Paul in some parts of that Epistle speaks to the Corinthians, he cannot pretend that he wishes it unwritten". There, too, we have shown that I Corinthians is replete with material which must have had the impact as it were of a rod upon the backs of the Corinthian Christians, and the writing of which must have cost one as warm-hearted and affectionate as the Apostle Paul much anguish.

No less distinguished a commentator than Plummer provides, in his writings, an illustration of the dangers of inconsistency and stultification which beset the man who too stringently presses a hypothesis. With reference to what Paul says in our present passage he comments: "It is quite clear that he had written a letter about which he had misgivings and regrets; he could have wished that he had not written it. It is difficult to agree with those who think that he could ever have had such feelings about I Corinthians. Could he for a moment have regretted having

---

[8] ’Εξ ἡμῶν—a loss "having its origin in me".

written such a letter? There must have been another letter of a much more painful character". If, however, we turn to the commentary on I Corinthians of which Plummer and Robertson are the joint-authors, but of which, as Bishop Robertson states in the Preface, the greater part is the work of Plummer, we there find it asserted that "warmth of affection, *as well as warmth of remonstrance and censure*, characterize the epistle *throughout*", that by contrast Philippians is "unclouded by any reproach or suspicion", and that "the sympathy is combined with *anxious solicitude*, and alternates with *indignant remonstrance*".[9] Indeed, in commenting on 10:9 below ("that I may not seem as if I would terrify you by my letters") Plummer makes the significant admission that "the strict injunctions about fornicators in the first letter (1 Cor. v. 9), and the severe sentence on the incestuous person in 1 Cor. (v. 3–5), would justify the expression 'terrifying by my letters' without the addition of another severe letter". This being so, there seems to be justification for concluding that the letter to which the Apostle alludes in II Cor. 7:8 (and in 2:3f.) is none other than I Corinthians. It is worthwhile remembering, too, Tertullian's assessment of I Corinthians as having been written, "as a whole, *not with ink, but with gall*".[10] Where Plummer and others appear to have gone wrong is in supposing that it was *the letter* as such that Paul regretted, so that he would, had it been possible, have retracted it; whereas the text makes it plain that it was not the letter (which as a faithful apostle he had felt it his duty to write) which he regretted, but *the sorrow* which it was bound to cause its recipients, for their distress was his distress also. That, however, it turned out to be sorrow "unto repentance", sorrow "after a godly sort", was a matter for rejoicing both to them and to him.

7:10

For godly sorrow worketh repentance unto salvation, a repentance which bringeth no regret: but the sorrow of the world worketh death.

Godly sorrow in its outworking leads to repentance-unto-salvation.[11] All commentators appear to understand the Apostle

---

[9] Robertson and Plummer, *Commentary on I Corinthians* (I.C.C., Edinburgh, 1911), p. xlvi—italics mine.

[10] Tertullian, *De Pudicitia*, XIV.

[11] ᾿Αμεταμέλητον, an adjective of two terminations, could be taken with either μετάνοιαν or σωτηρίαν. The Vulgate, Theophylact, Ambrose, Augustine,

to mean that this repentance-unto-salvation brings no regret *to those who experience it.* This is, of course, a truism. But we do not hesitate to take a different line and to affirm it as our judgment that a closer consideration of the context demands that we should understand Paul to mean that the repentance-unto-salvation of the Corinthians, although born of sorrow, was something which *he, their Apostle,* could not regret. He *had* regretted the necessity for sending them a letter which would make them sorry (v. 8); but that their sorrow had brought forth the fruit of repentance-unto-salvation was something in no way to be regretted. This understanding of Paul's language preserves the integrity of the passage in both thought and expression.

As Calvin points out, the Apostle is not commending repentance as though it were the ground of salvation—which would amount to a most un-Pauline doctrine of justification by works. Paul's concern here is not with the ground of salvation, which is the pure grace of God in Christ, but with the commendation of repentance, itself a sign of the grace of God in operation, because of the fruit which it produces. In the case of the members of the Corinthian church, the nature of their response to Paul's letter was in itself a sure indication that they were, as they professed to be, genuine Christians, and not dissemblers.

Besides godly sorrow, however, there is a different kind of sorrow which Paul calls "the sorrow of the world", and which works out its fulfilment in death. He makes use of a similar concept in Rom. 7:13 where he speaks of *sin* as working out its fulfilment in death.[12] The sorrow of the world, indeed, is not something distinct from sin; on the contrary, it partakes of the very essence of sin. It is not sorrow because of the heinousness of sin as rebellion against God, but sorrow because of the painful

---

Herveius, Meyer, Bengel, Alford, Hodge, and others connect it with σωτηρίαν; but the majority of commentators, and also the English versions, are more likely to be correct in connecting it with μετάνοιαν. We would suggest, however, that it is more satisfactory still to take it as qualifying the whole phrase μετάνοιαν εἰς σωτηρίαν. This sense may be aptly conveyed by the use of hyphens: "repentance-unto-salvation which is not to be regretted".

[12] Ἡ ἁμαρτία . . . κατεργαζομένη θάνατον. The distinction in our verse between ἐργάζεται = "works" or "produces" and κατεργάζεται = "works out" or "produces its fulfilment in" should probably be preserved. The latter may be explained as an intensive compound designed to emphasize the inevitability of the outworking in death of the sorrow of the world.

and unwelcome consequences of sin. Self is its central point; and self is also the central point of sin. Thus the sorrow of the world manifests itself in self-pity rather than in contrition and turning to God for mercy. The sorrow of the world may be very bitter and intense, like that of Esau who sorrowed with many tears over his lost birthright but found no place of repentance (Heb. 12:16f.). David also suffered extreme sorrow because of his sin, but his sorrow was directed to God in deep penitence. Acknowledging his guilt and unworthiness, he cried to God for forgiveness: "Wash me thoroughly from mine iniquity and cleanse me from my sin; for I acknowledge my transgressions and my sin is ever before me. Against Thee, Thee only have I sinned ..." (Psa. 51:2ff.). His was truly godly sorrow—centred in God and His holiness. And such godly sorrow is transmuted into godly joy—the joy of God's salvation and the praise of His goodness (Psa. 51:12ff.). The sorrow of the world, on the other hand, culminates in the weeping and gnashing of teeth of judgment (Mt. 13:42, 50; 25:30); it earns the wages of sin (Rom. 6:23). Had this been the sorrow displayed by the Corinthians, they would thereby have shown themselves to be unbelievers and hypocrites. That Paul wrote to them as he did (and as he does in our present epistle) is a proof of his conviction that they are truly members of Christ and temples of the Holy Spirit.

7:11

For behold, this selfsame thing, that ye were made sorry after a godly sort, what earnest care it wrought in you, yea what clearing of yourselves, yea what indignation, yea what fear, yea what longing, yea what zeal, yea what avenging! In everything ye approved yourselves to be pure in the matter.

The exclamation "Behold!" with which the Apostle introduces this sentence carries the ring of his exultation and suggests that the Corinthian scene as described by Titus is vividly pictured in his mind. There is no need for him to theorize as it were in the abstract, for in themselves as a Christian community they have practical first-hand knowledge and a compelling illustration of this very thing about which he is speaking, namely, sorrow which is according to God and the worthy fruits which it produces.

273

This is apparent from the notable degree of eager application [13] they have evinced, in contrast to their former carelessness and indifference. And Paul goes on to mention half-a-dozen forms in which this eager application of theirs has manifested itself—exoneration, indignation, fear, longing, zeal, and requital. The repeated "yea what ..." before each noun [14] powerfully conveys the impression that Paul is at this moment writing in a mood of exalted delight; the news brought by Titus has raised him from the trough of his former apprehensiveness to the crest of a great wave of consolation.

We cannot be certain of the precise significance in the given circumstances of each of the different aspects of the Corinthians' response to Paul's letter listed here, but a consideration of the available data leads us to suggest that they may best be interpreted in the following manner: *Clearing of themselves*—the Greek noun [15] means a defence of oneself in the face of a charge. The Corinthians had been roused to give an account of themselves, whereas previously in their apathy and inactivity it had mattered little to them whether or not they seemed to be guilty of complicity in the wrong that had been committed. *Indignation*—with themselves, rather than against the one who had sinned (as Chrysostom, Alford, etc., take it), because of the scandal they had permitted to continue unchecked in the church and the consequent affront to the holy Name of God. This indignation may be equated with the mourning mentioned in verse 7. *Fear*—not so much of God here (though that was undoubtedly present) as of Paul, lest with the authority divinely delegated to him he should come to them "with a rod" (I Cor. 4:21) as the messenger of God's judgment. *Longing*—(as in v. 7) to be reunited with him who had brought the gospel to them, to welcome him as their own genuine apostle, and to see the restoration of their former relationship of trust and affection. *Zeal*—(again as in v. 7) for Paul, for the honouring

---

[13] Σπουδή, translated "earnest care" in our version.

[14] An effective rendering of the repeated ἀλλά in the original, combined with the continuation of the πόσην with which σπουδήν was linked. Note the similar repetitive use of ἀλλά in I Cor. 6:11.

[15] Ἀπολογία. Hodge interprets the term in the sense of its modern English equivalent ("apology") as indicating that the Corinthians had *apologized* to Paul for their misconduct. This, however, does not seem to have been a meaning which the Greek noun bore.

of his apostolic authority and the repudiation of those intruders who had sought to usurp his authority, and for the imitation of his example in assiduously applying themselves to the cause of Christ. *Avenging*—or, better, requital,[16] that is, seeing that justice is done by bringing the guilty person to book and subjecting him to ecclesiastical discipline, and thus putting their house in order (cf. I Cor. 5:5, 13).

When Paul says, "in every respect you established yourselves to be pure in the matter", he means either that they (that is, as throughout this passage, the members of the Corinthian church as a whole, but not necessarily without exception) were innocent in that they had had no share in the impurity that had been committed—though they were to blame for not having taken immediate disciplinary action against the offender—or that *now*, having taken action and having shown godly sorrow, the past was put right and they were in a state of purity so far as this affair was concerned. The latter seems to us the more suitable interpretation. There is no necessity for him to specify here the nature of this unpleasant affair, since it is all too familiar to them. Hence he just refers to it as "the matter", or "the affair".[17]

7:12

> So although I wrote unto you, I wrote not for his cause that did the wrong, nor for his cause that suffered the wrong, but that your earnest care for us might be made manifest unto you in the sight of God.

The modern reader may find it strange that the Apostle should say that the letter in question was not written because of the one who had done the wrong or because of the one who had suffered the wrong, for it seems plain that the commission of this particular misdeed was one of the occasions of his writing it. But, so far from being guilty of inconsistency, Paul, as Plummer points out, is here exhibiting an accepted Hebrew mode of thought and language whereby, when one of two alternatives is negatived, it does not mean that it is negatived absolutely, "but only in comparison with the other alternative, which is much more important". Thus Hos. 6:6, "I will have mercy, and not

---

[16] ʼEϰδίϰησις.
[17] Tὸ πρᾶγμα.

275

sacrifice", is not a prohibition of sacrifice, but an assertion of the greater importance of mercy. So also here Paul is not denying that he had in mind the perpetrator of the offence, or the one who had suffered directly because of the offence, when he composed the letter; but he is affirming a major and more important reason which lay behind his writing of it, namely, that the earnestness of the Corinthians on his behalf might become apparent to themselves in the sight of God. In other words, he hoped by this letter to bring home to them a clear realization of their true relationship to him, as being in reality bound to him by the deepest bonds of affection and loyalty. To a greater or lesser degree the trouble-makers in Corinth had succeeded in casting a cloud over this relationship; but none the less he was the spiritual father of that church and he trusted that his letter would remind its members of that fact and fan the spark of devotion which, he was sure, still glowed within their hearts. Thus the cloud of disloyalty and disrespect would be removed and the true and proper emotions of their hearts be revealed to them—not, however, before Paul, as though his concern was for the repair of his wounded dignity rather than for the glory of God, but *in the sight of God*, for it was nothing less than their spiritual integrity which was at stake.[18]

That the purpose behind the sending of this earlier epistle, as expressed here by Paul, accords well with the purpose of the sending of our present I Corinthians is evident from what is said in I Cor. 4:14ff. where the Apostle explains that that letter was written, not to shame the Corinthians, but to admonish them *as his beloved children*; they may have countless tutors in Christ, but he alone is *their father who in Christ Jesus begat them through the gospel*; and so he beseeches them to be imitators of him, that is,

---

[18] The reading τὴν σπουδὴν ἡμῶν τὴν ὑπὲρ ὑμῶν, "our (Paul's) earnest care for you (the Corinthians)", though less unexpected than that followed by our version, must be rejected as an early "correction" of the text.

Plummer wishes the phrase ἐνώπιον τοῦ θεοῦ to be taken with ἔγραψα, but this can hardly be right since it is too far removed from that verb to suggest a natural connection with it. The expression should rather be understood in connection with the words which immediately precede it: "that your earnestness on my behalf in the presence of God might be manifested to you"—that is to say, if they search their hearts as before God then the true state of their feelings towards Paul will be made plain to them: in God's light they will see things as they really are.

as children who copy the example and receive the instruction of their father; moreover, with this in view he had sent to them Timothy, who also was his "beloved and faithful child in the Lord", to remind them of his ways which are in Christ. The fault for which he reproves them, not once but several times (4:6, 18, 19; 5:2, 6ff.), is that of being "puffed up", that is, of behaving like arrogant and rebellious children who flout parental authority. This is manifested in their factiousness, with which he has been dealing in the first four chapters, and in the litigiousness and disorderliness which he rebukes in the sixth and subsequent chapters, but most of all in their failure to take disciplinary action against the one who was guilty of the appalling sin with which the fifth chapter is concerned. By their behaviour in this connection they showed that they had failed in their duty to purge out the leaven (which puffs up) of malice and wickedness (5:6–8).

Once again, then, we insist that, rather than posit some lost intermediate letter or seek to cancel the loss by destroying the unity of II Corinthians, it is both reasonable and satisfactory to identify the letter to which Paul here refers again with our present First Epistle to the Corinthians. The offender in question is then the man guilty of incest and the person offended his outraged father. Until modern times this was how the universal Church understood Paul's words—with the exception of Tertullian who, because of his rigorist view that no fornicator could ever be restored to the communion of the Church, held that the Apostle must have been referring to some offence less serious than that of incest.[19] The opinion of Tertullian and also the modern theories that the person offended was Paul himself or Timothy or some other individual, now unknown, have already been discussed in the commentary on 2:5 above. We need say no more here than that it is a serious disability of such suppositions, in all their various forms, that they are no more than suppositions, lacking the support either of the exegesis or of the tradition of the historic Church. Conjecture is, of course, a legitimate exercise, provided it is not assigned an authority above its station, and at times is almost inevitable, as certain passages of this epistle show well enough—for example, the question con-

---

[19] Tertullian, *De Pudicitia*, XIIIff.

cerning the identity of the "brothers" mentioned in 8:18, 22f., 9:3, and 12:18, and the problem of the nature of the "affliction" mentioned in 1:8 and of the "thorn in the flesh" of which Paul speaks in 12:7. But where there is an absence of new and supporting archaeological discoveries, novelties which attempt to run counter to the stream of centuries must always be held suspect.

7:13

Therefore we have been comforted: and in our comfort we joyed the more exceedingly for the joy of Titus, because his spirit hath been refreshed by you all.

"Therefore we have been comforted": [20] Paul takes up again what he has said in verse 6, the intervening verses having filled out the cause and substance of the comfort he had received. And the resulting joy was all the greater because of the happiness and encouragement Titus had experienced in their midst when he came to Corinth. (See commentary above on the final clause of v. 7.) That Titus had been made to rejoice by the way they had responded to the letter he carried meant double joy for Paul.[21] The assertion that Titus's spirit had been refreshed *by them all* implies that, in contrast to the divisions and factions for which Paul had had to reprove them, the members of the Corinthian church had shown real unity in their welcome of his emissary. This implication is strengthened by the reference in verse 15 to "the obedience of you all". Titus must have entertained serious misgivings as to the kind of reception he would be accorded in Corinth where schisms, self-glorying, and false teaching had been disrupting the life of the church. Indeed, it had been necessary for Paul to admonish the Corinthians to see that Timothy should, if he came to Corinth, be permitted to do so without fear and that no man should despise him (I Cor. 16:10f.). It is possible, as Denney suggests, that Timothy's

---

[20] Παρακεκλήμεθα, perfect tense: "we have been comforted and continue to be so".

[21] Περισσοτέρως μᾶλλον, "the more exceedingly"; for other examples in the New Testament of the pleonasm, a comparative + μᾶλλον, cf. Mk. 7:36, Phil. 1:23. This combination is classical, being found in Homer, Herodotus, Aeschylus, Sophocles, Euripides, Plato, and Aristotle. Similarly a superlative was sometimes combined with μάλιστα.

courage had failed him, and that Titus had taken his place as Paul's emissary to Corinth. Be that as it may, Titus, so far from meeting with hostile rebuffs, was refreshed in spirit [22] by the whole church—a dénouement which brought the Apostle Paul intense joy.

7:14

For if in anything I have gloried to him on your behalf, I was not put to shame; but as we spake all things to you in truth, so our glorying also which I made before Titus was found to be truth.

The great confidence of Paul's glorying on behalf of the Corinthians, already mentioned in verse 4 (cf. 1:14), is illustrated here, for Titus was one to whom he had spoken with pride concerning them. So confident was he that they had been the recipients of a work of divine grace that, no matter what their failings and aberrations for the moment, he did not hesitate to assure others that at heart they were right towards himself and towards God. On this he had, as it were, staked his good faith, and with this commendation of them ringing in his ears Titus had ventured to come to Corinth. The event had not proved Paul wrong; their conduct had not put him to shame. This, in fact, was a further testimony to the consistency of the Apostle's character and the reliability of his word, which he had been constrained to defend in the early part of this epistle: just as his speech had always been truthful when he had been with them in Corinth, so now his glorying on their behalf in the presence

---

[22] Ἀναπέπαυται τὸ πνεῦμα αὐτοῦ—the perfect indicates that at the time of writing Titus was still in a state of refreshment. The same expression is used by Paul in I Cor. 16:18: ἀνέπαυσαν γὰρ τὸ ἐμὸν πνεῦμα καὶ τὸ ὑμῶν. Cf. Philem. 7: τὰ σπλάγχνα τῶν ἁγίων ἀναπέπαυται διὰ σοῦ, and 20: ἀνάπαυσόν μου τὰ σπλάγχνα ἐν Χριστῷ, where τὰ σπλάγχνα corresponds to and is in general synonymous with τὸ πνεῦμα here. (Note the occurrence of τὰ σπλάγχνα in v. 15 of our context.)

The textual evidence is overwhelmingly in favour of the reading ἐπὶ δὲ τῇ παρακλήσει ἡμῶν. The TR reading in which δέ is placed after περισσοτέρως (which necessitates the punctuation before περισσοτέρως instead of before ἐπί) and in which ὑμῶν is found instead of ἡμῶν, is followed by AV: "Therefore we were comforted in your comfort: yea, and exceedingly the more joyed we for the joy of Titus..." It was easy for copyists to confuse ἡμῶν and ὑμῶν.

of Titus [23] had also proved to be true. Thus even his generous praise of the Corinthians is a gentle and affectionate reproof to them for ever having allowed themselves to doubt his veracity and sincerity. And now even the most recalcitrant of them could not fail to see that his love for them was absolutely genuine, of the kind which, as he had previously written to them, "beareth all things, believeth all things, hopeth all things, endureth all things" (I Cor. 13:7).

Paul's attitude shows how excellent a director of their spiritual interests he is: not hesitating to reprove what is amiss, but yet warmly and sympathetically encouraging them in the true emotions of those whose hearts are regenerate, which is the best way of ensuring that their past errors will not be repeated. A minister who keeps the main end in view, the glorious goal to which he wishes to guide his people, will realize that to be truly faithful in his dealings with them means to encourage them lovingly in that which is good as well as to correct and discipline them when they fall into sin. He will never despair of them, but will make them his boast, even when he appears to have least cause for doing so. In this way he displays confidence, not in man (except as the vessel of the Holy Spirit), but in God and in the triumphant nature of His grace.

7:15

> And his affection is more abundantly toward you, while he remembereth the obedience of you all, how with fear and trembling ye received him.

The Apostle encourages the Corinthians still further by informing them that the unanimity of their obedience and the proper manner in which they had received his emissary were things which Titus did not forget and which had won for them the overflowing affection of his heart.[24] The obedience of

---

[23] 'Επὶ Τίτου. The preposition here has the sense of "before" or "in the presence of" (Latin, coram)—an occasional classical usage. Other New Testament examples are found in Mk. 13:9, Acts 25:9, I Cor. 1:1, 6.

[24] On τὰ σπλάγχνα, translated "affection" here, see note on 6:12 above. It is doubtful whether περισσοτέρως, translated "more abundantly" here, should in fact be given a comparative force. As both the New Testament and the papyri show, the superlative form was obsolescent in apostolic times, its

Christian men before those whom God has set over them as pastors and teachers is something of vital importance for the well-being and prosperity of the Church of Christ. Where there is indiscipline Christ's cause cannot fail to suffer; and indiscipline may frequently be attributed not only to turbulent and uncouth spirits within the congregation or to the seductive influence of false leaders, but also to insufficient seriousness and dignity on the part of the pastor himself. No matter what difficulties may be encountered, a due appreciation, on both sides, of the solemnity of his calling and office will lead to a spirit of mutual confidence and affection between pastor and people. The truth of this was demonstrated by the visit of Titus to the Corinthians. They received him "with fear and trembling"—that is, with respect for him who was their Apostle's representative, in contrast to the contempt for Paul which the trouble-makers in their midst had been seeking to plant in their minds, and with anxiety lest they should fall short of their duty of confident submission to his authority who in all his dealings with them had displayed unimpeachable trustworthiness and single-mindedness. The expression may also very well indicate the apprehension which the Corinthians felt lest Paul should shortly come to them and mete out discipline of the kind which their recent misdemeanours justly deserved.

"This passage teaches what is the right way of receiving the ministers of Christ", says Calvin. "It is assuredly not sumptuous banquets, nor luxurious clothing, nor effusive and honorific salutations, nor theatrical applause that gratify the upright and faithful pastor. But when the doctrine of salvation is received with reverence from his mouth, when the authority which belongs to him for the edification of the Church is secure, when the people submit themselves to his discipline so that by his ministry they may be governed under the banner of Christ, then his cup of joy is full."

In this context, of course, the phrase "fear and trembling" carries no suggestion whatever of subjection to some form of tyranny or authoritarianism. Moreover, if, in the sense which

---

place frequently being supplied by the comparative form (cf. Mt. 18:1; I Cor. 13:13). So here the meaning is probably: "he feels the most abundant affection for you". See note on 2:4 above.

we have explained, it is a mark of the obedient congregation, it is also a mark of the earnest minister of the gospel; for Paul himself had originally come to these same Corinthians "in fear and in much trembling" (I Cor. 2:3)—conscious, that is, of the awful magnitude of the task which had been entrusted to him by God, and realizing his own abject inadequacy in the face of the forces of evil which were arrayed against him. He, too, like every true minister, was a man under authority, owing allegiance to the Supreme Lord (Acts 22:10) and obedience to the heavenly vision (Acts 26:19); but doing so with trembling, because of his own weakness, yet with unassailable confidence, because of the all-prevailing power of God.

7:16

I rejoice that in everything I am of good courage concerning you.

The affectionate reception which the Corinthians had accorded Titus and their response of obedience to his letter had confirmed Paul in his attitude of confidence and good courage in respect of them.[25] And his good courage looks ahead also: they will not fail him, he is confident, over his appeal for sacrificial giving for the relief of their impoverished fellow-Christians in Jerusalem (chs. 8 and 9); and he is emboldened, further, to embark in the concluding chapters of the epistle (10–13) on a stern denunciation of the false apostles who had invaded Corinth and who were intent on overthrowing his authority. This brief verse, indeed, provides a perfect transition to all that follows. It is the delicate pin around which the whole of the epistle pivots.

---

[25] 'Ἐν ὑμῖν, "in respect of you". For another example in Paul's writings of ἐν meaning "in respect of" see Gal. 4:20, ἀπορούμαι ἐν ὑμῖν, "I am perplexed in respect of you".

PAUL'S COLLECTION FOR THE POOR CHRISTIANS AT JERUSALEM

In these two chapters the Apostle Paul turns to an entirely new subject—that of the collection of alms for the poverty-stricken saints in Jerusalem. It is a subject which he understandably approaches with a great deal of delicacy and, perhaps, a certain amount of embarrassment. Yet, though the change both in subject and in tone is marked, and though stylistically the composition is in these chapters less fluent than in those that have preceded, it is plain that the new theme is introduced at the most appropriate point, and indeed that the ground has been carefully prepared for its introduction. There is, as Plummer observes, "no good reason for suspecting that these two chapters are part of another letter, different from both the first seven chapters and the last four. They follow the seventh chapter quite naturally, and the change of tone is thoroughly intelligible". The change of tone, in fact, is precisely attributable to the change of subject, which, to quote Plummer again, "causes a sudden cessation of this overflowing enthusiasm and generosity of language". It is suggested, further, that the rapid changes of feeling of which "the Epistle is full" are "perhaps caused in some cases by breaks in the times of dictating". With these comments and conclusions we concur; and we would add, what should be obvious, that they are no less applicable to the final four chapters of our epistle which Plummer and numerous others wish to assign to some other epistle, largely on the grounds that they differ in style, tone, and subject-matter from the rest of II Corinthians. We are convinced, however, and shall hope in the course of this commentary to have shown, that the structure of the whole epistle as we now possess it is quite intelligible and its parts well enough, if at times somewhat abruptly, articulated.

For us, far removed in time from the circumstances in which this epistle was written, the theme of a collection of money for poor Christians may seem at first glance to be of little more than minor importance. But (as we shall soon see) it was evidently not so for the Apostle; and the reasons for this we must now investigate so that we may have a proper perspective of the significance of this matter for the growing Church of the first generation after Pentecost.

283

From its very earliest days the Apostolic Church had been confronted with the problem of the extreme poverty of the Christian community in Jerusalem, the Church's mother-city. The preaching of the Apostles on the day of Pentecost (May 26, A.D. 30) and on subsequent days had been attended by the conversion of thousands of souls (see Acts 2:41, 4:4). The material cost to the majority of this great number must have been immense. Coming as they did from the background of Jewish fervour and exclusivism, it needs no demonstration that they must have become, in consequence of their conversion, the victims of social and economic ostracism, ecclesiastical excommunication, and national disinheritance. Their business enterprises must in most cases have collapsed in ruins and family bonds been heart-breakingly severed. The situation to which this led was met by the touching and spontaneous manner in which the members of this young but numerous fellowship demonstrated their oneness of heart and soul by sharing their possessions and resources with each other (Acts 4:32ff.). Many interpreters, ancient (including Augustine) and modern, have propounded the strange view that this community of goods was the (or a) *cause* of the impoverishment of the Jerusalem Christians, as though it were a mistaken and even harmful venture. But surely it is far more reasonable to understand it as an *effect* of the want of the majority, a measure spontaneously designed to counteract as far as possible the prevailing indigence, and successfully so, for the time being at least, as the context shows (v. 34). Luke, moreover, utters no word of disapproval or disappointment; on the contrary, he records that "great grace was upon them all" (v. 33).

In the rapidly increasing Church, however, it very soon became apparent that the care of the poor called for control and direction of a more systematic nature. Accordingly (probably in the year A.D. 32) the seven deacons were appointed to supervise this charitable work. Thus the first distinct step in the organization of the primitive Church was occasioned, as Ramsay points out, by the pressure of poverty.[1] If we take A.D. 34 as the date of Paul's conversion, it was three years later, in A.D. 37, that he first visited Jerusalem (cf. Acts 9:26, Gal. 1:18) and witnessed for himself the material poverty of the Christians there. It is of particular interest, in connection with our present subject, that the purpose of his next visit (c. A.D. 46) was to bring, in company with Barnabas, alms from the Christians of Antioch for "the

---

[1] W. M. Ramsay, *St. Paul the Traveller and the Roman Citizen* (10th edn., London, 1908), pp. 372f.

brethren that dwelt in Judea" (Acts 11:27ff.). On the occasion of his third Jerusalem visit—which took place c. A.D. 51, fourteen years after the first (Gal. 2:1)—he attended the Council of Jerusalem (Acts 15:22), at which it was agreed that he and Barnabas should take the gospel to the Gentiles (Gal. 2:9). At the same time, Paul tells us, James, Peter, and John expressed the desire that he and Barnabas should remember the poor—meaning in particular, no doubt, the poor Christians in Jerusalem —"which very thing", Paul adds, "I was also zealous to do" (Gal. 2:10). As Lightfoot comments on this verse: "His past care for their poor prompted this request from the elder Apostles. His subsequent zeal in the same cause was the answer to their appeal".

The next specific reference to the collection of money for the relief of the Christians at Jerusalem is found near the end of I Corinthians. There Paul instructs the Corinthians (as he had also previously instructed the Galatians) to lay aside some money, according to the prosperity of each individual, on every first day of the week, telling them that in due course, after his arrival in Corinth, he would make arrangements for this money to be taken to Jerusalem (I Cor. 16:1ff.). The matter is taken up again at greater length in the two chapters of our present epistle which we are now about to consider, and from which it is seen that the members of the Macedonian churches had responded with the utmost generosity to Paul's appeal for funds. The year after writing II Corinthians (that is, c. A.D. 58) he informs the Romans that he is going to Jerusalem taking with him contributions from Macedonia and Achaia (of which Corinth was the capital city) for "the poor among the saints" there (Rom. 15:25ff.). This was the occasion of his fifth journey to Jerusalem (a fourth having taken place some four years previously, as Acts 18:22 indicates), and it was undertaken, as Paul explained to Felix, the governor of Caesarea, "to bring alms to my nation, and offerings" (Acts 24:17).

This brief survey, based on such evidence as the New Testament affords, helps to show how important a part the relief of the impoverished Jerusalem Christians played in the Apostle's activities. It was a matter which engaged his attention throughout these crowded years of travelling and evangelism. The logic of the situation is seen by him to reside in the fact that the church at Jerusalem is the Mother-Church of Christendom; it is from her that the message of the gospel has radiated out to the Gentile world, bringing eternal and spiritual blessings not to be measured in terms of the material values of this temporal age. In this sense, then, Gentile Christians are debtors to the believers in Jerusalem, who are the original believers; "for", explains Paul, "if the Gentiles have been made partakers of their spiritual things, they owe it to them also to minister unto them in carnal things" (Rom. 15:27; cf. I Cor. 9:11). Indeed, that is the very least they can do in acknowledgment of their spiritual indebtedness. "It is impossible to exaggerate the importance of the collection which he made for the poor in Jerusalem—which was not so much for 'the *poor* in Jerusalem' as for 'the poor in *Jerusalem*'", says Karl Schmidt. "Paul here recognized an obligation. It was not just a case of charity, though that came into it. Still less can it be called a piece of diplomacy on Paul's part. No: it shows a sense of duty on Paul's part, and of his respect for the men who first constituted God's *ecclesia* in Christ." [2]

We may be sure, further, that Paul regarded these acts of charitable giving as expressions of the organic unity of the Church, which is the body of Christ. They afforded tangible evidence to the world that in Christ the middle wall of partition between Jew and Gentile had indeed been broken down. This, in turn, would react powerfully in favour of the furtherance of the gospel and would administer an effective setback to judaizers on the one hand and hellenizers on the other, by whom the unity and welfare of the early Church were threatened. As the Jews of the dispersion year by year sent their contributions to the temple at Jerusalem, thereby proclaiming, though scattered, their national and religious unity, so the bringing of these contributions to Jerusalem would throw into relief that unity which transcends all other unities, the everlasting oneness in Christ of those who are "an elect race, a royal priesthood, a holy nation, a people for God's own possession", the living stones of a holy temple for the offering up of "spiritual sacrifies acceptable to God through Jesus Christ" (I Pet. 2:9, 5, Eph. 2:20ff.). Little wonder, therefore, that the Apostle urgently besought the Christians at Rome to strive together with him in prayer for the success of this enterprise (Rom. 15:30f.). "It is not then surprising", as Tasker says, "that two whole chapters of this Epistle should be occupied with this subject, and that the writer should deal with it so thoroughly and with such insight that we have here what might be aptly called a philosophy of Christian giving, which has lessons to teach the Church in every age".

---

[2] K. L. Schmidt, *The Church* (*Bible Key Words*, No. II, from Kittel TWNT, London, 1950), p. 13.

8:1, 2

Moreover, brethren, we make known to you the grace of
God which hath been given to the churches of Macedonia;
how that in much proof of affliction the abundance of their
joy and their deep poverty abounded unto the riches of
their liberality.

The Apostle's tone now becomes gently admonitory. Though
confident in his hopes of their response, he wishes to incite the
Corinthians to action by bringing to their notice the splendid
example set by the churches of Macedonia. There is, however,
no harsh note: he affectionately addresses them as his brethren,
and he speaks not of something which the Macedonians have
achieved, as though by some superior quality of character, but of
the grace of God which was given and which, rather than any
personal quality, was the mainspring of their generosity. There
is no question of human resources, but only of divine grace; and
that same grace was equally available to the Christians in Corinth.
Verses 10 and 11 indicate that they had made a start with the
project of the collection but thereafter had allowed it to lapse,
so that there is need for Paul to incite them to complete what they
had commenced. There is no evidence that this failure was due
to any fundamental deficiency of enthusiasm or of generosity on
their part (see commentary on 11:9 below). It may more probably
be attributed to the baneful influence of the false apostles who
must have found it to their advantage to bring the collection
to a halt, so that the money might be diverted to their own
ever-open pockets, and who also turned it into an opportunity
to assail Paul's integrity by insinuating that his motives in
promoting it were suspect (cf. 12:17). Thus, it would seem the
charitable impulse had been arrested. The Apostle, with the skill
and gentleness of a wise parent, now coaxes them to apply themselves once again to this worthy undertaking.

Paul speaks here of "the grace of God given in the churches
of Macedonia"—that is, the twofold grace of joy and generosity
(v. 2) granted to and displayed by the Macedonian believers.
Origen, Erasmus, Bachmann, and some others have wrongly
understood Paul to mean "the grace of God given *to me*" [3]. The

---

[3] As though ἐμοί should be supplied.

sense is given in verse 7 below, where Paul expresses the desire that the Corinthians should abound in this grace also, just as they abound in other graces. The grace granted to the Macedonians had been all the more noticeable because of the circumstances in which they had contributed to this cause. So far from enjoying conditions of material wealth and prosperity which would have enabled them to subscribe without discomfort, they gave in circumstances of the severe testing of affliction [4] and rock-bottom poverty.[5] Their own impoverishment was extreme; they were already, as it were, scraping the bottom of the barrel. But, regardless of this, they gave with joy and liberality. The effectiveness of Paul's description of this situation is enhanced by the use of a double paradox: in the midst of testing *affliction* the Macedonian Christians knew an abundance of *joy*, and their rock-bottom *poverty* they had used as an opportunity for abounding in the *wealth* of generosity. In this they had shown themselves to be truly Christlike.

The example of the Macedonians is a practical proof that true generosity is not the prerogative of those who enjoy an adequacy of means. The most genuine liberality is frequently displayed by those who have least to give. Christian giving is estimated in terms not of quantity but of sacrifice. Thus the widow who cast her two mites into the treasury gave more than all the others together, because they gave "of their superfluity", at no real cost to themselves, whereas she gave "all that she had, even all her living" (Mk. 12:41ff.). In the case of the members of the Macedonian churches, the fires of affliction and poverty had uncovered and refined the precious ore of joy and generosity. Indeed, this had been their commendation from the beginning, for when Paul first came to Thessalonica they had "received the word in much affliction with joy of the Holy Spirit", so that they "became an example to all that believe in Macedonia *and in Achaia*" (I Thess. 1:6f.; cf. 2:14, 3:3f., II Thess. 1:4f., Phil.

---

[4] 'Εν πολλῇ δοκιμῇ θλίψεως. For the significance of the noun δοκιμή see note on 2:9 above.

[5] 'Η κατὰ βάθους πτωχεία αὐτῶν—"their down-to-depth poverty" (Plummer), κατὰ βάθους forming an adjectival unit. An early variant of κατὰ βάθους was κατὰ βάθος (found in P[46] and a few other MSS), but the latter is likely to have been a scribal simplification or slip, and is an improbable substitute for an adjective proper. Κατὰ βάθους is certainly far more graphic and pointed.

1:29). That now, after a lapse of some years, Paul can still commend them as an example to the Christian world speaks eloquently of the constancy of their faith and the consistency of their conduct, with which the tardiness of the Corinthians in promoting the collection (a further symptom, no doubt, of the unloving spirit which, as I Corinthians shows, had fallen like a blight upon their internal relationships) stood out in obvious contrast.

The Macedonian churches of which we have knowledge through the New Testament are those at Philippi, Thessalonica, and Berea. "They were", as Lightfoot says, "baptized with the baptism of suffering, and this suffering was the result both of poverty and of persecution"; accordingly, we find that "there is no warning against the temptations of wealth, no enforcement of the duties of the rich, in the Epistles to the Thessalonians or Philippians".[6] Truly, then, their liberality on behalf of their fellow-Christians at Jerusalem, whose material lack was even more pressing than their own, was a manifestation of the grace of God operating in a notable manner in their midst.[7]

8:3—5

For according to their power, I bear witness, yea and beyond their power, they gave of their own accord, beseeching us with much entreaty in regard of this grace and the fellowship in the ministering to the saints: and this, not as we had hoped, but first they gave their own selves to the Lord, and to us through the will of God.

These three verses constitute one continuous sentence in the original, as follows: "For in accordance with their ability, I

---

[6] J. B. Lightfoot, *Biblical Essays*, pp. 247ff.

[7] The noun ἁπλότης, translated "liberality" in our version, means "simplicity", "single-mindedness", and hence true open-heartedness and generosity towards others in which there is *no duplicity* of motive. In the New Testament it is used only by Paul. Here and in 9:11, 13 it has the force of "generosity", with the implication we have mentioned. In 11:3, however, it is used in its fundamental sense of "simplicity", and in Eph. 6:5 and Col. 3:22 we find the phrase "singleness of heart" *(ἁπλότης τῆς καρδίας)*. The association of simplicity with liberality is well brought out in Rom. 12:8: "He that giveth, let him do it with singleness of purpose" *(ὁ μεταδιδούς, ἐν ἁπλότητι)*. Cf. the comment of Herveius: *non enim duplici, sed simplici corde dederunt.* For a similar and contemporary use of ἁπλότης = generosity, see Josephus, *Antiq.*, VII, xiii, 4 and cf. Tacitus, *Hist.*, III, 86 where *simplicitas* has the same sense.

testify, indeed, contrary to their ability, of their own accord, with much entreaty beseeching of us the favour, namely, fellowship in the ministry to the saints, and not just as we had expected, but they gave their own selves first to the Lord and to us by the will of God". Despite the opinion of many commentators, it is unnecessary to postulate an elliptical construction here. The verb "gave" governs the whole statement.[8] It is, however, a long and characteristically Pauline sentence: as he dictates, ideas occur to him one after the other in appreciation of the generosity of the Macedonian Christians, so that the appearance of the main verb is delayed. In translating, it is helpful to introduce the verb early on as well as in the late position where it occurs in the Greek, as RSV does: "For they gave according to their means, as I can testify, and beyond their means, of their own free will, begging us earnestly for the favour of taking part in the relief of the saints—and this, not as we expected, but first they gave themselves to the Lord and to us by the will of God".[9]

The Macedonian churches had contributed "according to their ability", says Paul; but he then paradoxically adds: "indeed, contrary to their ability".[10] The meaning of this paradox is that, because of their extreme poverty, the amount collected by them was not huge in quantity; a man possessing only ten pounds cannot be expected to contribute a hundred pounds, for ten pounds is the absolute limit of his ability. In this sense, the Macedonians had given "according to their ability". But the proportion of his goods which a person gives is generally determined by a twofold consideration: (i) a reckoning of the basic necessities for his own immediate existence, and (ii) prudence in setting aside at least something as a measure of security against future needs and emergencies. Such circumspection is justifiable and reasonable. The Macedonians, however, poor though they

---

[8] Ἔδωκαν, dederunt: Hoc verbum totam periochae structuram sustinet (Bengel).

[9] Allo takes ὅτι in parallel with the preceding ὅτι (v. 2) as introducing a further statement after γνωρίζομεν (v. 1); but it is preferable to interpret it, with the majority of translators and commentators, as the conjunction "because" or "for" (Vulgate, quia), introducing an explanation of what has just previously been said.

[10] Κατά + accusative and παρά + accusative stand here in strict antithesis to each other; cf. Rom. 11:24, κατὰ φύσιν, "according to nature", ... παρὰ φύσιν, "contrary to nature". The usage is thoroughly classical.

were, had shown a complete disregard of their own requirements, both present and future. It is in this sense that, impelled by love and compassion for brethren in Christ whom they had never seen, they had given "contrary to their ability". And this was a noteworthy token of their refusal to take anxious thought for the morrow because of their confident dependence on God, who as the Heavenly Father, knows His children's needs even before they ask Him and will not fail to supply those needs from the boundless storehouse of His grace (12:9; Mt. 6:8, 25ff.; Phil. 4:19).

Tyrannical coercion or extortion may, of course, bring it about that people give contrary to their ability. But there was no question (however much his adversaries might have insinuated it) of the Apostle having in any way exerted pressure upon the Macedonian churches in order to extract money from them. On the contrary, they had given spontaneously, "of their own accord". Indeed, what is more, it is apparent that Paul had actually forborne to ask them for any contribution to the collection, no doubt having concluded that churches so poverty-stricken as those in Macedonia could not be expected to spare of their meagre goods for others—for they had *besought* him "with much entreaty" to grant them the favour of a share in this ministration to the saints at Jerusalem. As Chrysostom remarks, it was they, not Paul, who did the begging.[11]

---

[11] Τὴν χάριν is the direct object after δεόμενοι: "begging the favour from us". Ambrosiaster and a few minuscules read δέξασθαι ἡμᾶς after τοὺς ἁγίους, a reading which requires both "favour" (χάριν) and "fellowship" (κοινωνίαν) to be understood as referring to the amount contributed by the Macedonian churches: "begging *us to accept* their charity (χάριν) and participation (κοινωνίαν) in the ministration to the saints". But the textual evidence demands the rejection of this addition—though it is interesting to find it recurring in the Modern Greek version of the New Testament: παρακαλοῦντες ἡμᾶς μετὰ πολλῆς παρακλήσεως νὰ δεχθῶμεν τὴν χάριν καὶ τὴν κοινωνίαν ... In his earlier letter Paul had used χάρις to describe the Corinthian contribution (I Cor. 16:3), and it seems to have this force also in verses 6 and 19 of our present chapter. Our version (= RV) apparently interprets it in this sense in the present verse, treating τὴν χάριν καὶ τὴν κοινωνίαν as accusatives of respect: "beseeching us in regard of this grace and the fellowship ..." But, as we have said, it is preferable to understand τὴν χάριν as the direct object after δεόμενοι, that is, "the favour" which the Macedonians sought from Paul. The καί may then be taken as epexegetic (Plummer): "begging from us the favour, *namely*, participation in the ministration ...", or τὴν χάριν καὶ τὴν

But there was still a further element of surprise in the manner of their giving: not only had they contributed contrary to their ability, and spontaneously at that, but—something Paul had not expected—they had first given their own selves to the Lord and to him. First and foremost, their giving had been a giving of themselves; from this their gifts of money followed as a natural consequence. Bengel and others have understood "first" here to mean that they gave themselves first in time, that is, before giving their money. Alford, Stanley, Hodge, Plummer and others have taken it to indicate first in importance. But it is better to combine these two interpretations: their giving of themselves was first in time as well as first in importance. Without self-giving there is no profound self-sacrifice. The latter is the expression, the manifestation, of the former.

A third view is that of the Latin authors and Denney and Allo, who take Paul to mean that the Macedonians gave themselves, first to the Lord, then to him; but this sense seems to us less than satisfactory and not really warranted by the text.[12] They did not give themselves twice; for in giving themselves to the Lord they also at the same time placed themselves at the disposal of Paul, the Lord's Apostle. As parallels to this mode of expression ("to the Lord and to us") Calvin draws attention to Acts 15:28: "it seemed good to the Holy Spirit and to us", and Ex. 14:31: "the people believed in the Lord and in His servant Moses", remarking that "when God orders or enjoins anything through some person it is common for Him to associate His minister with Himself in the authority of commanding no less than in obedience". The servant is nothing apart from his master, nor the instrument apart from its wielder. Thus the Macedonians gave themselves to the Lord and to Paul—and the emphasis is on the giving of *themselves*.[13] In accordance with the teaching and example of the Lord Himself and in accordance with the logic of redemption

---

κοινωνίαν may be treated as a hendiadys (Allo): "the favour of taking part in . . .," which is how RSV renders it, and which amounts to the same thing. Χάρις, then, is used with four different connotations in this chapter: of the grace of God (v. 1), of a favour sought (v. 4), of a charitable gift freely contributed by men (vv. 6, 19), and of thanks given to God (v. 16).

[12] Had Paul intended this sense, one would have expected πρῶτον, "first", to be balanced by ἔπειτα, "afterwards", as in the Vulgate: *primum Domino, deinde nobis*, where *deinde* is an insertion.

[13] The position of ἑαυτούς is emphatic.

they renounced any claim to themselves (Mk. 8:34ff.; I Cor. 6:19f.). They held themselves and their few goods in readiness to perform what was right "by the will of God". In a word, all is done in humble and cheerful submission to the sovereignty of the divine will.

Paul's reference here is general, to the members of the Macedonian churches as a whole, rather than, as some, including Bernard, Plummer, and Allo, have suggested, to particular Macedonians, such as Sopater, Aristarchus, Secundus, Epaphroditus, Jason, Gaius, and Demas, who may have offered themselves as collectors and propagandists in connection with this charitable project or for the task of evangelism.

8:6

> Insomuch that we exhorted Titus, that as he had made a beginning before, so he would also complete in you this grace also.

In consequence of [14] the remarkable liberality of the Macedonians Paul is encouraged to make arrangements for the carrying forward of the collection of alms in Corinth under the supervision of Titus. This charitable work had already been inaugurated by Titus on the occasion of a previous visit. But when had this been? I Cor. 16:1ff. shows that "the collection for the saints" was already at the time of the writing of the former epistle a matter concerning which the Apostle could speak without having to offer any explanation as to what it implied, apart from giving advice regarding questions of method and procedure. Indeed, the formula with which the subject is there introduced—"Now concerning ..."—in all probability indicates that it was a matter on which the Corinthians themselves had requested practical instruction (cf. the occurrence of the same formula in 7:1, 25, 8:1, 12:1), and therefore that the collection was something which had been started in Corinth at a time prior to the writing of I Corinthians. This in turn means that Titus, who, as Paul tells his readers here, had been responsible for making a beginning of this collection among the Corinthians, must have visited their city on some occasion prior to the writing of I Corinthians. It

---

14 'Εἰς τό ... introduces the consequence to which the preceding consideration leads.

is possible that he had been the bearer, or one of the bearers, of the epistle, now lost, mentioned in I Cor. 5:9. It is probable, moreover, that Titus was one of "the brethren" mentioned in I Cor. 16:11f. who, it would seem, had carried our present I Corinthians to its destination, as he was also one of the bearers of II Corinthians—indeed, it is certain if, as we believe, the letter mentioned in II Cor. 2:4 and 7:8ff. is the same as I Corinthians.[15] Assuming this reconstruction to be correct, Titus had visited Corinth at least twice previously to the writing of our present epistle, and the inauguration by him of the collection took place on some occasion prior to the writing of I Corinthians.

Bachmann, Allo, and others have propounded the view that the clause "as he had made a beginning before" refers, not to the commencement of the collecting work, but more generally to valuable services rendered by Titus in restoring a spirit of harmony and loyalty in the Corinthian church. It is true that he had been especially successful in his relations with the Corinthians, at any rate during his latest visit, and it was for this reason, no doubt, that Paul had such confidence in entrusting to him the delicate duty of supervising the collection among the members of that church for the relief of the Jerusalem Christians. But the more natural and proper interpretation of this clause, within its particular context, is that which takes it to refer to a beginning which Titus had previously made at Corinth in organizing the collection. It is Paul's desire that he should now carry this work through to completion.

Paul speaks of it as "this grace", that is, this work of charity. Already, then, in the first half-dozen verses of this chapter the word "grace" (*charis*) has been used with three different, though not unrelated connotations: (i) of grace given by God—verse 1, (ii) of a favour sought from the Apostle—verse 4, and (iii) of a charitable gift contributed by men to their fellows—verse 6, cf. verse 19. To these a fourth will later be added, namely, (iv) that of thanksgiving—verse 16, cf. 9:15. The source of all grace is God, who with Christ freely bestows upon us all things (Rom. 8:32); the expression of that grace in human relationship his Christian charity; and the response to that grace is thanksgiving

---

[15]   Cf. verses 18 and 22 of our present chapter, where Titus is named in connection with another "brother"; and see Lightfoot's discussion of the Mission of Titus to the Corinthians in *Biblical Essays*, pp. 273ff.

to God. The returning of thanks is the returning of grace. In our present verse (and in v. 19) the word "grace" both points back to the source—Christian charity is made possible by and is the logical outworking of God's grace in the human situation —and also carries the idea of a thankoffering which, in ministering to those who are in dire need, is nothing less than a reflection of the grace of our Lord Jesus Christ (v. 9).

Expounding this verse, Chrysostom has a fine passage concerning the gift of liberality ("this grace"): "Greater is this gift", he says, "than to raise the dead; for it is far greater to feed Christ when an hungred than to raise the dead by the name of Jesus. ... Almsgiving when it is done with willingness and with bountifulness, when you deem yourself not to give but to receive, when done as if you were benefited, as if gaining and not losing, is indeed a grace—but not otherwise. ... And why, O man, are you at all downhearted? For fear lest your gold should diminish? If such are your thoughts, do not give at all. If you are not quite certain that it is multiplied for you in heaven, do not bestow. But you seek your recompense here: why? Let your alms be alms, and not traffic".

8:7

> But as ye abound in everything, in faith, and utterance, and knowledge, and in all earnestness, and in your love to us, see that ye abound in this grace also.

If the example of liberality set by the Macedonians provided an incentive to the Corinthians, so also, and even more so, did the fact, on the ground of which Paul now exhorts them,[16] that in Corinth the Christians abounded in everything: God had withheld no good thing from them, but had bestowed on them an abundance of spiritual gifts, as is obvious from a perusal of I Corinthians. In that earlier letter Paul had spoken thankfully of the grace of God which had been given them in Christ Jesus and rejoiced, as here, that *in everything* they were enriched in Him (I Cor. 1:4f.). In the same place, too, he makes specific mention

---

16   As Alford remarks, the ἀλλά ("but") with which the verse commences marks the transition to an exhortation. Cf. Winer-Moulton, *Grammar of New Testament Greek* (3rd edn., Edinburgh, 1882), p. 551. Other examples of this usage will be found in Mt. 9:18; Mk. 9:22, 16:7; Lk. 7:7; Acts 9:6, 10:20, 26:16.

of "utterance" and "knowledge". (In the latter part of that epistle, especially chapters 12 to 14, the charismata in the diversity of their manifestation receive careful attention.) Here the list is expanded by the addition of "faith", "earnestness", and "love".

According to Plummer, "faith" here signifies "faith in Christ, such as every believer has". It seems preferable, however, to take it as referring to that faith of which the Apostle speaks in I Corinthians as belonging to the charismatic gifts of the Spirit, that is, wonder-working faith (I Cor. 12:9; cf. 13:2), rather than as saving faith. It was particularly in these charismatic gifts that the Corinthian church abounded.

"Utterance" and "knowledge" should be understood as belonging to the same class of gifts, the former probably referring to a power of utterance in the declaration of Christian truth, rather than to the gift of tongues, which is treated as a different gift in I Corinthians. "Utterance" here [17] would seem to correspond to "prophecy" there (I Cor. 12:10). It may, however, be connected with the "word (utterance) of wisdom" [18] and the "word (utterance) of knowledge" [19] (I Cor. 12:8), both of which were charismatic gifts enjoyed at Corinth. It is apparent that the gift of knowledge was closely associated with that of utterance, for such knowledge was bestowed in order that it might be imparted to others for their edification. Hence their combination in I Cor. 12:8 and their conjunction both here and in I Cor. 1:5.

The Corinthians were further distinguished for "every kind of earnestness", though in some instances, as the earlier epistle shows again, this had been misdirected and disorderly. Certainly, since the recent visit of Titus with Paul's admonitory letter their earnestness had reached new heights of integrity (7:11). Earnestness, of course, is not one of the charismatic gifts vouchsafed to some but not to all; it is a quality which should be characteristic of every follower of Christ.

And the same is true of "love", the greatest of all Christian virtues (I Cor. 13, Gal. 5:22), which, because of their overestimation of the more spectacular gifts, the Corinthians had failed to cultivate as they should in their relationships with each other. Indeed, it is likely that the correct reading here is not "in your

---

[17] Λόγος.

[18] Λόγος σόφιας.

[19] Λόγος γνώσεως.

love to us", but "in our love to you", or, more literally, "in the love from us which is in you";[20] so that the love in which they abounded was not their own but that of the Apostle for them. They were narrowed in their own affections, whereas his heart was enlarged toward them (6:11f.). It is noticeable that love and affection are not mentioned in the passage 7:5–16 as having been shown or expressed by them; yet the tenor of the passage suggests strongly that it was real love, still perhaps inarticulate, which was the motive force behind their godly sorrow and repentance. The love from their Apostle was indeed in them; what he desired was that they should open wide their own hearts and let this love shine forth, thus meeting love with love and as it were repaying him in like coinage (6:13, 7:2). The Apostle's reminder to them of the gifts and virtues with which they had been blessed acts as an incentive to them to abound also in the grace of generosity of which the Macedonian churches had provided so remarkable an example. Should they fail in this respect, it would falsify his boast that they abound *in everything*. A gentler and more urbane method of incitement to generosity it would be difficult to imagine!

8:8

I speak not by commandment, but as proving through the earnestness of others the sincerity also of your love.

It is not Paul's intention to enforce this collection on the Corinthians. They are free to do as they wish, for he is not dictating a course of action which they are bound to follow. That genuine love which demonstrates itself in liberality cannot, in fact, be the product of compulsion from without. And so Paul continues to coax them with affectionate diplomacy.[21] The

---

[20] The early reading τῇ ἐξ ἡμῶν ἐν ὑμῖν ἀγάπῃ (which is found in P46 Codex Vaticanus, Origen, etc.) is adopted by Westcott and Hort, Nestlé, and Allo. It is to be preferred to τῇ ἐξ ὑμῶν ἐν ἡμῖν ἀγάπῃ, both because it is the more difficult of the two (both are strongly attested), and also because, as we have indicated above, it suits the factual context better.

[21] Κατ' ἐπιταγήν is, as Plummer observes, a Pauline phrase. The same negative form is used by him in I Cor. 7:6. In the positive form it is always associated with the divine will: by command *of God* (see Rom. 16:26; I Tim. 1:1; Tit. 1:3)—as no doubt is also the case when Paul uses it with a negative. The noun ἐπιταγή seems to belong to later Greek, being found in Polybius and Diodorus Siculus.

expression, "I speak not by way of commandment", draws attention in an incidental manner to the fact of Paul's apostolic authority: he is one who, in accordance with his divine commission, is entitled to command and to exercise authority in the Church of Christ. Only one who is in a position to command can say, "I speak not by way of commandment". Such authority, however, is administered neither officiously nor by personal caprice, but in obedience to the revealed will of God, and to the glory of God alone.

The purpose of what Paul writes at this point is to put the Corinthian Christians to the test (which is the proper force of the verb "prove" [22] here). By means of the zeal of others, namely, the Christians of Macedonia, who themselves had come through the severe testing of affliction with flying colours (v. 2), he is making proof of the genuineness of their love also. This indeed is a sharp spur to them to give concrete evidence of warm-hearted liberality comparable to that of the Macedonian churches. Not that the Apostle is encouraging a spirit of rivalry between Corinth and Macedonia: he is implying rather that the wonderful liberality of the Macedonians in the face of their own extreme poverty (v. 1) should be an example and an incentive to the Corinthians to show a liberality of comparable quality. Nowhere is the *quantity* contributed even mentioned, for that is beside the point. One church may without inconvenience be able to give an amount which another can raise only at the cost of great self-sacrifice. It is the spirit of devoted and single-minded generosity that matters and by which alone God measures and assesses the act of giving. What He weighs is not the outward amount, but the inward motive, or, as Paul puts it here, "the genuineness of your love".[23]

---

[22] Δοκιμάζειν. The verb occurs again in verse 22 and in 13:5.

[23] Τὸ τῆς ὑμετέρας ἀγάπης γνήσιον. Here τὸ γνήσιον is a substantival adjective such as Paul uses effectively elsewhere—for example, τὸ μωρὸν τοῦ θεοῦ (I Cor. 1:25), τὸ χρηστὸν τοῦ θεοῦ (Rom. 2:4). Cf. Moule, *An Idiom Book of New Testament Greek*, pp. 96f.

Allo wishes to understand διὰ τῆς ἑτέρων σπουδῆς as meaning "through the zeal of the Corinthians for others", thus treating ἑτέρων as an objective genitive. The clause could then be translated: " . . . by means of your zeal for others putting to the proof the genuineness also of your love". This is possible, but the usual rendering, which treats ἑτέρων as a subjective genitive referring to the Macedonians, is both more appropriate to the context and

8:9

> For ye know the grace of our Lord Jesus Christ, that, though
> he was rich, yet for your sakes he became poor, that ye
> through his poverty might become rich.

At this point the Apostle adduces the supreme argument for
Christian liberality: the self-giving and self-impoverishment of
the Son of God on man's behalf. This example is one that no
Christian can gainsay; hence Paul introduces it with the declaration, "ye know". It is something with which the Corinthian
believers are fully acquainted, both externally, through the
proclamation to them of this great truth, and internally, by the
personal experience of its reality. The expression of a generous
spirit by sacrificial giving is itself an evidence of the grace of God
actively and fruitfully at work in an individual heart or within
a Christian community (v. 1), for sacrificial giving is of the very
essence of divine grace. In a certain sense it could be said that
the Macedonian Christians, whose circumstances (but not their
hearts!) were so straitened, had made others rich by their poverty,
which by their giving they had voluntarily aggravated. But what
they did is infinitely surpassed by what Christ has done. Grace,
as Hodge says, is "unmerited, spontaneous love"; and the grace
of our Lord Jesus Christ is the very perfection of grace and the
sum and source of all graces. None other has impoverished himself as He did. He, the first-begotten before every creature,
through whom all things visible and invisible were created, and
in whom all things consist (Col. 1:15ff., Jn. 1:1ff.), He whose
was the ineffable divine glory before the world was and from all
eternity (Jn. 17:5, Heb. 1:3), He who is one with the Father
(Jn. 10:30): He it was who emptied Himself, humbling Himself
by His incarnation, assuming the role of a servant, and becoming
obedient unto death, even the death of the cross (Phil. 2:6ff.)
From highest heaven He descended to Calvary and the grave.
None was richer than He; none became poorer than He.

---

also more natural, especially as ὑμετέρας in the second phrase (which is
equivalent to ὑμῶν) strongly suggests a contrast with ἑτέρων in the first phrase:
" . . . by means of the zeal of *others* putting to the proof the genuineness also
of *your* love". This, further, gives due force to the καί, whereas on Allo's
interpretation the καί is somewhat redundant. Nor is the καί copulative
(as AV). It serves to heighten the contrast between ἑτέρων and ὑμετέρας.

All this and much more it meant for our Lord Jesus Christ to become poor. And, Paul explains to the Corinthians, it was "for *your* sakes".[24] The significance of Christ's self-impoverishment is grasped only in a manner that is intensely *personal*: it was all, adds Paul, "so that *you* [25] through His poverty might become rich". The logic implicit in the statement of this great truth is too obvious for anyone to miss it: if He did all this for me, then nothing I give or do for Him can be too much; such love constrains me; redeemed at incalculable cost, I am no longer my own; all that was mine is now His, for Him to make use of in accordance with His holy purposes.

"He wished to become poor for a time for you", writes Herveius, "in order that you might become partakers of His everlasting riches. ... If therefore He who is the Creator and Lord of all submitted to poverty for you, why do you not for love of Him contribute part of your riches for His needy members? He was rich. For whence are men rich? By gold, silver, family, land. But all things were made through Him (Jn. 1). What then is richer than He, through whom riches have been made, and also those things which are not true riches? For to Him we owe the riches of intellect, memory, life, bodily health, our senses, and the strength of our members. For indeed when these are sound then even paupers are rich. Through Him also come those greater riches, faith, piety, justice, charity, morality. For no man possesses these things except through Him who justifies the wicked. ... Moreover, it is not said that He became poor when He had been rich, but that He became poor when He *was* rich. For He assumed poverty, yet did not lose His riches. Inwardly He was rich, outwardly poor. His deity was hidden in His riches, His manhood was apparent in His poverty. And so we have been enriched by His poverty, since in His blood the sackcloth of our sins has been torn to shreds. Through that blood we have cast away the rags of iniquity in order that we may be invested with the robe of immortality. Lest therefore we should

---

[24] The position of δι' ὑμᾶς is emphatic. The aorist ἐπτώχευσεν refers back to the event of Christ's incarnation. Moule (*Idiom Book*, p. 11) lists it as an example of an ingressive aorist, representing, according to J. H. Moulton's definition (*Grammar of New Testament Greek*, Vol. I, p. 109), "the point of entrance".

[25] Once again the position of ὑμεῖς is emphatic.

fear His riches, not daring in our beggarly state to approach Him, He showed Himself poor, that is, God deigned to be born as man, abasing the greatness of His power, so that He might make available to men the riches of His divinity and cause them to partake of the divine nature."

The pre-existence of Christ is, as Plummer observes, plainly taught here. Neither here nor elsewhere does Paul seek to explain or defend the truth of Christ's pre-existence. Nor does he present it tentatively as a theological inference or working hypothesis. It would have been felt unnatural to apologize for the affirmation of so essential an element of apostolic Christianity. Thus Jesus Christ is the Son who was *sent*, the One who *came* into the world, the Word who *became* flesh, the Lord who for our sakes impoverished Himself. The Apostles felt none of the embarrassment which is displayed by some modern scholars who, because of a preconceived antipathy to "supernaturalism", would prefer to dismiss this doctrine, or at any rate to draw its teeth by explaining it on the subjective level as an "assumption", an "inevitable deduction from Paul's conception of the exalted Christ", and a "mighty speculation" (Strachan). Indeed, it has become so fashionable to depreciate the objectivity of truth and to denounce "propositional religion" that pronouncements asserting or implying the eternal Godhead of Christ have been reduced to existential value-judgments, expressing, subjectively and not dogmatically, the significance of Christ at a particular moment in an individual's experience. If Christ helps me (I am told), I may assign Him the significance, valid for my subjective experience only, of "Lord" or "God"; I may say that He is God's Son because He helps me, but no longer may I be so objective as to say that He helps me because He is God's Son.[26] For the New Testament, however, the subjective experience of Christ's power is not and cannot be divorced from the objective reality of His essential Deity. His saving work does not exist apart from His theanthropic person. This is the solid foundation of Paul's soteriology here; and it is the soild foundation of the whole of the theology of the New Covenant.

---

[26] See R. Bultmann, *Essays Philosophical and Theological* (London, 1955), p. 280.

8 : 10

And herein I give my judgment: for this is expedient for
you, who were the first to make a beginning a year ago,
not only to do, but also to will.

This verse is closely linked in its form to verse 8: there Paul
says that he is not issuing a *command* to the Corinthians; here he
explains further that what he is offering is his own personal
judgment concerning this matter.[27] It is understandable that some
commentators speak of verse 9 as parenthetical, but to do so is
somewhat misleading, for verse 9 is in fact *central* to Paul's whole
argument. It constitutes the logical summit of this question. If
the Apostle does not command, surely the example of Christ
does. Having reminded the Corinthians of "the grace of our
Lord Jesus Christ", all that is necessary is for him to propound
his own judgment founded upon the recollection of this crucial
action of redemptive history.

God's grace in Christ, then, is central in a just consideration
of this matter of Christian giving; and it is also *conclusive*, as is
shown by the sentence with which this section of the epistle ends:
"Thanks be to God for His unspeakable gift" (9:15). All giving
that is genuinely Christian is the free and spontaneous response
to the inescapable logic of the divine goodness. It is in *love* that
the divine law is fulfilled (Rom. 13:10). Again, the question
previously addressed by the Apostle to these same Corinthians:
"What hast thou that thou didst not receive?" (I Cor. 4:7), sets
things in the same clear perspective. The Christian has no absolute
proprietary rights to his goods, be they material or spiritual, as
though they were of his own making. All is of grace.

In the case of the Corinthians there is, moreover, a further
logical consideration. Already, during the previous year, they
had made a start with the collection.[28] Judging from the present

---

[27] There is a similar contrast between ἐπιταγή ("command") and γνώμη
("judgment") in I Cor. 7:25.

[28] Some commentators take the prefix προ- in προενήρξασθε to mean that
the Corinthians began to collect *before the Macedonians* (as our version seems to
imply); others suggest that it indicates *before any mention of the matter to them
by Paul*. But it seems unlikely that, had either of these comparisons been
intended, the author would have left it to be inferred. As with προενήρξατο
in verse 6, the prefix should be taken to indicate a general temporal priority
—the collection had been started at Corinth on an occasion previous to the

context, it would seem that their original zeal in this enterprise had flagged and indeed that, whether through natural apathy or through mistrust of Paul planted in their hearts by the false teachers in their midst, they had permitted the matter to lapse into inactivity. Paul's appeal to them to abound also in the grace of liberality was therefore not inappropriate for the additional reason that they had already given evidence of generous intentions by initiating a benevolent fund in Corinth. Was it not fitting and reasonable that they should now complete what they had begun? As verse 6 indicates, the earlier commencement of this charitable project had been instigated by Titus. Fired by his enthusiasm, the Corinthians had responded with a will: the action which they took was based upon the best of intentions.[29]

The chronological designation, "last year", is particularly tantalizing: it could have told us so much, if only we knew with certainty the time when Paul was writing this letter and also what calendar he was following; for he might have been using any one of a variety of calendar reckonings. Thus there was the Roman year which, like our own, began on the first day of January; there was the Jewish ecclesiastical year, beginning in the spring; the Jewish civil year, beginning, like the Macedonian, Syrian, and other Oriental years, at the autumnal equinox; and the Athenian year, reckoned in olympiads, beginning at the summer solstice. Widely divergent opinions on this question have been expressed by different scholars. In our judgment, it is almost certain that Paul, the Roman citizen and traveller in the Roman empire, would ordinarily have followed the Roman calendar, except in his more direct dealings with Jewish circles. If this is so, and if, as seems probable, this epistle was written

---

time of writing. And in this present verse the time is more precisely designated by the addition of ἀπὸ πέρυσι, "last year". The beginning made by Titus (v. 6) coincides with the beginning made by the Corinthians (v. 10). Ἀπὸ πέρυσι does not mean "a year ago" (AV, RV), but "from last year" (ab anno priore, Vulgate); the former would mean twelve months ago, whereas the latter could cover virtually any length of time from one to twenty-three months, depending on the time of year when the letter was actually written. If, as is probable, Paul was writing these words in the autumn (of A.D. 57?), then the Corinthian collection would have been initiated not less than some nine months and up to as much as twenty-one months previously.

[29] Note the distinction, brought out by the tenses, between an act, ποιῆσαι (aorist) and a disposition, θέλειν (present).

in the latter part of A.D. 57, then "last year" must refer to some time in A.D. 56 when Titus had visited Corinth and, with the cooperation of the Corinthian Christians, made a start with the collection there. This would have been on some occasion prior to the writing of I Corinthians, and the occasion in question may well have been connected, as we have already suggested (see commentary above on v. 6), with the conveyance to the Corinthian church of the "lost" epistle to which reference is made in I Cor. 5:9. Should this theory be right, then the sequence of events may be reconstructed as follows: some time in A.D. 56 Paul had sent a letter from Ephesus by the hand of Titus to the Corinthians (I Cor. 5:9); the latter had replied, requesting advice on certain matters, amongst them that of "the collection for the saints" (I Cor. 16:1); this, together with other serious news he had received concerning their affairs, led to the writing of our present I Corinthians, from Ephesus again, probably in the earlier part of A.D. 57; Titus was a bearer of this letter; thereafter, anxious for news of the reaction to this important epistle, Paul had left Ephesus and travelled by way of Troas into Macedonia where he met Titus returning from his mission to Corinth; the news now brought by Titus caused Paul to write at once another letter (our present II Corinthians) which Titus then carried back to Corinth; shortly afterwards Paul paid his third visit to Corinth (II Cor. 12:14, 13:1, Acts 20:2).

8 : 11, 12

But now complete the doing also; that as there was the readiness to will, so there may be the completion also out of your ability. For if the readiness is there, it is acceptable according as a man hath, not according as he hath not.

Having reminded the Corinthians that during the previous year they had been the first to make a start with the collection, Paul exhorts them now to carry it through to completion. The implication is that they had allowed this enterprise to be interrupted or set aside, which in turn was symptomatic of a lack of application, if not indeed of a defect of the will, on their part. The ready and eager spirit with which they had shown their willingness to undertake this charitable task should now be matched by action in completing it. The doing of a thing is the only proper proof and expression of the willingness to do it. It is not Paul's intention, however, that the collection should be an oppressive burden to them. They are expected to give, like the Macedonians, according to their power; but Paul does not suggest that they should emulate the Macedonians by giving contrary to their power (see v. 3 above). To do the latter must always be unexpected, and is a signal mark of divine grace. In any case, as Paul explains, readiness, when it is present, is acceptable in accordance with the measure of its ability, not in accordance with what is impossible.[30] In his previous letter the Apostle had made it clear that he desired the giving of the Corinthians to this cause to be regular and systematic—each man setting aside on every first day of the week a sum corresponding to the measure of his own prosperity (I Cor. 16:2). Thus little by little a worthy amount would have accumulated without embarrassment to themselves. Suspicion of their Apostle (injected by the false apostles in their midst), however, and internal divisions and quarrels had caused them to be far from consistent in applying this scheme.

8 : 13, 14

> For I say not this that others may be eased and ye distressed; but by equality: your abundance being a supply at this present time for their want, that their abundance also may become a supply for your want; that there may be equality.

The Apostle is careful to explain to the Corinthians the "mechanics" of this operation. He does not intend that the relief of the saints at Jerusalem should be at the cost of hardship to those in Corinth, but it is his wish that things should work in

---

[30] Προθυμία should be understood as the personified subject of both ἔχῃ and ἔχει (as in Vulgate) and it is unnecessary to supply, as do AV and RV, "a man" (= τις) as subject. In verses 11 and 12 the verb ἔχειν should be taken in the sense of "to be able". This is, of course, a familiar usage, though less common without an ensuing infinitive. Cf., however, Homer, *Odys.*, XV, 281: οἷα κ'ἔχωμεν, "as far as we may be able"; *Iliad*, XVII, 354: ἀλλ' οὔπως ἔτι εἶχε, "but he was not yet able"; Sophocles, *Elec.*, 1379: ἐξ οἵων ἔχω, "as far as I am able", "according to my ability". The last example is similar in construction to ἐκ τοῦ ἔχειν here in verse 11, which again the context shows to be similar in meaning to καθὸ ἐὰν ἔχῃ in verse 12. Other examples in the New Testament of this usage of ἔχειν = "to be able" are found in Mt. 18:25; Lk. 7:42, 14:28; Acts 4:14, 25:26; Eph. 4:28; II Pet. 1:15.

accordance, as it were, with a law of equilibrium.[31] Under present circumstance the Corinthian Christians are enjoying a degree of material prosperity which is denied to their brethren in Jerusalem, and so the comparative abundance of the former must be extended in brotherly generosity to the want of the latter. The balance will, however, be restored should a time come when the Jerusalem church is comparatively prosperous and the Corinthian church in need; for then the extension of the abundance of the one to the want of the other will be repeated, only this time in the reverse direction. And so, by this spirit of reciprocity, a principle of equality is operative in the universal Christian fraternity.[32]

We cannot agree with Stanley that "the context and the probabilities of the case make it more likely" that by "others" here Paul means the churches of Macedonia, for if one thing is clear from the context it is that Paul is not thinking in terms of an equality of *giving*, as though Achaia by carrying through their project should share, and thus ease, the burden being borne by Macedonia. How could he mean this when a few sentences before (vv. 1ff.) he had commended the astonishing self-sacrifice of the Macedonians, who themselves were the opposite of affluent, as a manifest sign of the grace of God active in their midst? As Hodge points out, what Paul is advocating here "is not agrarianism, nor community of goods", for in the New Testament all giving is voluntary and the fruit of love. Its object is the relief of want, not an artificial equalization of property. There is, moreover, "a special obligation resting on the members of Christ to relieve the wants of their fellow-believers"; for while, as Paul tells the Galatians (6:10), we are to do good to all men, irrespective of their religious views, yet we have a particular responsibility to assist those who are of the household of faith. And, finally, Paul guards elsewhere against the possibilities of abuse: an able-bodied man who is unwilling to work deserves to go without; he

---

31 'Εξ ἰσότητος, "according to equality". This usage of ἐκ is the same as that in verse 11: ἐκ τοῦ ἔχειν, "according to ability".

32 In verse 14 the verb γίνεται should be understood after τὸ ὑμῶν περίσσευμα: "on this present occasion your abundance is extended to their want, in order that (on some future occasion) their abundance may in turn (καί) be extended to your want". Γίνεσθαι εἰς means "to be extended to"; cf. Gal. 3:14.

must not expect others to supply his daily bread for him (II Thess. 3:10). There is no justification for the presumption that a wealthier Christian, simply because he is a brother in Christ, should support an idle member of the church. Religious parasitism has no place in the New Testament. "Thus", concludes Hodge, "the Scriptures avoid, on the one hand, the injustice and destructive evils of agrarian communism, by recognizing the right of property and making all almsgiving optional; and on the other, the heartless disregard of the poor by inculcating the universal brotherhood of believers, and the consequent duty of each to contribute of his abundance to relieve the necessities of the poor. At the same time they inculcate on the poor the duty of self-support to the extent of their ability. They are commanded 'with quietness to work, and to eat their own bread'. Could these principles be carried out, there would be among Christians neither idleness nor want."

8:15

As it is written, He that gathered much had nothing over; and he that gathered little had no lack.

The quotation is from Ex. 16:18 where the context is that of the daily gathering by the Israelites of the manna in the wilderness.[33] It admirably illustrates Paul's point here about the principle of equality. Every day the members of each tent were to gather manna for their needs. Some, such as those who were young and vigorous, gathered more than the prescribed omer; others, perhaps through age or infirmity, gathered less. But all that had been gathered was then put together and equitably measured out to each member. And so there was an equality, which in this case meant also a sufficiency, of daily bread for all. Any who attempted selfishly to hoard the manna found that it went bad and became unserviceable either to themselves or to

---

[33] The quotation, which corresponds to the LXX version with slight variations (LXX: οὐκ ἐπλεόνασεν ὁ τὸ πολύ, καὶ ὁ τὸ ἔλαττον οὐκ ἠλαττόνησεν, II Cor. 8:15: ὁ τὸ πολὺ οὐκ ἐπλεόνασεν, καὶ ὁ τὸ ὀλίγον οὐκ ἠλαττόνησεν), leaves συλλέξας to be supplied after ὁ τὸ πολύ and ὁ τὸ ὀλίγον — "he who gathered much" and "he who gathered little" — from the context of Ex. 16:18. This would seem to indicate that Paul assumed familiarity on the part of his readers with this passage from the Pentateuch.

others. In this way covetousness was condemned and brotherly love and mutual aid encouraged. This principle for the sharing of the manna is applied by the Apostle, says Christopher Wordsworth, "as a practical lesson to the members of the Christian Church. They are all inmates of the same spiritual tent, travellers together through the wilderness of this world to the same heavenly Canaan. It is God who rains down the manna of His bounty in their temporal wealth. What they gather is *His*. And they may *not* gather only for *themselves*". All selfishly hoarded wealth corrupts, and leads to inequalities which ought never to exist, least of all in the Christian community.

Some commentators, such as Strachan and Plummer, have missed the point of this quotation and consequently fail to find Paul's application of it particularly relevant or enlightening. Allo, in common with other Roman Catholic scholars, wishes us to believe that Paul's meaning is that the material benefits received by the Jerusalem Christians from Corinth are counterbalanced or equalled by spiritual benefits received by the Corinthian Christians from Jerusalem. The further refinement of such an exegesis, which Alford rightly censures as a "monstrous perversion", teaches that the surplus merits of the saints may be purchased for a material price. Paul's thought at this point is concerned, as the quotation from Ex. 16:18 helps to emphasize, with the principle of reciprocity between Christians with respect to such material goods as they may enjoy. When, elsewhere, he speaks of material things being given in return for spiritual things (for example, Rom. 15:27, I Cor. 9:11), by spiritual things he means, not any supposed justifying merits of the saints, but the blessings of the gospel administered through Christ's servants, who have a right to expect some provision for their material needs to be made by those to whom they minister. Nowhere is there any suggestion that spiritual benefits are obtainable for material payment. On the contrary, it was a concept which was altogether alien to the apostolic mind, as the incident with Simon the sorcerer clearly shows (Acts 8:18ff.).

"The Lord", says Calvin with reference to the Christian Church, "has not prescribed to us an omer nor any other measure according to which the food of each day is to be regulated; but He has commended to us frugality and temperance, and it is forbidden that anyone should go to excess, taking advantage of his abundance. Let those, then, who have riches, whether left by inheritance or acquired by industry and labours, consider that their opulence is not intended as a means to intemperance and luxury but for the relief of the needs of their brethren. For whatever we possess is *manna*, from whatever quarter it comes. ... And as in the case of any who, either through greed or through distrust, hoarded the manna, what was laid up immediately putrefied, so we may not doubt that riches which are heaped up to the disadvantage of our brethren are accursed and will soon perish. ... I acknowledge", he adds, "that there has not been enjoined upon us an equality of such a kind as to make it unlawful for the rich to live in any greater degree of elegance than the poor; but an equality is to be observed to the extent that no one should go hungry, and no one should withhold his abundance to the detriment of others".

The question of equality in the New Testament is an important one. It is, of course, a fundamental truth that God is no respecter of persons. All men enjoy an equality of creaturehood. Indeed, the distinction between God as Sovereign Creator and man as His subject creature is of ultimate and constitutional significance. Since the fall, moreover, there is an equality of sinnerhood. Mankind is regarded as a community of sinners: in this respect "there is no distinction, for all have sinned and come short of the glory of God" (Rom. 3:22f.). Again, in redemption the classifications of this world have no significance: "there is no distinction between Jew and Greek, for the same Lord is Lord of all, and is rich unto all that call upon Him" (Rom. 10:12). The only final distinction made by the New Testament where mankind is concerned is that between the saved and the lost. But while the members of the redeemed society are "all one in Christ Jesus" (Gal. 3:28), that does not mean that from the social and economic standpoint they are regarded as or intended to be an undifferentiated mass. Unity is never equated with uniformity. Thus in the one Church there are diversities of gifts and diversities of ministries. There is one body, a true organic whole, but many members. Some are richer than others; some have many talents, others few; some are masters, some servants; some are parents, some children. Paul was far from being a sociological revolutionary, for he realized that the truest principle of social reform is that of the gospel and spirit of Christ. He

309

realized, too, that because of sin human society, including even the redeemed community, is marked by imperfection and that the ideal society will be achieved only hereafter, in the renewed creation. It is interesting to find that he does not instruct Philemon to release Onesimus, but to receive him back *as a Christian brother*. The acceptance of these terms means inevitably the disintegration of slavery. But it is not a corollary that the master-servant or employer-employee relationship is wrong and unchristian. Nor is it necessarily a relationship of inequality, for if it were Paul would not be able to exhort masters to render to their servants "justice and *equality*" (Col. 4:1): though socially the master is above the servant, yet under the gospel the whole relationship is embraced by the practical expression of brotherly unity in Christ Jesus.

So too in the distribution of material goods, Christian equality is expressed by the generous ministration of their means by those who are better off (in the instance before us, the Corinthian Christians) for the relief of those who are enduring economic hardship (the Christians in Jerusalem). That the Apostle is not demanding a communization of wealth is evident, both from the impracticability of any such scheme in our present world of change and uncertainty, and (because of this) from his envisagement of a future situation in which the Jerusalem Christians may be in a position to minister to the material wants of their brethren in Corinth. The equality proclaimed by Paul is that of the effective display of mutual respect and affection between fellow-creatures and fellow-sinners who by the grace of God have become fellow-believers in Jesus Christ and fellow-citizens of the kingdom of heaven.

8 : 16, 17

> But thanks be to God, who putteth the same earnest care for you into the heart of Titus. For he accepted indeed our exhortation; but being himself very earnest, he went forth unto you of his own accord.

Paul gives thanks to God that his own earnest care for the Corinthians is shared no less intensely by Titus. Indeed, he regards this solicitude in the heart of Titus as a gift from God and therefore as itself a sign of *God's* gracious concern for them and their well-being. Once again we see with what tact and skill the Apostle conducts this approach to the Corinthian Christians on a matter of great delicacy. It is their money that Titus is coming to collect, but, he assures them, Titus is impelled by zeal *for them*; it is not just a case of concern for the Jerusalem Christians. And his zeal is *the same*—the same, that is, as Paul entertains for them—namely, that they should abound in liberality as well as in all other spiritual graces (cf. v. 7). Evidence of this, for which Paul is so grateful to God, is seen in the manner in which Titus had welcomed [34] Paul's proposal that he should undertake this commission. In point of fact, deep down he was [35] too eager to go to need any exhortation,[36] so much so that it could be said that he had in reality set out for Corinth of his own accord.[37]

8 : 18, 19

And we have sent together with him the brother whose praise in the gospel is spread through all the churches; and not only so, but who was also appointed by the churches to travel with us in the matter of this grace, which is ministered by us to the glory of the Lord, and to show our readiness.

Who was "the brother" whom Paul sent with Titus to Corinth? All we know for certain is what we are told here, namely, that his praise in the gospel extended through all the churches, and that the churches (whether the churches in general

---

[34]   Ἐδέξατο, "he welcomed", rather than the comparatively colourless "he accepted".

[35]   Ὑπάρχων.

[36]   This is how Alford brings out the force of the comparative σπουδαιότερος. It may well, however, be another instance of a comparative used for a superlative, which is how our English version understands it. See note on 7:15 above.

[37]   The great majority of commentators interpret ἐξῆλθε here and συνεπέμψαμεν in verses 18 and 22 as epistolary or anticipatory aorists: what is about to take place at the time of writing the letter, namely, the setting out of Titus and his companions for Corinth, will have taken place at the time when the letter is read by its recipients. Allo, however, maintains that we should understand these aorists to indicate that when Paul was writing these words Titus and his companions had not only left Macedonia but were already in Corinth. We shall examine this question and its implications in the commentary on 12:18 below.

of Judea, Asia Minor, and Macedonia, or the churches of one particular area, is not specified) had selected him to be Paul's travelling-companion in conveying the money collected to Jerusalem. Anything further than this belongs to the realm of conjecture, and the fact that, in a manner of speaking, almost as many names have been suggested as there are scholars to conjecture them is in itself proof sufficient that such definite knowledge as we possess is inadequate for anything approaching a firm conclusion to be reached.

THE IDENTITY OF "THE BROTHER" MENTIONED IN 8:18

A brief consideration of the various individuals who have been felt to have some claim to identification with the brother here mentioned is, however, not without some value, inconclusive though it may be. That the "brother" in question was one of two who accompanied Titus is apparent from verses 22 and 23 below. The anonymity of these two brethren at least emphasizes the fact that Titus was Paul's official delegate and representative. Their presence with Titus was a precaution against malicious slander where so delicate a matter as the collection of money was concerned, a guarantee of the probity of both Titus and Paul.

In both ancient and modern times the claims of *Luke* to be the "brother" designated here have had many supporters, amongst whom Origen, Ephraem, Eusebius, Jerome, Ambrose, Anselm, Grotius, Olshausen, Wordsworth, Plummer, Bachmann, and Strachan may be mentioned. Tasker regards it as "a not improbable guess". This opinion became enshrined in one form of the subscription added at the end of this epistle, namely: "The second epistle to the Corinthians was written from Philippi of Macedonia, through Titus and Luke". But the inferior quality of the documentary evidence for this subscription [38] means that it cannot be treated as an authentic record of historical fact. It seems likely that the chief reason for the identification by later generations of "the brother" with Luke was Paul's assertion here that his "praise in the gospel extended through all the churches", which was taken to be a reference to the Apostle's travelling companion as the author of the Third Gospel. This, however, is now acknowledged to be inadmissible, because it may be regarded as certain that Luke's Gospel had not yet been composed when Paul was writing this epistle; nor does Paul elsewhere use the

---

[38] Far more authoritative is the brief πρὸς Κορινθίους β found in ℵ, B, etc.

term "gospel" of a written document, but only of the message of Jesus Christ and its proclamation. This interpretation is mentioned by Chrysostom and is preserved in the Collect of St. Luke's Day in the English Book of Common Prayer, which speaks of "Luke the Physician, whose praise is in the Gospel".

In favour of Luke as the individual intended it may be said that he, perhaps more than any other person, could at this time be described as Paul's "travelling companion" [39], and that he accompanied Paul to Jerusalem with the money that was in due course collected (as the plural pronoun "we" in Acts 21:15, 17 suggests). It has also been thought that the abandonment of the first person plural ("we") form of narrative in Acts 20:1ff. —which mentions events belonging to the period of this epistle— indicates that Luke had left the Apostle in order, *ex hypothesi*, to accompany Titus to Corinth. The passage might equally well indicate, however, that Paul left Luke in Macedonia, followed Titus to Greece, and subsequently rejoined Luke in Philippi, whence they sailed for Troas (Acts 20:6). If Luke was in fact closely involved in the organization of this fund at Corinth, it would seem surprising that he should have passed over the matter in silence in the Acts, giving the briefest possible account of the Apostle's movements, and virtually none of his motives, at this time. But, be that as it may, the balance of opinion is, if anything, in favour of the identification of Luke with the "brother" to whom Paul here refers, and the strength of the tradition to this effect has also to be taken into account.

Chrysostom, Theodoret, Theophylact, Luther, Calvin, and others have supposed that *Barnabas* is the person intended. Barnabas, it is true, had also been one of Paul's travelling companions, but they had parted from each other because of the disagreement over Mark (Acts 15:39). There is no evidence to suggest that Barnabas was with Paul at this time or that he accompanied him to Jerusalem with the collection; nor, had he been sent on this mission to Corinth, is it likely that he would have been placed in a position of subordination to Titus. A few minuscules, indeed, associate Barnabas as a bearer of this epistle with Luke and Titus in the concluding subscription.

Another person who could appropriately be described as Paul's travelling companion was *Silas*; but it is hardly credible that one who had previously laboured with the Apostle in the evangelization of Corinth (1:19; Acts 18:5), and who consequently must have been well known to the Corinthians, would have been

---

[39] Συνέκδημος ἡμῶν.

anonymously referred to as "the brother" by Paul when writing to these same Corinthians.

Precisely the same remarks are applicable to *Timothy*, who had formerly come down with Silas from Macedonia to Corinth in order to assist Paul with the evangelistic work there. Timothy, indeed, is described specifically (but not anonymously) as "the brother" in the opening salutation of our epistle; but the fact that Paul associates him with himself in the salutation shows not merely that Timothy was with Paul when the epistle was written, but, further, that he remained behind with Paul when the letter was sent.

Zahn, Windisch, and others have favoured the name of *Aristarchus*, who in Acts 19:29 is (together with Gaius) expressly described as one of Paul's travelling companions. He was, moreover, one of those who accompanied the Apostle on the journey back to Jerusalem with the collection (Acts 20:4).[40] Later he was with Paul on the eventful voyage to Rome (Acts 27:2), where he became his fellow-prisoner (Col. 4:10). These considerations make him an attractive candidate for identification with the "brother" who accompanied Titus to Corinth on the occasion in question. There is, however, one incapacitating factor: Aristarchus was a Macedonian of Thessalonica (Acts 19:29, 20:4, 27:2), and Paul's words to the Corinthians a little farther on in our epistle (9:4) indicate that neither of the companions of Titus on this mission was a Macedonian—the bare possibility that Paul might follow bringing with him some Macedonians should ensure that the Corinthians, even if only for appearance's sake, would not be dilatory in completing the collection. This spur to their zeal would have been without point had a Macedonian emissary preceded the Apostle.

Sopater of Berea and *Secundus* of Thessalonica, who are also in the list of Paul's companions given in Acts 20:4, have also been proposed; but, like Aristarchus, the fact that they were Macedonians rules them out. The same disability attaches to *Gaius*, assuming that the Gaius mentioned in Acts 19:29 as a Macedonian is one and the same with the Gaius of Acts 20:4 (in which case the Western text which describes him as coming from the Macedonian town of Doberus is to be preferred to the better authenicated reading which makes him a native of Derbe; but if the latter reading is correct, then the Gaius of 19:29 would appear to be a different person from the Gaius of 20:4).

---

[40] On balance, the textual evidence is against the inclusion of the limiting phrase "as far as Asia" in Acts 20:4. It is omitted in ℵ, B, and the Vulgate.

The name of *Mark* has been put forward by some; but the available evidence makes it improbable that he was associated with Paul at this particular time—though he had been with him previously (Acts 12:25, 13:5, 13) and would be with him again at a later period (Col. 4:10; II Tim. 4:11; Philem. 24).

To return to the list given in Acts 20:4 of those who accompanied Paul with the collection to Jerusalem, *Tychicus* and *Trophimus*, who were both "of Asia", and the latter more specifically a native of Ephesus (Acts 21:29), would alone appear not to be disqualified from fulfilling the role of the "brethren" referred to here and in verses 22f. From II Tim. 4:20 we learn that Trophimus set out with Paul on his final journey to Rome, but that owing to illness had to be left behind at Miletus. Paul's bond of friendship and confidence with Tychicus is clearly displayed elsewhere in his letters. Thus he is commended to the Ephesians as "the beloved brother and faithful minister in the Lord" (Eph. 6:21) and to the Colossians as "the beloved brother and faithful minister and fellow-servant in the Lord" (Col. 4:7), and it is apparent that Paul placed such trust in him that he was in the habit of sending him as his emissary and the bearer of his epistles to different churches or persons (cf. Eph. 6:21f.; II Tim. 4:12; Col. 4:7f.; Tit. 3:12). In view of all this, Tychicus is as likely as any to have been one of those chosen by Paul to travel with Titus on this mission to Corinth.

It remains only to mention the opinion of some, among them Souter,[41] that the "brother" of whom Paul speaks was in fact a literal brother of Titus. Apart, however, from the inadvisability of entrusting so delicate a business as the handling of charitable money to men who were linked to each other by close family ties, this exegesis would demand that "our brother" in verse 22 should be taken to mean literally a blood-brother of Paul's (as has even been suggested), which would almost inevitably have opened the door for the renewal of malicious slanders by the Apostle's antagonists in Corinth. One of Paul's main considerations, however, was the need to avoid giving any possible ground for suspicion or mistrust of any kind as this project was carried through to completion. The natural and only satisfactory way of understanding the term "brother" in this context is to interpret it to mean a fellow-believer or brother in Christ, in accordance with what has become a perfectly normal usage in the early Church, recurring many scores of times in the Acts and the Epistles. Otherwise it would seem necessary to maintain that Timothy,

---

[41] A. Souter, *Expository Times*, Vol. XVIII, pp. 285, 335ff.

Sosthenes, Epaphroditus, Tychicus, Onesimus, and Philemon were literal brothers of Paul (cf. I Cor. 1:1; II Cor. 1:1; Phil. 2:25; Col. 1:1, 4:7, 9; I Thess. 3:2; Philem. 1, 20, etc.), which would be an absurdity.

As in the appointment of the seven "deacons" to attend to matters of business and charity the Apostles had recognized the need for choosing "men of good report", that is, men who would be above suspicion (Acts 6:3), so now Paul writes on behalf of the worth and integrity of Titus and his two companions. Verses 16 to 24 constitute, in effect, a letter of commendation (cf. 3:1) of the three to the Corinthian church. Nor was it a case of the two brethren mentioned in this passage having been selected by Paul alone (which again might have been seized on and mischievously interpreted by his opponents in Corinth): they had been appointed [42] by the churches (no doubt the churches of Asia Minor) to travel with Paul for the prosecution of this charitable project.[43] The decision was not that of one man, nor of one church, but of the churches in general, so much so that Paul is able to describe the two brethren concerned as "the messengers of the churches" (v. 23). Paul, therefore, was not open to any accusation that he was seeking gain or glory for himself. The appointment was with a view both to the glory of God and to the expediting of the Apostle's task in making effective arrangements for the collection. The former may be defined as its ultimate, the latter as its proximate, aim.[44]

---

[42] Reference to verses 23f. indicates that what is said here in verse 19 of the one's appointment also applies to the other. Χειροτονηθείς seems to be an instance of a participle used for the indicative (=ἐχειροτονήθη). For other possible occurrences of this construction in our epistle see note on 4:8f. above. Χειροτονεῖν, which occurs only twice in the New Testament, namely, here and in Acts 14:23, means properly to stretch out the hand for the purpose of voting, then in a general sense to choose or elect, and thus to nominate or appoint. The contemporary usage of the verb indicates that in New Testament times it had the meaning simply of "to appoint", and consequently that it is due to a later misinterpretation to take it to mean "to ordain". Both here and in Acts 14:23 the verb signifies the selection and appointment of the person or persons in question, and not an act of ordination by laying on of hands.

[43] Or "with this grace" (AV), as bearers of the money contributed —the TR (σὺν τῇ χάριτι ταυτῇ) can now claim the support of P⁴⁶ and ℵ.

[44] Πρὸς τὴν τοῦ Κυρίου δόξαν καὶ προθυμίαν ἡμῶν is a difficult expression because, as Allo remarks, the preposition πρός introduces two concepts, "the glory of God" and "our readiness", which seem to belong to two different orders of ideas. The preposition points to the object or purpose towards which the appointment of the "brother" is directed. Accordingly, "to *promote* the glory of God and our readiness" brings out its force. We would suggest that

8 : 20, 21

> Avoiding this, that any man should blame us in the matter
> of this bounty which is ministered by us: for we take thought
> for things honourable not only in the sight of the Lord, but
> also in the sight of men.

Paul shrinks from giving others any excuse, however far-
fetched, for slanderous imputations where money matters are
concerned. Malicious gossip elaborated from some avoidable
though innocent circumstance can do great harm to the cause
of Christ. As Calvin says, "there is nothing which is more apt
to lay one open to sinister imputations than the handling of
public money". Hence the extreme care with which the Apostle
arranges the conduct of this collection: he himself does not collect
the money, but this task is committed to Titus, whom the Corinthians love and trust, and to two others who are messengers, not
of Paul, but of the churches; and even when he takes the money
contributed to Jerusalem it will be in the company of a group
of men who represent various churches (Acts 20:4). The importance, in monetary affairs, of having a name for integrity
not only before God, but also before men, is confirmed by the
Apostle by means of an allusion to Prov. 3:4, which speaks of
finding "favour and good repute in the sight of God and man".[45]
A similar allusion to Prov. 3:4 for the purpose of enjoining the
same principle is found in Rom. 12:17.

Paul was not, of course, moved by any self-centred concern for
the praise and approval of his fellow-men. It was really the name

the full nuance of Paul's thought here is that this brother's appointment
by the churches would, by introducing an independently delegated "official"
of the highest reputation, remove from the fractious any possible excuse for
suspicion or slander of this undertaking, in this way promoting God's glory
and at the same time Paul's willingness and preparedness for carrying the
collection through to a successful conclusion. In other words, this expression
must be understood in connection not only with what precedes, but also
with what follows on immediately in the next verse, in which the Apostle
speaks of his carefulness to avoid any shadow of mistrust.

[45] Paul's language is close to that of the LXX: καὶ προνοοῦ καλὰ ἐνώπιον
Κυρίου καὶ ἀνθρώπων, but he gives emphasis to his argument that a good name
is important before men as well as before God by his repetition of ἐνώπιον with
the formula οὐ μόνον ... ἀλλὰ καί: "not only in the sight of the Lord, but
also in the sight of men".

of Christ for which he was jealous, not his own name except in so far as it was bound up with the reputation of his Master. Had not the Lord Himself said: "Blessed are ye when men shall reproach you and persecute you and say all manner of evil against you falsely, for My sake" (Mt. 5:11)? The Apostle was no stranger to this form of persecution by slander, and in Corinth in particular he had been assailed in this manner. It was one aspect of his fellowship in the sufferings of Christ (Phil. 3:10), who Himself had patiently endured the revilings of hostile men and false witnesses against His good name (cf. I Pet. 2:23). But nowhere does the New Testament suggest that a Christian may be careless and unconcerned about his reputation for personal integrity; for always he must remember that he is no longer living to himself (5:15; Rom. 14:7), that in a real sense in his own reputation the reputation of Christ and His Church is at stake, and accordingly that he should abstain from anything which has even the appearance of evil (I Thess. 5:22). Consistently with this principle, Paul forbore to accept financial support from the Corinthians during the time of his ministry in their midst, so that, by giving no opportunity for malicious misrepresentation where money was concerned, he might "cause no hindrance to the gospel of Christ" (I Cor. 9:12). So also here, Paul is careful to avoid [46] giving any man an occasion for blaming him in the matter of this bounty [47] which he is supervising.

---

[46] *Στελλόμενοι* should probably be explained as a nautical metaphor here, which is how Wordsworth takes it, following Wettstein. In nautical parlance it meant to furl or shorten sail, when coming to shore or in order to avoid danger in navigation. Cf. Homer, *Iliad*, I, 433: *ἱστία μὲν στείλαντο*; also *Odys.*, XVI, 353, where the active form of the verb is used: *ἱστία τὲ στέλλοντας*. The verb is used again by Paul in II Thess. 3:6 with the same force as here. He takes precautions "to avoid the injurious effect of a gale of calumny from suspicious men", says Wordsworth; and, with reference to *ἁδρότητι* (see next note), he adds: "St. Paul compares himself to a mariner, sailing with a rich cargo of spiritual merchandise and Christian beneficence towards Jerusalem; and he says that he so pilots the vessel, as to decline the winds of envious censure, to which, on account of the riches of his freight, he was exposed". The nominative plural participle should be construed with *συνεπέμψαμεν* (v. 18), though some scholars treat it as an instance of an absolute participle. See note on 4:12 above.

[47] *Ἁδρότης* is a noun formed from the adjective *ἁδρός* which properly means "thick" or "bulky", and hence "full grown" or "abundant". Thus *ἁδρότης* has the sense of "wealth" or "abundance" (*ubertas*). The use of the

8 : 22

> And we have sent with them our brother, whom we have
> many times proved earnest in many things, but now much
> more earnest, by reason of the great confidence which he
> hath in you.

The identity of this second "brother" whom Paul sent with
Titus to Corinth is, like that of the first, shrouded in anonymity.
The field of conjecture is practically identical with that which
we have already surveyed in connection with the first "brother"
(see commentary on verses 18f. above), and what we have said
there about the various individuals who have been proposed may
be taken as equally applicable in this case. Paul simply says of
Titus's second companion that in many things and at many
times he had put him to the test and proved him earnest, which
indicates the great confidence he had in him, and also that the
eagerness of this brother to undertake this mission to Corinth
had been increased because of the great confidence which he [48]
had in the Corinthians. As many commentators point out, this
confidence of his does not imply that he had previously been in
Corinth and was familiar with the members of the church there,
but probably that his confidence in them rested on the good
reports concerning them which he had heard from the lips of
Paul and Titus. Had he been known to the Corinthians through
previous personal association with them, it is hardly likely that
Paul would have referred to him in this cryptic and anonymous
manner—a consideration which, therefore, would seem to invalidate the claims put forward on behalf of individuals, such as
Silas, Timothy, and Apollos, who were well known to the Corinthians. (The fact that Paul refers to "Apollos the brother" in
I Cor. 16:12 shows, if anything, that had Apollos been meant
here his name would have been included.)

---

term here may be taken both as a compliment and as an incitement to the
Corinthians—a compliment because it implies that their character is such as
to cause Paul to expect that they will give generously, and an incitement to
them in consequence not to disappoint this expectation.

[48] That is, the brother, rather than Paul (AV, Calvin, Beza, etc.).

8 : 23, 24

Whether any inquire about Titus, he is my partner and my
fellow-worker to you-ward; or our brethren, they are the
messengers of the churches, they are the glory of Christ.
Show ye therefore unto them in the face of the churches the
proof of your love, and of our glorying on your behalf.

Paul envisages some contentious person asking the Corinthians who these three emissaries are and by what authority they
have come to collect money. Respecting Titus, the answer is that
his standing is that of the partner of their own apostle and his
fellow-worker in bringing the gospel to them. Respecting the
other two, they are, firstly, "our brothers" in the faith, and as
such should be made to feel at home in the Corinthian church;
secondly, they are "messengers of the churches"—literally
"apostles of the churches": apostles, that is, in the general, non-
official sense of the word, indicating that they had been selected
and *sent forth* by the churches for this particular purpose (the
word seems to be used in this more general sense of Paul and
Barnabas in Acts 14:4, 14 and of Epaphroditus in Phil. 2:25)—
and as such should be welcomed with respect and attention; and,
thirdly, they are "the glory of Christ", and as such will bring the
light and victory of the risen Lord into their midst. Thus in this
threefold testimonial we may discern an ascending scale of
commendation. The precise significance of Paul's description of
them as "the glory of Christ" is difficult to ascertain. Many commentators take it to mean that their lives are such as to reflect
faithfully the glory of their Saviour. Filson suggests that "by
reason of their character and work they bring praise to their
Lord". Somewhat similarly, Stanley connects it in thought with
verse 19 above and 9:13 below in which the ministration of the
collection is envisaged as being to the glory of the Lord, and says
that "it seems to imply that the glory of Christ would in an
especial manner be shown to the Jewish Christians by the zeal
of the Gentile Christians in their behalf". The phrase, however,
may mean simply that the two emissaries are a credit to Christ.[49]

Since, therefore, the three of them come with such credentials,
it is only reasonable that Paul should expect and exhort the Corinthians to accord them a clear demonstration of their love and of

---

[49] This is one of the numerous senses which δόξα may bear.

the qualities and graces which had caused him to boast on their behalf. In other words, he is appealing to them to be true to themselves and not to disappoint the high opinion and hopes which he entertains of them. But more than that, for it is not only their Apostle who is watching them expectantly, but also the churches whom the emissaries represent, and indeed the Christian world as a whole. Hence their reception of Titus and the two brothers should reflect a consciousness that their actions and reactions are taking place as it were in the presence and under the scrutiny of the churches.[50]

NOTE ON THE SECTION 9:1–5

Some scholars have propounded the theory that the first five verses of this chapter constitute a section which is not a genuine part of the original epistle, but a fragment of some other letter which, whether by accident or design, has been inserted at this point. It is affirmed that whereas the conjunction "for" with which the chapter is introduced indicates a logical link with the immediately preceding matter, no such connection can be found between the end of chapter 8 and the beginning of chapter 9; it is suggested, further, that this section (or the letter from which it is supposed to have become detached) is addressed to the whole district of Achaia (cf. v. 2) rather than to the church located in Corinth; and it is maintained that things already said in chapter 8 are unnecessarily repeated in this chapter. Once again, however, we are confronted with a hypothesis which is entirely without the support of external evidence or of any tradition; and the pillars with which its advocates seek to support it may be seen, upon examination, to be without solidity.

That there is in fact a very close connection in thought between the closing section of chapter 8 and the opening section of chapter 9 has been recognized by many excellent commentators. Plummer, for instance, says not only that the conjunction "for" is "very intelligible", but also that "if the division between the chapters had not been so misplaced, no one would have proposed to separate ix. 1–5 from viii. 6–24". We may summarize the sequence of thought in the following way: Paul is sending Titus and two other brethren to supervise the collection at Corinth, and he asks that they may be given an appropriate welcome

---

[50] 'Εις πρόσωπον is probably a Semitism = לִפְנֵי, "in the presence of". See the note on ἐν προσώπῳ, 2:10 above.

(8:16–24); for there is no need for him to write telling them to give of their means for the Christians in Jerusalem, since he knows that they had already taken the initiative in this matter the previous year; accordingly he is sending on the three delegates in advance to see that everything is in readiness for his own arrival in Corinth a little later on, when he comes to receive from them the money they have collected (9:1–5). Regarding the mention of Achaia rather than Corinth in verse 2, it is sufficient to turn back to the opening salutation of this epistle, which shows that it was addressed not merely to "the church of God which is at Corinth", but also in fact to "all the saints which are in the whole of Achaia" (1:1), so that there is quite certainly nothing incongruous about the mention here of Achaia, which is the inclusive term. And as for the alleged repetitions, they are less real than apparent, for Paul's purpose now, in this chapter, is to emphasize in a way that he has not done before the blessings that are attached to generous giving. In any case, as Denney aptly remarks, "the statements, *e.g.* in vv. 3–5, would be quite unintelligible if we had not chap. viii. 16–24 to explain them".

9 : 1, 2

For as touching the ministering to the saints, it is superfluous for me to write to you: for I know your readiness, of which I glory on your behalf to them of Macedonia, that Achaia hath been prepared for a year past; and your zeal hath stirred up very many of them.

The particular form of "ministering" [51] of which Paul speaks here, namely, provision for the needs of distressed and destitute fellow-Christians, may be traced back, within the framework of the apostolic Church, to its origin in the appointment of the seven deacons, or ministers,[52] which in turn was a development from the "daily ministration"[53] of charity which had become a necessity after Pentecost in the rapidly growing church at Jerusalem (Acts 6:1ff.). The appointment of these seven deacons did not, of course, have the effect of removing the responsibility of contributing philanthropically to the needs of less fortunate fellow-believers from the shoulders of the ordinary Christian man and woman, as the passage we are now considering, together with

---

[51] Διακονία.

[52] Διάκονοι.

[53] Διακονία.

numerous other places in the New Testament, makes abundantly clear. What it did effect was the removal of the responsibility for the detailed organization and supervision of such charity from the shoulders of the Apostles, so that they might be free to concentrate their energies on the ministry of the Word (Acts 6:2–4). This charitable ministry is the duty and privilege of every Christian whose material resources make it possible for him to participate in it, in however small a measure. As Calvin says, "when we relieve the brethren in this way we do nothing more than discharge a ministry that is due to them".

It should be remembered that Paul, having lived for eighteen months in their midst (Acts 18:11), had a first-hand knowledge of the Corinthians. Their willingness in responding to the needs of others was something about which he gloried to the Macedonians. As the present tense [54] shows, this glorying of his on their behalf was not a thing of the past which more recent developments had caused him to abandon; he was doing it constantly, even at the time of writing this letter. To conclude that what Paul writes here is in any sense at variance with his injunction given to the Corinthians in the earlier epistle (I Cor. 1:31) and soon to be repeated in this epistle (10:17), that he who glories should glory only in the Lord (cf. Jer. 9:23), would be to misunderstand the situation, for Paul's glorying here is neither in men nor in human achievements as such, but in the grace of God manifested in and through the lives of men. Thus he has already gloried to the Corinthians of the amazing liberality of the Macedonians, but in doing so he has attributed everything to "the grace of God which hath been given in the churches of Macedonia" (8:1). True Christian giving flows from the prior giving of God's grace, and Paul's glorying concerning the Corinthians is essentially a glorying in the goodness of God.

The substance of Paul's boast to the Macedonians is: "Achaia has been prepared since last year".[55] This statement must be interpreted in association with what he has previously said in 8:10ff., which indicates that the Corinthians had made a start with the collection, but that the enterprise had not been brought

---

[54] Καυχῶμαι.

[55] The ὅτι should probably be taken as recitative, introducing the direct speech that the Apostle had used to the Macedonians. On the significance of ἀπὸ πέρυσι, see note on 8:10 above.

to completion. The readiness of which Paul speaks here is there described as "the readiness to will" (8:11): their preparedness was preparedness of purpose, but as yet only of partial fulfilment. All that was now needed was the incentive which the coming and supervision of Titus and his two companions would give, so that on Paul's arrival all the gifts should be gathered in, ready to be conveyed by him to the church at Jerusalem.

To suggest, as some have done, that the Apostle was craftily, and without regard to the requirements of strict honesty, playing the Macedonians and the Corinthians against each other in order to increase the size of the collection, is to show an astonishing insensitiveness to the character of Paul as it is plainly revealed in his own letters and in the Acts of the Apostles. True though it is that he here speaks of boasting to the Macedonians that Achaia has been *prepared* since last year, and that a few lines further on, in verse 4, he speaks of the possibility of finding the Corinthians *unprepared* when he himself arrives from Macedonia, yet the context makes it clear, as we have already explained, that what he means is that it will be most regrettable if their preparedness of intention, which led to the commencement of the good work, has not been crowned with the preparedness of completion when he comes, accompanied as he may well be by a number of Macedonian Christians; for this would mean the disappointment both of his own confidence and also of the expectations of the Macedonian churches. How can it be supposed that the Apostle who has so strenuously maintained his honour and his utter sincerity in both word and action (1:12–18, 2:17, 4:2) should now in this same epistle speak of having engaged in subterfuge and untruthfulness, as though a good end justifies a less than honourable means? Such inconsistency within the scope of a single letter would argue, at the very least, a lack of intelligence incompatible with the man we know Paul to have been; and, far worse, it would be more than sufficient to undermine the integrity of character and conscience which he has protested before both God and man. The situation that had arisen had been shaped by the development of events: the previous year the Corinthians had shown their enthusiasm by initiating this charitable enterprise; their enthusiasm had acted as a spur to many of the Macedonians; but, unlike the Macedonians, the Corinthians had failed to complete what they had so enthusiastically begun; the zeal of the Macedonians should now in turn be a spur to the Corinthians to bring this undertaking to full fruition in readiness for Paul's arrival.

9 : 3, 4

> But I have sent the brethren, that our glorying on your behalf may not be made void in this respect; that, even as I said, ye may be prepared: lest by any means, if there come with me any of Macedonia and find you unprepared, we (that we say not ye) should be put to shame in this confidence.

From what Paul now says it is plain that he was assured that his boasting on behalf of the Corinthians would not be proved hollow, excepting possibly in one respect,[56] namely, the question concerning the completion of the collection which they had undertaken and their consequent readiness for his arrival. It was not so much a question of their readiness to give, but rather of the need for efficient planning to get the money in. Thus Plummer comments: "He is not afraid that they will refuse to give, but he is afraid that they may be dilatory for want of organization. It will produce a bad impression if the money is not ready when it is wanted. He carefully limits his anxiety to this 'particular'".

Paul envisages the possibility that some Macedonians (those, no doubt, designated to travel with the money collected by the Macedonian churches) may accompany him to Corinth. Tasker may well be right in declaring that Paul's language here, although it appears hypothetical to us, is in fact under the influence of Semitic idiom, and actually means that a number of Macedonians will quite definitely come with him. (As parallel instances of such a usage he cites Jn. 12:32 and I Jn. 2:28.) If that is so, then we may suppose that the Apostle was waiting in Macedonia, not merely to give the Corinthians an opportunity for completing their charitable undertaking, but at the same time to enable the Macedonians to make the final arrangements concerning their own collection, now completed (perhaps the selection by the congregations of suitable men to travel with Paul to Jerusalem), before he came on with the latter to Corinth. It would be most unfortunate, and a source of embarrassment both to himself

---

[56] Ἐν τῷ μέρει τούτῳ (3:10, ἐν τούτῳ τῷ μέρει) = "in this respect", or, more literally, "in this part of the whole"; cf. Col. 2:16, ἐν μέρει ἑορτῆς, "in respect of a feast".

and (he delicately suggests) to the Corinthians, if these Macedonians whose zeal had been fired by the earlier enthusiasm of the Corinthians should arrive in Achaia to find the collection there in a state of disorganization.

It was this situation which, as he points out in the next verse, convinced Paul of the necessity of sending Titus and the other two brethren on ahead so that this business might be efficiently supervised. We may deduce from what Paul says here that neither of the brethren who accompanied Titus was a Macedonian, for otherwise there would have been little point in the admonition concerning the regrettable effect that a discovery of Corinthian unreadiness would have on any Macedonians who came with him. This means, further, that of those mentioned in Acts 20:4 as Paul's travelling companions the names of Sopater the Berean and of Aristarchus and Secundus the Thessalonians may be eliminated from the list of individuals who might possibly have gone on ahead with Titus. But, of course, Sopater, Aristarchus, and Secundus may well have been the Macedonians who came on later with Paul to Corinth. It is certainly plain from what Paul says here that he intended to follow Titus to Corinth and, from what he says hereafter, that this was to be his third visit to that city (cf. 10:2, 12:14, 13:1f.). When he does come he wants the Corinthians to be fully prepared, so that his great confidence[57] in them may be vindicated. If they fail him in this, it is a reflection on them, not on him. Indeed, Paul's confidence in the Corinthians is an excellent example of true Christian love in action—that love which "believeth all things, hopeth all things" (I Cor. 13:7).

9:5

> I thought it necessary therefore to entreat the brethren, that they would go before unto you, and make up beforehand your aforepromised bounty, that the same might be ready as a matter of bounty, and not of extortion.

As we have already seen (8:20f.), prudence dictated that Paul should not organize the collection at Corinth in person, in

---

[57] 'Υπόστασις ("confidence") is properly a basis, foundation, support (*substantia*, Vulgate), hence reality, a ground of hope or confidence, and hence assurance, resolution, confidence, which is the force here, and which is a meaning the noun bears in Polybius (IV, 1, 10) and Diodorus Siculus (I, 6). Cf. II Cor. 11:17; Heb. 3:14, 11:1.

order that the tongues of slanderers might be silenced. Hence Titus and two others, who were officially appointed delegates of the churches, were sent on ahead to attend to this matter. Paul now explains that another important reason for his being preceded by these three, here collectively referred to as "the brethren", was that all might be settled and in good order in anticipation of his arrival. In this way the boasts which he had made on behalf of the Corinthians would be seen, especially by any Macedonians in his party, to be justified and the Corinthian Christians would prove themselves to be both equal to their reputation and faithful to their promises, having completed the enterprise to which they had so purposefully set their hands during the previous year. The three emissaries were to go before and to organize to completion before Paul's arrival the collection which had been promised before by the Corinthians.[58] In this way all would be arranged in a state of excellent order and the promise of the Corinthians would be honoured in the sight of the churches and to the glory of God.

Our examination of these first five verses of chapter 9 has shown that they are not at all superfluous, but supplementary to what was said in 8:16-24 concerning the mission of the advance-party of three who preceded Paul to Corinth. There is no instance of purposeless repetition. And the concluding phrases of verse 5 act as an effective bridge to what follows (as we shall now see), so that 9:1-5 is isolated in thought and argument neither from what precedes nor from what ensues.

By saying that their gift is to be characteristic of a blessing [59]

---

[58] Note the threefold repetition of the prefix προ-: προέλθωσιν ... προκαταρτίσωσι ... προεπηγγελμένην. The verb προκαταρτίζειν means "to organize beforehand", "to bring into good order beforehand", which would seem to confirm that the chief problem at Corinth in connection with this charitable project was that of organization, not unwillingness to give generously. I Corinthians affords evidence in several respects of a serious lack of orderliness in the Corinthian church.

[59] Εὐλογία is the LXX rendering of the Hebrew בְּרָכָה, and is found with the same sense as here of a bountiful gift in Gen. 33:11; Josh. 15:19; Judg. 1:15. We do not doubt that the Apostle is indulging in a highly felicitous play on words: in I Cor. 16:1 he has used the term λογία, "collection"; and here the term εὐλογία suggests the thought that he desires it to be "a really fine collection" (εὐ-λογία), which will indeed be a blessing, εὐλογία (cf. Windisch).

327

and not of covetousness [60] Paul means that it is to come from an expansive and not a grudging spirit: their giving is to be expressive of a desire to be a blessing to others and not of cupidity which is preoccupied with selfish grasping and gain rather than with the needs of the unfortunate. As Herveius observes, "giving is called avarice when it is done with a grasping and niggardly and sad heart, but a blessing when it is done with a generous and eager heart". This note provides an appropriate introduction to the next section, which is an eloquent encomium of the blessedness of Christian liberality.

9:6

> But this I say, He that soweth sparingly shall reap also sparingly; and he that soweth bountifully shall reap also bountifully.

"The point is this",[61] that the man who sows in a niggardly manner [62] will inevitably reap a niggardly harvest, and, on the same principle, the man who sows generously [63] will reap a

---

[60] Πλεονεξία is rendered "extortion" in our version and "exaction" in RSV, but on both philological and contextual grounds the AV rendering "covetousness" (Vulgate, avaritia) is to be preferred. "Extortion" would imply a forcible or compulsory extraction of money by the Apostle, whereas any activity implied in πλεονεξία here should be associated with the Corinthians, as is the case in the parallel and contrasting εὐλογία. The use of πλεονεξία is pregnant. Thus Arndt and Gingrich explain it as indicating here "a gift that is grudgingly granted by avarice". Tasker rightly points out that "there is no suggestion that either the apostle or his envoys would ever apply force to extract from the Corinthians money they were unwilling to give".

[61] RSV. Τοῦτο δέ, used absolutely here, may correspond to τοῦτο δέ φημί or τοῦτο δέ λέγω, which Paul uses on occasions for the purpose of introducing an important piece of doctrinal instruction (see I Cor. 7:29, 15:50; Gal. 3:17; I Thess. 4:15). But the τοῦτο not only draws attention to what follows, it also forms a link with what has preceded: "In connection with this question of giving either generously or grudgingly, the point is this, that he who sows sparingly, etc ..."

[62] Φειδομένως, an adverb formed from the present participle, occurs only here in biblical literature and elsewhere only in Plutarch (Alex., XXXV, 7) and Cosmas and Damian (XXXIV, 70). There is an instance of the verb φείδεσθαι with the meaning of "to be miserly" as early as the sixth century B.C., in Theognis (Fragm., I, 931). This sense well suits φειδομένως here = "in a miserly manner". Cf. also the expression δώρων δὲ ὁ φειδόμενος in the LXX rendering of Prov. 21:14.

[63] Ἐπ' εὐλογίαις stands here in direct contrast to φειδομένως and must be given the opposite meaning, that is, "generously", "bountifully". This

generous harvest. The important lesson which Paul is urging upon the Corinthians at this point is that *to give is to sow*. What is given is not lost, but, like the seed sown by the farmer, contrary to all appearances it possesses the potency of life and increase. At the same time it is important to remember that, as the whole context shows, the Apostle is speaking of the quality, not the quantity, of giving. The source of giving is not the purse, but the heart, as the next verse makes clear. The poor widow who gave two common mites, the least of all gifts in quantity, none the less, because she gave her whole living, gave more than all the others together who, out of their superfluity, gave silver and gold at no cost to themselves (Mk. 12:41ff.). It was she who gave, and sowed, bountifully, not they. This principle had already received expression in Prov. 11:24ff.: "There is that scattereth, and increaseth yet more; and there is that withholdeth more than is meet, but it tendeth only to want. The liberal soul shall be made fat; and he that watereth shall be watered also himself. ... He that trusteth in his riches shall fall". The sphere of giving, then, presents no exception to the inexorable rule, valid in the moral no less than in the agricultural realm, that a man reaps according to the manner of his sowing, which Paul enunciates in Gal. 6:7ff. The thought of the text we are considering is in complete harmony with his exhortation there: "Let us not be weary in well-doing; for in due season we shall reap, if we faint not. So then, as we have opportunity, let us work that which is good toward all men, and especially toward them that are of the household of faith". Calvin comments well that "whenever fleshly reason calls us back from doing good through fear of loss, we should immediately oppose it with this shield: *But the Lord declares that we are sowing*".

The teaching of Christ concerning the blessedness of giving amply confirms what the Apostle says here. Even so slight a deed as the giving of a cup of cold water to "one of these little ones" will not remain unrewarded (Mt. 10:42; cf. Lk. 6:38).

---

usage of ἐπί gives the expression an adverbial force, answering to the adverb φειδομένως. A precisely similar combination is found in the Oxyrhynchus papyri: κακοτρόπως καὶ ἐπὶ ῥᾳδιουργίᾳ (Grenfell and Hunt, 237), VI, 21. Εὐλογία should be understood in the same sense as in the preceding verse, namely, a gift freely and spontaneously bestowed and thus constituting a blessing to the recipient.

To feed the hungry, give drink to the thirsty, shelter the stranger, clothe the naked, tend the sick, or befriend the captive is a mark of those who inherit the kingdom and elicits the commendation: "Inasmuch as ye did it unto one of these My brethren, even these least, ye did it unto Me" (Mt. 25:34ff.). This, again, accords with the wisdom of the Old Testament, which affirms that "he that hath pity upon the poor lendeth unto Jehovah, and his good deed will He pay him again" (Prov. 19:17). This principle of reaping in accordance with what has been sown is thus seen to belong to the moral no less than to the physical structure of God's universe. Goodness brings its own reward and indeed leads to an increase of goodness. Nowhere, however, does Scripture propose the gaining of rewards as a motive for goodness. Giving for the sake of gain ceases to be goodness flowing from a simple and unselfish heart; it is then that very form of giving which the Apostle deprecates here—giving which is governed by covetousness. But the man who gives ungrudgingly for the blessing of others may rejoice in the knowledge that in doing so he is sowing seed which will produce a harvest of blessing for himself.

9:7

> Let each man do according as he hath purposed in his heart: not grudgingly, or of necessity: for God loveth a cheerful giver.

As we have said previously, the true measure of a gift is not its external magnitude but the internal state of the giver's heart. There must be real freedom in Christian giving, each individual making the decision in his own heart how much he ought to give. It is far from Paul's intention that a "quota scheme" or a "means test" should be imposed upon the Corinthians. To part with money in a charitable cause and then to grieve over its loss [64] is not to give but to grudge. To contribute under compulsion, whether of superior authority or of public opinion, is likewise no act of Christian giving. Grudging or sorrowful giving manifests itself in a variety of ways. One particular instance had occurred

---

[64] Ἐκ λύπης, translated "grudgingly" in our version, means literally "of sorrow", that is, from a heart made sorrowful at the thought of parting with money.

330

in the Jerusalem church itself, when Ananias and Sapphira resorted to a subterfuge, keeping back for themselves a portion of the money they had received through the sale of their land, while seeking to deceive others into believing that they were contributing the whole amount (Acts 5:1ff.). They were under no compulsion whatever to give the whole; the money was entirely within their power; but their hearts were intent not on bringing blessing to others but on fabricating a reputation for themselves, and so they acted a lie, with disastrous results. Their object was getting rather than giving. Genuine, free, unremorseful giving is, however, as Paul reminds his readers here, distinguished by the mark of cheerfulness.[65] In it the giver finds real pleasure. It is for him, quite literally, an *exhilarating* experience. And the happiness and openness of his heart will be reflected in the happiness and openness of his face.

9:8

And God is able to make all grace abound unto you; that ye, having always all sufficiency in everything, may abound unto every good work.

The power of God, than which there can be nothing more powerful, is operative also in the sphere of Christian giving, for this too is a sphere of His grace. Thus, as we have seen, the exceptional liberality of the Macedonian churches was attributed by Paul to the grace of God which they had received (8:1). It afforded incontrovertible evidence of God's ability triumphing over and through human inability, of His power being made perfect in their weakness. Indeed, the place given in these two chapters to the all-prevailing sufficiency of divine grace is adequate

---

[65] "God loveth a cheerful giver"— *ἱλαρὸν γὰρ δότην ἀγαπᾷ ὁ θεός*—is a further instance of Paul's familiarity with the LXX, for it is an evident allusion to Prov. 22:9, *ἄνδρα ἱλαρὸν καὶ δότην ἀγαπᾷ ὁ θεός*. It may be remarked that, while *εὐλογεῖ* for *ἀγαπᾷ* is the better attested LXX reading, Paul's use of the latter may be taken to indicate that it was the reading known to him and the one accepted in his day, rather than, as Plummer suggests, that his failure to write *εὐλογεῖ* points to a lapse of memory.

Ἱλαρός is *hapax legomenon* in the New Testament, but in Rom. 12:8 the noun *ἱλαρότης* is found in a somewhat similar context: "He that giveth, let him do it with liberality *(ἐν ἁπλότητι)*; ... he that showeth mercy, with cheerfulness *(ἐν ἱλαρότητι)*".

to show that in their spiritual emphasis they are essentially in harmony with the main theme pervading the epistle. And what God did for the Macedonians He is able to do for the Corinthians. His grace is always abundant and enriching; it always leads to increase, not decrease—even when it involves parting with one's possessions!—so much so, indeed, that the overwhelming consequence of God's making *all* grace abound to them is that they, "in *all* things at *all* times having *all* sufficiency, may abound to *all* good work".[66] God's giving of His grace is the complete opposite of grudging and forced. In responding to it by generous and cheerful giving the Christian finds not only that, contrary to human probability, he yet has a sufficiency for his own needs, but, far more, that he is so enriched by divine grace as to be able constantly to abound in every kind of good work. The inexhaustible resources of the grace of God made available in Christ mean that this exuberant life in which the Christian "always abounds in the work of the Lord" (I Cor. 15:58) is a practical and joyful reality for the man of faith.

9:9

As it is written, He hath scattered abroad, he hath given to the poor; his righteousness abideth for ever.

The quotation, which corresponds exactly with the Septuagint version, is from Ps. 112:9, a psalm which describes the blessedness of "the man that feareth Jehovah, that delighteth greatly in His commandments" (v. 1). The words cited read like the epitaph of a philanthropist: "He scattered abroad" (the very expression is eloquent of his open-handed liberality), "he gave to the poor; his righteousness abides for ever". The metaphor is still that of the sower, as the next verse shows even more clearly. By his apprehensive niggardliness the miser may accumulate a great fortune; but his heart will be pinched and poverty-stricken and he will be a stranger to joy and blessedness. Christian generosity, on the other hand, may involve denying oneself certain things which the man of the world regards as amenities normal and even necessary to civilized living; but such denial of self for the benefit of others enlarges the heart to receive a

---

[66] Notice the highly effective accumulation of "alls": ... πᾶσαν ... παντὶ πάντοτε πᾶσαν ... πᾶν.

rich benison of contentedness and launches one into the limitless sea of divine grace where we learn experimentally that God does indeed supply every need of those who trust in Him (cf. Phil. 4:11, 19; I Tim. 6:6–10). Far from philanthropy being overlooked in the theocracy of Israel, or being regarded as merely a subject for poetic eulogy, it was in fact quite clearly *commanded* in the civic code: "Thou shalt not harden thy heart, nor shut thy hand from thy poor brother. ... I command thee, saying, Thou shalt surely open thy hand unto thy brother, to thy needy, and to thy poor, in thy land" (Deut. 15:7–11; cf. Lev. 25:35). Paul here, and the New Testament in general, in enjoining the Christian responsibility of liberality and care of those who are in distress is doing no more than continue the charitable teaching of the law, the prophets, and the poets of the Old Testament, while at the same time recognizing (as is amply evident from the two chapters now before us) that the Christian believer has, if anything, an added incentive and obligation because he is the beneficiary of the supreme gift of God's redeeming grace in and through His Son Jesus Christ. "Freely ye received: freely give" (Mt. 10:8) is the proper logic of his generosity.

The "righteousness" which the psalmist praises is that of right conduct, of kindness and beneficence, towards one's fellowmen. It is precisely the righteousness of which Christ Himself speaks in Mt. 6:1 where it is synonymous with almsgiving. There is certainly no suggestion that almsgiving, commendable though it is, is a means of justification before God, for such an interpretation would have been entirely alien to mind of the Apostle. Liberality is not a means to but rather an outward expression of righteousness. In Scripture the righteous man may be discerned by, *inter alia*, his generous concern for the poor and afflicted: he is a genuine philanthropist. The unrighteous man, on the other hand, will betray himself by his harshness to those who are in need, and by his grasping self-centredness. When, however, an unrighteous man is by God's grace transformed into a righteous man one of his first responsibilities is the cause of the needy. Hence the apostolic admonition in Eph. 4:28: "Let him that stole steal no more; but rather let him labour, working with his hands the thing that is good, that he may have whereof to give to him that hath need". As always, of course, it is possible for a man with an unrighteous heart to simulate the external manifestations of this righteousness, and thus to acquire a false reputation for righteousness among men. It was this form of hypocritical ostentation which Christ so sternly denounced when He warned His hearers against *"doing righteousness"* in order to be seen of men: such outward pretension may indeed win the praise of men, but those who indulge in it have no reward with the Heavenly Father, who infallibly discerns the true intents of their hearts. Almsgiving that is performed in secret, however, that is, free from vanity and with unselfish simplicity of purpose, brings an eternal reward (Mt. 6:1ff.). Once again we see that it is the heart of the giver that matters, as distinct from the quantity or the outwardness of the giving.

In an eloquent homily at this point Chrysostom develops the lesson of disinterested liberality from the example of the widow of Zarephath (I Kings 17:8ff.) who, in providing for Elijah in his need, ran the risk "not of poverty only, but even of death and extinction, and not only of herself, but of her son also". She outstripped the hospitality of Abraham, for he had *a herd* from which to fetch a tender calf (Gen. 18:7), whereas she had but *a handful* of meal. Her excellence is seen in that, "for the sake of the stranger, she spared not her son even, and that too though she looked not for things to come. But we", says Chrysostom, "though a heaven exists, though a hell is threatened, though (which is greater than all) God has done such great things for us, and is made glad and rejoices over such things, sink back supinely. Not so, I beseech you: but let us scatter abroad, let us give to the poor as we ought to give. ... For it is not possible that lust of wealth and righteousness should dwell together; they have their tents apart".

9 : 10

> And he that supplieth seed to the sower and bread for food, shall supply and multiply your seed for sowing, and increase the fruits of your righteousness.

The Apostle characteristically magnifies the grace of God yet further: not only is liberality a sign of God's grace given and also a sowing of seed which, by God's grace, will produce a harvest, but the seed itself, the wherewithal for sowing, is also supplied by God. Thus all is of God and His grace (5:18). The Christian, in fact, has nothing which he has not received—a truth of which the Corinthians had been reminded before (I Cor. 4:7). Once again we find Paul echoing the words of Scripture. In the first place, there is a reminiscence of Isa. 55:10 "... seed for the sower and bread for the eater". One man sows and another man eats the fruits of that sowing; but it is ultimately God who provides both the seed for sowing and the bread for eating. Moreover, what is a fundamental law of the natural realm points to or illustrates, as we have seen, an underlying principle of Christian philanthropy. Outwardly the seed may be small and insignificant, but inwardly its potential is immense. The seed which God supplies must be scattered, it must be sown beneath the ground, that is, it must become to all appearances lost, before its potential can be realized and the manifold blessing of a harvest enjoyed. A single seed contains the germ of a whole tree, which in turn bears many fruits, in each of which is fresh seed. The Macedonians had given out of deep poverty, and no doubt the amount they had collected was quantitatively small, especially when compared with the needs of the Christians at Jerusalem. But such seed as God had supplied they had sown in liberality, knowing that He who is the Lord of the annual miracle of the harvest will take what is in man's eyes a ludicrously inadequate quantity and multiply and increase it until it becomes a full blessing to great multitudes—as the same Lord demonstrated when He miraculously fed the five thousand from the insignificant offering of an unknown boy (Jn. 6:5ff.). So also will He increase the fruits of the Corinthians' righteousness, that is, give a manifold harvest of blessing to their generosity.[67] Here there seems to be another reminiscence of an Old Testament text, this time of the Septuagint version of Hosea 10:12. No doubt Paul had in mind the general tenor of this verse which fits in well with what he is saying here, and which may be summarized: "Sow for yourselves in righteousness, reap according to kindness; ... seek Jehovah until the fruits of righteousness come for you".[68]

---

[67] On the significance of the term "righteousness" here, see the commentary on the preceding verse.

[68] With reference to the expression "fruits of righteousness", γενήματα δικαιοσύνης, the term γένημα was used of the produce or yield of a harvest, and particularly of the fruit or juice of the grape-vine; cf. ἀμπέλου γένημα (Isa. 32:12, LXX), γένημα τῆς ἀμπέλου (Mk. 14:25; Mt. 26:29; Lk. 22:18), and also οἴνου γένημα and οἰνικὸν γένημα in the papyri.

9 : 11, 12

Ye being enriched in everything unto all liberality, which worketh through us thanksgiving to God. For the ministration of this service not only filleth up the measure of the wants of the saints, but aboundeth also through many thanksgivings unto God.

Liberality,[69] in accordance with the simile of sowing and harvesting, is an enriching activity for the giver as well as for the recipient. Indeed, what Paul says here indicates that the experience of enrichment precedes and is preparatory to the act of benefaction. Christian giving is the outward expression of a heart already rich in generosity. We cannot agree with the opinion of Hodge that the Apostle is here speaking of worldly rather than of inward or spiritual riches. Chrysostom seems to us to have gauged Paul's intention far more accurately when he says that "in things which are necessary he allows them to seek for nothing more than need requires, but in spiritual things counsels them to get for themselves a large superabundance". And not the least of the fruits of the harvest which Christian liberality yields is the rendering of thanksgiving to God by those who have benefited from the generosity of their fellow-believers —thanksgiving *to God*, let it be noted, for while there is of course gratitude to their human benefactors, the proper completion of the process is above all gratitude to God who graciously bestows not only the harvest but also the original seed of liberality.

By saying that the liberality of the Corinthians produces "through us" thanksgiving to God Paul would seem to have in mind his particular function as a kind of middle-man through whom the collection was to be conveyed from Greece to Jerusalem. Somewhat similar is his earlier reference (in 8:19f.) to this charitable project as being ministered by himself.[70]

---

[69] On the significance of ἁπλότης see note on 8:2 above.

[70] There are three ways of explaining the nominative participle πλουτιζόμενοι in verse 11: (i) as parallel with ἔχοντες in verse 8, treating verses 9 and 10 as a parenthesis (so AV, Bengel, Westcott and Hort)—but the thought of verse 11 follows on just as naturally after verse 10 as after verse 8; (ii) as a participle standing absolutely in the place of a finite verb (Allo; cf. δοξάζοντες, verse 13—see note there) with a force that is imperative (J. H. Moulton, *Grammar*, Vol. I, p. 181) or optative (Lightfoot, on Col. 3:16); (iii) as a simple anacoluthon, a nominative plural having been dictated, whereas strict grammar

Liberality is nothing less than a public service within the community of believers (though the outreach of Christian generosity is not limited to believers). It is a ministry which is open to all.[71] And, as verse 12 shows, it has a twofold effect: first, *material*—it fills up what is lacking to their poorer brethren of the necessities of life;[72] but, second, there is a *spiritual* overflow [73] of praise and gratitude to God. Christian giving, therefore, not only ministers to the physical needs of men, which in itself calls forth the blessing and approval of God, but it causes men to glorify God, which is a result far more wonderful than any material benefit conferred; for when men glorify God they then behave as they were created to behave. And the generosity of the Corinthian believers, Paul confidently assures them, will

---

would have required a genitive plural to agree with the antecedent (Plummer, etc.). Whichever of these explanations is preferred, Paul's meaning remains perfectly clear.

[71] The noun διακονία is used of a similar charitable ministration in Acts 12:25. Τῆς λειτουργίας is a genitive of apposition. The use of this term here is consistent with the use, in verse 10, of χορηγεῖν, a classical term meaning originally to lead a chorus, then to supply the money for the provision of a chorus at the public festivals, a costly business which was regarded as the principal of the Athenian public offices, and hence to supply in abundance. There, it is true, it is God who supplies bountifully, but only that the Corinthians may minister in turn to their needy brethren. This charitable ministration is indeed a public benefaction (λειτουργία = λαός or λεώς + ἔργον), but here within the setting of the Christian community, not the political state. Cf. Rom. 15:27 where Paul uses the verb λειτουργεῖν with reference to this same contribution from Macedonia and Achaia. In the LXX λειτουργία and λειτουργεῖν are used in connection with the functions of priests and Levites in the sanctuary, and this connotation is reflected in the New Testament in Lk. 1:23, Heb. 8:2 (λειτουργός), 9:21, 10:11. Deissmann draws attention to the fact that the papyri show that these terms were "commonly used in Egypt in the ceremonial sense", and in particular of the services of the Serapeum (*Bible Studies*, pp. 140f.). Λειτουργία and λειτουργός are used of the Christian ministry (Acts 13:2; Rom. 15:6), of the ministry of angels (Heb. 1:7 = Ps. 104:4 and Heb. 1:14, λειτουργικὰ πνεύματα), and also of civil magistrates (Rom. 13:6). Their use in Phil. 2:25, 30 is akin in meaning to our present verse, only there it is a question of ministering to Paul's needs. On λειτουργία in Phil. 2:17 see Lightfoot's valuable note. The development in the post-apostolic Church of ideas of sacramental sacrifice caused the term λειτουργία (*liturgy*) to be misapplied in its Old Testament connotation to the ministration of the eucharist.

[72] Προσαναπληροῦν, to add something (προσ-) so as to bring up (-ανα-) to a state of fulness (-πληροῦν).

[73] Περισσεύειν.

cause *many* to do precisely this. Thus the Apostle enthusiastically but tenderly leads the Corinthians on until, with him, they have risen to that spiritual height from which they are able to see Christian giving in the splendid sweep of its true perspective— not as a burden which cramps life and engenders regret, but as a privilege of grace that enlarges and enriches the soul of the giver, relieves the wants of others, and in its outworking causes many to return praise to God.

9 : 13

Seeing that through the proving of you by this ministration they glorify God for the obedience of your confession unto the gospel of Christ, and for the liberality of your contribution unto them and unto all.

The effect of this collection, though it has not yet been brought to fulfilment, presents itself vividly to the mind of the Apostle, as though it were already completed and over. Not only does he foresee the Christians in Jerusalem rendering thanks to God for sending them help in time of need, but also glorifying Him for the proof that this collection will afford of the genuineness of the members of the Greek and Macedonian churches as followers with them of the one Lord and Master.[74] Faith, as the leader of the Jerusalem church himself taught, which does not manifest itself in works is dead, a mere empty profession; for works are an evidence of faith. A profession of faith which permits one to have a Christian brother or sister "naked and in lack of daily food", without *doing* anything about it, is completely meaningless (Jas. 2:14ff.). This collection will be a "work" which will give concrete evidence to the Christians at Jerusalem of the reality of the faith of the Gentile converts in the Greek peninsula. From the first there had been the obstacle of an ingrained reluctance

---

[74] On the meaning of δοκιμή see note on 2:9. Τῆς διακονίας is another genitive of apposition: it is this charitable ministration that provides proof of their genuine Christianity. Hence the expression διὰ τῆς δοκιμῆς τῆς διακονίας ταύτης means, "because of the proof of your genuineness which this ministration affords". Bengel's rendering of δοκιμή as *documentum* here is very neat.

Δοξάζοντες is a *nominativus pendens*—"one of the easiest of anacolutha" (J. H. Moulton, *Grammar*, Vol. I, p. 69). Both πλουτιζόμενοι in verse 11 and δοξάζοντες here are explained by J. H. Moulton as imperatival participles (*Ibid.*, p. 181).

on the part of Jewish converts to accept the genuineness of the response of Gentiles to the gospel. Thus the apostles and brethren of Judea had found it difficult to understand that Peter was right in taking the gospel to the Gentile household of Cornelius (Acts 11:1ff.). Even when, not long after, the eyes of their leaders were opened to recognize the universal character and import of the gospel, it is probable that many of the thousands of Jewish converts in Jerusalem, nurtured as they had been since early childhood on pharisaical doctrines of exclusivism, were unable to set aside completely their misgiving and dislike of the Gentile and to realize experimentally the full significance of the evangelical doctrine that all believers, Gentiles as well as Jews, are one in Christ Jesus, unitedly the seed of faithful Abraham, and heirs according to the promise of the covenant (Gal. 3:16ff.). For Gentile converts to come to the aid of Jewish converts would be a tangible and compelling proof to the latter of the genuineness of the former in their Christian profession, and an undeniable expression to each other and to the world of their true unity in Christ. It would be the parable of the Good Samaritan enacted and extended; for with the Samaritans the Jews had no dealings (Jn. 4:9), but with the Gentiles mere contact meant, according to rabbinical tradition, contamination and the need for ceremonial cleansing (cf. Mk. 7:3ff.). The deed of the Good Samaritan, therefore, would be seen by the believers in Jerusalem to have been carried a stage further by the believers in Greece, so as to become the merciful action of the "Good Gentile".

It is possible also that reports of disorders in worship and doctrine at Corinth (cf. I Corinthians *passim*) had caused Christians in Jerusalem to doubt the reality of the profession of the church members there. This collection would help to silence these suspicions and to establish their genuineness and sincerity as fellow-believers. Hence Paul speaks here of the saints at Jerusalem glorifying God because of this evidence of the Corinthians' obedience to their profession of the gospel of Christ,[75] as

---

[75] This seems to be the proper meaning of the expression ἐπὶ τῇ ὑποταγῇ τῆς ὁμολογίας ὑμῶν εἰς τὸ εὐαγγέλιον τοῦ Χριστοῦ. As Hodge remarks, to treat τῆς ὁμολογίας as a genitive of the object, "obedience to your confession", gives the best sense. The same force of the genitive with the synonym ὑπακοή is found a little further down in the phrase ὑπακοὴ τοῦ Χριστοῦ (10:5), which connotes "obedience to Christ".

well as of the single-minded generosity of their fellowship.[76] By their action the Corinthians will exhibit the true unity and catholicity of the Church. They minister, it is true, to the believers in Jerusalem, but in doing so they minister to all believers everywhere. The part always affects the whole. In Christ's Body, the Church, there is no schism: one member in ministering to another member inevitably ministers to the whole body (cf. I Cor. 12:25ff.). The relationships of one local church with another are also and always relationships within and of the Church universal. This grand concept is an integral part of the Apostle's thought here. It explains the very special importance which he attached to this collection as demonstrating the spirit of genuine *ecumenicity*, which knows no longer any middle wall of partition, whether of race, language, colour, or culture, between those who through faith in Christ Jesus have become members of the household of God and fellow-heirs of the heavenly glory (cf. Eph. 2:11ff.).

9 : 14

> While they themselves also, with supplication on your behalf, long after you by reason of the exceeding grace of God in you.

A further notable effect of the collection is foreseen in the offering of prayer, that spontaneous answer of heart to heart before God, by the Jerusalem Christians on behalf of those whom they formerly had shunned. They now long after them (Paul's language is still proleptic), being drawn towards them by deep affection and fellow-feeling [77]—not, however, merely because they

---

[76] Ἀπλότης has here, if anywhere, its proper force of singleness of purpose leading to liberality in giving to others. The use of κοινωνία, "fellowship" (translated "contribution" in our version), should be noted. Paul uses it again of this same collection in Rom. 15:26. It implies the demonstration in this practical way of the communion of the saints, which is more than the word "contribution" or "distribution" (AV) or "*communicatio*" (Vulgate) would suggest.

[77] The construction of the phrase καὶ αὐτῶν δεήσει ὑπὲρ ὑμῶν ἐπιποθούντων ὑμᾶς has been the subject of much dispute. The suggestion that δεήσει is dependent on περισσεύουσα in verse 12 has little to commend it, nor can it satisfactorily be regarded as a dative governed (as are τῇ ὑποταγῇ and ἀπλότητι) by ἐπί in verse 13. It is preferable *either* to treat δεήσει as a separate dative after δοξάζοντες in the preceding verse—"glorifying God for your obedience

have received material assistance from them, but above all else because of the superabundant grace of God bestowed on the Corinthians, of which this gift is a pledge. And so, once again, all is of grace: the liberality of the Corinthians no less than of the Macedonians (8:1), and the fruits of that liberality.

This passage gives eloquent witness to the great faith which Paul placed in his Corinthian converts: he speaks of their generosity not as a problematical possibility of the future but as a present reality. We are struck, too, by the noble perspectives of his vision: he already sees as a reality the benefaction of the Corinthian church, the thanksgivings of the Jerusalem Christians, their glorifying of God, and their response of prayer and affection for their Gentile brothers in Christ. This would indeed be a splendid consummation of the tireless labours in the cause of the gospel of him who before had himself been a Hebrew of the Hebrews, belonging to the strictest sect of the Pharisees (cf. 11:22; Phil. 3:5; Acts 23:6, 26:5), but who now, by the grace and calling of God, had become the Apostle to the Gentiles (cf. Gal. 1:16, 2:7–9; Acts 9:15). Paul the Apostle was in his own dynamic history the very focal concentration of Christian ecumenicity.

That his confidence in the Corinthians was not disappointed is apparent from Rom. 15:25f. where Paul writes of being about to go to Jerusalem to minister to the saints there, since it has been "the good pleasure of Macedonia and Achaia to make a certain contribution for the poor among the saints that are at Jerusalem"; and of particular interest in this connection is the testimony of Clement of Rome who, writing to the members of this same church before the end of the first century, reminds them that they had formerly been *"more glad to give than to receive* and content with the provisions which God supplies", and that they had been given "an insatiable desire of doing good", and had "not repented of any good deed, but were ready unto every good work".[78]

---

and liberality . . . and by their prayer on your behalf as they long after you" —which gives good sense and grammatical coherence (Vg., AV); *or* to explain αὐτῶν . . . ἐπιποθούντων as a genitive absolute (as in our version, also Meyer, Plummer, Allo, etc.), in which case the genitive is a further anacoluthon, since strictly speaking the participle should have been in the nominative case, agreeing with δοξάζοντες (but in the Greek of the New Testament age inconsistent genitive absolutes have become almost a common usage).

[79] Clem. Rom., *Ep. ad Cor.*, ii.

9 : 15

Thanks be to God for his unspeakable gift.

Gratitude to God for His wonderful gift which defies all human description brings to an end all debate on the question of giving. Some commentators have understood Paul to be expressing gratefulness for the grace of Christian liberality or for the excellent gospel fruit of racial reconciliation and spiritual cooperation between Jew and Gentile, but we have no doubt that the gift to which he is here referring is God's unique gift of His only Son to be the Saviour of mankind—"the divine gift which inspires all gifts" (Tasker). Instinctively the redeemed mind feels that this is Paul's meaning when, with characteristic spontaneousness, he offers thanks to God for that gift which is inexpressible. Paul himself provides the best comment on his meaning here in his moving rhetorical question written not long afterwards in the Epistle to the Romans: "He that spared not His own Son, but delivered Him up for us all, how shall He not also with Him freely give us all things?" God's giving of His beloved Son for us is the supreme gift, infinitely transcending all human giving. Hence it is giving which is unspeakable: human language is utterly inadequate to express or explain it. But the human heart can *experience* it as a glorious, transforming reality, and then, as with Paul here, nothing is more natural than to pour forth praise and thanksgiving to God for it. At the same time, of course, all that Paul has been saying in these two chapters is most intimately associated with this maximum gift. The Christian's eternal salvation rests solely upon the foundation of God's unspeakable gift: what could be more proper than that he should give freely and bountifully to others? This is the logic of redemption: "Beloved, if God so loved us, we also ought to love one another" (I Jn. 4:11).

342

The authenticity of Chapters 10 to 13

We now come to the last main section of the epistle. Many modern commentators maintain that these concluding four chapters are so different in tone and content from those that precede that they cannot reasonably be held to belong to the same letter. This question has been discussed in the Introduction (pp. xxii ff.), where we have argued, in opposition to the hypothesis of their discontinuity with what has preceded, that these chapters in fact constitute an integral and original part of our epistle. It is true that this final section is largely (though by no means entirely) polemical in character; but its tone is tempered by both humility and humour. And the marked change in tone is to be attributed to the fact that the Apostle's sternest remarks refer not to the Corinthians in general but to the unscrupulous false teachers who were seeking to undermine his authority and to corrupt their faith, and to those of the Corinthians who were allowing themselves to be misled by these intruders. Besides, it is not difficult to show that important passages in this concluding section are plainly very much of a piece with themes and matters that have been introduced in the earlier chapters (see Introduction). In Allo's judgment, indeed, "the connections with the first part, chapters 1–7, arise in such great numbers that they can scarcely be counted; and this is a clear indication that the third part and the first both relate to the same period and the same situation".

Yet, polemical in tone though this section may be, Paul's ultimate purpose in writing these chapters was irenic rather than polemical: he hoped that by writing sternly now things would be put right in Corinth so that it would not be necessary for him to assert his authority when he came to them (cf. 13:10). But, unlike the previous occasion when in order to spare them he had forborne to visit them (1:23), this time he is definitely coming and, if things have not been put right, he will not spare (12:20–13:2).

Regarding the coherence of II Corinthians, the sequence is as follows: Paul explains that his plan to visit Corinth earlier had been set aside in order to spare them; he had, however, crossed from Troas to Macedonia in his impatience to meet Titus with news from Corinth (1:23–2:13); there follows the great "parenthesis" (2:14–7:4), and then the resumption of the account of his meeting with Titus (7:5–16); next he informs them that he is sending Titus with two brethren to organize the collection to its conclusion (chs. 8 and 9); and now, finally, he is preparing the way for his own coming to Corinth close on the heels of Titus and the two brethren (chs. 10–13), prior to his journeying to Jerusalem with the collection. The "skeleton" of the epistle is thus well articulated from beginning to end.

As for the abrupt change of subject and tone at this point, we shall content ourselves by quoting the wise observations which Denney offers: "The last four chapters of the Second Epistle to the Corinthians stand as manifestly apart as the two about the collection. A great deal too much has been made of this undeniable fact. If a man has a long letter to write, in which he wishes to speak of a variety of subjects, we may expect variations of tone, and more or less looseness of connection. If he has something on his mind which it is difficult to speak about, but which cannot be suppressed, we may expect him to keep it to the end, and to introduce it perhaps with awkward emphasis. The scholars who have argued, on the ground of extreme difference of tone, and want of connection, that chapters x–xiii of this Epistle were originally a separate letter, either earlier (Weisse) or later (Semler) than the first seven chapters, seem to have overlooked these obvious considerations. If Paul stopped dictating for the day at the end of chap. ix—if he even stopped for a few moments in doubt how to proceed to the critical subject he had still to handle—the want of connection is sufficiently explained; the tone in which he writes, when we consider the subject, needs no justification".

10 : 1

Now I Paul myself entreat you by the meekness and gentleness of Christ, I who in your presence am lowly among you, but being absent am of good courage toward you.

It is with the tone of authority, implicit rather than overtly asserted, that this section opens: "I Paul myself ..." But if there is a note of firmness there is also the ring of affection. The Apostle's address is that of entreaty, and his spirit that of meekness and gentleness. The Paul wielding apostolic authority to denounce the false apostles whose object is to destroy that authority and seduce his children in the faith from the pure gospel is the same Paul whose heart is enlarged with love for the Corinthians

344

(6:11; cf. 11:11ff.). There is a parallel situation in the Epistle to the Galatians, where the Apostle addresses the members of the Galatian church: "Behold, I Paul say unto you ..." There, as here, it is loving concern for his converts that impels him to speak in the sternest terms of those who are hindering, troubling, and unsettling them (Gal. 5:2, 7, 10, 12; cf. here vv. 10 and 11, and 11:3, 12–15). As Denney well says, *I Paul myself* "is not only the grammatical subject of the sentence, but if one may say so, the subject under consideration; it is the very person whose authority is in dispute who puts himself forward deliberately in this authoritative way". But his whole approach is that of confidence coupled with humility; for his confidence is no more self-sufficiency in these final chapters than it is in the earlier ones. It is founded solely upon the grace of God who saved him and commissioned him to be His apostle (cf. 12:1–12).

Paul therefore introduces this final section of the epistle, so difficult for him to write, not with any sign of exasperation or irascibility, but with the tone of entreaty, and, further, entreaty "by the meekness and gentleness of Christ"; that is to say, the spirit and example of Christ provide the norm which should govern all Christian conduct, and not least when an occasion may demand firmness and even severity. Our Lord had proclaimed His own meekness and lowliness of heart (Mt. 11:29), which indeed had been foretold by the prophet Zechariah (9:9; cf. Mt. 21:5), and He had also declared the blessedness of those that are meek (Mt. 5:5). The whole redemptive act of Christ's coming to suffer and to die was one of self-humiliation, and Christ's followers are logically called upon by Paul to show the same spirit (Phil. 2:5ff.) and to let their gentleness be known to all men (Phil. 4:5). The popular misconception that meekness and gentleness are incompatible with sternness is refuted by the example of Christ Himself, who not only could imperiously drive the grasping money-changers out of the temple with a scourge (Jn. 2:14ff.), but could also denounce false teachers and hypocrites in the severest possible terms (cf. Mt. 23). Such severity did not annul His gentleness; on the contrary, it was generated by the loving depths of His compassion for the lost, as is shown, for example, by the way in which the prolonged and unsparing denunciation of Mt. 23 is brought to a conclusion by one of the tenderest and most moving of all His utterances.

So, too, here Christlike meekness and gentleness must not be misunderstood as though they are incongruous with sternness in refuting the propaganda of false teachers who are attacking the foundations of the divine gospel that Paul had faithfully communicated to the Corinthians (cf. 11:3f.). In harmony with the supreme example of Him who is the Church's Lord, plain-spoken severity in the face of spiritual imposture becomes everyone whose concern is for the truth of God and the salvation of souls. Paul utters strictures no less uncompromising when meeting a comparable situation in Galatia, not long after this (cf. Gal. 1:6ff.)—yet the Epistle to the Galatians is by no means devoid of the spirit of meekness and gentleness (cf. 5:22f., 6:1ff.). To describe our present passage, as Plummer does, as "bitter and vehement", and therefore to suggest that this opening appeal to the meekness and gentleness of Christ "reads somewhat strangely", reflects the prejudice which attachment to a particular hypothesis (namely, that these four chapters belong elsewhere) can produce. And as for Plummer's comment that we might have expected Paul to say "Jesus" when speaking of the earthly life of Christ, we believe that had he foreseen the extent to which the fashionable theology of our day would develop the distinction between "the historical Jesus" and "the risen Christ", in such a way as to obscure the New Testament teaching of the actual resurrection of Jesus from the dead, we believe he would have expressed himself more circumspectly.

In writing the words, "who in your presence am lowly among you, but being absent am of good courage toward you", the Apostle is, as Chrysostom points out, ironically echoing the slander which his enemies in Corinth had maliciously invented against him: they had been saying that when present he was mild and timid, but when absent full of boldness, like a craven dog that barks loudly at a safe distance.[1] As is common with

---

[1] Κατὰ πρόσωπον, which our version renders as "in your presence" and RSV as "face to face", balances ἀπών, "when absent", in the second limb of the clause, and similarly ἐν ὑμῖν balances εἰς ὑμᾶς. There is, it is true, a measure of tautology between κατὰ πρόσωπον and ἐν ὑμῖν, which causes Alford to translate: "who *in personal appearance* am mean among you" (cf. Vg., *in facie*); but it is a rendering which we feel bound to reject, (i) because of the balance of the phrases to which we have referred—indeed, in every respect the two limbs are perfectly balanced, κατὰ πρόσωπον μέν corres-

slanderers, Paul's opponents had taken a truth and distorted it into an untruth: in his earlier letter he had reminded the Corinthians that he had come with the gospel to them "in weakness and in fear and in much trembling", but that in striking contrast to his weakness was the amazing power of God demonstrated through his preaching of the crucified Saviour (I Cor. 2:3ff.). He had not forced himself on them with bovine aggressiveness. But, weak and fearful though he had been, the evident power of the Spirit manifested through his ministry, and as a result experienced by them, was also the seal for all to acknowledge upon his apostolic authority. In our epistle too, as we have already repeatedly seen, and as we shall see again in this final section (especially 11:21—12:10), the almighty power of God, paradoxically magnified and conveyed through the inadequate and frail human vessel which He chooses and uses, is a major and pervasive theme. Paul's diffidence, his realization of his own utter insufficiency for the stupendous task which God had entrusted to him, his humility, and his forbearance were twisted by his detractors into a despicable charge of cowardice and impotence when present (as though the demonstration of the divine power counted for nothing) and of hypocritical boldness, by the medium of letter-writing, when he was at a safe remove from them. In this respect also a close link with the early part of the epistle may be discerned (cf. 1:12ff.).

---

ponding to ἄπων δέ, ταπεινός to θαρρῶ, and ἐν ὑμῖν to εἰς ὑμᾶς, (ii) because the reference here is to Paul's demeanour, not to his physical appearance —though it is apparent a little further on that this latter was also subject to the derision of his calumniators (v. 10), and (iii) because the expression κατὰ πρόσωπον, when used in this way elsewhere always means "face to face" or "present in person", and not "in physical appearance" (cf. Lk. 2:31, Acts 3:13, 25:16, Gal. 2:11, and references in II Macc., Josephus, Polybius, Plutarch, and the inscriptions and papyri given in Arndt and Gingrich, *sub* πρόσωπον, 1, c, δ). The same usage also holds good for the classical authors: cf. Thucydides, I, 106, Xenophon, *Cyr.* I, vi, 43, VI, iii, 35. In Gen 25:18 the LXX has κατὰ πρόσωπον for עַל פְּנֵי. This usage in pagan authors shows that it is not properly a semitism, though the Old Testament prepositional expressions may well have influenced the New Testament writers to some extent (see J. H. Moulton, *Grammar*, Vol. II, p. 466). The inscriptions show that κατὰ πρόσωπον was also a technical term in judicial phraseology = *coram*, which is its force here (see Moulton and Milligan).

10 : 2, 3

Yea, I beseech you, that I may not when present show courage with the confidence wherewith I count to be bold against some, who count of us as if we walked according to the flesh. For though we walk in the flesh, we do not war according to the flesh.

Paul resumes the entreaty of the previous verse, only still more appealingly, for he now *beseeches* the Corinthians,[2] earnestly desiring them so to set things in order that he may not be forced on arrival to demonstrate that he is capable not only of writing stern letters but also of acting with severity when present in their midst; for it is his firm intention to deal boldly with "some" who have expressed the opinion [3] that he is "walking according to the flesh". In Rom. 8:4f. Paul declares that those who walk according to the flesh mind the things of the flesh, that is, their living is not centred in God but governed by self-interest. In our epistle he has already (1:17) alluded to the accusation of his enemies that it was his custom to make plans "according to the flesh" (yet another link between the earlier part and these concluding chapters of the letter).[4] Both there and here the integrity of the Apostle's character is impugned: he writes one thing and does another, and such a man is not merely inconsistent but thoroughly unreliable. This imputation Paul constantly repudiates. If necessity requires, they will find that his deed is as good as his word. But he takes no delight in being severe, and accordingly begs the Corinthians to ensure that, in expectation

---

[2] Bengel, however, suggests "God" as the object of δέομαι ("I pray God that . . ."), as though equivalent to εὔχομαι δὲ πρὸς τὸν θεόν in 13:7, but there can be little doubt that "you" *(ὑμᾶς)* is the intended object here, as it is the expressed object of παρακαλῶ in verse 1.

[3] The Vulgate, Luther, Bengel, and others treat λογίζομαι as a passive here (cf. Rom. 4:4f.): " . . . the confidence wherewith *I am reckoned* (that is, by my opponents) to be bold against some". But, though this rendering would certainly be to the point, it is improbable that Paul would have written λογίζομαι (passive) followed by λογιζομένους (middle) in the same clause, and it is preferable to treat both words as being in the middle voice. Paul then is declaring, with a note of irony, his own intentions: " . . . the confidence wherewith I reckon to be bold against some who reckon of us as if we walked according to the flesh".

[4] For a discussion of the expression "according to the flesh" *(κατὰ σάρκα)* see commentary on 5:16 above.

of his arrival, his personal integrity and apostolic authority are acknowledged by all. "It is the duty of a good pastor to draw his sheep on calmly and kindly", says Calvin, "so that many suffer themselves to be governed, rather than to coerce them with violence. I acknowledge, indeed, that severity is sometimes necessary; but we must always set out with gentleness, and persevere in it, so long as the hearer shows himself tractable. Severity is the extreme remedy. ... For as men should be drawn, as far as is in our power, rather than driven, so, when mildness proves to be ineffective with those who are hard and refractory, it then becomes necessary to resort to rigour; otherwise it will not be moderation, or impartiality, but culpable cowardice."

Paul, however, though he does not walk "according to the flesh", yet he does walk "in the flesh", that is, in the element of flesh, living his life, like every other man, subject to the laws and limitations which are common to human flesh. While, therefore, in this context the expression "according to the flesh" has a distinctively ethical connotation, in the phrase "in the flesh" the term "flesh" is used in a neutral sense to denote the medium of man's present corporeal existence; for the life lived by faith is still a life lived in the flesh (Gal. 2:20); it is in our mortal flesh that the victorious life of Jesus is manifested (4:11). In this latter sense the flesh is the equivalent of the frail earthen vessel which contains the divine glory (4:7), of our outward man which is decaying (4:16), and of the earthly house of our tabernacle which is dissolved in death (5:1). But for Paul to walk *according to* the flesh would have meant the contradiction at the very roots of his being of the power of the gospel which he preached and by which both he and the Corinthian converts had been saved and transformed. Herein lies the danger and the subtlety of the charge that had been made against him. The follower of Christ cannot allow his conduct to be controlled by the considerations of expediency and self-seeking which were characteristic of his unregenerate state, when he walked according to the flesh, not according to the Spirit (cf. Rom. 8:4ff.; Gal. 5:16ff.). For the new man in Christ this principle "according to the flesh" is one of the old things that have passed away (5:17). To revert to it is nothing less than an undoing of the gospel.

At this point, however, the Apostle leaves the more general figure of *walking* in favour of the affirmation that he does not *wage war* according to the flesh, thereby introducing an admonitory note; for he is about to engage in battle. That the Christian life is not merely a walk but a warfare is, indeed, a favourite theme with him (cf. Eph. 6:11ff.; I Tim. 1:18; II Tim. 2:3f., 4:7, and in our epistle (6:7)—a warfare against evil and error and the powers of darkness, and therefore against those who seek, as his enemies at Corinth were doing, to overthrow the truth and to gainsay the gospel of Jesus Christ.

10 : 4

(For the weapons of our warfare are not of the flesh, but mighty before God to the casting down of strongholds).

The military metaphor just introduced (see previous verse) is now developed by the Apostle. A man who engages in warfare [5] must have weapons with which to fight. The satanic forces against which the soldiers of Christ's army contend are not forces of flesh and blood; therefore to attempt to withstand them with weapons of the flesh would be nothing short of folly. The armour of Saul, though splendid in the eyes of men, cannot avail to overcome the Philistine giant. Only the panoply *of God* will serve for this purpose (Eph. 6:11ff.). Only spiritual weapons are divinely powerful for the overthrow of the fortresses of evil. This constitutes an admonition to the Church and particularly to her leaders, for the temptation is ever present to meet the challenge of the world, which is under the sway of the evil one, with the carnal weapons of this world—with human wisdom and philosophy, with the attractions of secular entertainment, with the display of massive organization. Not only do such weapons fail to make an impression on the strongholds of Satan, but a secularized Church is a Church which, having adopted the standards of the world, has ceased to fight and is herself overshadowed by the powers of darkness.

But this verse also constitutes a promise to the Church, for it is constantly true of those weapons with which the Holy Spirit

---

[5] Στρατείας is, on the textual evidence, to be preferred to στρατιας, though the support for the latter is not slight. If στρατιας is adopted, it should be accented στρατίας = στρατείας (of which it is a variant form), not στρατιᾶς = "army"; cf. Deissmann, *Bible Studies*, pp. 181f.

has supplied her that they are *divinely powerful* [6] for the destruction of these very strongholds.[7] When engaging the enemy with these weapons the Church is assured of victory. And what precisely are these mighty weapons? They are the weapons, scorned by the world and yet most feared by the powers of darkness, of truth, righteousness, evangelism, faith, salvation, the Word of God, and prayer, enumerated by Paul in Eph. 6:14ff. They are the very weapons which he wielded in the unremitting warfare that he was called upon to wage as Christ's apostle, which enabled him at last to testify that he had fought the good fight, and which won for him the victor's crown of righteousness (II Tim. 4:7f.).

10:5

> Casting down imaginations, and every high thing that is exalted against the knowledge of God, and bringing every thought into captivity to the obedience of Christ.

The strongholds which the Christian assails and overthrows with his spiritual weapons are now more precisely defined, and it is noticeable that they belong to the realm of will and intellect, that is, to the spirit of man in separation from the Spirit of God. This we know to be diagnostically sound, in respect of human psychology and physiology as well as of the religious life, for a

---

[6] In the expression δυνατὰ τῷ θεῷ the dative has been variously explained, for example, as a *dativus commodi* = "for God", or as meaning "before God", "in God's sight", or "in God's judgment". We prefer, however, to regard it as a semitism, or at any rate as reflecting the influence of the LXX, and to translate δυνατὰ τῷ θεῷ as "divinely powerful" (Beza, Moffatt). In the Old Testament לֵאלֹהִים sometimes has this superlative force—for example, Jonah 3:3, πόλις μεγάλη τῷ θεῷ, "an exceedingly great city "(that is, great to God and therefore exceedingly great); cf. Acts 7:20, ἀστεῖος τῷ θεῷ, "exceedingly fair". There is an interesting parallel in Modern Greek in which the prefix θεο- is used to convey a superlative force (cf. J. H. Moulton, *Grammar*, Vol. II, p. 443, who, however, prefers to treat τῷ θεῷ here as a *dativus commodi*; F. F. Bruce, *The Acts of the Apostles*, London, 1951, *sub* 7:20, p. 167).

[7] Πρὸς καθαίρεσιν ὀχυρωμάτων: it is possible that when writing this phrase Paul had the LXX of Prov. 21:22 in mind—πόλεις ὀχυρὰς ἐπέβη σοφὸς καὶ καθεῖλε τὸ ὀχύρωμα ἐφ᾽ ᾧ ἐπεποίθησαν οἱ ἀσεβεῖς, "a wise man scales strong cities and casts down the stronghold in which the ungodly trusted"; cf. also Prov. 10:29, LXX: ὀχύρωμα ὁσίου φόβος κυρίου, "the fear of the Lord is a stronghold of the upright man", and Lam. 2:2, I Macc. 5:65, 8:10.

man's inner motives are the fount of his action; mind and will determine his conduct; and his attitudes are the effect of the presuppositions of his philosophy of things. This is true of all men without exception, but what Paul says here must have come with special force to the Corinthians who breathed the Greek atmosphere of pride in human wisdom and philosophy. To the Greek of Paul's day, who epitomized the worshipper of human wisdom, the word of the Cross was mere foolishness. None the less the Apostle did speak wisdom, the only ultimate wisdom, a wisdom, however, not of this world and therefore unknown to the intellectual leaders of this world whose wisdom is that of fallen and rebellious human reason. Sin in fact so blinds the human mind that the "natural" unregenerate man not only does not but cannot know the things of the Spirit of God, because they are spiritually discerned; and what the wise man of this world cannot receive he dismisses as foolishness. Only the new man in Christ possesses the mind of Christ, who Himself is the wisdom of God (see I Cor. 1:22–25, 2:1–16).

Hence it is that the Christian warfare is aimed at the casting down of the reasonings [8] which are the strongholds whereby the unbelieving mind seeks to fortify itself against the truths of human depravity and divine grace, and at the casting down also of every proud bulwark raised high against the knowledge of God. This metaphor emphasizes the defiant and mutinous nature of sin: sinful man does not wish to know God; he wishes himself to be the self-sufficient centre of his universe. The knowledge of God is available to him, indeed he cannot escape from it: it is a knowledge which is constitutional to him, for he himself is God's creature, made, moreover, in the image of his Creator; it is a knowledge which the whole created order clearly and ceaselessly proclaims, witnessing as it does to the eternal power and godhead of the Creator (cf. Ps. 19:1–4; Rom. 1:19f.); and it is a knowledge livingly and graciously revealed in Christ Jesus, preserved in Holy Scripture, and presented in the preaching of the gospel (cf. 4:6). But sinful man rebels against this knowledge of God. He holds down the truth in unrighteousness. Knowing God, he refuses to glorify Him as God. His senseless heart is darkened, so that, though professing himself to be wise, he becomes a fool.

---

[8] Margin. Λογισμοί here = the reasonings or rationalizations of self-centred man.

In short, he exchanges the truth of and about God for a lie. It is thus that Paul incisively analyses the intellectual motives of unbelief in Rom. 1:18–25. And this analysis reveals, starkly and precisely, the nature of the high tower raised against the knowledge of God within which proud unregenerate man immures himself. But, unless it is cast down by the gospel of God's grace in Christ Jesus, his tower becomes his tomb.

Not only are strongholds and high towers cast down, but prisoners are taken captive in the Christian warfare. These prisoners are the thoughts—the cogitations and intentions—of man's mind, and they are led captive, every one of them, into [9] the obedience of Christ. In this way the genuine Christian position is established. The rebellion of the human heart is quelled, the truth of God prevails, and the divine sovereignty is acknowledged. The capture, moreover, proves to be a radical liberation, for only in unconditional surrender to God, his Creator, Redeemer, and Judge, is man's freedom to be found.

Unfortunately, while the thinking of regenerate man is in principle entirely subjected to the obedience of Christ, in practice it is not always entirely so. The philosophies and sophistries of the "natural" man are frequently permitted to usurp a position of influence in the redeemed intellect. This was the case with some of the Corinthian believers who, through failure to submit their thinking consistently to the obedience of Christ, were being deceived by the specious logic of the false apostles whose teaching differed fundamentally from that delivered to them by Paul, their true and authentic apostle (cf. 11:2ff.). Paul is determined to expose the perversity of mind and will of such impostors. He earnestly desires that the members of the Corinthian church may learn what it means to bring both mind and will into complete submission to, and therefore harmony with, the mind and will of Christ.[10]

---

[9] *Εἰς,* as though into the victor's territory.

[10] *Νόημα* is "thought" or "mind". As thinking controls conduct so it also has the meaning of "intention", and, in a pejorative sense, "device" or "scheme", as in 2:11 where *νοήματα* = the devices or schemings of Satan. Here, however (*pace* Plummer and others), *νόημα* should be given its more general, neutral force, so that *πᾶν νόημα* = "every thought of whatever kind", or, as Alford paraphrases, combining the ideas of intellect and will, "every intention of the mind". Better still, perhaps, *νόημα* might be understood to

10 : 6

> And being in readiness to avenge all disobedience, when your obedience shall be made full.

Moffatt suggestively treats this verse as a continuation of the military metaphors of the preceding verses, and translates as follows: "I am prepared to court-martial anyone who remains insubordinate, once your submission is complete".[11] As apostolic commander of the Christian forces at Corinth, Paul is now holding himself in readiness to arraign and punish every case of disobedience and treachery. But his affection and gentleness are shown again here in his assertion that he will take action against disobedience when the obedience of the Corinthians has been fulfilled. This indicates two things: firstly, that the punishment he administers will not be indiscriminate, for the true-hearted will have ample opportunity for displaying their loyalty by openly taking their stand with him; and, secondly, that he confidently anticipates that the response at Corinth will be one of obedience, although there may be a few defiant spirits who will attempt to continue their opposition to his authority and message.

So far, in fact, is this verse from reading "oddly *after* vii. 4, 16" (as Plummer thinks: "There he is enthusiastic about them; here their obedience is still incomplete") that the Apostle's attitude here is in excellent accord with what he says there. The good courage and confidence towards the Corinthians expressed in

---

denote here the perceptive or intellective centre of man's being, as in 3:14 where Paul speaks of the νοήματα of the Jews being hardened, and 4:4 where the νοήματα of unbelievers are said to be blinded by Satan. Cf. Phil. 4:7 where νόημα is distinguished from καρδία, the affective centre of man's being.

Καθαιροῦντες, αἰχμαλωτίζοντες, and (in the next verse) ἔχοντες may be explained as being in series with περιπατοῦντες in verse 3, in which case verse 4 is grammatically a parenthesis (AV, RV, Westcott and Hort, Souter). Since however, verse 4 in no way interrupts the train of thought, but rather is integral to it, these participles may better be explained as absolute participles, standing for the indicative. See note on 4:8f. above and compare θλιβόμενοι in 7:5, χειροτονηθείς in 8:19, ἐνδεικνύμενοι in 8:24, πλουτιζόμενοι in 9:11, and δοξάζοντες in 9:13. With reference to the unity of our epistle, Allo remarks that this indicates a stylistic affinity with the preceding chapters.

11 'Εν ἑτοίμῳ ἔχειν is a phrase which is also found in Polybius and Philo. The common classical construction of the adverb with ἔχειν (= the adjective with εἶναι) is found in 12:14, ἑτοίμως ἔχω.

chapter 7 are certainly implied here in his stated expectation
that they will bring their obedience to completion. He does not
doubt that his authority will be fully acknowledged by them
when he comes to their city. Any who persist in disobedience he
will no longer count in their number.[12]   Like the antichrists
spoken of in I Jn. 2:18f., such persons are not of them, they are
not true members of Christ's Church at Corinth, and they will
not continue with them. "What can be more tender than the
compassion of the Apostle?" asks Chrysostom, "who because he
saw his own mixed up with aliens desires indeed to inflict the
blow, but forbears, and restrains his indignation until the former
shall have withdrawn, that he may smite the latter alone—yea,
rather, not even these; for he therefore threatens this, and says
he is desirous to separate unto punishment them alone, so that
they also being amended by fear may change, and he let loose
his anger against no one".

10:7

Ye look at the things that are before your face. If any man
trusteth in himself that he is Christ's, let him consider this
again with himself, that, even as he is Christ's, so also are we.

You are looking at things in a thoroughly superficial manner,
Paul says to the Corinthians (if we accept the rendering of our
version). If they would but look into their hearts [13] and face the
irrefutable facts of their spiritual experience, they would perforce
have to acknowledge that Paul was in truth their own genuine
apostle and reject the unsubstantial claims of those spurious
apostles who had intruded themselves into their community.
The sentence may, however, be taken as interrogative (as in
AV, RV margin): "Are you looking on the outward appearance
of things?" But it seems much the best to treat it, with Vulgate
and RSV, as an imperative: "Look at what is before your eyes"
—that is, "Face the obvious facts", the facts so well known to
them regarding Paul and his apostleship. Paul refers ironically
to "anyone who is self-persuaded that he is of Christ" and advises
such a person that reflection will show that Paul himself is no

---

12   In the clause ὅταν πληρωθῇ ὑμῶν ἡ ὑπακοή the position of ὑμῶν is one
of emphasis: "when *your* obedience shall be fulfilled".
13   Cf. 5:12, where πρόσωπον is opposed to καρδία.

less so—an effective use of understatement. The reference in the singular here to "any man" does not necessarily imply that Paul had only one adversary in mind at this point, for it becomes apparent from what he says later on that there was a plurality of these false teachers in Corinth (cf., for example, 11:13, 22).

The precise significance of the claim to be "Christ's" must remain in doubt. It is not improbable that those who made it boasted that they had heard and followed Christ during His earthly ministry and were thus so to speak in a dominical succession, which according to them reflected adversely on Paul, who, presumably, could make no such claim. (See, however, commentary on 5:16 above.) It may well be, also, that those who pretended to the supposed advantage of being "of Christ" had been the inaugurators and leaders of the "Christ-faction" in Corinth (I Cor. 1:12—"I am of Christ"). But Paul none the less had seen and been instructed by the Lord Christ, only in a manner more intimate and vital than was guaranteed by any mere casual encounter after the flesh. The gospel he preached had been received by him by revelation directly from the risen Master Himself (Gal. 1:11f.). Well might he have repeated at this point the appeal to his Corinthian converts made in the earlier epistle: "Am I not an apostle? am I not free? have I not seen Jesus our Lord? are ye not my work in the Lord? If to others I am not an apostle, yet at least I am to you: for the seal of mine apostleship are ye in the Lord" (I Cor. 9:1f.).

PAUL'S ADVERSARIES AT CORINTH

It seems appropriate at this juncture to inquire somewhat more fully into the character of the adversaries with whom Paul is now joining battle. But our method in doing so cannot be other than conjectural, by way of inference from such hints and implications as offer themselves in the course of this epistle. The following is the picture which we believe may be pieced together with some degree of reasonableness.

(i) *They were intruders from without.* They had needed letters of commendation (3:1), and even resorted to *self*-commendation (10:12), in order to cover over the illegitimacy of their invasion of another man's territory (10:13ff.); and they had come to the church in Corinth, where they did not belong, preaching another Jesus (11:4).

(ii) *They made special claims to superior authority.* They proclaimed

356

themselves to be "super-apostles" (11:5), despising and depre-
ciating the apostolic authority of Paul. But Paul shows that even
to have known Christ after the flesh guarantees nothing; the
vital necessity is to be a new man *in Christ* (5:16f.). So far from
being that, these men were false apostles, ministers of Satan, who
had disguised themselves as ministers of righteousness (11:13ff.).
(iii) *They were judaizers.* To have known Christ after the flesh
would suggest the probability that they had come from Palestine
and more particularly from Jerusalem, the geographical source
and centre of Christianity. They were Hebrews, Israelites claiming
succession from Abraham (11:22). They proclaimed a message
different from that communicated to the Corinthians by Paul
(11:4, 15). They had sought to bring the Corinthian Christians
under bondage to the Mosaic dispensation (3:6ff., 11:15).
(iv) *They were libertines,* who encouraged indiscriminate promis-
cuous relations with unbelievers in both social and religious life,
which could only lead to "defilement of flesh and spirit" and to
the negation of that holy witness which should distinguish the
Church of Christ (6:14–7:1, 12:21).
(v) *They were "gnostics"* who exalted their own philosophy of
knowledge (*gnosis*) against the knowledge of God (10:5) and who
gloried in fleshly wisdom (1:12). In opposition to their false
theory of esoteric knowledge Paul affirmed the uniqueness and
supremacy of "the light of the knowledge of the glory of God in
the face of Jesus Christ" which shines in every believing heart
(4:6, cf. 2:14), and found it necessary to assert, in answer to
their calumnies, that, however inexpert he might be in speech,
he was not so in knowledge (11:6).
(vi) *They were mercenary-minded.* Their alleged interest in the
gospel was prompted by selfish commercial greed as they moved
from church to church like itinerant parasites reckoning on the
gullibility of the communities to which they attached themselves.
Paul reminds the Corinthians, by way of contrast, that he had
preached the gospel to them for nothing and in everything had
kept himself from being burdensome to them (11:7, 9, 12:13–18).
Having regard to the importance which these false apostles
might seem to have attached to eloquence and the rhetorical art,
Allo concludes that, though judaizers, they were not of Palestinian
origin, but came from a background of Greek culture and were
thus probably Hellenistic Jews of the Diaspora. It is his opinion
that the doctrine they preached was a kind of syncretistic Jewish-
pagan-Christian gnosis, and that they had fostered the perpetua-
tion of the "Christ-party" as a convenient vehicle for their
erroneous teaching.

Windisch, however, does not agree that these intruders were judaizers, but follows Lütgert and Schlatter in regarding them as the leaders of a "spiritual" gnostic-libertine movement which had originated in Palestine. Käsemann (ZNTW, 1942, pp. 45ff.) champions the view that the description of "superlative apostles" used by Paul in 11:5 and 12:11 is in fact a reference to the genuine and original apostles in Jerusalem, and not to the false apostles who had invaded the Corinthian church. Others have held that Paul's opponents at Corinth were authentic emissaries of the Twelve in Jerusalem. But Munck observes that, had that been the case, Paul could hardly have described them as ministers of Satan (11:15) at the moment when he was urging the Corinthians to contribute generously for the relief of the poverty-stricken Jerusalem church.

Whether Munck's own assessment is any more satisfactory is open to some doubt. He takes a benevolent view of these opponents: they were not judaizers, he avers; and their doctrine, of which, according to him, we know nothing, cannot have been false doctrine, "as Paul refrains from any attack on them on that point". They were, in his opinion, a few Jewish Christians, who were apostles—"either emissaries of other churches or missionaries sent by Christ"—and were not really Paul's opponents at all. What had embarrassed Paul was the fact that they came when they did. "They could have chosen no worse moment", for their attitude and conduct were in conflict with Paul's picture of the true apostle, and their presence threatened the church with disruption. They were failing to manifest the apostolic marks of humility and suffering, and so were "a temptation to apostasy", just at the moment when Paul believed he had re-established his apostolic authority among the Corinthians. While, then, we are invited to "reject the charge that they preached a different gospel from his", we are told that "their demeanour showed that they were serving Satan by their apostleship, and that their gospel was therefore a false message" (Munck, *op. cit.*, pp. 184ff.). This interpretation seems to us to raise more problems than it sets out to solve and to come very near to contradicting itself. The whole tenor of the context is, in our judgment, against it. But, as we have said, every opinion concerning the character and identity of these false apostles is ventured only in the realm of conjecture. Each man's judgment must be formed, and then no more than in a tentative manner, in accordance with the probabilities to which such straws as may be discerned, rightly or wrongly, within the letter as a whole may seem to point.

10:8

For though I should glory somewhat abundantly concerning our authority (which the Lord gave for building you up and not for casting you down), I shall not be put to shame.

Paul's "glorying" was never hollow or self-centred; its substance was that of the word and work of God. In glorying to Titus on behalf of the Corinthians he had not been put to shame, but his glorying was found to be truth, as also all that he had spoken to the Corinthians themselves was truth (7:14, cf. 4:2, 6:7). So now Paul, as a man of truth, is able to say that should he glory somewhat more than hitherto [14] he will not be put to shame. He is, in fact, preparing the way for a "boastful" section which, though, as is apparent throughout, far from congenial to him, is necessary for the purpose of vindicating his own apostolic authority and the integrity of the work at Corinth (see especially 11:5–12:13). The fundamental reason for his confidence was that his authority had been *given* him *by the Lord*. It was not an authority he had usurped or assumed to himself. It was not *human* authority, but actually *the Lord's* authority. Hence he was in no sense guilty of infringing the precept, so much emphasized by him, that he who glories should glory in the Lord (v. 17, I Cor. 1:31). On the occasion of his conversion the living Jesus Himself had appointed him a minister and a witness both of the things then revealed to him and also of the things yet to be revealed to him (Acts 26:16).

Moreover, the authority which Paul had received was given him for the purpose of building up (edification) and not, as would be the disastrous result of submitting to the pretended authority of those false apostles who had invaded the Corinthians'

---

[14] We prefer to give a genuine comparative force to περισσότερόν τι, "somewhat more" (cf. Vg, *amplius quid*, and AV) rather than the indefinite force of our version, "somewhat abundantly". The sense is: "Even though I should boast a bit more than I should ordinarily regard as fitting or have done previously, yet anything I say will be strictly in accordance with the truth". Stanley, less satisfactorily, relates the comparison to what has just been said in the preceding verse: "I truly belong to Christ: for even if my boast extended beyond this *(περισσότερον)*, it would still be true". There is much to commend the rendering of RSV, "even if I boast a little too much of our authority . . .", which conveys a feeling of Paul's distaste for glorying which involves his own person and status.

359

ranks, for casting down. To acknowledge the "authority" of the latter would inevitably lead to strife and disunity and the destruction of their fellowship in Christ (cf. 12:20). But the true work of the gospel is always constructive. Hence Paul's admonition, previously given to the Corinthians, that all things done in the Church should conduce to edification (I Cor. 14:26), and his assurance to them later in our own epistle that everything he writes is for their edifying (12:19).

Having spoken in verses 4 and 5 of casting down strongholds and imaginations, Paul is not contradicting himself by saying here that his authority was given him for building up and not for casting down. For one thing, the unsound fabrications of the rebellious mind must be cleared away before the evangelical work of edification can begin; and, for another, ruthless deceivers who by their infiltration into the Church's ranks are casting down the Christian edifice must authoritatively be opposed and ejected if the work of edification is to continue. Chrysostom observes that the casting down of imaginations "is itself a special form of edification—removing hindrances, detecting the unsound, and laying the true together in the building".

Origen, facing in the third century a not dissimilar situation in his conflict with the pagan philosopher Celsus, draws on Paul's imagery in this passage to excellent effect. After aptly quoting the word of God to Jeremiah: "See, I have this day set thee over the nations and over the kingdoms, to pluck up and to break down and to destroy and to overthrow, to build and to plant" (Jer. 1:10), he goes on to say: "We need words now which will root out of every wounded soul the reproaches uttered against the truth by this treatise of Celsus, or which proceed from opinions like his. And we need also thoughts which will pull down all edifices based on false opinions, and especially the edifice raised by Celsus in his work, which resembles the building of those who said, "Come, let us build us a city, and a tower whose top shall reach to heaven" (Gen. 11:4). Yea, we even require a wisdom which will throw down all high things that rise against the knowledge of God, and especially that height of arrogance which Celsus displays against us. And in the next place, as we must not stop with rooting out and pulling down the hindrances which have just been mentioned, but must, in room of what has been rooted out, plant the plants

360

of God's husbandry, and in place of what has been pulled down rear up the building of God, and the temple of His glory,—we must for that reason pray also to the Lord, who bestowed the gifts named in the book of Jeremiah, that He may grant even to us words adapted both for building up the temple of Christ and for planting the spiritual law."[15]

In 13:10 Paul refers again to "the authority which the Lord gave me for building, and not for casting down"; but the conjecture that the relative clause (placed in parenthesis in our version to clarify the meaning) in our verse is an importation from 13:10 is entirely unnecessary, for it is perfectly understandable, rather than inherently improbable as the conjecture presupposes, that the Apostle should have used this particular expression twice within this particular context (which extends to 13:10).

10:9—11

That I may not seem as if I would terrify you by my letters. For, His letters, they say, are weighty and strong; but his bodily presence is weak, and his speech of no account. Let such a one reckon this, that, what we are in word by letters when we are absent, such are we also in deed when we are present.

Verse 9 is intended ironically: assertively though he may speak about his apostolic authority (given him, however, as he has just reminded his readers, for building them up), yet he has no intention[16] of terrifying them out of their wits[17] by the letters he writes, as though putting on a show[18] of authority from a safe distance. This is an effective thrust, for the picture of Paul, whom they knew so well, acting the part of a distant despot

---

[15] Origen, *Con. Cels.*, IV, i; cf. V, i.

[16] The ἵνα expresses Paul's intention (ironically stated), and ἵνα μὴ δόξω may be translated here, "it is not my intention that I should seem . . ."

[17] Ἐκφοβεῖν is an intensive compound: to "terrify" or "frighten to distraction", and is *hapax legomenon* in the New Testament, though frequent in the LXX. It conveys an ironically exaggerated echo of the calumny of Paul's opponents.

[18] Δοκεῖν ὡς ἄν, "to give the appearance as it were . . ." J. H. Moulton sees in the use of ὡς ἄν here a foreshadowing of the idiom of Modern Greek, in which ἄν = "if", and renders it "as it were" (*Grammar*, Vol. I, p. 167).

terrorizing them by his correspondence must have struck the Corinthians as altogether ridiculous. As a riposte to the calumnies of those who were defaming him in Corinth it was both adroit and legitimate. The particular slander in question was in fact most damaging to his authority. It was being said[19] that between the tone of his letters and the manner of his conduct when present there existed the greatest discrepancy, that the former was impressive and forceful, whereas the latter was marked by weakness and indecision. The charge, in short, was one of radical inconsistency and inconstancy. (Cf. the comparable accusation implied in 1:13, to the effect that what he wrote and what he did were two different things.)

It is improbable that the mention here of Paul's bodily presence is intended to refer to his physical appearance, except possibly by innuendo. It may well be that in physique Paul was unimpressive (see commentary on 1:1 above). But, though small in stature and marked by the sufferings which he so constantly endured for Christ's sake, it is unlikely that one who was so inured to incessant hardship and journeying could be described as a weakling. The accusation was rather of a moral character, and therefore much more damaging to the authority he claimed than the ridicule of any merely physical disabilities. Like so many who judge things according to the outward display of this world, Paul's opponents interpreted meekness as weakness, forbearance as cowardice, and gentleness as indecision (cf. v. 1; and see commentary on 11:21 below)—or at least they had sought to induce the Corinthians to place this interpretation on Paul's character.

And they also sought to disparage Paul's "oratory". The Greek veneration of human wisdom and of eloquence for the sake of eloquence made it relatively simple for his calumniators in Corinth to pour scorn on his unprofessional manner of speaking

---

[19] The texts of Westcott and Hort, Nestlé, and Souter reflect the balance of the textual evidence in favour of φησίν (singular) rather than φασίν (plural). The singular may indicate that one opponent in particular—cf. τις (v. 7) and ὁ τοιοῦτος (v. 11)—was responsible for this calumny. Most commentators, however, treat it as indefinite, that is, = "people say" (equivalent to the French on dit). The plural φασίν, if right, would also have this force, as in Vg., inquiunt, and AV and RV, "they say", that is, "certain unspecified people are saying" or "it is being said".

in public, unadorned as it was by the polished refinements and artificialities of the academic rhetorician. Paul, however, was not concerned with superficial finesse which charms the ear without touching the heart, but with the communication of saving truth. It was for this reason that he had resolutely eschewed the arts and devices of the orator in bringing the gospel to Corinth (I Cor. 2:1-5; and see comments below on 11:6). Anything that might distract his hearers' attention from or overlay the dynamic truth of his message was to be avoided at all costs. It was essential that their faith should stand, "not in the wisdom of men, but in the power of God".

Chrysostom and many others have treated verse 10 as a parenthesis, and, putting a full stop at the end of verse 8, have linked verse 11 grammatically to verse 9, as apodosis to protasis, thus: "In order that I may not seem as if I would terrify you by my letters, let such a one reckon this, etc. ..." But, although this may help to resolve a grammatical problem (which is a matter of minor importance when we remember that it is the epistolary style of Paul with which we are dealing), it does not improve the sense; for verse 11 is closely associated in thought with the calumny that has just been cited in verse 10. Such a calumniator[20] is given due warning that Paul on paper and Paul when present are not two incompatibles. The Apostle is here defending the constancy, at all times, of his character. The allusion to his being present should not be limited in scope to his coming visit, though that is as a matter of course embraced in the general statement. It was, naturally, essential for his authority that his personal integrity and consistency should be both acknowledged and established. No traducement of a man's authority is more dangerous than that which accuses him of insincerity, fickleness, and inability to translate his words into action. It is this serious charge which Paul now faces and repudiates: what he is in word, through his letters, when absent he is also in deed when present (cf. v. 2). The gentleness and paternal compassion of Paul are such that it will give him no pleasure to come to Corinth with a rod (I Cor. 4:21); should, however, the situation require it, he will not spare when he comes, but will enforce his authority to the full against any who resist him (13:2, 10).

---

[20] Ὁ τοιοῦτος. See preceding note.

10:12

> For we are not bold to number or compare ourselves with certain of them that commend themselves: but they themselves, measuring themselves by themselves, and comparing themselves with themselves, are without understanding.

Paul now indulges in a note of sarcasm. Though defending his own boldness and disavowing the timidity of cowardice, he declares with strong irony that there are, however, limits to his boldness: he would not be so daring as to put himself on an equality or even to compare himself[21] with certain individuals whose daring is so extraordinary that they rest their authority upon *self*-commendation! That is a boldness with which he does not compete! Always Paul was acutely conscious that, *in himself*, he was utterly unworthy of God's call to apostleship, that everything he was he owed entirely to the sovereign grace of God (cf. 12:11; I Cor. 15:9f., 3:6f.; Eph. 3:7f.). His commendation, his authority, was of God, not of men, and least of all of self. Indeed, in spiritual matters self-commendation is self-condemnation. As Tasker observes, "the point Paul is making is that self-praise is dispraise". But these men are so puffed up with arrogant ambition and self-esteem that self is their only measure of authority and their sole standard of comparison. And this, so far from being a recommendation of their worth, unmasks them as impostors lacking any understanding of the character and qualities of genuine Christian apostleship and service. Thus the very accusation of self-commendation which, with the purpose of diverting attention from their own misdemeanours and discrediting the Corinthians' true apostle, they had maliciously

---

[21]   It is difficult to reproduce in English the play on words in the expression ἐγκρῖναι ἢ συγκρῖναι. Plummer suggests "pair or compare". Bengel renders into Latin, "*aequiparare aut comparare*". Ἐγκρῖναι is to adjudge as being *within* the class of, and thus as being on an equality with, someone or something else. Συγκρῖναι is to judge in company *with* someone or something else, and thus to compare for purposes of classification. Those who, like these false apostles, measure and compare themselves with themselves show that in reality they have no standard of comparison at all. Of particular significance, in view of the following verses, is the fact that the verb ἐγκρίνειν was also used of admitting persons as competitors in the athletic games. This may well have been the metaphor in Paul's mind at this point (cf. Xenophon, *Hell.*, IV, i, 40 and Aristides, *Panath.*, 109). We would suggest, then, that ἐγκρῖναι ἢ συγκρῖναι may effectively be rendered "compete or compare".

hurled at Paul (cf. 3:1, 5:12) recoils with crippling force upon the heads of these intruders.[22]

10 : 13, 14

But we will not glory beyond our measure, but according to the measure of the province which God apportioned to us as a measure, to reach even unto you. For we stretch not ourselves overmuch, as though we reached not unto you: for we came even as far as unto you in the gospel of Christ.

The polemic against those who, with no justification whatever, had intruded themselves into the Corinthian church is still further intensified. Not only had they employed self-commendation in seeking to usurp Paul's apostolic authority, but they

---

[22] Some documents omit the last two words of this verse and the first two of the next: οὐ συνιᾶσιν ἡμεῖς δέ. This has the effect of altering the whole import of 12ᵇ and of running it on grammatically into the next verse, thus: "but we, measuring ourselves by ourselves and comparing ourselves with ourselves, will not glory beyond measure...", the pronouns then being treated as first instead of third person plural. The sense would then be somewhat as follows: "our standard is in ourselves, what God has made us by His call to apostleship, and we are not concerned with the judgment of others concerning us". The omission of the four words in question, however, must be regarded as an attempt by some later hand to facilitate the reading, in which οὐ συνιᾶσιν (or συνιοῦσιν) was felt to be a difficulty. Apart from the balance of the textual evidence, which favours their retention, it is most improbable that the words would have been *inserted* into the text.

Some, accepting the reading συνιουσιν, have interpreted 12ᵇ in the first person singular by treating it as a participle *(συνίουσιν)* agreeing with ἑαυτοῖς: "we measure ourselves by ourselves and compare ourselves with ourselves, without understanding though we be (that is, in the eyes of our adversaries)". But this construction, as has been pointed out, would require the article before οὐ συνίουσιν (thus: τοῖς οὐ συνίουσιν). Another suggestion has been that οὐ συνίουσιν should be referred to Paul's opponents, while the preceding pronouns are understood as being first person plural, thus: "we measure ourselves by ourselves and compare ourselves with ourselves, not with those who are wise (that is, in their own judgment)". But in this case the article would be required between οὐ and συνίουσιν (thus: οὐ τοῖς συνίουσιν). In either of these cases μετροῦντες and συγκρίνοντες would be explained as participles standing absolutely for the indicative. The difficulty seems to have arisen through treating the subject of 12ᵇ as first person plural (= Paul) instead of third person plural (= Paul's adversaries), which at once leads to the need either for interpreting συνιουσιν as a dative plural participle or for the omission of the four words already indicated if συνιουσιν is read as the third person plural of the present indicative *(= συνιᾶσιν)*.

had also invaded a territory to which they had no right of entry. "I, however," says Paul pointedly, "will not glory in things that have not been measured out for me".[23] The picture Paul has in mind is that of a course measured out by God for each of His servants—and, more particularly here for each of His apostles. These intruders, however, had not been chosen of God; no sphere or track had been divinely marked out for them, certainly not in Corinth. The claims they were boastfully making were, therefore, entirely without foundation. Paul, on the other hand, confines his glorying to what are its only legitimate limits, namely, the course of evangelism which God, not self, had so clearly marked out for him and which, in the dispensation of God's strategic will, had brought him even as far as Corinth (the farthest point West which he had so far reached with the gospel). In coming to the Corinthians he had not overrun the prescribed limits, as would have been the case had the course appointed him by God not reached as far as them. The others who had come to them were unauthorized interlopers who had illegally trespassed on the lane marked out, not for them, but for him. Apart from other considerations, this was apparent from the indisputable fact that it was Paul who had first arrived in Corinth with the gospel of Christ.[24] The circumstance that these others who posed as apostles had reached Corinth *after* Paul should have caused the Corinthians to suspect that they were illegitimate competitors, and this suspicion should have been confirmed by the realization that they preached another Jesus and offered a different gospel (11:4). It was Paul, not these others, who had laid the foundation and who, as their spiritual father, had begotten them in the gospel (I Cor. 3:10, 4:15).

Lightfoot understands the image in these verses to be "taken from surveying and mapping out a district, so as to assign to different persons their respective parcels of ground".[25] It seems to us more probable, however, that the metaphor is that of the

---

[23] Εἰς τὰ ἄμετρα.

[24] Φθάνειν should be given its full meaning of "to arrive first", "to come before others". Paul uses it with the same force in I Thess. 4:15: "we . . . shall in no wise precede *(οὐ μὴ φθάσωμεν)* them that are fallen asleep". This force of φθάνειν, normal in classical Greek, is well attested in both literary and non-literary sources of the New Testament period.

[25] J. B. Lightfoot, commenting on the meaning of κανών in Gal. 6:16.

athletic contests, for which Corinth, with its Isthmian Games, was renowned. In the games a course or lane was measured out for each of the runners, which was marked by a line ("canon")[26]. The lane measured out by God for Paul was one which led him to Corinth; whereas his opponents had not been admitted by God to any lane, let alone one which led to Corinth. Hence they were disqualified as "competitors".

10 : 15, 16

> Not glorying beyond our measure, that is, in other men's labors; but having hope that, as your faith groweth, we shall be magnified in you according to our province unto further abundance, so as to preach the gospel even unto the parts beyond you, and not to glory in another's province in regard of things ready to our hand.

Those intruders who, having no appointed course of their own, trespass on the territory marked out by God for someone else are precisely the ones who boast of the labours of others as though they were their own. To an extreme degree they are "meddlers in other men's matters", "alien bishops".[27]   But it was by the unremitting labours of Paul himself that the Corinthian church had been founded. It was he, and none other, who in Christ Jesus had begotten its members through the gospel (I Cor. 4:15). Yet these others had made a completely unwarranted invasion of his Corinthian territory, they had arrogantly claimed

---

[26]   Cf. Jul. Pollux, III, 15, τὸ μέτρον τοῦ πηδήματος κανών, and see note on the meaning of ἐγκρῖναι in verse 12 above.

Κανών is probably derived from the Hebrew קָנֶה = "reed" or "cane", and hence a measuring rod; cf. *κάννα*, Latin, *canna*. It commonly signified a rule or standard, and in the ancient Church was used of the rule or standard of faith. In his epistle to the Corinthians Clement of Rome uses κανών in much the same sense as Paul does here, when, after speaking of the variety of distinct ministerial offices and of the ordinances proper to the layman, he calls upon each one of them not to transgress the appointed limit, the prescribed measure, of his service *(τὸν ὡρισμένον τῆς λειτουργίας αὐτοῦ κανόνα—Ep. ad Cor.*, XLI).

In the expression, τὸ μέτρον τοῦ κανόνος οὗ ἐμέρισεν ἡμῖν ὁ θεὸς μέτρου, the relative pronoun οὗ is attracted into the case of its antecedent κανόνος, and μέτρου stands in apposition to οὗ. This is well brought out by our English version: "the measure of the province which God apportioned to us as a measure".

[27]   *Ἀλλοτριεπίσκοποι*, I Pet. 4:15.

for themselves the credit which belonged solely to him (not, however, that Paul would have spoken in terms of credit) as though it was they who had first brought the genuine gospel to Corinth, they were trespassing on a harvest-field which, under God, was his and not at all theirs, they had instigated despicable slanders against his personal character and apostolic authority, and by their false teaching they were threatening the very foundation of truth upon which Christ's church at Corinth was constructed. This being so, it is not surprising that Paul felt and expressed himself strongly about such persons.

In accordance with his divine commission, Paul regarded himself as a pioneer missionary of the gospel, and particularly to the Gentiles. When, after writing this present epistle, he had travelled on to Corinth, he wrote from there (probably in the first part of the year 58 A.D.) to explain to the Christians in Rome, whom he hoped to visit, that his aim was to preach the gospel where Christ was not already named, so that he might not build upon another man's foundation (Rom. 15:20), thereby indicating that it was not his intention to "invade" their territory, to which God in His wise grace had already brought an apostolic messenger, and further, that his constant purpose was to move on to places and cities which had not yet been reached by the gospel. His outlook was ever dynamic and progressive, in irreconcilable contrast to the parasitic mentality of the false apostles who had battened on the Corinthian church. The hardships of the course appointed for him did not make him wish to withdraw from the contest. On the contrary, he was determined at all costs to finish his course and to press on towards the goal (Acts 20:24; II Tim. 4:7; Phil. 3:14). And the end of the course marked out for him was not yet: it had brought him as far as Corinth, but it stretched on beyond that milestone to farther horizons. Hence the hope which he here expresses that, as the faith of the Corinthians grows, so he will become free to increase the measure of his apostolic course beyond Corinth to more distant parts which are as yet without the gospel. A spiritually unsettled state of affairs in Corinth constitutes a hindrance to his moving on further afield.[28] Their love and loyalty and their

---

[28] Ἐν ὑμῖν μεγαλυνθῆναι κατὰ τὸν κανόνα ἡμῶν εἰς περισσείαν is a difficult clause, the significance of which is anything but clear in our English version ("that . . . we shall be magnified in you according to our province

establishment in the faith not only give joy to him as their spiritual father, but also have the effect of liberating him in his apostolic capacity for carrying the good tidings of salvation to others who are still, as they once were, in the darkness and bondage of unbelief.

It was far from Paul's practice to invade, or cut into, the appointed course of someone else and to boast of achievements which he found ready to hand as though they were his own.[29] Certainly, their Apostle's far-reaching vision, as set before them here, must have acted as another incentive, and an impelling one, to the Corinthian Christians to set their house in order and to give proof of spiritual maturity so that he might be liberated to advance beyond them and make fresh conquests for the gospel of Christ. Their need was to capture his vision for themselves and to see that they too, though, it was true, a geographically localized community, were integrally bound up with the realization of that dynamic vision. And this same vision, so truly catholic and ecumenical, is no less essential for the local Christian communities and congregations of every generation, our own included, if the temptation to narrow-hearted inward-looking insularity, by which every such community or congregation is

---

unto further abundance"). Paul is still employing the athletic metaphor: his hope is that as their faith reaches a stage of maturity so he will be enlarged among them; that is to say, his way forward is at present blocked or narrowed because they still need his oversight and attention. But he cannot regard Corinth as the end or goal of his course. The growth of their faith will, as it were, clear the way before him so that he can continue his course beyond them. The reference to his enlargement (μεγαλυνθῆναι) relates to the track which God has marked out for him (κατὰ τὸν κανόνα ἡμῶν) and its objective is the preaching of the gospel to those in more distant parts (εἰς περισσείαν, εἰς τὰ ὑπερέκεινα ὑμῶν εὐαγγελίσασθαι).

'Υπερέκεινα is not, as Plummer suggests, a term coined by Paul; it is, as J. H. Moulton says (*Grammar of New Testament Greek*, Vol. II, p. 326), "simply ὑπὲρ ἐκεῖνα turned into one word", and is "guaranteed to be good Κοινή by the strictures of Thomas Magister". It is a synonym of the classical ἐπέκεινα. According to Thomas Magister (14th century), ἐπέκεινα ῥήτορες λέγουσιν ... ὑπερέκεινα δὲ μόνοι οἱ σύρφακες — "rhetoricians say ἐπέκεινα ... but only the rabble say ὑπερέκεινα" (155, 7).

[29] Tasker rightly criticizes the AV rendering ("not to boast in another man's line of things made ready to our hand") of οὐκ ἐν ἀλλοτρίῳ κανόνι εἰς τὰ ἕτοιμα καυχήσασθαι as "unusually clumsy", and the Revised Version (ASV = ERV) is not much better. The sense is more aptly reproduced by RSV: "without boasting of work already done in another's field."

constantly threatened, is to be abhorred and overcome. The local church in which this temptation is not abhorred and overcome actually becomes a hindrance to the spread of the good news. It degenerates into a religious club and is in danger of having its candlestick removed (Rev. 2:5).

Paul's purpose of preaching the gospel in places where Christ had not yet been named included at or about this time the project of a pioneering journey, via Rome, to Spain (Rom. 15:24, 28). That this project was in fact fulfilled is strongly suggested by Clement of Rome who, writing to the Corinthians towards the end of the first century, asserts that Paul travelled to the farthest limit of the West.[30] This being so, it may be concluded that the Corinthians responded to Paul's appeal by putting things to rights in their own church, and thus helped to clear the way for him to proceed on westwards beyond them with the gospel.

It is worth repeating that the Apostle's controversy in these concluding chapters is plainly not with the general membership of the Corinthian church, to whom he looks with confidence, but with those intruders who are seeking to impose themselves and their dangerous doctrines upon them, and thereby to usurp the authority which rightly belongs to him. "We should notice", says Allo, "that he utters no reproach against the community; on the contrary, Paul is counting on them for the unlimited extension of his apostolate."

10 : 17, 18

But he that glorieth, let him glory in the Lord. For not he that commendeth himself is approved, but whom the Lord commendeth.

In this epistle, where, with a view to authenticating his apostleship, it is necessary for him to say so much about himself and his labours and to expose the imposture of those who had come to Corinth posing as apostles, it is apparent that Paul is

---

[30] Clement of Rome, *Ep. ad Cor.*, V: ἐπὶ τὸ τέρμα τῆς δύσεως. For citations from Strabo and Velleius Paterculus supporting this understanding of Spain as the western boundary of the world in Paul's day, see Lightfoot, *The Apostolic Fathers*, Part I, Vol. II, (London, 1890), p. 30.

constantly aware of the danger of laying himself open to mis-understanding, or more particularly to perverse and malicious misinterpretation by those who are intent on denigrating his character as a Christian. It is these opponents in Corinth who have been boasting and taking the credit for work which is not theirs at all; but it does not follow that Paul wishes to arrogate to himself the praise and the credit for this work as though they are due to him. Far from it; and to make this unmistakeably plain he adds an admonition from the Old Testament Scriptures: "He that glorieth, let him glory in the Lord". He had previously used the same citation in I Cor. 1:31, introducing it there with the words, "according as it is written". It is in fact a free con-densation of what is said in Jer. 9:24, a passage which emphasizes that, so far from finding cause for boasting in wisdom or might or wealth, man's only legitimate cause for glorying is in knowing and acknowledging the sovereignty of God. In and of himself man can find no justification for boasting. Anything, therefore, which may have been achieved through Paul's efforts in Corinth is to be attributed to the grace of God alone. Hence the key-note of Paul's apostolic life: "not I, but Christ"; and this is the key-note of every genuine Christian life.

In the Christian Church, indeed, self-commendation should be viewed with suspicion as a mark of disqualification. God's commendation of a person is shown, not by verbal boasts, but by the testimony of the consciences of those who have experienced the blessing attendant upon that person's labours and by the continuing and increasing fruits of his labours (cf. 4:2, 5:11). The occurrence of division and heresy, deplorable though they are, may at least be said to have this function within the con-glomerate of good and bad which forms the visible Church on earth, that it serves to draw a distinction from time to time between those who are true and those who are false. Thus Paul has already written in his earlier letter to the Corinthians: "There must also be heresies among you, that they which are approved may be made manifest among you" (I Cor. 11:19). As for him-self, Paul appeals, not to self-commendation, nor to human approbation, but to the judgment of the Lord, "who will both bring to light the hidden things of darkness and make manifest the counsels of the hearts; and then shall each man have his praise from God" (I Cor. 4:4f.). The application of this principle

371

to ourselves is well stated by Calvin: "Let us therefore", he writes, "leaving off all other things, aim exclusively at this—that we may be approved by God and may be satisfied to have His approbation alone, as it justly ought to be regarded by us as of more value than all the applauses of the whole world."

With regard to the quotation of verse 17, Bachmann and others have drawn attention to the manner in which the New Testament writers apply or transfer to Christ references in the Old Testament to Jehovah (= "the Lord"), as Paul does here and in I Cor. 1:31 (cf. also I Cor. 2:16, 10:22; Rom. 10:13; Phil. 2:11). This is done without embarrassment or explanation, as something entirely natural, and is a significant pointer to the fundamental apostolic belief in the pre-existence of Christ in the unity of the eternal Godhead.

11:1

> Would that ye could bear with me in a little foolishness: but indeed ye do bear with me.

Having stated the principle that it is not self-commendation but only the commendation of God which makes a man approved, Paul now craves the indulgence of the Corinthians while he speaks at some length concerning himself. It is not self-esteem that causes him to do so, but the menace to the Corinthian believers of those who, claiming a spurious authority and inflated with self-importance, have intruded themselves and their erroneous teachings into the sphere of his apostolic jurisdiction. To suggest that this humblest of God's servants was moved by injured pride to write as he now does is to show a complete misconception of the situation. It is concern, loving anxious concern, for the spiritual welfare of those who are his children in Christ which moves him so strongly—so much so that he is prepared to appear to indulge in what he calls "a little foolishness", by speaking about himself, in order to counteract the impact of the intruders who in their foolishness have been extolling themselves. That this is an exercise distasteful to the Apostle is obvious. Hence his desire that the Corinthians will bear with him, followed by the confidence afforded by the remembrance that they already are such as bear with him; so that he need not fear from them a misconstruction of his motives.[31] Here, again, his confidence in the Corinthians, his "boldness" on their behalf (cf. 7:4, 14, 16; 8:24; 9:2ff.), shines clearly through. All that he writes is for their sakes, not for his own glory (12:19). "He that remembers sin which God remembers not", comments Chrysostom, "and who therefore says that he is unworthy of the very name of the Apostles, even by the most insensate is seen clearly not to be saying what he is now going to say, for the sake of glory ... but he looked to one thing, the salvation of his hearers."

11:2

> For I am jealous over you with a godly jealousy: for I espoused you to one husband, that I might present you as a pure virgin to Christ.

The ultimate reason for the "foolishness" of speaking here about himself to the Corinthians, for which he has requested their forbearance, is that as their spiritual parent he views them in the perspective of eternity. He is jealous over them as one who has a special, almost a proprietary, interest in them and their affairs. "Those souls are jealous which burn ardently for those they love, and jealousy can in no other way be begotten than out of a vehement affection", says Chrysostom. But, again, Paul's jealousy over the Corinthians is not a merely human jealousy of selfish possessiveness; it is *of God.*[32] Jealousy for his own reputation among men is very far removed from the Apostle's mind. His jealousy is directed outwards and as it were protectively over the Corinthians as its object, and, being one with that jealousy which God has for those who are His, it is centred in God and the honour of His supreme Name. Indeed, Paul wishes

---

[31] The Vulgate, AV, RV, RSV, Calvin, Beza, Bengel, Allo, and numerous others treat ἀνέχεσθε here as an imperative: "nay indeed bear with me", regarding it as giving greater force to the wish that has just been expressed. We do not hesitate, however, to prefer, with Chrysostom, Alford, Hodge, Plummer, etc., and our own version, to understand ἀνέχεσθε as indicative, which is much better suited to the ἀλλὰ καί which precedes it: "but indeed you do already bear with me". It expresses once more the tone of confidence in the Corinthians. In reminding himself of this the Apostle reassures not only himself but them also. An imperative added to a wish demanding the same thing is really redundant here.

[32] Θεοῦ ζῆλος, which is well rendered "godly jealousy" in our version.

them to see that theirs is a particularly intimate and sacred relationship with God, a relationship which he was instrumental in bringing about. They were his work in the Lord, and the seal of his apostleship in the Lord; he had begotten them through the gospel (I Cor. 9:1f., 4:15). And as it is the father's right to give his daughter in marriage to an approved bridegroom, so he, their spiritual father, had given them in betrothal to one husband, a Divine Husband. The betrothal of a maiden implies purity and faithfulness; she is committed to the one man to whom she is engaged to be married. "By adding the word *one* Paul stresses the truth that, just as the marriage relationship is exclusive, so believers in Christ owe an exclusive loyalty to Him" (Tasker). It is, moreover, the father's prerogative to present the bride to her husband on the wedding-day: accordingly, the Apostle anticipates with joy the presentation of his Corinthian converts as a faithful and undefiled virgin to Christ when, at His parousia, He takes His bride to Himself and brings her to that eternal home which He has gone to prepare. It is then that the marriage of the Lamb with His Church will be celebrated amidst the rejoicing of heaven (cf. Mt. 22:1ff., 25:1ff.; Jn. 3:29, 14:2f.; Eph. 5:22ff.; Rev. 19:7ff., 21:2, 9).

In the Old Testament, of course, Israel, God's chosen people, is frequently spoken of as the spouse of Jehovah (cf. Isa. 54:5f., 62:5; Jer. 3:14; Ezek. 16:8; Hos. 2:19f.); and unfaithfulness to the Lord is denounced as spiritual adultery (cf. Judg. 2:17, 8:27; I Chron. 5:25; Ps. 106:39; Jer. 3:1; Ezek. 6:9, 16:15ff.; Hos. 4:12, etc.; and cf. in the New Testament Jas. 4:4). To members of the Church in the setting of the notoriously dissolute society of Corinth Paul's words here must have come with particular force. Indeed, when we bear in mind the former immoral manner of life of many of Paul's Corinthian converts (see the outspoken passage in I Cor. 6:9-11) we can but join with Allo in marvelling at his apostolic boldness and hope in refashioning them into spiritual virgins. No longer, he admonishes them, can they regard themselves as their own, for by divine redemption they now belong to Christ (I Cor. 3:23, 6:19f.); He is their one Husband, and in anticipation of the coming of the Bridegroom they are under obligation to preserve unsullied their virginity (cf. I Jn. 3:3); and Paul, their father in the gospel, jealously desires to present them as a pure and faithful bride to Christ on that great day.

374

In the Apostle's language here we may discover further evidence of the identification of Christ in the New Testament with Jehovah in the Old Testament (cf. commentary on 10:17 above). It belongs to the essence of apostolic christology that Christ, who is the Husband of God's people under the new dispensation, is none other than Jehovah, who is the Husband of His people under the former dispensation, and therefore that He is Himself very God of very God, who became man and suffered for our redemption, and who, as the risen, ascended, and glorified Lord, is the ever-living Bridegroom of those who are His. The inference is clear, also, that the Church of the New Testament, which is the bride of Christ, is continuous with the Church of the Old Testament, which is the bride of Jehovah. Hence Paul elsewhere describes the Church as "the Israel of God" (Gal. 6:16; cf. Gal. 3:7ff., 29; Rom. 2:29, 4:9ff., 9:6ff.; Phil. 3:3).

Allo rightly observes that the imagery of this verse shows that "Paul was very far from despising marriage since he makes it the symbol of the ideal consummation". Yet the calumny still strangely persists in circles which are hostile to Christianity that Paul forbade marriage, and that therefore had his teaching been universally followed the human race would have been faced with extinction!

11:3

But I fear, lest by any means, as the serpent beguiled Eve in his craftiness, your minds should be corrupted from the simplicity and the purity that is toward Christ.

Paul is concerned because he perceives that the Corinthian converts, though betrothed to the one Bridegroom, are in grave danger of being seduced into unfaithfulness by the impostors who have invaded their community. Aware that Satan, the father of all lying (Jn. 8:44), is ever active in opposition to the Word of God, he is afraid lest they should be completely deceived [33] as Eve, the first bride, was by the craftiness of the serpent acting

---

[33] Ἐξηπάτησεν should probably be taken as an intensive compound; cf. I Tim. 2:14: "Adam was not deceived (ἠπατήθη), but the woman being completely deceived (ἐξαπατηθεῖσα) hath fallen into transgression". This seems to indicate that the compound verb is deliberately used by Paul to describe that original deception which Eve suffered.

375

as the instrument of him who is himself described as "that old Serpent" (Rev. 12:9, 20:2). That these false teachers are tools and emissaries of Satan, serpent-like in the versatility of their cunning,[34] is implicit in what Paul says here, and is explicitly stated in verses 13 to 15 below: the manner in which they deceitfully disguise themselves as ministers of righteousness betrays the operation within them of the subtle power of their master Satan whose custom it is to transform himself into an angel of light. Like him, they appear in friendly and alluring guise, but, like him again, they contradict the Word of God and lead their victims to spiritual disaster, described here by Paul as the corruption of their minds, that is, of their whole outlook, volitional as well as intellectual.[35] They are distracted from the simplicity —that is, wholeheartedness, singleness of devotion, freedom from duplicity [36]—and from the purity which a faithful bride should maintain towards the one to whom she is betrothed.[37] The enmity between the seed of the serpent and the Seed of the woman continues unremittingly until the day of judgment, and mankind will continue to suffer from and be threatened by the evil effects of the first sin of the first woman until, at Christ's coming, the new creation is fully realized and the former things are passed away.

---

[34] Πανουργία. See note on 4:2 above.

[35] See note on νόημα, 10:5 above.

[36] See note on ἁπλότης, 8:2 above.

[37] Εἰς τὸν Χριστόν = "toward Christ" here rather than "in Christ" (AV, Calvin). The preposition indicates the centre toward and into which "the simplicity and purity" are directed: they are Christocentric. Paul is still speaking in terms of the relationship of the virgin church to the one to whom she is betrothed.

Τῆς ἁπλότητος καὶ τῆς ἁγνότητος is the best attested reading, being present in P46 as well as other important early documents. In some documents the order is reversed—something which could easily have happened when nouns so similar in appearance and sound were being copied. The evidence for the omission of καὶ τῆς ἁγνότητος is impressive enough, however, to have caused editors of the standing of Westcott and Hort and Nestlé to have suspicions regarding the originality of the phrase. On the other hand, τῆς ἁγνότητος is frequently found by itself in Lucifer and Augustine, and Ambrosiaster has τῆς ἁγνότητος τοῦ θεοῦ. The similarity of the two terms explains the confusion in the readings. We concur with Allo's judgment that an error of haplography is more likely to have occurred than one of dittography.

11:4

For if he that cometh preacheth another Jesus, whom we did not preach, or if ye receive a different spirit, which ye did not receive, or a different gospel, which ye did not accept, ye do well to bear with him.

In verse 1 the Apostle has requested the Corinthians to bear with him in a little "foolishness" as he speaks of himself; and now the ironical note struck there is intensified as he reminds them that they bear well enough with someone who comes to them with a message the content of which is subversive of the teaching he had himself given them.[38] The designation "he that cometh" may indicate the leader of the false teachers who had invaded the Corinthian church, but in view of the fact that there were several of such ministers of Satan it seems preferable to understand the expression, as most commentators do, in a generic sense. The designation itself is charged with ironical significance, since "he that cometh" is the direct antithesis of the title of apostle, which means "he that is sent". They posed, indeed, as apostles of Christ (v. 13), but, unlike Paul, Christ had neither commissioned nor sent them: they had simply *come*, unsent and without divine authorization; and therefore they were no apostles. They had come preaching a Jesus other than Him whom Paul had preached—a "Jesus", perhaps, who was son of man but not Son of God, crucified but not risen, of David's royal line but not the universal and everlasting King of Glory. (It is difficult to believe that Hodge can be right in his view that Paul means here "another person than the son of Mary". The proclamation of a person quite other than Jesus of Nazareth as the true saviour of man would hardly have beguiled the Corinthians.) And the reception of this "other Jesus" meant the

---

[38] Καλῶς ἀνέχεσθε: "You bear well enough with him". Our English version, "ye do well to bear with him", though no doubt intended to convey the overtone of irony, scarcely succeeds in doing so. The AV, "ye might well bear with him", reflects a reading (Vg, *recte pateremini*), which is not only less well attested but is also less well suited to the preceding present indicatives— —κηρύσσει . . . λαμβάνετε— which state the *facts* of the case, not a mere conjecture. A number of commentators have suggested that this verse should be understood in an interrogative sense: " . . . do ye well to bear with him?"; but the majority of scholars are agreed that the sense of irony running through this passage calls for a direct categorical statement here.

reception of a spirit different from that which they had received through Paul's ministry—a spirit, perhaps, of the world, that is, of human wisdom and gnosis (I Cor. 2:12), a spirit of bondage (Rom. 8:15; Gal. 2:4, 4:24; Col. 2:20ff.) and enslavement to spurious or outmoded ordinances, especially of a judaizing nature, a spirit of fear associated with the observance of the latter and with the questioning of their eternal security in Christ (II Tim. 1:7; Rom. 8:15). The spirit they had received through Paul's ministry, however, was very different—a spirit of liberty (3:17; Gal. 2:4, 5:1), a spirit of love, joy, and peace (Gal. 5:22; Rom. 14:17), a spirit of power (II Tim. 1:7; Eph. 3:20; Col. 1:11)—the sum of the blessings, in other words, of the outpoured Third Person of the Holy Trinity (cf. I Cor. 1:4ff.). In short, the "gospel" which these false teachers were seeking to impose upon them was quite different from the gospel they had accepted through the preaching of Paul.[39] There is only *one* gospel of our Lord and Saviour Jesus Christ, and upon any, be he even an angel from heaven, who proclaims a different gospel Paul does not hesitate to pronounce an anathema (Gal. 1:6ff.), for such a person cannot be other than an impostor and a minister of damnation. And such were these self-commending interlopers. Their presence·threatened destruction to the church in Achaia. How, then, could Paul be expected to speak calmly of them? It was essential that by severely denouncing them and exposing their deceits he, as a faithful pastor, should warn the flock of Christ and rescue it from the peril in which it was placed.

11:5

For I reckon that I am not a whit behind the very chiefest apostles.

The thrust of Paul's thought is: "You bear well enough with an intruder such as I have just described (v. 4); then I ask you at least to bear with me (v. 1), for I reckon that I am in no way inferior to super-apostles of his kind". We concur

[39] In the sequence ἄλλον Ἰησοῦν .. πνεῦμα ἕτερον ... εὐαγγέλιον ἕτερον the change from ἄλλος to ἕτερος is marked in our English version, which reads: "another Jesus ... a different spirit ... a different gospel". In its strict sense ἕτερος means "the other (of two)"; but where the context does not support this precise sense ἕτερος is indistinguishable in meaning from ἄλλος and the two terms may be used interchangeably, as seems to be the case here (see Moulton

with the opinion of most modern commentators that Paul is not referring to the authentic apostles, but to the impostors who had invaded his Corinthian territory falsely claiming to be apostles of Christ (v. 13). To have heard them commend themselves, one would have thought that these "comers" (v. 4) were something even grander than apostles. Paul's description of them here is vibrant with sarcasm: they are, if one believes all that they say about themselves, "extra-super-apostles".[40] The verses that follow show how well he comes out of a comparison with them and their practices.

The possibility that the commentators of earlier centuries were right in understanding Paul to be speaking here of the true apostles cannot, of course, be ruled out. Thus Chrysostom holds that he is referring to the very chiefest, the innermost circle, of the Twelve, namely, Peter, James, and John; and this view has been acceptable to Calvin, Bengel, Hodge, and many others of more recent times. Paul is then saying to the Corinthians in effect: "You bear well enough with these intruding deceivers; surely, then, you will bear with me who, if you take into account my calling by the Lord, my spiritual gifts, my labours, and my character, can stand comparison with the very topmost of those who are genuine apostles". Of his apostolic commission and authority he has no doubts; nor, in their consciences, have they.

Those, however, who, maintaining this interpretation, have pressed this verse as an argument against the Roman Catholic doctrine of the supremacy of Peter seem to us to do so without legitimate reason, for, if it be granted that Paul's reference here is to Peter and the others, it is yet certain that he is very far

---

and Milligan and Arndt and Gingrich *sub* ἕτερος). That Paul could use ἄλλος and ἕτερος with precise regard to their distinctive nuances is well shown in Gal. 1:6f.

As Plummer remarks, "the aorists, ἐκηρύξαμεν, ἐλάβετε, ἐδέξασθε, refer to the time when the Apostle converted the Corinthians".

[40] Ὑπερλίαν is found only here and in 12:11 in biblical Greek, and otherwise twice in Eustathius (12th century). As year by year fresh light is thrown on the language of the New Testament, it becomes increasingly difficult to regard as probable the suggestion, made by Allo and Plummer, and favoured by Tasker, that Paul coined the term for his present purpose. It is more likely to have been a colloquialism in current use. Cf. note on κατενάρκησα, verse 9 below.

from thinking in terms of apostolic *supremacy*. This would be totally out of character in the case of one who regarded himself as "the least of the apostles" and "not meet to be called an apostle" (I Cor. 15:9). Far less is there justification for the misuse of this verse by the Tübingen school to support their hypothesis of an apostolic feud between Paul and Peter. Of course, if the reference is to the false apostles in Corinth then the question of any kind of comparison with Peter cannot even arise here.

In favour of the interpretation for which we have expressed preference it may be said that for Paul ironically to reckon up his worth in comparison of these false apostles is far more consonant with the satirical vein of the passage,[41] and is also germane to his immediate concern which is with these impostors rather than with any of the Twelve. Besides, the particular points of comparison supplied in the following verses are not applicable as between Paul on the one hand and Peter, James, and John on the other: could it be said that the latter were more skilled in rhetoric than he was? or that the knowledge revealed to Christ's true apostles was susceptible of degrees of comparison? or that Peter and the others were not content with a humble existence or were burdensome to the churches in a way that Paul was not? We conclude, therefore, that "these superlative apostles" (RSV) of our present verse (and also of 12:11) with whom Paul is comparing himself are to be identified with the "false apostles" of verse 13 below.

11:6

> But though I be rude in speech, yet am I not in knowledge; nay, in every way have we made this manifest unto you in all things.

Paul's language here reflects the accusations brought against him by the rival "apostles" who had invaded the Corinthian church. To the sophisticated Greek mind skill in rhetoric and philosophy provided a commendation superior to all others for the man who wished to gain a following; and these false teachers endeavoured to trade upon this mentality. No doubt they sought to commend themselves by some display of rhetorical art

---

[41] Even the word ὑπερλίαν has a satirical ring.

and by the presentation of a philosophical-religious gnosis (know-ledge) calculated to appeal to the Greek mind; and in doing so they drew attention to the deficiencies of Paul in these respects, hoping thereby to discredit him.   In his earlier letter Paul had already exposed the incompatibility of artificial eloquence and human philosophy with the style and content of Christian preaching.   To the unregenerate Greeks the latter was mere foolishness.   But Paul knew that their hearts were darkened by sin and that in professing themselves to be wise it was they who had in fact become fools; he knew that the gospel, the word of the Cross, was the wisdom of God and the power of God unto salvation to every believing heart; and so in coming to Corinth he properly eschewed the devices of the rhetorician and the wisdom-expert.   As a minister of the gospel, the alluring tricks of oratory and the persuasive arguments of philosophy were not his stock in trade (see I Cor. 1:18–2:5; Rom. 1:21ff.).   Yet in bringing them the gospel of Jesus Christ he was indeed bringing them wisdom, a wisdom, it is true, not of this fallen world (though *for* this fallen world), but the only true wisdom, the wisdom *of God* (I Cor. 2:6ff.).

Paul, accordingly, is prepared to concede, doubtless with a suspicion of irony, that he is unversed in the refinements of the rhetorical art.[42]   He cannot offer the professional polish and verbal virtuosity of those who have passed through the schools of rhetoric.   It would, however, be a mistake to conclude from this that he was necessarily a poor or clumsy speaker.   While the Athenian philosophers called him a "babbler", yet they took him to the Areopagus, which was either the famous forum for public speaking or, more probably, the supreme council of Athens [43] to hear more of what he had to say (Acts 17:16ff.).   The contrast

---

[42]   'Ιδιώτης τῷ λόγῳ, "a layman in speech".   The ἰδιώτης was the private individual as opposed to the public personage, and hence the unskilled (cf. *imperitus*, Vg here), the uninstructed (cf. I Cor. 14:16, 23f.), the non-professional man.   In view of the divergence of opinion over the identity of the ὑπερλίαν ἀπόστολοι (see comments on previous verse) it is of considerable interest to find Peter and John described by the Sanhedrin as ἰδιῶται (Acts 4:13)—on that occasion, however, not from the Greek but from the Jewish, that is, professional rabbinical, point of view.

[43]   See N. B. Stonehouse, *Paul Before the Areopagus* (Grand Rapids, 1957), pp. 8ff.; F. F. Bruce, *Commentary on the Book of the Acts* (Grand Rapids, 1954), pp. 351f.; Arndt and Gingrich, under "Areopagus".

in its essence is between rhetoric *and preaching*. The former is superficial, artificial, formal, ephemeral, attractive to the ears, but unrelated to the depth of human need; the latter is direct, serious, earnest, directed to heart and mind and will, related to eternal issues, concerned with the message rather than with the method of its utterance. The former is applauded, for it conduces to human adulation; the latter is unapplauded, for it brings men face to face with God.

But, whatever might be his deficiencies as a speaker, Paul is unable to concede that there is any inadequacy in his knowledge. He knows, with the absolute certainty of the Holy Spirit's inner witness, that the only genuine gnosis is to be found in the revelation of Jesus Christ, in whom are hid all the treasures of wisdom and knowledge (Col. 2:3). And this, despite the entice-ments of the false apostles in their midst, was something of which his Corinthian converts were fully aware: he had made it manifest to them among all men, and it was precisely by his despised *preaching* that he had done so. In contrast, then, to the gnosis of the religious philosophers, Paul's gnosis was not of an esoteric nature, reserved for the élite and fortunate few who had been accorded initiation into its secrets. His aim was to make it manifest *among all men*,[44] in accordance with his explicit commis-sion to be a witness for Christ unto all men of what he had seen and heard (Acts 22:15, 26:16ff.; cf. Mk. 16:15; Acts 1:8).

11 : 7

> Or did I commit a sin in abasing myself that ye might be exalted, because I preached to you the gospel of God for nought?

The intensity of the irony mounts as the Apostle inquires whether by preaching God's gospel to them without accepting any remuneration he has been guilty of committing a sin. The immediate connection of thought is with the term translated

---

[44] We prefer with RV to translate ἐν πᾶσιν as "among all men", that is, publicly, not secretly, rather than "in all things", as in our version and in AV, which makes ἐν πᾶσιν practically tautologous with ἐν παντί.

Φανερώσαντες is another case of a participle used absolutely, in this instance for the indicative (see note on 4:8f. above). The object is unstated. Allo, Lietzmann, Plummer, and others take it that τὴν γνῶσιν is implied. Equally well it may be that Paul intended his readers to understand the object more "rude" in the preceding verse,[45] the proper force of which in this context is "amateur" or "non-professional". Among the Greeks the accredited rhetorician or philosopher was a "professional" man who charged for his services and lived by his art. For a speaker to refuse remuneration, or not to demand it, would at once cause his listeners, such was the sophistication of their outlook, to suspect him of being spurious, a mere *poseur*, and his teaching as worthless. Thus Antipho told Socrates, who used to make no charge for his teaching,[46] that if he considered his conversation to be worth anything he would demand for it no less remuneration than it was worth, and accordingly that, just though he might be, because he deceived nobody through covetousness, wise he could not be, since he had no knowledge that was of any value.[47] Professional philosophers, or sophists, who sold their wisdom for money were a familiar feature in Greek society in Socrates' day and even more so in the Hellenistic period.[48] What we have here, then, is the echo of another and most despicable accusation fabricated by the false teachers who had trespassed on his territory in Corinth: it is Paul, they were whispering, who is not genuine; his teaching is so worthless that he does not dare to accept payment for it; a man who has so little confidence in his proclamation, and who so obviously declares himself to be the unskilled amateur, is unworthy the credence of intelligent people.

And so Paul puts the question as to whether he had committed a sin by breaking the "law" that a teacher's worth is to be estimated in proportion to the remuneration he receives for his performance. It is certainly true, as he had explained to the Corinthians in his earlier letter (I Cor. 9:3–18), that, consonant both with the law of Moses (see Deut. 25:4) and the precept of Christ (see Mt. 10:10), those who proclaim the gospel have a

---

broadly with reference to what he has just said, thus: "But *that in knowledge I I am no ἰδιώτης* I made manifest to you ...." The variant readings φανερωθέντες and φανερωθείς may be dismissed as scribal alterations intended to simplify the sense = "Nay, in every way I was made manifest unto you"; cf. AV and Vg: *manifestatus sum vobis.*

[45]   'Ιδιώτης.
[46]   Cf. Plato, *Apol.* 19DE.
[47]   Xenophon, *Mem.* I, vi.
[48]   Cf. Xenophon, *loc. cit.,* Plato, *Apol.* 19E–20A, Aristotle, *Eth. Nic.* IX, i, 5–7.

right to live of the gospel. But, though he might with complete legitimacy have done so, Paul forbore to avail himself of that right. As he reminds the Corinthians here, he humbled himself, accepting the status of a common artisan, because he sustained himself by his own manual labour rather than afford even a semblance of truth to those who would like to suggest that in preaching the gospel he was impelled by mercenary motives.

So far, indeed, was Paul from feeling that by preaching the gospel he was placing others in his debt, that he felt rather that by so doing he was himself discharging a debt (Rom. 1:14ff.). It was to the gospel of the grace of God in Christ that he himself owed absolutely everything. Freely he had received, freely he would give (Mt. 10:8), forgoing even the right which was his to be supported by those to whom he ministered—"for", he explained, "if I preach the gospel, I have nothing to glory of; for necessity is laid upon me; for woe is unto me if I preach not the gospel". This was not a task which he could as it were meritoriously take up and voluntarily lay down: it was a stewardship entrusted to him, and, by a paradox incomprehensible to the spirit of this age, he described it as his reward that, when he preached the gospel, he should make the gospel without charge, so as not to use to the full his right in the gospel (I Cor. 9:16ff.).

Furthermore, the purpose of this self-abasement was their exaltation: through his preaching of the gospel they were raised from the death of sin and from the degradation of their former ways and caused to sit in heavenly places in Christ Jesus (Eph. 2:6). How, then, could he have committed a sin in doing what he did? and how could they, who had experienced the transforming truth and power of his message, ever doubt the genuineness of his apostolic mission to them? The authenticity of his character and ministry was indelibly stamped on the heart and conscience of every believer (cf. 4:2).

It was in the course of his second missionary journey that Paul first visited Corinth and founded the church there (52 A.D.). There he lived and worked with Aquila at the craft of tentmaking so that he might be free to preach the gospel without charge to others (Acts 18:1ff.); and there he remained for eighteen months instructing the Corinthians in the Word of God (Acts 18:11). It was during that period that he wrote the two earliest of his extant letters, those to the Thessalonians, to whom he had brought the gospel a short while previously. From these letters it is apparent that when in Thessalonica he had adhered to this same practice of supporting himself. "Ye remember, brethren", he writes, "our labor and travail: working night and day, that we might not burden any of you, we preached unto you the gospel of God" (I Thess. 2:9). And again: "Neither did we eat bread for nought at any man's hand, but in labor and travail, working night and day, that we might not burden any of you: not because we have not the right ..." (II Thess. 3:8f.). Some years later, during the latter part of his third missionary journey, when saying farewell to the Ephesian elders at Miletus, he reminds them that this, once more, had been his practice when ministering in their midst: "I coveted no man's silver or gold or apparel", he says. "Ye yourselves know that these hands ministered unto my necessities"; and at the same time he recalled the Lord's saying that "it is more blessed to give than to receive" (Acts 20:34f.). We may conclude, therefore, that it was Paul's custom, when preaching or teaching in a place, to accept no gifts at the hands of the local people, even though such independence might mean real hardship to himself (see commentary below on v. 9).

11:8

I robbed other churches, taking wages of them that I might minister unto you.

It is a bold military metaphor which Paul employs here. The salary or ration-money [49] which was his due as an apostle he had obtained by pillaging or despoiling [50] other places which, in the course of his missionary campaign he had already conquered for the gospel. The purpose of the metaphor is to emphasize what he has just been saying, namely, that the Corinthians had received the gospel without even having been obliged to make provision for the support of him who had ministered it to them. While, however, they had been quite unencumbered, other churches had contributed towards his "wages". Inevitably this carries the implication that the Corinthian church was in this

---

[49] Ὀφώνιον (ὄψον + ὠνέομαι) = a soldier's "money for buying rations", hence also "rations" or "wages"; cf. Deissmann, *Bible Studies*, p. 266, also Arndt and Gingrich; and see Lk. 3:14 and I Cor. 9:7.

[50] Συλάω = to "pillage" or "plunder"; cf. Vg: *expoliavi*.

respect *indebted* to those other churches that had generously helped to supply Paul's "wages". This overtone (which is reinforced in the next verse by the specific reference to the generosity of the Macedonian Christians) constitutes a harmonic link with what he has previously said about the example set by the churches of Macedonia in the matter of the collection for the poor saints at Jerusalem (8:1ff.). Once again, the "earnestness of others" (8:8) is set before the Corinthians; and in this we may discern another internal strand uniting these last four chapters to those which precede them.

There is, of course, no question of Paul having in any literal sense "robbed" or extorted money from other churches against their will for his own maintenance. The "robbery" consisted of his acceptance of their gifts at a time when he was not actually ministering in their midst, and when, accordingly, he could not expect maintenance from them as of right; from which it is apparent that, while being careful to avoid giving any possible ground for suspicion that his bringing of the gospel to a place was in any way a commercial enterprise on his part, he was not unwilling to accept the unsolicited love-gifts from elsewhere of those who were his children in the gospel, and who in this way were able to share the burden of bringing, or sending, the good news to communities who as yet had not heard it.

In this sense, then, it was possible to speak of his "campaign" in Achaia as having been at least in some measure "financed" by the "spoils" of his earlier victorious campaigns in other places. Nor was this "spoiling" for the purpose of personal indulgence in unnecessary luxuries. "Wages" received were applied by the Apostle simply for the provision of the bare necessities of existence. They were a contribution to the basic rations of a soldier making new conquests in the name of his King.

11:9

> And when I was present with you and was in want, I was not a burden on any man; for the brethren, when they came from Macedonia, supplied the measure of my want; and in everything I kept myself from being burdensome unto you, and so will I keep myself.

The extreme precariousness, humanly speaking, of the Apostle's livelihood is thrown into quite startling relief by this revelation that when he was in Corinth he had actually been in want; he had not, for some while, possessed the wherewithal even for providing the bare necessities of existence. And yet, even so, he had consistently persevered in his determination to accept no remuneration from those to whom he was ministering. The Corinthians had not had to support him like some dead weight on their resources.[51] This, we may be sure, was in strong contrast to his rivals who had subsequently arrived in Corinth, and who, because they lived as parasites on the Christian community, demanding full maintenance and more, had the effect of a numbing weight on the attenuated economy of the church and its members.

But God had not forgotten His servant in the time of his need, for brethren had arrived in Corinth from Macedonia with a gift which made good that which Paul was lacking.[52] The names

---

[51]   The fundamental force of the verb καταναρκάω may be gathered from the uncompounded form ναρκάω which means "to grow numb"; hence our English derivatives narcosis and narcotic (cf. Gen. 32:26, 33 LXX). The rendering of οὐ κατενάρκησα οὐδενός by our English version as "I was not a burden on any man" corresponds to the Latin of Jerome in the Vulgate, nulli onerosus fui. According to Jerome (Epistle to Algasia), καταναρκάω is one of many words used by Paul which he had acquired from the language of his own city (Tarsus) and province (Cilicia) and which was still in common usage amongst the Cilicians in the fourth century. The meaning of οὐ κατενάρκησα ὑμᾶς he gives as non gravavi vos. This throws an interesting and important light on the vocabulary of the New Testament. A word which is rare in Greek literature—καταναρκάω is found only in a couple of passages in Hippocrates and Philodemus—may none the less have been widely used in common speech, so that the literary usage of a word cannot be regarded as a reliable guide to the spoken usage of that word in the living language of a particular period. The numerous rare words and even hapax legomena, therefore, which Paul uses in this epistle should not necessarily be interpreted as a mark of his virtuosity in the Greek language, but should more reasonably lead us to suppose that such words were commonly employed in the language of his day and were accordingly perfectly familiar to his readers, to all of whom, humble as well as educated, it was his desire to speak intelligibly. It is very easy to forget that Greek literature as it has in the main come down to us is but one particularized aspect of the Greek language, and not always the most illuminating aspect at that. This is becoming increasingly evident with the progress of research into the mass of non-literary material of the New Testament era which is now available.

[52]   Προσανεπλήρωσαν means properly "they filled up in addition", the prefix προς signifying something added. This may indicate (which seems likely) that the gift from Macedonia supplemented the amount which Paul

of these brethren are not given since those to whom Paul was writing already knew them. It is by no means improbable that they were Silas and Timothy. These two had accompanied Paul from Asia Minor to Macedonia; Paul had gone on without them from Berea to Athens, where they later rejoined him (Acts 15:40, 16:1ff., 17:14ff.); thence he had travelled on to Corinth, though having first, it seems, sent Silas and Timothy back to Macedonia —the latter, as we know, to establish and strengthen the Thessalonians in the faith (I Thess. 3:1ff.); and subsequently these two brethren had come down from Macedonia and joined the Apostle in Corinth (Acts 18:5; II Cor. 1:19). If they are the brethren intended in our present verse, then we may well suppose that they had brought with them a love-gift from the Macedonian Christians which had served to supplement the meagre and inadequate income from Paul's handicraft of tentmaking. Thus what Paul says here confirms the testimony he has already given to the remarkable generosity of the Macedonian churches in chapter 8. The Philippians in particular seem to have shown unusual liberality in ministering to the Apostle's material needs: even when he was in Thessalonica, that is, still on Macedonian soil, they had sent him gifts on two occasions, and another after his departure southwards from Macedonia (Phil. 4:15ff.); and then ten years later (some years after our present letter was written), so constant was their affection for him, they despatched a further present by the hand of Epaphroditus to Rome, where he was awaiting trial before the emperor (Phil. 4:18).

Not only had Paul kept himself from being burdensome to the Corinthians in the past, but it was his firm determination to continue to do so during future visits to them, convinced as he was of the importance for himself, in the special circumstances of his pioneering task, of remaining financially independent of those to whom he was ministering spiritual things.

Calvin, surprisingly, seems to have misunderstood the thrust of the Apostle's argument at this point. Paul is not reproaching the Corinthians for not having contributed towards his subsistence when he was with them, as though the poorer Macedonians by their gift had put them to shame. "Ah, how few

---

had been able to earn with his own hands, or that it was a gift additional to one or more previous gifts from the same source.

'Macedonians' there are in the present day", exclaims the
Reformer, "and on the other hand how many 'Corinthians' you
may find everywhere!" Chrysostom, too, treats this verse as an
accusation against the Corinthians: "Great the excess, of the
one in negligence, of the other in zeal!" he says; "for these sent
to him even when at a great distance, and those did not even
support him when amongst them". But the whole point is that
when ministering in Corinth Paul, in accordance with his pre-
determined course of conduct, refused to allow the Corinthians
to contribute to his material requirements, though, as the next
two verses suggest (see below), they had in fact wished to do so.
The explanation of his independence is offered not as a rebuke
to the Christians at Corinth but as a rebuttal of the calumnies
which were being spread abroad by his enemies.

11 : 10, 11

As the truth of Christ is in me, no man shall stop me of this
glorying in the regions of Achaia. Wherefore? because I
love you not? God knoweth.

The Apostle's declaration here should perhaps be described
as an asseveration rather than as an oath. The literal rendering
of his words is: "The truth of Christ is in me (when I say) that ..."
(cf. Rom. 9:1). As it is his great mission in life to propagate the
truth of Christ, so it is essential that his own language and conduct
should be in conformity with the example of absolute truthfulness
set by Christ. His glorying is in the resolution to ensure that the
gospel, which he had received at no cost to himself and which
he was under obligation of debt to proclaim to others, should
be ministered by him to others without cost. This glorying he
will not permit to be blocked or stifled.[53] It is not difficult to
infer that Paul's rivals in Achaia criticized this practice of his
because, in fact, it put them at a disadvantage. Their "gospel"
provided them with an income, a livelihood; and that, compared

---

[53] Literally: "This glorying shall not be stopped as far as I am concerned"
(εἰς ἐμέ). Plummer proposes to understand the metaphor implicit in φραγήσεται
of the blocking or barricading of a road (cf. Hos. 2:6, Lam. 3:9, LXX)
in preference to Chrysostom's application of it to the damming of a river
(cf. Prov. 25:26, Judith 16:3, LXX). Elsewhere in the New Testament it is
used of mouths being stopped (Rom. 3:19, Heb. 11:33). In each case the
central idea is that of blockage.

with Paul's obvious and utter disinterestedness, cast the shadow of suspicion on their motives. And so they fabricated the further despicable calumny that Paul's independence, his refusal to accept the gifts offered by the Corinthians, was an indication that he was lacking in love for them. They twisted his disinterestedness into unconcern. It was, they said or whispered, the symptom of a cold heart and indicated a haughty and loveless spirit of detachment.

There were no depths to which these intruders were unwilling to descend in order to alienate the Apostle from his dearly loved children in the gospel. Hence Paul's question here: "Wherefore? because I love you not?" and his protestation: "God knoweth!" It is a real cry from the heart. Words and explanations and justifications are out of place when the relationship of love involved is that between a father and his children. Before God both he and they need no persuasion that this accusation is a cruel and damnable falsehood. No man on earth had a warmer and more devoted heart than the Apostle Paul. Love was the impulse of his whole life and ministry as Christ's Apostle. And so he leaves this shocking and monstrous insinuation that he has no love for them to the judgment of God, who knows and will vindicate the truth. And in doing so he also leaves it to their consciences.

11 : 12

> But what I do, that I will do, that I may cut off occasion from them that desire an occasion; that wherein they glory, they may be found even as we.

The proper force of this verse is not clear from our English version. Paul's words may be rendered in the following way: "But what it is my practice to do (namely, to refuse remuneration from those to whom I am ministering) that I will also continue to do, in order that I may remove the opportunity from those that desire an opportunity for being found on a level with me in the work in which they boast". In other words, it is the aim of Paul's rivals in Corinth to bring him on to an equality with themselves by inducing him, in one way or another, to accept remuneration for his ministry. Thus one of the more obvious disadvantages under which they laboured would be removed.

Paul, however, is not deceived by their devices, and is more determined than ever to maintain his practice of independence, for the additional reason now that thereby he will deprive these impostors of the occasion they seek for the removal of the inequality which is apparent between his and their practice in this respect. It was, of course, open to them to bring about an equality by following Paul's example and refusing to accept any kind of payment for their services; but this, it is evident, was a method which could not commend itself to minds as mercenary and insincere as theirs.

Other interpretations of this verse are based upon what is, in our judgment, a misunderstanding of the syntax, whereby Paul is made to say: "I shall continue my practice of financial independence ... in order that they may be found even as we in the thing in which they glory". That is to give the verse a sense exactly the opposite of that which we have proposed above; namely, it is he (not his rivals) who wishes an equality to be established between himself and them. The reasons assigned to the Apostle for this alleged desire for equality with his rivals may be summarized under two alternative headings: *either* (i) that these rivals themselves gave their services gratuitously and wished to engineer matters in such a way that Paul should accept payment for his ministrations, so that thereby they might score an advantage over him; Paul, however, is determined to remain on a level with them in this and not to let them steal a march on him (Chrysostom, Theophylact, Calvin, Grotius, etc.); *or* (ii) that by his example of disinterestedness Paul hoped to shame his opponents, who outwardly boasted pecuniary independence ("that wherein they glory") but in reality were leading a parasitic existence, into the abandonment of their mercenary outlook and thus, as it were, to raise them to his own level of genuine independence (Theodoret, Aquinas, Meyer, etc.). These explanations, however, scarcely suit the context, whereas that which we have proposed (in company with Tasker, Allo, Plummer, Lietzmann, and others) gives excellent sense which is at the same time appropriate to the context. Paul's boasting (and it must be remembered that he has asked the Corinthians to bear with him in a little "foolishness"—verse 1) is that he preached the gospel to them at no charge (vv. 7 to 10), whereas, by way of contrast, one feature of the boasting of his opponents ("that wherein they glory") is that their acceptance of remuneration is a sign of their apostleship (see commentary on v. 7 above). Yet the contrast is an uncomfortable one for them, and so they desire an occasion for inducing Paul to abandon his custom and to accept payment as they do, so that the disadvantage forced upon them by the present contrast may be removed.[54]

11 : 13

For such men are false apostles, deceitful workers, fashioning themselves into apostles of Christ.

The moment has come for Paul to drop the veil of irony and to speak in the plainest possible terms in denunciation of these would-be "super-apostles" who have invaded his territory in Achaia. Men of this sort are in fact *false* apostles, impostors whose aim is to usurp the apostolic authority. They are like those who, at a later date, set themselves up in Ephesus and called themselves apostles, but were not, and were found to be false (Rev. 2:2). They perform their destructive work with deceit, treachery, and cunning,[55] similar to the "vain talkers and deceivers, specially they of the circumcision, ... men who overthrow whole houses, teaching things which they ought not, for filthy lucre's sake", against whom Paul warned Titus (Titus

---

[54] In effect, the interpretation of this verse depends on whether the second ἵνα clause is dependent, like the first, on ποιήσω or on the immediately preceding τῶν θελόντων ἀφορμήν. If the former, then some interpretation such as we have rejected above becomes necessary, for Paul is then saying: "I will continue my policy of independence, in order that I may cut off occasion from those who desire occasion, so that (I may bring it about that) they may be found even as I in the thing in which they glory". This interpretation, however, leaves ἀφορμήν adrift as an undefined term, and is also exegetically unsuited to the context. There can be little doubt that the second ἵνα clause is not in series with the first but is dependent on τῶν θελόντων ἀφορμήν. Paul is then saying: "I will continue my policy of independence, in order that I may cut off occasion from those who desire an occasion for (the purpose of) being found even as I in the thing in which they glory". This is an altogether natural way of taking the Greek, it defines the term ἀφορμήν adequately, and it gives a sense which is excellently suited to the context. 'Ἀφορμή, incidentally, is yet another military term meaning properly a base for the launching of operations, and thence a point of departure, "springboard", occasion, opportunity, or pretext.

[55] All these ideas are implicit in the adjective δόλιος, which is *hapax legomenon* in the New Testament.

1:10f.), and to those who were causers of division and strife in
the church at Rome, contrary to the apostolic teaching, and
who are described by Paul as men who "serve not our Lord Jesus
Christ, but their own belly", and who "by their smooth and fair
speech ... beguile the hearts of the innocent" (Rom. 16:17f.).

For the purpose of achieving their subversive ends these
intruders even assume the guise of apostles of Christ. They pose
as something which they are not,[56] and in doing so they deceive
those who through gullibility or inexperience are more ready to
give credence to plausible impostors than to remember the sound
teaching and the warnings of him who is their true apostle. If
this was the case in the primitive New Testament Church it is
no less so in our own day when we see the Church split into
fragments by sectarianism and when an individual has only to
make the most preposterous claims for himself in order to gain
an enthusiastic and undiscerning following. In every age the
Church is under urgent necessity to be proof against false apostles
by remembering and holding fast to the doctrine of those who
are Christ's true apostles—that doctrine, in a word, which we
possess in the writings of the New Testament.

11 : 14, 15

> And no marvel; for even Satan fashioneth himself into an
> angel of light. It is no great thing therefore if his ministers
> also fashion themselves as ministers of righteousness; whose
> end shall be according to their works.

In view of the fact that it is the custom of Satan to masquerade
as an angel of light [57] there is little cause for surprise that his

---

[56] Μετασχηματίζειν means "to transform", as in Phil. 3:21 where Paul
uses it to describe the transformation of our present bodies into the likeness
of Christ's glorified body. In I Cor. 4:6 the verb is used in a special sense of
transferring the application of a particular point by a figure or device of speech.
In the middle voice, as here, it means to disguise oneself, to change one's
appearance, to masquerade as someone else, while one's true nature remains
unaltered. So also in the next verse which speaks of Satan changing his
appearance into that of an angel of light. (Cf. Arndt and Gingrich.) These
are the only occasions on which the verb occurs in the New Testament.

[57] Regarding Paul's mention of Satan disguising himself as an angel of
light, Allo's comment is to the point. This, he says, "has been taken as an
allusion to some pagan theophany (Schmiedel), or to the histories of Satan
in the Haggadah (such as the *Vita Adami*, 9, and the *Apocalypse of Moses*,

ministers should disguise themselves as ministers of righteousness. They are doing no more than following their master's deceitful example. According to our Lord Himself, Satan is the father of all lying and there is no truth in him (Jn. 8:44). So far indeed is he from being an angel of light that it is darkness which is his proper sphere (cf. Lk. 22:53; Eph. 6:12; Col. 1:13). To turn from the power of Satan unto God is to turn from darkness to light (Acts 26:18), as Paul himself learnt on that memorable day of his conversion when his encounter with the risen and glorified Saviour surrounded him with a heavenly light above the brightness of the midday sun (Acts 26:13). He knows at first hand what he is talking about, for it was then that he ceased to be a minister of Satan and became the apostle of Jesus Christ. God, in direct antithesis to Satan, "is light, and in Him is no darkness at all" (I Jn. 1:5). It is His recreative Word that dispels the darkness and causes the light of salvation to shine in our hearts (4:6), for light can have no communion with darkness (6:14).

Nothing could be more incongruous, therefore, than for Satan to pose as an angel of light; but he can do so only by falsehood, that is by the contradiction of God's Word, as he has done from the beginning, and by his lies he murders the souls of men. Thus in denying the truth of the Word of God and promising life to the sinner (Gen. 3:4, "Ye shall not surely die") he was both a liar and a murderer, for the seed of unbelief and disobedience which he sowed in the heart of man was also and inevitably the seed of death. Death follows on sin as inexorably as darkness follows the setting of the sun (cf. Jn. 8:44; Rom. 5:16, 6:23; Jas. 1:15; Eph. 2:1, 5).

It is not unlikely that in speaking of their pose as "ministers

---

17, v. Strack-Billerbeck). Syncretists like Windisch and others would readily believe this; but, as Plummer, Bachmann, and others rightly observe, there is no need to suppose that Paul is referring to any particular legend or history; his experience as an apostle, gained at Corinth and elsewhere, was sufficient for him to become acquainted with the customary practices of the Enemy". Bengel (together with others) draws attention to the present tense of the verb, μετασχηματίζεται—"Praesens: i.e. solet se transformare".

The descriptive genitive in the expression ἄγγελος φωτός may be due to Semitic influence. Thus Moule (*Idiom Book*, p. 175) suggests that here "ἄγγελον φωτός perhaps = ἄγγελον φωτεινόν". Arndt and Gingrich interpret it as meaning "an angel (from the kingdom) of light" (*sub μετασχηματίζω*).

of righteousness" Paul is obliquely alluding to the judaistic emphasis in the teaching of the false apostles at Corinth. As many places in the epistles of Paul show, such judaizers constituted a serious threat to true Christianity in the primitive Church. He himself had been, prior to his conversion, a zealous advocate of that righteousness which is according to the works of the law; but his conversion had meant precisely the renunciation of any claim to a meritorious righteousness of his own and the appropriation, through faith in Christ, of the righteousness which is of God (Phil. 3:6, 9). Thus he had proclaimed to his audience in Pisidian Antioch that by Christ "every one that believeth is justified from all things, from which ye could not be justified by the law of Moses" (Acts 13:39). "If righteousness is through the law, then Christ died for nought", he admonishes the Galatians (Gal. 2:21). The Jews, he tells the Romans, "being ignorant of God's righteousness, and seeking to establish their own, did not subject themselves to the righteousness of God" (Rom. 10:3)— an observation which may be said to be applicable also to the judaizers who troubled the Church with their distortion of the doctrine of grace. And so the Corinthians were reminded by him that it is in Christ alone, thanks to His having been made sin for us, that we may become the righteousness of God (5:21 above; cf. I Cor. 1:30). Paul, indeed, is their genuine minister of righteousness, not these intruders who are impostors and perverters of the saving grace of the gospel.

Concerning these false apostles, he adds that their "end shall be according to their works". It is characteristic of Paul to comment in this way of the ultimate destiny of those who wilfully oppose or pervert the gospel of Jesus Christ. Thus in Phil. 3:18f. he speaks of "enemies of the cross of Christ, whose end is perdition"; in Rom. 3:8 of misrepresenters of his teaching, "whose condemnation is just"; and in II Tim. 4:14 he says of Alexander the coppersmith who did him much evil: "the Lord will render to him according to his works" (cf. also Rom. 6:21; II Thess. 1:8f.).

With Hodge's observation that God, whose judgments are according to the truth, "does not pass sentence ... on the mask, but on the man", and that "the end, i.e. the recompense of every man, shall not be according to his professions, not according to his own convictions or judgment of his character or conduct, not according to appearances or the estimate of men, but according to his works", we are of course in complete agreement (cf. Mt. 16:27; Rom. 2:6); but we cannot help suspecting a *double entendre* in the terminology which the Apostle uses here—a satirical innuendo, suggesting that these intruders, who vaunt themselves as "ministers of righteousness" and lay such emphasis on the necessity of "works" at the expense of free grace, will, as though by a kind of poetic justice, meet with an end "in accordance with their works". As they sow works, they will not fail to reap works!

11 : 16

I say again, Let no man think me foolish; but if ye do, yet as foolish receive me, that I also may glory a little.

Paul now resumes the theme which was introduced at the beginning of this chapter, that, namely, of his indulgence in the foolishness of boasting; but he requests that no one should conclude that he is in fact foolish, that is, ordinarily given to the folly of self-commendation. If, however, some among them insist on misjudging him, he at least has a right to expect that, since they have given a welcome to those foolish boasters who have invaded his territory in Corinth, they will receive him *also* as he engages in the foolishness of boasting for a short while. He is not asking of them any favour which they have not already accorded to the intruding false apostles. As he has explained, any glorying in which he indulges is not for his own sake, but for theirs, and for the sake of the purity of the gospel in their midst (vv. 2f.). The whole tenor of his language here, his obvious embarrassment in broaching such a subject, conveys the impression more powerfully than a mere disclaimer could do that to speak of himself, who he is and what he has done and endured, is something thoroughly distasteful to him. It does not come naturally to the man who has denied self and whose whole being is now taken up with the person and work of Christ. Nothing, in fact, could be more uncongenial to him. And so his very awkwardness here, as, in order to prick the balloon of these self-inflated deceivers who are undoing the work of the gospel in Corinth, he faces the necessity of commending himself in some measure, speaks volumes for his own genuine humility and sincerity.

11 : 17, 18

That which I speak, I speak not after the Lord, but as in foolishness, in this confidence of glorying. Seeing that many glory after the flesh, I will glory also.

The reason for Paul's embarrassment at this juncture is now given: self-commendation is not "after the Lord" but, the exact opposite, "after the flesh",[58] that is, typical of the old unregenerate nature whose values are dictated by the external, self-centred standards of this fallen world. It is most unlike Christ who has set us the supreme example of humility and self-abnegation (cf. Phil. 2:5ff.). To boast is a mark of folly, for the Christian has nothing which he has not received (I Cor. 4:7) and in the flesh "dwelleth no good thing" (Rom. 7:18). Paul, moreover, is one of those who "glory in Christ Jesus and have no confidence in the flesh" (Phil. 3:3). "Far be it from me to glory", he says to the Galatians, "save in the cross of our Lord Jesus Christ, through which the world hath been crucified unto me, and I unto the world" (Gal. 6:14). Paul, then, is no praiser of himself, and if he now speaks about himself it is not because of any love of worldly praise, but in the interests of the sacred cause to which he is committed. His object is not to draw attention to himself but to safeguard the gospel of which he is a minister by God's appointment. His *purpose*, therefore, is according to the Lord, though the utterance of self-praise for its own sake is not. "By itself indeed it is not 'after the Lord'", says Chrysostom, "but by the intention it becomes so. And therefore he said, 'that which I speak', not accusing the motive, but the words; since his aim is so admirable as to dignify the words also". Thus Paul is not really succumbing to the foolishness and vanity of self-esteem. Any appearance to the contrary remains only an appearance— he speaks "as in foolishness", not actually in it. Heart and conscience are not compromised.

When Paul says "I speak not after the Lord" the question of inspiration is not involved. The reference, as we have seen, is to the folly of self-laudation as being incompatible with the Lord's example of humility (cf. 10:1), not to the question of the fallibility or otherwise of his utterance. Therefore it is a

---

[58] *Κατὰ τὴν σάρκα.* See commentary on 5:16 above.

mistake, on the one hand, to suggest that the Apostle is at this point claiming to be uninspired, and, on the other hand, to decide that his inspiration is in need of defence. Plummer, for instance, who explains this clause by saying that Paul "does not claim Divine authority" for what he is now doing, that "it is not official", and that the meaning is that "it is the man rather than the Apostle who is speaking", has, in our judgment, missed the point. Moffatt, also, betrays the same misunderstanding when he renders it: "What I am now going to say is not inspired by the Lord". The expression "after the Lord" is equivalent in force to "after Christ" in Col. 2:8, "according to Christ Jesus" in Rom. 15:5, and "after God" in Eph. 4:24, and, as Sanday and Headlam point out, means "in accordance with the character or example of Christ".[59]

On the human level, Paul is not going to do any more than many others are doing—in reality, considerably less, for it is only *a little* boasting in which he proposes to indulge (vv. 1 and 16). Moreover, it is clear, as Tasker observes, "that Paul is going to meet his opponents on their own ground, and that the word *also* must be taken to imply 'after the flesh, as they do'".[60]

11 : 19, 20

For ye bear with the foolish gladly, being wise yourselves. For ye bear with a man, if he bringeth you into bondage, if he devoureth you, if he taketh you captive, if he exalteth himself, if he smiteth you on the face.

The situation of Corinth is full of irony. Paul has already asked the Corinthians to bear with him in a little foolishness, the foolishness, that is, of self-commendation (v. 1), and he has reminded them of the humiliation and indigence which, in stark contrast to the "super-apostles" who turned up after his departure, he endured as the result of his decision not to accept any

---

[59] Sanday and Headlam, *Commentary on Paul's Epistle to the Romans* (ICC, London, 1907), p. 396.

[60] 'Υπόστασις, verse 17, should be rendered "confidence", as in our version, its usage here being similar to that in 9:4. This opinion has the support of Allo, Lietzmann, Plummer, Alford, Calvin, etc. The term may also, however, be assigned the meaning of "subject" or "matter", and this sense is favoured here by Moffatt ("this business of boasting"), Bachmann, Olshausen, Erasmus (*argumentum*), and the Vulgate (*substantia*).

payment for his ministerial labours (vv. 5ff.). Now he points out that they, or at any rate some among them, have in fact shown themselves remarkably tolerant to the foolish (that is, the boastful false apostles) in the way they have submitted not only to the boasting but even to the depredations of these parasitical intruders who have battened on their community. "You, being men of good sense, bear quite happily with senseless persons",[61] he says, intending it not as a gibe but as a goad to them to shake themselves free from the tyranny of these impostors. An onlooker might almost have thought that the Corinthians in question were displaying, by their tolerance of this imposition, something of the impassive sagacity advocated by their own Stoic philosophers.[62]

Paul adds five examples of what it means to tolerate indignities imposed by someone else, as though by way of illustration ("for ye bear with a man if he bringeth you into bondage, etc."). But he is not speaking hypothetically, for the implication is so plain as to be almost explicit: he is describing what actually has been happening at Corinth. His indirect way of saying it is yet another indication of his constant consideration and affection for those to whom he had brought the gospel. It grieved him deeply to see them reduced by these intruders to a pitiable state of subjection.

(i) They were being brought into a state of utter bondage,[63] possibly to the ceremonial law of Judaism, as also happened in the Galatian church (Gal. 2:4, etc.); or it may be that an ascendancy over their souls is intended (cf. Moffatt's rendering: "assumes control of your souls"). Whatever the Apostle is alluding to, those over whom these ministers of Satan had established a supremacy had forfeited their Christian liberty. Well might he have written to them the words which before long he was to write to the Galatians: "For freedom did Christ set us free: stand fast therefore, and be not entangled again in a yoke of bondage" (Gal. 5:1).

---

[61] Φρόνιμος and ἄφρων were naturally employed as opposites; cf., for example, Plato, Soph. 247A.

[62] Zeno, the founder of the Stoic school, regarded φρόνησις, practical wisdom, as the source and sum of all the virtues.

[63] Καταδουλόω is an intensive compound; cf. Gal. 2:4

(ii) They were being swallowed up,[64] in the sense that the intruding "super-apostles" were living on them like parasites and growing fat at their expense, serving "not our Lord Christ, but their own belly" (Rom. 16:18; cf. Phil. 3:19). Thus Christ denounced the scribes as men "who devour [65] widows' houses". (iii) They were being taken captive, that is, ensnared in the trap laid for them by these interlopers. They had become their dupes. Indeed, 12:16, "I caught you"[66], would suggest that Paul, as a fisher of men (cf. Mk. 1:17), was their true and original "captor" and that they were accordingly a quite illegitimate "catch" for these false apostles.

(iv) They had stood by, as it were, and watched these impostors exalt themselves to a position of authority to which they held no title and from which they sought, like earthly potentates, to lord it over the Corinthian flock (cf. Mk. 10:42ff.; I Pet. 5:3). Light is thrown on Paul's meaning here by what he has already said, in 10:5, about "every high thing that is exalted [67] against the knowledge of God". The exaltation of these upstart "apostles" is essentially *self*-exaltation, carnal and worldly in character, though speciously disguised by a cloak of sanctimony.

(v) Members of the Corinthian church had even allowed themselves to be struck in the face. This may be meant in a figurative or metaphorical sense of enduring gross affronts from the lips of these overbearing intruders; and many commentators interpret it in this way. But it is more probable that Paul is alluding to instances of actual physical assault. It was not uncommon at that time for those who held positions of ecclesiastical authority to strike, or cause to be struck, on the mouth any whom they considered to be uttering impiety. Thus the high priest Ananias had commanded Paul to be struck (Acts 23:2; cf. I Cor. 4:11); and Paul had felt it necessary to enjoin that a man exercising the authority of a bishop should not be a striker (I Tim. 3:3; Titus 1:7). To submit to violence without thoughts of vengeance is, it is true, a mark of the Christian man, as our Lord Himself taught: "Resist not him that is evil; but whosoever smiteth thee

---

[64] *Κατεσθίειν* is another intensive compound. For examples of its use in the papyri see Moulton and Milligan.

[65] Οἱ *κατεσθίοντες*, Mt. 12:40 = Lk. 20:47, οἱ *κατεσθίουσι*.

[66] Ὑμᾶς ἔλαβον. Cf. εἴ τις λαμβάνει here.

[67] Ἐπαιρόμενον. Cf. ἐπαίρεται here.

on thy right cheek, turn to him the other also" (Mt. 5:39; cf. I Pet. 2:19f.). But the fault of the Corinthians was that they had accepted this indignity as though coming from men of apostolic authority, without discerning how utterly incongruous it was with the true spirit of Christ and His apostles, and thereby dishonouring Paul, whom in their hearts they knew to be Christ's genuine apostle, and the gospel which he had preached to them.

As we look back over nineteen centuries of the history of the Christian Church, we cannot help being struck by the manner in which for most of the time so many of its adherents seem to have been content lamely to tolerate the impositions and extortions of ecclesiastical despots whose lives are a contradiction of the meekness and gentleness of Christ and whose concern has been less for the souls of the perishing than for the buttressing of their own reputation in the eyes of the world. The Reformation of the sixteenth century was a breaking away from this dark spirit of tyranny and the recovery, through returning to the pure doctrine of the New Testament, of that liberty in the gospel which is the birthright of every Christian man.

11:21a

I speak by way of disparagement, as though we had been weak.

At this point Paul's satire reaches its peak: "I confess to my shame that I (when compared with these 'super-apostles')[68] have been weak". His rivals in Corinth had been saying that his presence when in Corinth was characterized by weakness (cf. 10:10), thereby, no doubt, wishing not only to disparage him, but also to justify the harshness of their own régime. To this Paul now offers the effective rejoinder that if tyranny, greed, falsity, arrogance, and violence are the marks of true Christian oversight, then he must admit shamefacedly that as an apostle

---

[68] The ἡμεῖς is emphatic and introduces a note of contrast. On the usage of ὡς ὅτι see note on 5:19 above. Its force here is either a plain "that", the ὡς being redundant, or "as people have been saying, that", in which case the sentence could be expanded as follows: "I confess to my shame that it is true (as people have been saying) that I have taken a weak line (when compared with these 'super-apostles')". The rendering of ὡς ὅτι by "as though" (our version and AV, and also Vg: *quasi*) does not seem to be justifiable.

to Corinth he has indeed been a failure and a weakling (cf. 1:24).[69]

The irony of this brief statement can hardly have failed to produce a profound effect in the feelings of the Corinthians as they remembered the time of Paul's ministry in their midst and contrasted his spirit with that of the men who had subsequently descended on them making such extravagant claims for themselves. With what contrite hearts they must have read all that he is now about to say, by way of reminder, concerning himself, realizing that, thanks to their tolerance of these impostors, it had become necessary for him, their own apostle and father in the gospel, to authenticate himself to them with such evident embarrassment!

11:21b

> Yet whereinsoever any is bold (I speak in foolishness), I am bold also.

The moment has come for Paul to speak out boldly in authentication of his apostleship, though still, as he is careful to remind the Corinthians yet again, speaking in "foolishness". But the comparison of himself with these false apostles has been forced upon him because of their deceitful calumnies and because of the toleration of these usurpers in the Corinthian church. Indeed, Paul has a record second to none in the service of Christ, allied to the testimony of a clear conscience (1:12), and consequently he has nothing to fear from comparison with any man. Not that he is entering into a boasting contest with his opponents merely for the sake of vindicating himself and routing them. That would have been the greatest worldly folly; for, as Paul incessantly preached, it is *before God* that we must be justified, not before men. And Christ, not self, was the concern of Paul the Apostle. No, it is for the Corinthians' sakes that he is now going to match boldness with boldness, so that, acknowledging afresh what they have been tempted to forget, namely, that he is their true gospeller, they may reject the false apostles and their

---

[69] Had κατὰ ἀτιμίαν λέγω here been intended as equivalent to πρὸς ἐντροπὴν ὑμῖν λέγω or πρὸς ἐντροπὴν ὑμῖν λαλῶ in I Cor. 6:5 and 15:34 respectively, we would, as Plummer says, have expected the addition of ὑμῶν after ἀτιμίαν. Our own version (ASV) of this sentence is singularly unenlightening.

teachings and abide in the pure Christian truth in which they had been so earnestly instructed by him, and also that he may have the joy of presenting them as a pure virgin to Christ, their only Bridegroom (v. 2).

11 : 22

Are they Hebrews? so am I.   Are they Israelites? so am I. Are they the seed of Abraham? so am I.

It is apparent from these three rhetorical questions that the false apostles who had invaded the Corinthian church were not Gentiles, but men who prided themselves and traded on their pure Hebrew stock.   There can be little doubt that they intended this particular aspect of their self-commendation to reflect adversely on Paul and presented it in such a way as to call into suspicion his own origins.   They came from Jerusalem, the very heart of Jewry, but he was born at Tarsus in the "foreign" territory of Cilicia.   Was it really credible that pure Hebrew blood ran in his veins? (cf. Acts 21:39, 22:3).   Was it not likely that he was an impostor, claiming what he did not possess?   In this respect it is of interest to find that the first-century Ebionites asserted categorically that Paul was in fact a Gentile by birth.[70] The truth was, of course, that the Apostle to the Gentiles was a Jew to the very last fibre of his being—born of unmixed Jewish ancestry, brought up in Jerusalem at the feet of Gamaliel, the most famous of Jewish rabbis, and, prior to his conversion, a fanatical nationalist, who lived as a Pharisee according to the strictest of the Jewish sects (Acts 22:3ff., 26:4f.).   His pedigree was unimpeachable: "circumcised the eighth day, of the stock of Israel, of the tribe of Benjamin, a Hebrew of the Hebrews; as touching the law, a Pharisee; as touching zeal, persecuting the Church; as touching the righteousness which is in the law, found blameless" (Phil. 3:5f.).

To Paul it was something thrilling to be in the midstream of God's age-old purposes for the whole of mankind through the chosen people of Israel, "whose is the adoption, and the glory, and the covenants, and the giving of the law, and the service of God, and the promises; whose are the fathers, and of whom is Christ concerning the flesh" (Rom. 9:4f.).   His deep affection

---

[70]   See Epiphanius *Haer.*, XXX, 16.

and fellow-feeling for his own people, who as a nation had rejected Jesus their long promised Messiah and Saviour, is nowhere more movingly displayed than in his confession: "I say the truth in Christ, I lie not, my conscience bearing witness with me in the Holy Ghost, that I have great sorrow and unceasing pain in my heart; for I could wish that I myself were anathema from Christ for my brethren's sake, my kinsmen according to the flesh" (Rom. 9:1–3). Paul himself, who formerly as a Pharisee had laid waste the Church of Christ (Acts 8:3) and who had been a blasphemer and a persecutor and injurious (I Tim. 1:13), now belonged to the "remnant according to the election of grace" (Rom. 11:5), "the Israel of God" (Gal. 6:16), which comprises Gentiles as well as Jews (Gal. 3:28; cf. Rom. 9:6). But he did not for that reason seek to renounce or cover up his origins, even though he no longer knew any man, not even himself, after the flesh (5:16), and even though these very things which previously had been gain to him he now counted loss for Christ (Phil. 3:4–8); for no man was more conscious than Paul of the unfolding of God's sovereign purposes not only in individual lives and situations, but throughout the whole range of human history, from its first beginnings to its ultimate end, purposes which in their redemptive scope were particularly bound up with the covenant of universal grace committed to his forebears of the elect nation.

The fleshly boasting of his adversaries in Corinth he could match, and more than match, giving glory only to the grace of God (I Cor. 15:10), because of the profound spiritual significance which his ancestry held for him. No less than they, he was a pure Hebrew by nationality, a member of the theocracy of Israel, and a descendant of Abraham. But to rely on these external associations, as he had once done, as though by a sort of *opus operatum* they by themselves ensured the promised blessings to which they pointed, was nothing other than confidence in the flesh (cf. Phil. 3:3ff.). It was to shut the door on grace. Precisely this same boast led the Pharisees, who proudly and complacently claimed that Abraham, and *ipso facto* God, was their father, to mock our Lord, because of the unusual circumstances of His birth, with the scornful taunt that He had been born of fornication, thereby implying that He was beyond the scope of God's favour. To this our Lord sternly replied that they, by their addiction to falsehood and hatred, showed that the fatherhood under which they really stood was that of the devil (Jn. 8:39ff.). In rejecting Jesus they were rejecting Him who is uniquely The Seed of Abraham (Gal. 3:16), in whom all the promises of God receive their clinching affirmation (1:20), and through union with whom alone the blessings of the Abrahamic covenant may be appropriated (Gal. 3:7ff., 26ff.). As Denney comments, "there was not an Israelite in the world prouder of his birth, with a more magnificent sense of his country's glories, than the Apostle of the Gentiles: and it provoked him beyond endurance to see the things in which he gloried debased, as they were debased, by his rivals—made the symbols of a paltry vanity which he despised, made barriers to the universal love of God by which all the families of the earth were to be blessed".

11:23

> Are they ministers of Christ? (I speak as one beside himself) I more; in labours more abundantly, in prisons more abundantly, in stripes above measure, in deaths oft.

Paul is not in reality conceding the claim of his opponents to be ministers of Christ, except by way of argument, so that by a comparison of his ministry with theirs it may be clear beyond all doubt how worthless is their pretension to this calling. He has already expressed his judgment of them in no uncertain terms: they are false apostles, impostors, ministers not of Christ but of Satan (vv. 13, 15). What, indeed, do they know of the fellowship of Christ's sufferings, these deceivers whose skin is so precious to them? What experience have they had of apostolic labours, imprisonments, beatings, and the rest? What it really means to be a minister of Christ is something entirely beyond the range of their awareness. Equality with the Apostle there might be in the matter of nationality and lineage; but that is as far as any equality goes. Here Paul moves into a different category. Where the ministry is concerned, his is something beyond their horizon.[71]

---

[71] Ὑπὲρ ἐγώ is the only instance of the adverbial use of ὑπέρ in the New Testament (cf. J. H. Moulton, *Grammar*, Vol. II, p. 326; Moule, *Idiom Book*, p. 64). The force of ὑπέρ (=Latin *super*) is superlative rather than comparative. Thus the meaning of ὑπέρ ἐγώ here is not fully conveyed by the rendering "I more". Paul is saying that as a minister of Christ he surpasses the pseudo-apostles altogether, he is beyond their range. Accordingly it is best to give

Again the Apostle feels it necessary to remind his readers that for a minister of Christ to speak in this way of what he has done and endured is madness. It is, on the face of it, incompatible with the meekness and humility of Christ (10:1), and the servant must be as his Master (cf. Lk. 6:40; Mt. 10:24f.; Jn. 15:20). And yet Paul is not in fact magnifying self in the passage which is now beginning—in this, too, there is complete disparity between himself and his adversaries—but he is magnifying, as he does throughout this epistle, the amazing grace of God which in the midst of afflictions and sufferings is sufficient for his every need. This is the climax towards which he is building up. The only thing of self which he in reality magnifies is his utter weakness and insufficiency (12:9f.). Thus all the glory belongs to the Lord and to the triumph of His grace.

As practically every commentator points out, the catalogue of Paul's sufferings which commences at this point (vv. 23 to 33) contains the mention of many experiences which are not recorded in the Acts of the Apostles, and therefore serves to remind us of how little we really know of the biographical details of his apostolic ministry. The book of the Acts, indeed, was not written for the purpose of recounting the lives and achievements of men, albeit apostles, but in order to draw attention to the sovereign activity of God the Holy Spirit in the founding and expansion of the Christian Church. On the other hand, there are incidents and experiences related in the Acts of the Apostles which do not find a place here. This catalogue, therefore, is not

---

the repeated περισσοτέρως a superlative force, remembering that in Hellenistic Greek there is a tendency for superlative forms to disappear. The Vulgate in fact translates the first περισσοτέρως by the superlative *plurimis*, but, with surprising inconsistency, the second by the comparative *abundantius*. See the notes on περισσοτέρως in 2:4 and 7:15 above. "We must not assume", says Plummer, "that the comparative adverb necessarily implies comparison *with his opponents* . . . It is possible that after ὑπὲρ ἐγώ they are altogether banished from consideration, and that περισσοτέρως means 'very abundantly' ".

Some have suggested that ὑπὲρ ἐγώ implies "I am something more than a minister of Christ", and therefore something more than those who claim to be ministers of Christ. But that the explanation which we have offered (and which has the support of the majority of commentators) is the right one "is clear from what follows, and because in Paul's language and estimation there was no higher title or service than that of ministers of Christ" (Hodge). Cf. Allo: "Paul certainly did not imagine that there was a title higher than minister of Christ' ".

exhaustive. It has all the marks of spontaneity. But it is quite definitely not incidental, nor is it competitive (though it is true that the way of hardship was not the way of his rivals); for suffering was an integral and authenticating aspect of Paul's apostolic ministry, and had been from the very first. Thus even at his conversion the Lord said to Ananias: "I will show him how many things he must suffer for My name's sake" (Acts 9:16), and in the year following the writing of this epistle Paul tells the elders from Ephesus: "The Holy Ghost testifieth unto me in every city, saying that bonds and afflictions abide me" (Acts 20:23). This section, moreover, provides a close link with the earlier part of the epistle, especially 4:7–12 and 6:4–10, thereby affording further evidence of the unity of II Corinthians. In fact, in 6:4ff. stripes, imprisonments, tumults, labours, watchings, and fastings are listed as things by which Paul was able to commend himself as a minister of God—the very things which he mentions in our present passage in authentication of himself as a minister of Christ.

Of Paul's abundant labours as Christ's minister it is unnecessary to speak here. No man in the history of the Christian Church has been more unflagging in evangelical toil and zeal. Of his imprisonments, five are recorded in the book of Acts: at Philippi (Acts 16:23), Jerusalem (Acts 22:29f., 23:10ff.), Caesarea (Acts 23:35, 24:23, 25:4, 26:32), and twice at Rome (Acts 28:16ff.; II Tim. 1:8). Of these, only the first had taken place when he was writing this epistle. This means that, prior to the composition of II Corinthians, he must have experienced imprisonments other than the one at Philippi which are not chronicled in the New Testament; and this is, if anything, confirmed by Clement of Rome, writing before the end of the first century, who says that Paul was in bonds no less than seven times.[72]

One occasion only is specified in the Acts on which stripes were inflicted on Paul (Acts 16:22f.—"many stripes"). That there were others is plain from the next verse.

The expression "in deaths oft" would be out of place in this starkly realistic catalogue if it were intended merely in a metaphorical sense. The experience described by the psalmist as being killed all the day long for the Lord's sake (Ps. 44:22,

---

[72] Clem. Rom., *Ep. ad Cor.*, V—ἑπτάκις δεσμὰ φορέσας.

quoted by Paul in Rom. 8:36) was an experience familiar to the Apostle and is never far from his thought in our present epistle (cf. 1:9f., 4:11, 5:1, 6:9; also I Cor. 15:30–32). There was the remarkable occasion when, after having been stoned by Jews at Lystra, he was dragged out of the city as dead, and then was miraculously raised up again in strength (Acts 14:19f.). This was an experience little if anything short of literal death. As to the frequency with which his life was seriously threatened, see Acts 9:23, 14:5, 16:22, 17:5, 13, 19:29ff., 21:30ff. Concerning the affliction which befell him in Asia, described as "so great a death", and deliverance from which could be explained only as the work of "God who raiseth the dead", see our commentary on 1:8ff. above.

11 : 24, 25

Of the Jews five times received I forty stripes save one. Thrice was I beaten with rods, once was I stoned, thrice I suffered shipwreck, a night and a day have I been in the deep.

These two verses form a parenthesis of particularity in the middle of a context of tribulations which are described in more general terms. Thus, from the point of view of structural sequence, verse 26, "in journeyings often ...", follows on from verse 24, "... in deaths oft".[73] But there is no interruption in the flow of thought, and the biographical information conveyed in this parenthesis, though penned with laconic brevity, is in all but two of the thirteen incidents mentioned unrecorded elsewhere in the New Testament. The particular sufferings enumerated here may have been intended as illustrations of what Paul means by the expression "in deaths oft" which he has just written. The terrible floggings he endured, the stoning, the shipwrecks, the buffeting in the deep, were all "living deaths" through which he had passed.

---

[73] Though in point of fact in the Greek the construction with ἐν is resumed only in verse 27. But the datives in verse 26 (ὁδοιπορίαις, etc.) may be treated as the equivalent of datives governed by ἐν, as in the Vulgate and English versions. This seems preferable, in this context, to Plummer's suggestion that the change should be marked in translation by the use of the preposition "by": "by journeyings often", etc. Alford treats ἐν as instrumental throughout this passage (v. 23–27) and in translating uses "by" when ἐν is both present and absent. Hodge also takes it in this way.

The occasions of the five scourgings suffered by Paul at the hands of the Jews can only be conjectured. Allo suggests that they might have occurred at Damascus (Acts 9:23), Jerusalem (Acts 9:29), Pisidian Antioch (Acts 13:50), Iconium (Acts 14:2, 5), and during his first months in Ephesus (Acts 19:9; cf. the fighting with "beasts" mentioned in I Cor. 15:32). The Mosaic law laid down that the maximum number of stripes which might be administered to a convicted man was forty (Deut. 25:1–3). The typical scrupulosity of the rabbis where the letter of the law was concerned led to the custom of inflicting one less than the forty stripes to ensure that the prescribed maximum was not by miscalculation exceeded and the sacred law infringed.[74] The place where the Jews administered this punishment in Paul's day was in the synagogue. Thus Christ had warned His disciples that they must expect to be scourged by the Jews in the synagogues (Mt. 10:17; Mk. 13:9; cf. Lk. 12:11, 21:12), and to the hypocritical Pharisees He had foretold: "Behold, I send unto you prophets and wise men and scribes: some of them shall ye kill and crucify; and some of them shall ye scourge in your synagogues, and persecute from city to city" (Mt. 23:34). Paul himself had been a leading agent in the literal fulfilment of this prophecy when, as Saul of Tarsus the Pharisee and persecutor, he had beaten Christian believers "in every synagogue" (Acts 22:20, 26:11). But now, as Paul the Apostle, he is numbered among those who are persecuted for Christ's sake (Mt. 5:11; Lk. 6:22).

Olshausen sees special point in Paul's specification that he suffered at the hands *of the Jews*, here and in verse 26 ("my countrymen"), suggesting that he thereby intended to impress upon his readers that in the kingdom of Christ to be of Jewish descent was not a special cause for glorying. It is an interesting suggestion, but in our opinion it is unlikely that the Jews are mentioned at these two points for this particular purpose, since a more obvious explanation lies ready to hand, namely, that the Jews are named here in order to distinguish them from the Gentiles. Thus the beatings with thirty-nine stripes in verse 24

---

[74] Cf. Mishnah *Maccoth* iii, 12, which in response to the inquiry as to how often the culprit should be smitten says, "forty less one"; and also Josephus, *Antt.* IV, viii, 21, who describes this punishment of forty stripes save one as most ignominious *(τιμωρία αἰσχίστη)* for a free man.

are *Jewish* beatings, while those with rods in verse 25 are *Gentile* beatings; and in verse 26 the perils from his own countrymen are offset by perils from the Gentiles which are mentioned immediately after.

Of the three occasions on which he was beaten with rods, that is, by Gentile magistrates, one only is recorded in the book of Acts. This was at Philippi, when many stripes were laid upon Paul and Silas (Acts 16:22f.). The other two receive no mention elsewhere. Ramsay expresses the opinion that "it is probable that the persecution which is mentioned in Antioch, and hinted at in Lystra, included beating by lictors" (i.e., Acts 13:50, 14:19).[75] But it is difficult to justify the description of such a conjecture as "probable". Paul, of course, was a Roman citizen and as such was technically protected by law against such floggings (cf. Acts 16:37f., 22:25ff.). His reference in I Thess. 2:2 to having been "shamefully treated" at Philippi almost certainly concerns the beating with rods administered to him, a Roman citizen, in that city by order of the magistrates (Acts 16:22f.). As Plummer says, "the fact that St Paul was thrice treated in this way is evidence that being a Roman citizen was an imperfect protection when magistrates were disposed to be brutal".

An account of the experience of stoning which the Apostle had survived is found in Acts 14:19f. That Paul did not rashly court persecution is shown by the fact that, prior to the occurrence of this assault at Lystra, he and Barnabas had made good their escape from Iconium when they learnt that their enemies were plotting to stone them there (Acts 14:5f.). Stoning was the customary Jewish method of carrying out the death penalty; accordingly, it was an experience from which death alone might be anticipated. Paul was probably stoned on the pretext that he had uttered blasphemy, as was the case with Stephen (Acts 6:11, 7:57f.), and with our Lord also when the Jews threatened to stone Him (Jn. 10:30f.); for according to the Mosaic law the blasphemer was to be put to death by stoning (Lev. 24:16).

The only shipwreck recorded in the Acts is that suffered by Paul at Malta, some three years after the writing of this epistle, when he was on his way to stand trial at Rome (Acts 27:39ff.).

---

[75] W. Ramsay, *St. Paul the Traveller and the Roman Citizen* (10th edition, London, 1908), pp. 106f.

Voyages in which the three shipwrecks referred to by Paul here might have occurred are:

the journey from Caesarea to Tarsus (Acts 9:30; cf. Gal. 1:21),
the journey from Tarsus to Antioch (Acts 11:25f.),
the journey from Seleucia to Salamis in Cyprus (Acts 13:4),
the journey from Paphos to Perga (Acts 13:13),
the journey from Attalia to Antioch (Acts 14:25f.),
the journey from Troas to Neapolis (Acts 16:11),
the journey from Berea to Athens (Acts 17:14f.),
the journey from Corinth to Ephesus (Acts 18:18f.),
and the journey from Ephesus to Caesarea (Acts 18:21f.)

—no less than nine voyages; and there are at least another nine voyages from place to place subsequent to the writing of II Corinthians and prior to the Malta shipwreck. Thus Paul was no stranger to the sea and its perils.

Presumably the night and day which he spent in the deep (an event which is not recorded elsewhere in the New Testament) was a result of one of the three shipwrecks just mentioned, and during this time no doubt he was tossed about by the waves while clinging to a spar or some other piece of wreckage, in imminent peril of drowning. Beyond doubt, this is how Paul's words must be understood. In the past, however, there have been some extraordinary interpretations of this statement. According to Theophylact, for example, there were some who maintained that the "deep" here spoken of by Paul was a certain well or subterranean pit [76] in which he was hidden after the peril at Lystra. More fanciful still is the opinion of Estius that, following a shipwreck, Paul was submerged and miraculously preserved without harm at the bottom of the sea for a night and a day before being delivered.[77]

---

[76] Φρέαρ.

[77] The term νυχθήμερον (literally, "night-day") effectively expresses the distinctive Hebrew custom of reckoning the day of twenty-four hours from evening to evening (cf. Lev. 23:32, "from even unto even shall ye keep your sabbath"). Unlike other peoples, the Jews calculated days, weeks, and years in relation to the moon—although, of course, the duration of a day is determined by the revolution of the earth in relation to the sun. As the crescent moon is visible only after sunset, the Jewish civil day was reckoned from sunset, not from sunrise; hence the concept of a day as a sequence from evening to morning and its description as "the evening and the morning" in Gen. 1:5ff. The term νυχθήμερον is hapax legomenon in the New Testament, and occurs

11 : 26, 27

In journeyings often, in perils of rivers, in perils of robbers, in perils from my countrymen, in perils from the Gentiles, in perils in the city, in perils in the wilderness, in perils in the sea, in perils among false brethren; in labour and travail, in watchings often, in hunger and thirst, in fastings often, in cold and nakedness.

It is unnecessary to suggest particular events which Paul might have had in mind when writing these words, because it is plain that his wish is to show how his whole life of apostleship has hitherto been fraught with perils, whether on his arduous journeys when unbridged torrents had somehow to be crossed and there was a constant threat of brigands lurking in untamed tracts, or during his sojourns in particular places, whether at the hands of his fellow-countrymen, no less frenzied than brigands, or of fanatical Gentile mobs, whether in centres of population or in the wild and deserted wastes which at times he traversed, whether on land or on sea, from savage beasts as well as from savage men—in no place and under no circumstances was he free from such perils; and the worst and most to be feared he mentions last of all, namely, false brethren. "The other dangers threatened life and limb and property", says Plummer, "but this one imperilled, and sometimes ruined, his work." Such false

again only in later literature. J. H. Moulton explains it as an adverbial form (*Grammar*, Vol. II, pp. 269, 283); but it is preferable to regard it as a noun, the direct object here of πεποίηκα. The adjective νυχθήμερος is found as early as the first century A.D. in Periplus Maris Erythraei (see Arndt and Gingrich). It is probable that our Lord used an equivalent Aramaic expression when He told the scribes and Pharisees that the Son of man would be three days and three nights in the heart of the earth (Mt. 12:40), that is, three νυχθήμερα or "night-days", a part being also spoken of as a whole. Thus He was crucified and buried on the day before the sabbath and rose from the dead on the day after the sabbath. In this way we see how Mt. 12:40 harmonizes with Christ's prophecy, recorded in the same Gospel (16:21), that He would be raised up on the third day (cf. Mk. 8:31, Lk. 9:32).

Although there may be a number of genuinely aoristic perfects in the New Testament, to treat πεποίηκα here as "a mere equivalent for ἐποίησα ... would only place the experience on a level with the others", says J. H. Moulton, in whose judgment the perfect πεποίηκα "recalls it as a memory specially vivid now". Plummer comments: "The change from aorists to perfect is not casual. The perf. shows that the dreadful experience is vividly before the Apostle's mind, and possibly indicates that the occurrence was recent".

brethren are his opponents in Corinth, who insinuate themselves into the Christian community, undermine his ministry of the gospel, and seek to rob believers of their liberty in Christ Jesus.

The "labour and travail" mentioned in verse 27 would seem to refer to Paul's toiling with his own hands at a craft in order not to be in any sense a financial burden on those to whom he was ministering, since the selfsame expression is used in I Thess. 2:9 and II Thess. 3:8 and in both cases this explanation is added (cf. 11:9, 12:16).

The "watchings" no doubt refer to activity far into the night while others were sleeping, "in order to make a livelihood from his trade, after days spent in apostolic ministry, or in order to reach distant stopping-places, or to conquer heaven by his prayers" (Allo).

The "hunger and thirst" may well correspond to the "being in want" alluded to earlier in verse 9, though their application here is not simply to his experience in Corinth but far more generally to what he endured in many different places and circumstances.

The "fastings" should not here be taken to refer to self-imposed religious disciplines, but rather to the forgoing of meals in order that his work as a minister of Christ might not be interrupted. Inspired by the example of his Master, the will of God was paramount in his life, far more important than food and drink, for the impulse of his whole ministry was the realization that "man shall not live by bread alone" and that his meat was to do the will of Him that had sent him, and to accomplish His work (Mt. 4:4; Jn. 4:34).

The climax of his human destitution is reached in the words "in cold and nakedness", words which speak volumes on their own. On an earlier occasion he had written to the Corinthians in much the same strain as here: "Even unto this present hour we both hunger and thirst, and are naked, and are buffeted, and have no certain dwelling-place, and we toil, working with our own hands ..." (I Cor. 4:11ff.; cf. Phil. 4:12). In the eyes of the world this life to which the service of Christ had led him, this daily living death (4:10ff.; Rom. 8:36), can be seen only as a disaster and a pitiable negation of all that it counts worthwhile. But that was not how Paul saw it, for he saw beyond the present sufferings to the glory ahead (Rom. 8:18); and he knew by constant experience that nothing, whether persecution or famine or nakedness or peril or sword, could separate him from the love of Christ (Rom. 8:35ff.). And this was so to the end, even when, on the eve of his martyrdom, in coldness and nakedness he pathetically requests Timothy to bring him the cloak which he had left at Troas (II Tim. 4:13) : even then his gaze was stedfastly fixed on the glory ahead (II Tim. 4:6ff.), for, in contrast to the wealthy fool of the parable, his treasure was in heaven and he was rich toward God (Lk. 12:21).

What Paul says in this present passage throws a strong beam of light on his earlier description of himself: "as sorrowful, yet alway rejoicing; as poor, yet making many rich; as having nothing, and yet possessing all things" (6:10). One is moved to wonder how much we who are Christ's ministers in our contemporary western civilization really know of these things—labours, persecutions, perils, watchings, want, cold, and nakedness—which the Apostle here sets forth as authenticating marks of his ministry. Is not the conclusion inescapable that less self-concern and less love of present security would mean greater apostolicity? But how many are there today who, with Paul, can say: "From henceforth let no man trouble me: for I bear branded on my body the marks of Jesus" (Gal. 6:17)?

11 : 28

> Besides those things that are without, there is that which presseth upon me daily, anxiety for all the churches.

There is, however, something more, something deeper, than outward afflictions which Paul is called upon to endure as a minister of Christ. The sufferings he has been constrained to mention in order to put his opponents to silence are in themselves externals, incidental in their significance, indeed beside the point except in so far as they are borne for Christ's honour (cf. Mt. 13:9).[78]

---

[78] The precise meaning of χωρὶς τῶν παρεκτός has been a matter of dispute. Elsewhere παρεκτός occurs as a preposition with the force of "besides" or "apart from" (Latin: *praeter*; cf. Mt. 5:32, Acts 26:29, and also references in Arndt and Gingrich and Moulton and Milligan), which is of course the force of the preposition which Paul uses here. To take τὰ παρεκτός to mean "the things which are without" (that is, as the equivalent of τὰ ἔξωθεν or τὰ ἔξω), as do Vg, AV, Bengel, etc., and our own version, makes the phrase

Paul is daily pressed [79] with anxiety for all the churches. That this anxiety was not faithless fussiness is shown over and over again by the serious problems, defections, and irregularities which occurred so distressingly in the different churches of the New Testament and which necessitated his visits and his letters and his constant prayers. This anxiety was based not only on

---

refer to the *outward* sufferings which Paul has just been enumerating, in contrast to the *inward* anxiety which he now mentions in this verse. So also Arndt and Gingrich propose "apart from what is external" as a possible meaning of χωρὶς τῶν παρεκτός. But, as Alford, Plummer, and Tasker observe, παρεκτός implies *exception*, not externality, and the Vulgate rendering *extrinsecus* therefore appears to be a misconception—a misconception which Denney fails to avoid, though he understands it figuratively as a reference to things which are of secondary or of incidental significance (that is, Paul's sufferings here). In view of the *exceptive* significance of παρεκτός the only really satisfactory meaning of the expression χωρὶς τῶν παρεκτός is "apart from the things that have not been mentioned". This is the interpretation of so early an exegete as Chrysostom, who comments: "the things left out are more than those enumerated", and of Tasker, Allo, Plummer, Alford, Hodge, and others among modern commentators. Chrysostom, indeed, places a full stop after παρεκτός, thereby making χωρὶς τῶν παρεκτός the concluding statement of the list of Paul's sufferings. It fits much better, however, as the opening statemeui of a new sentence, which otherwise would be too abrupt in its isolation.

[79] The noun ἐπίστασις is capable of a variety of meanings. Accordingly, a variety of interpretations of the expression ἡ ἐπίστασίς μοι ἡ καθ᾽ ἡμέραν have been proposed, of which the following may be mentioned:

(i) "My daily supervision or oversight", *sc.* of church affairs; cf. Xenophon, *Mem.*, I, v, 2, ἐπίστασις ἔργων, "superintendence (or supervision) of works";

(ii) "My daily attention", *sc.* to church affairs; cf. Aristotle, *Metaphys.*, XIII, ii, 17, *Phys.*, II, iv, 7, τουτ᾽ ἄξιον ἐπιστάσεως, Polybius, VIII, xxx, 13, XI, ii, 4, ἄξιος ἐπιστάσεως. In both these interpretations ἐπίστασις is the equivalent of ἐπιστασία.

(iii) "The daily onset or uprising or conspiring against me", which is the interpretation preferred by Moulton and Milligan and by Souter, in conformity with the meaning of ἐπίστασις in Acts 24:12; cf. II Macc. 6:3.

(iv) "The hindrance or delay or interruption which I experience daily", ἐπίστασις in this case having the meaning of being brought to a standstill, whence (i) and (ii), a stopping to examine or give attention to a thing; cf. Xenophon, *Anab.*, II, iv, 26, of the halting of an army, Sophocles, *Antig.*, 225, φροντίδων ἐπιστάσεις, "stoppages, interruptions of thought", Aristotle, *De Anima*, I, iii, 21, where it is the opposite of κίνησις, and Hippocrates, who uses the term medically of intestinal stoppage (195E) and of the staunching of blood (380).

(v) "The daily pressure of responsibility", as in our version: "that which presseth upon me daily", and as in the concise rendering of the Vulgate: *instantia mea cotidiana*. The following phrase, ἡ μέριμνα πασῶν τῶν ἐκκλησιῶν,

415

disturbing reports which came to his ears, but on his knowledge of the savage subtlety of the enemy of souls who, he realized, would stop at nothing in his attempts to overthrow the work of the gospel. Paul was certainly no perfectionist in his view of the state of Christ's Church here on earth. He knew that, as Christ Himself had forewarned (Mt. 18:7; Lk. 17:1), occasions of stumbling must come, that heresies and divisions were to be expected (I Cor. 11:19), that some would be seduced from the faith (I Tim. 4:1), that grievous wolves would—like his adversaries at Corinth—come in from without, not sparing the flock, and that even from the midst of the Christian community itself false leaders would arise (Acts 20:29f.).

Paul, therefore, laboured under no misapprehension concerning the forces of evil that are active in the world and in particular concentrate their attack on the churches of Christ. But at the same time his anxiety was not the outcome of an inadequate appreciation of the sovereignty of God over the world and over His Church. On the contrary, for no man had a clearer and grander perspective of the sovereign providence and majesty of Almighty God. It was precisely because by God's sovereign and

---

is then epexegetic, in apposition to ἐπίστασις. Arndt and Gingrich describe this sense of "pressure" for ἐπίστασις as "an outstanding possibility" here, and most commentators agree that it is to be preferred to the other possibilities. In our judgment it accords best with the context.

The textual evidence is overwhelmingly against the acceptance of the reading ἐπισύστασις of the Textus Receptus. This noun suggests a riotous concourse—as is the case with ἐπίστασις in Acts 24:12—which would seem unsuited to Paul's thought here as he has already, in the preceding verses, described the different kinds of violence he has suffered. This, however, is how Chrysostom understands it: "the tumults, the disturbances, the assaults of mobs, the onsets of cities". Luther, Estius, and Stanley understand it in a peaceful sense to refer to the daily concourse of people who crowded upon Paul and demanded his attention. Cf. also Beza's figurative interpretation: "that army pressing against me every day, namely, concern for all the churches."

As Plummer points out, μέριμνα means "care" in the sense of anxiety, not supervision or jurisdiction: "Therefore this does not mean that St. Paul claimed jurisdiction over all churches, whether founded by himself or not; he is not thinking of jurisdiction at all". The word μέριμνα appears to be radically connected with μερίζω, "divide", and μερίς, "a part or division". If so, its basic significance is that of division of thought and attention, distraction of purpose—a concept which is clearly brought out in Chrysostom's comment: "This was the chief thing of all, that his soul too was distracted and his thoughts divided".

gracious will he had been converted from his former ways and chosen to bear Christ's name "before the Gentiles and kings and the children of Israel", and to suffer for the sake of that name (Acts 9:15f.), that the care of the churches founded through his missionary labours pressed daily upon him. The honour of Christ's name is a supreme concern. To see Christ's name dishonoured in the Church of all places caused Paul the acutest grief. When the flock of Christ is ravaged by wolves the undershepherd cannot stand by impassively as though uninvolved in what is taking place. It is his duty immediately to come to their aid and to drive away the marauders, both for love of the flock and for the honour of his Master, the Good Shepherd, in whose strength he acts and to whom he is answerable for the work entrusted to his hands.

11 : 29

Who is weak, and I am not weak? who is caused to stumble, and I burn not?

The anxiety which the Apostle experiences for the churches is engendered not by lack of faith but by compassion. So sensitive is he to the fortunes of those who through his ministry have become his spiritual children, so conscious is he of the responsibility that has been laid upon him for them as Christ's apostle, that he cannot detach himself from their lot. It is not merely his sense of the essential corporateness of the Church of Christ, whereby the suffering of one member means the suffering of all (I Cor. 12:26), which causes Paul to be so full of sympathy and fellow-feeling for the Corinthians. It is something, if possible, even deeper, namely, compassion—the apostolic, pastoral compassion of identification—the compassion of the parent for the children he has begotten, of the shepherd for his frail sheep. As Christ's apostle and minister he cannot hold himself aloof from his people, as though he belonged to a different or higher order of existence. Like the high priests of old, he "can bear gently with the ignorant and erring, for that he himself is compassed with infirmity"; and like the great and unique High Priest Himself, he is touched with the feeling of their infirmities (Heb. 5:2, 4:16). Their weakness is felt as his weakness. Their frailty, so easily suffering offence, is his frailty also. The stumbling of one

417

of them causes him to burn with shame as though it were his own stumbling and to burn with indignation against the seducer who has made one of Christ's little ones to stumble (cf. Mk. 9:42, etc.). And so it should be with every faithful pastor of Christ's flock: he should lovingly identify himself with those who have been committed to his care, showing himself deeply anxious for their spiritual well-being, compassionate with them in their frailties and temptations, and resisting and resenting every one who seeks to entice them away from the purity of their devotion to Christ. This compassion is not of man: it is the divine compassion of Christ Himself, burning in the heart of His servant, and blazing forth in love to reach and to bind to the one Bridegroom the hearts of those to whom he ministers.

11 : 30

> If I must needs glory, I will glory of the things that concern my weakness.

This statement, though closely connected with what precedes (the catalogue of his persecutions and sufferings is nothing if not glorying in weakness), marks the beginning of a new section, in so far as it is possible and desirable to discern divisions in a homogeneous context. In our judgment, chapter 12 might more appropriately have started at this point than at the place where the chapter-division is traditionally made. The reasons for this opinion will become apparent in our exegesis of this and the following verses. The present verse is, indeed, in complete harmony with the whole tenor of this epistle, the outstanding and pervading feature of which is, on the one hand, the emphasis on the utter weakness of the human instrument and, on the other hand and in consequence, the magnification of the glorious grace and power of Almighty God (cf. 1:8ff., 2:12ff., 3:5, 4:7ff., 16ff., 5:1ff., 6:4ff., 7:5ff., 10:17f., 11:9f., 23ff., 12:1ff., 13:4). To give prominence, as Paul does in this epistle, to the frail earthen vessel, the decaying outward man, the disintegrating physical frame, the body absorbing persecution, is to glory of the things that concern his weakness. And here, at this point, the epistle begins to move to its climax, which is reached in 12:9f. This glorying in weakness, which is the obverse side of glorying in God's power, is now to be brought to its peak.

Even so, to speak of himself at all is still clearly distasteful to Paul: it is for him a question of "If I must needs glory ..." Circumstances have placed him under this necessity, but it is a necessity which he turns into an opportunity for stressing his own utter weakness and indeed inability for the performance of his apostolic task. As always, his testimony is: "By the grace of God I am what I am", and, "I laboured ..., yet not I, but the grace of God which was with me" (I Cor. 15:10). "The fact that he had thus continually to struggle and suffer", says Allo, "was proof sufficient that he was not a sort of divine or 'superhuman' being, but a poor 'earthen vessel' (4:7) all whose endurance is the result of being filled with the power of someone else, the power, namely, of Christ".

11:31

The God and Father of the Lord Jesus, he who is blessed for evermore, knoweth that I lie not.

Concerning the significance of the expression "the God and Father of the Lord Jesus" see commentary on 1:3 above, where the similar phrase "the God and Father of our Lord Jesus Christ" is used. There was no name or person to whom Paul could more solemnly appeal as a witness of his truthfulness than He who, under the title here assigned to Him, is his Creator, Redeemer, and Judge, the One "unto whom all hearts are open, all desires known, and from whom no secrets are hid".

Opinion is divided as to whether this solemn asseveration by Paul of his truthfulness refers to what precedes or to what follows. Tasker, for instance, understands it to apply to what he has already said: "This amazing record of his afflictions as an apostle of Christ", he comments, "might appear to those hearing it for the first time incredulous. The apostle, therefore, now calls God to witness that everything he has said bears the hall-mark of truth. There has been no inaccuracy and no over-statement". In our judgment, however, this adjuration relates not to the sufferings already enumerated in verses 23ff. (although it is, of course, fully applicable to them), which were to all intents and purposes public knowledge and scarcely open to dispute, but to Paul's assertion (in the immediately preceding verse) that it is the things concerning his weakness in which he glories and to the specific instances of this which he is now about to give, namely, his escape from Damascus and his "thorn in the flesh", concluding, at 12:9f., with the renewed emphasis on glorying and taking pleasure in his weaknesses.

Alford, in applying it to what follows—"to the strange history about to be related"—, surprises us by remarking: "It will be seen that I differ from all Commentators here, and cannot but think that they have missed the connection", since Calvin and others before him had in fact applied it in the same way. Thus Calvin comments that as Paul "was about to relate a singular feat, which, at the same time, was not well known, he confirms it by making use of an oath". As Plummer points out, "the strong language here and 1:23 is indirect evidence of the calumnies which were circulated about him; he said 'yes' when he meant 'no', or said both 'yes' and 'no' in one breath (1:17); he could not speak the truth". We may, then, perhaps be permitted to regard this as yet another strand of the internal evidence which points to the coherence of the latter with the former part of this epistle.

For the hebraistic formula, God "who is blessed for evermore", cf. Rom. 1:25, 9:5, and Mk. 14:61.

11 : 32, 33

In Damascus the governor under Aretas the king guarded the city of the Damascenes in order to take me: and through a window was I let down in a basket by the wall, and escaped his hands.

It cannot be denied that the incident related in so matter-of-fact a way in these two verses has the appearance of being an anticlimax—an appearance to which the accepted chapter-division at this place materially contributes, since it has the effect of making this incident the concluding item of all the experiences that have been catalogued from verse 23 onwards. Thus apportioned, it almost gives the reader the impression of an after-thought, as though, having passed from the catalogue of his afflictions endured as Christ's minister, Paul had suddenly remembered his escape from Damascus, and wished it to be recorded also, although dislocated from the earlier list. This is, indeed, the view of some, for example, Tasker and Moffatt; and it is, of course, a perfectly possible explanation. But if it was in fact an afterthought, we cannot help thinking that it would have been easy for Paul to have had it inserted at a suitable point in the catalogue which he had so recently dictated. There is, however, no evidence to suggest either that this was Paul's intention, or that as the result of some subsequent chance these two verses were removed to their present position from an original place within the previous catalogue—for example, at verse 26, as Windisch has suggested — or that, as a number of Continental scholars have proposed, they represent an interpolation by a later hand. Moreover, while it is true that the spontaneousness of the Apostle's temperament is frequently reflected in his literary style, it is doubtful whether we have an instance of this here. The obvious after-thought of I Cor. 1:16 can scarcely be cited as a parallel, since it in no way suggests a dislocation within its immediate context, with which it is thoroughly homogeneous.

In considering these two verses, then, it is desirable that we should endeavour to understand them within the context in which they are placed—and that context, it is important to remember, does not end with the modern chapter division, but continues on into the twelfth chapter. The temptation to "improve" the text by omitting verses 32 and 33, or by allocating them elsewhere, must be resisted. As Plummer remarks, "countless passages in letters and books would have been greatly improved if certain sentences had been omitted, and yet there is no doubt that the intrusive sentences are original"; and, what is more, "here we are not certain that the omission of the sentences would have been an improvement". Augustine praises the whole section from verse 16 onwards as an outstanding example of Paul's wisdom and eloquence—"wisdom is his guide, eloquence his attendant; he follows the first, the second follows him"—and then, after an analysis of the passage, writes: "I cannot sufficiently express how beautiful and delightful it is when after this outburst he rests himself, and gives the hearer rest, by interposing a slight narrative".[80] This solution to the particular question we are considering is, however, too superficial and subjective to be satisfactory.

---

[80]   Augustine, *De Doct. Christ.*, IV, vii, 12ff.

What, then, may we say about the narration of this experience at this particular point? In the first place, we may take it that this escape from Damascus held particular significance for the Apostle, for it was, as Calvin says, his first apprenticeship in persecution; it was the initiation of the new recruit into the front line of gospel warfare. But, secondly, it was an event which emphasized, at the very beginning of his ministry, his own abject weakness and frailty: Paul the Apostle who was ignominiously lowered in a fish-basket at dead of night in order to escape the Jewish enemies of the gospel was none other than the man who as Saul of Tarsus, the arrogant Jewish persecutor and blasphemer of Christ, had ostentatiously approached this same city of Damascus with authority from the high-priest to arrest and man-handle Christ's followers. The contrast between Saul of Tarsus and Paul the Apostle could not have been more striking, nor the contrast between his manner of approach to Damascus and his manner of exit from it. And, thirdly, may it not with good reason be inferred that Paul intended, by the mention of this experience here rather than within the framework of the earlier catalogue, to present it as an effective and contrasting prelude to the experience which he is now about to describe (12:2ff.)? The man who experienced the ineffable "ascent" even to the third heaven was the same man who had experienced the undistinguished "descent" from a window in the Damascus wall. Paul is determined to keep himself in true perspective, which is that of a weak and unworthy mortal who owes everything to the grace of Almighty God. Hence the relation of his rapture into the third heaven is hemmed in, as it were, on the one side by the narration of his inglorious escape in weakness from Damascus and, on the other, by the reference to the humiliating "thorn in the flesh" which he was called upon to endure (12:7ff.). We venture to suggest that, understood in this way within their immediate context, verses 32 and 33 are not inappropriate or misplaced, but full of significance, and that to see them as deliberately set down by the Apostle at this point in the epistle for the purpose which we have proposed is far more satisfactory than to explain them as an illogical after-thought interrupting the flow of his argument.

The question naturally arises as to whether it is justifiable for a Christian leader to flee from persecution, and if so, under what circumstances. Augustine offers the following observations: "When the Apostle Paul was 'let down in a basket through a window', to prevent his enemies from seizing him, and so escaped their hands, was the church in Damascus deprived of the necessary labours of Christ's servants? Was not all the service that was requisite supplied after his departure by other brethren settled in that city? For the Apostle had done this at their request, in order that he might preserve for the Church's good his life, which the persecutor on that occasion specially sought to destroy. Let those therefore who are servants of Christ, His ministers in word and sacrament, do what He has commanded or permitted. When any of them is specially sought for by persecutors, let him by all means flee from one city to another, provided that the Church is not thereby deserted, but that others who are not specially sought after remain to supply spiritual food to their fellow-servants, whom they know to be unable otherwise to maintain spiritual life".[81]

"Shall we make mention any more of goods, or even of wife, or city, or freedom, when we have seen him ten thousand times despising even life itself?" asks Chrysostom in his rhapsodic homily on the sufferings of Paul enumerated in this chapter. "The martyr dies once for all: but that blessed saint, in his one body and one soul, endured so many perils as were enough to disturb even a soul of adamant; and what things all the saints together have suffered in so many bodies, those all he himself endured in one. He entered into the world as if a race-course, and stripped himself of all, and so made a noble stand; for he knew the fiends that were wrestling with him. Wherefore also he shone forth brightly at once from the beginning, from the very starting-post, and even to the end he continued the same; yea, rather, he even increased the intensity of his pursuit as he drew nearer to the prize. ... Knowing then these things, let us also learn to be modest and not to boast at any time of wealth or other worldly things, but in the reproaches we suffer for Christ's sake, and in these only when need compels; for if there be nothing urging it let us not mention these even (lest we be puffed up), but our sins only."

---

[81] Augustine, *Ep.* CCXXVIII, to Honoratus.

THE MENTION OF ARETAS IN 11:32 AND PAULINE CHRONOLOGY

The incident of Paul's escape from Damascus is narrated by Luke in Acts 9:23–25 as well as by Paul himself here, and the two accounts, brief though they are, serve to supplement each other. Luke says that "when many days were fulfilled" the Jews in Damascus plotted to kill Paul and watched the gates day and night in order to achieve their object; but that Paul, having learned of the plot, was lowered from the wall of the city in a basket. Paul gives the further information that it was the governor or ethnarch[82] who guarded the city for the purpose of apprehending him. There is no discrepancy between Luke's assertion that the Jews watched the gates and Paul's that the city was guarded by the ethnarch: the ethnarch would have placed a guard to watch the city exits at the instigation of the Jews who constituted a numerous section of the city's population[83] and who no doubt themselves also assisted in the watching. Indeed, it is not unlikely that the ethnarch was himself a Jew and that the guard appointed by him was composed entirely of men of the Jewish race. The term *ethnarch* means literally a ruler of a tribe or race and was commonly used to denote a deputy governor or subordinate ruler responsible for a particular racial section of the population. Thus in the Maccabean period the Jewish High Priest Simon held the office of "ethnarch of the Jews" under the Syrian regime[84], and Augustus conferred this title on Herod's son Archelaus[85]. Strabo says that in Alexandria the Jews, who were numerous in that city, were granted an ethnarch "who governs the nation, and distributes justice to them, and takes care of their contracts and of the laws pertaining to them, as if he were the ruler of a free republic".[86] There is therefore no inherent improbability in the supposition that "the ethnarch of Aretas the king" mentioned by Paul in our text was himself a Jew with particular authority over the Jewish section of the population and that those detailed or permitted by him to watch the gates belonged to that race.

---

[82] Ὁ ἐθνάρχης.

[83] Josephus tells us that during the reign of Nero, and therefore in the course of Paul's apostleship, no less than ten thousand Jews were massacred in Damascus within a single hour (*Bell. Jud.*, II, xx, 2; and cf. VII, viii, 7, where he gives the number as 18,000).

[84] I Macc. 14:47, 15:1ff.; Josephus, *Antt.*, XIII, vi, 7.

[85] Josephus, *Antt.*, XVII, xi, 4; *Bell. Jud.*, II, vi, 3.

[86] Strabo, XVII, 798—quoted in Josephus, *Antt.*, XIV, vii, 2.

It is Paul's reference to Aretas, however, which is of special interest in connection with the chronology of his conversion and the commencement of his ministry.   Aretas IV was king of Nabatea, the territory east of Damascus whose capital was Petra. He succeeded Obodas II and reigned over the Nabatean kingdom from c. 9 B.C. to A.D. 40. On his accession he changed his name from Aeneas to Aretas, thereby appropriating a name that had become closely associated with the kingdom of Arabia Nabatea.[87]   In what sense, then, was it possible for Paul to speak of Aretas IV as king with authority to appoint on ethnarch with jurisdiction in Damascus?   To this question a precise answer cannot be given, but a reasonable solution may be suggested on the strength of such evidence as is available.   Thus it can hardly be without significance that during the principates of Caligula and Claudius, that is, from A.D. 37 to 54, there are no Damascene coins bearing the image of the Roman emperor, whereas prior to this period there are coins carrying the head of Augustus and Tiberius, and, subsequently to it, of Nero and his successors. This gap may be fortuitous, but it is far more probable that for the period A.D. 37 to 54 the government of Damascus had been granted by Rome to Aretas IV and those who followed him. If this assumption is correct, then Paul's escape from Damascus must be placed within the limits of the accession of Caligula, March, A.D. 37, on the one hand, and the death of Aretas, A.D. 40, on the other.

We are told by Josephus that when Herod Antipas, who had married the daughter of Aretas, divorced his wife in order to marry his own niece Herodias, Aretas for this reason, and also because of certain frontier disputes, declared war on Herod and, in A.D. 32, destroyed his army.   Herod thereupon appealed to Tiberius.   The emperor, incensed at the way Aretas had taken the law into his own hands, commanded the governor of Syria, Vitellius, to march against Aretas and to bring him either dead or alive to Rome.   Vitellius accordingly made preparations for war and in due course set out at the head of two legions for Petra. While, however, he was in Jerusalem *en route* news reached him of the death of Tiberius (which took place on March 16, A.D. 37),

---

[87] Josephus, *Antt*, XVI, ix, 4. The original form of the name is reflected in the rough breathing which is accepted by Nestlé and Westcott and Hort, though not by Souter. Ἀρέτας then corresponds to *Haritha* or *Charitheth* (חרתת). Deissmann (*Bible Studies*, pp. 183f.) concurs with Schürer's view that "the form Ἀρέτας undoubtedly has arisen under the influence of the Greek word ἀρετή" (*History of the Jewish People in the Time of Jesus Christ*, I, ii, p. 359).

and he immediately called off the campaign on the pretext that now that Caligula had succeeded Tiberius he no longer possessed authority for prosecuting the war.[88] But it was his own personal dislike of Herod Antipas which provided the real reason for abandoning this project [89]—a dislike which, it seems, he could count on Caligula to share with him. Caligula, indeed, treated Herod Antipas with the greatest disfavour, banishing him to Gaul, and granting the tetrarchy of Galilee to his rival, Herod Agrippa. It is not improbable, therefore, that he granted the government of Damascus to Antipas's other enemy, as he now was, Aretas IV, with whose kingdom that city had been closely associated in the past. This is the view propounded by Wieseler [90] and adopted by Schürer and the majority of scholars since.

The next question that arises is concerning the point at which Paul's escape from Damascus took place within the period A.D. 37 to 40. Luke provides us with two notes of time: (i) after his conversion Paul "was *certain days* with the disciples that were at Damascus" (Acts 9:19); and (ii) "when *many days* were fulfilled" Paul learnt of the Jewish plot to kill him and escaped in the manner described (Acts 9:23–25). There can be no reasonable doubt that the two periods described as "certain days" [91] and many days" [92] are distinct from each other, the former referring to a short and the latter to a long period of time. In the epistle to the Galatians Paul says that following upon his conversion he did not confer with flesh and blood, nor did he go up to Jerusalem to meet the apostles there, but went away into Arabia and then returned to Damascus. "Then after three years", he adds, "I went up to Jerusalem to visit Cephas" (Gal. 1:16–18); and while there he also saw James, the Lord's brother. Luke tells us that this visit to Jerusalem was made after the escape from Damascus (Acts 9:26). In company with most commentators we understand the "certain days" of Acts 9:19 to refer to the short interval between Paul's conversion and his departure into Arabia, and the "many days" of Acts 9:23 to refer to the interval of "three years" starting with his conversion and ending, after his return from Arabia, with his escape from Damascus.[93] The "three

---

[88] Josephus, *Antt.*, XVIII, v, 1–3.

[89] Josephus, *Ibid.*, iv, 5.

[90] Wieseler, *Chronologie des Apostolischen Zeitalters* (Göttingen, 1848), pp. 167ff.

[91] Ἡμέραι τινές.

[92] Ἡμέραι ἱκαναί.

[93] It is of interest to find that in I Kings 2:38f. a period of three years is described as "many days", יָמִים רַבִּים (Vg, *diebus multis*, Luther, "*lange zeit*"). The Septuagint, however, particularizes the expression as ἔτη τρία.

years", however, do not necessarily denote a full period of three years, since according to the Jewish method of reckoning a part of a year (or day) was customarily spoken of as a year (or day), so that "three years" might indicate any length of time from one full year plus a part of each year on either side to three full years.

From what has already been said it will be evident (assuming the proposed reconstruction to be correct) that the earliest date for Paul's escape from Damascus would have been shortly after Damascus came under the suzerainty of Aretas IV, that is, the spring of A.D. 37, and the latest date shortly before the death of Aretas, probably in the early part of A.D. 40 or possibly towards the end of A.D. 39, and that the event of Paul's conversion antedates his escape by a period of some one-and-a-half to three years. At the earliest, then, his conversion could have been in A.D. 34, and at the latest in A.D. 38.

A further piece of chronological information to which we have not yet referred is given by Paul in Gal. 2:1 where he says that after the space of fourteen years he went up again to Jerusalem, with Barnabas and Titus as his companions. But again, as with the "three years" of Gal. 1:18, we are faced with a double problem: firstly, does the period of fourteen years mean fourteen full years or twelve full years plus parts of two other years, one on either side? and, secondly, is this interval of fourteen years to be reckoned from the date of Paul's conversion or from the date of his first visit to Jerusalem? There seems little likelihood of this problem ever being finally resolved. If the period of "fourteen years" is to be reckoned from Paul's conversion, then it is probable that this visit to Jerusalem refers to his second visit to that city for the purpose of taking famine relief to the Christians there (Acts 11:29f.). If, however, it is to be reckoned from his first visit to Jerusalem, following his escape from Damascus, it is probable that Gal. 2:1 refers to his *third* visit to Jerusalem in order to attend the Apostolic Council (Acts 15), the famine visit being left out of account. It is unnecessary for us to mention the various solutions which have been offered to this problem by different scholars. It will suffice to refer readers to Bishop Lightfoot's essay on *the Chronology of St. Paul's Life and Epistles*,[94] Kirsopp Lake's excursus on *The Chronology of Acts*,[95] and C. H. Turner's article on "The Chronology of the New Testament" in *Hasting's Dictionary of the Bible*.[96]

---

[94]   *In Biblical Essays*, pp. 215ff.
[95]   In *The Beginnings of Christianity*, Vol. V, pp. 445ff.
[96]   Vol. I, especially pp. 415ff. See also W. M. Ramsay, *St. Paul the Traveller and the Roman Citizen*.

The uncertainties with which we have to deal are emphasized by the fact that estimates of the date of Paul's conversion vary over a whole decade, from A.D. 30 (Harnack) to A.D. 40 (Wieseler). Lightfoot, indeed, places it in A.D. 34 in the essay mentioned above (which was posthumously published from lecture notes) and in A.D. 36 in his commentary on Galatians (p. 102), the discrepancy being due in the main to his rejection of the Jewish method of reckoning in the former instance, and his acceptance of it in the latter. If one thing is obvious, it is that precision in fixing dates for Paul's conversion and the earlier part of his ministry is not possible, and that we must therefore be content with approximations. The mention of Aretas in the passage before us is one of the few pointers that we have.

12 : 1

I must needs glory, though it is not expedient; but I will come to visions and revelations of the Lord.

Paul's embarrassment increases as he is on the point of disclosing what was probably the most intimate and sacred of all his religious experiences as a Christian. This particular experience was, as far as we know, granted to no other person, least of all to his arrogant rivals in Corinth, who, it is likely, had been boasting of visions and revelations which they claimed to have received. The Apostle reiterates that he speaks of himself only because circumstances have compelled him to do so. For himself personally it remains all along an uncongenial and unprofitable duty.[97] Yet it would be wrong to conclude that Paul

---

[97] Cf. the RSV rendering: "I must boast; there is nothing to be gained by it, ..." There are so many variant readings for the opening clause of this verse that its original form must still be regarded as uncertain. The best attested, however, is that followed by our version and RSV, namely, καυχᾶσθαι δεῖ, οὐ συμφέρον μέν ... The reading καυχᾶσθαι δεῖ fits the context well, for it takes up positively what was stated in a conditional form in 11:30 —εἰ καυχᾶσθαι δεῖ. As for καυχᾶσθαι δέ, since the normal position of the particle δέ is after the first word of a clause, it is easy to understand that a copyist could inadvertently have dropped the iota when transcribing δεῖ and written καυχᾶσθαι δέ. The reading καυχᾶσθαι δή is probably attributable to the similarity in pronunciation between δεῖ and δή. But this could, of course, have operated in the opposite direction, and it must be admitted that καυχᾶσθαι δὴ οὐ συμφέρον μέν, ἐλεύσομαι δέ κτλ — "boasting, it is true, is unprofitable, but (compelled by circumstances) I will come to visions and revelations"—is not unattractive.

Κυρίου, "of the Lord", is commonly explained as a subjective genitive here:

is here *competing* with his antagonists in this matter of visions and revelations (as Allo, Strachan, and others have supposed). Nor is he claiming the privilege of contact with Christ through a supernatural mystical experience in order to counteract their claim to have known Christ after the flesh (as suggested, for example, by Baur; cf. 5:16). Such a contest would have been particularly barren, for claims to abnormal and private visionary experiences can be neither established nor refuted in debate. And, besides, had Paul wished to impress others in this way he could without difficulty have compiled a catalogue of "visions and revelations" which he had experienced, in much the same way as he had set down a catalogue of some of his sufferings endured as a minister of Christ (11:23ff.). No other apostle was so rich in the experience of visions and revelations.

It is important, moreover, to realize that Paul, consistently with what he has recently said (11:30), is still glorying in his weakness, and that his rapture of ineffable exaltation which he is about to narrate is a necessary prelude to his mention of what was his most obvious and disabling physical weakness, the "thorn in the flesh" with which he was afflicted (v. 7). To have omitted reference to his "thorn in the flesh" would have been to leave his flank wide open to the enemy. To include it required mention of this remarkable ecstatic experience of which, in a certain sense, his "thorn in the flesh" was a consequence. It is for this reason, then, that he now reveals what has hitherto humbly been withheld from public knowledge.

12:2

> I know a man in Christ, fourteen years ago (whether in the body, I know not; or whether out of the body, I know not; God knoweth), such a one caught up even to the third heaven.

So far is Paul from vaunting himself that, in describing an experience which his boastful adversaries would have welcomed for their own, he speaks of himself in the third person, almost as

---

the Lord is the source of the visions and revelations. It is not impossible, however, that a note of objectivity is intended as well, that is, that during the course of this experience Paul saw the risen and ascended Lord; cf. the vision of Stephen who, "being full of the Holy Spirit, looked up stedfastly into heaven, and saw the glory of God, and Jesus standing on the right hand of God" (Acts 7:55).

though he is speaking of someone else. It is only when he comes on to mention the humiliating "thorn in the flesh" that he returns to the use of the first person. Verse 7, indeed, shows beyond dispute that the "man" to whom he refers here is none other than himself. His modesty is further displayed by the way in which he quite frankly admits his ignorance as to whether or not the rapture in question was experienced in the body; and again by the implication that for the past fourteen years, since its occurrence, he had forborne to speak, let alone boast, to others about this unique privileged experience.

The event referred to took place fourteen years before the writing of this epistle, that is, about the year A.D. 44. Of Paul's visionary experiences recorded elsewhere we may rule out that of his conversion on the road to Damascus, which took place several years prior to A.D. 44, and about which, in any case, he delighted to speak (Acts 9:3ff., 22:6ff., 26:12ff.); that also of his trance during the first visit to Jerusalem following his escape from Damascus some three years after his conversion (Acts 22:17f.); and that of his second visit to Jerusalem (Acts 11:29f.) when, according to Gal. 2:2, he went up "by revelation", which should be placed probably a couple of years after A.D. 44. Both the vision of the man of Macedonia (Acts 16:9)—which is inappropriate to what he is describing here—and the vision he later saw in Corinth (Acts 18:9f.) took place a number of years after A.D. 44. Other occasions on which it has been suggested that Paul might have undergone the experience narrated here are those of his withdrawal into Arabia (Gal. 1:17) and his apparent death at Lystra as a result of stoning (Acts 14:19), when, so it is conjectured, his soul might have been caught up to heavenly places; but the former happened several years before and the latter several years after A.D. 44, and both accordingly must be eliminated as possibilities.

As far as we can estimate (and where so few data are available chronological reconstruction can be no more than tentative), in A.D. 44 Paul was probably in Antioch, where he spent a whole year (Acts 11:26). Some accordingly have inclined to the view that this ecstatic experience was closely connected with Paul's commissioning at Antioch as Apostle to the Gentiles, immediately prior to the commencement of his first missionary journey (Acts 13:1-4; see, for example, Allo, Zahn, Windisch, Plummer, Bachmann, Wordsworth). As, however, it is impossible to escape from the realm of conjecture, it is wise to be content with the passage before us, which affords the only precise information concerning this experience, especially as the Apostle himself evidently showed the greatest reserve in speaking about it at all. And the event alone is mentioned by him here, for the revelations granted him were in fact incommunicable to others (v. 4). We must learn what we can, then, from the things which he feels it right to divulge.

In the first place, Paul's uncertainty as to whether the rapture experienced was in the body or not indicates that a bodily rapture was not regarded by him as an impossibility. Indeed, the concept of bodily rapture formed an important element in his eschatological teaching. This is implicit in what he has already said in 5:1ff.; and it is explicit in what he had written some five years previously in his earliest extant epistle (I Thess. 4:15–17), where he affirms that at Christ's second advent the dead in Christ will first be raised and then those that are still alive will be caught up together with them to meet the Lord in the air. Doubtless this doctrine came to him "through revelation of Jesus Christ" (Gal. 1:12), who also had taught a rapture of Christians at His coming (cf. Mt. 24:40f.; Lk. 17:34f.; Jn. 14:3) —a revelation, though, that was communicable, in contrast to the revelation of which he is here speaking, which was incommunicable. There are two instances in the Old Testament of bodily rapture into heaven: that of Enoch (Gen. 5:24; cf. Heb. 11:5) and that of Elijah (II Kings 2:11; cf. Mk. 9:4). But the supreme and definitive precedent is that of the bodily ascension of Christ Himself into heaven, whither He has gone to prepare a place for those who are His (Jn. 14:2).

In the second place, it follows equally from what Paul says here that neither was an incorporeal rapture of the soul alone regarded by him as an impossibility. In fact, he has already in this epistle discussed the intermediate disembodied state of the soul between death and resurrection (5:1ff.), declaring that to be absent from the body, though an imperfect condition, is to be at home with the Lord, and thereby indicating that the intermediate condition of the soul is one of perceptive consciousness (cf. Phil. 1:23; Lk. 16:19ff.). If the experience he is now describing was one in which the soul was separated from the

431

body (and of this the Apostle cannot be certain), then it would provide confirmation of the inherent intuitive faculty of the human soul, if such confirmation were needed.

In the third place, we may conclude that by means of this ineffable experience Paul was granted a sight of the glory that lies ahead (as were, though under different circumstances, Peter, James, and John on the mount of transfiguration) and thereby fortified to endure patiently all the severe sufferings which awaited him in the prosecution of his ministry. Thus he was enabled to reckon that the sufferings of this present time are not worthy to be compared with the glory which shall at last be revealed to every "man in Christ" (Rom. 8:18; II Tim. 4:8).

It was not by virtue of some natural psychic propensity or any acquired capacity for mystical experience that Paul was caught up in this way, but by virtue of his being, through grace, a "man-in-Christ". And so too it is only the man-in-Christ who may anticipate exaltation to heavenly glory at the Lord's appearing. We find ourselves in radical disagreement with Allo when he declares, with reference to the occurrence which Paul is here narrating, that "we are assuredly on the terrain of the highest experience possible to mystical theology". It cannot be emphasized too strongly that what the Apostle is describing is an incomparable experience which has nothing to do with the questionable efforts and achievements of mysticism. Like the "thorn in the flesh" that followed, it was something unimagined and unsought by him.

THE THIRD HEAVEN

It remains to inquire what Paul means when he speaks of having been caught up into *the third heaven*. Belief in a hierarchical series of seven heavens is found in rabbinical teaching and also in Zoroastrianism, but whether it was prevalent in Paul's day is uncertain. It is difficult to discover any justification for Salmond's statement that "in view of the evidence, the most reasonable conclusion is that the conception of the heavens which pervades the Old Testament and the New Testament (not excepting the Pauline writings, though St. Paul mentions only the *third* heaven and *Paradise*) is that of a series of seven heavens".[98]

---

[98] S. D. F. Salmond, in HDB, II, p. 322. For the concept of a hierarchy of seven (or eight) heavens, cf. Irenaeus, *Adv. Haer.*, I, V, 2, xvii, 1, and

Nowhere does Scripture so much as hint at this number of heavens, and besides, as Irenaeus pointed out long ago, Paul "described that assumption of himself up to the third heaven as something great and pre-eminent",[99] which it certainly was not if there still remained four heavens beyond the one to which he was carried.

The fact that the plural form "heavens" [100] occurs in the New Testament is probably due to the influence of the Hebrew term *shamayim* [101] which is dual in form. The plural form is, in general, used interchangeably with the singular in the New Testament; and it is certainly worthy of remark that the plural is never used in the Fourth Gospel and the Apocalypse (with the single exception of Rev. 12:12, where there is a citation from the Septuagint), nor is it found in the writings of Paul's Jewish contemporaries Philo and Josephus. In Deut. 10:14 a distinction is made between "heaven" and "the heaven of heavens",[102] where the first "heaven" (or "heavens") should be understood of the *created* celestial, that is, non-terrestrial, order, and "the heaven of heavens" bespeaks the absolute transcendence of God's dwelling beyond the realm of creation (cf. I Kings 8:27). Accordingly, Ps. 68:33 speaks of God as riding upon "the heaven of heavens, which are of old", where the description of the heaven of heavens as being "of old" suggests an eternal realm which existed prior to creation. The distinction, then, is between the heavens, atmospheric and stellar, and that which is entirely other, limitless and unlocalized—between the created and the uncreated, the visible and the invisible, the material and the spiritual.

The probability is that Paul had in mind the conception of the heavens as threefold. Thus Bengel explains that the first heaven was that of the clouds, that is, of the earth's atmosphere, the second that of the stars (cf. the appearance of "the lights in the firmament of heaven" on the fourth day of creation, Gen. 1:14), and the third a heaven which is spiritual. But what we have said above concerning the Old Testament concept of a "heaven of heavens" would seem (if our interpretation is correct) to invalidate his conclusion that as the dual form of the Hebrew

---

xxx, 4, 5, Tertullian, *Adv. Valent.*, 20, Clement of Alexandria, *Strom.*, iv, 25, Origen, *De Princ.*, ii, 11, *Con. Cels.*, vi, 31, Epiphanius, *Haer.*, xxvi, 10, Augustine, *De Haer.*, i, 4.

[99] Irenaeus, *Adv. Haer.*, II, xxx, 7.
[100] Οὐρανοί.
[101] שָׁמַיִם.
[102] הַשָּׁמַיִם וּשְׁמֵי הַשָּׁמַיִם—the same dual form is used in each instance.

word *shamayim* indicates a twofold visible heaven, it was left to the New Testament to supply "the name of a *third* heaven, which the eye does not see".

When the author of the epistle to the Hebrews speaks of Christ as having "passed through the heavens" (4:14) and as having been "made higher than the heavens" (7:26) he is referring to the mighty expanse of the visible heavens and endeavouring to express the absolute exaltation and transcendence of Christ over the whole created order. As Bishop Westcott says: "Christ not merely ascended up to heaven in the language of space, but transcended the limitations of space. Thus we say that He 'entered into heaven' and yet is 'above the heavens'".[103] And again: "Under different aspects Christ may be said (1) to have been taken, or to have entered, 'into heaven' (Mark xvi. 19; Luke xxiv. 51; Acts i. 10f.; iii. 21; I Pet. iii. 22; c. ix. 24) and to be 'in heaven', Eph. vi. 9; and also (2) 'to have passed beyond the heavens' (Eph. vi. 10; c. iv. 14 note). The former phrase expresses His reception to the immediate presence of God: the latter His elevation above the limitations of sense".[104] Despite the assurances of Rudolf Bultmann and many other modern writers, it is not a simple question of a naïve, prescientific conception of a three-storeyed universe with which we are confronted in Scripture. The question is one of transcendence and pre-eminence, and this can only be expressed metaphorically by the use of "local" terms such as "above", "beyond", "higher", and so on, just as in our so-called scientific age they are necessarily also used metaphorically in everyday speech *and* in scientific language to express the ideas involved in gradation, comparison, and authority. Calvin, indeed, explains the number three implicit in our text in a purely symbolical sense: "The number *three* is made use of by way of eminence", he says, "to denote what is highest and most perfect". We may take it as certain that the Apostle, when he was caught up "even to the third heaven", was taken into the heavenly presence of the exalted and glorified Saviour—a transcendental and unparalleled experience by no means to be explained in ordinary terms of locality and space or equated with the ecstasies of the mystic or visionary. For this reason we find Augustine's comment, that "the intellectual vision of God, the cognition of God Himself, is called *the third heaven*",[105] unsatisfactory and too reminiscent of the contemplative philosophy of neoplatonism.

---

[103] B. F. Westcott, *Commentary on the Epistle to the Hebrews*, sub 4:14.
[104] B. F. Westcott, *op. cit.*, sub 7:26.
[105] Augustine, *Sup. Gen. ad Lit.*, 12.

12:3, 4

And I know such a man (whether in the body, or apart from the body, I know not; God knoweth), how that he was caught up into Paradise, and heard unspeakable words, which it is not lawful for a man to utter.

Opinion is divided as to whether the Apostle is here merely repeating and amplifying what he has just said in verse 2 or is describing a second and different, or additional, rapture. The "and" at the beginning of the sentence at least seems to indicate that he is narrating something additional to what has gone before. Yet the chronological information of verse 2—"fourteen years ago"—argues that Paul is here concerned with one particular experience. If "Paradise" is identical with "the third heaven", then what he now writes is repetitive: the term "Paradise" serves to define "the third heaven" more precisely. If, however, it is to be distinguished from "the third heaven", then he is adding something new to what he has already said: it is a further stage in the sequence of events. Clement of Alexandria,[106] Irenaeus,[107] Origen,[108] Oecumenius, Theophylact, Athanasius,[109] Jerome,[110] Hilary, Ambrosiaster, Primasius, Anselm, Erasmus, Bengel, Meyer, Wordsworth, Denney, and Plummer are among those who favour the view that Paul experienced two raptures, or two stages in the one rapture, first of all to the third heaven, and then from there to Paradise. It may be, however, that Alford is right in supposing that we have here a solemn repetition of the information of verse 2, "Paradise" being substituted for "the third heaven" as its equivalent, and the *additional* information being limited to what Paul now says about having heard unspeakable words. That "Paradise" and "the third heaven" are synonymous terms is the view also of Theodoret, Augustine,[111] Aquinas, Estius, Hodge, Bachmann, Windisch, Tasker, and most modern commentators, and also of Swete and Charles.[112] The

---

[106] Clement of Alexandria. *Strom.*, i, 5.
[107] Irenaeus, *Adv. Haer.*, II, lv.
[108] Origen, on Rom. 16.
[109] Athanasius, in *Apol.*
[110] Jerome, on Ezek. 28:13.
[111] Augustine, *Sup. Gen ad Lit.*, 12.
[112] Commenting on Rev. 2:7.

two places are identified with each other in the apocryphal *Revelation of Moses*, and sometimes also in the rabbinical literature.

PARADISE

Before forming a judgment on the questions that face us in this passage it is advisable to take into account the significance which was attached to the term "Paradise" in Scripture and in the early centuries of the Christian era. The word itself is probably Persian in origin, meaning an "enclosure", and hence a pleasure-garden or park. It should be noticed that in the Septuagint version of the Old Testament it is used to render the expression "garden of Eden".[113] In the New Testament it occurs only three times: (i) Lk. 23:43, where Christ assures the penitent thief, "Today thou shalt be with Me in Paradise"; (ii) our present text, and (iii) Rev. ii. 7, "To him that overcometh, to him will I give to eat of the tree of life, which is in the Paradise of God". It is evident that our own text and also Rev. 2:7 speak of a *heavenly* Paradise, and, further, that the tree of life mentioned in the latter links the original Paradise, which man lost because of sin, with the heavenly Paradise, wherein all blessedness is restored to mankind redeemed in Christ (cf. Rev. 22:1ff.). Hence we may conclude that the Paradise of II Cor. 12:4 is one and the same with the Paradise of Rev. 2:7. But what of the Paradise of Lk. 23:43? Does that refer to a quite different place or state, as some scholars have believed? Does it involve a *descent* to hades rather than an *ascent* to heaven? Such a view we find unacceptable. We do not hesitate to assert that the Paradise of which Christ spoke to the penitent thief is identical with that of our text and of Rev. 2:7. If our Lord descended to hades, it was to liberate the souls of the just who had been awaiting His triumph and thence to lead them to the heavenly Paradise won for them through His conquest on the Cross. It was there that the penitent thief was *with Him* on the day of his death. It was thither that Paul was transported in this rapture which he experienced. It is there that, after death, the souls of believers are *with Christ* even now (Phil. 1:23), rejoicing in His presence. (It should, of course, be remembered that in this context terms such as "ascent" and "descent" are symbolically diagrammatic rather than geographical.)

The early Fathers regarded Paradise as a place where the souls of believers congregated after death to await the bodily

---

[113] Thus in Gen. 2 and 3 גַּן עֵדֶן = παράδεισος (LXX).

resurrection at the end of this age. Origen, indeed, held it to be located somewhere on the earth's surface;[114] and this opinion was shared by the pseudepigraphical writers who in general believed it to be identical in locality with the original garden of Eden, to which certain privileged individuals had been admitted by God. Thus in the *Gospel of Nicodemus* Enoch, Elijah, and the penitent thief are found there, and Adam also enters in to join them, together with all the saints.[115] In the *Narrative of Joseph* the penitent thief alone is to dwell in Paradise until Christ's second appearing.[116] In the *Revelation of Esdras* God says to the prophet Esdras, "I will give rest in Paradise to the righteous", and there he is shown "Enoch and Elijah and Moses and Peter and Paul and Luke and Matthew, and all the righteous, and the patriarchs". In the *Revelation of Paul* Mary the mother of the Lord, Abraham, Isaac, and Jacob, "the righteous forefathers", and all the patriarchs from Abraham to Manasseh, Moses the lawgiver, the prophets Isaiah, Jeremiah, and Ezekiel, Noah, Enoch, and Elijah are encountered in Paradise, in that order. And in the *Revelation of Moses* Adam is raised into Paradise, "even to the third heaven" (an echo of our present passage) after his death. These are, of course, apocryphal writings, full of fancies and discrepancies; but they do at least supplement the unanimous voice of the Church of the early centuries that Paradise is a place of rest and bliss for those who enter it after death.

Our own judgment is that Paul is speaking of one rapture, not two, in these verses; but that, none the less, he is not merely repeating himself when he says that he was caught up into Paradise. The mention of Paradise gives added information. The Apostle was caught up "*as far as* [117] the third heaven": this specifies the "height" or "distance" of his rapture. Also, but not separately, he was caught up "*into* [118] Paradise": this specifies the "depth" of his rapture, and is a more precise disclosure of the particular "part" or nature of the third heaven into which he was taken. There, it may be presumed, he witnessed the state of the disembodied spirits of the redeemed who had been overtaken by death

---

[114] Origen, *De Princ.*, II, ix, 6.

[115] *Gospel of Nicodemus*, Part II ("The Descent of Christ into Hell"), chapters 9 and 10.

[116] *Narrative of Joseph*, chapter 3.

[117] Ἑώς.

[118] Εἰς.

—a blissful and desirable state, for they are "at home with the Lord" (5:8), but still an imperfect state until the day when their nakedness is covered by the assumption of the glorified and incorruptible resurrection body (see commentary above on 5:1ff.; and cf. I Cor. 15:42ff.; Phil. 3:20f.). Then at last redeemed humanity will shine forth in the full splendour of eternal Christlikeness.

We must emphasize again, however, that in attempting to understand and explain something of this experience which carried Paul, whether in body or in spirit, beyond the confines of this earth into the sphere of ultimate spiritual reality, we are able to employ only our own familiar mundane language, which in the nature of the case is incapable of describing with any adequacy things that transcend all mundane knowledge and comprehension. We may find it necessary to speak of Paradise as though it were a "locality" to be defined in terms of a heavenly "topography", whereas the truth is that we are stepping over the threshold of a quite different dimension, not of this world, infinite, eternal, spiritual, only dimly and distantly sensed by us in this earthly vale, and yet known with assurance by those who are Christ's to be the realm of their true home. In Holy Scripture the mists of our earthly existence are occasionally parted and we are permitted brief glimpses of the glory yet to be revealed. Paul, however, was granted the unique privilege of entry for a while, during the course of his earthly pilgrimage, into that very glory of heaven. That was an experience of things otherwise unseen by human eye, unheard by human ear, and unfelt by human heart this side of heaven (cf. I Cor. 2:9), and accordingly incommunicable to others.

Paradise, then, is not a shadowy waiting-room, but a blissful abode within the very courts of heaven itself. Its glory is that of the ultimate heavenly glory, namely, the glory of the presence of the Son of God (cf. Rev. 7:9ff., 22:1ff.). There, in the Paradise of God, the souls of the saints are at home with Christ, the last Adam (I Cor. 15:45). There they are beyond the reach of sin and suffering, without fear of being driven out, as happened in the first Paradise. There they await the crowning consummation of their redemption, which is the union of soul and resurrection body, when the new heavens and the new earth will be introduced and all God's purposes in creation finally and eternally fulfilled.

In Paradise Paul heard words unspeakable. This paradoxical language indicates that the revelation he received on this occasion was incapable of translation into human and earthly terminology. It was an ineffable communication intended for him alone, which also, even if it were possible, it was not lawful for him to repeat.[119] There was no question, therefore, of an esoteric form of Pauline doctrine or gnosis to be passed on only to an inner circle of selected initiates. The things which the Apostle received to communicate he communicated to all, speaking not in terms of man's philosophy but under the tuition of the Holy Spirit (I Cor. 2:11ff.). It may perhaps be that certain aspects of the truth he beheld in Paradise were in fact communicable in some measure and are reflected in the knowledge he was able to impart concerning the intermediate and final states of the Christian believer (for example, 5:1ff.; I Cor. 15:50ff.; Rom. 8:38f.; Phil. 1:21, 23; 3:20f.; I Thess. 4:13ff.; II Tim. 4:8). But the particular revelation which he mentions here could not be disclosed and was kept sacred between himself and God. In answer to the objection that this revelation, having been "buried in perpetual silence", seems consequently to serve no good purpose, Calvin explains that it took place "for the sake of Paul himself, for one who had such arduous difficulties awaiting him, enough to break a thousand hearts, required to be strengthened by special means that he might not give way, but might persevere undaunted". And Calvin deduces the further lesson that we "should not seek to know anything but what the Lord has seen good to reveal to His Church", and that we should be content "to let this be the limit of our knowledge".

Yet this extraordinary revelation, though not communicable to other ears, must have exercised an incalculable influence on Paul's whole ministry and apostleship, providing, it may be, a key to his astonishing zeal and indefatigable labours through which untold blessing flowed not only to his own generation but to every subsequent generation in the history of the Church. Though he was its sole recipient, its effects did not end in him.

---

[119] Οὐκ ἐξόν may also mean "it is not possible", and so Olshausen understands it here. But the meaning "it is not lawful" is preferable, firstly, because the adjective ἄρρητα, "unspeakable", has already indicated the impossibility of communicating what was heard, and, secondly, because ἔξεστι elsewhere in the New Testament (31 times) always seems to bear the meaning "it is lawful".

12 : 5, 6

On behalf of such a one will I glory: but on mine own behalf I will not glory, save in my weaknesses. For if I should desire to glory, I shall not be foolish; for I shall speak the truth: but I forbear, lest any man should account of me above that which he seeth me to be, or heareth from me.

Paul reiterates his determination to glory only in his weaknesses. There were certainly things in which, unlike his opponents, he could glory with perfect veracity; and if he were to do so he would not imitate their folly of self-esteem, for none realizes better than the Apostle that in self there is no cause whatever for glorying or commendation (cf. Rom. 7:18). Self-vaunting is not only foolish, but also false. It subverts the fundamental truth that to God alone is all glory due. Paul's glorying in the ineffable experience of fourteen years ago is a glorying in truth, not in self; indeed, that experience was so unique, so other-worldly, that he speaks of it as though it had happened to a different person. In any case, how could he take glory to himself for an experience which, being beyond every human capacity, was attributable only to the omnipotence of God—an experience, moreover, which had transported him into the glorious presence of his Saviour to whom as pre-eminent the redeemed will delight to ascribe honour and praise throughout eternity (cf. Rev. 5:12f.; Phil. 2:10f.)? And so he forbears to embark on that glorying which even he might recognize as legitimate, such as rejoicing over the wonderful privilege of his rapture into the third heaven; for he fears that to do so might lead others to form an estimate of him in excess of what they see him to be by his actions or hear him to be by his words, namely, a frail fellow-mortal of like passions with themselves (cf. Jas. 5:17).

In subsequent centuries, however, and indeed right up to the present day, many people have fallen into this very error which Paul sought to prevent, regarding him and the other Apostles of Christ as more than human and elevating them to a position which they would without hesitation have repudiated, notably blessed among men though they were. To see how *ordinary* they were in themselves, it is necessary only to read the account of them in the Gospels (or in Paul's case to heed his self-testimony, especially Rom. 7). To see how the power of the Holy Spirit can transform ordinary men into *extraordinary* men, it is necessary only to read the Acts of the Apostles. And it is ever the work of the Holy Spirit miraculously to transform human lives in this way. The very same power which was active in the lives of the Apostles is available in all its fulness for us today; and, as with them, the glory belongs entirely to God (10:17).[120]

12:7

And by reason of the exceeding greatness of the revelations, that I should not be exalted overmuch, there was given to me a thorn in the flesh, a messenger of Satan to buffet me, that I should not be exalted overmuch.

Here we arrive at the true purpose behind Paul's disclosure of his rapture to the third heaven: it was in order that, while glorying in weaknesses, he might expose and explain his greatest disability of all. And it is most remarkable how, by a kind of condign paradox, the explaining of his deepest humiliation requires the revealing of his highest exaltation, so that the very point where his adversaries hold him to be most contemptible is linked with an ineffable experience far outshining the tawdry tinsel of their vaunting. Thus by an unexpected justice the tables are turned against them and the hypocrisy of their position is exposed for all to see.

---

[120] Some have taken ὑπὲρ τοῦ τοιούτου as neuter, for example, Luther and Moffatt ("of an experience like that I am prepared to boast"); but (i) τοῦ τοιούτου here is most naturally taken as masculine corresponding to the masculine τὸν τοιοῦτον of verse 2, which is repeated in verse 3; (ii) ὑπὲρ τοῦ τοιούτου is balanced by ὑπὲρ ἐμαυτοῦ, and the former, like the latter, should be treated as personal; (iii) with καυχᾶσθαι, the preposition ὑπέρ ("on behalf of") is generally used of a person (cf. 7:14, ὑπὲρ ὑμῶν κεκαύχημαι, and 9:2, ὑπὲρ ὑμῶν καυχῶμαι), whereas the preposition ἐν ("in") is used of a thing; accordingly, in this same verse, when Paul speaks of glorying in weaknesses he passes from ὑπὲρ ἐμαυτοῦ to ἐν ταῖς ἀσθενείαις. So, too, ὑπὲρ τούτου at the beginning of verse 8 should be understood in a quasi-personal sense of the ἄγγελος Σατανᾶ (v. 7): "concerning this messenger of Satan", rather than impersonally: "concerning this thing", as in the English versions and the Vulgate (*propter quod*).

PAUL'S "THORN IN THE FLESH"

The problem of Paul's "thorn in the flesh" is another one of those questions which, on the evidence available, must remain unanswered. Over the centuries many solutions have been proposed, frequently with excessive confidence, but the plain fact is that it is impossible to escape from the realm of conjecture, which is by its nature the realm of inconclusiveness. Presumably those to whom the Apostle wrote knew well enough the character of this particular infirmity with which he was afflicted, but there is an absence of any firm tradition which might enable us to identify it. His silence concerning such symptoms as would have enabled a diagnosis to be made may have been a cause of exasperation to some curious souls. But we are convinced that this silence was in accordance with the mind of God and that therefore, as we shall endeavour to show, it is, and has always been, of more benefit to the Church to remain in ignorance on this matter than would have been the case had the nature of the affliction been fully known. Let us suppose that Paul had supplied specific details regarding his "thorn in the flesh", and that, of the sake of argument, it was some particular form of epilepsy; then subsequent generations of Christians, the great majority of whom have been free from this complaint, would have been inclined to dismiss the Apostle's problem as one remote from the reality of their own experience.

As things are, however, there has been a discernible tendency, as Bishop Lightfoot has pointed out, for interpreters in different periods of the Church's history to see "in the Apostle's temptation a more or less perfect reflection of the trials which beset their own lives".[121] This tendency, unconscious though it has been, is perfectly understandable. It has been an *instinctive* tendency, and there is no doubt that it has been a *right* tendency (though only, of course, a tendency and not a universal rule); for it is of the essence of Holy Scripture that it is profitable (II Tim. 3:16) and applicable in a truly dynamic and existential manner to every circumstance and to every age of the Church and of the individual Christian within the Church.

Is there a single servant of Christ who cannot point to some "thorn in the flesh", visible or private, physical or psychological, from which he has prayed to be released, but which has been given him by God to keep him humble, and therefore,

---

[121] J. B. Lightfoot, *Commentary on the Epistle to the Galatians*, pp. 186ff. See also Plummer, who seems to follow Lightfoot in this respect.

fruitful, in His service? And is not this the case to a special degree with those who have been called to be ministers of the gospel? Every believer must learn that human weakness and divine grace go hand in hand together. Hence Paul's "thorn in the flesh" is, by its very lack of definition, a type of every Christian's "thorn in the flesh", not with regard to externals, but by its spiritual significance.

We do not propose to swell the number of conjectures concerning the precise nature of Paul's "thorn in the flesh". The great diversity of solutions which have been offered from the early centuries onward is sufficient warning to those who may think that they have answered the problem—not, of course, that we regard the formulation of conjectures as illegitimate; but we do feel that in this instance history has proved that no amount of induction, however ingenious, is going to dispel the uncertainty with which the subject is enveloped.

The earliest reference is found in Tertullian who mentions that it was said that Paul's malady was earache or headache.[122] The tradition that it was headache is noticed also by Chrysostom, Pelagius, and Primasius, when commenting on this verse, and also by Jerome with reference to Gal. 4:13. Chrysostom, however, finds the suggestion that Paul's body was given over to Satan for the infliction of physical pain quite unacceptable, and, taking the term "Satan" in its general Hebrew sense of "adversary", understands this "messenger of Satan" by whom he was buffeted to signify "Alexander the coppersmith, the party of Hymeneus and Philetas, and all the adversaries of the word, those who contended with him and fought against him, those that cast him into prison, those that beat him, that led him away to death; for they did Satan's business". This view that Paul's "thorn in the flesh" refers to the endurance of outward persecutions has the support of Augustine, Theodore of Mopsuestia, Theodoret, Photius, and Theophylact, as well as of some of the Latin commentators—though in his homily on Psalm 99 Augustine understands it as "perhaps some bodily pain". Most recently, R. V. G. Tasker has shown an inclination to accept Chrysostom's explanation: "As there is nothing", he says, "which tends to elate a Christian evangelist so much as the enjoyment of spiritual experiences, and as there is nothing so calculated to deflate the spiritual pride which may follow them as the opposition he

---

[122] Tertullian, *De Pudic.*, xiii, 16.

encounters while preaching the Word, it is not unlikely that Chrysostom's interpretation is nearer the truth than any other".

The Vulgate rendering (or rather misrendering), "spur (or goad) of the flesh" (*stimulus carnis*) may have given rise, as Luther supposes, to the opinion that Paul was afflicted with impure temptations of the flesh—an opinion which prevailed in the medieval period and which continued to be generally approved by Roman Catholic writers. Cornelius à Lapide, in fact, writing in the seventeenth century, declares that the interpretation of Paul's affliction as the temptation of carnal lust was universally held by "the faithful", that is, in the Roman Catholic Church. This view is dismissed by Calvin as ridiculous. In the Reformer's judgment the reference is to "every kind of temptation with which Paul was exercised". Luther also, when commenting on Gal. 4:13, rejects the view that temptation to impurity is intended by Paul, or, for that matter, some physical ailment, and explains the "thorn in the flesh" of the various temptations and persecutions to which the Apostle was subject; though, as Lightfoot points out, in his later Table-Talk he speaks of spiritual trials only.

Of more recent hypotheses there are several that deserve mention. One is that Paul suffered from some severe form of ophthalmia. As evidence for this attention is drawn to Gal. 4:15 where Paul, who has just been speaking of "an infirmity of the flesh" (v. 13), says that the Galatians would, if possible, have plucked out their eyes and given them to him. It is further suggested that hints of defective eyesight may be discerned in Gal. 6:11, where the Apostle, when writing with his own hand, forms large letters; in Acts 23:5, where he fails to recognize the high priest; and in the temporary blindness associated with his conversion and accompanied, as some think, by a secretion because of the impression of scales falling from his eyes when his sight was restored (Acts 9:9, 18). Interesting though these suggestions may be, they are of very doubtful worth. The reference to Gal. 4:15 has more substance, though it is possible that Paul is speaking metaphorically when he says that the Galatians would, if possible, have plucked out their eyes and given them to him, that is to say, they would have done anything to assist him in whatever distress he was enduring. In our opinion, however, the qualification "if possible" points to a literal rather than a metaphorical sense, so that it is more probable that in this passage there is an allusion to an actual affliction of the eyes; but whether this was connected with the Apostle's "thorn in the flesh" it is impossible to determine.

Another theory that has found favour is that Paul suffered

444

from a form of epilepsy—a complaint which as it recurred would have been highly distressing both to him and to his friends. Other great men, such as Caesar, Muhammed, Cromwell, and Napoleon, have been cited as epileptics, but it is extremely questionable whether they were in fact such, and in any case modern medical knowledge, when related to what we know of Paul, leads to the conclusion that the symptoms of epilepsy are unlikely to have been those of his "thorn in the flesh".[123]

Perhaps no recent conjecture has aroused greater interest than that of Sir William Ramsay who strongly advocated the form of recurrent malarial fever which is known in the Eastern Mediterranean, and particularly in Pamphylia, as satisfying every symptom of Paul's infirmity deducible from the New Testament. "In some constitutions", he writes, "malaria fever tends to recur in very distressing and prostrating paroxysms, whenever one's energies are taxed for a great effort. Such an attack is for the time absolutely incapacitating: the sufferer can only lie and feel himself a shaking and helpless weakling, when he ought to be at work. He feels a contempt and loathing for self, and believes that others feel equal contempt and loathing. ... A strong corroboration is found in the phrase: 'a stake in the flesh', which Paul uses about his malady (II Cor. 12:7). That is the peculiar headache which accompanies the paroxysms: within my experience several persons, innocent of Pauline theorizing, have described it as 'like a red-hot bar thrust through the forehead'. As soon as fever connected itself with Paul in my mind, the 'stake in the flesh' impressed me as a strikingly illustrative metaphor; and the oldest tradition on the subject, quoted by Tertullian and others, explains the 'stake in the flesh' as a headache." Ramsay supposes that Paul contracted this fever on reaching Perga in Pamphylia, during his first missionary journey (Acts 13:13).[124] W. M. Alexander believes that the Apostle's complaint may be identified more specifically as Malta fever, which is accompanied by severe pain, nocturnal delirium, unsightly eruptions, and loss of hair, and which may be fatal in its effects.[125] This theory of intermittent paludinous fever is enthusiastically espoused by Allo, who maintains that it "accounts without a single difficulty for everything that Paul tells us concerning his malady".

---

[123] See Allo's discussion of this theory, pp. 316ff.

[124] W. M. Ramsay, *St. Paul the Traveller and the Roman Citizen*, pp. 94ff.; *The Church in the Roman Empire*, pp. 62ff.

[125] W. M. Alexander, "St. Paul's Infirmity", in *The Expository Times*, Vol. X (1904).

In our own day Ph. H. Menoud has advanced the novel hypothesis that the Apostle's "thorn in the flesh" was not a physical complaint at all, but was "the great sorrow and unceasing pain" which he experienced in his heart because of the unbelief of his Jewish compatriots (Rom. 9:1–3). He maintains that, while Paul often speaks of sufferings associated with the exercise of his apostolate, he never speaks of his state of health, and that nothing justifies the supposition that he was a sick man. "Sickness never intervenes to modify or disrupt his plans for travelling.[126] ... The missionary career of Paul, his boundless activity, his incessant journeyings, do not bespeak a valetudinarian." If our present verse refers to an illness, then, in M. Menoud's judgment, it conflicts with what Paul had previously written in I Cor. 11:30, where illness is conceived as a punishment with which God afflicts unworthy believers.[127] He understands the "thorn in the flesh" as a trial which was peculiar to the Apostle Paul. "All missionaries", he says, "are exposed to perils and persecutions; Paul alone suffers, in addition, the special trial which is the counterweight—as the context shows—of the exceptional revelations which he enjoyed." The solution he offers is, however, original rather than convincing.[128]

Many other solutions have been advanced, such as hysteria, hypochondria, gallstones, gout, rheumatism, sciatica, gastritis, leprosy, lice in the head, deafness, dental infection, neurasthenia, an impediment of the speech, and remorse for the tortures he had himself inflicted on Christians prior to his conversion; and no doubt there will be fresh proposals in years to come, for this is a matter which is unlikely to be regarded as closed while there are minds to speculate on it. As we have already indicated, while we do not wish to disparage sane speculation, we are convinced that the very anonymity of this particular affliction has been and is still productive of far wider blessing to the members of the Church universal than would have been the case had it been possible to identify with accuracy the specific nature of the disability in question.

---

[126] This sweeping statement is unwarranted; cf., for example, Gal. 4:13f., I Thess. 2:18, also 1:8 in our own epistle, and Paul's repeated allusions to "weaknesses", some at least of which were probably due to illness.

[127] The implication that this was Paul's doctrine concerning *all* illness that overtook Christians in whatever circumstances is inadmissible; cf., for example, I Tim. 5:23, Phil. 2:25ff.

[128] Ph. H. Menoud, *L'Echarde et L'Ange Satanique*, in *Studia Paulina* (*ut supra*), pp. 163ff.

The proper meaning of the Greek word [129] translated "thorn" in our English version is "stake" (as in the margin), or a sharpened wooden shaft.   In Hellenistic Greek, however, the modified meaning of thorn or splinter is found,[130] though not to the exclusion of the original meaning.   In Origen, indeed, we find the term used contemptuously by Celsus for the cross,[131] and Eustathius identifies "crosses" and "stakes".[132] We cannot agree with Stanley's inference, however, that Paul's metaphor is analogous to the expression "I am crucified with Christ" (Gal. 2:20); for it is evident that the Apostle has in mind the picture of impalement or transfixion rather than crucifixion.   What he says is, literally: "there was given to me a stake *for* the flesh",[133] rather than "*in* the flesh".   This is of importance from the point of view of exegesis: "in the flesh" would almost certainly indicate that the reference is to some *physical* affliction of the body; whereas "for the flesh" at least leaves this an open question.   It seems to us that Paul is thinking graphically of a body helplessly impaled. He sees himself as it were transfixed, painfully held down and humiliated, for the purpose, twice expressed, that he should not be exalted overmuch as a result of the surpassing wonder of the revelations he had been granted.

This stake for his flesh is further described as a "messenger (or angel) of Satan".   This, as we have seen, has been understood by some to signify that Paul is speaking of a person rather than a thing.   It need indicate no more, however, than that this stake for the flesh was satanic in origin, attributable to demonic agency, though permitted by God and overruled by Him for His servant's good.   As was the case with Job (Job 2:1ff.), God's gracious and restraining hand is never removed.   And as always, the Heavenly Father's chastening is "for our profit, that we may be partakers of His holiness" (Heb. 12:10).[134]

---

[129] Σκόλοψ.

[130] Cf. the Septuagint version of Num. 33:55, Ezek. 28:24, Hos. 2:6, and Ecclus. 43:19, and also the evidence in Moulton and Milligan and in Arndt and Gingrich.

[131] Origen, *Con. Cels.*, ii, 55, 68.

[132] Σταυροί, ὄρθα καὶ ἀπωξυμμένα ξύλα — οἱ δὲ αὐτοὶ σκόλοπες λέγονται.

[133] Σκόλοψ τῇ σαρκί, a *dativus incommodi*.

[134] The present tenses κολαφίζῃ and ὑπεραίρωμαι suggest that Paul is not alluding to some single attack or affliction in the past, but to a buffeting which he has constantly, or it may be recurrently, to endure.

The stake for the flesh, then, of which Paul is speaking may mean a "stake" for his physical frame, that is, a physical affliction, or a "stake" for the flesh understood in the ethical sense, that is, for the *carnal* nature, in which case either a physical or a psychological visitation may be intended. But the ethical sense is less likely here, in a narrative passage, since ordinarily Paul reserves it for a doctrinal-ethical context in which "the flesh" and "the Spirit" are set forth as opposing forces. If it is correct to associate (as is generally done) the Apostle's stake for the flesh with Gal. 4:13f., then the expression is certainly intended of a physical disability. "Ye know", he reminds the Galatians, "that because of an infirmity of the flesh I preached the gospel unto you the first time; and that which was a temptation to you in my flesh ye despised not, nor rejected; but ye received me as an angel of God, even as Christ Jesus". From this it may be deduced that when he first came to Galatia he was stopped short by a physical illness or infirmity; that this was of an unpleasant, indeed repulsive,[135] nature; and that consequently the Galatians were tempted to regard the Apostle with disgust. Is it possible that when he says that, in spite of this, they received him as a messenger (angel) of God [136] he had in mind at the same time that he was being buffeted by a messenger (angel) of Satan?[137] Whether this is so or not, in Galatia his journey was interrupted (though this was overruled by God so that as a result the gospel was preached to the Galatians) by an unpleasant and humiliating ailment. Was the stake for the flesh one and the same with the affliction which overtook him in Asia, weighing him down exceedingly, beyond his power, so that he despaired even of life (1:8)? And does he refer to the same thing when he tells the Thessalonians that, having wished to visit them once and again, it was Satan that hindered him on each occasion (I Thess. 2:18)? These are some of the interesting suggestions which have been proposed and which, although they inevitably fall short of certainty, are deserving of sympathetic consideration.[138]

---

135 The word rendered "rejected" means literally "spat out": ἐξεπτύσατε.

136 Ἄγγελος θεοῦ.

137 Ἄγγελος Σατανᾶ.

138 Westcott and Hort give it as their opinion that διό and the second ἵνα μὴ ὑπεραίρωμαι have come into the text as the result of a primitive error. The διό is in fact omitted in P⁴⁶, in numerous codices, in Latin and Syriac

12 : 8, 9a

Concerning this thing I besought the Lord thrice, that it might depart from me. And he said unto me, My grace is sufficient for thee: for my power is made perfect in weakness.

The three occasions on which Paul besought the Lord for deliverance were most probably associated with three separate and severe assaults of this messenger of Satan.[139] Three times, like the Lord Himself in the garden of Gethsemane, the Apostle

---

versions, and in Irenaeus, Origen, Chrysostom, and Augustine, and its removal would mean the solution of the main difficulty with which the Greek text confronts us. But, until further evidence is forthcoming, the canon *difficilior lectio potior* demands its inclusion. Our own English text reflects exactly the text without the διό. RV and Souter retain the διό, but suppose a lacuna in the construction after the preceding word ἀποκαλύψεων: "and by reason of the exceeding greatness of the revelations—wherefore, that I should not be exalted overmuch, there was given to me, etc." Westcott and Hort, Soden, and Nestlé, however while retaining the διό, follow ℵ, A, and B in making it the beginning of a new sentence which is a very natural usage for διό. In this case the phrase καὶ τῇ ὑπερβολῇ τῶν ἀποκαλύψεων belongs to verse 6, and the sense is as follows: " . . . but I forbear lest any man should account of me above that which he seeth me to be, or heareth from me, and (I forbear) by reason of the exceeding greatness of the revelations"; or, in accordance with Allo's proposal that the expression should be attached to the verb λογίσηται: " . . . but I forbear, lest any man should account of me above that which he seeth me to be or heareth from me and (should account of me) on the basis of the exceeding greatness of the revelations". More awkward is the suggestion of Lachmann that the phrase should go with the latter part of verse 5: " . . . but on mine own behalf I will not glory, save in my weaknesses . . . and by reason of the exceeding greatness of the revelations", treating verse 6 as parenthetical. But more awkward still is the proposal of Bachmann and others that διό should be omitted and verses 5 and 6 treated as a parenthesis. The διό, if it is retained, most naturally refers back to what immediately precedes. It should perhaps be regarded as an emphatic redundancy: "and because of the exceeding greatness of the revelations, for *that* reason, lest I should be exalted overmuch, there was given to me, etc."

The second ἵνα μὴ ὑπεραίρωμαι is merely repetitive and constitutes no real difficulty. It is far more likely to have dropped out as an unnecessary repetition —a good many documents do in fact omit it—than to have crept into the text. Paul repeats it in Plummer's view, "either through forgetfulness, or (more probably) because he wishes his readers not to forget the purpose of the σκόλοψ".

[139] Grammatically, ὑπὲρ τούτου refers to the ἄγγελος Σατανᾶ rather than the σκόλοψ τῇ σαρκί, as is indicated by the verb ἀφίστημι which is used of persons, not of things, throughout the New Testament. Cf. the use of the same verb in connection with the departing of the devil from Jesus in Lk. 4:13

made this petition, for, again as with the Lord, all outward circumstances suggested that Satan was about to score a crushing triumph. But the fearsome concentration of all the powers of darkness against God's Anointed One in Gethsemane and at Calvary was powerless to overthrow or in the slightest measure to frustrate the determined purpose of God. Indeed, the very raging of Satan himself was overruled and utilized by God for the achievement of the supreme victory of divine grace. So with the Apostle, what seems to be an incapacitating conquest by Satan's messenger is transformed into a triumph of grace and a vindication of the sovereignty of Almighty God.

The legitimacy of Paul's petitions was not in doubt. He longed to be free from these satanic assaults which threatened to cripple and thwart him in the prosecution of the apostolic work to which he had been called. And we can imagine with what compassion his petitions were received by the Lord, who Himself had been so savagely buffeted by Satan, and who Himself "in the days of his flesh offered up prayers and supplications with strong crying and tears unto Him that was able to save Him from death" (Heb. 5:7; cf. 4:15f.). The prayers of God's people are never unheard, and they are never unheeded; but every believer must learn the lesson that God's answer to a particular petition, as with Paul here, may be "No", plus the revelation of some better way. So the Lord grants His Apostle a very definite answer to his thrice-repeated supplication. The answer, however, does not come immediately, but only after the third occasion, which illustrates the Lord's own teaching that it is necessary to persevere trustingly in prayer (Lk. 11:8). Delay in answering is intended to test the earnestness of the petitioner and to emphasize his utter dependence upon the divine mercy. Nor should it be thought that a negative answer conflicts with the Lord's promise that he who keeps on asking will receive (Lk. 11:9f.). Not to receive what one asks for does not mean not to receive at all; for the Heavenly Father always and only gives *good* things, and especially the gift of the Holy Spirit, to them that ask Him (Mt. 7:11;

(ὁ διάβολος ἀπέστη ἀπ' αὐτοῦ); and see note on verse 5 above concerning the use of ὑπέρ with persons.

Chrysostom and Calvin understand τρίς ("three times") here symbolically as signifying "many times"; but there appears to be little justification for departing from the literal sense.

Lk. 11:13). Thus the Lord's answers to prayer are never negative, except in a superficial and proximate sense; for essentially and in the ultimate issue they are fully positive, and directed to the eternal blessing of His people.

The stake for the flesh, then, continued to afflict the Apostle. But while it remained so also did the force and validity of the Lord's answer to his supplication: "He hath said . . .," and what He has said remains unshakeably firm.[140] To this answer, in which the will of God is revealed, Paul submits. It is not a case of his *resigning* himself to it as to an unwelcome but inexorable fate. He *welcomes* it, "most gladly", with full existential eagerness. He commits himself to it without regret or reservation. As here, so always, God's answer to prayer is *dynamic*, and it demands and makes possible a dynamic response. Enthusiastic willingness for the will of God, whatever it may entail, is the mark of genuine faith. In the Christian perspective there is no place for the aimless non-resistance of dispirited resignation.

"My grace is sufficient for thee: for My power is made perfect in weakness". This is the summit of the epistle, the lofty peak from which the whole is viewed in true proportion. From this vantage-point the entire range of Paul's apostleship is seen in focus—his calling, his conversion, his weaknesses, his trials, and his labours, his conquests and his exaltations—all fall into place; and as the splendour of the sun lights up and transfigures the dark ravines of a great mountain, so the grace of God transfuses and triumphs over, and even through, what is least impressive in the Apostle's constitution. All is of grace (I Cor. 15:10); the glory belongs to the Lord alone (10:17); the divine power is supreme. Indeed, the abject weakness of the human instrument serves to magnify and throw into relief the perfection of the divine power in a way that any suggestion of human adequacy could never do. The greater the servant's weakness, the more conspicuous is the power of his Master's all-sufficient grace.

---

[140] Εἴρηκε—perfect tense, the significance of which is that the force of something done in the past continues in the present: thus the word spoken to Paul after his third petition abides with present power. Similarly, it is said of Christ's resurrection, ἐγήγερται (I Cor. 15:4), and of the word of Scripture our Lord declared γέγραπται (Mt. 4:4, 7, 10). Compare the perfect εἴρηκε here with the aorist παρεκάλεσα: Paul did beseech in the past, but he does so no more, for he has received an answer of permanent validity.

12 : 9b

> Most gladly therefore will I rather glory in my weaknesses,
> that the power of Christ may rest upon me.

In consequence of the great reassurance concerning the all-sufficiency of God's grace, Paul now, rather than plead for release from his stake for the flesh and other apparent disabilities, welcomes weaknesses and glories in them most gladly as a means to the realization of the power of Christ abiding on him. Nothing, of course, could be more incongruous than to saddle this great preacher of salvation by grace alone through faith alone (cf. Eph. 2:8) with the errors of a later ascetic theology which encouraged men to think that by means of self-inflicted bodily sufferings and indignities they could accumulate forgiveness of post-baptismal sins and justifying merit before God. That was a joyless theology of insecurity; whereas Paul's theology is one of unclouded joy and impregnable security precisely because of the complete adequacy of God's grace in Christ to meet and make good the complete inadequacy of sinful man in the presence of his holy Creator. The weaknesses which Paul welcomed were not self-induced: they were *given* him (v. 7), and with them was given also grace sufficient for him to triumph through a power not his own and to rejoice because Christ instead of self was being glorified.

The Apostle seems to have in mind a picture of the power of Christ descending upon him and taking up its abode in the frail tabernacle of his body during the course of his earthly pilgrimage (cf. 5:1), as the *shechinah* of the divine glory descended upon the mercy-seat in the tabernacle of Moses during the wilderness wanderings of the people of Israel on their way to the promised land. The presence of the *shechinah* was the guarantee of the presence of the God of the Covenant in the midst of His people, in all His favour, protection, and power.[141]

---

[141] Plummer, Stanley, Olshausen, and Hodge think that an allusion to the *shechinah* is possibly intended by the use of the verb ἐπισκηνόω. The Greek root σκην- was certainly suggestive of the Hebrew root שָׁכַן, "to abide"; cf. the occurrence of σκηνόω in the New Testament, used of the incarnate Christ dwelling among us men (Jn. 1:14) and of God dwelling with His redeemed in the heavenly glory (Rev. 7:15, 12:12, 13:6, 21:3), and also the messianic prophecies in Ezekiel (37:27, κατασκήνωσις, LXX) and Zechariah (2:10, κατασκηνήσω, LXX). "Such language", says J. H. Bernard, commenting

12 : 10

Wherefore I take pleasure in weaknesses, in injuries, in necessities, in persecutions, in distresses, for Christ's sake: for when I am weak, then am I strong.

These words afford further evidence of the unity and coherence of this epistle, for they are closely linked in thought with 4:7–10 and 6:4–10. The former passage shows how the exceeding greatness of the power of God is manifested and magnified by the entrusting of His glory to the fragile earthen vessels of our bodies; and the latter passage describes the patient endurance by God's ministers of every form of persecution and indignity. Now, in our present verse, the Apostle sums up all that has gone before by explaining that, because the divine power is made perfect in human weakness, he is well pleased with weaknesses, insults,[142] and afflictions of every kind. Human weakness provides the opportunity for divine power. Not that in itself the endurance of hardships and indignities is of value. As we have previously indicated, the concept, so pernicious in the Church at a later

on Jn. 1:14, "goes back to the thought of the σκηνή or tabernacle in the desert (Ex. 25:8, 9), where Yahweh dwelt with Israel. The verb σκηνοῦν would always recall this to a Jew. Philo says that the sacred σκηνή was a symbol of God's intention to send down to earth from heaven the perfection of His divine virtue (*Quis div. haer.* 23)". The term *shechinah*, שְׁכִינָה, is not found in the Old Testament, but by the first century A.D. it had become current in the Jewish vocabulary. J. T. Marshall writes that "there can be no reasonable doubt that the Greek word σκηνή (= 'Tabernacle') was from its resemblance in sound and meaning used by bilingual Jews for the Heb. *Shekinah*; *e.g.* in Rev. 21:3 'Behold the σκηνή of God is with men, and he will *tabernacle* (σκηνώσει) with them' " (HDB, IV, p. 489). In the language of the Septuagint "the word σκηνή represented both tabernacle and Shekinah", says Archbishop Ramsey. "Hence conceptions which are distinct in Hebrew and Aramaic literature became, in the Septuagint, fused into a unified imagery of God's glory and God's dwelling or tabernacling with His people. This unified imagery is the background of much of the thought of the writers of the New Testament" (*The Glory of God and the Transfiguration of Christ*, p. 20). It is probable that in using ἐπισκηνόω here Paul had this unified imagery in mind: the power of God (which is inseparable from His glory, as in the doxology appended to the Lord's Prayer by some authorities, Mt. 6:13) descends upon him and makes its abode in the frail tabernacle of his earthly body (cf. the Greek of 5:1 above) Ἐπισκηνόω is *hapax legomenon* in biblical Greek. It occurs in Polybius (IV, xviii, 8) with the sense of taking up quarters.

142   The phrase ἐν ὕβρεσιν, rendered "in injuries" in our version, is more precisely rendered "in insults" in RSV.

date, of courting martyrdom, of practising asceticism, and even of embracing dirt, disease, and destitution as means to the acquisition of favour before God, is diametrically opposed to the Apostle's mind and to the whole tenor of the gospel in the New Testament, for it is a concept governing a way of life *for one's own sake*, with a view to making oneself righteous and acceptable before God—a concept of works, not faith. The weaknesses and sufferings in which Paul takes pleasure are, on the contrary, those endured *for Christ's sake* by one who has already been fully and freely justified by the grace of God. Christ Himself pronounced the blessedness of those who endure reproaches, persecutions, and injustices *for His sake* (Mt. 5:11, 19:29, etc.). To welcome sufferings for any other reason is to miss that blessedness of which our Lord speaks.

The history of the Christian Church testifies plainly to the fact that blessing is never remote from affliction that is endured for Christ's sake. No less applicable to the Church in this twentieth century than to the Church of his own day is Chrysostom's observation that an examination of our present state will show "how great is the advantage of affliction; for now indeed that we are in the enjoyment of peace we have become supine and lax, and have filled the Church with countless evils; but when we were persecuted we were more soberminded and more earnest and more ready for church attendance and for hearing".

12:11, 12

> I am become foolish: ye compelled me; for I ought to have been commended of you: for in nothing was I behind the very chiefest apostles, though I am nothing. Truly the signs of an apostle were wrought among you in all patience, by signs and wonders and mighty works.

"Well, there it is, I have actually become foolish, much though I detest speaking of myself", the Apostle says in effect to the Corinthians as he sums up: "but that I should have indulged in the folly of glorying is really not my fault, but yours, for it is *you* who ought to have spoken in commendation of me, your apostle; but as you have kept silent I have been compelled to speak so that those super-apostles, to whom, nothing though I am in myself, I am in no way inferior, may be seen in their true light". Paul's glorying, as we have seen, was, paradoxically, disinterested, prompted not by self-esteem but by concern for the Corinthians who were in grave spiritual danger of being corrupted by the false apostles from "the simplicity and purity that is toward Christ" (11:3). They should never have allowed themselves to be deceived by these intruders, for they owed everything, under God, to Paul and his evangelical labours in their midst. And not only they but the world knew this: were they not his letters of commendation, "known and read of all men" (3:1f.)?

Plummer describes it as "strange" that Paul, who in 3:2 calls the Corinthians his commendatory letter, known and read of all men, "should now say that they had failed even to speak in his favour, when his enemies assailed him"; and so, in pursuance of the hypothesis that chapters 10 to 13 are incompatible with the earlier chapters, he declares that "all runs smoothly" on the assumption that these two passages belong to two different letters. On the contrary, however, we discern here a further mark of the integrity of the epistle in the form in which we possess it. Verse 11 links up in a perfectly coherent manner with what has already been written in 3:2: it is precisely because the Corinthians are Paul's letters of commendation, that is, because of the transformation of their lives by the gospel which Paul had brought to them, that they *ought* to have stood up for him in the face of his opponents. This is the *logic* behind the Apostle's rebuke here. His argument gains rather than loses force by reference to what he has previously said in 3:2.

Inconsistently with the inward testimony of their own consciences and the public testimony of their transformed lives, the Corinthians had failed to speak out in defence of Paul when invaders of his territory assailed his apostolic authority. Quite apart from questions of spiritual integrity and responsibility and even indebtedness, this was a grave failure in the basic loyalties of friendship. The simplest comparison would have been sufficient to convince them that these self-inflated "super-apostles"[143] were not his spiritual superiors—not that he made any claims for himself, for he was nothing and the grace of God everything (v. 9, I Cor. 15:10); but it was he who had been the instrument in God's hands for planting the seed of the gospel in their hearts

---

[143] On the significance of the expression οἱ ὑπερλίαν ἀπόστολοι see commentary on 11:5 above.

(though he that does the planting is not anything, but God who gives the increase: I Cor. 3:6f.), it was he who was their father in the faith (6:13, I Cor. 4:14), and it was he who had, as their spiritual father, espoused them to one husband, even Christ (11:2).

Not only this, but they had further proof of his apostleship in the nature of the *signs* manifested when he was with them in Corinth. As Hodge says, *"the signs of an apostle* were the insignia of the apostleship". These signs were confirmatory of the apostolic work and word, and therefore of the authenticity of the Apostles' mission. Thus we are told that, after Christ's ascension, the Apostles "went forth and preached everywhere, the Lord working with them and confirming the word by the signs that followed" (Mk. 16:20).[144] First and foremost was the sign of the changed lives that had resulted from Paul's preaching in Corinth. These changed lives are Paul's work in the Lord; they are the seal of his apostleship. "Are not ye my work in the Lord?" he asks the Corinthians believers. "If to others I am not an apostle, yet at least I am to you: for the seal of mine apostleship are ye in the Lord" (I Cor. 9:1f.). There is nothing more miraculous and wonderful than the conversion of a sinner to God; it is a veritable passing from death to life; it is a permanent transformation, not an ephemeral spectacle. Accordingly to distinguish other signs as "miraculous" (as though conversion were not) is misleading and contrary to the truth of scriptural realism; and this must be borne in mind when we come to consider the significance of the "signs and wonders and mighty works" which Paul goes on to mention in this same sentence.

But first of all it must be stated that another essential sign of an apostle is that of a transfigured Christlike life on the part of him who preaches the apostolic message. Nothing could be more openly contradictory of the claim to apostleship than for conduct to be incommensurate with profession. This sign of personal consistency was clearly manifested by Paul, who "was before a blasphemer and a persecutor and injurious" (I Tim.

---

[144] The authenticity of Mk. 16:9–20, of which this verse is the conclusion, as a genuine part of the Second Gospel is a matter of doubt. For a valuable discussion of this question see N. B. Stonehouse, *The Witness of Matthew and Mark to Christ* (Grand Rapids, 1944), pp. 86ff.; also, F. F. Bruce, "The End of the Second Gospel", *Evangelical Quarterly*, Vol. XII, No. 3 (July, 1945), pp. 169ff.

1:13), but whose life was now one of holiness and sincerity; and it is a sign to which he repeatedly appeals in our epistle (cf. 1:12, 2:17, 3:4ff., 4:2, 5:11, 6:3ff., 7:2, 10:13ff., 11:6, 23ff.).

Moreover, these signs of an apostle were wrought among the Corinthians *in all patience*—that is, with unremitting endurance of oppositions and hardships, with persistent perseverance in the prosecution of the apostolic ministry, and with the full reliability and constancy of the man of God, irrespective of the circumstances in which he might find himself. Despite the objections of some commentators, there is much to be said for the view of Chrysostom and Calvin that *patience* should be included among the apostolic insignia; and none gave a more notable example of patience in the face of the severest trials than did the Apostle Paul.

These "signs of an apostle" which were witnessed by the Corinthians were accompanied by "signs and wonders and mighty works". The "signs" now referred to must be distinguished from those previously mentioned, for they themselves constitute one of the "signs of an apostle". Further, "signs and wonders and mighty works (or powers)" should be taken together as a unit: each one of the three refers to a different aspect of what are ordinarily given the name of *miracles*. Thus, as Calvin says, Paul "calls them *signs* because they are not empty shows, but are appointed for the instruction of mankind—*wonders*, because they ought, by their novelty, to arouse men and strike them with astonishment—and *powers* or *mighty deeds*, because they are more signal tokens of divine power than what we behold in the ordinary course of nature". These same three terms are found in association in other places in the New Testament: Acts 2:22, where Paul declares that Jesus of Nazareth was a man approved of God "by mighty works (powers) and wonders and signs"; Heb. 2:4, where God is said to have borne witness "both by signs and wonders and by manifold powers and by gifts of the Holy Ghost"; Rom. 15:18f., where Paul speaks of those things which Christ wrought through him "in the power of signs and wonders"; and II Thess. 2:9, where it is foretold that the coming of "the lawless one" will be "with all power and signs and lying wonders". These passages demonstrate that in the New Testament the purpose of signs and wonders and powers is that of authentication, even when deceitfully imitated by satanic forces. Again, in the

Acts it is not uncommon to find signs and wonders mentioned together (cf. 2:43, 4:30, 5:12, 7:36, 14:3, and also 8:13 where signs and powers are linked); and in the Fourth Gospel, of course, the miracles of Jesus are consistently entitled "signs".

The signs and wonders and powers of which Paul reminds the Corinthians here may be understood, then, as a reference to such miracles as he was enabled to perform in their midst and also to the special charismatic gifts of the Spirit (cf. Heb. 2:4 quoted in the preceding paragraph) with which he himself was endowed and which were conferred on others through his ministry (cf. I Cor. 12–14).

It should be noticed that Paul does not say that *he* wrought these signs of an apostle, but that they "were wrought" among the Corinthians. This use of the passive is not merely a reflection of his modesty (Meyer); it amounts to a renunciation of any claim to be the worker of these signs. They were not within the range of human capabilities, but were realized and performed by the mighty power of God through Paul as the human instrument, so that the glory and merit belong entirely to God and not at all to him, apostle though he be.

12:13

> For what is there wherein ye were made inferior to the rest of the churches, except it be that I myself was not a burden to you? forgive me this wrong.

As Paul's ministry in Corinth had been attested by the signs of an apostle, why had the members of the church he had founded there given credence to others who, after his departure, appeared on the scene with apostolic pretensions, but without apostolic signs? Was it because they felt that there was some deficiency in his apostleship, so that they were in a position of inferiority when compared with other churches? Was it perhaps, he inquires ironically, because, unlike the parasitical intruders who had battened with numbing effect on them, he had forgone his ministerial prerogative of being sustained by those to whom he ministered (cf. I Cor. 9:11ff.)?[145] But this prerogative was not a *sign* of an apostle (if it were, his super-apostolic opponents

---

[145] On the significance of καταναρκάω see commentary and note on 11:9 above.

were well enough attested!); it was only a right, which he was free to claim or not as he wished. If this was wrongful, that he had not been a dead weight upon them, then he begs their forgiveness for it. Paul is not (as some commentators suggest) resorting to the weapon of sarcasm: it is not his purpose to make the Corinthians squirm, but to bring them to their senses, to help them to rid themselves of the narcotic effect produced on them by the false apostles who had invaded their community. The device he uses is that of affectionate irony. He is (as the next verse indicates) a father cajoling his children into a right frame of mind.

That Paul should find it necessary to return here and in the verses that follow to the discussion of the motives that had led him to avoid "being a burden" to the Corinthians (cf. 11:7ff. above) indicates how wickedly his slanderers had manufactured and misused to his disadvantage the opportunity of misinterpreting his customary abstention from this right.

12:14a

Behold, this is the third time that I am ready to come to you.

PAUL'S THIRD VISIT TO CORINTH

Paul is now in readiness for his third visit to Corinth. Titus, the carrier of II Corinthians, was to go on ahead, accompanied by the "messengers of the churches", to complete the collection for the poverty-stricken Christians at Jerusalem (8:16–24, 9:3–5). But if this was in fact to be Paul's *third* journey to Corinth, the question arises as to when and under what circumstances his *second* visit to that city took place, for in the Acts Luke records only two such visits.

This problem has led Beza, Grotius, Paley, Stanley, and others to maintain that the Apostle is saying no more here than that it is the third time that he has been *ready* to come to Corinth, but that this proposed visit would, if it came off, actually be only his second *visit*, since on a previous occasion when he had made preparations to include Corinth in his itinerary he had in the end altered his plans (see 1:15–17, 23 and I Cor. 16:7). Thus Stanley interprets Paul's words as follows: "'This is the third time that I am ready to travel to you. Once I have been actually' (i.e. on his first visit in Acts xviii. 1); 'a second time I intended to come' (i.e. according to the plan mentioned in

i. 15, 16); 'the third time, on the present occasion, I am now ready'". But if this interpretation is adopted here, then it must also be applied to what Paul says in 13:1 and 2, which involves a still less natural manipulation. Paley, indeed, confesses that he was at first "confounded by this text" (namely, 13:1) because it appeared to contradict his opinion that the Apostle had paid only one previous visit to Corinth [146]—in other words, the natural and apparent meaning of 13:1 ("This is the third time that I am coming to you") is that Paul had been twice before in Corinth; and so until modern times it and 12:14 had always been understood.

The unnaturalness of the hypothesis we are discussing is increased by the necessity to explain that prior to writing these words Paul had once come and had once intended (but failed) to come to Corinth; for if he is saying no more than "this is the third time that I am intending to come to you", the reasonable implication would be that twice before he had intended visits, both of which had failed to materialize—as, in fact, had happened with the Thessalonians, to whom he wrote: "We would fain have come unto you, I Paul once and again; and Satan hindered us" (I Thess. 2:18). As Alford points out, however, "the context has absolutely nothing to do with his *third preparation* to come, which would be a new element, requiring some explanation, as in I Thess. ii. 18", and "the natural and ... only true inference from the words here is, 'I am coming to you a third time,—I will not burden you this time, any more than I did at *my two previous visits*'. Our business in such cases", Alford adds, "is, not to wrest plain words to fit our preconceived chronology, but to adapt our *confessedly uncertain and imperfect history of the Apostle's life* to the data furnished by the plain honest sense of his Epistles". Bishop Lightfoot also maintains that 12:14 and 13:1, 2 "seem inexplicable under any other hypothesis" than that he had already paid two visits to Corinth.[147]

For Paul to speak of mere *intentions* which (*ex hypothesi*) are uncertain of fulfilment would, moreover, be out of character

---

[146] W. Paley, *Horae Paulinae* (London, 1820), pp. 127ff.

[147] J. B. Lightfoot, *Biblical Essays* p. 274. Plummer rightly observes that "the objection that ἑτοίμως ἔχω comes between τρίτον τοῦτο and ἐλθεῖν, and that therefore τρίτον τοῦτο cannot be taken with ἐλθεῖν, is baseless, as Acts xxi. 13 shows, where ἑτοίμως ἔχω comes between ἀποθανεῖν and ὑπὲρ τοῦ ὀνόματος".

with the whole tenor of this epistle, which is one of certainty and definiteness, and would have laid him open to the very charge, already rebutted so firmly by him, of fickleness, of planning according to the flesh, and of saying yea and nay in one breath (1:17f.). His earlier mention of his impending visit, in 9:4, is not couched in terms of uncertainty, and the same is the case with verses 20 and 21 of the present chapter and the opening of the next chapter.

The fact that in Acts Luke records only one visit by Paul to Corinth prior to the writing of II Corinthians does not necessarily conflict with what the Apostle says here about his impending *third* visit to that city. We have already seen, from the list of his experiences given in 11:23ff., that the history of the Acts is selective and by no means provides an exhaustive biography of the Apostle to the Gentiles. "Though the circumstance is not noticed by Luke", says Lightfoot,[148] "yet his silence is easily accounted for, supposing it intentional, when we reflect that his object was not to write a complete biography of St. Paul, but a history of the Christian Church, and he has accordingly selected out of his materials such facts only as throw light upon Christianity in all ages—*representative* facts, as we might call them; while on the other hand, if it be supposed that he was unacquainted with the circumstance, this supposition again is easily explained from the short duration of St. Paul's stay at Corinth, and the facility of intercourse between the two coasts of the Aegean".

In point of fact, what Paul says here is not the first indication in our epistle that he had already paid more than one visit to Corinth, for in 2:1 he tells the Corinthians that he had determined not to come to them again with sorrow, plainly implying that he had already paid them one sorrowful visit. This can refer only to a visit after the establishment of the Corinthian church, occasioned by conditions that had developed within that church which were a source of grief to him, and therefore after his first visit to Corinth for the purpose of founding a church there. This is, incidentally, a further indication of the integrity of our epistle. Verse 21 of our present chapter points to the same conclusion: "I fear", Paul says, "lest, when I come, God should *again* humble me before you".

---

[148] J. B. Lightfoot, *loc. cit.*

We may conjecture that this second visit to Corinth took place during the course of his three years' stay in Ephesus (which is mentioned retrospectively by the Apostle in Acts 20:31), that it was not only a sorrowful visit but also of brief duration, and that subsequently he wrote a letter, now lost, telling the Corinthian believers not to keep company with fornicators (I Cor. 5:9).

12 : 14b, 15

> And I will not be a burden to you: for I seek not yours, but you: for the children ought not to lay up for the parents, but the parents for the children. And I will most gladly spend and be spent for your souls. If I love you more abundantly, am I loved the less?

Those who stress the severity of the final four chapters of our epistle, as evidence for the hypothesis that these chapters belong elsewhere, seem predisposed to overlook the great tenderness and affection which time and again shine through so brightly, as we have already seen at 11:1-3, for instance, and 11:11 and 11:28f., and as is in a very notable manner the case here. What could be more genuinely tender and loving, what could be less austere, than the sentiments Paul expresses at this point? "On this my third visit to you", he says, "I will, as on previous occasions, refuse to be a numbing burden on you; because what I want is *you*, your own selves, not your money or your material goods. Remember, it is a duty of parents to provide for their children, not the other way round, and I am your father in the gospel; therefore *I* will do the spending and indeed will myself be utterly spent, not for the sake of any material returns, but for the sake of your souls."

With justice Denney has described this as "one of the most movingly tender passages in the whole Bible". It breathes the same spontaneous spirit of dedicated love that we have previously encountered in 6:11-13 and 7:1-4, where Paul, as here, speaks to them as a father to his children. "Our passage", says Allo, "though briefer [than 6:11ff.], is no less moving, and shows clearly that, in these polemical and at times threatening pages, the fundamental attitudes of the Apostle are precisely the same as in the earlier chapters." The complete congruity between this and the earlier passages provides another strand in the cord

462

which binds our epistle into a coherent whole. There too, as in these concluding chapters, he has stern things to say to those to whom he is writing (cf. 6:14ff.). But sternness and affection dwell together in a father's heart; they are not mutually exclusive. True parental love demands discipline, not indulgence. It cannot rejoice in unrighteousness (I Cor. 13:6).

Already Paul has affirmed that it is anything but lack of love which caused him to keep himself from being a burden to the Corinthians and to determine so to keep himself in the future (11:9–11). So now he repeats his determination not to be dependent on them for the supply of his physical wants, for the reason that his heart is set on winning them wholly for Christ (cf. 11:2). Any thought of winning material gain from them would endanger the full and undivided intensity of that purpose; and so he resolutely sets his face against exercising a privilege to which he had an indisputable title. He prefers and elects to exercise the privilege of a father, who is driven by love to give his substance and his very self for his children, seeking nothing in return but the response of their hearts. This is an expensive love, but he "most gladly" bears the cost, being willing not only to spend but even for the sake of their souls to be himself utterly expended.[149]

Furthermore, such is his fatherly love that, if it meets with an unworthy response, he will still expend himself wholeheartedly for their souls' sakes. Less love on their part will not diminish the greatness of his love for them; for it is not to himself that he wishes to bind them, but to Christ. The magnitude of his love for them is, indeed, a reflection of the love of Christ, who came not to be ministered unto, but to minister, and to expend His life a ransom for many (Mk. 10:45). It is *Christ's* love which constrains the servant of the gospel because it is the supremacy of love, far outshining every pastoral reflection of its splendour, redeemingly active on behalf not of those who "love less", but who because of sin do not love at all and are actually His enemies and haters (5:14; Rom. 5:6, 8, 10; I Jn. 4:10). It is love for souls, for persons, not things. And it is this love which burns inextinguishably in the breast of every faithful minister and

---

[149] The contrast between δαπανήσω, "I will spend", and the intensive compound ἐκδαπανηθήσομαι, "I will be utterly spent", should be observed.

messenger of the gospel of Jesus Christ—love first received and then expended—love that does not count the cost, that gives all and seeks no reward.

12 : 16

> But be it so, I did not myself burden you; but, being crafty, I caught you with guile.

Paul assumes that those to whom he is writing grant his point—"But let that be conceded: I did not make myself a financial burden to you". There is, however, yet another despicable calumny which his opponents have whispered in the ears of the Corinthians: "The very fact that he remained independent of your support when with you is suspicious", they suggest; "it was a device to make you believe that he is a man of integrity: but, crafty fox that he is by nature,[150] he has trapped you in another way, for it is obvious enough that, of the money you have sacrificed for the Jerusalem church, a sizeable sum will go into his own pocket. So he won't be any the poorer for his independence!" In the earlier part of this epistle Paul has already denied that he "walks in craftiness" (4:2), which may be taken as an allusion to this contumelious accusation of which he here speaks more plainly, and accordingly as a further thread of internal evidence pointing to the unity of the epistle.

Craftiness was, of course, characteristic of the Apostle's detractors, just as it is pre-eminently characteristic of Satan, whose ministers they were (11:15). As Satan beguiled Eve with his craftiness, so too these deceitful workers (11:13) were seeking to delude and pervert the Corinthian Christians whom Paul had betrothed to Christ (11:2f.). They entertained no scruples about living parasitically upon the Corinthians. But the fact that Paul consistently refused to accept financial support was an embarrassment to these rapacious intruders, and so they invented

---

[150] Ὑπάρχων πανοῦργος—"being by constitution crafty". This is a clear instance where ὑπάρχειν must be distinguished from εἶναι. Πανοῦργος, an adjective which is *hapax legomenon* in the New Testament, means "up to every trick", and therefore crafty and unscrupulous. Paul has already used the noun πανουργία, "unscrupulous cunning", twice in this epistle (4:2 and 11:3) and once in I Corinthians (3:19). He uses it again in Eph. 4:14 and it is also found in Lk. 20:23.

the lie that the Corinthians were falling into a cunningly laid trap [151] by contributing to the fund for the relief of the Jerusalem Christians. The fact was that they would dearly have liked to get their own fingers on that money; but, being unable to do this, they did the next most damaging thing, which was to ascribe to the one whose authority they wished to destroy the designs of their own evil hearts. As Calvin says, "it is customary for the wicked impudently to impute to the servants of God whatever they would themselves do, if they had it in their power".

12 : 17, 18

Did I take advantage of you by any one of them whom I have sent unto you? I exhorted Titus, and I sent the brother with him. Did Titus take any advantage of you? walked we not in the same spirit? walked we not in the same steps?

The Apostle answers this calumny by simply referring his Corinthian converts to the knowledge which they had by first-hand experience of his own character and of the character of those whom he had sent to supervise the collection. Had Titus, or the brother who accompanied him, or Paul through these emissaries, or Paul himself when he had been present in Corinth, defrauded them in any way or shown themselves greedy for gain?[152] To such an inquiry there could be but one answer: by conduct and character Paul, Titus, and "the brother" were beyond the slightest shadow of suspicion.[153]

---

[151] Ἔλαβον, "I caught you"; cf. λαμβάνει, 11:20—a metaphor, as Plummer points out, from hunting or fishing.

[152] Concerning the significance of πλεονεκτεῖν see note on 2:11 above.

[153] Of the four questions which Paul puts, the first two are introduced by μή, which shows that a negative answer is presupposed, and the second two by οὐ, which shows that a positive answer is presupposed.

It is commonly thought that in verse 17 we have an anacoluthon, the construction with τινα being uncompleted. Thus C. F. D. Moule (*Idiom Book*, p. 176) classifies τινα here as a redundant pronoun. "Hebrew and Aramaic use an indeclinable and genderless relative followed by a pronoun indicating its case and gender; and this construction has probably left its stamp on the New Testament ... II Cor. xii. 17, μή τινα ... δι᾽ αὐτοῦ ἐπλεονέκτησα, is," he says, "a well-known anacoluthon, and may possibly be due to the same Semitic way of handling pronouns, as it were retrospectively". In our opinion, however, if the Semitic idiom has left its mark here it is only incidentally. Instead of writing μὴ διά τινος ..., Paul writes μή τινα ... δι᾽ αὐτοῦ ...

For a discussion of the associations of Titus with the Corinthian church see the commentary above on 8:6 and 8:10, and also on 2:13. On at least two previous occasions Titus had been sent to Corinth by Paul, and it is apparent from the manner in which Paul speaks of him at different places in this epistle that the Corinthians had complete confidence in him and held him in high esteem. It is also apparent from what Paul says here that on the occasion when Titus had gone to initiate the collection at Corinth (8:6) he had not been alone, but, as was seemly in the conduct of matters involving the handling of money, a "brother", that is, a fellow-Christian, had been sent with him. Whether this brother is the same as the one mentioned in 8:18, who was now to accompany Titus to Corinth for the purpose of completing the collection, cannot be determined with certainty; but as the same designation ("the brother") is used both here and in 8:18 it is not improbable that the same person is meant.

There is no question of Paul's trying to "spread" the responsibility in the matter of this collection. On the contrary, he stands squarely on his own feet. It was at *his* instigation that Titus had gone to Corinth, and it was *he* again who was responsible for sending "the brother" with him.[154] The character of Titus and "the brother" in their conduct of affairs in Corinth reflected on the character of Paul who had sent them. They trusted Titus: well, in all reasonableness they must trust Paul equally. Had the behaviour of Titus aroused suspicions, then there would have been some ground for suspicions concerning Paul's motives. But they also knew Paul at first hand: he had given them no possible justification for mistrust; he had conducted himself in the same

---

The τινα is to be explained as an accusative of respect: "With respect to any one of those whom I have sent to you, did I outwit you through him for gain?" corresponding to the τι, which is an accusative of respect, in the next question: μή τι ἐπλεονέκτησεν ὑμᾶς Τίτος; — "with respect to any one thing did Titus outwit you for gain?" Paul's purpose in using this construction is one of emphasis: both τινα and τι are emphatically placed. He is challenging the Corinthians to name one single emissary who has defrauded them or one single instance of fraud on the part of Titus.

[154] The terminology here and in 8:17f. is similar: τὴν παράκλησιν ἐδέξατο ... συνεπέμψαμεν δὲ τὸν ἀδελφὸν μετ' αὐτοῦ (8:17f.) and παρεκάλεσα Τίτον, καὶ συναπέστειλα τὸν ἀδελφόν (here)—a further mark of the integrity of this epistle.

spirit and walked in the same steps of integrity and honour as had Titus. In other words, he, no less than his emissary, was completely blameless both in his motives and in his deeds.[155]

THE DESPATCH OF TITUS TO CORINTH

Allo wishes to give the aorists here ($\pi\alpha\varrho\epsilon\varkappa\dot{\alpha}\lambda\epsilon\sigma\alpha$, $\sigma\upsilon\nu\alpha\pi\dot{\epsilon}\sigma\tau\epsilon\iota\lambda\alpha$) and in 8:17 ($\dot{\epsilon}\xi\tilde{\eta}\lambda\theta\epsilon$, $\sigma\upsilon\nu\epsilon\pi\dot{\epsilon}\mu\psi\alpha\mu\epsilon\nu$) their full aoristic force: that is to say, he understands them to mean that at the time of writing Paul had already sent Titus and two other brethren to Corinth —as he now writes, his emissaries are in Corinth attending to the organization of the collection, and not by his side awaiting the completion of the epistle so that they may take it with them. In Allo's opinion this view of the situation is confirmed by Paul's use of the perfect $\dot{\alpha}\pi\dot{\epsilon}\sigma\tau\alpha\lambda\varkappa\alpha$, which he takes to indicate that those whom Paul has sent are even at this moment engaged on the task entrusted to them. This theory, however, introduces greater difficulties than it is supposed to remove. For one thing, it necessitates the postulation of an "appreciable interval" between the writing of the first seven chapters and the remainder of the epistle (an opinion previously propounded by Stanley and others), for it would seem from what Paul says at the conclusion of chapter 7 (particularly 7:15) that Titus was with him at that stage of the letter's composition. Allo supposes that at this juncture Titus and his two companions set off on their Corinthian mission, and that this explains the aorists of 8:17f.

It is further suggested that news of unfavourable criticism of the collection, and especially of Paul's motives in sending these three men to arrange its completion, reached the Apostle in Macedonia either before he had started to write chapter 8—in which case his eulogistic commendation of Titus and the two brethren, and his affirmation of his own uprightness, in 8:16–24 take on added meaning—or at any rate before he wrote 12:14–17 in which he repudiates the calumny imputing to him unscrupulous and deceitful motives (hence, argues Allo, the perfect $\dot{\alpha}\pi\dot{\epsilon}\sigma\tau\alpha\lambda\varkappa\alpha$ and the following aorists, the three emissaries being no longer with him).

But had there been this prolonged interruption in the com-

---

155 RV spells "Spirit" here with a capital S, and in his Greek edition Souter gives a capital initial to $\Pi\nu\epsilon\dot{\upsilon}\mu\alpha\tau\iota$, understanding it to refer to the Holy Spirit. But as "spirit" is parallel with "steps" it is preferable to refer it to the inner character and motives of the person, while the noun "steps" indicates, in all probability, the outward behaviour.

position of the epistle, and the development of a fresh situation in Corinth, it is all but certain that Paul would have spoken with much greater explicitness on the subject, explaining that since the despatch of Titus and his companions (during the writing of this epistle) an unfavourable report had reached him with which it was now necessary for him to deal. Windisch, indeed, who regards chapters 10 to 13 as a separate and later letter, supposes that Titus himself had returned from Corinth to Macedonia with news of the fortunes of his mission. Allo, however, being, like ourselves, convinced of the unity of II Corinthians as we possess it, finds this conjecture unacceptable; although his theory virtually has the effect of dividing II Corinthians into two separate letters occasioned by two distinct situations.

Another difficulty which Allo's hypothesis fails to resolve is that in 8:18ff. Paul speaks of having sent *two* companions with Titus, whereas here (12:18) he states that he sent only *one* ("the brother") with him. Of this Allo offers no convincing explanation. We believe, however, that there is a very simple explanation, namely, that in the two places Paul is referring to two different missions of Titus—here to an earlier mission in company with one other, and in chapter 8 to the immediately impending mission in company with two others. Here, in other words, we too interpret the aorists in a genuinely aoristic sense, not, however understanding them to signify that Titus had left Paul before this part of the epistle was written, but taking them (as befits the context) to refer to the Corinthians' previous experience of the character of Titus when, during the preceding year, he and the brother had initiated the collection among them. This particular difficulty is not resolved, of course, by treating, as so many commentators do, the aorists both in chapter 8 and here as epistolary aorists. But it is resolved by treating the aorists here as genuine aorists and in chapter 8 as epistolary or anticipatory aorists. In chapter 8 Paul employs the aorist tense because he is thinking there, not of the moment of writing, but by anticipation of the moment of the epistle's arrival and perusal in Corinth. To the Corinthian reader or hearer of the epistle the aorist tense is perfectly accurate (cf., for example, Eph. 6:21f. where ἔπεμψα is an undoubted example of the usage of an epistolary aorist by Paul). Similarly, the perfect ἀπέσταλκα in 12:17 is appropriate to cover Paul's "sendings" both past and immediate, especially as Titus, together, in all probability, with "the brother", was involved in both missions.

Further confirmation for his hypothesis is sought by Allo in the fact that the name of Titus is not mentioned in the concluding salutations of the epistle, which he takes to imply that he was no longer with Paul, but was already in Corinth. But Allo does not mention the additional fact, which is less convenient to his theory, that *no names at all* are mentioned in these final salutations —not even that of Timothy, who presumably was with Paul at the time of writing (cf. 1:1). But even if there had been a number of names there would have been a simple and adequate reason for the omission of the name of Titus since he, in accordance with a belief which may be described as certainly primitive, almost universal, and in harmony with the implications of the epistle, was the bearer of II Corinthians and accordingly would have given his own salutations in person upon arrival in Corinth with the letter.

Allo believes his to be the "only plausible" and least conjectural reconstruction; but we leave it to our readers to judge whether the interpretation we have proposed is not considerably less hypothetical and more straightforward than his.

12:19

Ye think all this time that we are excusing ourselves unto you. In the sight of God we speak in Christ. But all things, beloved, are for your edifying.

Paul is still anxious lest his defence of himself in these chapters should be misconstrued. If the Corinthians imagine that all along he has been as it were standing trial *before them*,[156] as though intent on the preservation of a good reputation for himself, they are very much mistaken. It is before *God's* tribunal that he stands and answers; and what he says is said not in himself, but in Christ, for, but for the grace of God in Christ, he would be, like any other unregenerate man, entirely without

---

[156] 'Υμῖν is emphatic by position. The sentence is probably interrogative, as in RSV, and as J. H. Moulton understands it: "Have you been thinking all along that I have been defending myself *before you*?" (*Grammar*, Vol. I, p. 118). It is interesting to find that P46 reads οὐ before πάλαι. This may be a case of assimilation to the two immediately preceding questions in verse 18, which are both introduced by οὐ. At least it indicates that in our earliest document this sentence was understood as interrogative.

The reading πάλαι has considerably better attestation than πάλιν, and the latter may well be an assimilation to 3:1. There is ample justification in the classical authors for the rendering of our English version: "all this time", and also for the use with πάλαι of the present in the sense of a perfect (which corresponds to idiomatic usage in a variety of modern languages).

defence (Rom. 1:20 [157]). Paul's standing, so far from being self-centred or self-sufficient, is vicariously christocentric. He has already defined his position more fully in his earlier epistle, where, with reference as here to his ministry, he has told the Corinthians: "With me it is a very small thing that I should be judged of you or of man's judgment: yea, I judge not mine own self; ... but he that judgeth me is the Lord" (I Cor. 4:3f.). And in the early part of our own epistle we have seen that he makes an affirmation identical with that which he makes here: "in the sight of God we speak in Christ" (2:17—yet another mark of congruity of the later with the earlier part of the epistle).

The Apostle adds the reminder, very lovingly expressed ("beloved"—only here and in 7:1 in this epistle: another uniting link) that all things are for their edification, for their building up in the faith, which, as he has already declared (10:8) and will declare again (13:10), is the very purpose for which the Lord has entrusted him with authority. It is *not* motives of self-esteem or self-protection that have driven him to speak as he has been doing of himself, but his own deep love for them and his devotion to their most vital interests.[158]

12:20

> For I fear, lest by any means, when I come, I should find you such as I would not, and should myself be found of you such as ye would not; lest by any means there should be strife, jealousy, wraths, factions, backbitings, whisperings, swellings, tumults.

As Chrysostom has observed, and many since, what the Apostle now has to say is softened by his manner of saying it. His spirit is that of a father's affectionate restraint, who will not pass judgment until he has seen the situation for himself. He utters, not denunciations, but misgivings "lest by any means" he should find a less than satisfactory state of affairs in Corinth

---

[157] Ἀναπολόγητος. Cf. ἀπολογούμεθα here. They were terms of the law-courts.

[158] Olshausen wishes to combine τὰ δέ into the single term τάδε, and to take τάδε πάντα—"all these things"—as the direct object of the verb λαλοῦμεν, thus giving one sentence instead of two: "In the sight of God in Christ I speak all these things, beloved, for your edifying". But the commonly accepted punctuation and word-division give a better and, one feels, a more truly Pauline effect.

on his arrival, which in turn would necessitate the stern exercise of his authority. He is unwilling meanwhile to adopt a tone of certainty regarding reports which have reached him, for he loves them, and "love hopeth all things" (I Cor. 13:7). What he fears to find is, in a word, professing Christians leading thoroughly carnal lives, and thereby contradicting the power of the faith they profess.

The sins which Paul mentions here and in the next verse are the very sins which occasioned the writing of I Corinthians. There we have a picture of the church at Corinth marred by jealousy and strife (I Cor. 3:3),[159] angry disputes leading to lawsuits (6:1ff.),[160] factions (1:11ff.),[161] revilings (5:11, 6:10),[162] swellings of pride (4:6, 18, 19, 5:2, 8:1, 13:4),[163] grave disorders (11:20ff., 14:26ff.),[164] and immorality (5:1, 10, 11, 6:9, 13, 18, 7:2)[165]. That only a minority of the church membership was likely to be involved in such misconduct may be inferred from what Paul has previously said in 2:5, 6 (see commentary *ad loc.*); but none the less for him who is their apostle and father in the faith this is a deplorable prospect and it is his earnest wish that anything which needs to be put right may be effectively dealt with in the interval between their receipt of this letter and his arrival in Corinth. Paternal love no more takes pleasure in finding a state of disobedience, even on the part of only a few, than it does in enforcing discipline with the rod (cf. I Cor. 4:21). But love cannot flourish in the presence of disorder and defiance; hence when need requires it must be displayed in timely correction (cf. Heb. 12:5ff.). It is Paul's longing, however, that the need will not arise, but that he may find any who have been causing trouble restored to a loyal and spiritual frame of mind at his coming to them. That he expresses his misgivings beforehand is a mark of his pastoral wisdom, because by so doing he provides them with an opportunity for themselves dealing with what is amiss prior to his arrival. The method of Paul's procedure here

---

159   *Ζῆλος καὶ ἔρις.* Cf. *ἔρις, ζῆλος* here.
160   Cf. *θυμοί* here.
161   Cf. *ἐριθείαι* here.
162   Cf. *καταλαλιαί* and *ψιθυρισμοί* here.
163   Cf. *φυσιώσεις* here.
164   Cf. *ἀκαταστασίαι* here.
165   Cf. *ἀκαθαρσία καὶ πορνεία καὶ ἀσελγεία,* verse 21.

should teach us, as Calvin remarks, "that mild remedies must always be resorted to by pastors, for the correction of faults, before they have recourse to extreme severity".

12 : 21

Lest again when I come God should humble me before you, and I should mourn for many of them that have sinned heretofore, and repented not of the uncleanness and fornication and lasciviousness which they committed.

Paul fears, further, lest on coming to Corinth he should find a spirit of unrepentance, which would be a cause to him, if not to those who are guilty, of humiliation and grief. And so it should be with every minister of Christ: Christlike, he identifies himself with his people; their joys are his joys, their sorrows his sorrows, their shame his shame; when they are made to stumble he burns (11:29). His chief concern is their soundness and their victory in Christ. Once before Paul had come to the Corinthians with sorrow and been humbled by the unfaithfulness that he found (2:1); and he shrinks from the repetition of this experience. Once before he had forborne to visit Corinth in order that he might spare them (1:23); but now he will certainly come and he will not spare (13:1f.). The time of forbearance is past. For their good, if the offenders will not repent, he will assert his apostolic authority to the full. A second humiliation would be damaging to the cause of Christ in Corinth,[166] so much so that, should the members of the unrepentant faction continue to defy him, he will have no alternative but to *mourn* over them as over those who are dead before God. The implication, as Filson observes, is that they will have to be excluded from the church.

The language of this verse suggests that numbers of those who in the past had been guilty of immoral conduct, characteristic of the viciousness of the surrounding unregenerate Corinthian society, did not *repent* of their past wickedness, presumably on

---

[166] Πάλιν should be understood in connection with ταπεινώσῃ (as AV and RSV), not with ἐλθόντος μου. Had Paul wished to emphasize his *coming* to them again, he would no doubt have said μὴ πάλιν ἐλθών in the previous verse; but, as Plummer remarks, he "often uses ἔρχομαι, without πάλιν, for 'coming back' ". What Paul fears here is a *second himiliation* on coming to Corinth.

the occasion when Paul had been humiliated before them (cf.
I Cor. 5:9), even if they then outwardly abandoned it.[167] This
showed that their heart was not right with God, that the root of
the matter was not in them, and that, instead of the fruit of the
Spirit, their lives were still productive of the works of the flesh.
"From within, out of the heart of men, evil thoughts proceed,
fornications, thefts, murders, adulteries, covetings, wickednesses,
deceit, lasciviousness, an evil eye, railing, pride, foolishness: all
these evil things", said Christ, "proceed from within, and defile
the man" (Mk. 7:21–23). "The works of the flesh", Paul writes
to the Galatians, "are these: fornication, uncleanness, lasciviousness, idolatry, sorcery, enmities, strife, jealousies, wraths, factions,
divisions, parties, envyings, drunkenness, revellings, and such
like" (Gal. 5:19–21). A comparison of these two lists with the
evil things mentioned in this and the preceding verse is instructive.
And Paul is in effect saying here to the Corinthians what he
actually did go on to say to the Galatians: "of which I forewarn
you even as I did forewarn you, that they who practise such
things shall not inherit the kingdom of God". The Christian
minister can only mourn for them as for those in whom there is
no life.

13:1

This is the third time I am coming to you. At the mouth
of two witnesses or three shall every word be established.

As Allo, Plummer, Lightfoot, Alford, Olshausen, Hodge,
and others point out, the opening sentence of this verse is capable
of only one natural and unforced meaning, namely, that Paul,
having already visited the Corinthians on two occasions is now
on the point of coming to them for the third time. An ambiguity
of sense is apparent to those alone who approach the sentence
with the preconception that Paul had previously paid only one

---

[167]   The force of the tenses here seems to be as follows: the perfect προημαρ-
τηκότων refers to persistence in sexual sin by members of the Corinthian
church during a previous period—a period subsequent to their baptism, not
prior to it (cf. especially I Cor. 5:1ff., 9ff., 6:9f., 16ff.), while the aorists
μετανοησάντων and ἔπραξαν show that they did not repent, presumably upon
receiving a visit or a letter from Paul, of their behaviour—whether they are
still so behaving is not determined, but it will be ascertained by Paul when
he comes to Corinth.

actual visit to Corinth, so that it becomes necessary to understand him to mean: "This is the third time that I am coming to you *in intention*". An even more unsatisfactory interpretation is that of Beza and some others, who wish to explain the comings in question as being of an *epistolary* nature, so that the two previous comings should be understood of Paul's two earlier epistles to the Corinthians, and the third, impending, coming of this present letter. The question of the number of Paul's visits to Corinth has already been discussed in the commentary above on 12:14.

The second sentence is in fact a citation from Deut. 19:15. As in Mt. 18:16, where it occurs in the teaching of Christ, Paul uses it without any introductory formula, such as "according as it is written". Allusions to the same judicial canon are to be found in I Tim. 5:19, Jn. 8:17, Heb. 10:28, and I Jn. 5:8. A man might not be condemned on the evidence of a single witness. The minimum number of witnesses was two; and three were preferable to two.

Consideration must be given to an ancient interpretation, found in Chrysostom and Theodoret, which has persisted up to the present day (see, for example, Calvin, Estius, Wordsworth, Stanley, Olshausen, Bousset, Godet, Lietzmann, Bachmann, Windisch, Strachan), according to which the Apostle is speaking of his comings to Corinth as witnesses against the offenders there: twice he has testified against them in this way; now his third visit will bring the number of such witnesses up to three—a number which, in conformity with the law acknowledged by all, cannot be gainsaid. Thus if there are some who think that the witness of his two previous visits accords only with the minimum number required, his third visit will have the effect of increasing that number to the maximum as defined, and therefore judgment must inevitably follow. This interpretation is the consequence of a presumed relationship between the two mentions of the number three—the third coming and the three witnesses. But, if correct, it would indicate, as some of its advocates admit, a somewhat whimsical if not fanciful (Bousset even says humorous) application of the Old Testament prescription by Paul. This, however, can hardly be regarded as in harmony with the context, which is one of stern resolution. Even if, without any relaxation of his seriousness, he is employing the anagogical method, which is Calvin's explanation, his meaning must almost certainly have been missed at least by the great majority of his readers, who would have understood the quotation in its literal sense. For them the plain fact remains that, however many times Paul may visit Corinth, his testimony still is that of only *one* witness, not of two or three.

We cannot doubt, therefore, that the literal understanding of this quotation is the correct one. The Apostle is forewarning the Corinthians that he will not hesitate to execute condign justice should the state of affairs require it during his forthcoming visit, but that everything will be carried through in strict accord with the principles of justice laid down in the Mosaic code and approved by Christ Himself as applicable to disputes within the Church (Mt. 18:16): an adequate number of witnesses will be called and their evidence considered before a charge is accepted as proven and sentence passed. Paul is saying in effect that he will deal with any such cases in a manner that is both scriptural and also sanctioned afresh by Christ. The abrupt quotation (which by this time was probably generally recognized as not only a pentateuchal but also a dominical precept) lends emphasis to his determination to take formal and effective action.

13 : 2

> I have said beforehand and I do say beforehand, as when I was present the second time, so now, being absent, to them that have sinned heretofore, and to all the rest, that, if I come again, I will not spare.

Both Plummer and Denney describe as grotesque the suggestion, required by the hypothesis of those who maintain that Paul has so far paid only one visit to Corinth, that the Apostle here means: "I have said beforehand and I do say beforehand, as if I were present with you a second time, although in fact I am now absent ...". It would be difficult to imagine language more clumsy and redundant.[168] Beyond doubt his meaning is: "I

---

[168] "Is it possible", asks Alford, "that the Apostle should have written so confusedly as to have said in the same sentence τρίτον τοῦτο ἔρχομαι and ὡς παρὼν τὸ δεύτερον, *both*, according to these interpreters, with reference to *the same journey?* And would he not even on such a hypothesis have said τὸ δεύτερον τοῦτο?" Allo remarks that "the article placed before δεύτερον itself indicates that the reference is to a well defined 'time', '*the* second time', not '*a* second time' ".

have said beforehand when I was present with you on my second visit, and I say beforehand when I am now absent from you ..." A literal translation would have helped to make it clear that the construction here is (as Bengel observes) that of a series of three pairs of phrases, the members of each pair being linked to each other by the copula "and", as follows:

I have said beforehand	and	I do say beforehand
↓		↓
when I was present the second time	and	now being absent
↓		↓
to them that have sinned heretofore	and	to all the rest

"Those that have sinned heretofore", then, refers to the church members who were leading sinful lives prior to and at the time of the Apostle's second visit; and "all the rest" refers to any whom he may find sinning when he now comes to them for the third time.[169]

On the occasion of his second visit he had said to the offenders: "If I come again, I will not spare", and this warning he repeats now that he is on the point of coming again to Corinth.[170] He makes it perfectly plain, therefore, that he is determined to take

---

[169] The reading of γράφω after νῦν (TR), an obvious later insertion, is reflected in the AV rendering: "I told you before, and I foretell you, as if I were present, the second time; and being absent now I write to them which heretofore have sinned ..." The punctuation shows that AV adroitly avoids any question concerning the number of visits to Corinth by understanding τὸ δεύτερον with προλέγω, not with πάρων. Without the addition of γράφω, however, this association of words can hardly stand. The perfect tense of προείρηκα should be noticed; it implies: "I have said before, and what I said then still holds good", and the temporal reference is doubtless to Paul's second or 'intermediate' visit to Corinth.

[170] In the clause ὅτι ἐὰν ἔλθω εἰς τὸ πάλιν, οὐ φείσομαι it is preferable to take ὅτι as recitative, introducing the direct speech of Paul's warning to the Corinthians when he was with them the second time: "If (or when) I come again, I will not spare". If, at the time when this warning was first uttered, there was a shade of uncertainty regarding a third visit implied in the use of ἐάν, there is none at all now: he is definitely coming again and he is going to act. In any case, as Tasker remarks, the particle ἐάν "often has the meaning 'when' as in Jn. xvi. 7 and I Jn. iii. 2", and thus does not necessarily convey a sense of doubt.

action against any who disregard his warning and despise his apostolic authority by continuing to misconduct themselves. But it is also apparent that the purpose of the issuing of this final warning is to allow them one more opportunity to repent and mend their ways; for he is still hopeful that they will respond with humility and obedience and so make it unnecessary for him to descend on them with a display of severity (cf. vv. 7 and 10).

13 : 3

> Seeing that ye seek a proof of Christ that speaketh in me; who to youward is not weak, but is powerful in you.

Paul has forewarned the rebellious spirits at Corinth that, if need be, he will not spare them when next he comes to their city; and the reason for the adoption of stern measures is one taken from their own proud lips: they have said that they would like some proof [171] that it is Christ who speaks in him, that is, that the authority to which he lays claim is truly apostolic. They shall indeed have what they demand, and it is themselves, not him, whom they will have to blame when he displays this proof in their midst to their confusion. It must be emphasized once again that Paul is not moved by self-concern. He willingly endures for Christ's sake any number of affronts and indignities against his own person. But when the genuineness of his apostleship is called in question that is something he dare not endure in silence, for it is no less than a challenge to the authority of Christ Himself, whose apostle he is through the will of God (1:1). As Denney says, "in challenging Paul to come and exert his authority, in defying him to come with a rod, in presuming on what they called his weakness, they were really challenging Christ".

Rebellion against an appointed minister is rebellion against the higher power that appointed him. Thus the rebellion of Korah against the authority of Moses was nothing less than rebellion against Jehovah Himself; and in the proof of his God-given authority by the punishment of any who remained un-repentant Paul might well have used the words of Moses: "Hereby ye shall know that Jehovah hath sent me to do all these works;

---

[171]   On the significance of δοκιμή see note on 2:9 above.

for I have not done them of mine own mind" (Num. 16:28). And just as Jehovah had not been weak, but powerful, in His dealings with the children of Israel, particularly in delivering them from the bondage of Pharaoh, in sustaining them as they journeyed through the wilderness, and in the signs wrought through His servant Moses, so too the Apostle reminds the Corinthians that Christ has dealt and continues to deal with them in strength, not weakness, as was evident in their deliverance from the tyranny of Satan, in God's daily provision for their need even in such a "wilderness" as Corinth, and in the "signs and wonders and mighty works" (12:21) which had been performed among them through him as Christ's apostle. Truly, they had proved the gospel of Christ to be "the power of God unto salvation" (Rom. 1:16). There was, as Plummer observes, "the amazing fact of 'saints' in such a city as Corinth".

Moreover, just as the Lord gave proof, through Moses, that He was not weak, but powerful, in the punishment of Korah and his fellow-rebels, so also would any in Corinth who remained unrepentant have proof that Christ, through Paul, was not weak, but powerful, against them.

13:4

> For he was crucified through weakness, yet he liveth through the power of God. For we also are weak in him, but we shall live with him through the power of God toward you.

Even [172] Christ, whose almighty power has been manifested in the transformation of lives in Corinth, was crucified through (out of a condition of) weakness; [173] for death is the ultimate weakness. And for Him who is the Prince of Life (Acts 3:15) death, and particularly the death of the cross, is the lowest depth of humiliation (Phil. 2:8). Yet the cross, that supreme spectacle of weakness, is the focal point of the power and purpose of the omnipotent God for the rescuing of fallen man from his own utter powerlessness. Christ, however, who once submitted to

---

[172] *Καὶ γάρ* occurs twice here. On the first occasion it is best translated "for even", and on the second "for also": "For even Christ was crucified through weakness ... For we also are weak in Him". Our English version fails to translate the first *καί*.

[173] *'Εξ ἀσθενείας.*

the weakness of the death of crucifixion, is now alive through the power of God. His resurrection from the dead is the supreme manifestation of power; and the gospel of this same crucified and risen Christ is, as the Corinthian believers know, the power of God unto salvation (Rom. 1:16). This they know as the result of the ministry of Paul, Christ's apostle to them. He had been to them the instrument of God's power, albeit in weakness and fear and much trembling (I Cor. 2:3). An instrument, in itself weak, indeed powerless, transmits the power of him who wields it. How weak an instrument Paul was in himself he has already repeatedly stressed in this epistle (cf. especially 1:8, 4:7ff., 6:4ff., 11:23ff., 12:5ff.); but it is a weakness *in Christ*, who Himself endured the fellow-suffering of our weakness (Heb. 4:15 [174]), and whose power is made perfect in our weakness (12:9). Moreover, the believer is united to Christ not only in the weakness of His death and burial, but also in the glorious power of His resurrection (Rom. 6:3ff.; cf. Phil. 3:10). Thus Paul is able to say to the Corinthians, as their apostle by the will of God, that he will live with Christ through the power of God in his approach to them;[175] that is to say, as with the risen Saviour all weakness is laid aside, so he will come to them with the irresistible power and authority of the living Christ.

It would be a misconception to understand Paul, when he says, "we shall live with Him", to be speaking eschatologically of the future resurrection to everlasting glory at the end of the age. As the context shows, the reference is limited to his impending visit to Corinth and concerns the power of the authority which he will exercise there against any who are disobedient. The Apostle discerns an analogy between the smaller, localized setting of his relations with the Corinthian church and the cosmic drama in which his Master Christ is the chief actor. The weakness of the cross at Christ's first advent is to be followed by the manifested

---

[174] Συμπαθῆσαι ταῖς ἀσθενείαις ἡμῶν.

[175] Εἰς ὑμᾶς, "toward you", should not be understood in association with δυνάμεως θεοῦ so much as with ζήσομεν. In fact, the words from ζήσομεν to θεοῦ really form a unit, so that the sense might be made more graphic by the use of hyphens: "but we shall live-with-Him-through-the-power-of-God toward you". The omission of εἰς ὑμᾶς in some documents no doubt reflects a misunderstanding of the proper association of this phrase with the rest of the sentence. Rightly understood, however, it is scarcely dispensable.

479

power of His majestic authority as King of kings and Lord of lords at His second advent, when He will appear as the Judge of the whole world (cf. Rev. 19:11ff.). All, as the Apostle has previously said, must be made manifest before the judgment-seat of Christ (5:10). Meanwhile the period between the Lord's two comings is the season of opportunity for all to avail themselves of the longsuffering of the Lord and to come to repentance (II Pet. 3:9). "The cross", writes Denney, "does *not* exhaust Christ's relation to sin; He passed from the cross to the throne, and when He comes again it is as Judge. It is the sin of sins to presume upon the cross. ... When Christ comes again *He* will not spare. The two things go together in Him: the infinite patience of the cross, the inexorable righteousness of the throne". So too Paul, who is one with his Master in the "weakness" of compassion and patience and longsuffering, desiring the repentance of all, is one with Him also in the "power" of authority and judgment. If his former visit appeared to be marked by weakness, the defiant ones in Corinth will find that his impending visit is marked by power.

13:5—7

> Try your own selves, whether ye are in the faith; prove your own selves. Or know ye not as to your own selves, that Jesus Christ is in you? unless indeed ye be reprobate. But I hope that ye shall know that we are not reprobate. Now we pray to God that ye do no evil; not that we may appear approved, but that ye may do that which is honourable, though we be as reprobate.

The trouble-makers have been inciting the Corinthians to demand proof that Christ speaks in Paul. In other words, they have been impugning his apostolic authority. But Paul tells his readers that it is they themselves that they must examine and put to the proof. If such self-examination reveals that they have experience of the grace of God, then that alone is proof irrefutable that it is none other than Christ who speaks in Paul, for it was precisely through his ministry in Corinth that they received the gospel and passed from death to life. He thus appeals to their self-knowledge, which of all knowledge is the most intimate and indisputable: if they know Jesus Christ to be in themselves, then they know, by simple logic, that He is in the one who proclaimed

Jesus Christ to them. The form of the question, "or do you not know yourselves,[176] that Jesus Christ is in you?" is mildly ironical, and its tone indicates Paul's confidence that they do know quite certainly [177] the indwelling presence of Christ in their lives. The sole awful alternative to such certain knowledge is that they are reprobates—put to the proof and rejected as spurious. This doubtless is always true of some within the Church; but it cannot be true of the Church as a whole. The very existence of the Church in Corinth testifies to the saving and transforming power of the gospel of Christ. The spiritual gifts and blessings they enjoy cannot be the experience of those who are reprobate. The Corinthian Christians are veritably Paul's epistle commendatory, addressed to the world at large (3:2); they are the seal of his apostleship in the Lord (I Cor. 9:2). The bar of their own consciences will substantiate the genuineness both of their own standing in Christ and of his authority as their apostle (cf. 4:2, 5:11).

So far, then, is Paul from expecting that the proof afforded by their self-examination and self-knowledge will disclose that they are Christless reprobates, that it is his definite hope that this same proof will confirm them in the knowledge that *he* is not without proof—in other words, that the proof they seek of Christ speaking in him (v. 3) they will find in their own saving relationship to Christ. "You know only too well that Jesus Christ is in you", he says in effect to them, "and by that very fact you know that you already have the proof of Christ speaking in me, through whom the message of Christ was brought to you."

Paul, however, is not without other means of convincing any who, under the influence of the reprobate false apostles, may persist in disregarding this inward proof and in challenging him to give proof openly of his apostolic authority. To such he will come in power, not weakness. They will find him a stern judge, not a helpless bystander. But to give proof of his authority in this way will afford him no pleasure. A father does not delight in the chastisement of his children, even when for their own good it becomes a necessity. Hence Paul's hope that the Corin-

---

[176] The words "as to" are not in the original.

[177] Ἐπιγινώσκετε is an intensive compound: "or do you not have a thorough knowledge of yourselves?"

thians will be persuaded by the adequate proof which they already possess within themselves, so that when he arrives in Corinth their attitude to him may be consistent with their own self-knowledge.

Hence his prayer that they may abstain from all evil and conduct themselves in an honourable manner befitting Christ's followers. The proof of his apostolic authority is not his objective, but their own well-being and well-doing. Indeed, if they respond (as he hopes they will) to his appeal, he will, when he now comes to Corinth, be like one without proof—that is, their obedience will make it unnecessary for him to give proof of his apostolic authority by dealing severely with them (cf. v. 10 below). It will, however, be only *as* or *like* one without proof—in the sense of outward display—for the proof will be there, none the less, but inwardly, in the hearts and consciences of his converts. Calvin, therefore, rightly points out that the particle "as" in verse 7 here is not superfluous, and that its significance is illustrated by Paul's use of it earlier in the epistle when he writes: "as deceivers, and yet true" (6:8).[178]

13 : 8, 9

For we can do nothing against the truth, but for the truth. For we rejoice when we are weak, and ye are strong: this we also pray for, even your perfecting.

A more coherent translation would read: "For we have no

---

[178] The force of Paul's argument in this passage (vv. 3 to 7) is clear in the Greek, but is difficult to convey in English translation. The sequence of the cognate terms δοκιμή, δοκιμάζω, δόκιμος, ἀδόκιμος is the key to the proper understanding of the argument: "Since you seek a proof (δοκιμήν, v. 3) of Christ speaking in me, you shall have it, for when I come again I will not spare . . . But it is your own selves, rather than me, whom you should put to the proof (δοκιμάζετε, v. 5). Can it really be that you do not know your own selves, that Christ Jesus is in you?—unless, and this is the sole alternative, you are without proof (ἀδόκιμοι, v. 5—that is, Christ Jesus is not in you). But it is my hope that you will know that I am not without proof (ἀδόκιμοι, v. 6—that is, of Christ speaking in me). I pray God, however, that you may not do what is wrong, not that I may be seen to have proof (δόκιμοι, v. 7 —that is, through coming to you with a rod); but that you may act honourably, and that I consequently may be like one without proof (ἀδόκιμοι, v.7—that is, since it will then be unnecessary for me to give proof of my authority by the use of the rod)". The corresponding sequence of terms in our English version

power [179] against the truth, but for the truth. For we rejoice when we are weak [180] and you are powerful" [181]. The conjunction "for" indicates that there is a close logical connection with what precedes. The train of thought is as follows: Should Paul come to Corinth and find everything in order, then he will have no occasion for giving the threatened proof of his apostolic authority by the adoption of stern measures, for there can be no power (in the sense of display of authority) against the truth, but only for (on behalf of) the truth. That is to say, a powerful demonstration of authority when the truth is established in a church would be a perversion of authority; for such a display of power is justified only when serious error and misconduct are present and require to be driven out so that the cause of the truth may be vindicated. It will be a matter of rejoicing to Paul, therefore, if the state of the church when he arrives in Corinth is such that he may be "weak", that is, under no necessity to enforce authority; for this will mean that the Corinthians are "powerful"—not merely in the sense that they give evidence of spiritual power (though this is inevitably involved), but more precisely in the sense that they have disciplined themselves, and thus obviated the necessity for him to come to them with a rod.

What Paul writes here throws particular light upon the office of the Christian pastor. He must not be so timid as to shrink from openly imposing discipline when circumstances demand it. But at the same time he must always remember that, in contrast to the great ones of this world who exercise their authority as tyrannical and domineering overlords, it is not his part to be

---

("proof", "prove", "approved", "reprobate"), though it is true that they are cognate terms, is inadequate to convey the force of the original. The particular difficulty lies in the translation of the adjectives δόκιμοι and ἀδόκιμοι, which "approved" and "reprobate" in their current usage scarcely match. It is doubtful whether the translator will find a neat solution to this problem.

[179] Οὐ γὰρ δυνάμεθα τι.

[180] Ἀσθενῶμεν.

[181] Δυνατοί. The sequence: δυνάμεθα ... ἀσθενῶμεν ... δυνατοί, must be interpreted in the light of the context (from v. 3 onwards), in which terms expressing "power" and "weakness" are used with precise reference to the exercise of authority. To translate οὐ δυνάμεθα τι as "we can do nothing" obscures this significance, which is essential to coherent exegesis. What Paul is saying is that he has no *power*, that is, there is no occasion for him to enforce his authority, except when the truth is being opposed.

overbearing. He must not allow authority to degenerate into authoritarianism. He must never forget that, in conformity with the teaching and example of Him who is the Head of the Church, he who would be great must be the minister and servant of all (Mk. 10:42ff.). An overbearing spirit, ambition for preferment, and notions of superiority must be shunned by him as the marks of hirelings and false leaders. Like Paul, he will rejoice when the spiritual well-being of his people is such that, so far as the display of his authority is concerned, he can move among them in "weakness".

Thoughts of personal eminence and position are far, then, from the Apostle's mind. His prayers are centred, not on himself, but on his spiritual children and their perfecting. He longs to see them fully integrated in the communion of the Church as their proper sphere of life and function, harmoniously and fruitfully articulated as members together in the body of Christ. The active force of the Greek noun which Paul uses here [182] is brought out by the rendering "perfecting" of our English version. The word denotes a correct articulating of limbs and joints in the body, a resetting of what has been broken and dislocated, and hence a restoration of harmonious and efficient functioning. It carries no suggestion of what is known theologically as "perfectionism".

13:10

For this cause I write these things while absent, that I may not when present deal sharply, according to the authority which the Lord gave me for building up, and not for casting down.

This verse brings to a conclusion the section of the epistle which began at 10:1. The theme there announced as it were in a minor key is now happily transposed into the major key: there he is accused of being bold and terrifying when absent, especially in his letters, but weak and innocuous when present; here he concludes his answer to this charge by saying that if he writes with sharpness when absent it is with the purpose of obviating the need for acting with sharpness when present. There is, however, no renunciation of authority on his part, but

[182] Κατάρτισις.

his conduct is governed by the principle that (as he has previously stated in 10:8) his authority has been entrusted to him by the Lord to be used for constructive, not destructive, ends. And so the Corinthians must understand that all that he does and says, whether present or absent, is directed towards the building up of themselves (12:19). His opponents in Corinth have in effect challenged him to come and give a display of force such as might impress the secular world, but which he well knows would do more to cast down than to build up the church there. He has indeed made it perfectly plain that this time he will come and exhibit his authority by inflicting stern punishment on any who deserve it; but he will be much happier (and so will they) if the effect of this strongly worded letter is such that when he comes he finds them "such as he would" (12:20), so that he may be with them in gentleness rather than severity. If there is punishment, it will be because it is merited; if there is no punishment, it will be because they have purged themselves of offences. In either case his authority will be acknowledged and their edification will be promoted. The decision now rests with them as to whether he is to come to them "with a rod or in love and a spirit of meekness" (cf. I Cor. 4:21).

13:11

Finally, brethren, farewell. Be perfected; be comforted; be of the same mind; live in peace: and the God of love and peace shall be with you.

In bringing the epistle to a close the Apostle addresses the members of the Corinthian church affectionately as brethren and exhorts them with a succession of staccato injunctions. The Greek word [1] translated "farewell" in our version may also, as the marginal reading indicates, mean "rejoice"; and this latter rendering seems to us to be the right one here, corresponding closely as it does with the exhortation in Phil. 3:1, "Finally, my brethren, rejoice in the Lord".[2] Christian joy is one of the foremost fruits of the Spirit (Gal. 5:22) and it should be a foremost mark of every Christian community. An incitement to rejoice, therefore, stands fittingly at the head of this sequence of exhortations, and has more point than a general expression of farewell. The rejoicing, it goes without saying, is not mere high-spiritedness or the superficial affectation of a jovial attitude to life, but is the manifestation of a serene and heavenward-looking disposition, arising from a deep and exhaustless centre of origin, for, as is apparent from Phil. 3:1 and 4:4, it is rejoicing *in the Lord.*

The admonition to "be perfected"[3] links up with Paul's prayer for the "perfecting"[4] of the Corinthians in verse 9, and it implies the need, not so much for individual sanctity (essential though that is), as for a united, properly articulated, and therefore harmoniously functioning together of the members of Christ's body in Corinth.

"Be comforted"[5] may, as Tasker suggests, be connected with what Paul has said in the opening part of the epistle (1:3ff.),

---

[1]   Χαίρετε.

[2]   II Cor. 13:11—λοιπόν, ἀδελφοί, Χαίρετε. Phil. 3:1—τὸ λοιπόν, ἀδελφοί μου, Χαίρετε ἐν Κυρίῳ.   Cf. 4:4.

[3]   Καταρτίζεσθε.

[4]   Κατάρτισις.

[5]   Παρακαλεῖσθε.

where the same verb is used in this sense. But it seems preferable to translate it here in its other sense, namely, "be admonished" or "heed my appeal" (RSV)—that is, respond to the plea which this epistle conveys.

To "be of the same mind"[6]—does not mean that individual judgment and opinion should be set aside, but that as fellow-Christians, with all their diversities of ability and temperament, they should be united in what is essential, namely, in the love and doctrine of Christ. It is Christian unity, not artificial uniformity or submission to the "mind" of an authoritarian officialdom, which binds together; and it is unity in depth arising from agreement in the *mind*[7], which in turn implies agreement in the *truth*. As Rom. 15:5 shows, this sameness of mind one with another is something which, human nature being what it is (even in the redeemed community where the "old man" ever lurks), Christians should look to God to grant, and which is qualified as being "according to Christ Jesus". That qualification, indeed, demarcates the only genuine basis for Christian unanimity.

Closely associated with the foregoing is the exhortation to "live in peace". Living in peace is, in fact, an outward consequence of the inward state of being of the same mind. The factions, envies, litigations, and disorders in public worship by which, as the earlier epistle testifies, the Corinthian church had been disfigured, and the disruptions induced by the intruding false apostles, were outward symptoms of inward disunity. Yet it is Christ's followers who, above all other people, should be both inwardly and visibly at one with each in love and fellowship. The Christian's warfare is with the enemy of souls and the powers of darkness, not with his fellow-believers.

The fact that the promise, "and the God of love and peace shall be with you", follows after the exhortations indicates that the Christian life is not one of passivity but of constant action (though not activism and restlessness). It is not by sitting with folded hands that we enter into the blessings of God, but by actively and purposefully promoting those dispositions which are in accordance with God's will for His people: rejoicing,

[6] *Τὸ αὐτὸ φρονεῖτε.*
[7] *Φρονεῖν.*

487

harmony, unity in the truth, living together in peace. It is true
that we look to God alone to supply the grace for their achievement; but it is the actual daily practice of love and peace that
ensures, from the human side, the realization of the promise that
the God of love and peace will be with us. The promise cannot
prevail where there is jealousy and strife.

13 : 12, 13

Salute one another with a holy kiss. All the saints salute you.

The singleness of heart and purpose to which Paul has just
exhorted the Corinthians may further be expressed or sealed by
an external token of affection. The kiss or embrace enjoined is
no mere social formality. It is "holy", and that means Christlike
and therefore absolutely sincere and pure. Like our handclasp
today, it is a symbol of mutual confidence, and, where the Corinthians are concerned, of the resolving of all their old divisions,
their joyful reconciliation with each other in Christ, and their
going forward together henceforth united in the fellowship and
the labour of the gospel to the glory of God.

Moreover, their unity at Corinth is but part of a still greater
unity—the unity in Christ of God's people everywhere. Hence
Paul conveys to them from Macedonia where he is writing the
greetings of *all* the saints, that is, all their fellow-Christians. Even
though the majority of the Corinthian and Macedonian Christians
have never met and are personally unknown to each other, yet
they are united *in Christ*, which is the supreme and transcendental
unity of redemption; they are members together in the one body
under the direction of the one Head; and they *will* meet, together
with all the saints of every age and clime, when the unity of Christ
and His people has its consummation in everlasting glory hereafter
(Rev. 7:9ff.).

13 : 14

The grace of the Lord Jesus Christ, and the love of God,
and the communion of the Holy Spirit, be with you all.

This final benediction is trinitarian in form, but spontaneously so. The doctrine of the Trinity is not, in fact, systematically
and as it were self-consciously formulated in the New Testament.

It is there, none the less, and indeed is one of the clearest inferences to be drawn from Scripture. Like other great doctrines of the faith, it is not, and could not be, a construction of unaided natural reason. The being of God, because of its transcendence, cannot be confined descriptively within the categories of man's mundane thought. In the New Testament the teaching of a trinitarian distinction within the Godhead is primarily practical in its impact. It is related to the human situation, for it is within the framework of redemption that it is disclosed to fallen man. And therefore it is a truth which is confirmed by the knowledge of the believer's experience. Hence Paul's mention of the grace, the love, and the fellowship that flow from the three Persons of the one God. The meaning of the Trinity is learnt (or one might more accurately say relearnt) in response, through personal faith, to what God, Father, Son, and Holy Spirit, have done for our redemption.

But the meaning of the Trinity is not exhausted by an understanding of the economy of redemption. It is a truth which defines an eternal relationship within the Godhead and which exists quite independently of man. The Triune God, as Scripture testifies, was active at the Creation; the glory of the Son is a glory of Trinitarian harmony enjoyed before the world was; the love of the Father for the Son existed in eternity before the foundation of the world (Jn. 17:5, 24). It is a truth which reveals the very constitution of the Godhead. However much, therefore, it transcends the limits of man's finite mind, to man, precisely because he is created in the divine image, the truth of the Trinity is, in this sense, a truth of his very constitution, and the foundation of all his knowledge of the being and mind of God. The revelation of the trinitarian nature of the Godhead is not, accordingly, the manifestation of a new truth, but the re-affirmation, in the very act of mercy (which is the act of re-creation), of the age-old foundation truth which man in his sin has sought to suppress. He who knows in his heart the saving activity of Father, Son, and Holy Spirit is in fact re-established in the truth of the Trinity and is restored to that divine image from which he had fallen.

Paul can write to the members of the Corinthian church as he does here because they have a first-hand experience of the operation of Father, Son, and Holy Spirit in their lives. Through God the Son as Mediator and Saviour they have returned to God the Father, and the sending forth of God the Holy Spirit into their hearts has enabled them to rejoice in this great spiritual reconciliation. It is through the grace of God in Christ that they have experienced the love of God the Father and been brought into the fellowship of God the Holy Spirit, which is the community of the new creation. This is a great threefold and yet unitary reality of abiding significance, the dynamic of which has transformed their whole being, both now and for ever. If it is not an abiding reality, then it is not a saving reality. Hence the Apostle's valedictory wish that they may all continuously know in their daily experience the presence of the grace, love, and fellowship of Son, Father, and Holy Spirit, the eternally blessed Triune God to whose sovereign goodness alone they owe their everlasting salvation.

INDEX OF PROPER NAMES

INDEX OF SCRIPTURE REFERENCES

OLD TESTAMENT

NEW TESTAMENT